**How to Use the Maps in *The Essential World History,*
2nd Edition**

Here are some basic map concepts that will help you to get
the most out of the maps in this textbook.

■ Always look at the scale, which allows you to determine the distance in
miles or kilometers between locations on the map.

■ Examine the legend carefully. It explains the colors and symbols used on
the map.

■ Note the locations of mountains, rivers, oceans, and other geographic
features, and consider how these would affect such human activities as
agriculture, commerce, travel, and warfare.

■ Read the map caption thoroughly. It provides important information,
sometimes not covered in the text itself, and poses a thought question to
encourage you to think beyond the mere appearance of the map and
make connections across chapters, regions, and concepts.

■ Several "spot maps" appear in each chapter, to allow you to view in detail
smaller areas that may not be apparent in larger maps. For example, a spot
map in Chapter 12 lets you zoom in on Charlemagne's Empire.

■ Many of the text's maps also carry a globe icon alongside the title, which
indicates that the map appears in interactive form on the text's website:

http://history.wadsworth.com/world

0-534-62823-0

www.wadsworth.com

www.wadsworth.com is the World Wide Web site for Wadsworth and is your direct source to dozens of online resources.

At *www.wadsworth.com* you can find out about supplements, demonstration software, and student resources. You can also send e-mail to many of our authors and preview new publications and exciting new technologies.

wadsworth.com
Changing the way the world learns®

THE ESSENTIAL WORLD HISTORY

VOLUME II: SINCE 1400

SECOND EDITION

WILLIAM J. DUIKER
THE PENNSYLVANIA STATE UNIVERSITY

JACKSON J. SPIELVOGEL
THE PENNSYLVANIA STATE UNIVERSITY

THOMSON ™

WADSWORTH

Australia • Canada • Mexico • Singapore • Spain
United Kingdom • United States

THOMSON

WADSWORTH

Publisher: Clark Baxter
Senior Development Editor: Sue Gleason
Assistant Editor: Paul Massicotte
Editorial Assistant: Richard Yoder
Technology Project Manager: Melinda Newfarmer
Executive Marketing Manager: Caroline Croley
Marketing Assistant: Mary Ho
Advertising Project Manager: Brian Chaffee
Project Manager, Editorial Production: Kimberly Adams
Print/Media Buyer: Doreen Suruki
Permissions Editor: Joohee Lee
Production Service: Orr Book Services

Text Designer: Diane Beasley
Photo Researcher: Sarah Evertson
Copy Editor: Mark Colucci
Illustrator: Maps.com
Cover Designer: Lisa Devenish
Cover Image: 19th century CE. Japan's first foreign mission headed by Prince Iwakura, Ambassador Extraordinary and Plenipotentiary, leaving Yokohama for the U.S. and Europe, Dec. 23, 1871. Coll. Ministry of Foreign Affairs, Tokyo. © Scala/Art Resource, NY
Compositor: New England Typographic Service
Printer: Quebecor World/Dubuque

For more information about our products, contact us at:
Thomson Learning Academic Resource Center
1-800-423-0563
For permission to use material from this text or product, submit a request online at http://www.thomsonrights.com

Any additional questions about permissions can be submitted by email to thomsonrights@thomson.com

Library of Congress Control Number: 2003117126

Student Edition: ISBN 0-534-62714-5

Instructor's Edition: ISBN 0-534-62716-1

Wadsworth Group/Thomson Learning
10 Davis Drive
Belmont, CA 94002-3098
USA

Asia
Thomson Learning
5 Shenton Way #01-01
UIC Building
Singapore 068808

Australia/New Zealand
Thomson Learning
102 Dodds Street
Southbank, Victoria 3006
Australia

Canada
Nelson
1120 Birchmount Road
Toronto, Ontario M1K 5G4
Canada

Europe/Middle East/Africa
Thomson Learning
High Holborn House
50/51 Bedford Row
London WC1R 4LR
United Kingdom

Latin America
Thomson Learning
Seneca, 53
Colonia Polanco
11560 Mexico D.F.
Mexico

Spain/Portugal
Paraninfo
Calle Magallanes, 25
28015 Madrid, Spain

ABOUT THE AUTHORS

WILLIAM J. DUIKER is liberal arts professor emeritus of East Asian studies at The Pennsylvania State University. A former U.S. diplomat with service in Taiwan, South Vietnam, and Washington, D.C., he received his doctorate in Far Eastern history from Georgetown University in 1968, where his dissertation dealt with the Chinese educator and reformer Cai Yuanpei. At Penn State, he has written extensively on the history of Vietnam and modern China, including the widely acclaimed *The Communist Road to Power in Vietnam* (revised edition, Westview Press, 1996), which was selected for a Choice Outstanding Academic Book Award in 1982–1983 and 1996–1997. Other recent books are *China and Vietnam: The Roots of Conflict* (Berkeley, 1987), *Sacred War: Nationalism and Revolution in a Divided Vietnam* (McGraw-Hill, 1995), and *Ho Chi Minh* (Hyperion, 2000). While his research specialization is in the field of nationalism and Asian revolutions, his intellectual interests are considerably more diverse. He has traveled widely and has taught courses on the History of Communism and Non-Western Civilizations at Penn State, where he was awarded a Faculty Scholar Medal for Outstanding Achievement in the spring of 1996.

To Yvonne,
for adding sparkle to this book, and to my life
W. J. D.

JACKSON J. SPIELVOGEL is associate professor emeritus of history at The Pennsylvania State University. He received his Ph.D. from The Ohio State University, where he specialized in Reformation history under Harold J. Grimm. His articles and reviews have appeared in such journals as *Moreana, Journal of General Education, Catholic Historical Review, Archiv für Reformationsgeschichte,* and *American Historical Review.* He has also contributed chapters or articles to *The Social History of the Reformation, The Holy Roman Empire: A Dictionary Handbook, Simon Wiesenthal Center Annual of Holocaust Studies,* and *Utopian Studies.* His work has been supported by fellowships from the Fullbright Foundation and the Foundation for Reformation Research. At Penn State, he helped inaugurate the Western civilization courses as well as a popular course on Nazi Germany. His book *Hitler and Nazi Germany* was published in 1987 (fourth edition, 2001). He is the author of *Western Civilization,* published in 1991 (fifth edition, 2003). Professor Spielvogel has won five major university-wide teaching awards. During the year 1988–1989, he held the Penn State Teaching Fellowship, the university's most prestigious teaching award. In 1996, he won the Dean Arthur Ray Warnock Award for Outstanding Faculty Member, and in 2000, received the Schreyer Honors College Excellence in Teaching Award.

To Diane,
whose love and support made it all possible
J. J. S

BRIEF CONTENTS

DETAILED CONTENTS

Part III   THE EMERGENCE OF NEW WORLD PATTERNS (1400–1800)   270

Part IV MODERN PATTERNS OF WORLD HISTORY (1800–1945) 390

Part V   TOWARD A GLOBAL CIVILIZATION? THE WORLD SINCE 1945   546

Chapter 26
Brave New World: Communism on Trial 568

Chapter 27
Europe and the Western Hemisphere Since 1945 589

Chapter 28
Challenges of Nation Building in Africa and the Middle East 610

DOCUMENT CREDITS

This page constitutes an extension of the copyright page. We have made every effort to trace the ownership of all copyrighted material and to secure permission from copyright holders. In the event of any question arising as to the use of any material, we will be pleased to make the necessary corrections in future printings. Thanks are due to the following authors, publishers, and agents for permission to use the material indicated.

CHRONOLOGIES

MAPS

discussed in the text are placed next to the discussions. Chapter outlines and focus questions, including analytical questions, at the beginning of each chapter help students with an overview and guide them to the main subjects of each chapter. A glossary of important terms and a pronunciation guide are included to enrich an understanding of the text.

After reexamining the entire book and analyzing the comments and reviews of many colleagues who have found the book to be a useful instrument for introducing their students to world history, we have also made a number of other changes for the second edition. In the first place, we have continued our effort to reduce the size of the book without affecting the quality of the material contained therein. As part of this effort, we have reorganized the material of five European chapters into three new chapters. These are Chapter 12, "The Making of Europe in the Middle Ages"; Chapter 13, "Renewal, Reform, and State Building in Europe"; and Chapter 17, "The West on the Eve of a New World Order." Moreover, Chapters 31 and 32 have been synthesized into a new Chapter 29, "Toward the Pacific Century?" We have also tried to delete excess words while retaining all essential material as well as the narrative thrust of the previous edition.

Second, we have sought to strengthen the global framework of the book, but not at the expense of reducing the attention assigned to individual regions of the world. The essays entitled "Reflection" that appear at the end of each of the five parts have been shortened slightly to accommodate the advice of many of our reviewers and to enable us to more concisely draw comparisons and contrasts across geographical, cultural, and chronological lines. Each Reflection section contains boxed essays, each highlighted with an illustration, to single out issues of particular importance to that period of history. Moreover, additional comparative material has been added to each chapter to help students be aware of similar developments globally. Among other things, this material includes new comparative sections, such as "Comparison of the Roman and Han Empires" in Chapter 5 and "Europe, China, and Scientific Revolutions" in Chapter 13, as well as comparative illustrations in each chapter. We hope that these techniques will assist instructors who wish to encourage their students to adopt a comparative approach to their understanding of the human experience.

Third, this new edition contains additional information on the role of women in world history. In conformity with our own convictions, as well as what we believe to be recent practice in the field, we have tried where possible to introduce such material at the appropriate point in the text, rather than to set aside separate sections devoted exclusively to women's issues.

Finally, a number of new illustrations, boxed documents, and maps have been added, and the bibliographies have been revised to take account of newly published material. The chronologies and maps have been fine-tuned as well, to help the reader locate in time and space the multitude of individuals and place names that appear in the book. To keep up with the ever-growing body of historical scholarship, new or revised material has been added throughout the book on many topics, including early civilizations around the world; the Aryans in India; the Zhou dynasty in China; Sparta; Alexander and the Mauryan Empire in India; Roman trade with China; comparison of Roman and Han Chinese empires; the first Americans; the Maya; first civilizations in South America; Islam; early civilizations in Africa; the spread of Buddhism; the Song dynasty in China; the Mongols; early Japan; the African slave trade; the Ottoman Empire; the Mughals; Ming China; Tokugawa Japan; the impact of Western expansion on indigenous peoples; the impact of the discovery of the Pacific Islands in the eighteenth century; the defeat of Napoleon; slave revolt in Haiti; how industrialized nations limited industrialization in their colonies; Latin America; Canada; the impact of World War I on Africa, East Asia, and the Pacific; the Russian Revolution; and the Asian theater of World War II. In addition, all of the chapters in Part V have been updated to bring our treatment of contemporary events up to the present.

Because courses in world history at American and Canadian colleges and universities follow different chronological divisions, a one-volume edition, a two-volume edition, and a volume covering events to 1400 are being made available to fit the needs of instructors. Teaching and learning ancillaries include:

Instructor's Manual and Test Bank Prepared by Eugene Larson, Los Angeles, Pierce College. Contains chapter outlines, class lecture/discussion topics, thought/discussion questions for primary sources (boxed documents), possible student projects, and examination questions (essay, identification, and multiple choice). Also available on the Instructor's Resource CD-ROM.

Instructor's Resource CD-ROM with ExamView® Includes the Instructor's Manual, Resource Integration Guide, *ExamView* computerized testing, and PowerPoint® slides with lecture outlines and images that can be used as offered or customized by importing personal lecture slides or other material. *ExamView* allows you to create, deliver, and customize tests and study guides (both print and online) in minutes with this easy-to-use assessment and tutorial system. It offers both a Quick Test Wizard and an Online Test Wizard that guide you step by step through the process of creating tests, while its "what you see is what you get" capability allows you to see the test you are creating on the screen exactly as it will print or display online. You can build tests of up to 250 questions with as many as 12 question types. Using *ExamView's* complete word-processing capabilities, you can enter an unlimited number of new questions or edit existing questions.

Map Acetates with Commentary for World History   Includes more than 100 four-color map images from the text and other sources. Map commentary for each map is prepared by James Harrison, Siena College. Three-hole punched and shrinkwrapped.

History Video Library   Includes Film For Humanities (these are available to qualified adoptions), CNN® videos, and Grade Improvement: Taking Charge of Your Learning.

CNN Videos for World History   Two- to five-minute CNN segments are easy to integrate into classroom discussions or as lecture launchers.

Sights and Sounds of History   Prepared by David Redles, Cuyahoga Community College. Short, focused video clips, photos, artwork, animations, music, and dramatic readings are used to bring life to historical topics and events which are most difficult for students to appreciate from a textbook alone. For example, students will experience the grandeur of Versailles and the defeat felt by a German soldier at Stalingrad. The video segments, each averaging 4 minutes long, make excellent lecture launchers. Available on VHS video.

Music CD-ROMs   Available to instructors on request, these CDs include music selections from the twelfth century to the present and can be used to enhance lectures. The Resource Integration Guide includes a correlation guide. Contact your local Thomson Wadsworth representative for further information.

Exploring the European Past: Text & Images   A Custom Reader for the Western Civilization coverage of the class. Written by leading educators and historians, this fully customizable reader of primary and secondary sources is enhanced with an online collection of visual sources, including maps, animations, and interactive exercises. Each reading also comes with an introduction and a series of review questions. To learn more, visit www.ThomsonCustom.com or call Thomson Custom Publishing at 1.800.355.9983.

History Interactive: A Study Tool   This valuable CD-ROM for students, prepared by Laura Wood and Michael Nichols of Tarrant County College. Includes a wealth of primary source documents; interactive maps and timelines; chapter summaries; multiple choice; essay questions; analysis of primary source documents; How to Read a Document; How to Read a Map; the World History Image Bank; simulations for World History; study tips for the narrative, maps, photographs, and documents; answers to text Focus questions and map questions; and sample H-Connect interactive modules. (Packaged for free with all new copies of the text.)

H-Connect: Interactive Explorations in World History   This CD-ROM and student guide feature interactive multimedia modules to complement any college-level world history course. The student guide provides a complete index to the interactive modules, as well as a correlation guide to *The Essential World History.* Contact your Thomson Wadsworth representative for more information.

Map Exercise Workbook   Prepared by Cynthia Kosso, Northern Arizona University. Has been thoroughly revised and improved. Contains over 20 maps and exercises, which ask students to identify important cities and countries. Also includes critical thinking questions for each unit. Available in two volumes.

World History MapTutor   This new mapping CD-ROM allows students to learn by manipulating maps through "locate and label" exercises, animations, and critical thinking exercises.

Migrations in Modern World History 1500–2000 CD-ROM   An interactive multimedia curriculum on CD-ROM by Patrick Manning and the World History Center. Includes over 400 primary source documents; analytical questions to help the student develop his/her own interpretations of history; timelines; and additional suggested resources, including books, films, and web sites.

Document Exercise Workbooks   Prepared by Donna Van Raaphorst, Cuyahoga Community College. Contains a collection of exercises based around primary source documents pertaining to world history.

The Journey of Civilization CD ROM for Windows   Prepared by David Redles, Cuyahoga Community College. This CD takes students on 18 interactive journeys through history. Enhanced with QuickTime movies, animations, sound clips, maps, and more, the journeys allow students to engage in history as active participants rather than as readers of past events.

Magellan World History Atlas   Available to bundle with any history text; contains 44 historical four-color maps in a practical 8″ × 10″ format.

Internet Guide for History, Third Edition   Prepared by John Soares. Provides newly revised and up-to-date Internet exercises by topic. Available at http://history.wadsworth.com.

Kishlansky, Sources in World History, Second and Third Editions   This reader is a collection of documents designed to supplement any world history text. Available in two volumes.

Web Tutor™ Toolbox   This content-rich, Web-based teaching and learning tool helps students succeed by taking the course beyond classroom boundaries to an anywhere, anytime environment. *Web Tutor* offers real-time access to a full array of study tools, including flashcards (with audio), practice quizzes, online tutorials, and Web links. Web Tutor also provides rich communication tools, including a course calendar, asynchronous discussion, "real-time" chat, and an integrated e-mail system. Available for Blackboard and WebCT.

InfoTrac® College Edition   An online university that lets students explore and use full-length articles from more than 900 periodicals for four months. When students log on with their personal ID, they will immediately see how easy it is to search. Students can print out the articles, which date back as far as four years.

The Wadsworth History Resource Center

http://history.wadsworth.com/

Features a career section, forum, and links to museums, historical documents, the World History Image Bank, and other fascinating sites. From the Resource Center you can access the book-specific web site, which contains the following: chapter by chapter tutorial quizzing, *InfoTrac* activities, Internet activities, interactive maps and time-lines, glossary, and hyperlinks for the student, and an online instructor's manual and downloadable PowerPoint files for the Instructor.

ACKNOWLEDGMENTS

Both authors gratefully acknowledge that without the generosity of many others, this project could not have been completed. William Duiker would like to thank Kumkum Chatterjee and On-cho Ng for their helpful comments about unfamiliar issues related to the history of India and premodern China. His long-time colleague Cyril Griffith, now deceased, was a cherished friend and a constant source of information about modern Africa. Art Goldschmidt has been of invaluable assistance in reading several chapters of the manuscript, as well as in unraveling many of the mysteries of Middle Eastern civilization. Finally, he remains profoundly grateful to his wife, Yvonne V. Duiker, Ph.D. She has not only given her usual measure of love and support when this appeared to be an insuperable task, but she has also contributed her own time and expertise to enrich the sections on art and literature, thereby adding life and sparkle to this, as well as the earlier edition of the book. To her, and to his daughters Laura and Claire, he will be forever thankful for bringing joy to his life.

Jackson Spielvogel would like to thank Art Goldschmidt, David Redles, and Christine Colin for their time and ideas and, above all, his family for their support. The gifts of love, laughter, and patience from his daughters, Jennifer and Kathryn, his sons, Eric and Christian, and his daughters-in-law, Liz and Laurie, were invaluable. Diane, his wife and best friend, provided him with editorial assistance, wise counsel, and the loving support that made a project of this magnitude possible.

Thanks to Wadsworth's comprehensive review process, many historians were asked to evaluate our manuscript. We are grateful to the following for the innumerable suggestions that have greatly improved our work:

Henry Abramson
  Florida Atlantic University
Eric H. Ash
  Wayne State University
William Bakken
  Rochester Community College
Suzanne Balch-Lindsay
  Eastern New Mexico University
Michael E. Birdwell
  Tennessee Technological University
Eileen Brown
  Norwalk Community College
Thomas Cardoza
  University of California, San Diego
Wade Dudley
  East Carolina University
E. J. Fabyan
  Vincennes University
Janine C. Hartman
  University of Connecticut
Sanders Huguenin
  University of Science and Arts of Oklahoma
C. Barden Keeler
  Gulf Coast High School
Marilynn Fox Kokoszka
  Orchard Ridge Campus, Oakland Community College
James Krippner-Martinez
  Haverford College

David Leinweber
  Oxford College, Emory University
Daniel Miller
  Calvin College
Michael Murdock
  Brigham Young University
Elsa A. Nystrom
  Kennesaw State University
Randall L. Pouwels
  University of Central Arkansas
Pamela Sayre
  Henry Ford Community College
Philip Curtis Skaggs
  Grand Valley State University
Laura Smoller
  University of Arkansas at Little Rock
Beatrice Spade
  University of Southern Colorado
Jeremy Stahl
  Middle Tennessee State University
Kate Transchel
  California State University, Chico
Lorna VanMeter
  Ball State University
Michelle White
  University of Tennessee at Chattanooga

The authors are truly grateful to the people who have helped us produce this book. We especially want to thank Clark Baxter, whose faith in our ability to do this project was inspiring. Sue Gleason thoughtfully guided the overall development of the second edition, and Paul Massicotte orchestrated the preparation of outstanding teaching and learning ancillaries. Mark Colucci and Pat Lewis were, as usual, outstanding copy editors. Sarah Evertson provided valuable assistance in obtaining permissions for the illustrations. We are grateful to the staff of New England Typographic Service for providing their array of typesetting and page layout abilities. John Orr, of Orr Book Services, was as cooperative and cheerful as he was competent in matters of production management.

A Note to Students about Languages and the Dating of Time

One of the most difficult challenges in studying world history is coming to grips with the multitude of names, words, and phrases in unfamiliar languages. Unfortunately, this problem has no easy solution. We have tried to alleviate the difficulty, where possible, by providing an English-language translation of foreign words or phrases, a glossary, and a pronunciation guide. The issue is especially complicated in the case of Chinese, since two separate systems are commonly used to transliterate the spoken Chinese language into the Roman alphabet. The Wade-Giles system, invented in the nineteenth century, was the most frequently used until recent years, when the pinyin system was adopted by the People's Republic of China as its own official form of transliteration. We have opted to use the latter, since it appears to be gaining acceptance in the United States, but the initial use of a Chinese word is accompanied by its Wade-Giles equivalent in parentheses for the benefit of those who may encounter the term in their outside reading.

In our examination of world history, we need also to be aware of the dating of time. In recording the past, historians try to determine the exact time when events occurred. World War II in Europe, for example, began on September 1, 1939, when Adolf Hitler sent German troops into Poland, and ended on May 7, 1945, when Germany surrendered. By using dates, historians can place events in order and try to determine the development of patterns over periods of time.

If someone asked you when you were born, you would reply with a number, such as 1985. In the United States, we would all accept that number without question, because it is part of the dating system followed in the Western world (Europe and the Western Hemisphere). In this system, events are dated by counting backward or forward from the birth of Christ (assumed to be the year 1). An event that took place 400 years before the birth of Christ would most commonly be dated 400 B.C. (before Christ). Dates after the birth of Christ are labeled as A.D. These letters stand for the Latin words *anno domini*, which mean "in the year of the Lord" (or the year of the birth of Christ). Thus an event that took place 250 years after the birth of Christ is written A.D. 250, or in the year of the Lord 250. It can also be written as 250, just as you would not give your birth year as A.D. 1985, but simply 1985.

Some historians now prefer to use the abbreviations B.C.E. ("before the common era") and C.E. ("common era") instead of B.C. and A.D. This is especially true of world historians who prefer to use symbols that are not so Western or Christian oriented. The dates, of course, remain the same. Thus, 1950 B.C.E. and 1950 B.C. would be the same year, as would A.D. 40 and 40 C.E. In keeping with the current usage by many world historians, this book will use the terms B.C.E. and C.E.

Historians also make use of other terms to refer to time. A decade is 10 years; a century is 100 years; and a millennium is 1,000 years. The phrase fourth century B.C.E. refers to the fourth period of 100 years counting backward from 1, the assumed date of the birth of Christ. Since the first century B.C.E. would be the years 100 B.C.E. to 1 B.C.E., the fourth century B.C.E. would be the years 400 B.C.E. to 301 B.C.E. We could say, then, that an event in 350 B.C.E. took place in the fourth century B.C.E.

The phrase fourth century C.E. refers to the fourth period of 100 years after the birth of Christ. Since the first period of 100 years would be the years 1 to 100, the fourth period or fourth century would be the years 301 to 400. We could say, then, for example, that an event in 350 took place in the fourth century. Likewise, the first millennium B.C.E. refers to the years 1000 B.C.E. to 1 B.C.E.; the second millennium C.E. refers to the years 1001 to 2000.

The dating of events can also vary from people to people. Most people in the Western world use the Western calendar, also known as the Gregorian calendar after Pope Gregory XIII who refined it in 1582. The Hebrew calendar, on the other hand, uses a different system in which the year one is the equivalent of the Western year 3760 B.C.E., considered by Jews to be the date of the creation of the world. Thus, the Western year 2003 will be the year 5763 on the Jewish calendar. The Islamic calendar begins year 1 on the day Muhammad fled Mecca, which is the year 622 on the Western calendar.

THEMES FOR UNDERSTANDING WORLD HISTORY

*I*n examining the past, historians often organize their material on the basis of themes that enable them to ask and try to answer basic questions about the past. The following ten themes are especially important.

1. *Political systems*. The study of politics seeks to answer certain basic questions that historians have about the structure of a society: How were people governed? What was the relationship between the ruler and the ruled? What people or groups of people (the political elites) held political power? What actions did people take to change their form of government? Historians also examine the causes and results of wars in order to understand the impact of war on human development.

2. *The role of ideas*. Ideas have great power to move people to action. For example, in the twentieth century, the idea of nationalism, which is based on a belief in loyalty to one's nation, helped produce two great conflicts—World War I and World War II. Together these wars cost the lives of more than fifty million people. The spread of ideas from one society to another has also played an important role in world history. From the earliest times, trade has especially served to bring different civilizations into contact with one another, and the transmission of religious and cultural ideas soon followed.

3. *Economics and history*. A society depends for its existence on certain basic needs. How did it grow its food? How did it make its goods? How did it provide the services people needed? How did individual people and governments use their limited resources? Did they spend more money on hospitals or military forces? By answering these questions, historians examine the different economic systems that have played a role in history.

4. *Social life and gender issues*. From a study of social life, we learn about the different social classes that make up a society. But we also examine how people dressed and found shelter, how and what they ate, and what they did for fun. The nature of family life and how knowledge was passed from one generation to another through education are also part of the social life of a society. So, too, are gender issues: What different roles did men and women play in their societies? How and why were those roles different?

5. *The importance of culture*. We cannot understand a society without looking at its culture, or the common ideas, beliefs, and patterns of behavior that are passed on from one generation to another. Culture includes both high culture and popular culture. High culture consists of the writings of a society's thinkers and the works of its artists. A society's popular culture is the world of ideas and experiences of ordinary people. Today the media have embraced the term *popular culture* to describe the most current trends and fashionable styles.

6. *Religion in history*. Throughout history, people have sought to find a deeper meaning to human life. How have the world's great religions, such as Hinduism, Buddhism, Judaism, Christianity, and Islam, influenced people's lives? How have these religions spread to create new patterns of culture?

7. *The role of individuals*. In discussing the role of politics, ideas, economics, social life, cultural developments, and religion, we have dealt with groups of people and forces that often seem beyond the control of any one person. But mentioning the names of Cleopatra, Queen Elizabeth I, Napoleon, and Hitler reminds us of the role of individuals in history. Decisive actions by powerful individuals have indeed played a crucial role in the course of history.

8. *The impact of science and technology*. For thousands of years, people around the world have made scientific discoveries and technological innovations that have changed our world. From the creation of stone tools that made farming easier to the advanced computers that guide our airplanes, science and technology have altered how humans have related to their world.

9. *The environment and history*. Throughout history, peoples and societies have been affected by the physical world in which they live. Climatic changes alone have been an important factor in human history. Peoples and societies, in turn, have also made an impact on their world. Human activities have affected the physical environment and even endangered the very existence of entire societies and species.

10. *The migration of peoples*. One characteristic of world history is an almost constant migration of peoples. Vast numbers of peoples abandoned their homelands and sought to live elsewhere. Sometimes the migration was peaceful. More often than not, however, the migration meant invasion and violent conflict.

Part III

THE EMERGENCE OF NEW WORLD PATTERNS

(1400–1800)

Beginning in the fifteenth century, a new force entered the world scene in the form of a revived Europe. The period of history known as the early modern era (1400–1800) was marked in Europe by an explosion of scientific knowledge and the appearance of a new secular ideology that emphasized the power of human beings to dominate nature and improve their material surroundings. After the breakdown of Christian unity in the Reformation era, Europeans engaged in a vigorous period of state building that resulted in the creation of independent monarchies in western and central Europe, which formed the basis for a new European state system.

The rise of early modern Europe had an immediate as well as a long-term impact on the rest of the world. The first stage began with the discovery of the Americas by Christopher Columbus in 1492 and the equally important voyages of Vasco da Gama and Ferdinand Magellan into the Indian and Pacific Oceans. These voyages and those that followed in this so-called Age of Discovery or Age of Exploration not only injected European sea power into new areas of the world but also vastly extended the maritime trade network until for the first time it literally encircled the globe. Some historians have characterized this period as the beginning of an era of European dominance.

Significant as it was, however, the emergence of Europe as a major player on the world stage was by no means the only important feature of this period. An excessive emphasis on the expanding European civilization tends to overlook the fact that other areas of the world were realizing impressive achievements of their own. Two great new Islamic empires, founded by the Ottomans in Turkey and the Safavids in Persia, arose in the Middle East, while a third, that of the Mughals, unified the Indian subcontinent for the first time in nearly two thousand years. Islam was now firmly established in Africa south of the Sahara and in Asia as far east as the Indonesian archipelago.

In most of Asia, the European revival had only minimal effects. Portuguese merchants reached the coast of China in the early sixteenth century and landed on the islands of Japan a generation later. Merchants and missionaries from various European countries were active in both countries by the end of the century. But the ruling authorities in China and Japan, like their counterparts in the mainland states in Southeast Asia, became increasingly wary of the impact of Europeans' activities on their own societies, and by the eighteenth century, the Western presence in the region had markedly declined.

The first thrust of European expansion, then, significantly changed the face of the world, but it did not firmly establish European dominance. China remained, in the eyes of many, the most advanced and most sophisticated civilization on earth, and its achievements were imitated by its neighbors and admired by philosophers in far-off Europe. The era of Muslim dominance over the seas had come to an end, but Islam was still a force to be reckoned with. The bulk of Africa remained essentially outside the purview of European influence.

Photo Vatican Museums

RENEWAL, REFORM, AND STATE BUILDING IN EUROPE

FOCUS QUESTIONS

- What were the main features of the Renaissance, and how did it differ from the Middle Ages?
- What were the main tenets of Lutheranism and Calvinism, and how did they differ from each other and from Catholicism?
- Why is the period between 1560 and 1650 in Europe called an age of crisis, and how did the turmoil contribute to the artistic and intellectual developments of the period?
- What was absolutism, and what were the main characteristics of the absolute monarchies that merged in France, Prussia, Austria, and Russia? Why did England follow a different path?
- ➤ What did Copernicus, Kepler, Galileo, and Newton contribute to a new vision of the universe, and how did their vision differ from the Ptolemaic conception of the universe? What was the significance of this new vision?

After the disintegrative patterns of the fourteenth century, Europe began a remarkable recovery known as the Renaissance, which encompassed a revival of arts and letters in the fifteenth century, and witnessed a religious renaissance in the sixteenth century known as the Reformation. The religious division of Europe (Catholics versus Protestants) that was a result of the Reformation was instrumental in beginning a series of wars that dominated much of European history from 1560 to 1650 and exacerbated the economic and social crises that were besetting the region.

One of the responses to the crises of the seventeenth century was a search for order. The most general trend was an extension of monarchical power as a stabilizing force. This development, which historians have called absolutism or absolute monarchy, was most evident in France during the flamboyant reign of Louis XIV, regarded by some as the perfect embodiment of an absolute monarch. In his memoirs, the duc de Saint-Simon, who had first-hand experience of French court life, said that Louis was "the very figure of a hero, so imbued with a natural but most imposing majesty that it appeared even in his most insignificant gestures and movements." The king's natural grace gave him a special charm: "He was as dignified and majestic in his dressing gown as when dressed in robes of state, or on horseback at the head of his troops." He was naturally kind, and "he loved truth, justice, order, and reason." His life was orderly: "Nothing could be regulated with greater exactitude than were his days and hours." His self-control was impeccable: "He did not lose control of himself ten times in his whole life, and then only with inferior persons." But even absolute monarchs had faults, and Saint-Simon had the courage to point them out: "Louis XIV's vanity was without limit or restraint," which led to his "distaste for . . . all independence of character and sentiment in others," as well as his "mistakes of judgment in matters of importance."

The seventeenth century in Europe also witnessed the Scientific Revolution, which brought Europeans a new way of viewing the universe and their place in it. In time, the Scientific Revolution would add to Europe's growing sense of power as changes in government, the economy, and the military enabled Europeans to move out into the global stage in a dramatic fashion. •

THE RENAISSANCE

People who lived in Italy between 1350 and 1550 or so believed that they had witnessed a rebirth of classical antiquity—the world of the Greeks and Romans. To them, this marked a new age, which historians later called the Renaissance (French for "rebirth") and viewed as a distinct period of European history, which began in Italy and then spread to the rest of Europe.

Renaissance Italy was largely an urban society. The city-states became the centers of Italian political, economic, and social life. Within this new urban society, a secular spirit emerged as increasing wealth created new possibilities for the enjoyment of worldly things.

A new view of human beings emerged as people in the Italian Renaissance began to emphasize individual ability. The fifteenth-century Florentine architect Leon Battista Alberti expressed the new philosophy succinctly: "Men can do all things if they will."[1] This high regard for human worth and for individual potential gave rise to a new social ideal: the well-rounded personality or "universal person" (l'uomo universale) who was capable of achievements in many areas of life.

Renaissance Society

After the severe economic reversals and social upheavals of the fourteenth century, the European economy gradually recovered as manufacturing and trade increased in volume. The Italians and especially the Venetians expanded their wealthy commercial empire, rivaled only by the increasingly powerful Hanseatic League, a commercial and military alliance of north German coastal towns. Not until the sixteenth century, when overseas discoveries gave new importance to the states facing the Atlantic, did the Italian city-states begin to suffer from the competitive advantages of the more powerful national territorial states.

In the Middle Ages, society was divided into three estates: the clergy, or first estate (which will be examined later in this chapter); the nobility, or second estate; and the peasants and inhabitants of the towns and cities, the third estate. Although this social order continued into the Renaissance, some changes also became evident.

Throughout much of Europe, the landholding nobles faced declining real incomes during most of the fourteenth and fifteenth centuries. Many members of the old nobility survived, however, and new blood also infused its ranks. By 1500, the nobles, old and new, who constituted between 2 and 3 percent of the population in most countries, managed to dominate society, as they had done in the Middle Ages, holding important political posts and serving as advisers to the king.

Except in the heavily urban areas of northern Italy and Flanders, peasants made up the overwhelming mass of the third estate—they constituted 85 to 90 percent of the total European population. Serfdom decreased as the manorial system continued its decline. Increasingly, the labor dues owed by a peasant to his lord were converted into rents paid in money. By 1500, especially in western Europe, more and more peasants were becoming legally free.

The remainder of the third estate were inhabitants of towns and cities, originally merchants and artisans. But by the fifteenth century, the Renaissance town or city had become more complex. At the top of urban society were the patricians, whose wealth from capitalistic enterprises

MARRIAGE NEGOTIATIONS

Marriages were so important in maintaining families in Renaissance Italy that much energy was put into arranging them. Parents made the choices for their children, for considerations that had little to do with the modern notion of love. This selection is taken from the letters of a Florentine matron of the illustrious Strozzi family to her son Filippo in Naples. The family's considerations were complicated by the fact that the son was in exile.

ALESSANDRA STROZZI TO HER SON FILIPPO IN NAPLES

[April 20, 1464] Concerning the matter of a wife [for Filippo], it appears to me that if Francesco di Messer Tanagli wishes to give his daughter, that it would be a fine marriage. . . . Now I will speak with Marco [Parenti, Alessandra's son-in-law], to see if there are other prospects that would be better, and if there are none, then we will learn if he wishes to give her [in marriage]. . . . Francesco Tanagli has a good reputation, and he has held office, not the highest, but still he has been in office. You may ask: "Why should he give her to someone in exile?" There are three reasons. First, there aren't many young men of good family who have both virtue and property. Secondly, she has only a small dowry, 1,000 florins, which is the dowry of an artisan [although not a small sum, either—senior officials in the government bureaucracy earned 300 florins a year]. . . . Third, I believe that he will give her away, because he has a large family and he will need help to settle them. . . .

[July 26, 1465] Francesco is a good friend of Marco and he trusts him. On S. Jacopo's day, he spoke to him discreetly and persuasively, saying that for several months he had heard that we were interested in the girl and . . . that when we had made up our minds, she will come to us willingly. [He said that] you were a worthy man, and that his family had always made good marriages, but that he had only a small dowry to give her, and so he would prefer to send her outside of Florence to someone of worth, rather than to give her to someone here, from among those who were available, with little money. . . . We have information that she is affable and competent. She is responsible for a large family (there are twelve children, six boys and six girls), and the mother is always pregnant and isn't very competent. . . .

[August 31, 1465] I have recently received some very favorable information [about the Tanagli girl] from two individuals. . . . They are in agreement that whoever gets her will be content. . . . Concerning her beauty, they told me what I had already seen, that she is attractive and well-proportioned. Her face is long, but I couldn't look directly into her face, since she appeared to be aware that I was examining her . . . and so she turned away from me like the wind. . . . She reads quite well . . . and she can dance and sing. . . .

So yesterday I sent for Marco and told him what I had learned. And we talked about the matter for a while, and decided that he should say something to the father and give him a little hope, but not so much that we couldn't withdraw, and find out from him the amount of the dowry. . . . May God help us to choose what will contribute to our tranquility and to the consolation of us all. . . .

[September 13, 1465] Marco came to me and said that he had met with Francesco Tanagli, who had spoken very coldly, so that I understand that he had changed his mind.

[Filippo Strozzi eventually married Fiametta di Donato Adimari in 1466.]

---

in trade, industry, and banking enabled them to dominate their urban communities economically, socially, and politically. Below them were the petty burghers—the shopkeepers, artisans, guildmasters, and guildsmen—who were largely concerned with providing goods and services for local consumption. Below these two groups were the propertyless workers earning pitiful wages and the unemployed, living squalid and miserable lives. These poor city-dwellers constituted 30 to 40 percent of the urban population.

FAMILY AND MARRIAGE IN RENAISSANCE ITALY

The family bond was a source of great security in the urban world of Renaissance Italy. To maintain the family, parents carefully arranged marriages, often to strengthen business or family ties. Details were worked out well in advance, sometimes when children were only two or three, and reinforced by a legally binding marriage contract (see the box above).

The father-husband was the center of the Italian family. He gave it his name, managed all finances (his wife had no share in his wealth), and made the crucial decisions that determined his children's lives. A father's authority over his children was absolute until he died or formally freed his children. In Renaissance Italy, children did not become adults on reaching a certain age; adulthood came only when the father went before a judge and formally emancipated them. The age of emancipation varied from early teens to late twenties.

The wife managed the household, a position that gave women a certain degree of autonomy in their daily lives. Most wives, however, also knew that their primary function was to bear children. Upper-class wives were frequently pregnant; Alessandra Strozzi of Florence, for example, who had been married at the age of sixteen, bore eight children in ten years. For women in the Renaissance, childbirth was a fearful occasion. Not only was it painful, but it could be deadly; possibly as many as one woman in ten died in childbirth.

The Intellectual Renaissance

The emergence and growth of individualism and secularism as characteristics of the Italian Renaissance are most noticeable in the intellectual and artistic realms. The most important literary movement associated with the Renaissance is humanism.

ITALIAN RENAISSANCE HUMANISM

Renaissance humanism was an intellectual movement based on the study of the classics, the literary works of Greece and Rome. Humanists studied the liberal arts—grammar, rhetoric, poetry, moral philosophy or ethics, and history—all based on the writings of ancient Greek and Roman authors. We call these subjects the humanities.

Petrarch (1304–1374), who has often been called the father of Italian Renaissance humanism, did more than any other individual in the fourteenth century to foster the development of Renaissance humanism. Petrarch sought to find forgotten Latin manuscripts and set in motion a ransacking of monastic libraries throughout Europe. He also began the humanist emphasis on the use of pure classical Latin. Humanists used the works of Cicero as a model for prose and those of Virgil for poetry. As Petrarch said, "Christ is my God; Cicero is the prince of the language."

In Florence, the humanist movement took a new direction at the beginning of the fifteenth century. The humanists who worked as secretaries for the city council of Florence took a new interest in civic life. They came to believe that it was the duty of an intellectual to live an active life for one's state. Humanists came to believe that their study of the humanities should be put to the service of the state.

Also evident in the humanism of the first half of the fifteenth century was a growing interest in classical Greek civilization. One of the first Italian humanists to gain a thorough knowledge of Greek was Leonardo Bruni, who became an enthusiastic pupil of the Byzantine scholar Manuel Chrysoloras, who taught in Florence from 1396 to 1400.

THE IMPACT OF PRINTING

The Renaissance witnessed the development of printing, which made an immediate impact on European intellectual life and thought. Printing from hand-carved wooden blocks had been done in the West since the twelfth century and in China even before that. What was new in the fifteenth century in Europe was multiple printing with movable metal type. The development of printing with movable type was a gradual process that culminated some time between 1445 and 1450; Johannes Gutenberg of Mainz played an important role in bringing the process to completion. Gutenberg's Bible, completed in 1455 or 1456, was the first true book produced using movable type.

By 1500, there were more than a thousand printers in Europe, who collectively had published almost forty thousand titles (between eight and ten million copies). Probably 50 percent of these books were religious—Bibles and biblical commentaries, books of devotion, and sermons.

The printing of books encouraged the development of scholarly research and the desire to attain knowledge. Printing also stimulated the development of an ever-expanding lay reading public, a development that had an enormous impact on European society. Printing allowed European civilization to compete for the first time with the civilization of China.

The Artistic Renaissance

Renaissance artists sought to imitate nature in their works of art. Their search for naturalism became an end in itself: to persuade onlookers of the reality of the object or event they were portraying. At the same time, the new artistic standards reflected the new attitude of mind in which human beings became the focus of attention, the "center and measure of all things," as one artist proclaimed.

The new Renaissance style was developed by Florentine painters in the fifteenth century. Especially important were two major developments. One emphasized the technical side of painting—understanding the laws of perspective and the geometrical organization of space and light. The second development was the investigation of movement and anatomical structure. The realistic portrayal of the human nude became one of the foremost preoccupations of Italian Renaissance art. By the end of the fifteenth century, Italian painters had created a new artistic environment. Many artists had mastered the new techniques for a scientific observation of the world around them and were now ready to move into new forms of creative expression. This marked the shift to the High Renaissance.

The High Renaissance was dominated by the work of three artistic giants, Leonardo da Vinci (1452–1519), Raphael (1483–1520), and Michelangelo (1475–1564). Leonardo carried on the fifteenth-century experimental tradition by studying everything and even dissecting human bodies in order to see how nature worked. But Leonardo stressed the need to advance beyond such realism and initiated the High Renaissance's preoccupation with the idealization of nature, an attempt to generalize from realistic portrayal to an ideal form.

At twenty-five, Raphael was already regarded as one of Italy's best painters. He was acclaimed for his numerous Madonnas, in which he attempted to achieve an ideal of beauty far surpassing human standards. He is well known for his frescoes in the Vatican Palace; his *School of Athens* reveals a world of balance, harmony, and order—the underlying principles of the art of the classical world of Greece and Rome.

Michelangelo, an accomplished painter, sculptor, and architect, was fiercely driven by a desire to create, and he worked with great passion and energy on a remarkable number of projects. Michelangelo was influenced by Neoplatonism, especially evident in his figures on the ceiling of the Sistine Chapel. These muscular figures reveal an ideal type of human being with perfect proportions. In good Neoplatonic fashion, their beauty is meant to be a reflection of divine beauty; the more beautiful the body, the more God-like the figure.

The State in the Renaissance

In the second half of the fifteenth century, attempts were made to reestablish the centralized power of monarchical governments after the political disasters of the fourteenth century. Some historians called these states the "new monarchies," especially those of France, England, and Spain (see Map 13.1).

WESTERN EUROPE

The Hundred Years' War left France prostrate. But the war had also developed a degree of French national feeling toward a common enemy that the kings could use to reestablish monarchical power. The development of a French territorial state was greatly advanced by King Louis XI (1461–1483), known as the Spider because of his wily and devious ways. Louis strengthened the use of the *taille*—an annual direct tax usually on land or property—as a permanent tax imposed by royal authority, giving him a sound, regular source of income, which created the foundations of a strong French monarchy.

The Hundred Years' War had also strongly affected the English. The cost of the war in its final years and the losses to the labor force strained the English economy. At the end of the war, England faced even greater turmoil when a civil war, known as the War of the Roses, erupted and aristocratic factions fought over the monarchy until 1485, when Henry Tudor established a new dynasty.

As the first Tudor king, Henry VII (1485–1509) worked to establish a strong monarchical government. Henry ended the private wars of the nobility by abolishing their private armies. By not overburdening the nobility and the middle class with taxes, Henry won their favor, and they provided him with much support.

Spain, too, experienced the growth of a strong national monarchy by the end of the fifteenth century. During the Middle Ages, several independent Christian kingdoms had emerged in the course of the long reconquest of the Iberian peninsula from the Muslims. Two of the strongest were Aragon and Castile. When Isabella of Castile (1474–1504) married Ferdinand of Aragon (1479–1516) in 1469, it was a major step toward unifying Spain. The two rulers worked to strengthen royal control of the government.

Ferdinand and Isabella also pursued a policy of strict religious uniformity. Spain possessed two large religious minorities, the Jews and the Muslims, both of which had been largely tolerated in medieval Spain. Increased persecution in the fourteenth century, however, led most Spanish Jews to convert to Catholicism. In 1492, Ferdinand and Isabella took the drastic step of expelling all professed Jews from Spain. Muslims, too, were then "encouraged" to convert to Catholicism, and in 1502,

MICHELANGELO, *CREATION OF ADAM*.   In 1508, Pope Julius II recalled Michelangelo to Rome and commissioned him to decorate the ceiling of the Sistine Chapel. This colossal project was not completed until 1512. Michelangelo attempted to tell the story of the Fall of Man by depicting nine scenes from the biblical Book of Genesis. In this scene, the well-proportioned figure of Adam, meant by Michelangelo to be a reflection of divine beauty, awaits the divine spark.

Photo Vatican Museums

MAP 13.1 Europe in the Fifteenth Century. By the second half of the fifteenth century, states in western Europe, particularly France, Spain, and England, had begun the process of modern state building. With varying success, they reined in the power of the church and nobles, increased their ability to levy taxes, and established effective government bureaucracies. ➤ *What aspects of Europe's political boundaries help explain why France and the Holy Roman Empire were often at war with each other?*

Isabella issued a decree expelling all professed Muslims from her kingdom.

CENTRAL AND EASTERN EUROPE

Unlike France, England, and Spain, the Holy Roman Empire failed to develop a strong monarchical authority. The failure of the German emperors in the thirteenth century ended any chance of centralized monarchical authority, and Germany became a land of hundreds of virtually independent states. After 1438, the position of Holy Roman Emperor was held in the hands of the Habsburg dynasty. Having gradually acquired a number of possessions along the Danube, known collectively as Austria, the house of Habsburg had become one of the wealthiest landholders in the empire and by the mid-fifteenth century had begun to play an important role in European affairs.

In eastern Europe, rulers struggled to achieve the centralization of territorial states. Religious differences troubled the area, as Roman Catholics, Eastern Orthodox Christians, and other groups, including the Mongols, confronted each other. In Poland, the nobles gained the upper hand and established the right to elect their kings, a policy that drastically weakened royal authority. In Hungary, King Matthias Corvinus (1458–1490) broke the power of the wealthy lords and created a well-organized central administration. After his death, his work was largely undone.

Since the thirteenth century, Russia had been under the domination of the Mongols. Gradually, the princes of Moscow rose to prominence by using their close relationship to the Mongol khans to increase their wealth and expand their possessions. During the reign of the great Prince Ivan III (1462–1505), a new Russian state was born.

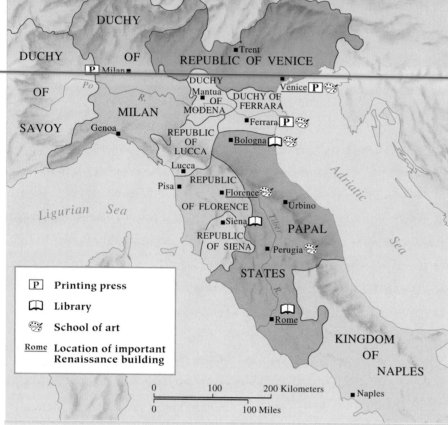

MAP 13.2 Renaissance Italy. Italy in the late fourteenth century was a land of five major states and numerous independent city-states. Increased prosperity and a supportive intellectual climate helped create the atmosphere for the middle and upper classes to "rediscover" Greco-Roman culture. Modern diplomacy is also a product of Renaissance Italy. ➤ *Could the presence of several other powers within easy marching distance make a ruler recognize the importance of diplomacy?*

- **P** Printing press
- 📖 Library
- 🎨 School of art
- <u>Rome</u> Location of important Renaissance building

Milan, located at the crossroads of the main trade routes from Italian coast cities to the Alpine passes, was one of the richest city-states in Italy. In the fourteenth century, members of the Visconti family established themselves as dukes of Milan and extended their power over all of Lombardy. In 1447, a *condottiere* (leader of a mercenary band) named Francesco Sforza conquered the city and became its new duke. Both Visconti and Sforza rulers worked to create the institutions of a strongly centralized territorial state.

The other major northern Italian state was the republic of Venice, which had grown rich from trade throughout the eastern Mediterranean and into northern Europe. A small oligarchy of merchant-aristocrats, who had become extremely wealthy through their commercial activities, ran the Venetian government on behalf of their own interests. Venice's commercial empire brought in enormous revenues and gave it the status of an international power.

The republic of Florence dominated the region of Tuscany. In the course of the fourteenth century, a small but wealthy merchant oligarchy gained control of the Florentine government and established Florence as a major territorial state in northern Italy. In 1434, Cosimo de' Medici (1434–1464) took control of the ruling oligarchy. Although the wealthy Medici family maintained republican forms of government for appearance's sake, it ran the government from behind the scenes.

The growth of powerful monarchical states led to trouble for the Italians and brought an end to the independence of the Italian states. Attracted by the riches of Italy, the French king Charles VIII (1483–1498) led an army of thirty thousand men into Italy and occupied the kingdom of Naples. Other Italian states turned for help to the Spanish, who gladly complied. For the next thirty years, the French and Spanish competed to dominate Italy. The terrible sack of Rome in 1527 by the armies of the Spanish king Charles I brought a temporary end to the Italian wars. Thereafter the Spaniards dominated Italy.

Ivan III annexed other Russian principalities and took advantage of dissension among the Mongols to throw off their yoke by 1480.

THE ITALIAN STATES

During the Middle Ages, Italy had failed to develop a centralized monarchical state. Moreover, the kingdom of Naples in the south was dominated by the French house of Anjou, Sicily was ruled by the Spanish house of Aragon, and the papacy remained in shaky control of much of central Italy as rulers of the Papal States. Lack of centralized authority had enabled numerous city-states in northern and central Italy to remain independent of any political authority. Three of them—Milan, Venice, and Florence—managed to become fairly well centralized territorial states (see Map 13.2).

Chronology

THE STATE IN THE RENAISSANCE

MACHIAVELLI AND THE NEW STATECRAFT

No one gave better expression to the Italians' preoccupation with political power than Niccolò Machiavelli (1469–1527), who wrote *The Prince* (1513), one of the most influential works on political power in the Western world. Machiavelli's major concerns in *The Prince* were the acquisition, maintenance, and expansion of political power as the means to restore and maintain order in his time. In the Middle Ages, many political theorists stressed the ethical side of a prince's activity—how a ruler ought to behave based on Christian moral principles. Machiavelli bluntly contradicted this approach: "For the gap between how people actually behave and how they ought to behave is so great that anyone who ignores everyday reality in order to live up to an ideal will soon discover he had been taught how to destroy himself, not how to preserve himself."[2] Machiavelli considered his approach far more realistic than that of his medieval forebears. Political activity, therefore, could not be restricted by moral considerations. The prince acts on behalf of the state and for the sake of the state must be willing to let his con-

science sleep. Machiavelli was among the first to abandon morality as the basis for the analysis of political activity.

THE REFORMATION OF THE SIXTEENTH CENTURY

The Protestant Reformation is the name given to the religious reform movement that divided the western church into Catholic and Protestant groups. Although Martin Luther began the Reformation in the early sixteenth century, several earlier developments had set the stage for religious change.

Prelude to Reformation

During the second half of the fifteenth century, the new classical learning of the Italian Renaissance spread to the European countries north of the Alps and spawned a movement called Christian humanism or Northern Renaissance humanism, whose major goal was the reform of Christendom. The Christian humanists believed in the ability of human beings to reason and improve themselves and thought that through education in the sources of classical, and especially Christian, antiquity, they could instill an inner piety or an inward religious feeling that would bring about a reform of the church and society. To change society, they believed, you must first change the human beings who compose it.

The most influential of all the Christian humanists was Desiderius Erasmus (1466–1536), who formulated and popularized the reform program of Christian humanism. He called his conception of religion "the philosophy of Christ," by which he meant that Christianity should be a guiding philosophy for the direction of daily life rather than the system of dogmatic beliefs and practices that the medieval church seemed to stress. No doubt his work helped prepare the way for the Reformation; as contemporaries proclaimed, "Erasmus laid the egg that Luther hatched."

Corruption in the Catholic church was another factor that encouraged people to want reform. Between 1450 and 1520, a series of popes—called the Renaissance popes—failed to meet the church's spiritual needs. The popes were supposed to be the spiritual leaders of the Catholic church but as leaders of the Papal States were all too often involved in worldly interests. Julius II (1503–1513), the fiery "warrior-pope," personally led armies against his enemies, much to the disgust of pious Christians, who viewed the pope as a spiritual leader. As one intellectual wrote, "How, O bishop standing in the room of the Apostles, dare you teach the people the things that pertain to war?" Many high church officials were also concerned with money and used their church offices as opportunities to advance their careers and their wealth, and many ordinary parish priests seemed ignorant of their spiritual duties.

While the leaders of the church were failing to meet their responsibilities, ordinary people were clamoring for meaningful religious expression and certainty of salvation. As a result, for some, the process of salvation became almost mechanical. Collections of relics grew as more and more people sought certainty of salvation through veneration of these relics. Frederick the Wise, elector of Saxony and Martin Luther's prince, had amassed over five thousand relics to which were attached indulgences that could reduce one's time in purgatory by 1,443 years. (An indulgence is a remission, after death, of all or part of the punishment due to sin.)

Martin Luther and the Reformation in Germany

Martin Luther was a monk and a professor at the University of Wittenberg, where he lectured on the Bible. Probably sometime between 1513 and 1516, through his study of the Bible, he arrived at an answer to a problem—the assurance of salvation—that had disturbed him since his entry into the monastery.

Catholic doctrine had emphasized that both faith and good works were required of a Christian to achieve personal salvation. In Luther's eyes, human beings, weak and powerless in the sight of an almighty God, could never do enough good works to merit salvation. Through his study of the Bible, Luther came to believe that humans are not saved through their good works but through faith in the promises of God, made possible by the sacrifice of Jesus on the cross. This doctrine of salvation, or justification by grace through faith alone, became the primary doctrine of the Protestant Reformation. Because Luther had arrived at this doctrine from his study of the Bible, the Bible became for Luther, as for all other Protestants, the chief guide to religious truth.

Luther did not see himself as a rebel, but he was greatly upset by the widespread selling of indulgences. Especially offensive in his eyes was the monk Johann Tetzel, who hawked indulgences with the slogan "As soon as the coin in the coffer [money box] rings, the soul from purgatory springs." Greatly angered, in 1517, Luther issued a stunning indictment of the abuses in the sale of indulgences—the Ninety-Five Theses. Thousands of copies were printed and quickly spread to all parts of Germany.

Unable to accept Luther's ideas, the church excommunicated him in January 1521. He had also been summoned in 1520 to appear before the imperial diet or Reichstag of the Holy Roman Empire, convened by the newly elected Emperor Charles V (1519–1556). Ordered to recant the heresies he had espoused, Luther refused and made the famous reply that became the battle cry of the Reformation:

> Unless I am convicted by Scripture and plain reason—I do not accept the authority of popes and councils, for they have contradicted each other—my conscience is captive to the Word of God. I cannot and I will not recant anything, for to go against conscience is neither right nor safe. Here I stand, I cannot do otherwise. God help me. Amen.[3]

Members of the Reichstag were outraged and demanded that Luther be captured and delivered to the emperor. But Luther's ruler, Elector Frederick of Saxony, stepped in and protected him.

During the next few years, Luther's religious movement became a revolution. Luther was able to gain the support of many of the German rulers among the three hundred or so states that made up the Holy Roman Empire. These rulers quickly took control of the churches in their territories. The Lutheran churches in Germany (and later in Scandinavia) quickly became territorial or state churches in which the state supervised the affairs of the church. As part of the development of these state-dominated churches, Luther also instituted new religious services to replace the Catholic Mass. These focused on Bible reading, preaching of the word of God, and song.

From its very beginning, the fate of Luther's movement was closely tied to political affairs. In 1519, Charles I, king of Spain and the grandson of Emperor Maximilian, was elected Holy Roman Emperor as Charles V. Charles V ruled over an immense empire, consisting of Spain and its overseas possessions, the traditional Austrian Habsburg lands, Bohemia, Hungary, the Low Countries, and the kingdom of Naples in southern Italy. Politically, Charles wanted to maintain his enormous empire; religiously, he hoped to preserve the unity of his empire in the Catholic faith.

However, the internal political situation in the Holy Roman Empire was not in Charles's favor. Germany was a land of several hundred territorial states. Although all owed loyalty to the emperor, in the Middle Ages these states had become quite independent of imperial authority. By the time Charles V was able to bring military forces to Germany in 1546, Lutheranism had become well established and the Lutheran princes were well organized. Unable to defeat them, Charles was forced to negotiate a truce. An end to religious warfare in Germany came in 1555 with the Peace of Augsburg. The division of Christianity was formally acknowledged; Lutheran states were to have the same legal rights as Catholic states. Although the German states were now free to choose between Catholicism and Lutheranism, the peace settlement did not recognize the principle of religious toleration for individuals. The right of each German ruler to determine the religion of his subjects was accepted, but not the right of the subjects to choose their own religion.

The Spread of the Protestant Reformation

With the Peace of Augsburg, what had at first been merely feared was now certain: the ideal of Christian unity was forever lost. The rapid spread of new Protestant groups made this a certainty.

⇒ WOODCUT: LUTHER VERSUS THE POPE. In the 1520s, after Luther's return to Wittenberg, his teachings began to spread rapidly, ending ultimately in a reform movement supported by state authorities. Pamphlets containing picturesque woodcuts were important in the spread of Luther's ideas. In the woodcut shown here, the crucified Jesus attends Luther's service on the left, while on the right, the pope is at a table selling indulgences.

CALVIN AND CALVINISM

John Calvin (1509–1564) was educated in his native France but after his conversion to Protestantism was forced to flee for the safety of Switzerland. In 1536, he published the first edition of the *Institutes of the Christian Religion*, a masterful synthesis of Protestant thought that immediately secured Calvin's reputation as one of the new leaders of Protestantism.

On most important doctrines, Calvin stood very close to Luther. He adhered to the doctrine of justification by faith alone to explain how humans achieved salvation. But Calvin also placed much emphasis on the absolute sovereignty of God or the all-powerful nature of God—what Calvin called the "power, grace, and glory of God." One of the ideas derived from his emphasis on the absolute sovereignty of God—predestination—gave a unique cast to Calvin's teachings. This "eternal decree," as Calvin called it, meant that God had predestined some people to be saved (the elect) and others to be damned (the reprobate). According to Calvin, "He has once for all determined, both whom He would admit to salvation, and whom He would condemn to destruction."[4] Although Calvin stressed that there could be no absolute certainty of salvation, his followers did not always make this distinction. The practical psychological effect of predestination was to

give later Calvinists an unshakable conviction that they were doing God's work on earth, making Calvinism a dynamic and activist faith.

In 1536, Calvin began working to reform the city of Geneva. He was able to fashion a tightly organized church order that employed both clergy and laymen in the service of the church. The Consistory, a special body for enforcing moral discipline, functioned as a court to oversee the moral life, daily behavior, and doctrinal orthodoxy of Genevans and to admonish and correct deviants. Citizens in Geneva were punished for such varied "crimes" as dancing, singing obscene songs, drunkenness, swearing, and playing cards.

Calvin's success in Geneva enabled the city to become a vibrant center of Protestantism. Following Calvin's lead, missionaries trained in Geneva were sent to all parts of Europe. Calvinism became established in France, the Netherlands, Scotland, and central and eastern Europe, and by the mid-sixteenth century, Calvin's Geneva stood as the fortress of the Reformation.

THE ENGLISH REFORMATION

The English Reformation was rooted in politics, not religion. King Henry VIII (1509–1547) had a strong desire to divorce his first wife, Catherine of Aragon, with whom the king had a daughter, Mary, but no male heir. He wanted to marry Anne Boleyn, with whom he had fallen in love. Impatient with the pope's unwillingness to grant him an annulment of his marriage, Henry turned to England's own church courts. As archbishop of Canterbury and head of the highest church court in England, Thomas Cranmer ruled in May 1533 that the king's marriage to Catherine was "absolutely void." At the beginning of June, Anne was crowned queen, and three months later, a child was born—a girl (the future queen Elizabeth I), much to the king's disappointment.

In 1534, at Henry's request, Parliament moved to finalize the break of the Church of England with Rome. The Act of Supremacy of 1534 declared that the king was "the only supreme head on earth of the Church of England," a position that gave him control of doctrine, clerical appointments, and discipline. Although Henry VIII had broken with the papacy, little change occurred in matters of doctrine, theology, and ceremony. Some of his supporters, including Archbishop Cranmer, sought a religious reformation as well as an administrative one, but Henry was unyielding. But he died in 1547 and was succeeded by his son, the underage and sickly Edward VI (1547–1553). During Edward's reign, Cranmer and others inclined toward Protestant doctrines were able to move the Church of England (or Anglican church) in a more Protestant direction. New acts of Parliament gave the clergy the right to marry and created a new Protestant church service.

Edward VI was succeeded by Mary (1553–1558), a Catholic who attempted to return England to Catholicism. Her actions aroused much anger, however, especially when "Bloody Mary" burned more than three hundred Protestant heretics. By the end of Mary's reign, England was more Protestant than it had been at the beginning.

The Catholic Reformation

By the mid-sixteenth century, Lutheranism had become established in Germany and Scandinavia and Calvinism in Switzerland, France, the Netherlands, and eastern Europe. In England, the split from Rome had resulted in the creation of a national church. The situation in Europe did not look particularly favorable to the Roman Catholic church. However, the Catholic church also underwent a revitalization in the sixteenth century, giving it new strength. There were three chief pillars of the Catholic Reformation: the Jesuits, a reformed papacy, and the Council of Trent.

The Society of Jesus, known as the Jesuits, was founded by a Spanish nobleman, Ignatius of Loyola (1491–1556). Loyola gathered together a small group of individuals who were recognized as a religious order by the pope in 1540. The new order was grounded on the principles of absolute obedience to the papacy, a strict hierarchical order for the society, the use of education to achieve its goals, and a dedication to engage in "conflict for God." A special vow of absolute obedience to the pope made the Jesuits an important instrument for papal policy. Jesuit missionaries proved singularly successful in restoring Catholicism to parts of Germany and eastern Europe.

A reformed papacy was another important factor in the development of the Catholic Reformation. The involvement of Renaissance popes in dubious financial undertakings and Italian political and military affairs had created numerous sources of corruption. It took the jolt of the Protestant Reformation to bring about serious reform. Pope Paul III (1534–1549) perceived the need for change and took the audacious step of appointing a reform commission to ascertain the church's ills. The commission's report in 1537 blamed the church's problems on the corrupt policies of popes and cardinals. It was also Paul III who formally recognized the Jesuits and began the Council of Trent.

In March 1545, a group of high church officials met in the city of Trent on the border between Germany and Italy and initiated the Council of Trent, which met intermittently from 1545 to 1563 in three major sessions. The final decrees of the Council of Trent reaffirmed traditional Catholic teachings in opposition to Protestant beliefs. Scripture and tradition were affirmed as equal authorities in religious matters; only the church could interpret Scripture. Both faith and good works were declared necessary for salvation. Belief in purgatory and in the use of indulgences was strengthened, although the selling of indulgences was prohibited.

After the Council of Trent, the Roman Catholic church possessed a clear body of doctrine and a unified church under the acknowledged supremacy of the popes. With a new spirit of confidence, the Catholic church entered a militant phase, as well prepared as the Calvinists to do battle for the Lord. An era of religious warfare was about to unfold.

EUROPE IN CRISIS, 1560–1650

Between 1560 and 1650, Europe experienced religious wars, revolutions and constitutional crises, economic and social disintegration, and a witchcraft craze. It was truly an age of crisis.

Politics and the Wars of Religion in the Sixteenth Century

By 1560, Calvinism and Catholicism had become militant religions dedicated to spreading the word of God as they interpreted it. Although their struggle for the minds and hearts of Europeans was at the heart of the religious wars of the sixteenth century, economic, social, and political forces also played an important role in these conflicts.

THE FRENCH WARS OF RELIGION (1562–1598)

Religion was central to the French civil wars of the sixteenth century. The growth of Calvinism had led to persecution by the French kings, but the latter did little to stop the spread of Calvinism. Huguenots (as the French Calvinists were called) constituted only about 7 percent of the population, but 40 to 50 percent of the French nobility became Huguenots, including the house of Bourbon, which stood next to the Valois in the royal line of succession. The conversion of so many nobles made the Huguenots a potentially dangerous political threat to monarchical power. Still, the Calvinist minority was greatly outnumbered by the Catholic majority, and the Valois monarchy was staunchly Catholic. At the same time, an extreme Catholic party, known as the ultra-Catholics, favored strict opposition to the Huguenots.

For thirty years, battles raged in France between Catholic and Calvinist parties. Finally, in 1589, Henry of Navarre, the political leader of the Huguenots and a member of the Bourbon dynasty, succeeded to the throne as Henry IV (1589–1610). Realizing, however, that he would never be accepted by Catholic France, Henry converted to Catholicism. With his coronation in 1594, the Wars of Religion finally came to an end. The Edict of Nantes in 1598 solved the religious problem by acknowledging Catholicism as the official religion of France while guaranteeing the Huguenots the right to worship and to enjoy all political privileges.

PHILIP II AND THE CAUSE OF MILITANT CATHOLICISM

The greatest advocate of militant Catholicism in the second half of the sixteenth century was King Philip II of Spain (1556–1598), the son and heir of Charles V. Philip's reign ushered in an age of Spanish greatness, both politically and culturally. Philip II had inherited from his father Spain, the Netherlands, and possessions in Italy and the New World. To strengthen his control, Philip insisted on strict conformity to Catholicism and strong monarchical authority. Achieving the latter was not an easy task, because each of the lands of his empire had its own structure of government.

Philip's attempt to strengthen his control in the Spanish Netherlands, which consisted of seventeen provinces (modern Netherlands and Belgium), soon led to a revolt. The nobles, who stood to lose the most politically, strongly opposed Philip's efforts. Religion also became a major catalyst for rebellion when Philip attempted to crush Calvinism. Violence erupted in 1566, and the revolt became organized, especially in the northern provinces, where the Dutch, under the leadership of William of Nassau, the prince of Orange, offered growing resistance. The struggle dragged on for decades until 1609, when a twelve-year truce ended the war, virtually recognizing the independence of the northern provinces. These seven northern provinces, which called themselves the United Provinces of the Netherlands, became the core of the modern Dutch state.

To most Europeans, Spain still seemed the greatest power of the age at the beginning of the seventeenth century, but the reality was quite different. The Spanish treasury was empty; the armed forces were obsolescent; and the government was inefficient. Spain continued to play the role of a great power, but real power had shifted to England.

THE ENGLAND OF ELIZABETH

When Elizabeth Tudor, the daughter of Henry VIII and Anne Boleyn, ascended the throne in 1558, England was home to fewer than four million people. Yet during her reign, the small island kingdom became leader of the Protestant nations of Europe and laid the foundations for a world empire.

Intelligent, cautious, and self-confident, Elizabeth moved quickly to solve the difficult religious problem she inherited from her half-sister, Queen Mary. Elizabeth's religious policy was based on moderation and compromise. She repealed the Catholic laws of Mary's reign, and a new Act of Supremacy designated Elizabeth as "the only supreme governor" of both church and state. The Church of England under Elizabeth was basically Protestant, but it was of a moderate bent that kept most people satisfied.

Caution and moderation also dictated Elizabeth's foreign policy. Gradually, however, Elizabeth was drawn into conflict with Spain. Having resisted for years the idea of invading England as too impractical, Philip II of Spain was finally persuaded to do so by advisers who assured him that the people of England would rise against their queen when the Spaniards arrived. A successful invasion of England would mean the overthrow of heresy and the return of England to Catholicism. Philip ordered preparations for a fleet of warships, the Armada, to spearhead the invasion of England.

The Armada was a disaster. The Spanish fleet that finally set sail had neither the ships nor the manpower that Philip had planned to send. Battered by a number of encounters with the English, the Spanish fleet sailed back to Spain by a northward route around Scotland and Ireland, where it was further pounded by storms.

Economic and Social Crises: Witchcraft Mania

The period of European history from 1560 to 1650 witnessed severe economic and social crises as well as political upheaval. Economic contraction began to be evident in some parts of Europe by the 1620s. In the 1630s and 1640s, as imports of silver from the Americas declined, economic recession intensified, especially in the Mediterranean area. Once the industrial and financial center of Europe in the age of the Renaissance, Italy was now becoming an economic backwater.

A WITCHCRAFT TRIAL IN FRANCE

Prosecutions for witchcraft reached their high point in the sixteenth and seventeenth centuries, when tens of thousands of people were brought to trial. In this excerpt from the minutes of a trial in France in 1652, we can see why the accused witch stood little chance of exonerating herself.

THE TRIAL OF SUZANNE GAUDRY

28 May, 1652. . . . Interrogation of Suzanne Gaudry, prisoner at the court of Rieux. . . . During interrogations on May 28 and May 29, the prisoner confessed to a number of activities involving the devil.

Deliberation of the Court—June 3, 1652

The undersigned advocates of the Court have seen these interrogations and answers. They say that the aforementioned Suzanne Gaudry confesses that she is a witch, that she had given herself to the devil, that she had renounced God, Lent, and baptism, that she has been marked on the shoulder, that she has cohabited with the devil and that she has been to the dances, confessing only to have cast a spell upon and caused to die a beast of Philippe Cornié. . . .

Third Interrogation, June 27

This prisoner being led into the chamber, she was examined to know if things were not as she had said and confessed at the beginning of her imprisonment.

—Answers no, and that what she has said was done so by force.

Pressed to say the truth, that otherwise she would be subjected to torture, having pointed out to her that her aunt was burned for this same subject.

—Answers that she is not a witch. . . .

She was placed in the hands of the officer in charge of torture, throwing herself on her knees, struggling to cry, uttering several exclamations, without being able, nevertheless, to shed a tear. Saying at every moment that she is not a witch.

The Torture

On this same day, being at the place of torture.

This prisoner, before being strapped down, was admonished to maintain herself in her first confessions and to renounce her lover.

—Says that she denies everything she has said, and that she has no lover. Feeling herself being strapped down, says that she is not a witch, while struggling to cry. . . . and upon being asked why she confessed to being one, said that she was forced to say it.

Told that she was not forced, that on the contrary she declared herself to be a witch without any threat.

—Says that she confessed it and that she is not a witch, and being a little stretched [on the rack] screams ceaselessly that she is not a witch.

Asked if she did not confess that she had been a witch for twenty-six years.

—Says that she said it, that she retracts it, crying that she is not a witch.

Asked if she did not make Philippe Cornié's horse die, as she confessed.

—Answers no, crying Jesus-Maria, that she is not a witch.

The mark having been probed by the officer, in the presence of Doctor Bouchain, it was adjudged by the aforesaid doctor and officer truly to be the mark of the devil.

Being more tightly stretched upon the torture rack, urged to maintain her confessions.

—Said that it was true that she is a witch and that she would maintain what she had said.

Asked how long she has been in subjugation to the devil.

—Answers that it was twenty years ago that the devil appeared to her, being in her lodgings in the form of a man dressed in a little cowhide and black breeches. . . .

Verdict

July 9, 1652. In the light of the interrogations, answers, and investigations made into the charge against Suzanne Gaudry, . . . seeing by her own confessions that she is said to have made a pact with the devil, received the mark from him, . . . and that following this, she had renounced God, Lent, and baptism and had let herself be known carnally by him, in which she received satisfaction. Also, seeing that she is said to have been a part of nocturnal carols and dances.

For expiation of which the advice of the undersigned is that the office of Rieux can legitimately condemn the aforesaid Suzanne Gaudry to death, tying her to a gallows, and strangling her to death, then burning her body and burying it here in the environs of the woods.

Population trends of the sixteenth and seventeenth centuries also reveal Europe's worsening conditions. The population of Europe increased from 60 million in 1500 to 85 million by 1600, the first major recovery of European population since the devastation of the Black Death in the mid-fourteenth century. However, records also indicate a decline of the population by 1650, especially in central and southern Europe. Europe's longtime adversaries—war, famine, and plague—continued to affect population levels. Europe's problems created social tensions, some of which became manifested in an obsession with witches.

Hysteria over witchcraft affected the lives of many Europeans in the sixteenth and seventeenth centuries. Perhaps more than 100,000 people were prosecuted throughout Europe on charges of witchcraft. As more and more people were brought to trial, the fear of witches, as well as the fear of being accused of witchcraft, escalated to frightening levels (see the box above).

Common people—usually those who were poor and without property—were more likely to be accused of witchcraft. Indeed, where lists are given, those mentioned most often are milkmaids, peasant women, and servant girls. In the witchcraft trials of the sixteenth and seventeenth centuries, more than 75 percent of the accused were women, most of them single or widowed and many over fifty years old.

That women should be the chief victims of witchcraft trials was hardly accidental. Nicholas Rémy, a witchcraft judge in France in the 1590s, found it "not unreasonable that this scum of humanity, i.e., witches, should be drawn chiefly from the feminine sex." To another judge, it came as no surprise that witches would confess to sexual experiences with Satan: "The Devil uses them so, because he knows that women love carnal pleasures, and he means to bind them to his allegiance by such agreeable provocations."[5]

By the mid-seventeenth century, the witchcraft hysteria had begun to subside. As governments grew stronger, fewer magistrates were willing to accept the unsettling and divisive conditions generated by the trials of witches. Moreover, by the end of the seventeenth and beginning of the eighteenth centuries, more and more people were questioning altogether their old attitudes toward religion and found it especially contrary to reason to believe in the old view of a world haunted by evil spirits.

Seventeenth-Century Crises

During the first half of the seventeenth century, a series of rebellions and civil wars rocked the domestic stability of many European governments. A devastating war that affected much of Europe also added to the sense of crisis.

The Thirty Years' War began in 1618 in the Germanic lands of the Holy Roman Empire as a struggle between Catholic forces, led by the Habsburg Holy Roman Emperors, and Protestant—primarily Calvinist—nobles in Bohemia who rebelled against Habsburg authority (see Map 13.3). What began as a struggle over religious issues soon became a wider conflict perpetuated by political motivations as both minor and major European powers—Denmark, Sweden, France, and Spain—entered the war. The competition for European leadership between the Bourbon dynasty of France and the Habsburg dynasties of Spain and the Holy Roman Empire was an especially important factor. Nevertheless, most of the battles were fought on German soil.

The war in Germany was officially ended in 1648 by the Peace of Westphalia, which proclaimed that all German states, including the Calvinist ones, were free to determine their own religion. The major contenders gained new territories, and France emerged as the dominant nation in Europe. The more than three hundred states that made up the Holy Roman Empire were recognized as independent states, and each was given the power to conduct its own foreign policy; this brought an end to the Holy Roman Empire as a political entity and ensured German disunity for another two hundred years. The Peace of Westphalia made it clear that political motives, not religious convictions, had become the guiding force in public affairs.

THE PRACTICE OF ABSOLUTISM

Many people responded to the crises of the seventeenth century by searching for order. An increase in monarchical power became an obvious means for achieving stability. The result was what historians have called absolutism or absolute monarchy. Absolutism meant that the sovereign power or ultimate authority in the state rested in the hands of a king who claimed to rule by divine right—the idea that kings received their power from God and were responsible to no one except God. Late sixteenth-century political theorists believed that sovereign power consisted of the authority to make laws, tax, administer justice, control the state's administrative system, and determine foreign policy.

France Under Louis XIV

France during the reign of Louis XIV (1643–1715) has traditionally been regarded as the best example of the practice of absolute monarchy in the seventeenth century. One of the keys to Louis's power was his control of the central policy-making machinery of government because it was part of his own court and household. The royal court located at Versailles served three purposes simultaneously: it was the personal household of the king, the location of central governmental machinery, and the place where powerful subjects came to find favors and offices for themselves and their clients. The greatest danger to Louis's personal rule came from the very high nobles and princes of the blood (the royal princes), who considered it their natural role to assert the policy-making role of royal ministers. Louis eliminated this threat by removing them from the royal council, the chief administrative body of the king, and enticing them to his court, where he could keep them preoccupied with court life and out of politics. Instead of the high nobility and royal princes, Louis relied for his ministers on nobles who came from relatively new aristocratic families. His ministers were expected to be subservient; "I had no intention of sharing my authority with them," Louis said.

Louis's domination of his ministers and secretaries gave him control of the central policy-making machinery of government and thus authority over the traditional areas of monarchical power: the formulation of foreign policy, the making of war and peace, the assertion of the secular power of the crown against any religious authority, and the ability to levy taxes to fulfill these functions. However, Louis had considerably less success with the internal administration of the kingdom.

The cost of building palaces, maintaining his court, and pursuing his wars made finances a crucial issue for Louis XIV. He was most fortunate in having the services of Jean-Baptiste Colbert (1619–1683) as controller general of finances. Colbert sought to increase the wealth and power of France by general adherence to mercantilism, a set of principles that dominated economic thought in the seventeenth century. According to the mercantilists, the prosperity of a nation depended on a plentiful supply of bullion (gold and silver). For this reason, it was desirable

to achieve a favorable balance of trade in which goods exported were of greater value than those imported, promoting an influx of gold and silver payments that would increase the quantity of bullion. Mercantilism focused on the role of the state, believing that state intervention in the economy was desirable for the sake of the national good.

The increase in royal power that Louis pursued led the king to develop a professional army numbering 100,000 men in peacetime and 400,000 in time of war. To achieve the prestige and military glory befitting an absolute king as well as to ensure the domination of his Bourbon dynasty over European affairs, Louis waged four wars between 1667 and 1713. His ambitions roused much of Europe to form coalitions that were determined to prevent the certain

Sun Kings, West and East

At the end of the seventeenth century, two powerful rulers dominated the affairs of their regions and saw themselves as "sun kings"—the sources of light for their people. On the left, Louis XIV, who ruled France from 1643 to 1715, is seen in a portrait by Hyacinth Rigaud that captures the king's sense of royal dignity and grandeur. On the right, Kangxi, who ruled China from 1661 to 1722, is seen in a nineteenth-century portrait that shows the ruler seated in majesty on his imperial throne.

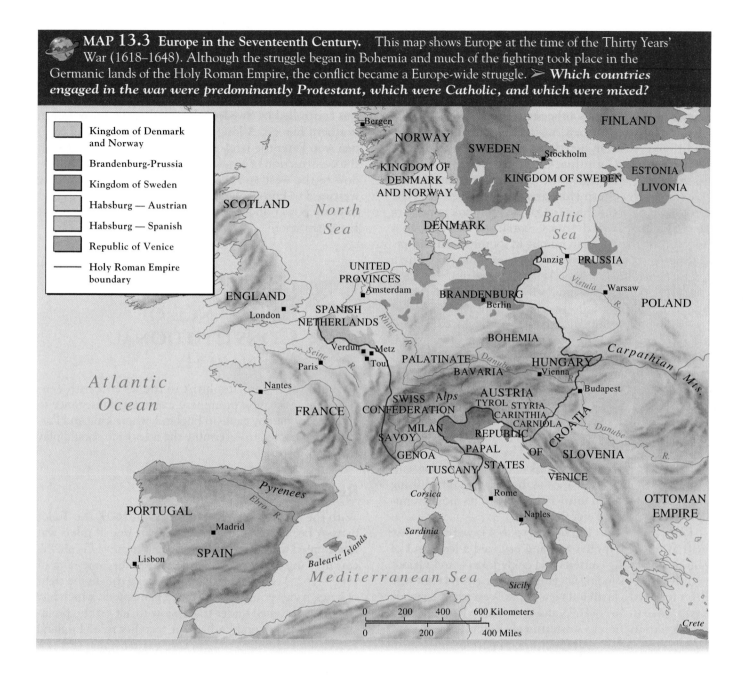

MAP 13.3 Europe in the Seventeenth Century. This map shows Europe at the time of the Thirty Years' War (1618–1648). Although the struggle began in Bohemia and much of the fighting took place in the Germanic lands of the Holy Roman Empire, the conflict became a Europe-wide struggle. ➤ *Which countries engaged in the war were predominantly Protestant, which were Catholic, and which were mixed?*

Legend:
- Kingdom of Denmark and Norway
- Brandenburg-Prussia
- Kingdom of Sweden
- Habsburg — Austrian
- Habsburg — Spanish
- Republic of Venice
- —— Holy Roman Empire boundary

destruction of the European balance of power by Bourbon hegemony. Louis left France impoverished and surrounded by enemies.

Absolutism in Central and Eastern Europe

During the seventeenth century, a development of great importance for the modern Western world took place with the appearance in central and eastern Europe of three new powers: Prussia, Austria, and Russia.

Frederick William the Great Elector (1640–1688) laid the foundation for the Prussian state. Realizing that the land he had inherited, known as Brandenburg-Prussia, constituted a small, open territory with no natural fron-

tiers for defense, Frederick William built an army of forty thousand men, making it the fourth largest in Europe. To sustain the army, Frederick William established the General War Commissariat to levy taxes for the army and oversee its growth. The commissariat soon evolved into an agency for civil government as well. The new bureaucratic machine became the elector's chief instrument to govern the state. Many of its officials were members of the Prussian landed aristocracy, the Junkers, who also served as officers in the all-important army.

In 1701, Frederick William's son Frederick officially gained the title of king. Elector Frederick III became King Frederick I; and Brandenburg-Prussia, simply Prussia. In the eighteenth century, Prussia emerged as a great power in Europe.

The Austrian Habsburgs had long played a significant role in European politics as Holy Roman Emperors. By the end of the Thirty Years' War, the Habsburg hopes of creating an empire in Germany had been dashed. In the seventeenth century, the house of Austria created a new empire in eastern and southeastern Europe.

The nucleus of the new Austrian Empire remained the traditional Austrian hereditary possessions: Lower and Upper Austria, Carinthia, Carniola, Styria, and Tyrol. To these had been added the kingdom of Bohemia and parts of northwestern Hungary. After the defeat of the Turks in 1687 (see Chapter 15), Austria took control of all of Hungary, Transylvania, Croatia, and Slovenia, thus establishing the Austrian Empire in southeastern Europe.

The Austrian monarchy, however, never became a highly centralized, absolutist state, primarily because it contained so many different national groups. The Austrian Empire remained a collection of territories held together by the Habsburg emperor, who was archduke of Austria, king of Bohemia, and king of Hungary. Each of these regions, however, had its own laws and political life.

A new Russian state had emerged in the fifteenth century under the leadership of the principality of Moscow and its grand dukes. In the sixteenth century, Ivan IV (1533–1584) became the first ruler to take the title of *tsar* (the Russian word for *caesar*). When Ivan's dynasty came to an end in 1598, it was followed by a period of anarchy that did not end until the Zemsky Sobor (national assembly) chose Michael Romanov as the new tsar, establishing a dynasty that lasted until 1917. One of its most prominent members was Peter the Great.

Peter the Great (1689–1725) was a towering, strong man at 6 feet 9 inches tall and enjoyed a low kind of humor—belching contests and crude jokes—and vicious punishments, including floggings, impalings, and roastings. Peter received a firsthand view of the West when he made a trip there in 1697–1698 and returned to Russia with a firm determination to westernize or Europeanize Russia. He was especially eager to borrow European technology in order to give him the army and navy he needed to make Russia a great power.

As could be expected, one of his first priorities was the reorganization of the army and the creation of a navy. Employing both Russians and Europeans as officers, he conscripted peasants for twenty-five-year stints of service to build a standing army of 210,000 men. Peter has also been given credit for forming the first Russian navy. To impose the rule of the central government more effectively throughout the land, Peter divided Russia into provinces. Although he hoped to create a "police state," by which he meant a well-ordered community governed in accordance with law, few of his bureaucrats shared his concept of duty to the state. Peter hoped for a sense of civic duty, but his own forceful personality created an atmosphere of fear that prevented it.

The object of Peter's domestic reforms was to make Russia into a great state and military power. His primary goal was to "open a window to the west," meaning an ice-free port easily accessible to Europe. This could only be achieved on the Baltic, but at that time, the Baltic coast was controlled by Sweden, the most important power in northern Europe. A long and hard-fought war with Sweden won Peter the lands he sought. In 1703, Peter began the construction of a new city, Saint Petersburg, his window to the west and a symbol that Russia was looking westward to Europe. Under Peter, Russia became a great military power and, by his death in 1725, an important European state.

ENGLAND AND THE EMERGENCE OF CONSTITUTIONAL MONARCHY

Not all states were absolutist in the seventeenth century. One of the most prominent examples of resistance to absolute monarchy came in England, where king and Parliament struggled to determine the roles each should play in governing England.

Revolution and Civil War

With the death of Queen Elizabeth I in 1603, the Tudor dynasty became extinct, and the Stuart line of rulers was inaugurated with the accession to the throne of Elizabeth's cousin, King James VI of Scotland, who became James I (1603–1625) of England. James espoused the divine right of kings, a viewpoint that alienated Parliament, which had grown accustomed under the Tudors to act on the premise that monarch and Parliament together ruled England as a "balanced polity." Then, too, the Puritans—Protestants within the Anglican church who, inspired by Calvinist theology, wished to eliminate every trace of Roman Catholicism from the Church of England—were alienated by the king's strong defense of the Anglican church. Much of England's gentry, mostly well-to-do landowners, had become Puritans, and this Puritan gentry formed an important and substantial part of the House of Commons, the lower house of Parliament. It was not wise to alienate these men.

The conflict that had begun during the reign of James came to a head during the reign of his son, Charles I (1625–1649). Charles also believed in divine-right monarchy, and religious differences also added to the hostility between Charles I and Parliament. Grievances mounted until England finally slipped into a civil war (1642–1648) won by the parliamentary forces, due largely to the New

Model Army of Oliver Cromwell, the only real military genius of the war. The New Model Army was composed primarily of more extreme Puritans known as the Independents, who, in typical Calvinist fashion, believed they were doing battle for God. As Cromwell wrote in one of his military reports, "Sir, this is none other but the hand of God; and to Him alone belongs the glory." We might give some credit to Cromwell; his soldiers were well trained in the new military tactics of the seventeenth century.

After the execution of Charles I on January 30, 1649, Parliament abolished the monarchy and the House of Lords and proclaimed England a republic or commonwealth. But Cromwell and his army, unable to work effectively with Parliament, dispersed it by force and established a military dictatorship. After Cromwell's death in 1658, the army decided that military rule was no longer feasible and restored the monarchy in the person of Charles II, the son of Charles I.

Restoration and a Glorious Revolution

Charles was sympathetic to Catholicism, and Parliament's suspicions were aroused in 1672 when Charles took the audacious step of issuing the Declaration of Indulgence, which suspended the laws that Parliament had passed against Catholics and Puritans after the restoration of the monarchy. Parliament forced the king to suspend the declaration.

The accession of James II (1685–1688) to the crown virtually guaranteed a new constitutional crisis for England. An open and devout Catholic, his attempt to further Catholic interests made religion once more a primary cause of conflict between king and Parliament. Parliamentary outcries against James's policies stopped short of rebellion because members knew that he was an old man and that his successors were his Protestant daughters Mary and Anne, born to his first wife. But on June 10, 1688, a son was born to James II's second wife, also a Catholic. Suddenly the specter of a Catholic hereditary monarchy loomed large. A group of prominent English noblemen invited the Dutch chief executive, William of Orange, husband of James's daughter Mary, to invade England. William and Mary raised an army and invaded England while James, his wife, and their infant son fled to France. With little bloodshed, England had undergone its "Glorious Revolution."

In January 1689, Parliament offered the throne to William and Mary, who accepted it along with the provisions of a bill of rights (see the box on p. 290). The Bill of Rights affirmed Parliament's right to make laws and levy taxes. The rights of citizens to keep arms and have a jury trial were also confirmed. By deposing one king and establishing another, Parliament had destroyed the divine-right theory of kingship (William was, after all, king by grace of

Parliament, not God) and asserted its right to participate in the government. Parliament did not have complete control of the government, but it now had the right to participate in affairs of state. Over the next century, it would gradually prove to be the real authority in the English system of constitutional monarchy.

 # EUROPEAN CULTURE

Art and intellectual activity experienced dramatic changes in the sixteenth and seventeenth centuries. Especially important in developing a new view of the world was the Scientific Revolution.

Art: The Baroque

The artistic movement known as the Baroque dominated the Western artistic world for a century and a half. The Baroque began in Italy in the last quarter of the sixteenth century and spread to the rest of Europe and Latin America. Baroque artists sought to harmonize the classical ideals of Renaissance art with the spiritual feelings of the

THE BILL OF RIGHTS

In 1688, the English experienced yet another revolution, a bloodless one in which the Stuart king James II was replaced by Mary, James's daughter, and her husband, William of Orange. After William and Mary had assumed power, Parliament passed a bill of rights that specified the rights of Parliament and laid the foundation for a constitutional monarchy.

THE BILL OF RIGHTS

Whereas the said late King James II having abdicated the government, and the throne being thereby vacant, his Highness the prince of Orange (whom it hath pleased Almighty God to make the glorious instrument of delivering this kingdom from popery and arbitrary power) did (by the device of the lords spiritual and temporal, and diverse principal persons of the Commons) cause letters to be written to the lords spiritual and temporal, being Protestants, and other letters to the several counties, cities, universities, boroughs, and Cinque Ports, for the choosing of such persons to represent them, as were of right to be sent to parliament, to meet and sit at Westminster upon the two and twentieth day of January, in this year 1689, in order to such an establishment as that their religion, laws, and liberties might not again be in danger of being subverted; upon which letters elections have been accordingly made.

And thereupon the said lords spiritual and temporal and Commons, pursuant to their respective letters and elections, being now assembled in a full and free representation of this nation, taking into their most serious consideration the best means for attaining the ends aforesaid, do in the first place (as their ancestors in like case have usually done), for the vindication and assertion of their ancient rights and liberties, declare:

1. That the pretended power of suspending laws, or the execution of laws, by regal authority, without consent of parliament is illegal.

2. That the pretended power of dispensing with the laws, or the execution of law by regal authority, as it hath been assumed and exercised of late, is illegal.

3. That the commission for erecting the late court of commissioners for ecclesiastical causes, and all other commissions and courts of like nature, are illegal and pernicious.

4. That levying money for or to the use of the crown by pretense of prerogative, without grant of parliament, for longer time or in other manner than the same is or shall be granted, is illegal.

5. That it is the right of the subjects to petition the king, and all commitments and prosecutions for such petitioning are illegal.

6. That the raising or keeping a standing army within the kingdom in time of peace, unless it be with consent of parliament, is against law.

7. That the subjects which are Protestants may have arms for their defense suitable to their conditions, and as allowed by law.

8. That election of members of parliament ought to be free.

9. That the freedom of speech, and debates or proceedings in parliament, ought not to be impeached or questioned in any court or place out of parliament.

10. That excessive bail ought not to be required, nor excessive fines imposed, nor cruel and unusual punishments inflicted.

11. That jurors ought to be duly impaneled and returned, and jurors which pass upon men in trials for high treason ought to be freeholders.

12. That all grants and promises of fines and forfeitures of particular persons before conviction are illegal and void.

13. And that for redress of all grievances, and for the amending, strengthening, and preserving of the laws, parliament ought to be held frequently.

---

sixteenth-century religious revival. In large part, Baroque art and architecture reflected the search for power that was characteristic of much of the seventeenth century. Baroque churches and palaces featured richly ornamented facades, sweeping staircases, and an overall splendor meant to impress people.

Baroque painting was known for its use of dramatic effects to arouse the emotions, especially evident in the works of Peter Paul Rubens (1577–1640), a prolific artist and an important figure in the spread of the Baroque from Italy to other parts of Europe. In his artistic masterpieces, bodies in violent motion, heavily fleshed nudes, a dramatic use of light and shadow, and rich sensuous pigments converge to express intense emotions.

A Golden Age of Literature in England

In England, writing for the stage reached new heights between 1580 and 1640. The golden age of English literature is often called the Elizabethan Era because much of the English cultural flowering occurred during Elizabeth I's reign. Of all the forms of Elizabethan literature, none expressed the energy and intellectual versatility of the era better than drama. And no dramatist is more famous or more accomplished than William Shakespeare (1564–1614).

Shakespeare was a "complete man of the theater." Although best known for writing plays, he was also an actor and a shareholder in the chief acting company of the time, the Lord Chamberlain's Company, which played

➤ PETER PAUL RUBENS, *THE LANDING OF MARIE DE'
MEDICI AT MARSEILLES.*   Peter Paul Rubens played a key role
in spreading the Baroque style from Italy to other parts of
Europe. *In The Landing of Marie de' Medici at Marseilles,* Rubens
made dramatic use of light and color, bodies in motion, and luxurious nudes to heighten the emotional intensity of the scene.
This was one of a cycle of twenty-one paintings dedicated to the
queen mother of France.

in various London theaters. Shakespeare is to this day
hailed as a genius. A master of the English language, he
imbued its words with power and majesty. And his technical proficiency was matched by incredible insight into
human psychology. Whether writing tragedies or come-
dies, Shakespeare exhibited a remarkable understanding
of the human condition (see the box on p. 292).

The Scientific Revolution

The Scientific Revolution ultimately challenged conceptions and beliefs about the nature of the external world
that had become dominant by the Late Middle Ages.
The Scientific Revolution taught Europeans to view the
universe in a new way.

TOWARD A NEW HEAVEN: A REVOLUTION
IN ASTRONOMY

The philosophers of the Middle Ages had used the ideas
of Aristotle, Ptolemy (the greatest astronomer of antiquity, who lived in the second century C.E.), and Christianity to construct the Ptolemaic or geocentric
conception of the universe. In this conception, the
universe was seen as a series of concentric spheres with a
fixed or motionless earth at its center. Composed of
material substance, the earth was imperfect and constantly
changing. The spheres that surrounded the earth were
made of a crystalline, transparent substance and moved in
circular orbits around the earth. The heavenly bodies,
which numbered ten in 1500, were pure orbs of light,
embedded in the moving, concentric spheres. Working
outward from the earth, the first eight spheres contained
the Moon, Mercury, Venus, the Sun, Mars, Jupiter, Saturn,
and the fixed stars. The ninth sphere imparted to the
eighth sphere of the fixed stars its daily motion, while
the tenth sphere was frequently described as the prime
mover that moved itself and imparted motion to the other
spheres. Beyond the tenth sphere was the Empyrean
Heaven—the location of God and all the saved souls. God
and the saved souls were at one end of the universe, then,
and humans were at the center. They had power over the
earth, but their real purpose was to achieve salvation.

Nicholas Copernicus (1473–1543), a native of Poland,
was a mathematician who felt that Ptolemy's geocentric
system failed to accord with the observed motions of the
heavenly bodies and hoped that his heliocentric (sun-
centered) conception would offer a more accurate explanation. Copernicus argued that the sun was motionless
at the center of the universe. The planets revolved around
the sun in the order of Mercury, Venus, the earth, Mars,
Jupiter, and Saturn. The moon, however, revolved around
the earth. Moreover, what appeared to be the movement
of the sun around the earth was really explained by the
daily rotation of the earth on its axis and the journey of
the earth around the sun each year. But Copernicus did
not reject the idea that the heavenly spheres moved in circular orbits.

The next step in destroying the geocentric conception and supporting the Copernican system was taken by
Johannes Kepler (1571–1630). A brilliant German mathematician and astronomer, Kepler arrived at laws of planetary motion that confirmed Copernicus's heliocentric
theory. In his first law, however, he contradicted Copernicus by showing that the orbits of the planets around the
sun were not circular but elliptical, with the sun at one
focus of the ellipse rather than at the center.

Kepler's work destroyed the basic structure of the
Ptolemaic system. People could now think in new terms
of the actual paths of planets revolving around the sun
in elliptical orbits. But important questions remained

WILLIAM SHAKESPEARE: IN PRAISE OF ENGLAND

William Shakespeare is one of the most famous playwrights in the Western world. He was a universal genius, outclassing all others in his psychological insights, depth of characterization, imaginative skills, and versatility. His historical plays reflected the patriotic enthusiasm of the English in the Elizabethan Era, as this excerpt from Richard II *illustrates.*

WILLIAM SHAKESPEARE, RICHARD II

This royal throne of kings, this sceptered isle,
This earth of majesty, this seat of Mars,
This other Eden, demi-Paradise,
This fortress built by Nature for herself
Against infection and the hand of war,
This happy breed of men, this little world,
This precious stone set in the silver sea,
Which serves it in the office of a wall
Or as a moat defensive to a house
Against the envy of less happier lands—
This blessed plot, this earth, this realm, this England,

This nurse, this teeming womb of royal kings,
Feared by their breed and famous by their birth,
Renowned for their deeds as far from home,
For Christian service and true chivalry,
As is the sepulcher in stubborn Jewry [the Holy Sepulcher in
   Jerusalem]
Of the world's ransom, blessed Mary's Son—
This land of such dear souls, this dear dear land,
Dear for her reputation through the world,
Is now leased out, I die pronouncing it,
Like a tenement or pelting farm.

England, bound in with the triumphant sea,
Whose rocky shore beats back the envious siege
Of watery Neptune, is now bound in with shame,
With inky blots and rotten parchment bonds.
That England, that was wont to conquer others,
Hath made a shameful conquest of itself.
Ah, would the scandal vanish with my life,
How happy then were my ensuing death!

---

unanswered. For example, what were the planets made of? An Italian scientist achieved the next important breakthrough to a new cosmology by answering that question.

Galileo Galilei (1564–1642) taught mathematics and was the first European to make systematic observations of the heavens by means of a telescope, inaugurating a new age in astronomy. Galileo turned his telescope to the skies and made a remarkable series of discoveries: mountains on the moon, four moons revolving around Jupiter, and sunspots. Galileo's observations seemed to destroy yet another aspect of the traditional cosmology in that the universe seemed to be composed of material similar to that of the earth rather than a perfect and unchanging substance.

Galileo's revelations, published in *The Starry Messenger* in 1610, made Europeans aware of a new picture of the universe. But the Catholic church condemned Copernicanism and ordered Galileo to abandon the Copernican thesis. The church attacked the Copernican system because it threatened not only Scripture but also an entire conception of the universe. The heavens were no longer a spiritual world but a world of matter.

By the 1630s and 1640s, most astronomers had come to accept the new heliocentric conception of the universe. Nevertheless, the problem of explaining motion in the universe and tying together the ideas of Copernicus, Galileo, and Kepler had not yet been done. This would be the work of an Englishman who has long been considered the greatest genius of the Scientific Revolution.

Born in 1642, Isaac Newton taught at Cambridge University, where he wrote his major work, *Mathematical Principles of Natural Philosophy*, known simply as the *Principia* by the first word of its Latin title. In the first book of the *Principia*, Newton defined the three laws of motion that govern the planetary bodies, as well as objects on earth. Crucial to his whole argument was the universal law of gravitation, which explained why the planetary bodies did not go off in straight lines but continued in elliptical orbits about the sun. In mathematical terms, Newton explained that every object in the universe is attracted to every other object by a force called gravity.

Newton had demonstrated that one mathematically proven universal law could explain all motion in the universe. At the same time, the Newtonian synthesis created a new cosmology in which the universe was seen as one huge, regulated machine that operated according to natural laws in absolute time, space, and motion. Newton's world-machine concept dominated the modern worldview until the twentieth century, when Albert Einstein's concept of relativity created a new picture of the universe.

EUROPE, CHINA, AND SCIENTIFIC REVOLUTIONS

An interesting question that arises is why the Scientific Revolution occurred in Europe and not in China. In the Middle Ages, China had been the most technologically advanced civilization in the world. After 1500, that dis-

MEDIEVAL CONCEPTION OF THE UNIVERSE. As this sixteenth-century illustration shows, the medieval cosmological view placed the earth at the center of the universe, surrounded by a series of concentric spheres. The earth was imperfect and constantly changing, while the heavenly bodies that surrounded it were perfect and incorruptible. Beyond the tenth and final sphere was heaven, where God and all the saved souls were located.

THE COPERNICAN SYSTEM. The Copernican system was presented in *On the Revolutions of the Heavenly Spheres*, published shortly before Copernicus's death. As shown in this illustration from the first edition of the book, Copernicus maintained that the sun was the center of the universe while the planets, including the earth, revolved around it. Moreover, the earth rotated daily on its axis.

tinction passed to the West. Historians are not sure why. Some have contrasted the sense of order in Chinese society with the competitive spirit existing in Europe. Others have emphasized China's ideological viewpoint that favored living in harmony with nature rather than trying to dominate it. One historian has even suggested that China's civil service system drew the "best and the brightest" into government service, to the detriment of other occupations.

CONCLUSION

In the next chapter, we will examine how the movement of Europeans outside of Europe began to change the shape of world history. But what had made this development possible? After all, the religious division of Europe had led to almost a hundred years of religious warfare complicated by serious political, economic, and social issues before Europeans finally admitted that they would have to accept different ways of worshiping God.

At the same time, the concept of a united Christendom, held as an ideal since the Middle Ages, had been irrevocably destroyed by the religious wars, enabling a system of nation-states to emerge in which power politics took on increasing significance. Within those states there slowly emerged some of the machinery that made possible a growing centralization of power. In those states called absolutist, strong monarchs with the assistance of their aristocracies provided the leadership for greater centralization. In all the major European states, a growing concern for power led to larger armies and greater conflict, stronger economies, and more powerful governments. From a global point of view, the political and economic power of Europeans was beginning to slowly outstrip that of other peoples.

The Scientific Revolution also represents a major turning point in modern civilization. With a new conception of the universe came a new conception of humankind. Europeans came to believe that by using only reason they could understand and dominate the world of nature. Combined with the eighteenth-century Enlightenment (see Chapter 17), the Scientific Revolution gave the West an intellectual boost that contributed to the increased confidence of Western civilization. Europeans—with their strong governments, prosperous economies, and strengthened military forces—began to dominate other parts of the world, leading to a growing belief in the superiority of their civilization.

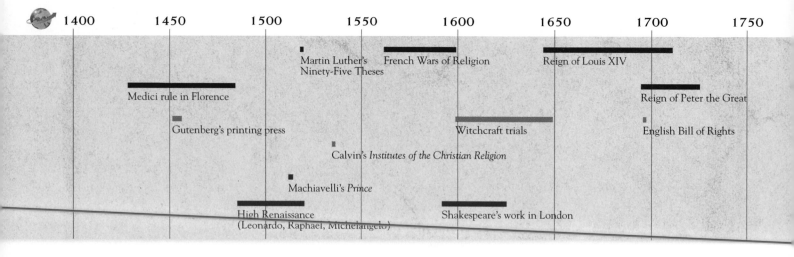

1400   1450   1500   1550   1600   1650   1700   1750

Martin Luther's Ninety-Five Theses

French Wars of Religion

Reign of Louis XIV

Medici rule in Florence

Reign of Peter the Great

Gutenberg's printing press

Witchcraft trials

English Bill of Rights

Calvin's *Institutes of the Christian Religion*

Machiavelli's *Prince*

High Renaissance (Leonardo, Raphael, Michelangelo)

Shakespeare's work in London

CHAPTER NOTES

1. Quoted in Jacob Burckhardt, *The Civilization of the Renaissance in Italy*, trans. S. G. C. Middlemore (London, 1960), p. 81.
2. Niccolò Machiavelli, *The Prince*, trans. David Wootton (Indianapolis, 1995), p. 48.
3. Quoted in Roland Bainton, *Here I Stand: A Life of Martin Luther* (New York, 1950), p. 144.
4. John Calvin, *Institutes of the Christian Religion*, trans. John Allen (Philadelphia, 1936), vol. 1, p. 228; vol. 2, p. 181.
5. Quoted in Joseph Klaits, *Servants of Satan: The Age of Witch Hunts* (Bloomington, Ind., 1985), p. 68.

SUGGESTED READING

General works on the Renaissance in Europe include D. L. Jensen, *Renaissance Europe*, 2d ed. (Lexington, Mass., 1991); P. Burke, *The European Renaissance: Centres and Peripheries* (Oxford, 1998); and J. R. Hale, *The Civilization of Europe in the Renaissance* (New York, 1994). For a good summary of literature on the Renaissance, see P. Burke, *The Renaissance* (New York, 1997).

Numerous facets of social life in the Renaissance are examined in J. R. Hale, *Renaissance Europe: The Individual and Society* (London, 1971). On family and marriage, see D. Herlihy, *The Family in Renaissance Italy* (St. Louis, 1974), and the valuable C. Klapisch-Zuber, *Women, Family, and Ritual in Renaissance Italy* (Chicago, 1985). Women are examined in M. L. King, *Women of the Renaissance* (Chicago, 1991).

Brief introductions to Renaissance humanism can be found in D. Kelley, *Renaissance Humanism* (Boston, 1991), and C. G. Nauert Jr., *Humanism and the Culture of Renaissance Europe* (Cambridge, 1995). The impact of printing is exhaustively examined in E. Eisenstein, *The Printing Press as an Agent of Change*, 2 vols. (New York, 1978). Good surveys of Renaissance art include R. Turner, *Renaissance Florence: The Invention of a New Art* (New York, 1997), and F. Hartt, *History of Italian Renaissance Art*, 4th ed. (Englewood Cliffs, N.J., 1994).

For a general work on the political development of Europe in the Renaissance, see J. H. Shennan, *The Origins of the Modern European State, 1450–1725* (London, 1974). The best overall study

of the Italian states is L. Martines, *Power and Imagination: City-States in Renaissance Italy* (New York, 1979). Machiavelli's life can be examined in Q. Skinner, *Machiavelli* (Oxford, 1981).

Basic surveys of the Reformation period include H. J. Grimm, *The Reformation Era, 1500–1650*, 2d ed. (New York, 1973); D. L. Jensen, *Reformation Europe*, 2d ed. (Lexington, Mass., 1990); G. R. Elton, *Reformation Europe, 1517–1559* (Cleveland, 1963); C. Lindberg, *The European Reformations* (Cambridge, Mass., 1996); and E. Cameron, *The European Reformation* (New York, 1991).

The classic account of Martin Luther's life is R. Bainton, *Here I Stand: A Life of Martin Luther* (New York, 1950). More recent works include J. M. Kittelson, *Luther the Reformer: The Story of the Man and His Career* (Minneapolis, 1986), and H. A. Oberman, *Luther: Man Between God and the Devil* (New York, 1992). Two worthwhile surveys of the English Reformation are A. G. Dickens, *The English Reformation*, 2d ed. (New York, 1989), and G. R. Elton, *Reform and Reformation: England, 1509–1558* (Cambridge, Mass., 1977). On John Calvin, see A. McGrath, *A Life of John Calvin: A Study in the Shaping of Western Culture* (Cambridge, Mass., 1990), and W. J. Bouwsma, *John Calvin* (New York, 1988). A good introduction to the Catholic Reformation can be found in M. R. O'Connell, *The Counter-Reformation, 1559–1610* (New York, 1974).

On the French Wars of Religion, see M. P. Holt, *The French Wars of Religion, 1562–1629* (New York, 1995), and R. J. Knecht, *The*

French Wars of Religion, 1559–1598, 2d ed. (New York, 1996). A good biography of Philip II is G. Parker, *Philip II*, 3d ed. (Chicago, 1995). Elizabeth's reign can be examined in C. Haigh, *Elizabeth I*, 2d ed. (New York, 1998). On the Thirty Years' War, see R. G. Asch, *The Thirty Years' War: The Holy Roman Empire and Europe, 1618–1648* (New York, 1997). A good general work on the period of the English Revolution is M. A. Kishlansky, *A Monarchy Transformed* (London, 1996). On England, see also W. A. Speck, *The Revolution of 1688* (Oxford, 1988).

Witchcraft hysteria can be examined in J. B. Russell, *A History of Witchcraft* (London, 1980), and B. P. Levack, *The Witch-Hunt in Early Modern Europe* (London, 1987).

For a brief account of seventeenth-century French history, see J. B. Collins, *The State in Early Modern France* (Cambridge, 1995). A solid and very readable biography of Louis XIV is J. B. Wolf, *Louis XIV* (New York, 1968). For a brief study, see P. R. Campbell, *Louis XIV, 1661–1715* (London, 1993). On the creation

of an Austrian state, see C. Ingrao, *The Habsburg Monarchy, 1618–1815* (Cambridge, 1994). F. L. Carsten, *The Origins of Prussia* (Oxford, 1954), remains an outstanding study of early Prussian history. Works on Peter the Great include M. S. Anderson, *Peter the Great*, 2d ed. (New York, 1995), and L. Hughes, *Russia in the Age of Peter the Great* (New Haven, Conn., 1998).

For a general survey of Baroque culture, see J. S. Held, *Seventeenth and Eighteenth Century Art: Baroque Painting, Sculpture, Architecture* (New York, 1971). The literature on Shakespeare is enormous. For a biography, see A. L. Rowse, *The Life of Shakespeare* (New York, 1963).

Four general surveys of the Scientific Revolution are A. G. R. Smith, *Science and Society in the Sixteenth and Seventeenth Centuries* (London, 1972); J. R. Jacob, *The Scientific Revolution: Aspirations and Achievements, 1500–1700* (Atlantic Highlands, N.J., 1998); S. Shapin, *The Scientific Revolution* (Chicago, 1996); and J. Henry, *The Scientific Revolution and the Origins of Modern Science* (New York, 1997).

INFOTRAC COLLEGE EDITION

Visit the source collections at infotrac.thomsonlearning.com and use the Search function with the following key terms.

Louis XIV	Reformation
Machiavelli	Renaissance
Martin Luther not King	Thirty Years' War

WORLD HISTORY RESOURCES

Visit the *Essential World History* Companion Web Site for resources specific to this textbook:

http://history.wadsworth.com/duikeressentials02/

The CD in the back of this book and the World History Resource Center at **http://history.wadsworth.com/world/** offer a variety of tools to help you succeed in this course, including access to quizzes; images; documents; interactive simulations, maps, and timelines; movie explorations; and a wealth of other sources.

The Art Archive, London

New Encounters: The Creation of a World Market

Focus Questions

- Why did Europeans begin to embark on voyages of discovery and expansion at the end of the fifteenth century?
- How did Portugal and Spain acquire their overseas empires, and how did their empires differ?
- How and why did the Europeans expand into Africa, and what were the main consequences of their presence there?
- What were the main features of the African slave trade, and what effects did it have on Africa?
- ➤ What were the main characteristics of Southeast Asian civilization, and how was it affected by the coming of Islam and the Europeans?

*W*hen, in the spring of 1498, a local official asked the Portuguese explorer Vasco da Gama why he had come all the way to India from his homeland in Europe, he replied simply, "Christians and spices." Da Gama might have been more accurate if he had reversed the order of his objectives. As it turned out, God was probably much less important than gold and glory to Europeans like himself who participated in the Age of Exploration that was already under way. Still, da Gama's comments at Calicut were an accurate forecast of the future, for his voyage inaugurated an extended period of European expansion into Asia, led by merchant adventurers and missionaries, that lasted several hundred years and had effects that are still felt today. Eventually it resulted in a Western takeover of existing trade routes in the Indian Ocean and the establishment of colonies throughout Asia, Africa, and Latin America. So complete did Western dominance seem that some historians assumed that the peoples of the non-Western world were mere passive recipients in this process, absorbing and assimilating the advanced knowledge of the

West and offering nothing in return. Historians writing about the period after 1500 often talked metaphorically about the "impact of the West" and the "response" of non-Western peoples.

That image of impact and response, however, is not an entirely accurate description of what took place between the end of the fifteenth century and the end of the eighteenth. Although European rule was firmly established in Latin America and the island regions of Southeast Asia, traditional governments and institutions elsewhere remained largely intact and in some areas, notably South Asia and the Middle East, displayed considerable vitality. Moreover, although da Gama and his contemporaries are deservedly famous for their contribution to a new era of maritime commerce that circled the globe, they were not alone in extending the world trade network and transporting goods and ideas from one end of the earth to the other. Islam, too, was on the march, blazing new trails into Southeast Asia and across the Sahara to the civilizations that flourished along the banks of the Niger River. In this chapter, we turn our attention to the stunning expansion in the scope and volume of commercial and cultural contacts that took place in the generations preceding and following da Gama's historic voyage to India, as well as to the factors that brought about this expansion. •

AN AGE OF EXPLORATION AND EXPANSION

The voyage of Vasco da Gama has customarily been seen as a crucial step in the opening of trade routes to the East. In fact, however, as has been pointed out in earlier chapters, the Indian Ocean had been a busy thoroughfare for centuries. The spice trade had been carried on by sea in the region since the days of the legendary Queen of Sheba, and Chinese junks had sailed to the area in search of cloves and nutmeg since the Tang dynasty. Then, during the early fifteenth century, Chinese fleets sailed into the Indian Ocean and all the way to the coast of East Africa in search of trade and alliances (see Chapter 16).

Islam and the Spice Trade

By the fourteenth century, a growing percentage of the spice trade was being transported in Muslim ships sailing from ports in India or the Middle East. Muslims, either Arabs or Indian converts, had taken part in the Indian Ocean trade for centuries, and by the thirteenth century, Islam had established a presence in seaports on the islands of Sumatra and Java and was gradually moving inland. In 1292, the Venetian traveler Marco Polo observed that Muslims were engaging in missionary activity in northern Sumatra: "This kingdom is so much frequented by the Saracen merchants that they have converted the natives to the Law of Mahomet—I mean the townspeople only, for the hill people live for all the world like beasts, and eat human flesh, as well as other kinds of flesh, clean or unclean."[1]

But the major impact of Islam came in the early fifteenth century with the rise of the new sultanate at Malacca, whose founder was a Muslim convert. With its strategic location astride the strait of the same name (see Map 14.1), Malacca was "a city that was made for commerce; . . . the trade and commerce between the different nations for a thousand leagues on every hand must come to Malacca,"[2] said a sixteenth-century Portuguese visitor. Within a few years, Malacca become the leading power in the region.

Unfortunately for the Muslim traders who had come to Southeast Asia for the spice trade, others would also covet that trade. The arrival of Vasco da Gama's fleet was a sure sign that others would soon follow.

A New Player: Europe

For almost a millennium, Catholic Europe had been confined to one area. Its one major attempt to expand beyond those frontiers, the Crusades, had largely failed. Of course, Europe had never completely lost contact with the outside world: the goods of Asia and Africa made their way into medieval castles, the works of Muslim philosophers were read in medieval universities, and the Vikings in the ninth and tenth centuries had even explored the eastern fringes of North America. Nevertheless, Europe's contacts with non-European civilizations remained limited until the fifteenth century, when Europeans began to embark on a remarkable series of overseas journeys. What caused European seafarers to undertake such dangerous voyages to the ends of the earth?

Europeans had long been attracted to the East. In the Middle Ages, myths and legends of an exotic land of great riches and magic were widespread. The most famous medieval travelers to the East were the Polos of Venice. In 1271, Nicolò and Maffeo, merchants from Venice, accompanied by Nicolò's son Marco, undertook the lengthy journey to the court of the great Mongol ruler Khubilai Khan (see Chapter 10). As one of the Great Khan's ambassadors,

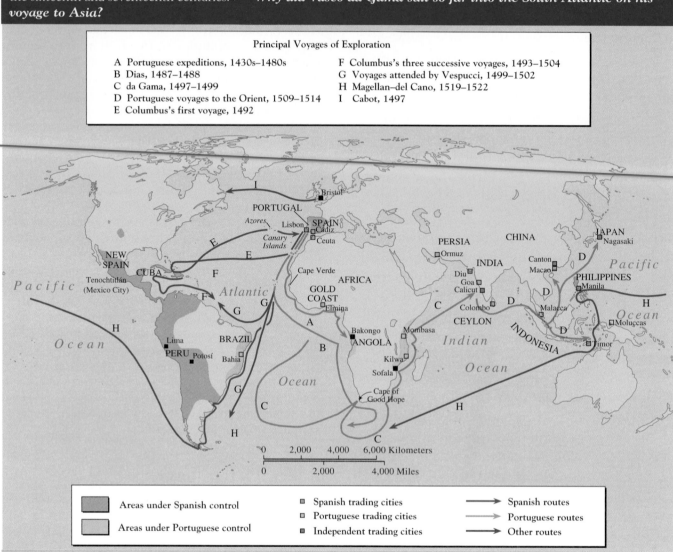

MAP 14.1 **European Voyages and Possessions in the Sixteenth and Seventeenth Centuries.** This map indicates the most important voyages launched by Europeans during their momentous Age of Exploration in the sixteenth and seventeenth centuries. ➤ *Why did Vasco da Gama sail so far into the South Atlantic on his voyage to Asia?*

Principal Voyages of Exploration

A Portuguese expeditions, 1430s–1480s
B Dias, 1487–1488
C da Gama, 1497–1499
D Portuguese voyages to the Orient, 1509–1514
E Columbus's first voyage, 1492

F Columbus's three successive voyages, 1493–1504
G Voyages attended by Vespucci, 1499–1502
H Magellan–del Cano, 1519–1522
I Cabot, 1497

Areas under Spanish control
Areas under Portuguese control

Spanish trading cities
Portuguese trading cities
Independent trading cities

Spanish routes
Portuguese routes
Other routes

Marco traveled to Japan as well and did not return to Italy until 1295. An account of his experiences, the *Travels*, proved to be the most informative of all the descriptions of Asia by medieval European travelers. Others, like the Franciscan friar John Plano Carpini, had preceded the Polos, but in the fourteenth century, the conquests of the Ottoman Turks and then the breakup of the Mongol Empire reduced Western traffic to the East. With the closing of the overland routes, a number of people in Europe became interested in the possibility of reaching Asia by sea.

An economic motive thus looms large in Renaissance European expansion (see Chapter 13). The rise of capitalism in Europe was undoubtedly a powerful spur to the process. Merchants, adventurers, and government officials had high hopes of finding precious metals and expanding the areas of trade, especially for the spices of the East. Spices continued to be transported to Europe via Arab intermediaries but were outrageously expensive. Adventurous Europeans did not hesitate to express their desire to share in the wealth. As one Spanish conquistador explained, he and his kind went to the New World to "serve God and His Majesty, to give light to those who were in darkness, and to grow rich, as all men desire to do."[3]

This statement expresses another major reason for the overseas voyages—religious zeal. A crusading mentality was particularly strong in Portugal and Spain, where the Muslims had largely been driven out in the Middle Ages. Contemporaries of Prince Henry the Navigator of Portugal said that he was motivated by "his great desire to make increase in the faith of our Lord Jesus Christ and to bring him all the souls that should be saved." Although most scholars believe that the religious motive was secondary to economic considerations, it would be foolish to overlook the genuine desire on the part of both explorers and conquistadors, let alone missionaries, to convert the heathen to Christianity. Hernán Cortés, the conqueror of Mexico, asked his Spanish rulers if it was not their duty to ensure that the native Mexicans were "introduced into and instructed in the holy Catholic faith."[4] Spiritual and secular affairs were closely intertwined in the sixteenth century. No doubt, grandeur and glory as well as plain intellectual curiosity and a spirit of adventure also played some role in European expansion.

If "God, glory, and gold" were the primary motives, what made the voyages possible? First of all, the expansion of Europe was a state enterprise, tied to the growth of centralized monarchies during the Renaissance. By the second half of the fifteenth century, European monarchies had increased both their authority and their resources and were in a position to turn their energies beyond their borders. That meant the invasion of Italy for France, but for Portugal, a state not strong enough to pursue power in Europe, it meant going abroad. The Spanish scene was more complex, since the Spanish monarchy was strong enough by the sixteenth century to pursue power both on the Continent and beyond.

At the same time, by the end of the fifteenth century, European states had a level of knowledge and technology that enabled them to achieve a regular series of voyages beyond Europe. Although the highly schematic and symbolic medieval maps were of little help to sailors, the *portolani,* or detailed charts made by medieval navigators and mathematicians in the thirteenth and fourteenth centuries, were more useful. With details on coastal contours, distances between ports, and compass readings, they proved of great value for voyages in European waters. But because the *portolani* were drawn on a flat scale and took no account of the curvature of the earth, they were of little use for longer overseas voyages. Only when seafarers began to venture beyond the coasts of Europe did they begin to accumulate information about the actual shape of the earth. By the end of the fifteenth century, cartography had developed to the point that Europeans possessed fairly accurate maps of the known world.

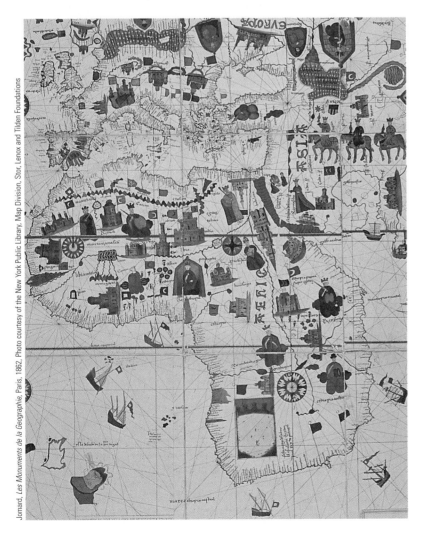

Jomard, Les Monuments de la Géographie, Paris, 1862, Photo courtesy of the New York Public Library, Map Division, Stor, Lenox and Tilden Foundations

➤ **A SIXTEENTH-CENTURY MAP OF AFRICA.** Advances in mapmaking also contributed to the European Age of Exploration. Here a section of a world map by the early-sixteenth-century Spanish cartographer Juan de la Cosa shows the continent of Africa. Note the drawing of the legendary Prester John, mentioned in Chapter 10, at the right, and the Portuguese caravels with their lateen sails in the South Atlantic Ocean. In the minds of Europeans at the time, the legend of Prester John had been identified with the Christian king of Ethiopia.

In addition, Europeans had developed remarkably seaworthy ships as well as new navigational techniques. European shipbuilders had mastered the use of the stern-post rudder (an import from China) and had learned how to combine the use of lateen sails with a square rig. With these innovations, they could construct ships mobile enough to sail against the wind and engage in naval warfare and also large enough to mount heavy cannons and carry a substantial amount of goods over long distances. Previously sailors had used a quadrant and their knowledge of the position of the polestar to ascertain their latitude. Below the equator, however, this technique was useless. Only with the assistance of new navigational aids such as the compass (a Chinese invention) and the astrolabe (an astronomical instrument used to measure the altitude of the sun and the stars above the horizon) were they able to explore the high seas with confidence.

The Portuguese Maritime Empire

Portugal took the lead in exploration when it began exploring the coast of Africa under the sponsorship of Prince Henry the Navigator (1394–1460). Prince Henry's motives were a blend of seeking a Christian kingdom as an ally against the Muslims, acquiring new trade opportunities for Portugal, and extending Christianity. In 1419, he founded a school for navigators on the southwestern coast of Portugal. Shortly thereafter, Portuguese fleets began probing southward along the western coast of Africa in search of gold. In 1441, Portuguese ships reached the Senegal River, just north of Cape Verde, and brought home a cargo of black Africans, most of whom were sold as slaves to wealthy buyers elsewhere in Europe. Within a few years, an estimated thousand slaves were shipped annually from the area back to Lisbon.

Continuing southward, in 1471 the Portuguese discovered a new source of gold along the southern coast of the hump of West Africa (an area that would henceforth be known to Europeans as the Gold Coast). To facilitate trade in gold, ivory, and slaves (some slaves were brought back to Lisbon and others were bartered to local merchants for gold), the Portuguese leased land from local rulers and built stone forts along the coast.

Hearing reports of a route to India around the southern tip of Africa, Portuguese sea captains continued their probing. In 1487, Bartolomeu Dias took advantage of westerly winds in the South Atlantic to round the Cape of Good Hope, but he feared a mutiny from his crew and returned home without continuing onward. Ten years later, a fleet under the command of Vasco da Gama rounded the cape and stopped at several ports controlled by Muslim merchants along the coast of East Africa, including Sofala, Kilwa, and Mombasa. Then da Gama's fleet crossed the Arabian Sea and arrived off the port of Calicut on the southwestern coast of India, on May 18, 1498. The Por-

AN EARLY JEWISH COMMUNITY IN INDIA. When Vasco de Gama arrived in the port city of Cochin, along the western coast of India, in 1498, he was surprised to discover the presence of a Jewish community that had been in the area since as early as the first century C.E. Jewish merchants from the Middle East had settled there to take part in the trading network that stretched westward from the Indian Ocean all the way to the Mediterranean Sea. Shown here is the entrance gate to the Jewish quarter in Cochin. Inside the gates are a number of commercial establishments and a synagogue that dates back to the fourteenth century.

tuguese crown had sponsored da Gama's voyage with the clear objective of destroying the Muslim monopoly over the spice trade, a monopoly that had been intensified by the Ottoman conquest of Constantinople in 1453 (see Chapter 15). Calicut was a major entrepôt on the long route from the Spice Islands to the Mediterranean Sea, but the ill-informed Europeans believed it was the source of the spices themselves. Although he lost two ships en route, da Gama's remaining vessels returned to Europe with their holds filled with ginger and cinnamon, a cargo that earned the investors a profit of several thousand percent.

During the next years, the Portuguese set out to gain control of the spice trade. In 1510, Admiral Afonso de Albuquerque established his headquarters at Goa, on the western coast of India south of present-day Bombay. From there, the Portuguese raided Arab shippers, provoking the following comment from an Arab source: "[The

THE PORTUGUESE CONQUEST
OF MALACCA

In 1511, a Portuguese fleet led by Afonso de Albuquerque attacked the Muslim sultanate at Malacca, on the west coast of the Malay peninsula. Occupation of the port gave the Portuguese control over the strategic Strait of Malacca and the route to the Spice Islands. In this passage, Albuquerque tells his men the reasons for the attack. Note that he sees control of Malacca as a way to reduce the power of the Muslim world. The relevance of economic wealth to military power continues to underlie conflicts among nations today. The Pacific War in the 1940s, for example, began as a result of a conflict over control of the rich resources of Southeast Asia.

THE COMMENTARIES OF THE GREAT AFONSO DE ALBUQUERQUE, SECOND VICEROY OF INDIA

Although there be many reasons which I could allege in favor of our taking this city and building a fortress therein to maintain possession of it, two only will I mention to you, on this occasion. . . .

The first is the great service which we shall perform to Our Lord in casting the Moors out of this country. . . . If we can only achieve the task before us, it will result in the Moors resigning India altogether to our rule, for the greater part of them—or perhaps all of them—live upon the trade of this country and are become great and rich, and lords of extensive treasures. . . . For when we were committing ourselves to the business of cruising in the Straits (of the Red Sea), where the King of Portugal had often ordered me to go (for it was there that His Highness considered we could cut down the commerce which the Moors of Cairo, of Mecca, and of Judah, carry on with these parts), Our Lord for his service thought right to lead us hither, for when Malacca is taken the places on the Straits must be shut up, and they will never more be able to introduce their spiceries into those places.

And the other reason is the additional service which we shall render to the King D. Manuel in taking this city, because it is the headquarters of all the spiceries and drugs which the Moors carry every year hence to the Straits without our being able to prevent them from so doing; but if we deprive them of this their ancient market there, there does not remain for them a single port, nor a single situation, so commodious in the whole of these parts, where they can carry on their trade in these things. . . . I hold it as very certain that if we take this trade of Malacca away out of their hands, Cairo and Mecca are entirely ruined, and to Venice will no spiceries be conveyed except that which her merchants go and buy in Portugal.

Portuguese] took about seven vessels, killing those on board and making some prisoner. This was their first action, may God curse them."[5] In 1511, Albuquerque attacked Malacca itself.

For Albuquerque, control of Malacca would serve two purposes. It could help to destroy the Arab spice trade network by blocking passage through the Strait of Malacca, and it could also provide the Portuguese with a way station en route to the Spice Islands and other points east (see the box above). After a short but bloody battle, the Portuguese seized the city and put the local Arab population to the sword. They then proceeded to erect a fort, a factory (a common term at the time for a warehouse), and a church.

The Spice Islands

From Malacca, the Portuguese launched expeditions farther east, to China and the Moluccas, then known as the Spice Islands. There they signed a treaty with a local sultan for the purchase and export of cloves to the European market. Within a few years, they had managed to seize control of the spice trade from Muslim traders and had garnered substantial profits for the Portuguese monarchy.

Why were the Portuguese so successful? Basically, their success was a matter of guns and seamanship. The first Portuguese fleet to arrive in Indian waters was relatively modest in size. It consisted of three ships and twenty guns, a force sufficient for self-defense and intimidation but not for serious military operations. Sixteenth-century Portuguese fleets were more heavily armed and were capable of inflicting severe defeats if necessary on local naval and land forces. The Portuguese by no means possessed a monopoly on the use of firearms and explosives, but they used the maneuverability of their light ships to maintain their distance while bombarding the enemy with their powerful cannons. Such tactics gave them a military superiority over lightly armed rivals that they were able to exploit until the arrival of other European forces several decades later.

Voyages to the "New World"

While the Portuguese were seeking access to the spice trade of the Indies by sailing eastward through the Indian Ocean, the Spanish attempted to reach the same destination by sailing westward across the Atlantic. Although the Spanish came to overseas discovery and exploration later than the Portuguese, their greater resources enabled them to establish a far grander overseas empire.

An important figure in the history of Spanish exploration was an Italian from Genoa, Christopher Columbus (1451–1506). Knowledgeable Europeans were aware that the world was round but had little understanding of its circumference or the extent of the continent of Asia. Convinced that the circumference of the earth was smaller than contemporaries believed and that Asia was larger, Columbus felt that Asia could be reached by sailing due west instead of eastward around Africa. After being rejected by the Portuguese, he persuaded Queen Isabella of Spain to finance his exploratory expedition, which reached the Americas in October 1492 and explored the coastline of Cuba and the northern shores of the neighboring island of Hispaniola. Columbus believed that he had reached Asia and in three subsequent voyages (1493, 1498, and 1502) sought in vain to find a route through the outer islands to the Asian mainland. In his four voyages, Columbus reached all the major islands of the Caribbean, which he called the Indies, as well as Honduras in Central America.

Although Columbus clung to his belief until his death, other explorers soon realized that he had discovered a new frontier altogether. State-sponsored explorers joined the race to the New World. A Venetian seafarer, John Cabot, explored the New England coastline of the Americas under a license from King Henry VII of England. The continent of South America was discovered accidentally by the Portuguese sea captain Pedro Cabral in 1500. Amerigo Vespucci, a Florentine, accompanied several voyages and wrote a series of letters describing the geography of the New World. The publication of these letters led to the use of the name "America" (after Amerigo) for the new lands.

The newly discovered territories were referred to as the New World, even though they possessed flourishing civilizations populated by millions of people when the Europeans arrived. But the Americas were new to the Europeans, who quickly saw opportunities for conquest and exploitation. The Spanish, in particular, were interested because in 1494 the Treaty of Tordesillas had divided the newly discovered world into separate Portuguese and Spanish spheres of influence. Thereafter the route east around the Cape of Good Hope was to be reserved for the Portuguese, while the route across the Atlantic (except for the eastern hump of South America) was assigned to Spain. The Spanish conquistadors were a hardy lot of mostly upper-class individuals motivated by a typical sixteenth-century blend of glory, greed, and religious crusading zeal. Although sanctioned by the Castilian crown, these groups were financed and outfitted privately, not by the government.

Their superior weapons, organizational skills, and determination brought the conquistadors incredible success. Beginning in 1519 with a small band of men, Hernán Cortés took three years to overthrow the mighty Aztec Empire in central Mexico, led by the chieftain Moctezuma

COLUMBUS LANDS IN THE NEW WORLD. In the log that he wrote during his first voyage to the Americas, Christopher Columbus noted that the peoples of the New World were intelligent and friendly, and relations between them and the Spanish were amicable at first. Later, however, the conquistadors began to mistreat the local people. Here is a somewhat imaginative painting of the first encounter from a European perspective. Note the upturned eyes of Columbus and several of his companions, suggesting that their motives were spiritual rather than material.

© North Wind Picture Archives

SPANISH ACTIVITIES IN THE AMERICAS

Christopher Columbus's first voyage to the Americas	1492
Last voyages of Columbus	1502–1504
Spanish conquest of Mexico	1519–1522
Francisco Pizarro's conquest of the Incas	1531–1536

(see Chapter 6). By 1550, the Spanish had gained control of northern Mexico. Between 1531 and 1536, another expedition led by a hardened and somewhat corrupt soldier, Francisco Pizarro (1470–1541), took control of the Inca Empire high in the Peruvian Andes. The Spanish conquests were undoubtedly facilitated by the previous arrival of European diseases, which had decimated the local population. Although it took another three decades before the western part of Latin America was brought under Spanish control (the Portuguese took over Brazil), already by 1535, the Spanish had created a system of colonial administration that made the New World an extension of the old—at least in European eyes.

Administration of the Spanish Empire in the New World

Spanish policy toward the inhabitants of the New World, whom the Europeans called Indians, was a combination of confusion, misguided paternalism, and cruel exploitation. Confusion arose over the nature of the Indians. Queen Isabella declared the Indians to be subjects of Castile and instituted the encomienda system, which permitted the conquering Spaniards to collect tribute from the natives and use them as laborers. In return, the holders of an encomienda were supposed to protect the Indians and supervise their spiritual and material needs. In practice, this meant that the settlers were free to implement the system as they pleased. Three thousand miles from Spain, Spanish settlers largely ignored their government and brutally used the Indians to pursue their own economic interests. Indians were put to work on sugar plantations and in the lucrative gold and silver mines. Forced labor, starvation, and especially disease took a fearful toll on Indian lives. With little or no natural resistance to European diseases, the Indians of America were ravaged by smallpox, measles, and typhus brought by the explorers and the conquistadors. Although scholarly estimates of native populations vary drastically, a reasonable guess is that at least half of the natives died of European diseases. On Hispaniola alone, out of an initial population of 100,000 natives when Columbus arrived in 1493, only 300 Indians survived by

1570. In 1542, largely in response to the publications of Bartolomé de Las Casas, a Dominican monk who championed the Indians (see the box on p. 304), the government abolished the encomienda system and provided more protection for the natives.

The chief organ of colonial administration was the Council of the Indies. The council nominated colonial viceroys, oversaw their activities, and kept an eye on ecclesiastical affairs in the colonies. Spanish possessions in the New World were initially divided between New Spain (Mexico, Central America, and the Caribbean islands), with its center in Mexico City, and Peru (western South America), with its capital at Lima. Each area was governed by a viceroy who served as the king's chief civil and military officer.

By papal agreement, the Catholic monarchs of Spain were given extensive rights over ecclesiastical affairs in the New World. They could nominate church officials, build churches, collect fees, and supervise the various religious orders that conducted missionary activities. Catholic monks had remarkable success converting and baptizing hundreds of thousands of Indians in the early years of the conquest. Soon after the missionaries came the establishment of dioceses, parishes, schools, and hospitals—all the trappings of a European society.

The Impact of European Expansion

The arrival of the Europeans had an enormous impact on both the conquerors and the conquered. The native American civilizations, which (as we discussed in Chapter 6) had their own unique qualities and a degree of sophistication rarely appreciated by the conquerors, were virtually destroyed, while the native populations were ravaged by diseases introduced by the Europeans. Ancient social and political structures were ripped up and replaced by European institutions, religion, language, and culture.

How does one evaluate the psychological impact of colonization on the colonizers? The relatively easy European success in dominating native peoples undoubtedly reinforced the conviction of Europeans in the inherent superiority of their civilization. The Scientific Revolution of the seventeenth century, to be followed by the era of imperialism a century later, then served to strengthen the Eurocentric perspective that has long pervaded Western civilization in its relationship with the rest of the world.

European expansion also affected the conquerors in the economic arena. Wherever they went in the Americas, Europeans sought gold and silver. One Aztec observer commented that the Spanish conquerors "longed and lusted for gold. Their bodies swelled with greed, and their hunger was ravenous; they hungered like pigs for that gold."[6] Rich silver deposits were found and exploited in Mexico and southern Peru (modern Bolivia). When the mines at Potosí in Peru were opened in 1545, the value of precious metals imported into Europe quadrupled. It has

LAS CASAS AND THE SPANISH TREATMENT
OF THE AMERICAN NATIVES

*B*artolomé de Las Casas (1474–1566) was a Dominican monk who participated in the conquest of Cuba and received land and Indians in return for his efforts. But in 1514, he underwent a radical transformation that led him to believe that the Indians had been cruelly mistreated by his fellow Spaniards. He spent the remaining years of his life (he lived to the age of ninety-two) fighting for the Indians. This section is taken from his most influential work, Brevísima Relación de la Destrucción de las Indias, known to English readers as The Tears of the Indians. This work was largely responsible for the legend of the Spanish as inherently "cruel and murderous fanatics." Many scholars today feel that Las Casas may have exaggerated his account to shock his contemporaries into action.

BARTOLOMÉ DE LAS CASAS, THE TEARS OF THE INDIANS

There is nothing more detestable or more cruel than the tyranny which the Spaniards use toward the Indians for the getting of pearl. Surely the infernal torments cannot much exceed the anguish that they endure, by reason of that way of cruelty; for they put them under water some four or five ells deep, where they are forced without any liberty of respiration, to gather up the shells wherein the Pearls are; sometimes they come up again with nets full of shells to take breath, but if they stay any while to rest themselves, immediately comes a hangman row'd in a little boat, who as soon as he hath well beaten them, drags them again to their labor. Their food is nothing but filth, and the very same that contains the Pearl, with small portion of that bread which that Country affords; in the first whereof there is little nourishment; and as for the latter, it is made with great difficulty, besides that they have not enough of that neither for sustenance; they lie upon the ground in fetters, lest they should run away; and many times they are drown'd in this labor, and are never seen again till they swim upon the top of the waves; oftentimes they also are devoured by certain sea monsters, that are frequent in those seas. Consider whether this hard usage of the poor creatures be consistent with the precepts which God commands concerning charity to our neighbor, by those that cast them so undeservedly into the dangers of a cruel death, causing them to perish without any remorse or pity, or allowing them the benefit of the Sacraments, or the knowledge of Religion; it being impossible for them to live any time under the water; and this death is so much the more painful, by reason that by the coarctation of the breast, while the lungs strive to do their office, the vital parts are so afflicted that they die vomiting the blood out of their mouths. Their hair also, which is by nature black, is hereby changed and made of the same color with that of the sea Wolves; their bodies are also so besprinkled with the froth of the sea, that they appear rather like monsters than men.

been estimated that between 1503 and 1650, some 16 million kilograms of silver and 185,000 kilograms of gold entered the port of Seville, fueling a price revolution that affected the Spanish economy.

But gold and silver were only two of the products sent to Europe from the New World. Into Seville flowed sugar, dyes, cotton, vanilla, and hides from livestock raised on the South American pampas. New agricultural products native to the Americas, such as potatoes, cacao, corn, manioc, and tobacco, were also imported. Because of its trading posts in Asia, Portugal soon challenged the Italian states as the chief entry point of the eastern trade in spices, jewels, silk, carpets, ivory, leather, and perfumes. Economic historians believe that the increase in the volume and area of European trade and the rise in fluid capital due to this expansion were crucial factors in producing a new era of commercial capitalism that represented the first step toward the world economy that has characterized the modern era.

European expansion, which was in part a product of European rivalries, also deepened those rivalries and increased the tensions among European states. Bitter conflicts arose over the cargoes coming from the New World and Asia. Although the Spanish and Portuguese were first in the competition, by the end of the sixteenth century, new competitors were entering the scene and beginning to challenge the dominance of the Iberian powers. The first to arrive were the English and the Dutch.

Why did Europeans risk their lives to explore new lands far from friendly shores? For some, expansion abroad brought hopes for land, riches, and social advancement. Although some wives accompanied their husbands abroad, many ordinary European women found new opportunities for marriage in the New World because of the lack of white women. In the violence-prone world of early Spanish America, a number of women also found themselves rich after their husbands were killed unexpectedly. In one area of Central America, women owned about 25 percent of the landed estates by 1700.

New Rivals

Portugal's efforts to dominate the trade of the Indian Ocean were never totally successful. The Portuguese lacked both the numbers and the wealth to overcome local resistance and colonize the Asian regions. Moreover, their massive investments in ships and laborers for their empire (hundreds of ships and hundreds of thousands of workers in shipyards and overseas bases) proved very costly. Disease, shipwreck, and battles took a heavy toll of life. The empire was simply too large and Portugal too small to maintain it, and by the end of the century, the Portuguese were being severely challenged by rivals.

The Spanish had established themselves in Asia in the early 1520s, when Ferdinand Magellan, seeking a western route to the Spice Islands across the Pacific Ocean, had sailed around the southern tip of South America, crossed the Pacific, and landed on the island of Cebu in the Philippine Islands. Although Magellan and some forty of his crew were killed in a skirmish with the local population, one of the two remaining ships sailed on to Tidor, in the Moluccas, and thence around the world via the Cape of Good Hope. In the words of a contemporary historian, they arrived in Cádiz "with precious cargo and fifteen men surviving out of a fleet of five sail."[7]

As it turned out, the Spanish could not follow up on Magellan's accomplishment, and in 1529, they sold their rights in Tidor to the Portuguese. But Magellan's voyage was not a total loss. In the absence of concerted resistance from the local population, the Spanish managed to consolidate their control over the Philippines, which eventually became a major Spanish base in the carrying trade across the Pacific.

The primary threat to the Portuguese toehold in Southeast Asia, however, came from the English and the Dutch. In 1591, the first English expedition to the Indies through the Indian Ocean arrived in London with a cargo of pepper. Nine years later, a private joint-stock company, the East India Company, was founded to provide a stable source of capital for future voyages. In 1608, an English fleet landed at Surat, on the northwestern coast of India. Trade with Southeast Asia soon followed.

The Dutch were quick to follow suit, and the first Dutch fleet arrived in India in 1595. In 1602, the Dutch East India Company was established under government sponsorship and was soon actively competing with the English and the Portuguese in the region.

The Dutch, the French, and the English also began to make inroads on Spanish and Portuguese possessions in the Americas. War and steady pressure from their Dutch and English rivals eroded Portuguese trade in both the West and the East, although Portugal continued to profit from its large colonial empire in Brazil. A formal administration system had been instituted in Brazil in 1549, and Portuguese migrants had established massive plantations there to produce sugar for export to the

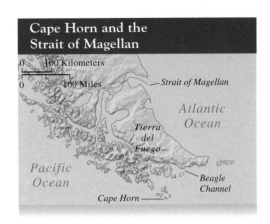

Cape Horn and the Strait of Magellan

Old World. The Spanish also maintained an enormous South American empire, but Spain's importance as a commercial power declined rapidly in the seventeenth century because of a drop in the output of the silver mines and the poverty of the Spanish monarchy.

The Dutch formed their own Dutch West India Company in 1621 to compete with Spanish and Portuguese interests in the Americas. But although it made some inroads in Portuguese Brazil and the Caribbean (see Map 14.2), the company's profits were never large enough to compensate for the expenditures. Dutch settlements were also established on the North American continent. The mainland colony of New Netherland stretched from the mouth of the Hudson River as far north as Albany, New York. In the meantime, French colonies appeared in the Lesser Antilles, and in Louisiana, at the mouth of the Mississippi River.

In the second half of the seventeenth century, however, rivalry and years of warfare with the English and the French (who had also become active in North America) brought the decline of the Dutch commercial empire in the New World. In 1664, the English seized the colony of New Netherland and renamed it New York, and the Dutch West India Company soon went bankrupt. In 1663, Canada became the property of the French crown and was administered like a French province. But the French failed to provide adequate men or money, allowing their continental wars to take precedence over the conquest of the North American continent. By the early eighteenth century, the French began to cede some of their American possessions to their English rival.

The English, meanwhile, had proceeded to create a colonial empire in the New World along the Atlantic seaboard of North America. The desire to escape from religious oppression combined with economic interests did make successful colonization possible, as the Massachusetts Bay Company demonstrated. The Massachusetts colony had only four thousand settlers in its early years, but by 1660, their number had swelled to forty thousand.

AFRICA IN TRANSITION

Although the primary objective of the Portuguese in rounding the Cape of Good Hope was to find a sea route to the Spice Islands, they soon discovered that profits were

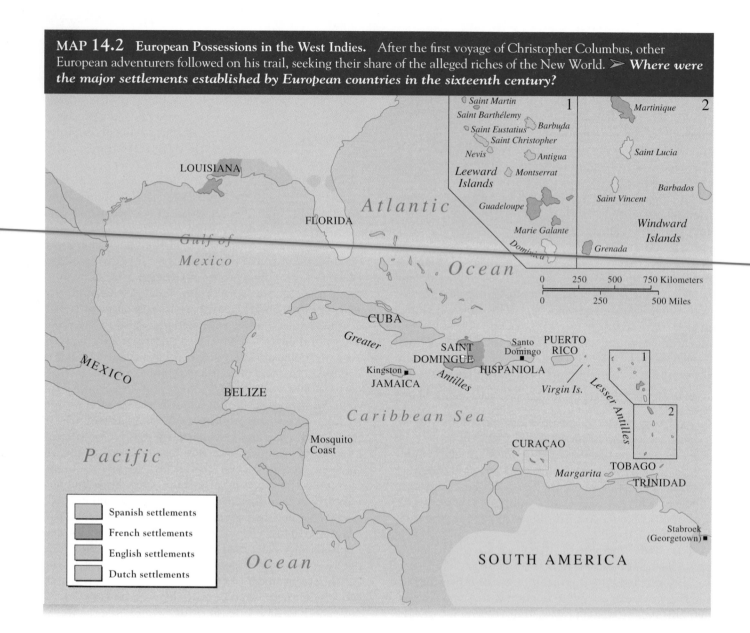

MAP 14.2 European Possessions in the West Indies. After the first voyage of Christopher Columbus, other European adventurers followed on his trail, seeking their share of the alleged riches of the New World. ➤ *Where were the major settlements established by European countries in the sixteenth century?*

LOUISIANA

FLORIDA

Atlantic

Gulf of
Mexico

Ocean

MEXICO

BELIZE

Pacific

Greater

CUBA

SAINT
DOMINGUE

Kingston
JAMAICA

Santo
Domingo

Antilles

PUERTO
RICO

HISPANIOLA

Virgin Is.

Lesser Antilles

Caribbean Sea

Mosquito
Coast

CURAÇAO

Margarita

TOBAGO

TRINIDAD

Ocean

SOUTH AMERICA

Stabroek
(Georgetown)

Saint Martin
Saint Barthélemy
Saint Eustatius   Barbuda
Saint Christopher
Nevis   Antigua
Leeward   Montserrat
Islands

Guadeloupe

Marie Galante

Dominica

1

Martinique   2

Saint Lucia

Saint Vincent   Barbados

Windward
Islands

Grenada

1

2

▢	Spanish settlements
▢	French settlements
▢	English settlements
▢	Dutch settlements

0   250   500   750 Kilometers
0   250   500 Miles

to be made en route, along the eastern coast of Africa. In the early sixteenth century, a Portuguese fleet seized a number of East African port cities, including Kilwa, Sofala, and Mombasa, and built forts along the coast in an effort to control the trade in the area. Above all, the Portuguese wanted to monopolize the trade in gold, which was mined by Bantu workers in the hills along the upper Zambezi River and then shipped to Sofala on the coast (see Chapter 8). For centuries, the gold trade had been monopolized by local Shona peoples at Zimbabwe. In the fifteenth century, it had come under the control of a Shona dynasty known as the Mwene Metapa. The Portuguese opened treaty relations with the Mwene Metapa, and Jesuit priests were eventually posted to the court in 1561. At first, the Mwene Metapa found the Europeans useful as an ally against local rivals, but by the end of the sixteenth century, the Portuguese had established a protectorate and

forced the local ruler to grant title to large tracts of land to European officials and private individuals living in the area. The Portuguese, however, lacked the personnel, the capital, and the expertise to dominate local trade, and in the late seventeenth century, a vassal of the Mwene Metapa succeeded in driving them from the plateau; his descendants maintained control of the area for the next two hundred years.

The first Europeans to settle in southern Africa were the Dutch. After an unsuccessful attempt to seize the Portuguese settlement on the island of Mozambique off the East African coast, in 1652 the Dutch set up a way station at the Cape of Good Hope to serve as a base for their fleets en route to the East Indies. At first, the new settlement was meant simply to provide food and other provisions to Dutch ships, but eventually it developed into a permanent colony. Dutch farmers, known as Boers and speak-

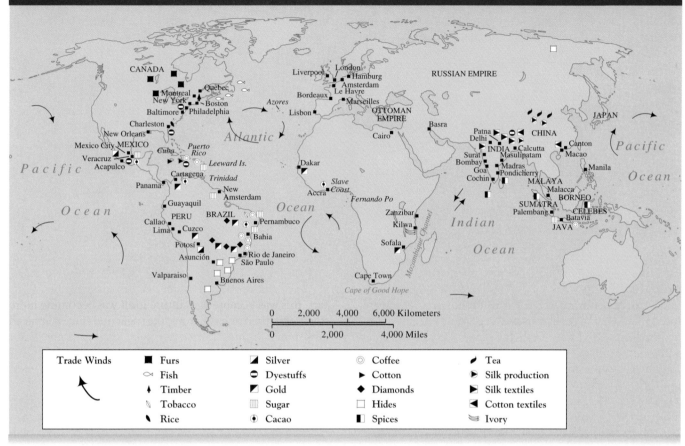

Trade Winds	■	Furs	◪	Silver	◎	Coffee	✒	Tea
	∾	Fish	⬭	Dyestuffs	►	Cotton	►	Silk production
	♦	Timber	◪	Gold	◆	Diamonds	◄	Silk textiles
	⬈	Tobacco	⦀	Sugar	□	Hides	◄	Cotton textiles
	➘	Rice	◉	Cacao	▮	Spices	〰	Ivory

the region than anywhere else in Asia. Daughters often had the same inheritance rights as sons, and family property was held jointly between husband and wife. Wives were often permitted to divorce their husbands, and monogamy was the rule rather than the exception. Although women were usually restricted to specialized work, such as making ceramics, weaving, or transplanting the rice seedlings into the main paddy fields, and rarely possessed legal rights equal to those of men, they enjoyed a comparatively high degree of freedom and status in most societies in the region and were sometimes involved in commerce.

 ## CONCLUSION

During the fifteenth century, Europeans burst onto the world scene. Beginning with the seemingly modest ventures of the Portuguese ships that sailed southward along the West African coast, the process accelerated with the epoch-making voyages of Christopher Columbus to the Americas and Vasco da Gama to the Indian Ocean in the

1490s. Soon a number of other European states had entered the scene, and by the end of the eighteenth century, they had created a global trade network dominated by Western ships and Western power that distributed foodstuffs, textile goods, spices, and precious minerals from one end of the globe to the other (see Map 14.4).

In less than three hundred years, the European Age of Exploration changed the face of the world. In some areas, such as the Americas and the Spice Islands, it led to the destruction of indigenous civilizations and the establishment of European colonies. In others, as in Africa, South Asia, and mainland Southeast Asia, it left native regimes intact but had a strong impact on local societies and regional trade patterns.

At the time, many European observers viewed the process in a favorable light. Not only did it expand world trade and foster the exchange of new crops and discoveries between the Old and the New Worlds (a process that will be discussed in the Reflection at the end of Part III), but it also introduced the message of Jesus Christ to "heathen peoples" around the globe. Most modern historians have been much more critical, concluding that European activities during the sixteenth and seventeenth centuries created a "tributary mode of production" based on European profits from unequal terms of trade that foreshadowed the exploitative relationship characteristic of the later colonial period. Other scholars have questioned that contention, however, and argue that although Western commercial operations had a significant impact on global trade patterns, they did not—at least not before the eighteenth century—freeze out non-European participants. Muslim merchants, for example, were long able to evade European efforts to eliminate them from the spice trade, and the trans-Saharan caravan trade was relatively unaffected by European merchant shipping along the West African coast.

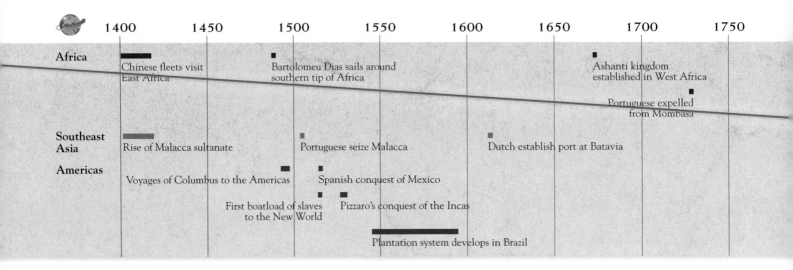

	1400	1450	1500	1550	1600	1650	1700	1750

Africa
Chinese fleets visit East Africa
Bartolomeu Dias sails around southern tip of Africa
Ashanti kingdom established in West Africa
Portuguese expelled from Mombasa

Southeast Asia
Rise of Malacca sultanate
Portuguese seize Malacca
Dutch establish port at Batavia

Americas
Voyages of Columbus to the Americas
Spanish conquest of Mexico
First boatload of slaves to the New World
Pizzaro's conquest of the Incas
Plantation system develops in Brazil

CHAPTER NOTES

1. Harry J. Benda and John A. Larkin, eds., *The World of Southeast Asia: Selected Historical Readings* (New York, 1967), p. 13.
2. J. H. Parry, *The European Reconnaissance: Selected Documents* (New York, 1968), p. 113, quoting from Armando Cortesão, *The Summa Oriental of Tomé Pires* (London, 1944), vol. 2, pp. 283–287.
3. Quoted in J. H. Parry, *The Age of Reconnaissance: Discovery, Exploration, and Settlement, 1450 to 1650* (New York, 1963), p. 33.
4. Quoted in Richard B. Reed, "The Expansion of Europe," in Richard DeMolen, ed., *The Meaning of the Renaissance and Reformation* (Boston, 1974), p. 308.

5. K. N. Chaudhuri, *Trade and Civilization in the Indian Ocean: An Economic History from the Rise of Islam to 1750* (Cambridge, 1985), p. 65.
6. Miguel Leon-Portilla, ed., *The Broken Spears: The Aztec Account of the Conquest of Mexico* (Boston, 1969), p. 51.
7. Quoted in Parry, *Age of Reconnaissance*, pp. 176–177.
8. Quoted in Basil Davidson, *Africa in History: Themes and Outlines* (London, 1968), p. 137.

SUGGESTED READING

Classic works on the period of European expansion include J. H. Parry, *The Age of Reconnaissance: Discovery, Exploration, and Settlement, 1450 to 1650* (New York, 1963); B. Penrose, *Travel and Discovery in the Renaissance, 1420–1620* (New York, 1962); and the brief work by J. H. Parry, *The Establishment of European Hegemony, 1415–1715* (New York, 1961). Also see K. M. Panikkar, *Asia and Western Dominance* (London, 1959), and H. Furber, *Rival Empires of Trade in the Orient, 1600–1800* (Minneapolis, 1976). For a more

critical interpretation, see E. Wolf, *Europe and the People Without History* (Berkeley, Calif., 1982), and A. G. Frank, *World Accumulation, 1492–1789* (New York, 1978).

On the technological aspects, see C. M. Cipolla, *Guns, Sails, and Empires: Technological Innovation and the Early Phases of European Expansion, 1400–1700* (New York, 1965); F. Fernandez-Armesto, ed., *The Times Atlas of World Exploration* (New York, 1991); and R. C. Smith, *Vanguard of Empire: Ships of Exploration in the*

Age of Columbus (Oxford, 1993); also see A. Pagden, *Lords of All the World: Ideologies of Empire in Spain, Britain, and France, c. 1500–c. 1800* (New Haven, Conn., 1995). For an overview on the impact of European expansion in the Indian Ocean, see K. N. Chaudhuri, *Trade and Civilization in the Indian Ocean: An Economic History from the Rise of Islam to 1750* (Cambridge, 1985). For a series of stimulating essays reflecting modern scholarship, see J. D. Tracy, *The Rise of Merchant Empires: Long-Distance Trade in the Early Modern World, 1350–1750* (Cambridge, 1990).

For a fundamental work on Spanish colonization, see J. H. Parry, *The Spanish Seaborne Empire* (New York, 1966). A recent work on the conquistadors is H. Thomas, *Conquest: Montezuma, Cortés, and the Fall of Old Mexico* (New York, 1993). The human effects of the interaction of New and Old World cultures are examined thoughtfully in A. W. Crosby, *The Columbian Exchange: Biological and Cultural Consequences of 1492* (Westport, Conn., 1972).

On Portuguese expansion, the fundamental work is C. R. Boxer, *The Portuguese Seaborne Empire, 1415–1825* (New York, 1969). For a more recent interpretation, see W. B. Diffie and G. D. Winius, *Foundations of the Portuguese Empire, 1415–1580* (Minneapolis, 1979). On the Dutch, see J. I. Israel, *Dutch Primacy in World Trade,* 1585–1740 (Oxford, 1989). The effects of European trade in Southeast Asia are discussed in A. Reid, *Southeast Asia in the Age of Commerce, 1450–1680* (New Haven, Conn., 1989).

On the African slave trade, the standard work is P. Curtin, *The African Slave Trade: A Census* (Madison, Wis., 1969). For more recent treatments, see P. Lovejoy, *Transformations in Slavery: A History of Slavery in Africa* (1983), and P. Manning, *Slavery and African Life* (Cambridge, 1990); H. Thomas, *The Slave Trade* (New York, 1997), provides a useful overview.

For a brief introduction to women's experiences during the Age of Exploration and global trade, see S. Hughes and B. Hughes, *Women in World History*, vol. 2 (Armonk, N.Y., 1997). For a more theoretical discussion of violence and gender in the early modern period, consult R. Trexler, *Sex and Conquest: Gendered Violence, Political Order, and the European Conquest of the Americas* (Ithaca, N.Y., 1995). The native American female experience with the European encounter is presented in R. Gutierrez, *When Jesus Came the Corn Mothers Went Away: Marriage, Sexuality and Power in New Mexico, 1500–1846* (Stanford, Calif., 1991), and K. Anderson, *Chain Her by One Foot: The Subjugation of Women in Seventeenth Century New France* (London, 1991).

INFOTRAC COLLEGE EDITION

Visit the source collections at infotrac.thomsonlearning.com and use the Search function with the following key terms.

African history   mercantilism

Christopher Columbus   Vasco da Gama

WORLD HISTORY RESOURCES

Visit the *Essential World History* Companion Web Site for resources specific to this textbook:

http://history.wadsworth.com/duikeressentials02/

The CD in the back of this book and the World History Resource Center at **http://history.wadsworth.com/world/** offer a variety of tools to help you succeed in this course, including access to quizzes; images; documents; interactive simulations, maps, and timelines; movie explorations; and a wealth of other sources.

© Sonia Halliday Photographs

Chapter 15

THE MUSLIM EMPIRES

FOCUS QUESTIONS

- Why are the Ottoman, Safavid, and Mughal Empires sometimes called "gunpowder empires," and how accurate is that characterization?
- What were the main characteristics of each of the Muslim empires, and in what ways were they similar?
- What contact did each of the Muslim empires have with Europeans, and how was each empire affected by that contact?
- What role did women play in each of the Muslim empires?
- ➢ How did each of the great Muslim empires come into existence, and why did they ultimately decline?

*O*ne of the primary objectives of European leaders in seeking a route to the Spice Islands was to lessen the political and economic power of Islam by reducing the Muslims' strong position in the global trade network. As we saw in Chapter 14, Portuguese fleets, followed by those of the Spanish, the English, and the Dutch, had some success in wresting control over the spice trade from Muslim shippers, although the latter were never totally driven out of the business. By the eighteenth century, the Indian Ocean had ceased to be an Arab preserve and had become, in some respects, a European lake.

Thus the European dream of controlling global trade markets had become a reality. But in the broader scheme of things, the goal of crippling the power of Islam was not entirely realized, for Europe's success had not been achieved by the collapse of its great rival. To the contrary, the Muslim world, which appeared to have entered a period of decline with the collapse of the Abbasid caliphate during the era of the Mongols, managed to revive in the shadow of Europe's Age of Exploration, a period that also saw the rise of three great Muslim empires. These powerful Muslim states—those of the Ottomans, the Safavids, and the Mughals—dominated the Middle East and the South Asian subcontinent and brought stability to a region that had been in turmoil for centuries. ●

THE OTTOMAN EMPIRE

The Ottoman Turks were among the various Turkic-speaking peoples who had spread westward from Central Asia in the ninth, tenth, and eleventh centuries. The first to dominate were the Seljuk Turks, who initially attempted to revive the declining Abbasid caliphate in Baghdad. Later they established themselves in the Anatolian peninsula at the expense of the Byzantine Empire. Turks served as warriors or administrators, while the peasants who tilled the farmland were mainly Greek.

In the late thirteenth century, a new group of Turks under the tribal leader Osman (1280–1326) began to consolidate their power in the northwestern corner of the Anatolian peninsula. At first, the Osman Turks were relatively peaceful and engaged in pastoral pursuits, but as the Seljuk Empire began to disintegrate in the early fourteenth century, they began to expand and founded the Osmanli (later to be known as Ottoman) dynasty.

The Ottomans gained a key advantage by seizing the Bosporus and the Dardanelles, between the Mediterranean and the Black Seas. The Byzantine Empire, of course, had controlled the area for centuries, serving as a buffer between the Muslim Middle East and the Latin West. The Byzantines, however, had been severely weakened by the sack of Constantinople in the Fourth Crusade (in 1204) and the Western occupation of much of the empire for the next half century. In 1345, Ottoman forces under their leader Orkhan I (1326–1360) crossed the Bosporus for the first time to support a usurper against the Byzantine emperor in Constantinople. Setting up their first European base at Gallipoli at the Mediterranean entrance to the Dardanelles, Turkish forces expanded gradually into the Balkans and allied with fractious Serbian and Bulgar forces against the Byzantines. In these unstable conditions, the Ottomans gradually established permanent settlements throughout the area, where Turkish beys (provincial governors in the Ottoman Empire; from the Turkish *beg*, "knight") drove out the previous landlords and collected taxes from the local Slavic peasants. The Ottoman leader now began to claim the title of sultan or sovereign of his domain.

In 1360, Orkhan was succeeded by his son Murad I, who consolidated Ottoman power in the Balkans and gradually reduced the Byzantine emperor to a vassal. Murad now began to build up a strong military administration based on the recruitment of Christians into an elite guard. Called Janissaries (from the Turkish *yeni cheri*, "new troops"), they were recruited from the local Christian population in the Balkans and then converted to Islam and trained as foot soldiers or administrators. One of the major advantages of the Janissaries was that they were directly subordinated to the sultanate and therefore owed their loyalty to the person of the sultan. Other military forces were organized by the beys and were thus loyal to their local tribal leaders.

The Janissary corps also represented a response to changes in warfare. As the knowledge of firearms spread in the late

MEHMET II, CONQUEROR OF CONSTANTINOPLE. Identified with the seizure of Constantinople from the Byzantine Empire in 1453, Mehmet II was one of the most illustrious Ottoman sultans. This Turkish miniature portrays Mehmet II with his handkerchief, a symbol of the supreme power of the Ottoman ruler. He is also smelling a rose, representing his cultural interests, especially as patron of the arts.

© Sonia Halliday Photographs

fourteenth century, the Turks began to master the new technology, including siege cannons and muskets. The traditional nomadic cavalry charge was now outmoded and was superseded by infantry forces armed with muskets. Thus the Janissaries provided a well-armed infantry who served both as an elite guard to protect the palace and as a means of extending Turkish control in the Balkans. With his new forces, Murad defeated the Serbs at the famous Battle of Kosovo in 1389 and ended Serbian hegemony in the area.

Under Murad's successor, Bayazid I (1389–1402), the Ottomans advanced northward, annexed Bulgaria, and slaughtered the flower of French cavalry at a major battle on the Danube. When Mehmet II (1451–1481) succeeded to the throne, he was determined to capture Constantinople. Already in control of the Dardanelles, he ordered the construction of a major fortress on the Bosporus just north of the city, which put the Turks in a position to strangle the Byzantines.

THE FALL OF CONSTANTINOPLE

F̶ew events in the history of the Ottoman Empire are more dramatic than the conquest of Constantinople in 1453. In this excerpt, the conquest is described by Kritovoulos, a Greek who later served in the Ottoman administration. Although the author did not witness the conquest itself, he was apparently well informed about the event and provides us with a vivid description.

KRITOVOULOS, *LIFE OF MEHMED THE CONQUEROR*

So saying, he [the Sultan] led them himself. And they, with a shout on the run and with a fearsome yell, went on ahead of the Sultan, pressing on up to the palisade. After a long and bitter struggle they hurled back the Romans [Byzantines] from there and climbed by force up the palisade. They dashed some of their foe down into the ditch between the great wall and the palisade, which was deep and hard to get out of, and they killed them there. The rest they drove back to the gate.

He had opened this gate in the great wall, so as to go easily over to the palisade. Now there was a great struggle there and great slaughter among those stationed there, for they were attacked by the heavy infantry and not a few others in irregular formation, who had been attracted from many points by the shouting. There the Emperor Constantine [Constantine XIII Paleologus], with all who were with him, fell in gallant combat.

The heavy infantry were already streaming through the little gate into the City, and others had rushed in through the breach in the great wall. Then all the rest of the army, with a rush and a roar, poured in brilliantly and scattered all over the City. And the Sultan stood before the great wall, where the standard also was and the ensigns, and watched the proceedings. The day was already breaking. . . .

The soldiers fell on them [the citizens] with anger and great wrath. For one thing, they were actuated by the hardships of the siege. For another, some foolish people had hurled taunts and curses at them from the battlements all through the siege. Now, in general they killed so as to frighten all the City, and to terrorize and enslave all by the slaughter.

When they had had enough of murder, and the City was reduced to slavery, some of the troops turned to the mansions of the mighty, by bands and companies and divisions, for plunder and spoil. Others went to the robbing of churches, and others dispersed to the simple homes of the common people, stealing, robbing, plundering, killing, insulting, taking and enslaving men, women, and children, old and young, priests, monks—in short, every age and class. . . .

After this the Sultan entered the City and looked about to see its great size, its situation, its grandeur and beauty, its teeming population, its loveliness, and the costliness of its churches and public buildings and of the private houses and community houses and those of the officials. . . . When he saw what a large number had been killed, and the ruin of the buildings, and the wholesale ruin and destruction of the City, he was filled with compassion and repented not a little at the destruction and plundering. Tears fell from his eyes as he groaned deeply and passionately: "What a city we have given over to plunder and destruction." . . .

As for the great City of Constantine, raised to a great height of glory and dominion and wealth in its own times, overshadowing to an infinite degree all the cities around it, renowned for its glory, wealth, authority, power, and greatness, and all its other qualities, it thus came to its end.

The last Byzantine emperor desperately called for help from the Europeans, but only the Genoese came to his defense. With eighty thousand troops ranged against only seven thousand defenders, Mehmet laid siege to Constantinople in 1453. In their attack on the city, the Turks made use of massive cannons with 26-foot barrels that could launch stone balls weighing up to 1,200 pounds each. The Byzantines stretched heavy chains across the Golden Horn, the inlet that forms the city's harbor, to prevent a naval attack from the north and prepared to make their final stand behind the 13-mile-long wall along the western edge of the city. But Mehmet's forces seized the tip of the peninsula north of the Golden Horn and then dragged their ships overland across the peninsula from the Bosporus and put them into the water behind the chains.

Finally, the walls were breached; the Byzantine emperor died in the final battle (see the box above).

Expansion of the Empire

With their new capital at Constantinople, renamed Istanbul, the Ottoman Turks were now a dominant force in the Balkans and the Anatolian peninsula. They now began to advance to the east against the Shi'ite kingdom of the Safavids in Persia (see "The Safavids" later in this chapter),

The Fall of Constantinople, 1453

Legend:
- Ottoman Empire, 1451
- Ottoman gains to 1481
- Ottoman gains to 1521
- Ottoman gains to 1566
- Area lost to Austria in 1699
- Battle sites

which had been promoting rebellion among the Anatolian tribal population and disrupting Turkish trade through the Middle East. After defeating the Safavids at a major battle in 1514, Emperor Selim I (1512–1520) consolidated Turkish control over Mesopotamia and then turned his attention to the Mamluks in Egypt, who had failed to support the Ottomans in their struggle against the Safavids. The Mamluks were defeated in Syria in 1516; Cairo fell a year later. Now controlling several of the holy cities of Islam, including Jerusalem, Mecca, and Medina, Selim declared himself to be the new caliph, or successor to Muhammad. During the next few years, Turkish armies and fleets advanced westward along the African coast, occupying Tripoli, Tunis, and Algeria and eventually penetrating almost to the Strait of Gibraltar (see Map 15.1).

The impact of Turkish rule on the peoples of North Africa was relatively light. Like their predecessors, the Turks were Muslims, and they preferred where possible to administer their conquered regions through local rulers. Central government direction was achieved through appointed pashas who collected taxes (and then paid a fixed percentage as tribute to the central government), maintained law and order, and were directly responsible to Istanbul. The Turks ruled from coastal cities like Algiers, Tunis, and Tripoli and made no attempt to control the interior beyond maintaining the trade routes through the Sahara to the trading centers along the Niger River. Meanwhile, local pirates along the Barbary Coast—the northern coast of Africa from Egypt to the Atlantic Ocean—competed with their Christian rivals in raiding the shipping that passed through the Mediterranean.

By the seventeenth century, the links between the imperial court in Istanbul and its appointed representatives in the Turkish regencies in North Africa had begun to decline. Some of the pashas were dethroned by local elites, while others, such as the bey of Tunis, became

Reign of Osman I	1280–1326
Ottoman Turks first cross the Bosporus	1345
Murad I consolidates Turkish power in the Balkans	1360
Ottomans defeat Serbian army at Kosovo	1389
Tamerlane defeats Ottoman army at Ankara	1402
Rule of Mehmet II (the Conqueror)	1451–1481
Turkish conquest of Constantinople	1453
Turks defeat Mamluks in Syria and seize Cairo	1516–1517
Reign of Suleyman I (the Magnificent)	1520–1566
Defeat of Hungarians at Battle of Mohács	1526
Defeat of Turks at Vienna	1529
Battle of Lepanto	1571

THE SIEGE OF VIENNA. After seizing the Byzantine capital of Constantinople in 1453, Turkish forces began advancing into southern Europe to extend the borders of the Ottoman Empire. By 1529, they had reached the gates of Vienna, capital of the Habsburg Empire, which they placed under siege. In this contemporary painting from the Topkapi Palace in Istanbul, Turkish forces across the Danube River have besieged the walled city, shown in the background. Despite the use of cannons, first introduced to the West by Ottoman forces during this campaign, the siege was unsuccessful.

hereditary rulers. Even Egypt, whose agricultural wealth and control over the route to the Red Sea made it the most important country in the area to the Turks, gradually became autonomous under a new official class of Janissaries.

TURKISH EXPANSION IN EUROPE

After their conquest of Constantinople in 1453, the Ottoman Turks tried to extend their territory in Europe. Under the leadership of Suleyman I the Magnificent (1520–1566), Turkish forces advanced up the Danube,

seizing Belgrade in 1521 and winning a major victory over the Hungarians at the Battle of Mohács on the Danube in 1526. Subsequently the Turks overran most of Hungary, moved into Austria, and advanced as far as Vienna, where they were finally repulsed in 1529. At the same time, they extended their power into the western Mediterranean and threatened to turn it into a Turkish lake until a large Turkish fleet was destroyed by the Spanish at Lepanto in 1571.

Under a new line of grand vezirs in the second half of the seventeenth century, the Ottoman Empire again took the offensive. By mid-1683, the Ottomans had marched through the Hungarian plain and laid siege to Vienna. Repulsed by a mixed army of Austrians, Poles, Bavarians, and Saxons, the Turks retreated and were pushed out of Hungary by a new European coalition. Although they retained the core of their empire, the Ottoman Turks would never again be a threat to Europe. Although the Turkish empire held together for the rest of the seventeenth and the eighteenth centuries, it would be faced with new challenges from the ever-growing Austrian Empire in southeastern Europe and the new Russian giant to the north.

The Nature of Turkish Rule

Like other Muslim empires in Persia and India, the Ottoman political system was the result of the evolution of tribal institutions into a sedentary empire. At the apex

© Sonia Halliday Photographs

success, war resumed in the 1620s, and a lasting peace was not achieved until 1638 (see Map 15.2).

Abbas the Great had managed to strengthen the dynasty significantly, and for a time after his death in 1629, it remained stable and vigorous. But succession conflicts plagued the dynasty. Partly as a result, the power of the more militant Shi'ites began to increase at court and in Safavid society at large. The intellectual freedom that had characterized the empire at its height was curtailed under the pressure of religious orthodoxy, and Iranian women, who had enjoyed considerable freedom and influence during the early empire, were forced to withdraw into seclusion and behind the veil. Meanwhile, attempts to suppress the religious beliefs of minorities led to increased popular unrest. In the early eighteenth century, Afghan warriors took advantage of local revolts to seize the capital of Isfahan, forcing the remnants of the Safavid ruling family to retreat to Azerbaijan, their original homeland. The Ottomans seized territories along the western border. Eventually order was restored by the military adventurer Nadir Shah Afshar, who launched an extended series of campaigns that restored the country's borders and even occupied the Mughal capital of Delhi (see "Twilight of the Mughals" later in this chapter). After his death, the Zand dynasty ruled until the end of the eighteenth century.

Safavid Politics and Society

Like the Ottoman Empire, Iran under the Safavids was a mixed society. The Safavids had come to power with the support of nomadic Turkic-speaking tribal groups, and leading elements from those groups retained considerable influence within the empire. But the majority of the population were Iranian; most of them were farmers or townspeople, with attitudes inherited from the relatively sophisticated and urbanized culture of pre-Safavid Iran. Faced with the problem of integrating unruly Turkic-speaking tribal peoples with the sedentary Persian-speaking population of the urban areas, the Safavids used the Shi'ite faith as a unifying force. The shah himself acquired an almost divine quality and claimed to be the spiritual leader of all Islam. Shi'ism was declared the state religion.

Although there was a landed aristocracy, aristocratic power and influence were firmly controlled by strong-minded shahs, who confiscated aristocratic estates when

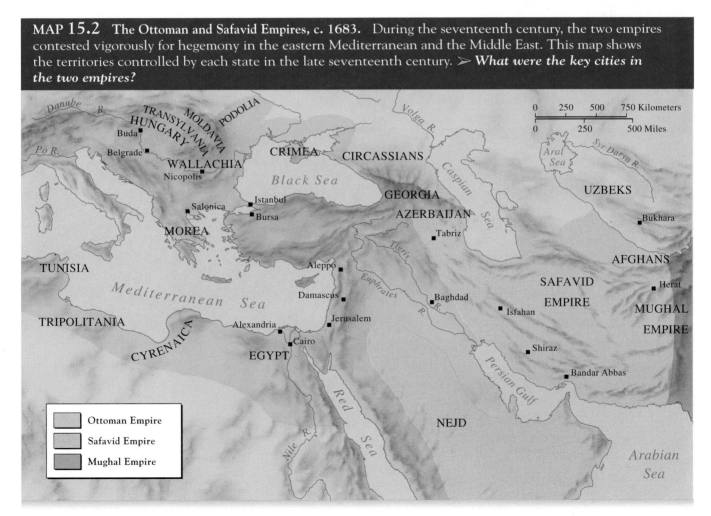

MAP 15.2 The Ottoman and Safavid Empires, c. 1683. During the seventeenth century, the two empires contested vigorously for hegemony in the eastern Mediterranean and the Middle East. This map shows the territories controlled by each state in the late seventeenth century. ➤ *What were the key cities in the two empires?*

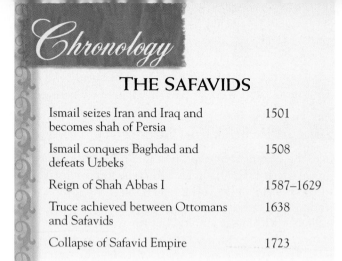

Chronology

THE SAFAVIDS

Ismail seizes Iran and Iraq and becomes shah of Persia	1501
Ismail conquers Baghdad and defeats Uzbeks	1508
Reign of Shah Abbas I	1587–1629
Truce achieved between Ottomans and Safavids	1638
Collapse of Safavid Empire	1723

he had the baker cooked in his own oven and the butcher roasted on a spit.

At its height, Safavid Iran was a worthy successor to the great Persian empires of the past, although it was probably not as wealthy as its Mughal and Ottoman neighbors to the east and west. Hemmed in by the sea power of the Europeans to the south and by the land power of the Ottomans to the west, the early Safavids had no navy and were forced to divert overland trade with Europe through southern Russia to avoid an Ottoman blockade. In the early seventeenth century, the situation improved when Iranian forces, in cooperation with the English, seized the island of Hormuz from Portugal and established a new seaport on the southern coast at Bandar Abbas. As a consequence, commercial ties with Europe began to increase.

Safavid Art and Literature

Persia witnessed an extraordinary flowering of the arts during the reign of Shah Abbas I. His new capital of Isfahan was a grandiose planned city with wide visual perspectives and a sense of order almost unique in the region. Shah Abbas ordered his architects to position his palaces, mosques, and bazaars around the Maydan-i-Shah, a mas-

possible and brought them under the control of the crown. Appointment to senior positions in the bureaucracy was by merit rather than birth.

The Safavid shahs took a direct interest in the economy and actively engaged in commercial and manufacturing activities, although there was also a large and affluent urban bourgeoisie. Like the Ottoman sultan, one shah regularly traveled the city streets incognito to check on the honesty of his subjects. When he discovered that a baker and butcher were overcharging for their products,

⟫• **THE ROYAL ACADEMY OF ISFAHAN.** Along with institutions such as libraries and hospitals, theological schools were often included in the mosque compound. One of the most sumptuous was the Royal Academy of Isfahan, built by the shah of Iran in the early eighteenth century. This view shows the large courtyard surrounded by arcades of student rooms, reminiscent of the arrangement of monks' cells in European cloisters.

© George Holton/Photo Researchers, Inc.

THE MUGHAL CONQUEST OF NORTHERN INDIA

*B*abur, the founder of the great Mughal dynasty, began his career by allying with one Indian prince against another and then turned on his ally to put himself in power, a tactic that had been used by the Ottomans and the Mongols before him (see Chapter 10). In this excerpt from his memoirs, Babur describes his triumph over the powerful army of his Indian enemy, the sultan Ibrâhim.

BABUR, MEMOIRS

They made one or two very poor charges on our right and left divisions. My troops making use of their bows, plied them with arrows, and drove them in upon their center. The troops on the right and the left of their center, being huddled together in one place, such confusion ensued, that the enemy, while totally unable to advance, found also no road by which they could flee. The sun had mounted spear-high when the onset of battle began, and the combat lasted till midday, when the enemy were completely broken and routed, and my friends victorious and exulting. By the grace and mercy of Almighty God, this arduous undertaking was rendered easy for me, and this mighty army, in the space of half a day, laid in the dust. Five or six thousand men were discovered lying slain, in one spot, near Ibrâhim. We reckoned that the number lying slain, in different parts of this field of battle, amounted to fifteen or sixteen thousand men. On reaching Agra, we found, from the accounts of the natives of Hindustân, that forty or fifty thousand men had fallen in this field. After routing the enemy, we continued the pursuit, slaughtering, and making them prisoners. . . .

It was now afternoon prayers when Tahir Taberi, the younger brother of Khalîfeh, having found Ibrâhim lying dead amidst a number of slain, cut off his head, and brought it in. . . .

In consideration of my confidence in Divine aid, the Most High God did not suffer the distress and hardships that I had undergone to be thrown away, but defeated my formidable enemy, and made me the conqueror of the noble country of Hindustân. This success I do not ascribe to my own strength, nor did this good fortune flow from my own efforts, but from the fountain of the favor and mercy of God.

---

sive rectangular polo ground. Much of the original city is still in good condition and remains the gem of modern Iran. The immense mosques are richly decorated with elaborate blue tiles. The palaces are delicate structures with unusual slender wooden columns. These architectural wonders of Isfahan epitomize the grandeur, delicacy, and color that defined the Safavid golden age. To adorn the splendid buildings, Safavid artisans created imaginative metalwork, tile decorations, and original and delicate glass vessels.

The greatest area of productivity, however, was in textiles. Silk weaving based on new techniques became a national industry. The silks depicted birds, animals, and flowers in a brilliant mass of color with silver and gold threads. Above all, carpet weaving flourished, stimulated by the great demand for Persian carpets in the West.

The long tradition of Persian painting continued in the Safavid era but changed from paintings to line drawings and from landscape scenes to portraits, mostly of young ladies, boys, lovers, or dervishes. Although some Persian artists studied in Rome, Safavid art was little influenced by the West. Riza-i-Abassi, the most famous artist of this period, created exquisite works on simple naturalistic subjects, such as an ox plowing, hunters, or lovers. Soft colors, delicacy, and flowing movement were the dominant characteristics of the painting of this era.

THE GRANDEUR OF THE MUGHALS

In retrospect, the period from the sixteenth to the eighteenth centuries can be viewed as a high point of traditional culture in India. The era began with the creation of one of the subcontinent's greatest empires—that of the Mughals. For the first time since the Mauryan dynasty, the entire subcontinent was united under a single government, with a common culture that inspired admiration and envy throughout the entire region.

The Mughal Empire reached its peak in the sixteenth century under the famed Emperor Akbar and maintained its vitality under a series of strong rulers for another century (see Map 15.3). Then the dynasty began to weaken, a process that was hastened by the increasingly insistent challenge of the foreigners arriving by sea. The Portuguese, who first arrived in 1498, were little more than an irritant. Two centuries later, however, Europeans began to seize control of regional trade routes and to meddle in the internal politics of the subcontinent. By the end of the eighteenth century, nothing remained of the empire but a shell. But some historians see the seeds of decay less in the challenge from abroad than in internal weakness—in the very nature of the dynasty itself, which was always more a heterogeneous collection of semiautonomous political forces than a centralized empire in the style of neighboring China.

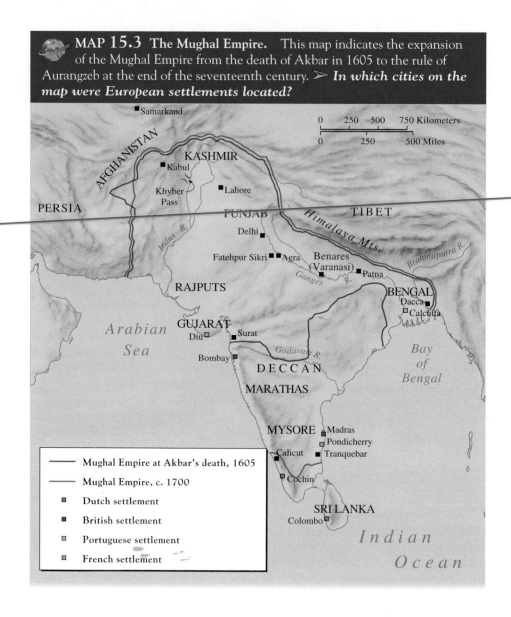

MAP 15.3 The Mughal Empire. This map indicates the expansion of the Mughal Empire from the death of Akbar in 1605 to the rule of Aurangzeb at the end of the seventeenth century. ➤ *In which cities on the map were European settlements located?*

Samarkand

AFGHANISTAN

KASHMIR

Kabul

Khyber Pass

Lahore

PERSIA

PUNJAB

TIBET

Indus R.

Delhi

Himalaya Mts.

Brahmaputra R.

Fatehpur Sikri ■ Agra

Benares (Varanasi)

Patna

Ganges R.

RAJPUTS

BENGAL

Dacca

Calcutta

Arabian Sea

GUJARAT

Diu □

Surat

Bombay

Godavari R.

Bay of Bengal

DECCAN

MARATHAS

MYSORE

Madras

Pondicherry

Calicut

Tranquebar

Cochin

SRI LANKA

Colombo

Indian Ocean

0   250   500   750 Kilometers
0   250   500 Miles

—— Mughal Empire at Akbar's death, 1605

—— Mughal Empire, c. 1700

■ Dutch settlement

■ British settlement

□ Portuguese settlement

□ French settlement

The Mughal Dynasty: A "Gunpowder Empire"?

When the Portuguese fleet led by Vasco da Gama arrived at the port of Calicut in the spring of 1498, the Indian subcontinent was still divided into a number of Hindu and Muslim kingdoms. But it was on the verge of a new era of unity that would be brought about by a foreign dynasty called the Mughals. Like so many recent rulers of northern India, the founders of the Mughal Empire were not natives of India but came from the mountainous region north of the Ganges River. The founder of the dynasty, known to history as Babur (1483–1530), had an illustrious pedigree. His father was descended from the great Asian conqueror Tamerlane, his mother from the Mongol conqueror Genghis Khan.

Babur had inherited a fragment of Tamerlane's empire in an upland valley of the Syr Darya River. Driven south by the rising power of the Uzbeks and then the Safavid

dynasty in Persia, Babur and his warriors seized Kabul in 1504 and, thirteen years later, crossed the Khyber Pass to India.

Following a pattern that we have seen before, Babur began his rise to power by offering to help an ailing dynasty against its opponents. Although his own forces were far smaller than those of his adversaries, he possessed advanced weapons, including artillery, and used them to great effect. His use of mobile cavalry was particularly successful against the massed forces, supplemented by mounted elephants, of his enemy. In 1526, with only twelve thousand troops against an enemy force nearly ten times that size, Babur captured Delhi and established his power in the plains of northern India (see the box on p. 329). Over the next several years, he continued his conquests in northern India, until his early death in 1530 at the age of forty-seven.

Babur's success was due in part to his vigor and his charismatic personality, which earned him the undying loyalty of his followers. His son and successor Humayun (1530–1556) was, in the words of one British historian, "intelligent but lazy." In 1540, he was forced to flee to Persia, where he lived in exile for sixteen years. Finally, with the aid of the Safavid shah of Persia, he returned to India and reconquered Delhi in 1555 but died the following year in a household accident, reportedly from injuries suffered in a fall after smoking a pipeful of opium.

Humayun was succeeded by his son Akbar (1556–1605). Born while his father was living in exile, Akbar was only fourteen when he mounted the throne. Illiterate but highly intelligent and industrious, Akbar set out to extend his domain, then limited to Punjab and the upper Ganges River valley. "A monarch," he remarked, "should be ever intent on conquest, otherwise his neighbors rise in arms against him. The army should be exercised in warfare, lest from want of training they become self-indulgent."[1] By the end of his life, he had brought Mughal rule to most of the subcontinent, from the Himalaya Mountains to the Godavari River in central India and from Kashmir to the mouths of the Brahmaputra and the Ganges. In so doing, Akbar had created the greatest Indian empire since the Mauryan dynasty nearly two thousand years earlier. It was an empire that appeared highly centralized from the outside but was actually a collection of semiautonomous principalities ruled by provincial elites and linked together by the overarching majesty of the Mughal emperor.

Akbar and Indo-Muslim Civilization

Although Akbar was probably the greatest of the conquering Mughal monarchs, like his famous predecessor Asoka, he is best known for the humane character of his rule. Above all, he accepted the diversity of Indian society and took steps to reconcile his Muslim and Hindu subjects.

Though raised an orthodox Muslim, Akbar had been exposed to other beliefs during his childhood and had little patience with the pedantic views of Muslim scholars at court. As emperor, he displayed a keen interest in other religions, not only tolerating Hindu practices in his own domains but also welcoming the expression of Christian views by his Jesuit advisers. Akbar put his policy of religious tolerance into practice by taking a Hindu princess as one of his wives, and the success of this marriage may well have had an effect on his religious convictions. He patronized classical Indian arts and architecture and abolished many of the restrictions faced by Hindus in a Muslim-dominated society.

During his later years, Akbar became steadily more hostile to Islam. To the dismay of many Muslims at court, he sponsored a new form of worship called the Divine Faith (Din-i-Ilahi), which combined characteristics of several religions with a central belief in the infallibility of all decisions reached by the emperor. The new faith aroused deep hostility in Muslim circles and rapidly vanished after his death.

Akbar also extended his innovations to the empire's administration. Although the upper ranks of the government continued to be dominated by nonnative Muslims, a substantial proportion of lower-ranking officials were Hindus, and a few Hindus were appointed to positions of importance. At first, most officials were paid salaries, but later they were ordinarily assigned sections of agricultural land for their temporary use; they kept a portion of the taxes paid by the local peasants in lieu of a salary. These local officials, known as zamindars, were expected to forward the rest of the taxes from the lands under their control to the central government.

The same tolerance that marked Akbar's attitude toward religion and administration extended to the Mughal legal system. While Muslims were subject to the Islamic codes (the Shari'a), Hindu law applied to areas settled by Hindus, who after 1579 were no longer required to pay the hated jizya, or poll tax on non-Muslims. Punishments for crime were relatively mild, at least by the standards of the day, and justice was administered in a relatively impartial and efficient manner.

Overall, Akbar's reign was a time of peace and prosperity. Although all Indian peasants were required to pay about one-third of their annual harvest to the state through the zamindars, the system was applied fairly, and when drought struck in the 1590s, the taxes were reduced or even suspended altogether. Thanks to a long period of relative peace and political stability, commerce and manufacturing flourished. Foreign trade, in particular, thrived as Indian goods, notably textiles, tropical food products, spices, and precious stones, were exported in exchange for gold and silver. Tariffs on imports were low. Much of the foreign commerce was handled by Arab traders, since the Indians, like their Mughal rulers, did not care for travel by sea. Internal trade, however, was dominated by large merchant castes, who also were active in banking and handicrafts.

Twilight of the Mughals

Akbar died in 1605 and was succeeded by his son Jahangir (1605–1628). During the early years of his reign, Jahangir continued to strengthen central control over the vast empire. Eventually, however, his grip began to weaken (according to his memoirs, he "only wanted a bottle of wine and a piece of meat to make merry"), and the court fell under the influence of one of his wives, the Persian-born Nur Jahan (see the box on p. 332). The empress took advantage of her position to enrich her own family and arranged for her niece Mumtaz Mahal to marry her husband's third son and ultimate successor, Shah Jahan. When Shah Jahan succeeded to the throne in 1628, he quickly demonstrated the single-minded quality of his grandfather (albeit in a much more brutal manner), ordering the assassination of all of his rivals in order to secure his position.

THE POWER BEHIND THE THRONE

During his reign as Mughal emperor, Jahangir (1605–1628) was addicted to alcohol and opium. Because of his weakened condition, his Persian wife Nur Jahan began to rule on his behalf. She also groomed his young son Khurram to rule as the future emperor Shah Jahan and arranged for him to marry her own niece Mumtaz Mahal, thereby cementing her influence over two successive Mughal rulers. During this period, Nur Jahan was the de facto ruler of India, exerting her influence in both internal and foreign affairs during an era of peace and prosperity. Although the extent of her influence was often criticized at court, her performance impressed many European observers, as these remarks by two English visitors attest.

NUR JAHAN, EMPRESS OF MUGHAL INDIA

If anyone with a request to make at Court obtains an audience or is allowed to speak, the King hears him indeed, but will give no definite answer of Yes or No, referring him promptly to Asaf Khan, who in the same way will dispose of no important matter without communicating with his sister, the Queen, and who regulates his attitude in such a way that the authority of neither of them may be diminished. Anyone then who obtains a favour must thank them for it, and not the King. . . .

Her abilities were uncommon; for she rendered herself absolute, in a government in which women are thought incapable of bearing any part. Their power, it is true, is sometimes exerted in the haram; but, like the virtues of the magnet, it is silent and unperceived. Nur Jahan stood forth in public; she broke through all restraint and custom, and acquired power by her own address, more than by the weakness of Jahangir. . . .

Her former and present supporters have been well rewarded, so that now most of the men who are near the King owe their promotion to her, and are consequently under . . . obligations to her. . . . Many misunderstandings result, for the King's orders or grants of appointments, etc., are not certainties, being of no value until they have been approved by the Queen.

During a reign of three decades, Shah Jahan maintained the system established by his predecessors while expanding the boundaries of the empire by successful campaigns in the Deccan Plateau and against Samarkand, north of the Hindu Kush. But Shah Jahan's rule was marred by his failure to deal with the growing domestic problems. He had inherited a nearly empty treasury because of Empress Nur Jahan's penchant for luxury and ambitious charity projects. Though the majority of his subjects lived in grinding poverty, Shah Jahan's frequent military campaigns and expensive building projects put a heavy strain on the imperial finances and compelled him to raise taxes. At the same time, the government did little to improve rural conditions. In a country where transport was primitive (it often took three months to travel the 600 miles between Patna, in the middle of the Ganges River valley, and Delhi) and drought conditions frequent, the dynasty made few efforts to increase agricultural efficiency or to improve the roads or the irrigation network. A Dutch merchant in Gujarat described conditions during a famine in the mid-seventeenth century:

As the famine increased, men abandoned towns and villages and wandered helplessly. It was easy to recognize their condition: eyes sunk deep in head, lips pale and covered with slime, the skin hard, with the bones showing through, the belly nothing but a pouch hanging down empty, knuckles and kneecaps showing prominently. One would cry and howl for hunger, while another lay stretched on the ground dying in misery; wherever you went, you saw nothing but corpses.[2]

In 1648, Shah Jahan moved his capital from Agra to Delhi and built the famous Red Fort in his new capital city. But he is best known for the Taj Mahal in Agra, widely considered to be the most beautiful building in India, if not in the entire world. The story is a romantic one—that the Taj was built by the emperor in memory of his wife Mumtaz Mahal, who had died giving birth to her thirteenth child at the age of thirty-nine. But the story has a less attractive side: the expense of the building, which employed twenty thousand masons over twenty years, forced the government to raise agricultural taxes, further impoverishing many Indian peasants.

Succession struggles returned to haunt the dynasty in the mid-1650s when Shah Jahan's illness led to a struggle for power between his sons Dara Shikoh and Aurangzeb. Dara Shikoh was described by his contemporaries as progressive and humane, but he apparently lacked political acumen and was outmaneuvered by Aurangzeb (1658–1707), who had Dara Shikoh put to death and then imprisoned his father in the fort at Agra.

Aurangzeb is one of the most controversial individuals in the history of India. A man of high principle, he attempted to eliminate many of what he considered to be India's social evils, prohibiting the immolation of widows on their husband's funeral pyre (*sati*), the castration of eunuchs, and the exaction of illegal taxes. With less success, he tried to forbid gambling, drinking, and prostitution. But Aurangzeb, a devout and somewhat doctrinaire Muslim, also adopted a number of measures that reversed the policies of religious tolerance established by his predecessors. The building of new Hindu temples was prohibited, and the Hindu poll tax was restored. Forced conversions to Islam were resumed, and non-Muslims were driven from the court. Aurangzeb's heavy-handed religious policies led to considerable domestic unrest and to a revival of Hindu fervor during the last years of his reign. A number of revolts also broke out against imperial authority.

During the eighteenth century, Mughal power was threatened from both within and without. Fueled by the growing power and autonomy of the local gentry and merchants, rebellious groups in provinces throughout the empire, from the Deccan to the Punjab, began to reassert local authority and reduce the power of the Mughal emperor to that of a "tinsel sovereign." Increasingly divided, India was vulnerable to attack from abroad. In 1739, Delhi was sacked by the Persians, who left it in ashes.

A number of obvious reasons for the virtual collapse of the Mughal Empire can be identified, including the draining of the imperial treasury and the decline in competence of the Mughal rulers. But it should also be noted that even at its height under Akbar, the empire was a loosely knit collection of heterogeneous principalities held together by the authority of the throne, which tried to combine Persian concepts of kingship with the Indian tradition of decentralized power. Decline set in when centrifugal forces gradually began to predominate over centripetal ones.

The Impact of Western Power in India

As we have seen, the first Europeans to arrive were the Portuguese. Although they established a virtual monopoly over regional trade in the Indian Ocean, they did not aggressively seek to penetrate the interior of the subcontinent. The situation changed at the end of the sixteenth century, when the English and the Dutch entered the scene. Soon both powers were in active competition with Portugal, and with each other, for trading privileges in the region.

Penetration of the new market was not easy. When the first English fleet arrived at Surat, a thriving port on the northwestern coast of India, in 1608, their request for trading privileges was rejected by Emperor Jahangir. Needing lightweight Indian cloth to trade for spices in the East Indies, the English persisted, and in 1616, they were finally permitted to install their own ambassador at the imperial court in Agra. Three years later, the first English factory was established at Surat.

During the next several decades, the English presence in India steadily increased while Mughal power gradually waned. By midcentury, additional English factories had been established at Fort William (now the great city of Calcutta) on the Hoogly River near the Bay of Bengal and at Madras on the southeastern coast. From there, English ships carried Indian-made cotton goods to the East Indies, where they were bartered for spices, which were shipped back to England.

English success in India attracted rivals, including the Dutch and the French. The Dutch abandoned their interests to concentrate on the spice trade in the middle of the seventeenth century, but the French were more persistent

THE MUGHAL ERA

Arrival of Vasco da Gama at Calicut	1498
Babur seizes Delhi	1526
Death of Babur	1530
Humayun recovers throne in Delhi	1555
Death of Humayun and accession of Akbar	1556
Death of Akbar and accession of Jahangir	1605
Arrival of English at Surat	1608
Reign of Emperor Shah Jahan	1628–1657
Foundation of English fort at Madras	1639
Aurangzeb succeeds to the throne	1658
Bombay ceded to England	1661
Death of Aurangzeb	1707
French capture Madras	1746
Battle of Plassey	1757

and established factories of their own. For a brief period, under the ambitious empire builder Joseph François Dupleix, the French competed successfully with the British. But the military genius of Sir Robert Clive, an aggressive British administrator and empire builder who eventually became the chief representative of the East India Company in the subcontinent, and the refusal of the French government to provide financial support for Dupleix's efforts eventually left the French with only their fort at Pondicherry and a handful of small territories on the southeastern coast.

In the meantime, Clive began to consolidate British control in Bengal, where the local ruler had attacked Fort William and imprisoned the local British population in the infamous Black Hole of Calcutta (an underground prison for holding the prisoners, many of whom died in captivity). In 1757, a small British force numbering about three thousand defeated a Mughal-led army over ten times that size in the Battle of Plassey. As part of the spoils of victory, the British East India Company exacted from the now-decrepit Mughal court the authority to collect taxes from extensive lands in the area surrounding Calcutta. Less than ten years later, British forces seized the reigning Mughal emperor in a skirmish at Buxar, and the British began to consolidate their economic and administrative control over Indian territory through the surrogate power of the now powerless Mughal court (see Map 15.4).

To officials of the East India Company, the expansion of their authority into the interior of the subcontinent

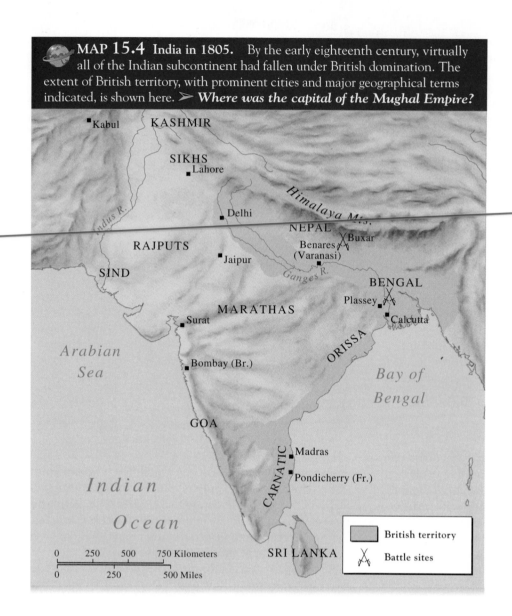

MAP 15.4 India in 1805. By the early eighteenth century, virtually all of the Indian subcontinent had fallen under British domination. The extent of British territory, with prominent cities and major geographical terms indicated, is shown here. ➤ *Where was the capital of the Mughal Empire?*

Kabul • **KASHMIR**

SIKHS
• Lahore

Indus R.

Himalaya Mts.

• Delhi

NEPAL
✕ Buxar
Benares
(Varanasi)

RAJPUTS
• Jaipur

SIND

Ganges R.

BENGAL
Plassey • ✕
Calcutta

MARATHAS
• Surat

ORISSA

*Arabian
Sea*

• Bombay (Br.)

*Bay of
Bengal*

GOA

*Indian
Ocean*

CARNATIC
• Madras
• Pondicherry (Fr.)

SRI LANKA

| | British territory |
| ✕ | Battle sites |

0 250 500 750 Kilometers
0 250 500 Miles

probably seemed like a simple commercial decision, a move designed to seek guaranteed revenues to pay for the increasingly expensive military operations in India. To historians, it marks a major step in the gradual transfer of all of the Indian subcontinent to the British East India Company and later, in 1858, to the British crown. The process was more haphazard than deliberate.

The company's takeover of vast landholdings, notably in the eastern Indian states of Orissa and Bengal, may have been a windfall for enterprising British officials, but it was a disaster for the Indian economy. In the first place, it resulted in the transfer of capital from the local Indian aristocracy to company officials, most of whom sent their profits back to Britain. Second, it hastened the destruction of once healthy local industries because British goods such as machine-made textiles were imported duty-free into India to compete against local products. Finally,

British expansion hurt the peasants. As the British took over the administration of the land tax, they also applied British law, which allowed the lands of those unable to pay the tax to be confiscated. In the 1770s, a series of massive famines led to the death of an estimated one-third of the population in the areas under company administration. The British government attempted to resolve the problem by assigning tax lands to the local revenue collectors (*zamindars*) in the hope of transforming them into English-style rural gentry, but many collectors themselves fell into bankruptcy and sold their lands to absentee bankers while the now landless peasants remained in abject poverty. It was hardly an auspicious beginning to "civilized" British rule.

As a result of such problems, Britain's rise to power in India did not go unchallenged. Astute Indian commanders avoided pitched battles with the well-armed British

As a primer for political leadership, the emperor's edict reflects the genius of Confucian philosophy at its best and has a timeless quality that applies to our age as well as to the golden age of the Qing dynasty.

Kangxi reigned during one of the most glorious eras in the long history of China. Under the Ming (1369–1644) and the early Qing (1644–1911) dynasties, the empire expanded its borders to a degree not seen since the Han and the Tang. Chinese culture was the envy of its neighbors and earned the admiration of many European visitors, including Jesuit priests and Enlightenment philosophers.

On the surface, China appeared to be an unchanging society patterned after the Confucian vision of a "golden age" in the remote past. Although few observers could have been aware of it at the time, however, China was changing—and rather rapidly.

A similar process was under way in neighboring Japan. A vigorous new shogunate called the Tokugawa rose to power in the early seventeenth century and managed to revitalize the traditional system in a somewhat more centralized form that enabled it to survive for another 250 years. But major structural changes were also taking place in Japanese society.

One of the many factors involved in the quickening pace of change in both countries was contact with the West, which began with the arrival of Portuguese ships in Chinese and Japanese ports in the first half of the sixteenth century. The Ming and the Tokugawa initially opened their doors to European trade and missionary activity. Later, however, Chinese and Japanese rulers became concerned about the corrosive effects of Western ideas and practices and attempted to protect their traditional societies from external intrusion. •

CHINA AT ITS APEX

In 1514, a Portuguese fleet dropped anchor off the coast of China, just south of the Pearl River estuary and present-day Hong Kong. It was the first direct contact between the Chinese Empire and the West since the arrival of the Venetian adventurer Marco Polo two centuries earlier, and it opened an era that would eventually change the face of China and, indeed, all the world.

From the Ming to the Qing

By the time the Portuguese fleet arrived off the coast of China, the Mongol Empire had long since disappeared. It had gradually weakened after the death of Khubilai Khan and was finally overthrown in 1368 by a massive peasant rebellion under the leadership of Zhu Yuanzhang, who had declared himself the founding emperor of a new Ming (Bright) dynasty and assumed the reign title of Ming Hongwu (Ming Hung Wu, or Ming Martial Emperor). The Ming inaugurated a new era of greatness in Chinese history. Under a series of strong rulers, China extended its rule into Mongolia and Central Asia. The Ming even briefly reconquered Vietnam, which, after a thousand years of Chinese rule, had reclaimed its independence following the collapse of the Tang dynasty in the tenth century. Along the northern frontier, the emperor Yongle (Yung Lo, 1402–1424) strengthened the Great Wall and pacified the nomadic tribespeople who had troubled China in previous centuries. A tributary relationship was established with the Yi dynasty in Korea.

The internal achievements of the Ming were equally impressive. When they replaced the Mongols in the fourteenth century, the Ming turned to traditional Confucian institutions as a means of ruling their vast empire. These included the six ministries at the apex of the bureaucracy, the use of the civil service examinations to select members of the bureaucracy, and the division of the empire into provinces, districts, and counties. As before, Chinese villages were relatively autonomous, and local councils of elders continued to be responsible for adjudicating disputes, initiating local construction and irrigation projects, mustering a militia, and assessing and collecting taxes.

The society that was governed by this vast hierarchy of officials was a far cry from the predominantly agrarian society that had been ruled by the Han. In the burgeoning cities near the coast and along the Yangtze River valley, factories and workshops were vastly increasing the variety and output of their manufactured goods. The population had doubled, and new crops had been introduced, greatly expanding the food output of the empire.

In 1405, in a splendid display of Chinese maritime might, Yongle sent a fleet of Chinese trading ships under the eunuch admiral Zhenghe (Cheng Ho) through the Strait of Malacca and out into the Indian Ocean; there they traveled as far west as the east coast of Africa, stopping on the way at ports in South Asia. The size of the fleet was impressive: it included nearly 28,000 sailors on sixty-two ships, some of them junks larger by far than any other oceangoing vessels the world had yet seen. China seemed about to become a direct participant in the vast trade network that

Courtesy of William J. Duiker

THE GREAT WALL OF CHINA. Although the Great Wall is popularly believed to be over two thousand years old, the part of the wall that is most frequently visited by tourists was a reconstruction undertaken during the early Ming dynasty as a means of protection against invasion from the north. Part of that wall, which was built to protect the imperial capital of Beijing from rampaging nomadic peoples to the north, is shown here.

extended as far west as the Atlantic Ocean, thus culminating the process of opening China to the wider world that had begun with the Tang dynasty.

Why the expeditions were undertaken has been a matter of some debate. Some historians assume that economic profit was the main reason. Others point to Yongle's native curiosity and note that the voyage—and the six others that followed it—returned not only with goods but also with a plethora of information about the outside world as well as with some items unknown in China (the emperor was especially intrigued by the giraffes and placed them in the imperial zoo).

Whatever the case, the voyages resulted in a dramatic increase in Chinese knowledge about the world and the

nature of ocean travel. They also brought massive profits for their sponsors, including individuals connected with Admiral Zhenghe at court. This aroused resentment among conservatives within the bureaucracy, some of whom viewed commercial activities with a characteristic measure of Confucian disdain.

Shortly after Yongle's death, the voyages were discontinued, never to be revived. The decision had long-term consequences and in the eyes of many modern historians marks a turning inward of the Chinese state, away from commerce and toward a more traditional emphasis on agriculture, away from the exotic lands to the south and toward the heartland of the country in the Yellow River valley. The imperial capital was moved from Nanjing, in central China, back to Beijing.

FIRST CONTACTS WITH THE WEST

Despite the Ming's retreat from active participation in the maritime trade, when the Portuguese arrived in 1514, China was in command of a vast empire that stretched from the steppes of Central Asia to the China Sea, from the Gobi Desert to the tropical rain forests of Southeast Asia. From the lofty perspective of the imperial throne in Beijing, the Europeans could only have seemed like an unusually exotic form of barbarian to be placed within the familiar framework of the tributary system, the hierarchical arrangement in which rulers of all other countries were regarded as "younger brothers" of the Son of Heaven. Indeed, the bellicose and uncultured behavior of the Portuguese so outraged Chinese officials that they expelled the Europeans, but after further negotiations, the Portuguese were permitted to occupy the tiny territory of Macao, a foothold they would retain until the end of the twentieth century.

Initially the arrival of the Europeans did not have much impact on Chinese society. Direct trade between Europe and China was limited, and Portuguese ships became involved in the regional trade network, carrying silk to Japan in return for Japanese silver.

More influential than trade, perhaps, were the ideas introduced by Christian missionaries. Among the most active and the most effective were highly educated Jesuits, who were familiar with European philosophical and scientific developments. Recognizing the Chinese pride in their own culture, the Jesuits attempted to draw parallels between Christian and Confucian concepts (for example, they identified the Western concept of God with the Chinese character for Heaven) and to show the similarities between Christian morality and Confucian ethics. European inventions such as the clock, the prism, and various astronomical and musical instruments impressed Chinese officials, hitherto deeply imbued with a sense of the superiority of Chinese civilization, and helped Western ideas win acceptance at court. An elderly Chinese scholar expressed his wonder at the miracle of eyeglasses:

THE ART OF PRINTING

Europeans obtained much of their early information about China from the Jesuits who served at the Ming court in the sixteenth and seventeenth centuries. Clerics such as the Italian Matteo Ricci (1552–1610) found much to admire in Chinese civilization. Here Ricci expresses a keen interest in Chinese printing methods, which at that time were well in advance of the techniques used in the West.

MATTEO RICCI, *THE DIARY OF MATTHEW RICCI*

The art of printing was practiced in China at a date somewhat earlier than that assigned to the beginning of printing in Europe, which was about 1405. It is quite certain that the Chinese knew the art of printing at least five centuries ago, and some of them assert that printing was known to their people before the beginning of the Christian era, about 50 B.C. Their method of printing differs widely from that employed in Europe, and our method would be quite impracticable for them because of the exceedingly large number of Chinese characters and symbols. . . .

Their method of making printed books is quite ingenious. The text is written in ink, with a brush made of very fine hair, on a sheet of paper which is inverted and pasted on a wooden tablet. When the paper has become thoroughly dry, its surface is scraped off quickly and with great skill, until nothing but a fine tissue bearing the characters remains on the wooden tablet. Then, with a steel graver, the workman cuts away the surface following the outlines of the characters until these alone stand out in low relief. From such a block a skilled printer can make copies with incredible speed, turning out as many as fifteen hundred copies in a single day. . . . This scheme of engraving wooden blocks is well adapted for the large and complex nature of the Chinese characters, but I do not think it would lend itself very aptly to our European type, which could hardly be engraved upon wood because of its small dimensions.

Their method of printing has one decided advantage, namely, that once these tablets are made, they can be preserved and used for making changes in the text as often as one wishes. Additions and subtractions can also be made as the tablets can be readily patched. . . . We have derived great benefit from this method of Chinese printing, as we employ the domestic help in our homes to strike off copies of the books on religious and scientific subjects which we translate into Chinese from the languages in which they were written originally. In truth, the whole method is so simple that one is tempted to try it for himself after once having watched the process. The simplicity of Chinese printing is what accounts for the exceedingly large numbers of books in circulation here and the ridiculously low prices at which they are sold.

White glass from across the Western Seas
Is imported through Macao:
Fashioned into lenses big as coins,
They encompass the eyes in a double frame.
I put them on—it suddenly becomes clear;
I can see the very tips of things!
And read fine print by the dim-lit window
Just like in my youth.[2]

For their part, the missionaries were much impressed with many aspects of Chinese civilization, and reports of their experiences heightened European curiosity about this great society on the other side of the world (see the box above).

THE MING BROUGHT TO EARTH

During the late sixteenth century, the Ming began to decline as a series of weak rulers led to an era of corruption, concentration of landownership, and ultimately peasant rebellions and tribal unrest along the northern frontier. The inflow of vast amounts of foreign silver led to an alarming increase in inflation. Then the arrival of the English and the Dutch disrupted the silver trade; silver imports plummeted, severely straining the Chinese economy by raising the value of the metal relative to that of copper.

Crop yields declined due to harsh weather, and the resulting scarcity reduced the ability of the government to provide food in times of imminent starvation. High taxes, provoked in part by increased official corruption, led to peasant unrest and worker violence in urban areas.

As always, internal problems were accompanied by unrest along the northern frontier. Following long precedent, the Ming had attempted to pacify the frontier tribes by forging alliances with them and granting trade privileges. One of the alliances was with the Manchus (also known as the Jurchen), the descendants of peoples who had briefly established a kingdom in northern China during the early thirteenth century. The Manchus, a mixed agricultural and hunting people, lived northeast of the Great Wall in the area known today as Manchuria.

At first, the Manchus were satisfied with consolidating their territory and made little effort to extend their rule south of the Great Wall. But during the first decades of the seventeenth century, a major epidemic devastated the population in many areas of the country. The suffering brought on by the epidemic helped spark a vast peasant revolt led by Li Zicheng (Li Tzu-ch'eng, 1604–1651), a postal worker in central China who had been dismissed from his job as part of a cost-saving measure by the imperial court. In the 1630s, Li managed to extend the revolt throughout the country and finally occupied the capital of Beijing in 1644.

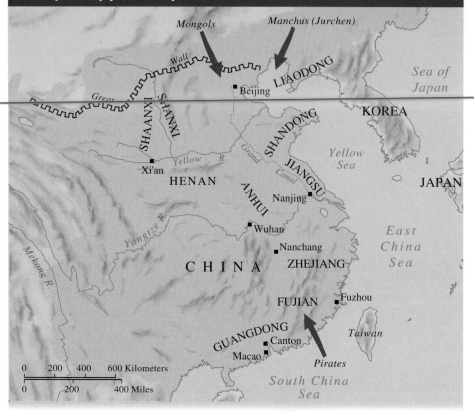

MAP 16.1 China and Its Enemies During the Late Ming Era. During the seventeenth century, the Ming dynasty faced challenges on two fronts, from China's traditional adversaries—nomadic groups north of the Great Wall—and from new arrivals—European merchants—who had begun to press for trading privileges along the southern coast. ➤ *How do these threats differ from those faced by previous dynasties in China?*

The last Ming emperor committed suicide by hanging himself from a tree in the palace gardens.

But Li was unable to hold his conquest. The overthrow of the Ming dynasty presented a great temptation to the Manchus. With the assistance of many military commanders who had deserted from the Ming, they conquered Beijing on their own (see Map 16.1). Li Zicheng's army disintegrated, and the Manchus declared the creation of a new dynasty with the reign title of the Qing (Ch'ing, or Pure). Once again, China was under foreign rule.

The Greatness of the Qing

The accession of the Manchus to power in Beijing was not universally applauded. Some Ming loyalists fled to Southeast Asia, but others continued their resistance to the new rulers from inside the country. To make it easier to identify the rebels, the government ordered all Chinese to adopt Manchu dress and hairstyles. All Chinese males were to shave their foreheads and braid their hair into a queue; those who refused were to be executed. As a popular saying put it, "Lose your hair or lose your head."[3]

But the Manchus eventually proved to be more adept at adapting to Chinese conditions than their predecessors, the Mongols. Unlike the latter, who had tried to impose their own methods of ruling, the Manchus adopted the Chinese political system (although, as we shall see, they retained their distinct position within it) and were gradually accepted by most Chinese as the legitimate rulers of the country.

Like all of China's great dynasties, the Qing was blessed with a series of strong early rulers who pacified the country, rectified many of the most obvious social and economic inequities, and restored peace and prosperity. For the Ming dynasty, these strong emperors had been Hongwu and Yongle; under the Qing, they would be Kangxi (K'ang Hsi) and Qianlong (Ch'ien Lung). The two Qing monarchs ruled China for well over a century, from the middle of the seventeenth century to the end of the eighteenth, and were responsible for much of the greatness of Manchu China.

Kangxi (1661–1722) was arguably the greatest ruler in Chinese history. Ascending to the throne at the age of seven, he was blessed with diligence, political astuteness, and a strong character and began to take charge of Qing administration while still an adolescent. During the six decades of his reign, Kangxi not only stabilized imperial rule by pacifying the restive peoples along the northern and western frontiers but also managed to make the dynasty acceptable to the general population. As an active patron of arts and letters, he cultivated the support of scholars through a number of major projects.

During Kangxi's reign, the activities of the Western missionaries, Dominicans and Franciscans as well as Jesuits, reached their height. The emperor was quite tolerant of the Christians, and several Jesuit missionaries became influential at court. Several hundred court officials converted to Christianity, as did an estimated 300,000 ordinary Chinese. But the Christian effort was ultimately undermined by squabbling among the Western religious orders over the Jesuit policy of accommodating local beliefs and practices in order to facilitate conversion. Jealous Dominicans and Franciscans complained to the pope, who issued an edict ordering all missionaries and converts to conform to the official orthodoxy set forth in Europe. At first, Kangxi attempted to resolve the problem by

SIXTEEN CONFUCIAN COMMANDMENTS

Although the Qing dynasty was of foreign origin, its rulers found Confucian maxims convenient for maintaining the social order. In 1670, the great emperor Kangxi issued the Sacred Edict to popularize Confucian values among the common people. The edict was read publicly at periodic intervals in every village in the country and set the standard for behavior throughout the empire.

KANGXI'S SACRED EDICT

1. Esteem most highly filial piety and brotherly submission, in order to give due importance to the social relations.
2. Behave with generosity toward your kindred, in order to illustrate harmony and benignity.
3. Cultivate peace and concord in your neighborhoods, in order to prevent quarrels and litigations.
4. Recognize the importance of husbandry and the culture of the mulberry tree, in order to ensure a sufficiency of clothing and food.
5. Show that you prize moderation and economy, in order to prevent the lavish waste of your means.
6. Give weight to colleges and schools, in order to make correct the practice of the scholar.
7. Extirpate strange principles, in order to exalt the correct doctrine.
8. Lecture on the laws, in order to warn the ignorant and obstinate.
9. Elucidate propriety and yielding courtesy, in order to make manners and customs good.
10. Labor diligently at your proper callings, in order to stabilize the will of the people.
11. Instruct sons and younger brothers, in order to prevent them from doing what is wrong.
12. Put a stop to false accusations, in order to preserve the honest and good.
13. Warn against sheltering deserters, in order to avoid being involved in their punishment.
14. Fully remit your taxes, in order to avoid being pressed for payment.
15. Unite in hundreds and tithing, in order to put an end to thefts and robbery.
16. Remove enmity and anger, in order to show the importance due to the person and life.

---

appealing directly to the Vatican, but the pope was uncompromising. After Kangxi's death, his successor began to suppress Christian activities throughout China.

Kangxi's achievements were carried on by his successors, Yongzheng (Yung Cheng, 1722–1736) and Qianlong (1736–1795). Like Kangxi, Qianlong was known for his diligence, tolerance, and intellectual curiosity, and he too combined vigorous military action against the unruly tribes along the frontier with active efforts to promote economic prosperity, administrative efficiency, and scholarship and artistic excellence. The result was continued growth for the Manchu Empire throughout much of the eighteenth century.

QING POLITICS

One reason for the success of the Manchus was their ability to adapt to their new environment. They retained the Ming political system with relatively few changes. They also tried to establish their legitimacy as China's rightful rulers by stressing their devotion to the principles of Confucianism. Emperor Kangxi ostentatiously studied the sacred Confucian classics and issued a "sacred edict" that proclaimed to the entire empire the importance of the moral values established by the master (see the box above).

Still, the Manchus, like the Mongols, were ethnically, linguistically, and culturally distinct from their subject population. The Qing attempted to cope with this reality by adopting a two-pronged strategy. On the one hand, the Manchus, representing less than 2 percent of the entire population, were legally defined as distinct from everyone else in China. The Manchu nobles retained their aristocratic privileges, while their economic base was protected by extensive landholdings and revenues provided from the state treasury. Other Manchus were assigned farmland and organized into military units, called banners, which were stationed as separate units in various strategic positions throughout China. These "bannermen" were the primary fighting force of the empire. Ethnic Chinese were prohibited from settling in Manchuria and were still compelled to wear their hair in a queue as a sign of submission to the ruling dynasty.

But while the Qing attempted to protect their distinct identity within an alien society, they also recognized the need to bring ethnic Chinese into the top ranks of imperial administration. Their solution was to create a system, known as dyarchy, in which all important administrative positions were shared equally by Chinese and Manchus. Meanwhile, the Manchus themselves, despite official efforts to preserve their separate language and culture, were increasingly assimilated into Chinese civilization.

CHINA ON THE EVE OF THE WESTERN ONSLAUGHT

In some ways, China was at the height of its power and glory in the mid-eighteenth century. But it was also under Qianlong that the first signs of the internal decay of the

Manchu dynasty began to appear. The clues were familiar ones. Qing military campaigns along the frontier were expensive and placed heavy demands on the imperial treasury. As the emperor aged, he became less astute in selecting his subordinates and fell under the influence of corrupt elements at court.

Corruption at the center led inevitably to unrest in rural areas, where higher taxes, bureaucratic venality, and rising pressure on the land because of the growing population had produced economic hardship. The heart of the unrest was in central China, where discontented peasants who had recently been settled on infertile land launched a revolt known as the White Lotus Rebellion (1796–1804). The revolt was eventually suppressed but at great expense.

Unfortunately for China, the decline of the Qing dynasty occurred just as China's modest relationship with the West was about to give way to a new era of military confrontation and increased pressure for trade. The first problems came in the north, where Russian traders seeking skins and furs

began to penetrate the region between Siberian Russia and Manchuria. Earlier the Ming dynasty had attempted to deal with the Russians by the traditional method of placing them in a tributary relationship. But the tsar refused to play by Chinese rules. His envoys to Beijing ignored the tribute system and refused to perform the kowtow (the ritual of prostration and knocking the head on the ground performed by foreign emissaries before the emperor), the classical symbol of fealty demanded of all foreign ambassadors to the Chinese court. Formal diplomatic relations were finally established in 1689, when the Treaty of Nerchinsk settled the boundary dispute and provided for regular trade between the two countries. Through such arrangements, the Manchus were able not only to pacify the northern frontier but also to extend their rule over Xinjiang and Tibet to the west and southwest (see Map 16.2).

Dealing with the foreigners who arrived by sea was more difficult. By the end of the seventeenth century, the English had replaced the Portuguese as the dominant force in Euro-

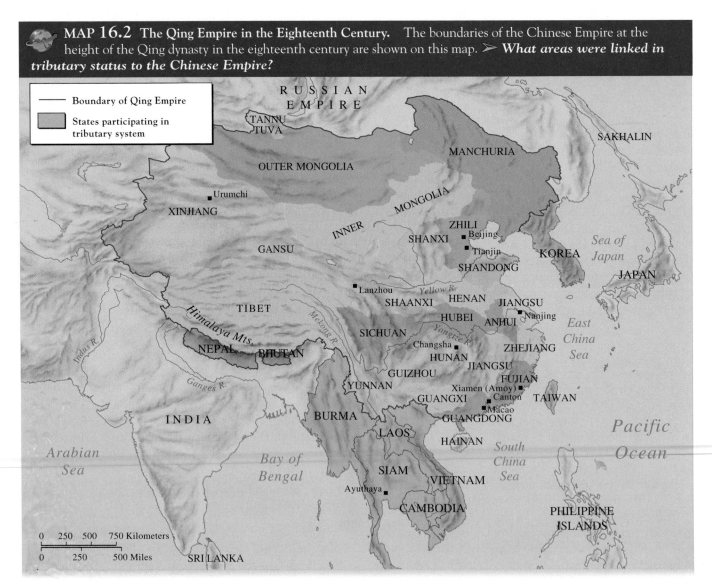

MAP 16.2 The Qing Empire in the Eighteenth Century. The boundaries of the Chinese Empire at the height of the Qing dynasty in the eighteenth century are shown on this map. ➤ *What areas were linked in tributary status to the Chinese Empire?*

Boundary of Qing Empire

States participating in tributary system

EUROPEAN WAREHOUSES AT CANTON. Aggravated by the growing presence of foreigners in the eighteenth century, the Chinese court severely restricted the movement of European traders in China. They were permitted to live only in a compound near Canton during the seven months of the trading season and could go into the city only three times a month. In this painting, the Dutch and British flags fly over the warehouses and residences of the foreign community, while Chinese sampans and junks sit anchored in the river.

pean trade. Operating through the East India Company, which served as both a trading unit and the administrator of English territories in Asia, the English established their first trading post at Canton in 1699. Over the next decades, trade with China, notably the export of tea and silk to England, increased rapidly. To limit contact between Chinese and Europeans, the Qing licensed Chinese trading firms at Canton to be the exclusive conduit for trade with the West. Eventually the Qing confined the Europeans to a small island just outside the city walls and permitted them to reside there only from October through March. *didn't trust foreigners*

For a while, the British tolerated this system, but by the end of the eighteenth century, the British government became restive at the uneven balance of trade between the two countries, which forced the British to ship vast amounts of silver bullion to China in exchange for its silks, porcelains, and teas. In 1793, a mission under Lord

Canton in the Eighteenth Century

Canton

EUROPEAN FACTORIES   *Pearl River*

Macartney visited Beijing to press for liberalization of trade restrictions. A compromise was reached on the kowtow (Macartney was permitted to bend on one knee as was the British custom), but Qianlong expressed no interest in British manufactured products. An exasperated Macartney compared the Chinese Empire to "an old, crazy, first-rate man-of-war" that had once awed its neighbors "merely by her bulk and appearance" but was now destined under incompetent leadership to be "dashed to pieces on the shore."[4] With his contemptuous dismissal of the British request, the emperor had inadvertently sowed the seeds for a century of humiliation.

Changing China

During the Ming and Qing dynasties, China remained a predominantly agricultural society; nearly 85 percent of its people were farmers. But although most Chinese still lived in rural villages, the economy was undergoing a number of changes.

THE POPULATION EXPLOSION

In the first place, the center of gravity was continuing to shift steadily from the north to the south. In the early centuries of Chinese civilization, the administrative and

The Art Archive/Marine Museum Stockholm/Dagli Orti (A)

Chronology

CHINA DURING THE EARLY MODERN ERA

Rise of Ming dynasty	1369
Voyages of Zhenghe	1405–1433
Portuguese arrive in southern China	1514
Matteo Ricci arrives in China	1601
Li Zicheng occupies Beijing	1644
Manchus seize China	1644
Reign of Kangxi	1661–1722
Treaty of Nerchinsk	1689
First English trading post at Canton	1699
Reign of Qianlong	1736–1795
Lord Macartney's mission to China	1793
White Lotus Rebellion	1796–1804

economic center of gravity was clearly in the north. By the early Qing, the economic breadbasket of China was located along the Yangtze River and regions to the south. One concrete indication of this shift occurred during the Ming dynasty, when Emperor Yongle ordered the renovation of the Grand Canal to facilitate the shipment of rice from the Yangtze delta to the food-starved north.

Moreover, the population was beginning to increase rapidly. For centuries, China's population had remained within a range of 50 to 100 million, rising in times of peace and prosperity and falling in periods of foreign invasion and internal anarchy. During the Ming and the early Qing, however, the population increased from an estimated 70 to 80 million in 1390 to over 300 million at the end of the eighteenth century. There were probably several reasons for this population increase: the relatively long period of peace and stability under the early Qing; the introduction of new crops from the Americas, including peanuts, sweet potatoes, and maize; and the planting of a new species of faster-growing rice from Southeast Asia.

Of course, this population increase meant much greater population pressure on the land, smaller farms, and a razor-thin margin of safety in case of climatic disaster. The imperial court attempted to deal with the problem through a variety of means, most notably by preventing the concentration of land in the hands of wealthy landowners. Nevertheless, by the eighteenth century, almost all the land that could be irrigated was already under cultivation, and the problems of rural hunger and landlessness became increasingly serious.

SEEDS OF INDUSTRIALIZATION

Another change that took place during the early modern period in China was the steady growth of manufacturing and commerce. Taking advantage of the long era of peace and prosperity, merchants and manufacturers began to expand their operations beyond their immediate provinces. Commercial networks began to operate on a regional and sometimes even a national basis, as trade in silk, metal and wood products, porcelain, cotton goods, and cash crops like cotton and tobacco developed rapidly. Foreign trade also expanded as Chinese merchants set up extensive contacts with countries in Southeast Asia.

Although this rise in industrial and commercial activity resembles the changes occurring in western Europe, China and Europe differed in several key ways. In the first place, members of the bourgeoisie in China were not as independent as their European counterparts. In China, trade and manufacturing remained under the firm control of the state. In addition, political and social prejudices against commercial activity remained strong. Reflecting an ancient preference for agriculture over manufacturing and trade, the state levied heavy taxes on manufacturing and commerce while attempting to keep agricultural taxes low.

One of the consequences of these differences was a growing technological gap between China and Europe. The Chinese reaction to European clockmaking techniques provides an example. In the early seventeenth century, the Jesuit Matteo Ricci introduced advanced European clocks driven by weights or springs. The emperor was fascinated and found the clocks more reliable than Chinese methods of keeping time. Over the next decades, European timepieces became a popular novelty at court, but the Chinese expressed little curiosity about the technology involved, provoking one European to remark that playthings like cuckoo clocks "will be received here with much greater interest than scientific instruments or *objets d'art*."[5]

Daily Life in Qing China

Daily life under the Ming and early Qing dynasties continued to follow traditional patterns. As in earlier periods, Chinese society was organized around the family. The ideal family unit in Qing China was the joint family, in which as many as three or even four generations lived under the same roof. When sons married, they brought their wives to live with them in the family homestead. Unmarried daughters would also remain in the house. Aging parents and grandparents remained under the same roof and were cared for by younger members of the household until they died. This ideal did not always correspond to reality, however, since many families did not possess sufficient land to support a large household.

The family continued to be important in early Qing times for much the same reasons as in earlier times. As a labor-intensive society based primarily on the cultivation of rice, China needed large families to help with the harvest and to provide security for parents too old to work in the fields. Sons were particularly prized, not only because they had strong backs but also because they would raise their own families under the parental roof. With few opportunities for employment outside the family, sons had little choice but to remain with their parents and help on the land. Within the family, the oldest male was king, and his wishes theoretically had to be obeyed by all family members. Marriages were normally arranged for the benefit of the family, often by a go-between, and the groom and bride were usually not consulted. Frequently they did not meet until the marriage ceremony. Under such conditions, love was clearly a secondary consideration. In fact, it was often viewed as detrimental since it inevitably distracted the attention of the husband and wife from their primary responsibility to the larger family unit.

Although this emphasis on filial piety might seem to represent a blatant disregard for individual rights, the obligations were not all on the side of the children. The father was expected to provide support for his wife and children and, like the ruler, was supposed to treat those in his care with respect and compassion. All too often, however, the male head of the family was able to exact his privileges without performing his responsibilities in return.

Beyond the joint family was the clan. Sometimes called a lineage, a clan was an extended kinship unit consisting of dozens or even hundreds of joint and nuclear families linked together by a clan council of elders and a variety of other common social and religious functions. The clan served a number of useful purposes. Some clans possessed lands that could be rented out to poorer families, or richer families within the clan might provide land for the poor. Since there was no general state-supported educational system, sons of poor families might be invited to study in a school established in the home of a more prosperous relative. If the young man succeeded in becoming an official, he would be expected to provide favors and prestige for the clan as a whole.

THE ROLE OF WOMEN

In traditional China, the role of women had always been inferior to that of men. A sixteenth-century Spanish visitor to South China observed that Chinese women were "very secluded and virtuous, and it was a very rare thing for us to see a woman in the cities and large towns, unless it was an old crone." Women were more visible, he said, in rural areas, where they frequently could be seen working in the fields.[6]

The concept of female inferiority had deep roots in Chinese history. This view was embodied in the belief that only a male would carry on sacred family rituals and that men alone had the talent to govern others. Only males could aspire to a career in government or scholarship. Within the family system, the wife was clearly subordinated to the husband. Legally she could not divorce her husband or inherit property. The husband, however, could divorce his wife if she did not produce male heirs, or he could take a second wife as well as a concubine for his pleasure. A widow suffered especially, because she had to either raise her children on a single income or fight off her former husband's greedy relatives, who would coerce her to remarry since, according to the law, they would then inherit all of her previous property and her original dowry.

Female children were less desirable because of their limited physical strength and because their parents would be required to pay a dowry to the parents of their future husband. Female children normally did not receive an education, and in times of scarcity when food was in short supply, daughters might even be put to death.

Though women were clearly inferior to men in theory, this was not always the case in practice. Capable women often compensated for their legal inferiority by playing a strong role within the family. Women were often in charge of educating the children and handled the family budget. Some privileged women also received training in the Confucian classics, although their schooling was generally for a shorter time and less rigorous than that of their male counterparts. A few produced significant works of art and poetry.

Cultural Developments

During the late Ming and the early Qing dynasties, traditional culture in China reached new heights of achievement. With the rise of a wealthy urban class, the demand for art, porcelain, textiles, and literature grew significantly.

THE RISE OF THE CHINESE NOVEL

During the Ming dynasty, a new form of literature arose that eventually evolved into the modern Chinese novel. Although considered less respectable than poetry and nonfiction prose, these groundbreaking works (often written anonymously or under pseudonyms) were enormously popular, especially among well-to-do urban dwellers.

Written in a colloquial style, the new fiction was characterized by a realism that resulted in vivid portraits of Chinese society. Many of the stories sympathized with society's downtrodden—often helpless maidens—and dealt with such crucial issues as love, money, marriage, and power. Adding to the realism were sexually explicit passages that depicted the private side of Chinese life. Readers delighted in sensuous tales that, no matter how pornographic, always professed a moral lesson; the villains were punished and the virtuous rewarded.

The Dream of the Red Chamber is generally considered China's most distinguished popular novel. Published in

➤ **THE TEMPLE OF HEAVEN.**   This temple, located in the capital city of Beijing, is one of the most important historical structures in China. Built in 1420 at the order of the Ming emperor Yongle, it served as the location for the emperor's annual ceremony appealing to Heaven for a good harvest. Yongle's temple burned to the ground in 1889 but was immediately rebuilt according to the original design.

1791, it tells of the tragic love between two young people caught in the financial and moral disintegration of a powerful Chinese clan. The hero and the heroine, both sensitive and spoiled, represent the inevitable decline of the Chia family and come to an equally inevitable tragic end, she in death and he in an unhappy marriage to another.

THE ART OF THE MING AND THE QING

During the Ming and the early Qing, China produced its last outpouring of traditional artistic brilliance. Although most of the creative work was modeled on past examples, the art of this period is impressive for its technical perfection and breathtaking quantity.

In architecture, the most outstanding example is the Imperial City in Beijing. Building on the remnants of the palace of the Yuan dynasty, the Ming emperor Yongle ordered renovations when he returned the capital to Beijing in 1421. Succeeding emperors continued to add to the palace, but the basic design has not changed since the

Ming era. Surrounded by high walls, the immense compound is divided into a maze of private apartments and offices and an imposing ceremonial quadrangle with a series of stately halls for imperial audiences and banquets. The grandiose scale, richly carved marble, spacious gardens, and graceful upturned roofs also contribute to the splendor of the "Forbidden City."

The decorative arts flourished in this period, especially the intricately carved lacquerware and the boldly shaped and colored cloisonné, a type of enamelwork in which colored areas are separated by thin metal bands. Silk production reached its zenith, and the best-quality silks

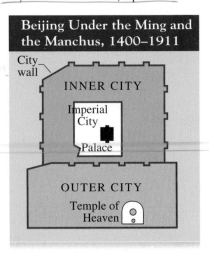

Courtesy of William J. Duiker

THE IMPERIAL CITY IN BEIJING. During the fifteenth century, the Ming dynasty erected an immense imperial city on the remnants of the palace of Khubilai Khan in Beijing. Surrounded by $6\frac{1}{2}$ miles of walls, the enclosed compound is divided into a maze of private apartments and offices; it also includes an imposing ceremonial quadrangle with stately halls for imperial audiences and banquets. Because it was off-limits to commoners, the compound was known as the Forbidden City.

were highly prized in Europe, where chinoiserie, as Chinese art of all kinds was called, was in vogue. Perhaps the most famous of all the achievements of the Ming era was its blue-and-white porcelain, still prized by collectors throughout the world.

During the Qing dynasty, artists produced great quantities of paintings, mostly for home consumption. Inside the Forbidden City in Beijing, court painters worked alongside Jesuit artists and experimented with Western techniques. Most scholarly painters and the literati, however, totally rejected foreign techniques and became obsessed with traditional Chinese styles. As a result, Qing painting became progressively more repetitive and stale.

TOKUGAWA JAPAN

At the end of the fifteenth century, the traditional Japanese system was at a point of near anarchy. With the decline in the authority of the Ashikaga shogunate at Kyoto, clan rivalries had exploded into an era of warring states. Even at the local level, power was frequently diffuse. The typical daimyo (great lord) domain had often become little more than a coalition of fief-holders held together by a loose allegiance to the manor lord. Nevertheless, Japan was on the verge of an extended era of national unification and peace under the rule of its greatest shogunate—the Tokugawa.

The Three Great Unifiers

The process began in the mid-sixteenth century with the emergence of three very powerful political figures, Oda Nobunaga (1568–1582), Toyotomi Hideyoshi (1582–1598), and Tokugawa Ieyasu (1598–1616). In 1568, Oda Nobunaga, the son of a samurai and a military commander under the Ashikaga shogunate, seized the imperial capital of Kyoto and placed the reigning shogun under his domination. During the next few years, the brutal and ambitious Nobunaga attempted to consolidate his rule throughout the central plains by defeating his rivals and suppressing the power of the Buddhist estates, but he was killed by one of his generals in 1582 before the process was complete. He was succeeded by Toyotomi Hideyoshi, a farmer's son who had worked his way up through the ranks to become a military commander. Hideyoshi located his capital at Osaka, where he built a castle to accommodate his headquarters, and gradually extended his power outward to the southern islands of Shikoku and Kyushu (see Map 16.3). By 1590, he had persuaded most of the daimyo on the Japanese islands to accept his authority and created a national currency. Then he invaded Korea in an abortive effort to export his rule to the Asian mainland.

Despite their efforts, however, neither Nobunaga nor Hideyoshi was able to eliminate the power of the local daimyo. Both were compelled to form alliances with some daimyo in order to destroy other more powerful rivals.

A PRESENT FOR LORD TOKITAKA

The Portuguese introduced firearms to Japan in the six-teenth century, and Japanese warriors were quick to explore the possibilities of these new weapons. In this passage, the daimyo of a small island off the southern tip of Japan receives an explanation of how to use the new weapons and is fascinated by the results. Note how Lord Tokitaka attempts to understand the procedures in terms of traditional Daoist beliefs.

THE JAPANESE DISCOVER FIREARMS

"There are two leaders among the traders, the one called Murashusa, and the other Christian Mota. In their hands they carried something two or three feet long, straight on the outside with a passage inside, and made of a heavy substance. The inner passage runs through it although it is closed at the end. At its side there is an aperture which is the passageway for fire. Its shape defies comparison with anything I know. To use it, fill it with powder and small lead pellets. Set up a small . . . target on a bank. Grip the object in your hand, compose your body, and closing one eye, apply fire to the aperture. Then the pellet hits the target squarely. The explosion is like lightning and the report like thunder. Bystanders must cover their ears. . . . This thing with one blow can smash a mountain of silver and a wall of iron. If one sought to do mischief in another man's domain and he was touched by it, he would lose his life instantly. Needless to say this is also true for the deer and stag that ravage the plants in the fields."

Lord Tokitaka saw it and thought it was the wonder of wonders. He did not know its name at first nor the details of its use. Then someone called it "iron-arms," although it was not known whether the Chinese called it so, or whether it was so called only on our island. Thus, one day, Tokitaka spoke to the two alien leaders through an interpreter: "Inca-pable though I am, I should like to learn about it." Whereupon, the chiefs answered, also through an interpreter: "If you wish to learn about it, we shall teach you its mysteries." Tokitaka then asked, "What is its secret?" The chief replied: "The secret is to put your mind aright and close one eye." Tokitaka said: "The ancient sages have often taught how to set one's mind aright, and I have learned something of it. If the mind is not set aright, there will be no logic for what we say or do. Thus, I understand what you say about setting our minds aright. However, will it not impair our vision for objects at a distance if we close an eye? Why should we close an eye?" To which the chiefs replied: "That is because concentration is important in everything. When one concentrates, a broad vision is not necessary. To close an eye is not to dim one's eyesight but rather to project one's concentration farther. You should know this." Delighted, Tokitaka said: "That corresponds to what Lao Tzu has said, 'Good sight means seeing what is very small.'"

That year the festival day of the Ninth Month fell on the day of the Metal and the Boar. Thus, one fine morning the weapon was filled with powder and lead pellets, a target was set up more than a hundred paces away, and fire was applied to the weapon. At first the people were astonished; then they became frightened. But in the end they all said in unison: "We should like to learn!" Disregarding the high price of the arms, Tokitaka purchased from the aliens two pieces of the firearms for his family treasure. As for the art of grinding, sifting, and mixing of the powder, Tokitaka let his retainer, Shinokawa Shoshiro, learn it. Tokitaka occupied himself, morning and night, and without rest in handling the arms. As a result, he was able to convert the misses of his early experiments into hits—a hundred hits in a hundred attempts.

At the conclusion of his conquests in 1590, Toyotomi Hideyoshi could claim to be the supreme proprietor of all registered lands in areas under his authority. But he then reassigned those lands as fiefs to the local daimyo, who declared their allegiance to him. The daimyo in turn began to pacify the countryside, carrying out extensive "sword hunts" to disarm the population and attracting samurai to their service. The Japanese tradition of decentralized rule had not been overcome.

After Hideyoshi's death in 1598, Tokugawa Ieyasu, the powerful daimyo of Edo (modern Tokyo), moved to fill the vacuum. Neither Hideyoshi nor Oda Nobunaga had claimed the title of shogun, but Ieyasu named himself shogun in 1603, initiating the most powerful and long-lasting of all Japanese shogunates. The Tokugawa rulers completed the restoration of central authority begun by Nobunaga and Hideyoshi and remained in power until 1868, when a war dismantled the entire system. As a contemporary phrased it, "Oda pounds the national rice cake, Hideyoshi kneads it, and in the end Ieyasu sits down and eats it."[7]

Opening to the West

The unification of Japan took place almost simultaneously with the coming of the Europeans. Portuguese traders sailing in a Chinese junk that may have been blown off course by a typhoon had landed on the islands in 1543. Within a few years, Portuguese ships were stopping at Japanese ports on a regular basis to take part in the regional trade between Japan, China, and Southeast Asia. The first Jesuit missionary, Francis Xavier, arrived in 1549.

Initially the visitors were welcomed. The curious Japanese were fascinated by tobacco, clocks, spectacles, and other European goods, and local daimyo were interested in purchasing all types of European weapons and armaments (see the box above). Oda Nobunaga and Toyotomi

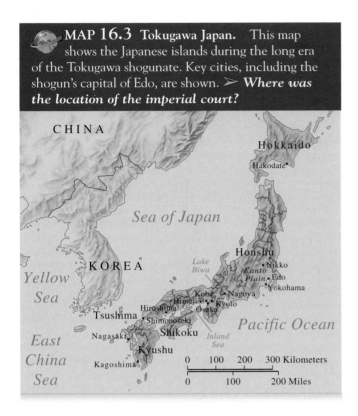

MAP 16.3 Tokugawa Japan. This map shows the Japanese islands during the long era of the Tokugawa shogunate. Key cities, including the shogun's capital of Edo, are shown. ➤ *Where was the location of the imperial court?*

Hideyoshi found the new firearms helpful in defeating their enemies and unifying the islands. The effect on Japanese military architecture was particularly striking as

local lords began to erect castles on the European model, many of which still exist today.

The missionaries also had some success in converting a number of local daimyo, some of whom may have been motivated in part by the desire for commercial profits. By the end of the sixteenth century, thousands of Japanese in the southernmost islands of Kyushu and Shikoku had become Christians. But papal claims to the loyalty of all Japanese Christians and the European habit of intervening in local politics soon began to arouse suspicion in official circles. Missionaries added to the problem by deliberately destroying local idols and shrines and turning some temples into Christian schools or churches.

Inevitably, the local authorities reacted. In 1587, Toyotomi Hideyoshi issued an edict prohibiting further Christian activities within his domains. Japan, he declared, was "the land of the Gods," and the destruction of shrines by the foreigners was "something unheard of in previous ages."[8] The Jesuits were ordered to leave the country within twenty days. Hideyoshi was careful to distinguish missionary from trading activities, however, and merchants were permitted to continue their operations (see the box on p. 354).

The Jesuits protested the expulsion, and eventually Hideyoshi relented, permitting them to continue proselytizing so long as they were discreet. But he refused to repeal the edicts, and when the aggressive activities of newly arrived Spanish Franciscans aroused his ire, he ordered the execution of nine missionaries and a number of their

⟫ THE PORTUGUESE ARRIVE AT NAGASAKI. Portuguese traders landed in Japan by accident in 1543. In a few years, they arrived regularly, taking part in a regional trade network between Japan, China, and Southeast Asia. In these panels done in black lacquer and gold leaf, we see a late-sixteenth-century Japanese interpretation of the first Portuguese landing at Nagasaki.

TOYOTOMI HIDEYOSHI EXPELS THE MISSIONARIES

When Christian missionaries in sixteenth-century Japan began to interfere in local politics and criticize traditional religious practices, Toyotomi Hideyoshi issued an edict calling for their expulsion. In this letter to the Portuguese viceroy in Asia, Hideyoshi explains his decision. Note his conviction that Buddhists, Confucianists, and followers of Shinto all believe in the same God and his criticism of Christianity for rejecting all other faiths.

TOYOTOMI HIDEYOSHI, LETTER TO THE VICEROY OF THE INDIES

Ours is the land of the Gods, and God is mind. Everything in nature comes into existence because of mind. Without God there can be no spirituality. Without God there can be no way. God rules in times of prosperity as in times of decline. God is positive and negative and unfathomable. Thus, God is the root and source of all existence. This God is spoken of by Buddhism in India, Confucianism in China, and Shinto in Japan. To know Shinto is to know Buddhism as well as Confucianism.

As long as man lives in this world, Humanity will be a basic principle. Were it not for Humanity and Righteousness, the sovereign would not be a sovereign, nor a minis-ter of a state a minister. It is through the practice of Humanity and Righteousness that the foundations of our relationships between sovereign and minister, parent and child, and husband and wife are established. If you are interested in the profound philosophy of God and Buddha, request an explanation and it will be given to you. In your land one doctrine is taught to the exclusion of others, and you are not yet informed of the [Confucian] philosophy of Humanity and Righteousness. Thus there is no respect for God and Buddha and no distinction between sovereign and ministers. Through heresies you intend to destroy the righteous law. Hereafter, do not expound, in ignorance of right and wrong, unreasonable and wanton doctrines. A few years ago the so-called Fathers came to my country seeking to bewitch our men and women, both of the laity and clergy. At that time punishment was administered to them, and it will be repeated if they should return to our domain to propagate their faith. It will not matter what sect or denomination they represent—they shall be destroyed. It will then be too late to repent. If you entertain any desire of establishing amity with this land, the seas have been rid of the pirate menace, and merchants are permitted to come and go. Remember this.

Japanese converts. When the missionaries continued to interfere in local politics, Tokugawa Ieyasu ordered the eviction of all missionaries in 1612.

At first, Japanese authorities hoped to maintain commercial relations with European countries even while suppressing the Western religion, but eventually they decided to prohibit foreign trade altogether and closed the two major foreign factories on the island of Hirado and at Nagasaki. The sole remaining opening to the West was at Deshima Island in Nagasaki harbor, where a small Dutch community was permitted to engage in limited trade with Japan (the Dutch, unlike the Portuguese and the Spanish, had not allowed missionary activities to interfere with their commercial interests). Dutch ships were permitted to dock at Nagasaki harbor only once a year and, after close inspection, were allowed to remain for two or three months.

Nagasaki and Hirado Island

Shimonoseki · Hirado · Nagasaki · KYUSHU · Pacific Ocean

0 — 150 Kilometers
0 — 100 Miles

Conditions on the island of Deshima itself were quite confining: the Dutch physician Engelbert Kaempfer complained that the Dutch lived in "almost perpetual imprisonment."[9] Nor were the Japanese free to engage in foreign trade. A small amount of commerce took place with China, but Japanese subjects of the shogunate were forbidden to leave the country on penalty of death.

The Tokugawa "Great Peace"

Once in power, the Tokugawa attempted to strengthen the system that had governed Japan for over three hundred years. They followed precedent in ruling through the *bakufu*, composed now of a coalition of daimyo, and a council of elders. But the system was more centralized than it had been previously. Now the shogunate government played a dual role. It set national policy on behalf of the emperor in Kyoto while simultaneously governing the shogun's own domain, which included about one-quarter of the national territory as well as the three great cities of Edo, Kyoto, and Osaka. As before, the state was divided into separate territories, called domains (*han*), which were ruled by a total of about 250 individual daimyo.

In theory, the daimyo were essentially autonomous since they were able to support themselves from taxes on their lands (the shogunate received its own revenues from its extensive landholdings). In actuality, the shogunate was able to guarantee daimyo loyalties by compelling daimyo to maintain two residences, one in their own domains and the other at Edo, and to leave their families in Edo as hostages for the daimyo's good behavior. Keeping up two residences also placed the Japanese nobility in a difficult economic position. Some were able to defray the high costs by concentrating on cash crops such as sugar, fish, and forestry products; but most were rice producers, and their revenues remained roughly the same throughout the period. The daimyo were also able to protect their economic interests by depriving their samurai retainers of their proprietary rights over the land and transforming them into salaried officials. The fief thus became a stipend, and the personal relationship between the daimyo and his retainers gradually gave way to a bureaucratic authority.

The Tokugawa also tinkered with the social system by limiting the size of the samurai class and reclassifying samurai who supported themselves by tilling the land as commoners. In fact, with the long period of peace brought about by Tokugawa rule, the samurai gradually ceased to be a warrior class and were required to live in the castle towns. As a gesture to their glorious past, samurai were still permitted to wear their two swords, and a rigid separation was maintained between persons of samurai status and the nonaristocratic segment of the population.

SEEDS OF CAPITALISM

The long period of peace under the Tokugawa shogunate made possible a dramatic rise in commerce and manufacturing, especially in the growing cities of Edo, Kyoto, and Osaka. By the mid-eighteenth century, Edo, with a population of more than one million, was one of the largest cities in the world. The growth of trade and industry was stimulated by a rising standard of living—driven in part by technological advances in agriculture and an expansion of arable land—and the voracious appetites of the aristocrats for new products.

Most of this commercial expansion took place in the major cities and the castle towns, where the merchants and artisans lived along with the samurai, who were clustered in neighborhoods surrounding the daimyo's castle. Banking flourished and paper money became the normal medium of exchange in commercial transactions. Merchants formed guilds not only to control market conditions but also to facilitate government control and the collection of taxes. Under the benign if somewhat contemptuous supervision of Japan's noble rulers, a Japanese merchant class gradually began to emerge from the shadows to play a significant role in the life of the Japanese nation. Some historians view the Tokugawa era as the first stage in the rise of an indigenous form of capitalism.

Eventually the increased pace of industrial activity spread beyond the cities into rural areas. As in Great Britain, cotton was a major factor. Cotton had been intro-

Chronology

JAPAN AND KOREA DURING THE EARLY MODERN ERA

First phonetic alphabet in Korea	Fifteenth century
Portuguese merchants arrive in Japan	1543
Francis Xavier arrives in Japan	1549
Rule of Oda Nobunaga	1568–1582
Seizure of Kyoto	1568
Rule of Toyotomi Hideyoshi	1582–1598
Edict prohibiting Christianity in Japan	1587
Invades Korea	1592
Death of Toyotomi Hideyoshi and withdrawal of army from Korea	1598
Rule of Tokugawa Ieyasu	1598–1616
Creation of Tokugawa shogunate	1603
Dutch granted permission to trade at Nagasaki	1609
Order evicting Christian missionaries	1612
Yi dynasty of Korea declares fealty to China	1630s
Christian uprising suppressed in Japan	1637
Dutch post at Nagasaki transferred to Hirado	1641

duced to China during the Song dynasty and had spread to Korea and Japan shortly thereafter. Traditionally, however, cotton cloth had been too expensive for the common people, who instead wore clothing made of hemp. Imports increased during the sixteenth century, however, when cotton cloth began to be used for uniforms, matchlock fuses, and sails. Eventually, technological advances reduced the cost, and specialized communities for producing cotton cloth began to appear in the countryside and were gradually transformed into towns. By the eighteenth century, cotton had firmly replaced hemp as the cloth of choice for most Japanese.

Not everyone benefited from the economic changes of the seventeenth and eighteenth centuries, however; the samurai were barred by tradition and prejudice from commercial activities. Most samurai still relied on their revenues from rice lands, which were often insufficient to cover their rising expenses; consequently they fell heavily into debt. Others were released from servitude to their lord and became "masterless samurai." Occasionally these unemployed warriors (known as *ronin*, or "wave men") revolted or plotted against the local authorities.

The effects of economic developments on the rural population during the Tokugawa era are harder to estimate. Some farm families benefited by exploiting the growing demand for cash crops. But not all prospered. Most peasants continued to rely on rice cultivation and were whipsawed between declining profits and rising costs and taxes (as daimyo expenses increased, land taxes often took up to 50 percent of the annual harvest). Many were forced to become tenants or to work as wage laborers on the farms of wealthy neighbors or in village industries. When rural conditions in some areas became desperate, peasant revolts erupted. According to one estimate, nearly seven thousand disturbances took place during the Tokugawa era.

Some Japanese historians, influenced by a Marxist view of history, have interpreted such evidence as an indication that the Tokugawa economic system was highly exploitative, with feudal aristocrats oppressing powerless peasants. Recent scholars, however, have tended to adopt a more balanced view, maintaining that in addition to agriculture, manufacturing and commerce experienced extensive growth. Some point out that although the population doubled in the seventeenth century, a relatively low rate for the time period, so did the amount of cultivable land, while agricultural technology made significant advances.

The relatively low rate of population growth probably meant that Japanese peasants were spared the kind of land hunger that many of their counterparts in China faced. Recent evidence indicates that the primary reasons for the relatively low rate of population growth were late marriage, abortion, and infanticide.

Life in the Village

The changes that took place during the Tokugawa era had a major impact on the lives of ordinary Japanese. In some respects, the result was an increase in the power of the central government at the village level. The shogunate increasingly relied on Confucian maxims advocating obedience and hierarchy to enhance its authority with the general population. Decrees from the *bakufu* instructed the peasants on all aspects of their lives, including their eating habits and their behavior. At the same time, the increased power of the government led to more autonomy from the local daimyo for the peasants. Villages now had more control over their local affairs.

At the same time, the Tokugawa era saw the emergence of the nuclear family (*ie*) as the basic unit in Japanese society. In previous times, Japanese peasants had few legal rights. Most were too poor to keep their conjugal family unit intact or to pass property on to their children. Many lived at the manorial residence or worked as servants in the households of more affluent villagers. Now, with farm income on the rise, the nuclear family took on the same form as in China, although without the joint family concept. The Japanese system of inheritance was based on primogeniture. Family property was passed on to the eldest son, although younger sons often received land from their parents to set up their own families after marriage.

Another result of the changes under the Tokugawa was that women were somewhat more restricted than they had been previously. The rights of females were especially restricted in the samurai class, where Confucian values were highly influential. Male heads of households had broad authority over property, marriage, and divorce; wives were expected to obey their husbands on pain of death. Males often took concubines or homosexual partners, while females were expected to remain chaste. The male offspring of samurai parents studied the Confucian classics in schools established by the daimyo, while females were reared at home, where only the fortunate might receive a rudimentary training in reading and writing Chinese characters. Some women, however, became accomplished poets and painters since, in aristocratic circles, female literacy was prized for enhancing the refinement, social graces, and moral virtue of the home.

Women were similarly at a disadvantage among the common people. Marriages were arranged, and as in China, the new wife moved in with the family of her husband. A wife who did not meet the expectations of her spouse or his family was likely to be divorced. Still, gender relations were more egalitarian than among the nobility. Women were generally valued as childbearers and homemakers, and both sexes worked in the fields. Coeducational schools were established in villages and market towns, and about one-quarter of the students were female. Poor families, however, often put infant daughters to death or sold them into prostitution.

Such attitudes toward women operated within the context of the increasingly rigid stratification of Japanese society. Deeply conservative in their social policies, the Tokugawa rulers established strict legal distinctions between the four main classes in Japan (warriors, artisans, peasants, and merchants). Intermarriage between classes was forbidden in theory, although sometimes the prohibitions were ignored in practice. Below these classes were Japan's outcasts, the *eta*. Formerly they were permitted to escape their status, at least in theory. The Tokugawa made their status hereditary and enacted severe discriminatory laws against them, regulating their place of residence, their dress, and even their hairstyles.

Tokugawa Culture

Under the Tokugawa, a vital new set of cultural values began to appear, especially in the cities. This innovative era witnessed the rise of popular literature written by and for the townspeople. With the development of woodblock printing in the early seventeenth century, literature became available to the common people, literacy levels rose, and lending libraries increased the accessibility of the printed word.

THE LITERATURE OF
THE NEW MIDDLE CLASS

The best examples of this new urban fiction are the works of Saikaku (1642–1693), considered one of Japan's finest novelists. Saikaku's greatest novel, *Five Women Who Loved Love*, relates the amorous exploits of five women of the merchant class. Based partly on real-life experiences, it broke from the Confucian ethic of wifely fidelity to her husband and portrayed women who were willing to die for love—and all but one eventually did. Despite the tragic circumstances, the tone of the novel is upbeat and sometimes comic, and the author's wry comments prevent the reader from becoming emotionally involved with the heroines' misfortunes.

In the theater, the rise of *Kabuki* threatened the long dominance of the *No* play, replacing the somewhat restrained and elegant thematic and stylistic approach of the classical drama with a new emphasis on violence, music, and dramatic gestures. Significantly, the new drama emerged not from the rarefied world of the court but from the new world of entertainment and amusement. Its very commercial success, however, led to difficulties with the government, which periodically attempted to restrict or even suppress it. Early *Kabuki* was often performed by prostitutes, and shogunate officials, fearing that such activities could have a corrupting effect on the nation's morals, prohibited women from appearing on the stage; at the same time, they attempted to create a new professional class of male actors to impersonate female characters on stage.

In contrast to the popular literature of the Tokugawa period, poetry persevered in its more serious tradition. The most exquisite poetry was produced in the seventeenth century by the greatest of all Japanese poets, Basho (1644–1694). He was concerned with the search for the meaning of existence and the poetic expression of his experience. With his love of Daoism and Zen Buddhism, Basho found answers to his quest for the meaning of life in nature, and his poems are grounded in seasonal imagery. The following are among his most famous poems:

> *The ancient pond*
> *A frog leaps in*
> *The sound of the water.*

> *On the withered branch*
> *A crow has alighted—*
> *The end of autumn.*

His last poem, dictated to a disciple only three days prior to his death, succinctly expressed his frustration with the unfinished business of life:

> *On a journey, ailing—*
> *my dreams roam about*
> *on a withered moor.*

Like all great artists, Basho made his poems seem effortless and simple. He speaks directly to everyone, everywhere.

TOKUGAWA ART

Art also reflected the dynamism and changes in Japanese culture under the Tokugawa regime. The shogun's order that all daimyo and their families live every other year in Edo set off a burst of building as provincial rulers competed to erect the most magnificent mansion. Furthermore, the shoguns themselves constructed splendid castles adorned with sumptuous, almost ostentatious decor and furnishings. And the prosperity of the newly rising merchant class added fuel to the fire. Japanese paintings, architecture, textiles, and ceramics all flourished during this affluent era.

Although Japan was isolated from the Western world during much of the Tokugawa era, Japanese art was enriched by ideas from other cultures. Japanese pottery makers borrowed both techniques and designs from Korea to produce handsome ceramics. The passion for "Dutch learning" inspired Japanese to study Western medicine, astronomy, and languages and also led to experimentation with oil painting and Western ideas of perspective and the interplay of light and dark. Europeans desired Japanese lacquerware and metalwork, inlaid with ivory and mother-of-pearl, and especially the ceramics, which were now as highly prized as those of the Chinese.

Perhaps the most famous of all Japanese art of the Tokugawa era is the woodblock print. Genre painting, or representations of daily life, began in the sixteenth century and found its new mass-produced form in the eighteenth-century woodblock print. The now literate mercantile class was eager for illustrated texts of the amusing and bawdy tales that had circulated in oral tradition. Some prints depict entire city blocks filled with people, trades, and festivals, while others show the interiors of houses; thus they provide us with excellent visual documentation of the times. Others portray the "floating world" of the entertainment quarter, with scenes of carefree revelers enjoying the pleasures of life.

One of the most renowned of the numerous block-print artists was Utamaro (1754–1806), who painted erotic and sardonic women in everyday poses, such as walking down the street, cooking, or drying their bodies after a bath. Hokusai (1760–1849) was famous for *Thirty-Six Views of Mount Fuji*, a new and bold interpretation of the Japanese landscape.

KOREA: THE HERMIT KINGDOM

While Japan was gradually moving away from its agrarian origins, the Yi dynasty in Korea was attempting to pattern its own society on the Chinese model. The dynasty had been founded by the military commander Yi Song Gye in the late fourteenth century and immediately set out to establish close political and cultural relations with the Ming dynasty. From their new capital at Seoul, located on the Han River in the center of the peninsula, the Yi rulers accepted a tributary relationship with their powerful neighbor and engaged in the wholesale adoption of Chinese institutions and values. As in China, the civil service examinations tested candidates on their knowledge of the Confucian classics, and success was viewed as an essential step toward upward mobility.

There were differences, however. As in Japan, the dynasty continued to restrict entry into the bureaucracy to members of the aristocratic class, known in Korea as the *yangban* (or "two groups," the civilian and military). At the same time, the peasantry remained in serflike conditions, working on government estates or on the manor holdings of the landed elite. A class of slaves (*chonmin*) labored on government plantations or served in certain occupations, such as butchers and entertainers, considered beneath the dignity of other groups in the population.

Popular Culture: East and West

By the eighteenth century, a popular culture distinct from the elite culture of the nobility was beginning to emerge in the urban worlds of both the East and the West. At the top right is a scene from the "floating world," as the pleasure district in Edo, Japan, was called. Seen here are courtesans, storytellers, jesters, and various other entertainers. Below is a scene from the celebration of Carnival on the Piazza Sante Croce in Florence, Italy. Carnival was a period of festivities before Lent, mostly celebrated in Roman Catholic countries. Carnival became an occasion for indulgence in food, drink, games, and practical jokes.

Eventually Korean society began to show signs of independence from Chinese orthodoxy. In the fifteenth century, a phonetic alphabet for writing the Korean spoken language (*hangul*) was devised. Although it was initially held in contempt by the elites and used primarily as a teaching device, eventually it became the medium for private correspondence and the publishing of fiction for a popular audience. At the same time, changes were taking place in the economy, where rising agricultural production contributed to a population increase and the appearance of a small urban industrial and commercial sector, and in society, where the long domination of the

yangban class began to weaken. As their numbers increased and their power and influence declined, some *yangban* became merchants or even moved into the ranks of the peasantry, further blurring the distinction between the aristocratic class and the common people.

In general, Korean rulers tried to keep the country isolated from the outside world, but they were not always successful. The Japanese invasion under Toyotomi Hideyoshi in the late sixteenth century had a disastrous impact on Korean society. A Manchu force invaded northern Korea in the 1630s and eventually compelled the Yi dynasty to grant allegiance to the new imperial government in Beijing. Korea was relatively untouched by the arrival of European merchants and missionaries, although information about Christianity was brought to the peninsula by Koreans returning from tribute missions to China, and a small Catholic community was established there in the late eighteenth century.

☙ CONCLUSION

When Christopher Columbus sailed from southern Spain in his three ships in August 1492, he was seeking a route to China and Japan. He did not find it, but others soon did. In 1514, Portuguese ships arrived on the coast of southern China. Thirty years later, a small contingent of Portuguese merchants became the first Europeans to set foot on the islands of Japan.

At first, the new arrivals were welcomed, if only as curiosities. Eventually several European nations established trade relations with China and Japan, and Christian missionaries of various religious orders were active in both countries and in Korea as well. But their success was short-lived. Europeans eventually began to be perceived as detrimental to law and order, and during the seventeenth century, the majority of the foreign merchants and missionaries were evicted from all three countries. From that time until the middle of the nineteenth century, China, Japan, and Korea were relatively little affected by events taking place beyond their borders.

That fact deluded many observers into the assumption that the societies of East Asia were essentially stagnant, characterized by agrarian institutions and values reminiscent of those of the feudal era in Europe. As we have seen, however, that picture is misleading, for all three countries were changing and by the early nineteenth century were quite different from what they had been three centuries earlier.

Ironically, these changes were especially marked in Tokugawa Japan, an allegedly "closed country," where traditional classes and institutions were under increasing strain, not only from the emergence of a new merchant class but also from the centralizing tendencies of the powerful Tokugawa shogunate. Some historians have seen strong parallels between Tokugawa Japan and early modern Europe, which gave birth to centralized empires and a strong merchant class during the same period. The image of the monarchy is reflected in a song sung at the shrine of Toyotomi Hideyoshi in Kyoto:

Who's that
Holding over four hundred provinces
In the palm of his hand
And entertaining at a tea-party?
It's His Highness
So mighty, so impressive![10]

By the beginning of the nineteenth century, then, powerful tensions, reflecting a growing gap between ideal and reality, were at work in both Chinese and Japanese society. Under these conditions, both countries were soon forced to face a new challenge from the aggressive power of an industrializing Europe.

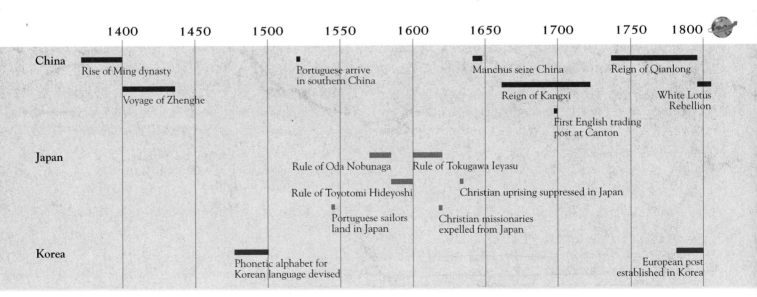

	1400	1450	1500	1550	1600	1650	1700	1750	1800
China	Rise of Ming dynasty			Portuguese arrive in southern China		Manchus seize China		Reign of Qianlong	
		Voyage of Zhenghe					Reign of Kangxi		White Lotus Rebellion
							First English trading post at Canton		
Japan				Rule of Oda Nobunaga	Rule of Tokugawa Ieyasu				
				Rule of Toyotomi Hideyoshi		Christian uprising suppressed in Japan			
					Portuguese sailors land in Japan	Christian missionaries expelled from Japan			
Korea			Phonetic alphabet for Korean language devised					European post established in Korea	

CHAPTER NOTES

1. From Jonathan D. Spence, *Emperor of China: Self-Portrait of K'ang Hsi* (New York, 1974), pp. 143–144.
2. Richard Strassberg, *The World of K'ang Shang-jen: A Man of Letters in Early Ch'ing China* (New York, 1983), p. 275.
3. Lynn Struve, *The Southern Ming, 1644–1662* (New Haven, Conn., 1984), p. 61.
4. J. L. Cranmer-Byng, *An Embassy to China: Lord Macartney's Journal, 1793–1794* (London, 1912), p. 340.
5. Daniel J. Boorstin, *The Discoverers: A History of Man's Search to Know His World and Himself* (New York, 1983), p. 63.
6. C. R. Boxer, ed., *South China in the Sixteenth Century* (London, 1953), p. 265.
7. Chie Nakane and Sinzaburo Oishi, eds., *Tokugawa Japan* (Tokyo, 1990), p. 14.
8. Quoted in Jurgis Elisonas, "Christianity and the Daimyo," in John Whitney Hall, ed., *The Cambridge History of Japan,* vol. 4 (Cambridge, 1991), p. 360.
9. Engelbert Kaempfer, *The History of Japan: Together with a Description of the Kingdom of Siam, 1690–1692,* vol. 2 (Glasgow, 1906), pp. 173–174.
10. Quoted in Ryusaku Tsunda et al., *Sources of Japanese Tradition* (New York, 1964), p. 313.

SUGGESTED READING

For a general overview of this period in East Asian history, see volumes 8 and 9 of F. W. Mote and D. Twitchett, eds., *The Cambridge History of China* (Cambridge, 1976), and J. W. Hall, ed., *The Cambridge History of Japan,* vol. 4 (Cambridge, 1991).

For information on Chinese voyages into the Indian Ocean, see P. Snow, *The Star Raft: China's Encounter with Africa* (Ithaca, N.Y., 1988). Also see Ma Huan, *Ying-hai Sheng-lan: The Overall Survey of the Ocean's Shores* (Bangkok, 1996), an ocean survey by a fifteenth-century Chinese cataloger.

On the late Ming, see J. D. Spence, *The Search for Modern China* (New York, 1990), and L. Struve, *The Southern Ming, 1644–1662* (New Haven, Conn., 1984). On the rise of the Qing, see F. Wakeman Jr., *The Great Enterprise: The Manchu Reconstruction of Imperial Order in Seventeenth-Century China* (Berkeley, Calif., 1985). On Kangxi, see J. D. Spence, *Emperor of China: Self-Portrait of K'ang Hsi* (New York, 1974). Social issues are discussed in S. Naquin and E. Rawski, *Chinese Society in the Eighteenth Century* (New Haven, Conn., 1987). Also see J. D. Spence and J. Wills, eds., *From Ming to Ch'ing* (New Haven, Conn., 1979). For a very interesting account of Jesuit missionary experiences in China, see L. J. Gallagher, ed. and trans., *China in the Sixteenth Century: The Journals of Matthew Ricci, 1583–1616* (New York, 1953). For brief biographies of Ming-Qing luminaries such as Wang Yangming, Zheng Chenggong, and Emperor Qianlong, see J. E. Wills Jr., *Mountains of Fame: Portraits in Chinese History* (Princeton, N.J., 1994).

The best surveys of Chinese literature are Liu Wu-chi, *An Introduction to Chinese Literature* (Bloomington, Ind., 1966); S. Owen, *An Anthology of Chinese Literature: Beginnings to 1911* (New York, 1996); and V. Mair, *The Columbia Anthology of Traditional Chinese Literature* (New York, 1994). For a concise and comprehensive introduction to the Chinese art of this period, see M. Sullivan, *The Arts of China,* 4th ed. (Berkeley, Calif., 1999); C. Clunas, *Art in China* (Oxford, 1997); and M. Tregear, *Chinese Art,* rev. ed. (London, 1997). For the best introduction to the painting of this era, see Yang Xin et al., *Three Thousand Years of Chinese Paintings* (New Haven, Conn., 1997).

On Japan before the rise of the Tokugawa, see J. W. Hall et al., eds., *Japan Before Tokugawa: Political Consolidation and Economic Growth* (Princeton, N.J., 1981). See also M. E. Berry, *Hideyoshi* (Cambridge, Mass., 1982), the first biography of this fascinating figure in Japanese history. On the first Christian activities, see G. Elison, *Deus Destroyed: The Image of Christianity in Early Modern Japan* (Cambridge, Mass., 1973), and C. R. Boxer, *The Christian Century in Japan, 1549–1650* (Berkeley, Calif., 1951).

On the Tokugawa era, see H. Bolitho, *Treasures Among Men: The Fudai Daimyo in Tokugawa Japan* (New Haven, Conn., 1974), and R. B. Toby, *State and Diplomacy in Early Modern Japan: Asia in the Development of the Tokugawa Bakufu* (Princeton, N.J., 1984). See also R. N. Bellah, *Tokugawa Religion: The Values of Pre-Industrial Japan* (New York, 1957), and C. I. Mulhern, ed., *Heroic with Grace: Legendary Women of Japan* (Armonk, N.Y., 1991). Three other worthwhile studies are S. Vlastos, *Peasant Protests and Uprisings in Tokugawa Japan* (Berkeley, Calif., 1986); H. Ooms, *Tokugawa Ideology: Early Constructs, 1570–1680* (Princeton, N.J., 1985); and C. Nakane, ed., *Tokugawa Japan: The Social and Economic Antecedents of Modern Japan* (Tokyo, 1990).

For a brief introduction to women in the Ming and Qing dynasties as well as the Tokugawa era, see S. Hughes and B. Hughes, *Women in World History,* vol. 2 (Armonk, N.Y., 1997). To witness Chinese village life in 1670, consult the classic J. D. Spence, *The Death of Woman Wang* (New York, 1978). For women's literacy in seventeenth-century China, see D. Ko, *Teachers of the Inner Chambers: Women and Culture in Seventeenth Century China* (Stanford, Calif., 1994). Most valuable is the collection of articles edited by G. L. Bernstein, *Re-Creating Japanese Women, 1600–1945* (Berkeley, Calif., 1991).

On Japanese literature of the Tokugawa era, see D. Keene, *World Within Walls: Japanese Literature of the Pre-Modern Era, 1600–1867* (New York, 1976). Of special value for the college student are D. Keene's *Anthology of Japanese Literature* (New York, 1955), *The Pleasures of Japanese Literature* (New York, 1988), and *Japanese Literature: An Introduction for Western Readers* (London, 1953). For an introduction to Basho's life, poems, and criticism, consult the stimulating *Basho and His Interpreters: Selected Hokku with Commentary* (Stanford, Calif., 1991), by M. Ueda.

For the most comprehensive and accessible overview of Japanese art, see P. Mason, *Japanese Art* (New York, 1993). For a concise introduction to Japanese art of the Tokugawa era, see J. Stanley-Baker, *Japanese Art* (London, 1984).

InfoTrac College Edition

Visit the source collections at infotrac.thomsonlearning.com and use the Search function with the following key terms.

China history   Qing

Japan history   Tokugawa

Ming China

World History Resources

Visit the *Essential World History* Companion Web Site for resources specific to this textbook:

http://history.wadsworth.com/duikeressentials02/

The CD in the back of this book and the World History Resource Center at **http://history.wadsworth.com/world/** offer a variety of tools to help you succeed in this course, including access to quizzes; images; documents; interactive simulations, maps, and timelines; movie explorations; and a wealth of other sources.

© Réunion des Musées Nationaux/Art Resource, NY

THE WEST ON THE EVE OF A NEW WORLD ORDER

CHAPTER OUTLINE

- THE ENLIGHTENMENT
- ECONOMIC CHANGES AND THE SOCIAL ORDER
- CHANGING PATTERNS OF WAR: GLOBAL CONFRONTATION
- COLONIAL EMPIRES AND REVOLUTION IN THE WESTERN HEMISPHERE
- TOWARD A NEW POLITICAL ORDER: ENLIGHTENED ABSOLUTISM
- THE FRENCH REVOLUTION
- THE AGE OF NAPOLEON
- CONCLUSION

FOCUS QUESTIONS

- Who were the leading figures of the Enlightenment, and what were their main contributions?
- What changes occurred in the European economy in the eighteenth century, and to what degree were these changes reflected in social patterns?
- How did Spain and Portugal administer their American colonies, and what were the main characteristics of Latin American society in the eighteenth century?
- What do historians mean by the term *enlightened absolutism*, and to what degree did eighteenth-century Prussia, Austria, and Russia exhibit its characteristics?
- What were the causes, the main events, and the results of the American Revolution and the French Revolution? Which aspects of the French Revolution did Napoleon preserve, and which did he destroy?
- ➤ In what ways were the American Revolution, the French Revolution, and the seventeenth-century English revolutions alike? In what ways were they different?

istorians have often portrayed the eighteenth century as the final phase of Europe's old order, before the violent upheaval and reordering of society associated with the French Revolution. The old order—still largely agrarian, dominated by kings and landed aristocrats, and grounded in privileges for nobles, clergy, towns, and provinces—seemed to continue a basic pattern that had prevailed in Europe since medieval times. However, just as a new intellectual order based on rationalism and secularism was emerging in Europe, demographic, economic, social, and political patterns were beginning to change in ways that proclaimed the emergence of a modern new order.

A key factor in the emergence of the new world order was the French Revolution. On the morning of July 14, 1789, a Parisian mob of some eight thousand men and women in search of weapons streamed toward the Bastille, a royal armory filled with arms and ammunition. The Bastille was also a state prison, and although it held only seven prisoners at the time, in the eyes of these angry Parisians, it was a glaring symbol of the government's despotic policies. It was defended by the marquis de Launay and a small garrison of 114 men. The attack on the Bastille began in earnest in the early afternoon, and after three hours of fighting, de Launay and the garrison surrendered. Angered by the loss of ninety-eight protesters, the victors beat de Launay to death, cut off his head, and carried it aloft in triumph through the streets of Paris. When King Louis XVI was told the news of the fall of the Bastille by the duc de La Rochefoucauld-Liancourt, he exclaimed, "Why, this is a revolt." "No, Sire," replied the duke. "It is a revolution."

The French Revolution has been portrayed as a major turning point in European political and social history, as a time when the institutions of the old regime were destroyed and a new order was created based on individual rights, representative institutions, and a concept of loyalty to the nation rather than the monarch. The revolutionary upheavals of the era, especially in France, did create new liberal and national political ideals, summarized in the French revolutionary slogan "Liberty, Equality, Fraternity," that transformed France and then spread to other European countries and the rest of the world. •

🎵 THE ENLIGHTENMENT

The impetus for political and social change in the eighteenth century stemmed in part from the Enlightenment. The Enlightenment was a movement of intellectuals who were greatly impressed with the accomplishments of the Scientific Revolution. When they used the word *reason*—one of their favorite words—they were advocating the application of the scientific method to the understanding of all life. All institutions and all systems of thought were subject to the rational, scientific way of thinking if people would only free themselves from the shackles of past, worthless traditions, especially religious ones. If Isaac Newton could discover the natural laws regulating the world of nature, they too, by using reason, could find the laws that governed human society. This belief in turn led them to hope that they could make progress toward a better society than the one they had inherited. *Reason, natural law, hope, progress*—these were the buzzwords in the heady atmosphere of eighteenth-century Europe.

The Path to Enlightenment

Major sources of inspiration for the Enlightenment were two Englishmen, Isaac Newton and John Locke. Newton contended that the world and everything in it worked like a giant machine. Enchanted by the grand design of this world-machine, the intellectuals of the Enlightenment were convinced that by following Newton's rules of reasoning, they could discover the natural laws that governed politics, economics, justice, and religion.

John Locke's theory of knowledge also made a great impact. In his *Essay Concerning Human Understanding*, written in 1690, Locke denied the existence of innate ideas and argued instead that every person was born with a *tabula rasa*, a blank mind:

> Let us then suppose the mind to be, as we say, white paper, void of all characters, without any ideas. How comes it to be furnished? Whence comes it by that vast store which the busy and boundless fancy of man has painted on it with an almost endless variety? Whence has it all the materials of reason and knowledge? To this I answer, in one word, from experience. . . . Our observation, employed either about external sensible objects or about the internal operations of our minds perceived and reflected on by ourselves, is that which supplies our understanding with all the materials of thinking.[1]

By denying innate ideas, Locke's philosophy implied that people were molded by their environment, by whatever they perceived through their senses from their surrounding world. By changing the environment and subjecting people to proper influences, they could be changed and a new society created. And how should the environment be changed? Newton had paved the way: reason enabled enlightened people to discover the natural laws to which all institutions should conform.

The Philosophes and Their Ideas

The intellectuals of the Enlightenment were known by the French term *philosophes*, although they were not all French and few were philosophers in the strict sense of the term.

They were literary people, professors, journalists, economists, political scientists, and above all, social reformers. Although it was a truly international and cosmopolitan movement, the Enlightenment also enhanced the dominant role being played by French culture; Paris was its recognized capital. Most of the leaders of the Enlightenment were French. The French philosophes, in turn, affected intellectuals elsewhere and created a movement that touched the entire Western world, including the British and Spanish colonies in America.

To the philosophes, the role of philosophy was not just to discuss the world but to change it. A spirit of rational criticism was to be applied to everything, including religion and politics. Spanning almost a century, the Enlightenment evolved with each succeeding generation, becoming more radical as new thinkers built on the contributions of their predecessors. A few individuals, however, dominated the landscape so completely that we can gain insight into the core ideas of the philosophes by focusing on the three French giants—Montesquieu, Voltaire, and Diderot.

MONTESQUIEU

Charles de Secondat, the baron de Montesquieu (1689–1755), came from the French nobility. His most famous work, *The Spirit of the Laws,* was published in 1748. In this comparative study of governments, Montesquieu attempted to apply the scientific method to the social and political arena to ascertain the "natural laws" governing the social and political relationships of human beings. Montesquieu distinguished three basic kinds of government: republic, monarchy, and despotism. Montesquieu used England as an example of monarchy, and it was his analysis of England's constitution that led to his most lasting contribution to political thought—the importance of checks and balances achieved by means of a separation of powers. He believed that England's system, with its separate executive, legislative, and judicial powers that served to limit and control each other, provided the greatest freedom and security for a state. The translation of his work into English two years after publication ensured its being read by American political leaders, who eventually incorporated its principles into the U.S. Constitution.

VOLTAIRE

The greatest figure of the Enlightenment was François-Marie Arouet, known simply as Voltaire (1694–1778). Son of a prosperous middle-class family from Paris, he studied law, although he achieved his first success as a playwright. Voltaire was a prolific author and wrote an almost endless stream of pamphlets, novels, plays, letters, philosophical essays, and histories.

Voltaire was especially well known for his criticism of traditional religion and his strong attachment to the ideal of religious toleration. As he grew older, Voltaire became ever more strident in his denunciations. "Crush the infamous thing," he thundered repeatedly—the infamous thing being religious fanaticism, intolerance, and superstition.

Throughout his life, Voltaire championed not only religious tolerance but also deism, a religious outlook shared by most other philosophes. Deism was built on the Newtonian world-machine, which implied the existence of a mechanic (God) who had created the universe. To Voltaire and most other philosophes, the universe was like a clock, and God was the clockmaker who had created it, set it in motion, and allowed it to run according to its own natural laws.

DIDEROT

Denis Diderot (1713–1784) was the son of a skilled craftsman from eastern France who became a freelance writer so that he could be free to study and read in many subjects and languages. One of Diderot's favorite topics was Christianity, which he condemned as fanatical and unreasonable. As he grew older, his literary attacks on Christianity grew more vicious. Of all religions, Christianity, he averred, was the worst, "the most absurd and the most atrocious in its dogma."

Diderot's most famous contribution to the Enlightenment was the *Encyclopedia,* or *Classified Dictionary of the Sciences, Arts, and Trades,* a twenty-eight-volume compendium of knowledge that he edited and referred to as the "great work of his life." Its purpose, according to Diderot, was to "change the general way of thinking." It did precisely that in becoming a major weapon of the philosophes' crusade against the old French society. The contributors included many philosophes who attacked religious intolerance and advocated a program for social, legal, and political improvements that would lead to a society that was more cosmopolitan, more tolerant, more humane, and more reasonable. The *Encyclopedia* was sold to doctors, clergymen, teachers, lawyers, and even military officers, thus spreading the ideas of the Enlightenment.

TOWARD A NEW "SCIENCE OF MAN"

The Enlightenment belief that Newton's scientific methods could be used to discover the natural laws underlying all areas of human life led to the emergence in the eighteenth century of what the philosophes called a "science of man," or what we would call the social sciences. In a number of areas, such as economics, politics, and education, the philosophes arrived at natural laws that they believed governed human actions.

Adam Smith (1723–1790) has been viewed as one of the founders of the modern discipline of economics. Smith believed that individuals should be left free to pursue their own economic self-interest. Through the actions of these individuals, all society would ultimately benefit. Consequently the state should in no way interrupt the free play of natural economic forces by government regulations on the economy but should leave it alone, a doctrine that subsequently became known as *laissez-faire* (French for "leave it alone").

Smith gave to government only three basic functions: it should protect society from invasion (army), defend its citizens from injustice (police), and keep up certain public works, such as roads and canals, that private individuals could not afford.

THE LATER ENLIGHTENMENT

By the late 1760s, a new generation of philosophes who had grown up with the worldview of the Enlightenment began to move beyond their predecessors' beliefs. Most famous was Jean-Jacques Rousseau (1712–1778), whose political beliefs were presented in two major works. In his *Discourse on the Origins of the Inequality of Mankind*, Rousseau argued that people had adopted laws and governors in order to preserve their private property. In the process, they had become enslaved by government. What, then, should people do to regain their freedom? In his celebrated treatise *The Social Contract*, published in 1762, Rousseau found an answer in the concept of the social contract. In a social contract, an entire society agreed to be governed by its general will. Each individual might have a particular will contrary to the general will, but if the individual put his particular will (self-interest) above the general will, he should be forced to abide by the general will. "This means nothing less than that he will be forced to be free," said Rousseau, because the general will was not only political but also ethical; it represented what the entire community ought to do.

Another influential treatise by Rousseau was his novel *Émile*, one of the Enlightenment's most important works on education. Rousseau's fundamental concern was that education should foster, rather than restrict, children's natural instincts. Rousseau's own experiences had shown him the importance of the emotions. What he sought was a balance between heart and mind, between emotion and reason.

But Rousseau did not necessarily practice what he preached. His own children were sent to orphanages, where many children died at a young age. Rousseau also viewed women as "naturally" different from men. In Rousseau's *Émile*, Sophie, Émile's intended wife, was educated for her role as wife and mother by learning obedience and the nurturing skills that would enable her to provide loving care for her husband and children. Not everyone in the eighteenth century, however, agreed with Rousseau.

THE "WOMAN QUESTION" IN THE ENLIGHTENMENT

For centuries, many male intellectuals had argued that the nature of women made them inferior to men and made male domination of women necessary and right. Female thinkers in the eighteenth century, however, provided suggestions for improving the conditions of women. The strongest statement for the rights of women was advanced by the English writer Mary Wollstonecraft (1759–1797), viewed by many as the founder of modern European feminism.

In her *Vindication of the Rights of Woman*, written in 1792, Wollstonecraft pointed out two contradictions in the views of women held by some Enlightenment thinkers. To argue that women must obey men, she said, was contrary to the beliefs of the same individuals that a system based on the arbitrary power of monarchs over their subjects or slave owners over their slaves was wrong. The subjection of women to men was equally wrong. In addition, she argued that the Enlightenment was based on an ideal of reason innate in all human beings. If women have reason, then they too are entitled to the same rights that men have. Women, Wollstonecraft declared, should have equal rights with men in education and in economic and political life as well (see the box on p. 366).

Culture in an Enlightened Age

Although the Baroque style that had dominated the seventeenth century continued to be popular, by the 1730s, a new style affecting decoration and architecture known as Rococo had spread throughout Europe. Unlike the Baroque, which stressed power, grandeur, and movement, Rococo emphasized grace, charm, and gentle action. Rococo rejected strict geometrical patterns and had a fondness for curves; it liked to follow the wandering lines of natural objects, such as seashells and flowers. It made much use of interlaced designs colored in gold with delicate contours and graceful arcs. Highly secular, its lightness and charm spoke of the pursuit of pleasure, happiness, and love.

Some of Rococo's appeal is evident already in the work of Antoine Watteau (1684–1721), whose lyrical views of aristocratic life, refined, sensual, and civilized, with gentlemen and ladies in elegant dress, revealed a world of upperclass pleasure and joy. Underneath that exterior, however, was an element of sadness as the artist revealed the fragility and transitory nature of pleasure, love, and life.

HIGH CULTURE

Historians have grown accustomed to distinguishing between a civilization's high culture and its popular culture. High culture is the literary and artistic culture of the educated and wealthy ruling classes; popular culture is the written and unwritten culture of the masses, most of which has traditionally been passed down orally. By the eighteenth century, European high culture reflected the learned tastes of theologians, scientists, philosophers, intellectuals, poets, and dramatists, for all of whom Latin remained a truly international language.

Especially noticeable in the eighteenth century was an expansion of both the reading public and publishing.

THE RIGHTS OF WOMEN

Mary Wollstonecraft responded to an unhappy childhood in a large family by seeking to lead an independent life. Few occupations were available for middle-class women in her day, but she survived by working as a teacher, chaperone, and governess to aristocratic children. All the while, she wrote and developed her ideas on the rights of women. This excerpt was taken from her Vindication of the Rights of Woman, *written in 1792. This work led to her reputation as the foremost British feminist thinker of the eighteenth century.*

MARY WOLLSTONECRAFT, VINDICATION OF THE RIGHTS OF WOMAN

It is a melancholy truth—yet such is the blessed effect of civilization—the most respectable women are the most oppressed; and, unless they have understandings far superior to the common run of understandings, taking in both sexes, they must, from being treated like contemptible beings, become contemptible. How many women thus waste life away the prey of discontent, who might have practiced as physicians, regulated a farm, managed a shop, and stood erect, supported by their own industry, instead of hanging their heads surcharged with the dew of sensibility, that consumes the beauty to which it at first gave luster. . . .

Proud of their weakness, however, [women] must always be protected, guarded from care, and all the rough toils that dignify the mind. If this be the fiat of fate, if they will make themselves insignificant and contemptible, sweetly to waste "life away," let them not expect to be valued when their beauty fades, for it is the fate of the fairest flowers to be admired and pulled to pieces by the careless hand that plucked them. In how many ways do I wish, from the purest benevolence, to impress this truth on my sex; yet I fear that they will not listen to a truth that dear-bought experience has brought home to many an agitated bosom, nor willingly resign the privileges of rank and sex for the privileges of humanity, to which those have no claim who do not discharge its duties. . . .

Would men but generously snap our chains, and be content with rational fellowship instead of slavish obedience, they would find us more observant daughters, more affectionate sisters, more faithful wives, and more reasonable mothers—in a word, better citizens. We should then love them with true affection, because we should learn to respect ourselves; and the peace of mind of a worthy man would not be interrupted by the idle vanity of his wife.

Whereas French publishers issued three hundred titles in 1750, about sixteen hundred were being published yearly in the 1780s. Although many of these titles were still geared for small groups of the educated elite, many were also directed to the new reading public of the middle classes, which included women and even urban artisans.

An important aspect of the growth of publishing and reading in the eighteenth century was the development of magazines for the general public. Great Britain saw 25 different periodicals published in 1700, 103 in 1760, 158 in 1780. Along with magazines came daily newspapers. The first was printed in London in 1702, but by 1780, thirty-seven other English towns had their own newspapers.

POPULAR CULTURE

The distinguishing characteristic of popular culture is its collective nature. Group activity was especially common in the festival, a broad name used to cover a variety of celebrations: community festivals in Catholic Europe that celebrated the feast day of the local patron saint; annual festivals, such as Christmas and Easter, that go back to medieval Christianity; and Carnival, which was celebrated in the Mediterranean world of Spain, Italy, and France as well as in Germany and Austria.

Indeed, the ultimate festival was Carnival, which began after Christmas and lasted until the start of Lent, the forty-day period of fasting and purification leading up to Easter. Because during Lent people were expected to abstain from meat, sex, and most recreations, Carnival was a time of great indulgence when heavy consumption of food and drink were the norm. It was a time of intense sexual activity as well. Songs with double meanings that would ordinarily be considered offensive could be sung publicly at this time of year. A float of Florentine "keymakers," for example, sang this ditty to the ladies: "Our tools are fine, new and useful. We always carry them with us. They are good for anything. If you want to touch them, you can."

ECONOMIC CHANGES AND THE SOCIAL ORDER

The eighteenth century in Europe witnessed the beginning of economic changes that ultimately had a strong impact on the rest of the world.

New Economic Patterns

Europe's population began to grow around 1750 and continued to increase steadily. The total European population was probably around 120 million in 1700, 140 million in

⟡ ANTOINE WATTEAU, *THE PILGRIMAGE TO CYTHERA*.   Antoine Watteau was one of the most gifted painters in eighteenth-century France. His portrayal of aristocratic life reveals a world of elegance, wealth, and pleasure. In this painting, Watteau depicts a group of aristocratic pilgrims about to depart the island of Cythera, where they have paid homage to Venus, the goddess of love.

1750, and 190 million in 1790. A falling death rate was perhaps the most important reason for this population growth. Of great significance in lowering death rates was the disappearance of bubonic plague, but so was diet. More plentiful food and better transportation of food supplies led to improved nutrition and relief from devastating famines.

More plentiful food was in part a result of improvements in agricultural practices and methods in the eighteenth century, especially in Britain, parts of France, and the Low Countries. Food production increased as more land was farmed, yields per acre increased, and climate improved. Also important to the increased yields was the cultivation of new vegetables, including two important American crops, the potato and maize (Indian corn). Both had been brought to Europe from the Americas in the sixteenth century.

In European industry in the eighteenth century, the most important product was textiles, most of which were still produced by master artisans in guild workshops. But a shift in textile production to the countryside was spreading to many rural areas of Europe by the "putting-out" or "domestic" system in which a merchant-capitalist entrepreneur bought the raw materials, mostly wool and flax, and "put them out" to rural workers who spun the raw material into yarn and then wove it into cloth on simple looms. Capitalist-entrepreneurs sold the finished product, made a profit, and used it to purchase materials to manufacture more. This system became known as the "cottage industry" because the spinners and weavers did their work on spinning wheels and looms in their own cottages.

In the eighteenth century, overseas trade boomed. Some historians speak of the emergence of a true global economy, pointing to the patterns of trade that interlocked Europe, Africa, the Far East, and the Americas (see Map 14.4 in Chapter 14). One such pattern involved the influx of gold and silver into Spain from its colonial American empire. Much of this gold and silver made its way to Britain, France, and the Netherlands in return for manufactured goods. British, Dutch, and French merchants in turn used their profits to buy tea, spices, silk and cotton goods from China and India to sell in Europe. Another important source of trading activity involved the plantations of the Western Hemisphere. The plantations were worked by African slaves and produced tobacco, cotton, coffee, and sugar, all products in demand by Europeans.

Commercial capitalism created enormous prosperity for some European countries. By 1700, Spain, Portugal, and the Dutch Republic, which had earlier monopolized overseas trade, found themselves increasingly overshadowed by France and England, which built enormously profitable colonial empires in the course of the eighteenth century. After the French lost the Seven Years' War in 1763, Britain emerged as the world's strongest overseas trading nation, and London became the world's greatest port.

European Society in the Eighteenth Century

The pattern of Europe's social organization, first established in the Middle Ages, continued well into the eighteenth century. Society was still divided into the traditional "orders" or "estates" determined by heredity.

Because society was still mostly rural in the eighteenth century, the peasantry constituted the largest social group, about 85 percent of Europe's population. There were rather wide differences within this group, however, especially between free peasants and serfs. In eastern Germany, eastern Europe, and Russia, serfs remained tied to the lands of their noble landlords. In contrast, peasants in Britain, northern Italy, the Low Countries, Spain, most of France, and some areas of western Germany were largely free.

The nobles, who constituted only 2 to 3 percent of the European population, played a dominating role in society. Being born a noble automatically guaranteed a place at the top of the social order, with all its attendant special privileges and rights. Nobles, for example, were exempt from many forms of taxation. Since medieval times, landed aristocrats had functioned as military officers, and eighteenth-century nobles held most of the important offices in the administrative machinery of state and controlled much of the life of their local districts.

Townspeople were still a distinct minority of the total population except in the Dutch Republic, Britain, and parts of Italy. At the end of the eighteenth century, about one-sixth of the French population lived in towns of two thousand people or more. The biggest city in Europe was London, with a million inhabitants; Paris was a little more than half that size.

Many cities in western and even central Europe had a long tradition of patrician oligarchies that continued to control their communities by dominating town and city councils. Just below the patricians stood an upper crust of the middle classes: nonnoble officeholders, financiers and bankers, merchants, wealthy *rentiers* who lived off their investments, and important professionals, including lawyers. Another large urban group was the lower middle class, made up of master artisans, shopkeepers, and small traders. Below them were the laborers or working classes and a large group of unskilled workers who served as servants, maids, and cooks at pitifully low wages.

CHANGING PATTERNS OF WAR: GLOBAL CONFRONTATION

The philosophes condemned war as a foolish waste of life and resources in stupid quarrels of no value to humankind. Despite their words, the rivalry among states that led to costly struggles remained unchanged in the European world of the eighteenth century. Europe consisted of a number of self-governing, individual states that were chiefly guided by the self-interest of the ruler. And as Frederick the Great of Prussia said, "The fundamental rule of governments is the principle of extending their territories."

In 1740, a major conflict erupted over the succession to the Austrian throne. King Frederick II of Prussia took advantage of the succession of a woman, Maria Theresa (1740–1780), to the throne of Austria by invading Austrian Silesia. The War of the Austrian Succession (1740–1748) was fought in three areas of the world. In Europe, Prussia seized Silesia from Austria while France occupied the Austrian Netherlands. In Asia, France took Madras in India from the British, and in North America, the British captured the French fortress of Louisbourg at the entrance to the Saint Lawrence River. By 1748, all parties were exhausted and agreed to a peace treaty that guaranteed the return of all occupied territories to their original owners, with the exception of Silesia.

The Seven Years' War: A Global Conflict

Maria Theresa refused to accept the loss of Silesia and prepared for its return by working diplomatically to separate Prussia from its chief ally, France. In 1756, Austria achieved a diplomatic revolution. French-Austrian rivalry had existed since the late sixteenth century. But two new rivalries now replaced the old one: the rivalry of Britain and France over colonial empires and the rivalry of Austria and Prussia over Silesia. France abandoned Prussia and allied with Austria. Russia, which saw Prussia as a major hindrance to Russian goals in central Europe, joined the new alliance. In turn, Great Britain allied with Prussia. These new alliances now led to another worldwide war.

Again there were three major areas of conflict: Europe, India, and North America. In Europe, the British and Prussians fought the Austrians, Russians, and French. With his superb army and military skill, Frederick the Great of Prussia was able for some time to defeat the Austrian, French, and Russian armies. Eventually, however, his forces were gradually worn down and faced utter defeat until a new Russian tsar, Peter III, withdrew Russian troops from the conflict. A stalemate ensued, ending the European conflict in 1763. All occupied territories were returned, and Austria officially recognized Prussia's permanent control of Silesia.

The struggle between Britain and France in the rest of the world had more decisive results. In India, the French had returned Madras to Britain after the War of the Austrian Succession, but the struggle continued. Ultimately, the British under Robert Clive won out, not because they had better forces but because they were more persistent. By the Treaty of Paris in 1763, the French withdrew and left India to the British.

By far the greatest conflicts of the Seven Years' War took place in North America. French North America (Canada and Louisiana) was thinly populated and run by the French government as a vast trading area. British North America had come to consist of thirteen colonies on the eastern coast of the present United States. They were thickly populated, containing about 1.5 million people by 1750, and were also prosperous.

British and French rivalry in North America finally led to war. Despite initial French successes, the British went on to seize Montreal, the Great Lakes area, and the Ohio valley. The French were forced to make peace. By the Treaty of Paris, they ceded Canada and the lands east of the Mississippi to England. Their ally Spain transferred Spanish Florida to British control; in return, the French gave their Louisiana territory to the Spanish. By 1763, Great Britain had become the world's greatest colonial power.

COLONIAL EMPIRES AND REVOLUTION IN THE WESTERN HEMISPHERE

The colonial empires in the Western Hemisphere were an integral part of the European economy in the eighteenth century and became entangled in the conflicts of the European states. Nevertheless, the colonies of Latin America and British North America were developing along lines that sometimes differed significantly from those of Europe.

The Society of Latin America

In the sixteenth century, Portugal came to dominate Brazil while Spain established a colonial empire in the New World that included Central America, most of South America, and parts of North America. Within the lands of Central and South America, a new civilization arose that we have come to call Latin America (see Map 17.1).

Latin America was a multiracial society. Already by 1501, Spanish rulers allowed intermarriage between Europeans and native American Indians, whose offspring became known as *mestizos*. In addition, over a period of three centuries, possibly as many as eight million African slaves were brought to Spanish and Portuguese America to work the plantations. Mulattoes—the offspring of Africans and whites—joined mestizos and descendants of whites, Africans, and native Indians to produce a unique multiracial society in Latin America.

THE ECONOMIC FOUNDATIONS

Both the Portuguese and the Spanish sought to profit from their colonies in Latin America. One source of wealth came from the abundant supplies of gold and silver. The Spaniards were especially successful, finding supplies of gold in the Caribbean and New Granada (Colombia) and silver in Mexico and the viceroyalty of Peru. Most of the gold and silver was sent to Europe, and little remained in the New World to benefit the people whose labor had produced it.

Although the pursuit of gold and silver offered prospects of fantastic financial rewards, agriculture proved to be a more abiding and more rewarding source of prosperity for Latin America. A noticeable feature of Latin American agriculture was the dominant role of the large landowner. Both Spanish and Portuguese landowners created immense estates, which left the Indians either to work as peons—native peasants permanently dependent on the landowners—on their estates or as poor farmers on marginal lands. This system of large landowners and dependent peasants has remained one of the persistent features of Latin American society. By the eighteenth century, both Spanish and Portuguese landowners were producing primarily for sale abroad.

Trade was another avenue for the economic exploitation of the American colonies. Latin American colonies became sources of raw materials for Spain and Portugal as gold, silver, sugar, tobacco, diamonds, animal hides, and a number of other natural products made their way to Europe. In turn, the mother countries supplied their colonists with manufactured goods.

THE STATE AND THE CHURCH IN COLONIAL LATIN AMERICA

Portuguese Brazil and Spanish America were colonial empires that lasted over three hundred years. The difficulties of communication and travel between the New World and Europe made the attempts of the Spanish and Portuguese monarchs to provide close regulation of their empires virtually impossible, which left colonial officials in Latin America with much autonomy in implementing imperial policies. However, the Iberians tried to keep the most important posts of colonial government in the hands of Europeans. Beginning in the mid-sixteenth century, the Portuguese monarchy began to assert its control over Brazil by establishing the position of governor-general. To rule his American empire, the king of Spain appointed a viceroy, the first of which was established for New Spain (Mexico) in 1535. Another viceroy was appointed for Peru in 1543. In the eighteenth century, two additional viceroyalties—New Granada and La Plata—were added. All of the major government positions were held by Spaniards.

From the beginning of their conquest of the New World, Spanish and Portuguese rulers were determined to Christianize the native peoples. This policy gave the Catholic church an important role to play in the New World—a role that added considerably to church power. Catholic missionaries fanned out to different parts of the Spanish Empire. To facilitate their efforts, missionaries brought Indians together into villages where the natives could be converted, taught trades, and encouraged to grow crops. Their missions enabled missionaries to control the lives of the Indians and keep them docile.

The Catholic church constructed hospitals, orphanages, and schools, which instructed Indian students in the

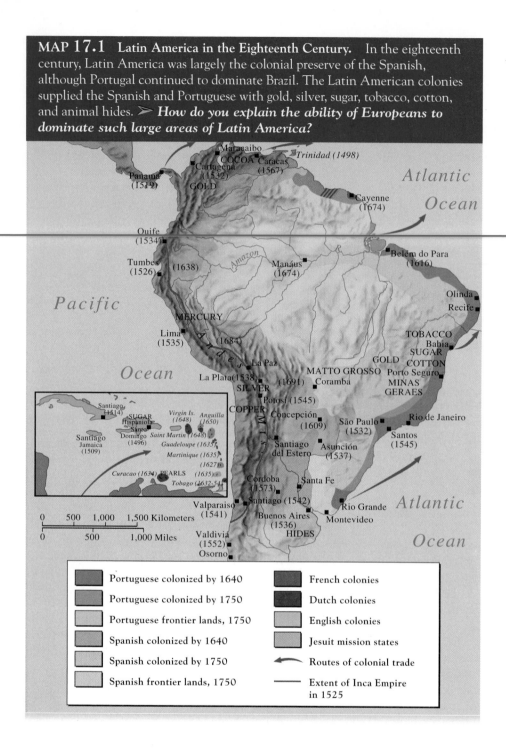

MAP 17.1 Latin America in the Eighteenth Century. In the eighteenth century, Latin America was largely the colonial preserve of the Spanish, although Portugal continued to dominate Brazil. The Latin American colonies supplied the Spanish and Portuguese with gold, silver, sugar, tobacco, cotton, and animal hides. ➤ *How do you explain the ability of Europeans to dominate such large areas of Latin America?*

Portuguese colonized by 1640
Portuguese colonized by 1750
Portuguese frontier lands, 1750
Spanish colonized by 1640
Spanish colonized by 1750
Spanish frontier lands, 1750
French colonies
Dutch colonies
English colonies
Jesuit mission states
← Routes of colonial trade
— Extent of Inca Empire in 1525

rudiments of reading, writing, and arithmetic. The church also provided outlets for women other than marriage. Nunneries were places of prayer and quiet contemplation, but women in religious orders, many of them of aristocratic background, often lived well and operated outside their establishments by running schools and hospitals. Indeed, one of these nuns, Sor Juana Inés de la Cruz (1651–1695), was one of seventeenth-century Latin America's best-known literary figures. She wrote poetry and prose and urged that women be educated.

British North America

In the eighteenth century, Spanish power in the New World was increasingly challenged by the British. (The United Kingdom of Great Britain came into existence in 1707, when the governments of England and Scotland were united; the term *British* came into use to refer to both English and Scots.) In eighteenth-century Britain, the king or queen and Parliament shared power, with Parliament gradually gaining the upper hand. The monarch

SOR JUANA INÉS DE LA CRUZ. Nunneries in colonial Latin America gave women—especially upper-class women—some opportunity for intellectual activity. As a woman, Juana Inés de la Cruz was denied admission to the University of Mexico. Consequently she entered a convent, where she wrote poetry and plays until her superiors forced her to focus on less worldly activities.

chose ministers who were responsible to the crown and who set policy and guided Parliament. Parliament had the power to make laws, levy taxes, pass budgets, and indirectly influence the monarch's ministers.

Growing trade and industry led to a growing middle class in Britain that favored expansion of trade and world empire. These people found a spokesman in William Pitt the Elder, who became prime minister in 1757 and expanded the British Empire by acquiring Canada and India in the Seven Years' War.

THE AMERICAN REVOLUTION

At the end of the Seven Years' War in 1763, Great Britain had become the world's greatest colonial power. In North America, Britain controlled Canada and the lands east of the Mississippi. After the Seven Years' War, British policy makers sought to obtain new revenues from the colonies to pay for British army expenses in defending the colonists. An attempt to levy new taxes by the Stamp Act of 1765 led to riots and the law's quick repeal.

The Americans and British had different conceptions of empire. The British envisioned a single empire with Parliament as the supreme authority throughout. The Americans, in contrast, had their own representative assemblies. They believed that neither king nor Parliament should interfere in their internal affairs and that no tax could be levied without the consent of their own assemblies.

Crisis followed crisis in the 1770s until 1776, when the colonists decided to declare their independence from the British Empire. On July 4, 1776, the Second Continental Congress approved a declaration of independence written by Thomas Jefferson. A stirring political document, the Declaration of Independence affirmed the Enlightenment's natural rights of "life, liberty, and the pursuit of happiness" and declared the colonies to be "free and independent states absolved from all allegiance to the British crown." The war for American independence had formally begun.

Of great importance to the colonies' cause was their support by foreign countries who were eager to gain revenge for earlier defeats at the hands of the British. French officers and soldiers served in the American Continental Army under George Washington as commander in chief. When the army of General Cornwallis was forced to surrender to a combined American and French army and French fleet under Washington at Yorktown in 1781, the British decided to call it quits. The Treaty of Paris, signed in 1783, recognized the independence of the American colonies and granted the Americans control of the territory from the Appalachians to the Mississippi River.

BIRTH OF A NEW NATION

The thirteen American colonies had gained their independence; but a fear of concentrated power and concern for their own interests caused them to have little enthusiasm for establishing a united nation with a strong central government, and so the Articles of Confederation, ratified in 1781, did not create one. A movement for a different form of national government soon arose. In the summer of 1787, fifty-five delegates attended a convention in Philadelphia to revise the Articles of Confederation. The convention's delegates—wealthy, politically experienced, and well educated—rejected revision and decided instead to devise a new constitution.

The proposed United States Constitution established a central government distinct from and superior to governments of the individual states. The central or federal government was divided into three branches, each with some power to check the functioning of the others.

A president would serve as the chief executive with the power to execute laws, veto the legislature's acts, supervise foreign affairs, and direct military forces. Legislative power was vested in the second branch of government, a bicameral legislature composed of the Senate, elected by the state legislatures, and the House of Representatives, elected directly by the people. A supreme court and other courts "as deemed necessary" by Congress provided the third branch of government. They would enforce the Constitution as the "supreme law of the land."

The Constitution was approved by the states—by a slim margin. Important to its success was a promise to add a bill of rights to the Constitution as the new government's first piece of business. Accordingly, in March 1789, the new Congress enacted the first ten amendments to the Constitution, ever since known as the Bill of Rights. These guaranteed freedom of religion, speech, press, petition, and assembly, as well as the right to bear arms, protection against unreasonable searches and arrests, trial by jury, due process of law, and protection of property rights. Many of these rights were derived from the natural rights philosophy of the eighteenth-century philosophes and the American colonists. Is it any wonder that many European intellectuals saw the American Revolution as the embodiment of the Enlightenment's political dreams?

TOWARD A NEW POLITICAL ORDER: ENLIGHTENED ABSOLUTISM

There is no doubt that Enlightenment thought had some impact on the political development of European states in the eighteenth century. The philosophes believed in natural rights, which were thought to be inalienable privileges that ought not to be withheld from any person. These natural rights included equality before the law, freedom of religious worship, freedom of speech and press, and the right to assemble, hold property, and pursue happiness.

But how were these natural rights to be established and preserved? Most philosophes believed that people needed to be ruled by an enlightened ruler. What, however, made rulers enlightened? They must allow religious toleration, freedom of speech and press, and the rights of private property. They must foster the arts, sciences, and education. Above all, they must obey the laws and enforce them fairly for all subjects. Only strong monarchs seemed capable of overcoming vested interests and effecting the reforms society needed. Reforms then should come from above (from absolute rulers) rather than from below (from the people).

Many historians once assumed that a new type of monarchy emerged in the later eighteenth century, which they called "enlightened despotism" or "enlightened abso-

lutism." Monarchs such as Frederick II of Prussia, Catherine the Great of Russia, and Joseph II of Austria supposedly followed the advice of the philosophes and ruled by enlightened principles. Recently, however, scholars have questioned the usefulness of the concept of "enlightened absolutism." We can determine the extent to which it can be applied by examining the major "enlightened absolutists" of the later eighteenth century.

Prussia

Frederick II, known as Frederick the Great (1740–1786), was one of the best-educated and most cultured monarchs in the eighteenth century. He was well versed in Enlightenment thought and even invited Voltaire to live at his court for several years. A believer in the king as the "first servant of the state," Frederick the Great was a conscientious ruler who enlarged the Prussian army (to 200,000 men) and kept a strict watch over the bureaucracy.

For a time, Frederick seemed quite willing to make enlightened reforms. He abolished the use of torture except in treason and murder cases and also granted limited freedom of speech and press, as well as complete religious toleration. However, he kept Prussia's rigid social structure and serfdom intact and avoided any additional reforms.

The Austrian Empire of the Habsburgs

The Austrian Empire had become one of the great European states by the beginning of the eighteenth century. Yet it was difficult to rule because it was a sprawling empire composed of many different nationalities, languages, religions, and cultures (see Map 17.2).

Joseph II (1780–1790) believed in the need to sweep away anything standing in the path of reason. As he said, "I have made Philosophy the lawmaker of my empire, her logical applications are going to transform Austria." Joseph's reform program was far-reaching. He abolished serfdom, abrogated the death penalty, and established the principle of equality of all before the law. Joseph produced drastic religious reforms as well, including complete religious toleration.

Joseph's reform program proved overwhelming for Austria, however. He alienated the nobility by freeing the serfs and alienated the church by his attacks on the monastic establishment. Even the serfs were unhappy, unable to comprehend the drastic changes inherent in Joseph's policies. His successors undid many of his reforms.

Russia Under Catherine the Great

Catherine II the Great (1762–1796) was an intelligent woman who was familiar with the works of the philosophes and seemed to favor enlightened reforms. She invited the French philosophe Diderot to Russia and, when he arrived, urged him to speak frankly "as man to man." He did, outlining a far-reaching program of political and financial reform. But Catherine was skeptical about impractical theories, which, she said, "would have turned everything in my kingdom upside down." She did consider the idea of a new law code that would recognize the principle of the equality of all people in the eyes of the law. But in the end, she did nothing, knowing that her success depended on the support of the Russian nobility. In 1785, she gave the nobles a charter that exempted them from taxes. Catherine's policy of favoring the landed nobility led to even worse conditions for the Russian peasants and a rebellion that soon faltered and collapsed. Catherine responded by even greater measures against the peasantry.

Above all, Catherine proved a worthy successor to Peter the Great in her policies of territorial expansion westward into Poland and southward to the Black Sea. Russia spread southward by defeating the Turks. Russian expansion westward occurred at the expense of neighboring Poland. In three partitions of Poland, Russia gained about 50 percent of Polish territory.

Of the rulers we have discussed, only Joseph II sought truly radical changes based on Enlightenment ideas. Both Frederick II and Catherine II liked to talk about enlightened reforms, and they even attempted some. But the policies of neither seemed seriously affected by Enlightenment thought. Necessities of state and maintenance of the existing system took precedence over reform. Indeed, many historians maintain that Joseph, Frederick, and Catherine were all primarily guided by a concern for the power and well-being of their states. In the final analysis, heightened state power was used to create armies and wage wars to gain more power.

It would be foolish, however, to overlook the fact that the ability of enlightened rulers to make reforms was also limited by political and social realities. Everywhere in Europe, the hereditary aristocracy was still the most powerful class in society. As the chief beneficiaries of a system based on traditional rights and privileges for their class, they were not willing to support a political ideology that trumpeted the principle of equal rights for all. The first

MAP 17.2 Europe in 1763. By the middle of the eighteenth century, five major powers dominated Europe—Prussia, Austria, Russia, Britain, and France. Each sought to enhance its power both domestically, through a bureaucracy that collected taxes and ran the military, and internationally, by capturing territory or preventing other powers from capturing territory. ➤ *Given the distribution of Prussian and Habsburg holdings, in what areas of Europe were they most likely to compete for land and power?*

serious challenge to their supremacy would come in the French Revolution, an event that blew open the door to the modern world of politics.

 THE FRENCH REVOLUTION

The year 1789 witnessed two far-reaching events, the beginning of a new United States of America under its revamped Constitution and the eruption of the French Revolution. Compared to the American Revolution a decade earlier, the French Revolution was more complex, more violent, and far more radical in its attempt to reconstruct both a new political and a new social order.

Background to the French Revolution

The root causes of the French Revolution must be sought in the condition of French society. Before the Revolution, France was a society grounded in privilege and inequality. Its population of 27 million was divided, as it had been since the Middle Ages, into three orders or estates.

SOCIAL STRUCTURE OF THE OLD REGIME

The first estate consisted of the clergy and numbered about 130,000 people who owned approximately 10 percent of the land. Clergy were exempt from the *taille*, France's chief tax. Clergy were also radically divided: the higher clergy, stemming from aristocratic families, shared the interests of the nobility, while the parish priests were often poor and from the class of commoners.

The second estate was the nobility, composed of about 350,000 people who owned about 25 to 30 percent of the land. The nobility had continued to play an important and even crucial role in French society in the eighteenth century, holding many of the leading positions in the government, the military, the law courts, and the higher church offices. The nobles sought to expand their power at the expense of the monarchy and to maintain their control over positions in the military, church, and government. Common to all nobles were tax exemptions, especially from the *taille*.

The third estate, or the commoners of society, constituted the overwhelming majority of the French population. They were divided by vast differences in occupation, level of education, and wealth. The peasants, who alone constituted 75 to 80 percent of the total population, were by far the largest segment of the third estate. They owned about 35 to 40 percent of the land, although their landholdings varied from area to area and over half had little or no land on which to survive. Serfdom no longer existed on any large scale in France, but French peasants still had obligations to their local landlords that they deeply resented. These "relics of feudalism," or aristocratic privileges, were obligations that

survived from an earlier age and included the payment of fees for the use of village facilities, such as the flour mill, community oven, and winepress.

Another part of the third estate consisted of skilled craftspeople, shopkeepers, and other wage earners in the cities. In the eighteenth century, a rise in consumer prices greater than the increase in wages left these urban groups with a noticeable decline in purchasing power. Their daily struggle for survival led many of these people to play an important role in the Revolution, especially in Paris.

About 8 percent of the population, or 2.3 million people, constituted the bourgeoisie or middle class, who owned about 20 to 25 percent of the land. This group included merchants, industrialists, and bankers who controlled the resources of trade, manufacturing, and finance and benefited from the economic prosperity after 1730. The bourgeoisie also included professional people— lawyers, holders of public offices, doctors, and writers. Many members of the bourgeoisie had their own set of grievances because they were often excluded from the social and political privileges monopolized by nobles. At the same time, remarkable similarities existed at the upper levels of society between the wealthier bourgeoisie and the nobility. By obtaining public offices, wealthy middle-class individuals could enter the ranks of the nobility.

Moreover, the new political ideas of the Enlightenment proved attractive to both the aristocracy and the bourgeoisie. Both elites, long accustomed to a new socioeconomic reality based on wealth and economic achievement, were increasingly frustrated by a monarchical system resting on privileges and on an old and rigid social order based on the concept of estates. The opposition of these elites to the old order led them ultimately to drastic action against the monarchical regime. In a real sense, the Revolution had its origins in political grievances.

OTHER PROBLEMS FACING THE FRENCH MONARCHY

The inability of the French monarchy to deal with new social realities was exacerbated by specific problems in the 1780s. Although France had enjoyed fifty years of economic expansion, bad harvests in 1787 and 1788 and the beginnings of a manufacturing depression resulted in food shortages, rising prices for food and other goods, and unemployment in the cities. The number of poor, estimated at almost one-third of the population, reached crisis proportions on the eve of the Revolution.

The immediate cause of the French Revolution was the near collapse of government finances. Costly wars and royal extravagance drove French governmental expenditures ever higher. On the verge of a complete financial collapse, the government of Louis XVI (1774–1792) was finally forced to call a meeting of the Estates-General, the French parliamentary body that had not met since 1614. The Estates-General consisted of representatives from the three orders of French society. In the elections for the Estates-General, the government had ruled that the third estate should get double representation (it did, after all, constitute 97 percent of the population). Consequently, while both the first estate (the clergy) and the second estate (the nobility) had about three hundred delegates each, the third estate had almost six hundred representatives, most of whom were lawyers from French towns.

From Estates-General to National Assembly

The Estates-General opened at Versailles on May 5, 1789. It was troubled from the start with the question of whether voting should be by order or by head (each delegate having one vote). Traditionally, each order would vote as a group and have one vote. That meant that the first and second estates could outvote the third estate two to one. The third estate demanded that each deputy have one vote. With the assistance of liberal nobles and clerics, that would give the third estate a majority. When the first estate declared in favor of voting by order, the third estate responded dramatically. On June 17, 1789, the third estate declared itself the "National Assembly" and decided to draw up a constitution. This was the first step in the French Revolution because the third estate had no legal right to act as the National Assembly. But this audacious act was soon in jeopardy, as the king sided with the first estate and threatened to dissolve the Estates-General. Louis XVI now prepared to use force.

The common people, however, saved the third estate from the king's forces. On July 14, a mob of Parisians stormed the Bastille, a royal armory, and proceeded to dismantle it, brick by brick. Louis XVI was soon informed that the royal troops were unreliable. Louis's acceptance of that reality signaled the collapse of royal authority; the king could no longer enforce his will. The fall of the Bastille had saved the National Assembly.

At the same time, popular revolts broke out throughout France, both in the cities and in the countryside.

Behind the popular uprising was a growing resentment of the entire landholding system, with its fees and obligations. The fall of the Bastille and the king's apparent capitulation to the demands of the third estate now led peasants to take matters into their own hands. Peasant rebellions occurred throughout France, serving as a backdrop to the Great Fear, a vast panic that spread like wildfire through France in July and August. The greatest impact of the agrarian revolts and Great Fear was on the National Assembly meeting in Versailles.

Revolution and Revolt in France and China

Both France and China experienced revolutionary upheaval at the end of the eighteenth century and well into the nineteenth century. In both countries, common people often played an important role. At top is a scene from the storming of the Bastille in 1789. This early success ultimately led to the overthrow of the monarchy. At the bottom is a scene from one of the struggles during the Taiping Rebellion, a major peasant revolt in the mid-nineteenth century in China. An imperial Chinese army is shown recapturing the city of Nanjing from Taiping rebels in 1864.

Musee de la Revolution Francais, Vizille, France/Visual Arts Library, London/Bridgeman Art Library

The Art Archive/School of Oriental & African Studies/Eileen Tweedy

DECLARATION OF THE RIGHTS OF MAN AND THE CITIZEN

*O*ne of the important documents of the French Revolution, the Declaration of the Rights of Man and the Citizen was adopted in August 1789 by the National Assembly. The declaration affirmed that "men are born and remain free and equal in rights," that governments must protect these natural rights, and that political power is derived from the people.

DECLARATION OF THE RIGHTS OF MAN AND THE CITIZEN

The representatives of the French people, organized as a national assembly, considering that ignorance, neglect, and scorn of the rights of man are the sole causes of public misfortunes and of corruption of governments, have resolved to display in a solemn declaration the natural, inalienable, and sacred rights of man, so that this declaration, constantly in the presence of all members of society, will continually remind them of their rights and their duties. . . . Consequently, the National Assembly recognizes and declares, in the presence and under the auspices of the Supreme Being, the following rights of man and citizen:

1. Men are born and remain free and equal in rights; social distinctions can be established only for the common benefit.
2. The aim of every political association is the conservation of the natural and imprescriptible rights of man; these rights are liberty, property, security, and resistance to oppression.
3. The source of all sovereignty is located in essence in the nation; no body, no individual can exercise authority which does not emanate from it expressly.
4. Liberty consists in being able to do anything that does not harm another person. . . .
6. The law is the expression of the general will; all citizens have the right to concur personally or through their representatives in its formation; it must be the same for all, whether it protects or punishes. All citizens being equal in its eyes are equally admissible to all honors, positions, and public employments, according to their capabilities and without other distinctions than those of their virtues and talents.
7. No man can be accused, arrested, or detained except in cases determined by the law, and according to the forms which it has prescribed. . . .
10. No one may be disturbed because of his opinions, even religious, provided that their public demonstration does not disturb the public order established by law.
11. The free communication of thoughts and opinions is one of the most precious rights of man: every citizen can therefore freely speak, write, and print. . . .
12. The guaranteeing of the rights of man and citizen necessitates a public force; this force is therefore instituted for the advantage of all, and not for the private use of those to whom it is entrusted. . . .
14. Citizens have the right to determine for themselves or through their representatives the need for taxation of the public, to consent to it freely, to investigate its use, and to determine its rate, basis, collection, and duration.
15. Society has the right to demand an accounting of his administration from every public agent.
16. Any society in which guarantees of rights are not assured nor the separation of powers determined has no constitution.
17. Property being an inviolable and sacred right, no one may be deprived of it unless public necessity, legally determined, clearly requires such action, and then only on condition of a just and prior indemnity.

Destruction of the Old Regime

One of the first acts of the National Assembly was to destroy the relics of feudalism and aristocratic privilege. On the night of August 4, 1789, the National Assembly voted to abolish the rights of landlords and the fiscal exemptions of nobles, clergy, towns, and provinces. On August 26, the National Assembly adopted the Declaration of the Rights of Man and the Citizen (see the box above). This charter of basic liberties affirmed the demise of aristocratic privileges by proclaiming an end to exemptions from taxation, freedom and equal rights for all men, and access to public office based on talent. All citizens were to have the right to take part in the legislative process. Freedom of speech and the press were coupled with the outlawing of arbitrary arrests.

The declaration also raised another important issue. Did its ideal of equal rights for all men also include women? Many deputies insisted that it did, provided that, as one said, "women do not hope to exercise political rights and functions." Olympe de Gouges, a playwright, refused to accept this exclusion of women from political rights. Echoing the words of the official declaration, she penned the Declaration of the Rights of Woman and the Female Citizen, in which she insisted that women should have all the same rights as men. The National Assembly ignored her demands.

In the meantime, Louis XVI, who had remained inactive at Versailles, refused to accept the decrees on the abolition of feudalism and the declaration of rights. On October 5, thousands of Parisian women, described by one eyewitness as "detachments of women . . . armed with broomsticks, lances, pitchforks, swords, pistols and muskets," marched to Versailles and forced the king to accept the new decrees. The crowd now insisted that the royal family return to Paris. On October 6, the king complied. As a goodwill gesture, he brought along wagonloads of flour from the palace stores, escorted by women armed with pikes (some of which held the severed heads of the king's guards) singing, "We are bringing back the baker, the baker's wife, and the baker's boy" (the king, queen, and their son). The king became virtually a prisoner in Paris.

Because the Catholic church was seen as an important pillar of the old order, it too was reformed. Most of the lands of the church were seized. The new Civil Constitution of the Clergy was put into effect. Both bishops and priests were to be elected by the people and paid by the state. The Catholic church, still an important institution in the life of the French people, now became an enemy of the Revolution.

By 1791, the National Assembly had finally completed a new constitution that established a limited constitutional monarchy. There was still a monarch (now called "king of the French"), but the new Legislative Assembly was to make the laws. The Legislative Assembly, in which sovereign power was vested, was to sit for two years and consist of 745 representatives chosen by an indirect system of election that preserved power in the hands of the more affluent members of society. Only active citizens (men over the age of twenty-five paying in taxes the equivalent of three days' unskilled labor) could vote for electors (men paying taxes equal in value to ten days' labor). This relatively small group of fifty thousand electors then chose the deputies.

By 1791, the old order had been destroyed. However, many people—including Catholic priests, nobles, lower classes hurt by a rise in the cost of living, peasants who remained opposed to dues that had still not been abandoned, and political clubs like the Jacobins who offered more radical solutions to France's problems—opposed the new order. The king also made things difficult for the new government when he sought to flee France in June 1791 and almost succeeded before being recognized, captured, and brought back to Paris. In this unsettled situation, under a discredited and seemingly disloyal monarch, the new Legislative Assembly held its first session in October 1791. France's relations with the rest of Europe soon led to Louis's downfall.

On August 27, 1791, the monarchs of Austria and Prussia, fearing that revolution would spread to their countries, invited other European monarchs to use force to reestab-lish monarchical authority in France. Insulted by this threat, the Legislative Assembly declared war on Austria on April 20, 1792. The French fared badly in the initial fighting, and a frantic search for scapegoats began. As one observer noted, "Everywhere you hear the cry that the king is betraying us, the generals are betraying us, that nobody is to be trusted; . . . that Paris will be taken in six weeks by the Austrians. . . . We are on a volcano ready to spout flames."[2] Defeats in war coupled with economic shortages in the spring led to renewed political demonstrations, especially against the king. In August 1792, radical political groups in Paris took the king captive and forced the Legislative Assembly to suspend the monarchy and call for a national convention, chosen on the basis of universal male suffrage, to decide on the future form of government. The French Revolution was about to enter a more radical stage.

The Radical Revolution

In September 1792, the newly elected National Convention began its sessions. Dominated by lawyers and other professionals, two-thirds of its deputies were under forty-five, and almost all had gained political experience as a result of the Revolution. Almost all distrusted the king. As a result, the convention's first step on September 21 was to abolish the monarchy and establish a republic. On January 21, 1793, the king was executed, and the destruction of the old regime was complete. But the execution of the king created new enemies for the Revolution both at home and abroad while strengthening those who were already its enemies.

In Paris, the local government, known as the Commune, whose leaders came from the working classes, favored radical change and put constant pressure on the convention, pushing it to ever more radical positions. Moreover, the National Convention still did not rule all of France. Peasants in the west and inhabitants of France's major provincial cities refused to accept the authority of the convention.

A foreign crisis also loomed large. By the beginning of 1793, after the king had been executed, most of Europe—an informal coalition of Austria, Prussia, Spain, Portugal, Britain, the Dutch Republic, and even Russia—aligned militarily against France. Grossly overextended, the French armies began to experience reverses, and by late spring, France was threatened with invasion. If the invasion was successful, both the Revolution and the revolutionaries would be destroyed and the old regime reestablished.

A NATION IN ARMS

To meet these crises, the convention gave broad powers to an executive committee of twelve known as the Committee of Public Safety, which came to be dominated by Maximilien Robespierre. For a twelve-month period, from 1793 to 1794, the Committee of Public Safety took control of France. To save the Republic from its foreign foes, the committee decreed a universal mobilization of the nation on August 23, 1793:

> Young men will fight, young men are called to conquer. Married men will forge arms, transport military baggage and guns and will prepare food supplies. Women, who at long last are to take their rightful place in the revolution and follow their true destiny, will forget their futile tasks: their delicate hands will work at making clothes for soldiers; they will make tents and they will extend their tender care to shelters where the defenders of the *Patrie* [nation] will receive the help that their wounds require. Children will make lint of old cloth. It is for them that we are fighting: children, those beings destined to gather all the fruits of the revolution, will raise their pure hands toward the skies. And old men, performing their missions again, as of yore, will be guided to the public squares of the cities where they will kindle the courage of young warriors and preach the doctrines of hate for kings and the unity of the Republic.[3]

In less than a year, the French revolutionary government had raised an army of 650,000; by September 1794, it numbered 1,169,000. The Republic's army was the largest ever seen in European history. It now pushed the allies back across the Rhine and even conquered the Austrian Netherlands.

The French revolutionary army was an important step in the creation of modern nationalism. Previously wars had been fought between governments or ruling dynasties by relatively small armies of professional soldiers. The new French army was the creation of a "people's" government; its wars were now "people's" wars. The entire nation was to be involved in the war. But when dynastic wars became people's wars, warfare increased in ferocity and lack of restraint. The wars of the French revolutionary era opened the door to the total war of the modern world.

REIGN OF TERROR

To meet the domestic crisis, the National Convention and the Committee of Public Safety launched the "Reign of Terror." Revolutionary courts were instituted to protect the Republic from its internal enemies. In the course of nine months, sixteen thousand people were officially killed under the blade of the guillotine—a revolutionary device for the quick and efficient separation of heads from bodies. The Committee of Public Safety held that this bloodletting was only temporary. Once the war and the domestic emergency were over, they would be succeeded by a "republic of virtue" in which the Declaration of the Rights of Man and the Citizen would be fully implemented.

Revolutionary armies were set up to bring recalcitrant cities and districts back under the control of the National Convention. The Committee of Public Safety decided to make an example of Lyons, which had defied the authority of the National Convention. By April 1794, some 1,880 citizens of Lyons had been executed. When the guillotine proved too slow, cannon fire was used to blow condemned men into open graves. A German observed:

> Whole ranges of houses, always the most handsome, burnt. The churches, convents, and all the dwellings of the former patricians were in ruins. When I came to the guillotine, the blood of those who had been executed a few hours beforehand was still running in the street. . . . I said to a group of sansculottes [radicals] that it would be decent to clear away all this human blood. Why should it be cleared? one of them said to me. It's the blood of aristocrats and rebels. The dogs should lick it up.[4]

The National Convention also pursued a policy of dechristianization. A new calendar was instituted in which years were no longer numbered from the birth of Christ

➤ WOMEN PATRIOTS. Women played a variety of roles in the events of the French Revolution. This picture shows a women's patriotic club discussing the decrees of the National Convention, an indication that some women became highly politicized by the upheavals of the Revolution.

but from September 22, 1792, the first day of the French Republic. The new calendar also eliminated Sundays and church holidays. In Paris, the cathedral of Notre-Dame was designated the Temple of Reason; in November 1793, a public ceremony dedicated to the worship of reason was held in the former cathedral in which patriotic maidens adorned in white dresses paraded before a "temple of reason" where the high altar once stood.

Reaction and the Directory

By the summer of 1794, the French had been successful on the battlefield against their foreign foes, making the Terror less necessary. But the Terror continued because Robespierre, who had become a figure of power and authority, became obsessed with purifying the body politic of all the corrupt. Many deputies in the National Convention were fearful, however, that they were not safe while Robespierre was free to act and gathered enough votes to condemn him. Robespierre was guillotined on July 28, 1794.

After the death of Robespierre, a reaction set in as more moderate middle-class leaders took control. The Reign of Terror came to a halt, and the National Convention reduced the power of the Committee of Public Safety. Churches were allowed to reopen for public worship. In addition, a new constitution was created in August 1795 that reflected the desire for a stability that did not sacrifice the ideals of 1789. Five directors—the Directory—acted as the executive authority.

The period of the Revolution under the government of the Directory (1795–1799) was an era of stagnation and corruption, a materialistic reaction to the sacrifices that had been demanded in the Reign of Terror. At the same time, the government of the Directory faced political enemies from both the left and the right of the political spectrum. On the right, royalists who wanted to restore the monarchy continued their agitation. On the left, radical hopes of power were revived by continuing economic problems. Battered from both sides, unable to solve the country's economic problems, and still carrying on the wars inherited from the Committee of Public Safety, the Directory increasingly relied on the military to maintain its power. This led to a coup d'état in 1799 in which the popular military general Napoleon Bonaparte seized power.

THE AGE OF NAPOLEON

Napoleon dominated both French and European history from 1799 to 1815. He was born in 1769 in Corsica shortly after France had annexed the island. The young Napoleon was sent to France to study in one of the new military schools and was a lieutenant when the Revolution broke out in 1789. The Revolution and the European war that followed gave him new opportunities, and Napoleon rose quickly through the ranks. In 1794, at the age of only twenty-five, he was made a brigadier general by the Committee of Public Safety. Two years later, he commanded the French armies in Italy, where he won a series of victories and returned to France as a conquering hero (see the box on p. 380). After a disastrous expedition to Egypt, Napoleon returned to Paris, where he participated in the coup that gave him control of France. He was only thirty years old.

After the coup of 1799, a new form of the Republic—called the Consulate—was proclaimed in which Napoleon, as first consul, controlled the entire executive authority of government. He had overwhelming influence over the legislature, appointed members of the administrative bureaucracy, commanded the army, and conducted foreign affairs. In 1802, Napoleon was made consul for life, and in 1804, he returned France to monarchy when he had himself crowned as Emperor Napoleon I.

NAPOLEON AND
PSYCHOLOGICAL WARFARE

*I*n 1796, at the age of twenty-seven, Napoleon Bonaparte was given command of the French army in Italy, where he won a series of stunning victories. His use of speed, deception, and surprise to overwhelm his opponents is well known. In this selection from a proclamation to his troops in Italy, Napoleon also appears as a master of psychological warfare.

NAPOLEON BONAPARTE, PROCLAMATION TO FRENCH TROOPS IN ITALY (APRIL 26, 1796)

Soldiers:

In a fortnight you have won six victories, taken twenty-one standards [flags of military units], fifty-five pieces of artillery, several strong positions, and conquered the richest part of Piedmont [in northern Italy]; you have captured 15,000 prisoners and killed or wounded more than 10,000 men. . . . You have won battles without cannon, crossed rivers without bridges, made forced marches without shoes, camped without brandy and often without bread. Soldiers of liberty, only republican troops could have endured what you have endured. Soldiers, you have our thanks! The grateful Patrie [nation] will owe its prosperity to you. . . .

The two armies which but recently attacked you with audacity are fleeing before you in terror; the wicked men who laughed at your misery and rejoiced at the thought of the triumphs of your enemies are confounded and trembling.

But, soldiers, as yet you have done nothing compared with what remains to be done. . . . Undoubtedly the greatest obstacles have been overcome; but you still have battles to fight, cities to capture, rivers to cross. Is there one among you whose courage is abating? No. . . . All of you are consumed with a desire to extend the glory of the French people; all of you long to humiliate those arrogant kings who dare to contemplate placing us in fetters; all of you desire to dictate a glorious peace, one which will indemnify the Patrie for the immense sacrifices it has made; all of you wish to be able to say with pride as you return to your villages, "I was with the victorious army of Italy!"

Domestic Policies

One of Napoleon's first domestic policies was to establish peace with the oldest and most implacable enemy of the Revolution, the Catholic church. In 1801, Napoleon arranged a concordat with the pope that recognized Catholicism as the religion of a majority of the French people. In return, the pope agreed not to raise the question of the church lands confiscated in the Revolution. As a result of the concordat, the Catholic church was no longer an enemy of the French government.

Napoleon's most enduring domestic achievement was his codification of the laws. Before the Revolution, France had some three hundred local legal systems. During the Revolution, efforts were made to prepare a single code of laws for the entire nation, but it remained for Napoleon to bring the work to completion in the famous Civil Code. This preserved most of the revolutionary gains by recognizing the principle of the equality of all citizens before the law, the abolition of serfdom and feudalism, and religious toleration. Property rights were protected, and the interests of employers were safeguarded by outlawing trade unions and strikes.

At the same time, the Civil Code strictly curtailed the rights of some people. During the radical phase of the French Revolution, new laws had made divorce an easy process for both husbands and wives and allowed sons and daughters to inherit property equally. Napoleon's Civil Code undid these laws. Divorce was still allowed but was made more difficult for women to obtain. Women were now "less equal than men" in other ways as well. When they married, their property came under the control of their husbands, and in lawsuits, they were treated as minors.

Napoleon also developed a powerful, centralized administrative machine and worked hard to develop a bureaucracy of capable officials. Early on, the regime showed that it cared little whether the expertise of officials had been acquired in royal or revolutionary bureaucracies. Promotion, whether in civil or military offices, was to be based not on rank or birth but on ability only. This principle of a government career open to talent was, of course, what many bourgeois had wanted before the Revolution.

In his domestic policies, then, Napoleon both destroyed and preserved aspects of the Revolution. Liberty had been replaced by an initially benevolent despotism that grew increasingly arbitrary as the demands of war overwhelmed Napoleon and the French. The Civil Code, however, preserved the equality of all citizens before the law. The concept of careers open to talent was also a gain of the Revolution that Napoleon preserved.

Napoleon's Empire and the European Response

When Napoleon became consul in 1799, France was at war with a second European coalition of Russia, Great Britain, and Austria. Napoleon realized the need for a pause and made a peace treaty in 1802. But war was renewed in 1803 with Britain, who was soon joined by Austria, Russia, and Prussia in the Third Coalition. In a series of battles from

THE CORONATION OF NAPOLEON. In 1804, Napoleon restored monarchy to France when he had himself crowned as emperor. In the coronation scene painted by Jacques-Louis David, Napoleon is shown crowning his wife, the empress Josephine, while the pope looks on. The painting shows Napoleon's mother seated in the box in the background, even though she was not at the ceremony.

1805 to 1807, Napoleon's Grand Army defeated the Austrian, Prussian, and Russian armies, giving Napoleon the opportunity to create a new European order.

THE GRAND EMPIRE

From 1807 to 1812, Napoleon was the master of Europe. His Grand Empire was composed of three major parts: the French Empire, dependent states, and allied states (see Map 17.3). The French Empire, the inner core of the Grand Empire, consisted of an enlarged France extending to the Rhine in the east and including the western half of Italy north of Rome. Dependent states were kingdoms under the rule of Napoleon's relatives; these came to include Spain, the Netherlands, the kingdom of Italy, the Swiss Republic, the Grand Duchy of Warsaw, and the Confederation of the Rhine (a union of all German states except Austria and Prussia). Allied states were those defeated by Napoleon and forced to join his struggle against Britain; these included Prussia, Austria, Russia, and Sweden.

Within his empire, Napoleon sought acceptance of certain revolutionary principles, including legal equality, religious toleration, and economic freedom. As he explained to his brother Jerome after he had made him king of the new German state of Westphalia:

What the people of Germany desire most impatiently is that talented commoners should have the same right to your esteem and to public employments as the nobles, that any trace of serfdom and of an intermediate hierarchy between the sovereign and the lowest class of the people should be completely abolished. The benefits of the Code Napoléon, the publicity of judicial procedure, the creation of juries must be so many distinguishing marks of your monarchy. . . . What nation would wish to return under the arbitrary Prussian government once it had tasted the benefits of a wise and liberal administration? The peoples of Germany, the peoples of France, of Italy, of Spain all desire equality and liberal ideas. I have guided the affairs of Europe for many years now, and I have had occasion to convince myself that the buzzing of the privileged classes is contrary to the general opinion. Be a constitutional king.[5]

MAP 17.3 Napoleon's Grand Empire. Napoleon's Grand Army won a series of victories against Britain, Austria, Prussia, and Russia that gave the French emperor full or partial control over much of Europe by 1807. ➤ *On the Continent, what is the overall relationship between distance from France and degree of French control, and how can you account for this?*

In the inner core and dependent states of his Grand Empire, Napoleon tried to destroy the old order. Nobility and clergy everywhere in these states lost their special privileges. He decreed equality of opportunity with offices open to talent, equality before the law, and religious toleration. This spread of French revolutionary principles was an important factor in the development of liberal traditions in these countries.

Napoleon hoped that his Grand Empire would last for centuries; it collapsed almost as rapidly as it had been formed. Two major reasons explain this: Great Britain and nationalism. As long as Britain ruled the waves, it was not subject to military attack. Napoleon hoped to invade Britain, but he could not overcome the British navy's decisive defeat of a combined French-Spanish fleet at Trafal-

gar in 1805. To defeat Britain, Napoleon turned to his Continental System. Put into effect between 1806 and 1808, it attempted to prevent British goods from reaching the European continent in order to weaken Britain economically and destroy its capacity to wage war. But the Continental System failed. Allied states resented it; some began to cheat and others to resist. New markets in the Middle East and in Latin America gave Britain new outlets for its goods.

The second important factor in the defeat of Napoleon was nationalism. This political creed had arisen during the French Revolution in the French people's emphasis on solidarity against other peoples. Nationalism involved the unique cultural identity of a people based on common language and national symbols. French nationalism had made possible the mass armies of the revolutionary and Napoleonic eras. But Napoleon's conquests aroused nationalism in two ways: by making the French hated oppressors and thus arousing the patriotism of others in opposition to French nationalism and by showing the people of Europe what nationalism was and what a nation in arms could do. It was a lesson not lost on other peoples and rulers. A Spanish uprising against Napoleon's rule, aided by British support, kept a French force of 200,000 pinned down for years.

THE FALL OF NAPOLEON

The beginning of Napoleon's downfall came in 1812 with his invasion of Russia. The refusal of the Russians to remain in the Continental System left Napoleon with little choice. Although aware of the risks in invading such a huge country, he also knew that if the Russians were allowed to challenge the Continental System unopposed, others would soon follow suit. In June 1812, he led his Grand Army of more than 600,000 men into Russia. Napoleon's hopes for victory depended on quickly defeating the Russian armies, but the Russian forces retreated and refused to give battle, torching their own villages and countryside to keep Napoleon's army from finding food. When the Russians did stop to fight at Borodino, Napoleon's forces won an indecisive and costly victory. When the remaining troops of the Grand Army arrived in Moscow, they found the city ablaze. Lacking food and supplies, Napoleon abandoned Moscow late in October and made a retreat across Russia in terrible winter conditions. Only 40,000 of the original 600,000 men managed to arrive back in Poland in January 1813.

This military disaster led other European states to rise up and attack the crippled French army. Paris was captured in March 1814, and Napoleon was sent into exile on the island of Elba, off the coast of Italy. Meanwhile the Bourbon monarchy was restored in the person of Louis XVIII, the Count of Provence, brother of the executed king. Louis XVII, son of Louis XVI, had died in prison at age ten. Napoleon, bored on Elba, slipped back into France. When troops were sent to capture him, Napoleon opened his coat and addressed them: "Soldiers of the 5th regiment, I am your Emperor. . . . If there is a man among you would kill his Emperor, here I am!" No one fired a shot. Shouting "Vive l'Empereur! Vive l'Empereur," the troops went over to his side, and Napoleon entered Paris in triumph on March 20, 1815.

The powers that had defeated him pledged once more to fight him. Having decided to strike first at his enemies, Napoleon raised yet another army and moved to attack the allied forces stationed in what is now Belgium. At Waterloo on June 18, Napoleon met a combined British and Prussian army under the duke of Wellington and suffered a bloody defeat. This time, the victorious allies exiled him to Saint Helena, a small, forsaken island in the South Atlantic. Only Napoleon's memory continued to haunt French political life.

CONCLUSION

Everywhere in Europe at the beginning of the eighteenth century, the old order remained strong. Nobles, clerics, towns, and provinces all had privileges. Everywhere in the eighteenth century, monarchs sought to enlarge their bureaucracies to raise taxes to support the large standing armies that had originated in the seventeenth century. The existence of five great powers, with two of them (France and England) embattled in the East and in the Western Hemisphere, ushered in a new scale of conflict; the Seven Years' War can legitimately be viewed as the first world war. Although the wars changed little on the European continent, British victories enabled Great Britain to emerge as the world's greatest naval and colonial power. Everywhere in Europe, increased demands for taxes to support these conflicts led to attacks on the privileged orders and a desire for change not met by the ruling monarchs. At the same time, sustained population growth and dramatic changes in finance, trade, and industry created tensions that undermined the traditional foundations of the old order. The inability of that old order to deal meaningfully with these changes led to a revolutionary outburst at the end of the eighteenth century that brought the old order to an end.

The revolutionary era of the late eighteenth century was a time of dramatic political transformations. Revolutionary upheavals, beginning in North America and continuing in France, spurred movements for political liberty and equality. The documents promulgated by these revolutions, the Declaration of Independence and the Declaration of the Rights of Man and the Citizen, embodied the fundamental ideas of the Enlightenment and created a liberal political agenda based on a belief in popular sovereignty—the people as the source of political power—and the principles of liberty and equality. Liberty meant, in theory, freedom from arbitrary power as well as the freedom to think, write, and worship as one chose. Equality meant equality in rights and equality of opportunity based on talent rather than wealth or status at birth. In practice, equality remained limited; property owners had greater opportunities for voting and officeholding, and women were still not treated as the equals of men.

The French Revolution set in motion a modern revolutionary concept. No one had foreseen or consciously planned the upheaval that began in 1789, but thereafter, radicals and revolutionaries knew that mass uprisings by the common people could overthrow unwanted elitist governments. For these people, the French Revolution became a symbol of hope; for those who feared such changes, it became a symbol of dread. The French Revolution became the classical political and social model for revolution. At the same time, the liberal and national political ideals created by the Revolution dominated the political landscape for well over a century. A new era had begun, and the world would never be the same.

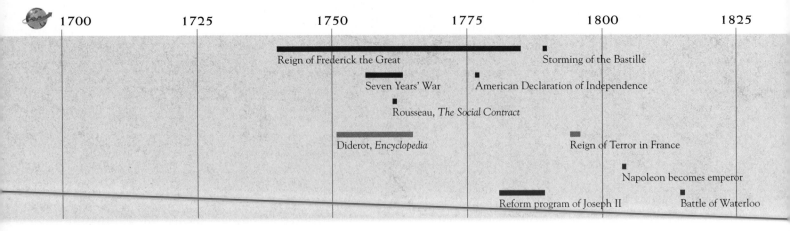

1700   1725   1750   1775   1800   1825

Reign of Frederick the Great

Storming of the Bastille

Seven Years' War   American Declaration of Independence

Rousseau, *The Social Contract*

Diderot, *Encyclopedia*

Reign of Terror in France

Napoleon becomes emperor

Reform program of Joseph II   Battle of Waterloo

CHAPTER NOTES

1. John Locke, *An Essay Concerning Human Understanding* (New York, 1964), pp. 89–90.
2. Quoted in William Doyle, *The Oxford History of the French Revolution* (Oxford, 1989), p. 184.
3. Quoted in Leo Gershoy, *The Era of the French Revolution* (Princeton, N.J., 1957), p. 157.
4. Quoted in Doyle, *Oxford History of the French Revolution*, p. 254.
5. Quoted in J. Christopher Herold, ed., *The Mind of Napoleon* (New York, 1955), pp. 74–75.

SUGGESTED READING

Two sound, comprehensive surveys of eighteenth-century Europe are I. Woloch, *Eighteenth-Century Europe* (New York, 1982), and M. S. Anderson, *Europe in the Eighteenth Century* (London, 1987).

Good introductions to the Enlightenment can be found in U. Im Hof, *The Enlightenment* (Oxford, 1994); D. Goodman, *The Republic of Letters: A Cultural History of the French Enlightenment* (Ithaca, N.Y., 1994); and D. Outram, *The Enlightenment* (Cambridge, 1995). A more detailed synthesis can be found in the two volumes by P. Gay, *The Enlightenment: An Interpretation* (New York, 1966–1969). For a short, popular survey on the French philosophes, see F. Artz, *The Enlightenment in France* (Kent, Ohio, 1968). On women in the eighteenth century, see N. Z. Davis and A. Farge, eds., *A History of Women: Renaissance and Enlightenment Paradoxes* (Cambridge, Mass., 1993), and O. Hufton, *The Prospect Before Her: A History of Women in Western Europe, 1500–1800* (New York, 1998).

A readable general survey on the arts and literature is M. Levy, *Rococo to Revolution* (London, 1966). An important study on popular culture is P. Burke, *Popular Culture in Early Modern Europe* (New York, 1978).

On the European nobility in the eighteenth century, see J. Dewald, *The European Nobility 1400–1800* (Cambridge, 1996), and H. M. Scott, *The European Nobility in the Seventeenth and Eighteenth Centuries* (London, 1995). On European cities, see J. de Vries, *European Urbanization, 1500–1800* (Cambridge, Mass., 1984). The

warfare of this period is examined in M. S. Anderson, *War and Society in Europe of the Old Regime, 1615–1789* (New York, 1988).

For a brief survey of Latin America, see E. B. Burns, *Latin America: A Concise Interpretative History*, 4th ed. (Englewood Cliffs, N.J., 1986). More detailed works on colonial Latin American history include S. J. Stein and B. H. Stein, *The Colonial Heritage of Latin America* (New York, 1970), and J. Lockhardt and S. B. Schwartz, *Early Latin America: A History of Colonial Spanish America and Brazil* (New York, 1983). A history of the revolutionary era in America can be found in R. Middlekauff, *The Glorious Cause: The American Revolution, 1763–1789* (New York, 1982), and C. Bonwick, *The American Revolution* (Charlottesville, Va., 1991).

On enlightened absolutism, see H. M. Scott, ed., *Enlightened Absolutism: Reform and Reformers in Late Eighteenth-Century Europe* (Ann Arbor, Mich., 1990). Good biographies of some of Europe's monarchs include R. Asprey, *Frederick the Great: The Magnificent Enigma* (New York, 1986); I. De Madariaga, *Catherine the Great: A Short History* (New Haven, Conn., 1990); and T. C. W. Blanning, *Joseph II* (New York, 1994).

A well-written introduction to the French Revolution can be found in W. Doyle, *The Oxford History of the French Revolution* (Oxford, 1989). For the entire revolutionary and Napoleonic eras, see O. Connelly, *The French Revolution and Napoleonic Era*, 3d ed. (Fort Worth, Tex., 2000), and D. M. G. Sutherland, *France, 1789–1815: Revolution and Counter-Revolution* (London, 1985). Two

POPULATION EXPLOSION

etween 1700 and 1800, Europe, China, and to a lesser degree India and the Ottoman Empire experienced a dramatic growth in population. In Europe, the population grew from 120 million people to almost 200 million by 1800; China, from less than 200 million to 300 million during the same period.

Four factors were important in causing this population explosion. First, better growing conditions, made possible by an improvement in climate, affected wide areas of the world and enabled people to produce more food. Summers in both China and Europe were warmer beginning in the early eighteenth century. Second, by the eighteenth century, people had begun to develop immunities to the epidemic diseases that had caused such widespread loss of life between 1500 and 1700. The spread of people by ship after 1500 had led to devastating epidemics. For example, the arrival of Europeans in Mexico led to smallpox, measles, and chickenpox among a native population that had no immunities to European diseases. In 1500, between 11 and 20 million people lived in the area of Mexico; by 1650, only 1.5 million remained. Gradually, however, people developed immunities to these diseases.

⟫ **FESTIVAL OF THE YAM.** The spread of a few major food crops made possible new sources of nutrition to feed more people. The importance of the yam to the Ashanti people of West Africa is evident in this celebration of a yam festival at harvest time in 1817.

© The Art Archive/Eileen Tweedy

A third factor in the population increase came from new food sources. As a result of the Columbian exchange (see the box on p. 387) American food crops—such as corn, potatoes, and sweet potatoes—were brought to other parts of the world, where they became important food sources. China had imported a new species of rice from Southeast Asia that had a shorter harvest cycle than that of existing varieties. These new foods provided additional sources of nutrition that enabled more people to live for a longer time. At the same time, land development and canal building in the eighteenth century also enabled government authorities to move food supplies to areas threatened with crop failure and famine.

Finally, the use of new weapons based on gunpowder allowed states to control larger territories and ensure a new degree of order. The early rulers of the Qing dynasty, for example, pacified the Chinese Empire and ensured a long period of peace and stability. Absolute monarchs achieved similar goals in a number of European states. Less violence led to fewer deaths at the same time that an increase in food supplies and a decrease in death from diseases were occurring, thus making possible in the eighteenth century the beginning of the world population explosion that persists to this day.

1650	1700	1750	1800

■ Dutch way station established at Cape of Good Hope

■ Founding of the kingdom of Ashanti

■ Portuguese expelled from Mombasa

■ Collapse of Safavids

■ Battle of Plassey

Reign of Kangxi

■ Lord Macartney's mission to China

Development of absolutism—Reign of Louis XIV

Enlightened absolutism

American Revolution

French Revolution

MODERN PATTERNS OF WORLD HISTORY

(1800–1945)

The period of world history from 1800 to 1945 was characterized, above all, by two major developments: the growth of industrialization and Western domination of the world. The two developments were, of course, interconnected. The Industrial Revolution became one of the major forces of change in the nineteenth century as it led Western civilization into the industrial era that has characterized the modern world. Beginning in Britain, it spread to the Continent and the Western Hemisphere in the course of the nineteenth century. At the same time, the Industrial Revolution created the technological means, including new weapons, by which the West achieved domination of much of the rest of the world by the end of the nineteenth century.

Europeans had begun to explore the world in the fifteenth century, but even as late as 1870, they had not yet completely penetrated North America, South America, or Australia. In Asia and Africa, with a few notable exceptions, the Western presence was limited to trading posts. Between 1870 and 1914, Western civilization expanded into the rest of the Americas and Australia, while the bulk of Africa and Asia was divided into European colonies or spheres of influence. Two major events explain this remarkable expansion: the migration of many Europeans to other parts of the world due to population growth and the revival of imperialism, which was made possible by the West's technological advancement. Beginning in the 1880s, European states began an intense scramble for overseas territory. This revival of imperialism—or the "new imperialism," as some have called it—led Europeans to carve up Asia and Africa.

Boehringer Collection: The Mariners' Museum, Newport News, VA

The new imperialism had a dramatic effect on Africa and Asia as European powers competed for control of the two continents. Latin America was the exception, as it was able in the course of the nineteenth century to achieve political independence from its colonial rulers and embark on the building of independent nations. Nevertheless, like the Ottoman Empire, Latin America still remained subject to commercial penetration by Western merchants. Another part of the world that escaped total domination by the West was East Asia, where China and Japan were able to maintain national independence during the height of the Western onslaught at the end of the nineteenth century.

Many Asian and African leaders resented Western attitudes of superiority and demanded human dignity for the indigenous people, but they nevertheless adopted the West's own ideologies for change. One of these—nationalism, with its emphasis on the right of people to have their own nations—was used to foster independence movements wherever native people suffered under foreign oppression. Colonial peoples soon learned the power of nationalism, and in the twentieth century, nationalism would become a powerful force in the rest of the world as nationalist revolutions moved through Asia, Africa, and the Middle East. Moreover, the exhausting struggles of two world wars sapped the power of the European states, and the colonial powers no longer had the energy or the wealth to maintain their colonial empires after World War II.

Chapter 18

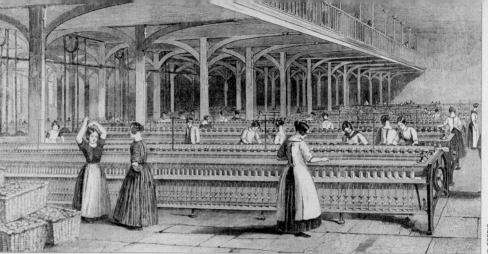
© CORBIS

THE BEGINNINGS OF MODERNIZATION: INDUSTRIALIZATION AND NATIONALISM, 1800–1870

FOCUS QUESTIONS
- What were the basic features of the new industrial system created by the Industrial Revolution, and what effects did the new system have on urban life, social classes, family life, and standards of living?
- What were the major ideas associated with conservatism, liberalism, and nationalism, and what role did each ideology play in Europe and Latin America between 1800 and 1870?
- What were the causes of the revolutions of 1848, and why did these revolutions fail?
- What actions did Cavour and Bismarck take to bring about unification in Italy and Germany, respectively, and what role did war play in their efforts?
- What were the main characteristics of Romanticism and Realism?
- ➤ In what ways were intellectual and artistic developments related to the political and social forces of the age?

he French Revolution dramatically and quickly altered the political structure of France, and the Napoleonic conquests spread many of the revolutionary principles in an equally rapid and stunning fashion to other parts of Europe. New ideologies of change, especially liberalism and nationalism, products of the upheaval initiated in France, had become too powerful to be contained. The forces of change called forth revolts that periodically shook the West and culminated in a spate of revolutions in 1848. Some of the revolutions and revolutionaries were successful; most were not. And yet by 1870, many of the goals sought by the liberals and nationalists during the first half of the nineteenth century seemed to have been achieved. National unity became a reality in Italy and Germany, and many Western states developed parliamentary features.

During the late eighteenth and early nineteenth centuries, another revolution—an industrial one—transformed the economic and social structure of Europe and spawned the industrial era that has characterized modern world history. The period of the Industrial Revolution witnessed a quantum leap in industrial production accompanied by a shift of much of the workforce from the home and the workshop to the new industrial workplace—the factory. Many early factories were dreadful places with difficult working conditions. Reformers, appalled at these conditions, were especially critical of the treatment of married women. One reported: "We have repeatedly seen married females, in the last stage of pregnancy, slaving from morning to night beside these never-tiring machines, and when . . . they were obliged to sit down to take a moment's ease, and being seen by the manager, were fined for the offense." But there were other examples of well-run factories. William Cobbett described one in Manchester in 1830: "In this room, which is lighted in the most convenient and beautiful manner, there were five hundred pairs of looms at work, and five hundred persons attending those looms; and, owing to the goodness of the masters, the whole looking healthy and well-dressed."

Although the Industrial Revolution took decades to spread, it was truly revolutionary in the way it fundamentally changed Europeans and ultimately the world. •

THE INDUSTRIAL REVOLUTION AND ITS IMPACT

The enormous leap in industrial production triggered by the Industrial Revolution relied largely on coal and steam, which replaced wind and water as new sources of energy and power to drive laborsaving machines. In turn, these machines called for new ways of organizing human labor to maximize the benefits and profits from the new machines; factories replaced shop and home workrooms. During the Industrial Revolution, Europe shifted from an economy based on agri-culture and handicrafts to an economy based on manufacturing by machines and automated factories. Large numbers of people moved from the countryside to cities to work in the new factories. The creation of a wealthy industrial middle class and a huge industrial working class (or proletariat) substantially transformed traditional social relationships.

The Industrial Revolution in Great Britain

The Industrial Revolution began in Britain in the 1780s. Improvements in agricultural practices in the eighteenth century led to a significant increase in food production. British agriculture could now feed more people at lower prices with less labor; even ordinary British families did not have to use most of their income to buy food, giving them the wherewithal to purchase manufactured goods. At the same time, rapid population growth in the second half of the eighteenth century provided a pool of surplus labor for the new factories of the emerging British industry.

A crucial factor in Britain's successful industrialization was the ability to produce cheaply the articles in greatest demand. The traditional methods of the cottage industry could not keep up with the growing demand for cotton clothes throughout Britain and its vast colonial empire. This problem led British cloth manufacturers to seek and accept the new methods of manufacturing that a series of inventions provided. In so doing, these individuals ignited the Industrial Revolution.

CHANGES IN TEXTILE PRODUCTION

The invention of the flying shuttle made weaving on a loom faster and enabled weavers to double their output. This created shortages of yarn until James Hargreaves's spinning jenny, perfected by 1768, allowed spinners to produce yarn in greater quantities. Edmund Cartwright's loom, powered by water and invented in 1787, allowed the weaving of cloth to catch up with the spinning of yarn. It was now more efficient to bring workers to the machines and organize their labor collectively in factories located next to rivers and streams, the sources of power for these early machines.

What pushed the cotton industry to even greater heights of productivity was the invention of the steam engine. In the 1760s, a Scottish engineer, James Watt (1736–1819), built an engine powered by steam that could pump water from mines three times as quickly as previous engines. In 1782, Watt developed a rotary engine that could turn a shaft and thus drive machinery. Steam power could now be applied to spinning and weaving cotton, and before long, cotton mills using steam engines were multiplying across Britain. Fired by coal, these steam engines could be located anywhere.

The new boost given to cotton textile production by technological changes became readily apparent. In 1760, Britain had imported 2.5 million pounds of raw cotton, which was farmed out to cottage industries. In 1787, the British imported 22 million pounds of cotton; most of it was spun on machines, some powered by water in large mills. By 1840, some 366 million pounds of cotton—now Britain's most important product in value—were being imported. By this time, British cotton goods were sold everywhere in the world.

OTHER TECHNOLOGICAL CHANGES

The British iron industry was radically transformed during the Industrial Revolution. A better quality of iron came into being in the 1780s when Henry Cort developed a system called puddling, in which coke, derived from coal, was used to burn away impurities in pig iron (crude iron) and produce an iron of high quality. A boom then ensued in the British iron industry. In 1740, Britain produced 17,000 tons of iron; by the 1840s, over 2 million tons; and by 1852, almost 3 million tons, more than the rest of the world combined.

The new high-quality wrought iron was in turn used to build new machines and ultimately new industries. In 1804, Richard Trevithick pioneered the first steam-powered locomotive on an industrial rail line in south Wales. It pulled 10 tons of ore and seventy people at 5 miles per hour. Better locomotives soon followed. Engines built by George Stephenson and his son proved superior, and it was Stephenson's *Rocket* that was used on the first public railway line, which opened in 1830, extending 32 miles from Liverpool to Manchester. *Rocket* sped along at 16 miles per hour. Within twenty years, locomotives had reached 50 miles per hour, an incredible speed to contemporary travelers. By 1840, Britain had almost 6,000 miles of railroads.

The railroad was an important contribution to the success and maturing of the Industrial Revolution. Railway construction created new job opportunities, especially for farm laborers and peasants who had long been accustomed to finding work outside their local villages. Perhaps most important, the proliferation of a cheaper and faster means of transportation had a ripple effect on the growth of the industrial economy. As the prices of goods fell, markets grew larger; increased sales meant more factories and more machinery, thereby reinforcing the self-sustaining aspect of the Industrial Revolution, a fundamental break with the traditional European economy. Continuous, self-sustaining economic growth came to be accepted as a fundamental characteristic of the new economy.

THE INDUSTRIAL FACTORY

Another visible symbol of the Industrial Revolution was the factory. From its beginning, the factory created a new labor system. Factory owners wanted to use their new machines constantly. Workers were therefore obliged to work regular hours and in shifts to keep the machines producing at a steady rate. Early factory workers, however, came from rural areas, where they were used to a different pace of life. Peasant farmers worked hard, especially at harvest time, but they were also used to periods of inactivity.

Early factory owners therefore had to create a system of work discipline in which employees became accustomed

Textile Factories, West and East

The development of the factory changed the relationship between workers and employers as workers were encouraged to adjust to a new system of discipline that forced them to work regular hours under close supervision. At the top is an 1851 illustration that shows women working in a British cotton factory. The factory system came later to the rest of the world than it did in Britain. Shown on the bottom is one of the earliest industrial factories in Japan, the Tomioka silk factory, built in the 1870s. Note that, although women are doing the work in both factories, the managers are men.

© CORBIS

Laurie Platt Whitney, Inc.

to working regular hours and doing the same work over and over. Of course, such work was boring, and factory owners resorted to tough methods to accomplish their goals. They issued minute and detailed factory regulations. For example, adult workers were fined for a wide variety of minor infractions, such as being a few minutes late for work, and dismissed for more serious misdoings, especially drunkenness, which set a bad example for younger workers and also courted disaster in the midst of dangerous machinery. Employers found that dismissals and fines worked well for adult employees; in a time when great population growth had produced large masses of unskilled labor, dismissal meant disaster. Children were less likely to understand the implications of dismissal, so they were sometimes disciplined more directly—often by beating. As the nineteenth century progressed, the second and third generations of workers came to view a regular workweek as a natural way of life.

By the mid-nineteenth century, Great Britain had become the world's first and richest industrial nation. Britain was the "workshop, banker, and trader of the world." It produced one-half of the world's coal and manufactured goods; its cotton industry alone in 1850 was equal in size to the industries of all other European countries combined.

The Spread of Industrialization

From Great Britain, industrialization spread to the continental countries of Europe and the United States at different times and speeds during the nineteenth century. First to be industrialized on the Continent were Belgium, France, and the German states (see Map 18.1). Their governments

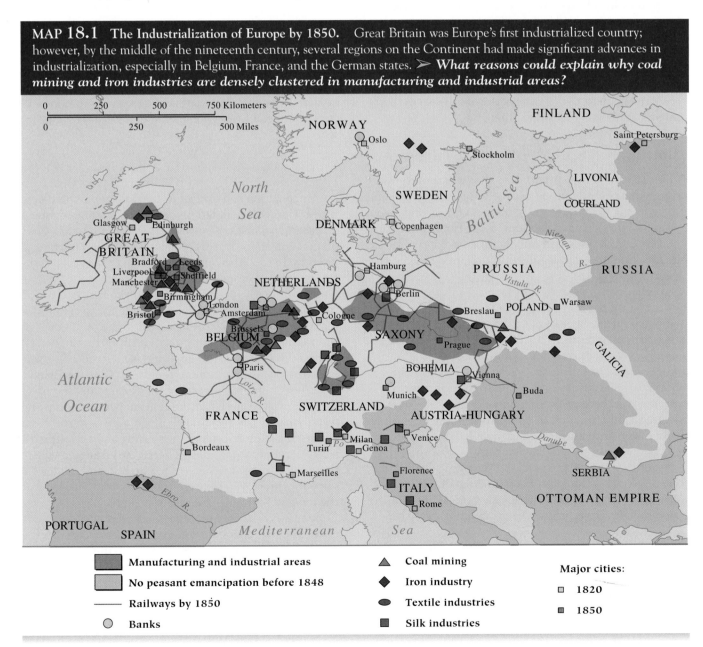

MAP 18.1 **The Industrialization of Europe by 1850.** Great Britain was Europe's first industrialized country; however, by the middle of the nineteenth century, several regions on the Continent had made significant advances in industrialization, especially in Belgium, France, and the German states. ➤ *What reasons could explain why coal mining and iron industries are densely clustered in manufacturing and industrial areas?*

were especially active in encouraging the development of industrialization. For example, the governments set up technical schools to train engineers and mechanics and provided funds to build roads, canals, and railroads. By 1850, a network of iron rails had spread across Europe.

The Industrial Revolution also transformed the new nation in North America, the United States. In 1800, six out of every seven American workers were farmers, and there were no cities with more than 100,000 people. By 1860, however, the population had sextupled to 30 million people (larger than Great Britain), nine U.S. cities had populations over 100,000, and only 50 percent of American workers were farmers.

In sharp contrast to Britain, the United States was a large country. Thousands of miles of roads and canals were built linking east and west. The steamboat facilitated transportation on the Great Lakes, Atlantic coastal waters, and rivers. Most important in the development of an American transportation system was the railroad. Beginning with 100 miles in 1830, by 1860 there were over 27,000 miles of railroad track covering the United States. This transportation revolution turned the United States into a single massive market for the manufactured goods of the Northeast, the early center of American industrialization.

Limiting the Spread of Industrialization

Before 1870, the industrialization that was transforming western and central Europe and the United States did not extend in any significant way to the rest of the world. Even in eastern Europe, industrialization lagged far behind. Russia, for example, was still largely rural and agricultural, ruled by an autocratic regime that preferred to keep the peasants in serfdom.

In other parts of the world where they had established control (see Chapter 20), newly industrialized European states pursued a deliberate policy of preventing the growth of mechanized industry. India provides an excellent example of how some of the rapidly industrializing nations of Europe worked to thwart the spread of the Industrial Revolution to their colonial dominions. In the eighteenth century, India had become one of the world's greatest exporters of cotton cloth produced by hand labor. In the first half of the nineteenth century, much of India fell under the control of the British East India Company. With British control came inexpensive British factory-produced textiles, and soon thousands of Indian spinners and handloom weavers were unemployed. British policy encouraged Indians to export their raw materials while buying British-made goods.

The Social Impact of the Industrial Revolution

Eventually the Industrial Revolution revolutionized the social life of Europe and the world. This change was already evident in the first half of the nineteenth century in the growth of cities and the emergence of new social classes.

POPULATION GROWTH AND URBANIZATION

Population increases had already begun in the eighteenth century, but they became dramatic in the nineteenth century. In 1750, the total European population stood at an estimated 140 million; by 1850, it had almost doubled to 266 million. The key to the expansion of population was the decline in death rates throughout Europe. Wars and major epidemic diseases, such as plague and smallpox, became less frequent, which led to a drop in the number of deaths. Thanks to the increase in the food supply, more people were better fed and more resistant to disease.

Throughout Europe, cities and towns grew dramatically in the first half of the nineteenth century, a phenomenon related to industrialization. By 1850, especially in Great Britain and Belgium, cities were rapidly becoming home for many industries. With the steam engine, factory owners could locate their manufacturing plants in urban centers where they had ready access to transportation facilities and unemployed people from the country looking for work.

In 1800, Great Britain had one major city, London, with a population of 1 million, and six cities with populations between 50,000 and 100,000. Fifty years later, London's population had swelled to 2,363,000, and there were nine cities with populations over 100,000 and eighteen cities with populations between 50,000 and 100,000. Over 50 percent of the British population lived in towns and cities by 1850. Urban populations also grew on the Continent, but less dramatically.

The dramatic growth of cities in the first half of the nineteenth century produced miserable living conditions for many of the inhabitants. Located in the center of most industrial towns were the row houses of the industrial workers. Rooms were not large and were frequently overcrowded, as a government report of 1838 in Britain revealed: "I entered several of the tenements. In one of them, on the ground floor, I found six persons occupying a very small room, two in bed, ill with fever. In the room above this were two more persons in one bed, ill with fever." Another report said: "There were 63 families where there were at least five persons to one bed; and there were some in which even six were packed in one bed, lying at the top and bottom—children and adults."[1]

Sanitary conditions in these towns were appalling; sewers and open drains were common on city streets: "In the centre of this street is a gutter, into which the refuse of animal and vegetable matters of all kinds, the dirty water from the washing of clothes and of the houses, are all poured, and there they stagnate and putrefy."[2] Unable to deal with human excrement, cities in the early industrial era smelled horrible and were extraordinarily unhealthy. Towns and cities were fundamentally death traps. As deaths outnumbered births in most large cities in the first half of the nineteenth century, only a constant influx of people from the country kept them alive and growing.

NEW SOCIAL CLASSES: THE INDUSTRIAL MIDDLE CLASS

The rise of industrial capitalism produced a new middle-class group. The bourgeoisie or middle class was not new; it had existed since the emergence of cities in the Middle Ages. Originally the bourgeois was the burgher or town dweller, active as a merchant, official, artisan, lawyer, or man of letters. As wealthy townspeople bought land, the original meaning of the word bourgeois became lost, and the term came to include people involved in commerce, industry, and banking as well as professionals such as teachers, physicians, and government officials.

The new industrial middle class was made up of the people who constructed the factories, purchased the machines, and figured out where the markets were. Their qualities included resourcefulness, single-mindedness, resolution, initiative, vision, ambition, and often, of course, greed. As Jedediah Strutt, a cotton manufacturer said, "Getting of money . . . is the main business of the life of men."

Members of the industrial middle class sought to reduce the barriers between themselves and the landed elite, but it is clear that they tried at the same time to separate themselves from the laboring classes below them. The working class was actually a mixture of different groups in the first half of the nineteenth century, but in the course of the nineteenth century, factory workers would form an industrial proletariat that constituted a majority of the working class.

NEW SOCIAL CLASSES: THE INDUSTRIAL WORKING CLASS

Early industrial workers faced wretched working conditions. Work shifts ranged from twelve to sixteen hours a day, six days a week, with a half hour for lunch and dinner. There was no security of employment and no minimum wage. The worst conditions were in the cotton mills, where temperatures were especially debilitating. One report noted that "in the cotton-spinning work, these creatures are kept, fourteen hours in each day, locked up, summer and winter, in a heat of from eighty to eighty-four degrees." Mills were dirty, dusty, and unhealthy.

Conditions in the coal mines were also harsh. Although steam-powered engines were used to lift coal from the mines to the top, inside the mines, men still bore the burden of digging the coal out while horses, mules, women, and children hauled coal carts on rails to the lift. Dangerous conditions, including cave-ins, explosions, and gas fumes, were a way of life. The cramped conditions in mines—tunnels were often only 3 or 4 feet high—and their constant dampness led to deformed bodies and ruined lungs.

Both children and women worked in large numbers in early factories and mines. Children had been an important part of the family economy in preindustrial times, working in the fields or carding and spinning wool at home. In the Industrial Revolution, however, child labor was exploited more than ever (see the box on p. 398). The owners of cotton factories found child labor very helpful. Children had a particular delicate touch as spinners of cotton. Their smaller size made it easier for them to move under machines to gather loose cotton. Moreover, children were more easily trained to do factory work. Above all, children represented a cheap supply of labor. In 1821, about half of the British population was under twenty years of age. Hence children made up an abundant supply of labor, and they were paid only about one-sixth to one-third of what a man was paid. In the cotton factories in 1838, children under eighteen made up 29 percent of the total workforce; children as young as seven worked twelve to fifteen hours per day, six days a week, in cotton mills.

By 1830, women and children made up two-thirds of the cotton industry's labor. However, as the number of children employed declined under the Factory Act of 1833, their places were taken by women, who came to dominate the labor forces of the early factories. Women made up 50 percent of the labor force in textile (cotton and woolen) factories before 1870. They were mostly unskilled laborers and were paid half or less of what men received.

REACTION AND REVOLUTION: THE GROWTH OF NATIONALISM

After the defeat of Napoleon, European rulers moved to restore much of the old order. This was the goal of the great powers—Great Britain, Austria, Prussia, and Russia—when they met at the Congress of Vienna in September 1814 to arrange a final peace settlement after the Napoleonic Wars. The leader of the congress was the Austrian foreign minister, Prince Klemens von Metternich (1773–1859), who claimed that he was guided at Vienna by the principle of legitimacy. To reestablish peace and stability in Europe, he considered it necessary to restore the legitimate monarchs who would preserve traditional institutions (see Map 18.2). This had already been done in France with the restoration of the Bourbon monarchy.

The peace arrangements of 1815 were but the beginning of a conservative reaction determined to contain the liberal and nationalist forces unleashed by the French Revolution. Metternich and his kind were representatives of the ideology known as conservatism. Most conservatives favored obedience to political authority, believed that organized religion was crucial to social order, hated

CHILD LABOR: DISCIPLINE IN THE TEXTILE MILLS

In the early Industrial Revolution, child labor was exploited more systematically than ever before. These selections are taken from the report of Sadler's Committee, commissioned in 1832 to inquire into the condition of child factory workers.

HOW THEY KEPT THE CHILDREN AWAKE

It is a very frequent thing at Mr. Marshall's [at Shrewsbury] where the least children were employed (for there were plenty working at six years of age), for Mr. Horseman to start the mill earlier in the morning than he formerly did; and provided a child should be drowsy, the overlooker walks round the room with a stick in his hand, and he touches that child on the shoulder, and says, "Come here." In a corner of the room there is an iron cistern; it is filled with water; he takes this boy, and takes him up by the legs, and dips him over head in the cistern, and sends him to work for the remainder of the day. . . .

What means were taken to keep the children to their work?—Sometimes they would tap them over the head, or nip them over the nose, or give them a pinch of snuff, or throw water in their faces, or pull them off where they were, and job them about to keep them waking.

THE SADISTIC OVERLOOKER

Samuel Downe, age 29, factory worker living near Leeds; at the age of about ten began work at Mr. Marshall's mill at Shrewsbury, where the customary hours when work was brisk were generally 5 A.M. to 8 P.M., sometimes from 5:30 A.M. to 8 or 9:

What means were taken to keep the children awake and vigilant, especially at the termination of such a day's labour as you have described?—There was generally a blow or a box, or a tap with a strap, or sometimes the hand.

Have you yourself been strapped?—Yes, most severely, till I could not bear to sit upon a chair without having pillows, and through that I left. I was strapped both on my own legs, and then I was put upon a man's back, and then strapped and buckled with two straps to an iron pillar, and flogged, and all by one overlooker; after that he took a piece of tow, and twisted it in the shape of a cord, and put it in my mouth, and tied it behind my head.

He gagged you?—Yes; and then he ordered me to run round a part of the machinery where he was overlooker, and he stood at one end, and every time I came there he struck me with a stick, which I believe was an ash plant, and which he generally carried in his hand, and sometimes he hit me, and sometimes he did not; and one of the men in the room came and begged me off, and that he let me go, and not beat me any more, and consequently he did.

You have been beaten with extraordinary severity?— Yes, I was beaten so that I had not power to cry at all, or hardly speak at one time. What age were you at that time?—Between 10 and 11.

---

revolutionary upheavals, and were unwilling to accept either the liberal demands for civil liberties and representative governments or the nationalistic aspirations generated by the French revolutionary era. After 1815, the political philosophy of conservatism was supported by hereditary monarchs, government bureaucracies, landowning aristocracies, and revived churches, both Protestant and Catholic. The conservative forces were dominant after 1815.

One method used by the great powers to maintain the new status quo they had constructed was the Concert of Europe, according to which Great Britain, Russia, Prussia, and Austria (and later France) agreed to meet periodically in conferences to take steps that would maintain the peace in Europe. Eventually the great powers adopted a principle of intervention that was based on their right to send armies into countries where there were revolutions, to restore legitimate monarchs to their thrones.

Forces for Change

Between 1815 and 1830, conservative governments throughout Europe worked to maintain the old order. However, powerful forces for change—liberalism and nationalism—were also at work. Liberalism owed much to the Enlightenment of the eighteenth century and the American and French Revolutions at the end of that century; it was based on the idea that people should be as free from restraint as possible.

Liberals came to hold a common set of political beliefs. Chief among them was the protection of civil liberties, or the basic rights of all people, which included equality before the law; freedom of assembly, speech, and the press; and freedom from arbitrary arrest. All of these freedoms should be guaranteed by a written document, such as the American Bill of Rights. In addition to religious toleration for all, most liberals advocated separation of church and state. Liberals also demanded the right of peaceful opposition to the government in and out of parliament and the making of laws by a representative assembly (legislature) elected by qualified voters. Many liberals believed, then, in a constitutional monarchy or constitutional state with limits on the powers of government in order to prevent despotism and in written constitutions that would guarantee these rights. Liberals were not democrats, however. They thought that the right to vote and hold office should be open only to men of property. As a political philosophy, liberalism was adopted by middle-class men, especially

MAP 18.2 Europe After the Congress of Vienna. The Congress of Vienna imposed order on Europe based on the principles of monarchical government and a balance of power. Monarchs were restored in France, Spain, and other states recently under Napoleon's control, and much territory changed hands, often at the expense of small and weak states. ➤ *How did Europe's major powers manipulate territory to decrease the probability that France could again threaten the Continent's stability?*

industrial middle-class men, who favored voting rights for themselves so that they could share power with the landowning classes.

Nationalism was an even more powerful ideology for change in the nineteenth century. Nationalism arose out of an awareness of being part of a community that has common institutions, traditions, language, and customs. This community is called a nation, and the primary political loyalty of individuals would be to the nation. Nationalism did not become a popular force for change until the French Revolution. From then on, nationalists came to believe that each nationality should have its own government. Thus the Germans, who were not united, wanted national unity in a German nation-state with one central government. Subject peoples, such as the Hungarians, wanted the right to establish their own autonomy rather than be subject to a German minority in the multinational Austrian Empire.

Nationalism, then, was a threat to the existing political order. A united Germany, for example, would upset the balance of power established at Vienna in 1815. Conservatives feared such change and tried hard to repress nationalism. The conservative order dominated much of Europe after 1815, but the forces of liberalism and nationalism, first generated by the French Revolution, continued to grow as that

second great revolution, the Industrial Revolution, expanded and brought in new groups of people who wanted change. In 1848, these forces for change erupted.

THE REVOLUTIONS OF 1848

Revolution in France was the spark for revolution in other countries. A severe industrial and agricultural depression beginning in 1846 brought untold hardship in France to the lower middle class, workers, and peasants, while the government's persistent refusal to lower the property qualification for voting angered the disenfranchised members of the middle class. When the government of King Louis-Philippe (1830–1848) refused to make changes, opposition grew and finally overthrew the monarchy on February 24, 1848. A group of moderate and radical republicans established a provisional government and called for the election by universal male suffrage of a "constituent assembly" that would draw up a new constitution.

The new constitution, ratified on November 4, 1848, established a republic (the Second Republic) with a single legislature elected to three-year terms by universal male suffrage and a president elected to a four-year term, also by universal male suffrage. In the elections for the presidency

REVOLUTIONARY EXCITEMENT: CARL SCHURZ
AND THE REVOLUTION OF 1848 IN GERMANY

The excitement with which German liberals and nationalists received the news of the February revolution in France and their own expectations for Germany are well captured in this selection from the Reminiscences *of Carl Schurz (1829–1906). Schurz made his way to the United States after the failure of the German revolution and eventually became a U.S. senator.*

CARL SCHURZ, *REMINISCENCES*

One morning, toward the end of February, 1848, I sat quietly in my attic-chamber, working hard at my tragedy of "Ulrich von Hutten" [sixteenth-century German humanist and knight], when suddenly a friend rushed breathlessly into the room, exclaiming: "What, you sitting here! Do you not know what has happened?"

"No; what?"

"The French have driven away Louis Philippe and proclaimed the republic."

I threw down my pen—and that was the end of "Ulrich von Hutten." I never touched the manuscript again. We tore down the stairs, into the street, to the market-square, the accustomed meeting-place for all the student societies after their midday dinner. Although it was still forenoon, the market was already crowded with young men talking excitedly. There was no shouting, no noise, only agitated conversation. What did we want there? This probably no one knew. But since the French had driven away Louis Philippe and proclaimed the republic, something of course must happen here, too. . . .

The next morning there were the usual lectures to be attended. But how profitless! The voice of the professor sounded like a monotonous drone coming from far away. What he had to say did not seem to concern us. The pen that should have taken notes remained idle. At last we closed with a sigh the notebook and went away, impelled by a feeling that now we had something more important to do—to devote ourselves to the affairs of the fatherland. And this we did by seeking as quickly as possible again the company of our friends, in order to discuss what had happened and what was to come. In these conversations, excited as they were, certain ideas and catchwords worked themselves to the surface, which expressed more or less the feelings of the people. Now had arrived in Germany the day for the establishment of "German Unity," and the founding of a great, powerful national German Empire. In the first line the convocation of a national parliament. Then the demands for civil rights and liberties, free speech, free press, the right of free assembly, equality before the law, a freely elected representation of the people with legislative power, responsibility of ministers, self-government of the communes, the right of the people to carry arms, the formation of a civic guard with elective officers, and so on—in short, that which was called a "constitutional form of government on a broad democratic basis." Republican ideas were at first only sparingly expressed. But the word *democracy* was soon on all tongues, and many, too, thought it a matter of course that if the princes should try to withhold from the people the rights and liberties demanded, force would take the place of mere petition. Of course the regeneration of the fatherland must, if possible, be accomplished by peaceable means. . . . Like many of my friends, I was dominated by the feeling that at last the great opportunity had arrived for giving to the German people the liberty which was their birthright and to the German fatherland its unity and greatness, and that it was now the first duty of every German to do and to sacrifice everything for this sacred object.

held in December 1848, Charles Louis Napoleon Bonaparte, the nephew of the famous French ruler, won a resounding victory.

News of the 1848 revolution in France led to upheaval in central Europe as well (see the box above). The Vienna settlement in 1815 had recognized the existence of thirty-eight sovereign states (called the Germanic Confederation) in what had once been the Holy Roman Empire. Austria and Prussia were the two great powers in terms of size and might; the other states varied considerably. In 1848, cries for change caused many German rulers to promise constitutions, a free press, jury trials, and other liberal reforms. In Prussia, King Frederick William IV (1840–1861) agreed to establish a new constitution and work for a united Germany.

The promise of unity reverberated throughout all the German states as governments allowed elections by universal male suffrage for deputies to an all-German parliament called the Frankfurt Assembly. Its purpose was to fulfill a liberal and nationalist dream—the preparation of a constitution for a new united Germany. But the Frankfurt Assembly failed to achieve its goal. The members had no real means of compelling the German rulers to accept the constitution they had drawn up. German unification was not achieved; the revolution had failed.

The Austrian Empire needed only the news of the revolution in Paris to erupt in flames in March 1848. The Austrian Empire was a multinational state, a collection of at least eleven ethnically distinct peoples, including Germans, Czechs, Magyars (Hungarians), Slovaks, Romanians, Serbians, and Italians, who had pledged their loyalty to the Habsburg emperor. The Germans, though only a quarter of the population, were economically dominant and played a leading role in governing Austria. In March, demonstrations in Buda, Prague, and Vienna led to the dismissal of Metternich, the Austrian foreign minister and the archsymbol of the conservative order, who fled abroad. In Vienna, revolutionary forces took control of the capital and demanded a liberal constitution. Hungary was given its own legislature and a separate national army.

Austrian officials had made concessions to appease the revolutionaries, but they were determined to reestablish firm control. As in the German states, they were increasingly encouraged by the divisions between radical and moderate revolutionaries and played on the middle-class fear of a working-class social revolution. By the end of October 1848, Austrian military forces had crushed radical rebels in Vienna, but it was only with the assistance of a Russian army of 140,000 men that the Hungarian revolution was finally put down in 1849. The revolutions in the Austrian Empire had failed.

So did revolutions in Italy. The Congress of Vienna had established nine states in Italy, including the Kingdom of Sardinia in the north, ruled by the house of Savoy; the Kingdom of the Two Sicilies (Naples and Sicily); the Papal States; a handful of small duchies; and the important northern provinces of Lombardy and Venetia, which were now part of the Austrian Empire. Italy was largely under Austrian domination, but a new movement for Italian unity known as Young Italy led to initially successful revolts in 1848. By 1849, however, the Austrians had reestablished complete control over Lombardy and Venetia, and the old order also prevailed in the rest of Italy.

Throughout Europe in 1848–1849, moderate, middle-class liberals and radical workers soon divided over their aims, and the failure of the revolutionaries to stay united soon led to the reestablishment of authoritarian regimes. In other parts of the Western world, revolutions took somewhat different directions.

Independence and the Development of the National State in Latin America

By the end of the eighteenth century, the ideas of the Enlightenment and the new political ideals stemming from the successful revolution in North America were beginning to influence the creole elites (descendants of Europeans who became permanent inhabitants of Latin America). The principles of the equality of all people in the eyes of the law, free trade, and a free press proved very attractive. Sons of creoles, such as Simón Bolívar and José de San Martín, who became leaders of the independence movement, even attended European universities, where they imbibed the ideas of the Enlightenment.

NATIONALISTIC REVOLTS

The creole elites soon began to use their new ideas to denounce the rule of the Iberian monarchs and the peninsulars (Spanish and Portuguese officials who resided in Latin America for political and economic gain). When Napoleon Bonaparte toppled the monarchies of Spain and Portugal, the authority of the Spaniards and Portuguese in their colonial empires was weakened, and between 1807 and 1825, a series of revolts enabled most of Latin America to become independent.

An unusual revolution preceded the main independence movements. Saint Domingue—the western third of Hispaniola—was a French sugar colony. Led by Toussaint L'Ouverture, a son of African slaves, over 100,000 black slaves rose in revolt and seized control of all of Hispaniola. On January 1, 1804, the western part of Hispaniola, now called Haiti, became the first independent state in Latin America.

Beginning in 1810, Mexico too experienced a revolt, fueled initially by the desire of the creole elites to overthrow the rule of the peninsulars. But when Indians and mestizos joined the revolt, both creoles and peninsulars, fearful of the masses, cooperated in defeating the popular revolutionary forces. Nevertheless, independence still came to Mexico, but it was now the conservative elites—both creoles and peninsulars—who decided to overthrow Spanish rule as a way of preserving their own power. They selected a creole military leader, Augustín de Iturbide, as the first emperor of Mexico in 1821.

Independence movements elsewhere in Latin America were the work of elites—primarily creoles—who overthrew Spanish rule and set up new governments that they could dominate. Two of the most prominent leaders were both members of the creole elite—José de San Martín of Argentina and Simón Bolívar of Venezuela.

By 1810, the forces of San Martín had freed Argentina from Spanish authority, while in Venezuela, Bolívar, hailed as the Liberator, led the bitter struggle for independence. San Martín, who believed that the Spaniards must be removed from all of South America if any nation was to be free, led his forces into Chile in 1817 and then in 1821 moved on to Lima, Peru, the center of Spanish authority. He was soon joined by Bolívar, who in 1824 assumed the task of crushing the last significant Spanish army. By then, Peru, Uruguay, Paraguay, Colombia, Venezuela, Argentina, Bolivia, and Chile had all become free states (see Map 18.3). In 1822, the Central American states had decided to ally themselves with Mexico, but one year later, they separated and became independent. In 1838 and 1839, the United Provinces of Central America divided into five republics: Guatemala, El Salvador, Honduras, Costa Rica, and Nicaragua. Earlier, in 1822, the prince regent of Brazil had declared Brazil's independence from Portugal.

THE DIFFICULTIES OF NATION BUILDING

The new Latin American nations, most of which began their existence as republics, faced a number of serious problems between 1830 and 1870. The wars for independence had themselves resulted in a staggering loss of population, of raw materials and foodstuffs for the industrializing nations of Europe and North America, exports, especially of wheat, tobacco, wools, sugar, coffee, and hides, to the North Atlantic countries increased noticeably. At the same time, the importation of finished consumer goods, especially textiles, also grew and caused a decline in industrial production in Latin America.

A fundamental underlying problem for all of the new Latin American nations was the persistent domination of society by the landed elites. Large estates remained the fact of Latin America's economic and social life. Land remained the basis of wealth, social prestige, and political power throughout the nineteenth century. Landed elites ran governments, controlled courts, and kept a system of inexpensive labor. These landowners made enormous profits growing single, specialized crops (such as coffee) for export, while the masses, unable to have land to grow basic food crops, experienced dire poverty.

Nationalism in the Balkans: The Ottoman Empire and the Eastern Question

The Ottoman Empire had long been in control of much of the Balkans in southeastern Europe. By the beginning of the nineteenth century, however, the Ottoman Empire was in decline, and authority over its outlying territories in the Balkans waned. As a result, European governments, especially those of Russia and Austria, began to take an active interest in the disintegration of the empire, which they called the "sick man of Europe."

When the Russians invaded the Ottoman provinces of Moldavia and Wallachia, the Ottoman Turks declared war on Russia on October 4, 1853. In the following year, on March 28, Great Britain and France, fearful of Russian gains, declared war on Russia. The Crimean War, as the conflict came to be called, was poorly planned and poorly fought. Heavy losses caused the Russians to sue for peace. By the Treaty of Paris, signed in March 1856, Russia agreed to allow Moldavia and Wallachia to be placed under the protection of all the great powers.

The Balkans in 1830

AUSTRIAN EMPIRE

MOLDAVIA AND WALLACHIA

BOSNIA

SERBIA

Danube

MONTENEGRO

Black Sea

BALKANS

Constantinople

OTTOMAN EMPIRE

GREECE

0   150   300 Kilometers

0   100   200 Miles

The Art Archive/Museo Nacional de Historia Lima/Dagli Orti

JOSÉ DE SAN MARTÍN. José de San Martín of Argentina was one of the famous leaders of the Latin American independence movement. His forces liberated Argentina, Chile, and Peru from Spanish authority. In this painting by Theodore Géricault, San Martín is shown leading his troops at the Battle of Chacabuco in Chile.

property, and livestock; at the same time, disputes arose between nations over their precise boundaries.

The new nations of Latin America began with republican governments, but they had no experience in ruling themselves. Soon after independence, strong leaders known as caudillos came into power. They ruled chiefly by military force and were usually supported by the landed elites. Many kept the new national states together.

Although political independence brought economic independence, old patterns were hard to extinguish. Instead of Spain and Portugal, Great Britain now dominated the Latin American economy. Old trade patterns soon reemerged. Because Latin America served as a source

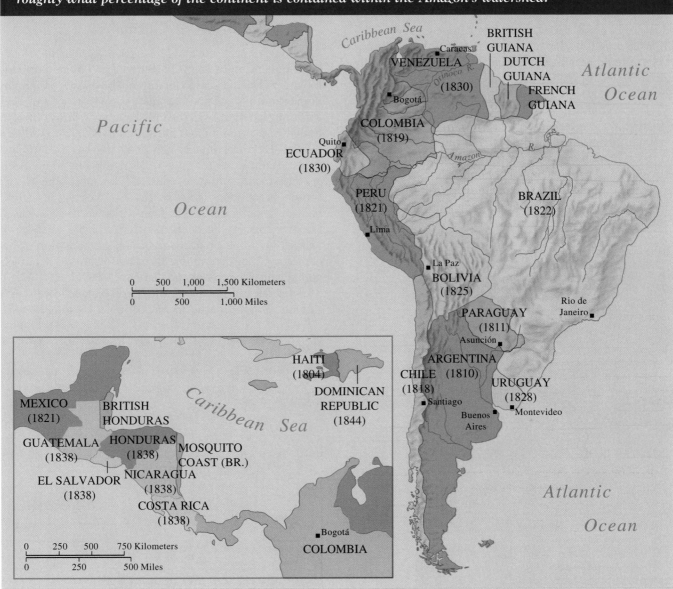

MAP 18.3 **Latin America in the First Half of the Nineteenth Century.** Latin American colonies took advantage of Spain's weakness during the Napoleonic Wars to fight for independence, beginning with Argentina in 1810 and spreading throughout the region over the next decade with the help of leaders like Simón Bolívar and José de San Martín. ➤ *How many South American countries are sources of rivers that feed the Amazon, and roughly what percentage of the continent is contained within the Amazon's watershed?*

The Crimean War destroyed the Concert of Europe. Austria and Russia, the two chief powers maintaining the status quo in the first half of the nineteenth century, were now enemies because of Austria's unwillingness to support Russia in the war. Russia, defeated and humiliated by the obvious failure of its armies, withdrew from European affairs for the next two decades. Great Britain, disillusioned by its role in the war, also pulled back from Continental affairs. Austria, paying the price for its neutrality, was now without friends among the great powers. This new international situation opened the door for the unification of Italy and Germany.

NATIONAL UNIFICATION AND THE NATIONAL STATE, 1848–1871

The revolutions of 1848 had failed, but within twenty-five years, many of the goals sought by liberals and nationalists during the first half of the nineteenth century were achieved. Italy and Germany became nations, and many European states were led by constitutional monarchs.

The Unification of Italy

The Italians were the first people to benefit from the breakdown of the Concert of Europe. In 1850, Austria was still the dominant power on the Italian peninsula. After the failure of the revolution of 1848–1849, more and more Italians looked to the northern Italian state of Piedmont, ruled by the royal house of Savoy, as their best hope to achieve the unification of Italy. It was, however, doubtful that the little state could provide the leadership needed to unify Italy until King Victor Emmanuel II (1849–1878) named Count Camillo di Cavour (1810–1861) prime minister in 1852.

As prime minister, Cavour pursued a policy of economic expansion that increased government revenues and enabled Piedmont to equip a large army. Cavour, allied with the French emperor, Louis Napoleon, defeated the Austrians and gained control of Lombardy. Cavour's success caused nationalists in some northern Italian states (Parma, Modena, and Tuscany) to overthrow their governments and join Piedmont.

Meanwhile, in southern Italy, Giuseppe Garibaldi (1807–1882), a dedicated Italian patriot, raised an army of a thousand volunteers called Red Shirts because of the color of their uniforms. Garibaldi's forces swept through Sicily and then crossed over to the mainland and began a victorious march up the Italian peninsula. Naples, and with it the Kingdom of the Two Sicilies, fell in early September. Ever the patriot, Garibaldi chose to turn over his conquests to Cavour's Piedmontese forces. On March 17, 1861, the new kingdom of Italy was proclaimed under a centralized government subordinated to the control of Piedmont and King Victor Emmanuel II (1861–1878) of the house of Savoy. The task of unification was not yet complete, however. Venetia in the north was taken from Austria in 1866. The Italian army annexed the city of Rome on September 20, 1870, and it became the new capital of the united Italian state.

The Unification of Germany

After the failure of the Frankfurt Assembly to achieve German unification in 1848–1849, more and more Germans looked to Prussia for leadership in the cause of German unification. Prussia had become a strong, prosperous, and authoritarian state, with the Prussian king in firm control of both the government and the army. In 1862, King William I (1861–1888) appointed a new prime minister, Count Otto von Bismarck (1815–1898). Bismarck has often been portrayed as the ultimate realist, the foremost nineteenth-century practitioner of *Realpolitik*—the "politics of reality." He said, "Not by speeches and majorities will the great questions of the day be decided—that was the mistake of 1848–1849—but by iron and blood."[3] Opposition to his domestic policy determined Bismarck on an active foreign policy, which led to war and German unification.

After defeating Denmark with Austrian help in 1864 and gaining control over the duchies of Schleswig and Holstein,

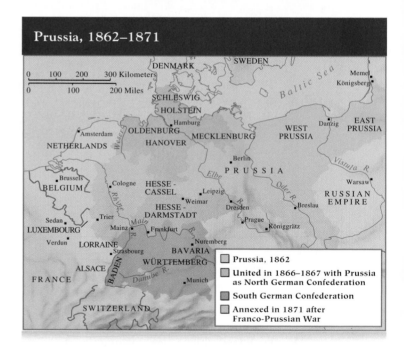

Bismarck created friction with the Austrians and goaded them into a war on June 14, 1866. The Austrians, no match for the disciplined Prussian army, were decisively defeated at Königgrätz on July 3. Prussia now organized the German states north of the Main River into the North German Confederation. The southern German states, largely Catholic, remained independent but signed military alliances with Prussia due to their fear of France, their western neighbor.

Prussia now dominated all of northern Germany. However, problems with France soon arose. Bismarck realized that France would never be content with a strong German state to its east because of the potential threat to French security. Bismarck goaded the French into declaring war on Prussia on July 15, 1870. The Prussian armies advanced into France, and at Sedan, on September 2, 1870, captured an entire French army and the French emperor Napoleon III himself. Paris capitulated on January 28, 1871. France had to give up the provinces of Alsace and Lorraine to the new German state, a loss that left the French burning for revenge.

Even before the war had ended, the southern German states had agreed to enter the North German Confederation. On January 18, 1871, in the Hall of Mirrors in Louis XIV's palace at Versailles, William I was proclaimed kaiser (emperor) of the Second German Empire (the first was the medieval Holy Roman Empire). German unity had been achieved by the Prussian monarchy and the Prussian army. The Prussian leadership of German unification meant the triumph of authoritarian, militaristic values over liberal, constitutional sentiments in the development of the new German state. With its industrial resources and military might, the new state had become the strongest power on the Continent. A new European balance of power was at hand.

Nationalism and Reform: Great Britain, France, the Austrian Empire, and Russia

Unlike nations on the Continent, Great Britain managed to avoid the revolutionary upheavals of the first half of the nineteenth century. In 1815, Great Britain was governed by the aristocratic landowning classes that dominated both houses of Parliament. But in 1832, to avoid the turmoil on the Continent, Parliament passed a reform bill that increased the number of male voters, chiefly members of the industrial middle class. By joining the industrial middle class to the landed interest in ruling Britain, Britain avoided revolution in 1848.

In the 1850s and 1860s, the liberal parliamentary system of Britain made both social and political reforms that enabled the country to remain stable. One of the other reasons for Britain's stability was its continuing economic growth. After 1850, middle-class prosperity was at last coupled with some improvements for the working classes as real wages for laborers increased more than 25 percent between 1850 and 1870. The British sense of national pride was well reflected in Queen Victoria (1837–1901), whose sense of duty and moral respectability reflected the attitudes of her age, which has ever since been known as the Victorian Age.

Events in France after the revolution of 1848 moved toward the restoration of monarchy. Four years after his election as president, Louis Napoleon restored an authoritarian empire. On December 2, 1852, Louis Napoleon assumed the title of Napoleon III (the first Napoleon had abdicated in favor of his son, Napoleon II, on April 6, 1814). The Second Empire had begun.

The first five years of Napoleon III's reign were a spectacular success. He took many steps to expand industrial growth. Government subsidies helped foster the rapid construction of railroads as well as harbors, roads, and canals. The major French railway lines were completed during Napoleon III's reign, and iron production tripled. In

⇒ **THE UNIFICATION OF GERMANY.** Under Prussian leadership, a new German empire was proclaimed on January 18, 1871, in the Hall of Mirrors in the Palace of Versailles. King William of Prussia became Emperor William I of the Second German Empire. Otto von Bismarck, the man who had been so instrumental in creating the new German state, is shown here, resplendently attired in his white uniform, standing at the foot of the throne.

Anton von Werner, Photo © Bildarchiv Preussischer Kulturbesitz, Berlin

DEVELOPMENTS IN EUROPE, 1800–1871

Great Britain	
Reform Act	1832
Queen Victoria	1837–1901

France	
Louis-Philippe	1830–1848
Abdication of Louis-Philippe	February 22–24, 1848
Establishment of Second Republic	November 1848
Election of Louis Napoleon as French president	December 1848
Emperor Napoleon III	1852–1870

Germany	
Germanic Confederation	1815
Frederick William IV of Prussia	1840–1861
Revolution in Germany	1848
Frankfurt Assembly	1848–1849
Unification of Germany	
King William I of Prussia	1861–1888
Danish War	1864
Austro-Prussian War	1866
Franco-Prussian War	1870–1871
German Empire proclaimed	January 18, 1871

Austrian Empire	
Revolt; Metternich dismissed	March 1848
Viennese rebels crushed	October 1848
Defeat of Hungarians with help of Russian troops	1849
Ausgleich: Dual Monarchy	1867

Italy	
Revolutions in Italy	1848
Unification of Italy	
Victor Emmanuel II	1849–1878
Count Cavour becomes prime minister of Piedmont	1852
Garibaldi's invasion of the Two Sicilies	1860
Kingdom of Italy proclaimed	March 17, 1861
Italy's annexation of Venetia	1866
Italy's annexation of Rome	1870

Russia	
Tsar Alexander II	1855–1881
Emancipation edict	March 3, 1861

Ottoman Empire	
Crimean War	1853–1856

the midst of this economic expansion, Napoleon III also undertook a vast reconstruction of the city of Paris. The medieval Paris of narrow streets and old city walls was destroyed and replaced by a modern Paris of broad boulevards, spacious buildings, an underground sewage system, a new public water supply, and gaslights.

In the 1860s, as opposition to his rule began to mount, Napoleon III began to liberalize his regime. He gave the Legislative Corps more say in affairs of state, including debate over the budget. Liberalization policies worked initially; in a plebiscite in May 1870 on whether to accept a new constitution that might have inaugurated a parliamentary regime, the French people gave Napoleon III a resounding victory. This triumph was short-lived, however. War with Prussia in 1870 brought Napoleon III's ouster, and a republic was proclaimed.

Although nationalism was a major force in nineteenth-century Europe, one of the region's most powerful states, the Austrian Empire, managed to frustrate the desire of its numerous ethnic groups for self-determination. After the Habsburgs had crushed the revolutions of 1848–1849, they restored centralized, autocratic government to the empire. But Austria's

defeat at the hands of the Prussians in 1866 forced the Austrians to deal with the fiercely nationalistic Hungarians.

The result was the negotiated Ausgleich, or Compromise, of 1867, which created the dual monarchy of Austria-Hungary. Each part of the empire now had its own constitution, its own legislature, its own governmental bureaucracy, and its own capital (Vienna for Austria and Budapest for Hungary). Holding the two states together were a single monarch—Francis Joseph (1848–1916) was emperor of Austria and king of Hungary—and a common army, foreign policy, and system of finances.

At the beginning of the nineteenth century, Russia was overwhelmingly rural, agricultural, and autocratic. The Russian imperial autocracy, based on soldiers, secret police, and repression, had withstood the revolutionary fervor of the first half of the nineteenth century. However, defeat in the Crimean War in 1856 led even staunch conservatives to realize that Russia was falling hopelessly behind the western European powers. Tsar Alexander II (1855–1881) decided to make serious reforms.

Serfdom was the most burdensome problem in tsarist Russia. On March 3, 1861, Alexander issued his eman-

in the industrial workforce. Working-class men argued that keeping women out of industrial work would ensure the moral and physical well-being of families. In reality, however, when their husbands were unemployed, women had to do low-wage work at home or labor part time in sweatshops to support their families.

The Second Industrial Revolution opened the door to new jobs for women. The development of larger industrial plants and the expansion of government services created a wide number of service and white-collar jobs. The increased demand for white-collar workers at relatively low wages coupled with a shortage of male workers led employers to hire women. Big businesses and retail shops needed clerks, typists, secretaries, file clerks, and salesclerks. The expansion of government services opened opportunities for women to be secretaries and telephone operators and to take jobs in health care and social services. Compulsory education necessitated more teachers, and the development of modern hospital services opened the way for an increase in nurses.

Many of the new white-collar jobs were far from exciting. The work was routine and, except for teaching and nursing, required few skills beyond basic literacy. Nevertheless, these jobs had distinct advantages for many women. For some middle-class women, the new jobs offered freedom from the domestic patterns expected of them. Most of them, however, were filled by working-class females who saw their opportunity to escape from the "dirty" work of the lower-class world.

Organizing the Working Classes

The desire to improve their working and living conditions led many industrial workers to form socialist political parties and socialist trade unions. These emerged after 1870, but the theory that made them possible had been developed more than two decades earlier in the work of Karl Marx. Marxism made its first appearance on the eve of the revolutions of 1848 with the publication of a short treatise titled *The Communist Manifesto*, written by two Germans, Karl Marx (1818–1883) and Friedrich Engels (1820–1895).

Marx and Engels began their treatise with the statement that "the history of all hitherto existing society is the history of class struggles." Throughout history, then, oppressor and oppressed have "stood in constant opposition to one another."[1] One group of people—the oppressors—owned the means of production and thus had the power to control government and society. Indeed, government itself was but an instrument of the ruling class. The other group, which depended on the owners of the means of production, were the oppressed.

In the industrialized societies of Marx's day, the class struggle continued. According to Marx, "Society as a whole is more and more splitting up into two great hostile camps, into two great classes directly facing each other: Bourgeoisie and Proletariat." Marx predicted that the struggle between the bourgeoisie and the proletariat would finally break into open revolution, "where the violent overthrow of the bourgeoisie lays the foundation for the sway of the proletariat." Marxism holds that the fall of the bourgeoisie "and the victory of the proletariat are equally inevitable."[2] For a while, the proletariat would form a dictatorship in order to organize the means of production. However, the end result would be a classless society, since classes themselves arose from the economic differences that have been abolished; the state—itself an instrument of the bourgeois interests—would wither away (see the box on p. 418).

In time, Marx's ideas were picked up by working-class leaders who formed socialist parties. Most important was the German Social Democratic Party (SPD), which emerged in 1875 and espoused revolutionary Marxist rhetoric while organizing itself as a mass political party competing in elections for the Reichstag (the lower house of parliament). Once in the Reichstag, SPD delegates worked to achieve legislation to improve the condition of the working class. When it received four million votes in the 1912 elections, the SPD became the largest single party in Germany.

Socialist parties emerged in other European states, although not with the kind of success achieved by the Geman Social Democrats. In 1889, leaders of the various socialist parties formed the Second International, an association of national socialist groups that would fight against capitalism worldwide. (The First International had failed in 1872.) The Second International took some coordinated actions—May Day (May 1), for example, was made an international labor holiday—but differences often wreaked havoc at the organization's congresses.

Marxist parties divided over the issue of revisionism. Pure Marxists believed in the imminent collapse of capitalism and the need for socialist ownership of the means of production. But others, called revisionists, rejected the revolutionary approach and argued that workers must organize mass political parties and work together with other progressive elements to gain reform. Evolution by democratic means, not revolution, would achieve the desired goal of socialism.

Another force working for evolutionary rather than revolutionary socialism was the development of trade unions. In Great Britain, unions won the right to strike in the 1870s. Soon after, the masses of workers in factories were organized into trade unions in order to use the instrument of the strike. By 1900, there were two million workers in British trade unions; by 1914, there were almost four million union members. Trade unions in the rest of Europe had varying degrees of success, but by the outbreak of World War I, they had made considerable progress in bettering both the living and the working conditions of workers.

THE CLASSLESS SOCIETY

In The Communist Manifesto, Karl Marx and Friedrich Engels projected the creation of a classless society as the final end product of the struggle between the bourgeoisie and the proletariat. In this selection, they discuss the steps by which that classless society would be reached.

KARL MARX AND FRIEDRICH ENGELS, *THE COMMUNIST MANIFESTO*

The first step in the revolution by the working class, is to raise the proletariat to the position of ruling class. . . . The proletariat will use its political supremacy to wrest, by degrees, all capital from the bourgeoisie; to centralize all instruments of production in the hands of the State, i.e., of the proletariat organized as the ruling class; and to increase the total of productive forces as rapidly as possible.

Of course, in the beginning, this cannot be effected except by means of despotic inroads on the rights of property, and on the conditions of bourgeois production; by means of measures, therefore, which appear economically insufficient and untenable, but which, in the course of the movement, outstrip themselves, necessitate further inroads upon the old social order, and are unavoidable as a means of entirely revolutionizing the mode of production.

These measures will of course be different in different countries.

Nevertheless, in the most advanced countries, the following will be pretty generally applicable:

1. Abolition of property in land and application of all rents of land to public purposes.
2. A heavy progressive or graduated income tax.
3. Abolition of all right of inheritance. . . .
5. Centralization of credit in the hands of the State, by means of a national bank with State capital and an exclusive monopoly.
6. Centralization of the means of communication and transport in the hands of the State.
7. Extension of factories and instruments of production owned by the State. . . .
8. Equal liability of all to labor. Establishment of industrial armies, especially for agriculture.
9. Combination of agriculture with manufacturing industries; gradual abolition of the distinction between town and country, by a more equable distribution of the population over the country.
10. Free education for all children in public schools. Abolition of children's factory labor in its present form. . . .

When, in the course of development, class distinctions have disappeared, and all production has been concentrated in the whole nation, the public power will lose its political character. Political power, properly so called, is merely the organized power of one class for oppressing another. If the proletariat during its contest with the bourgeoisie is compelled, by the force of circumstances, to organize itself as a class, if, by means of a revolution, it makes itself the ruling class, and, as such, sweeps away by force the old conditions of production, then it will, along with these conditions, have swept away the conditions for the existence of class antagonisms and of classes generally, and will thereby have abolished its own supremacy as a class.

In place of the old bourgeois society, with its classes and class antagonisms, we shall have an association, in which the free development of each is the condition for the free development of all.

THE EMERGENCE OF MASS SOCIETY

The rapid economic and social changes of the nineteenth century led to the emergence of mass society by the century's end. For the lower classes, mass society brought voting rights, an improved standard of living, and access to education. However, mass society also made possible the development of organizations that manipulated the populations of the nation-states. To understand this mass society, we need to examine some aspects of its structure.

The New Urban Environment

One of the most important consequences of industrialization and the population explosion of the nineteenth century was urbanization. In the course of the nineteenth century, more and more people came to live in cities. In 1800, city dwellers constituted 40 percent of the population in Britain, 25 percent in France and Germany, and only 10 percent in eastern Europe. By 1914, urban residents had increased to 80 percent of the population in Britain, 45 percent in France, 60 percent in Germany, and 30 percent in eastern Europe. The size of cities also expanded dramatically, especially in industrialized countries. Between 1800 and 1900, London's population grew from 960,000 to 6.5 million and Berlin's from 172,000 to 2.7 million.

Urban populations grew faster than the general population primarily because of the vast migration from rural areas to cities. But cities also grew faster in the second half of the nineteenth century because health and the conditions of life in them were improving as urban reformers and city officials used new technology to ameliorate the urban landscape. In the 1840s, a number of urban reformers had pointed to filthy living conditions as the primary cause of deadly epidemic diseases in the cities. Cholera, for example, had ravaged Europe in the early 1830s and

1840s, especially in the overcrowded cities. Following the advice of reformers, city governments set up boards of health to improve the quality of housing. New building regulations required running water and an internal drainage system for all new buildings.

Essential to the public health of the modern European city was the ability to bring in clean water and to expel sewage. The problem of fresh water was solved by a system of dams and reservoirs that stored the water and aqueducts and tunnels that carried it from the countryside to the city and into individual dwellings. Gas heaters in the 1860s, and later electric heaters, made regular hot baths available to many people. The treatment of sewage was also improved by building mammoth underground pipes that carried raw sewage far from the city for disposal. The city of Frankfurt, Germany, for example, began its program for sewers with a lengthy public campaign featuring the slogan "From the toilet to the river in half an hour."

Middle-class reformers also focused on the housing needs of the working class. Overcrowded, disease-ridden slums were seen as dangerous not only to physical health but also to the political and moral health of the entire nation. V. A. Huber, a German housing reformer, wrote in 1861: "Certainly it would not be too much to say that the home is the communal embodiment of family life. Thus the purity of the dwelling is almost as important for the family as is the cleanliness of the body for the individual."[3] To Huber, good housing was a prerequisite for stable family life, and without stable family life, society would fall apart.

Early efforts to attack the housing problem emphasized the middle-class, liberal belief in the efficacy of private enterprise. Reformers such as Huber believed that the building of model dwellings renting at a reasonable price would force other private landlords to elevate their housing standards. A fine example of this approach was the work of Octavia Hill (see the box on p. 420). As the number and size of cities continued to mushroom, governments by the 1880s concluded that private enterprise could not solve the housing crisis. In 1890, a British law empowered local town councils to construct cheap housing for the working classes. More and more, governments were stepping into areas of activity that they would not have touched earlier.

The Social Structure of Mass Society

At the top of European society stood a wealthy elite, constituting but 5 percent of the population while controlling between 30 and 40 percent of its wealth. In the course of the nineteenth century, landed aristocrats had joined with the most successful industrialists, bankers, and merchants (the wealthy upper middle class) to form a new elite. Members of this elite, whether aristocratic or middle class in background, assumed leadership roles in government bureaucracies and military hierarchies. Marriage also united the two groups. Daughters of business tycoons gained titles, while aristocratic heirs gained new sources of cash. When the American Consuelo Vanderbilt married the duke of Marlborough, the new duchess brought $10 million to her husband.

The middle classes consisted of a variety of groups. Below the upper middle class was a group that included lawyers, doctors, and members of the civil service, as well as business managers, engineers, architects, accountants, and chemists benefiting from industrial expansion. Beneath this solid and comfortable middle group was a lower middle class of small shopkeepers, traders, manufacturers, and prosperous peasants.

Standing between the lower middle class and the lower classes were new groups of white-collar workers who were the product of the Second Industrial Revolution. They were the salespeople, bookkeepers, bank tellers, telephone operators, and secretaries. Though often paid little more than skilled laborers, these white-collar workers were committed to middle-class ideals.

The middle classes shared a certain lifestyle, the values of which dominated much of nineteenth-century society. The members of the middle class were especially active in preaching their worldview to their children and to the upper and lower classes of their society. This was especially evident in Victorian Britain, often considered a model of middle-class society. The European middle classes believed in hard work, which was open to everyone and guaranteed to have positive results. They were also regular churchgoers who believed in the good conduct associated with traditional Christian morality. The middle class was concerned with propriety, the right way of doing things, which gave rise to an incessant stream of books aimed at the middle-class market with such titles as *The Habits of Good Society* or *Don't: A Manual of Mistakes and Improprieties More or Less Prevalent in Conduct and Speech*.

Below the middle classes on the social scale were the working classes, who constituted almost 80 percent of the European population. Many of them were landholding peasants, agricultural laborers, and sharecroppers, especially in eastern Europe. The urban working class consisted of many different groups, including skilled artisans in such traditional trades as cabinetmaking, printing, and the making of jewelry and semiskilled laborers, who included such people as carpenters, bricklayers, and many factory workers. At the bottom of the urban working class stood the largest group of workers, the unskilled laborers. They included day laborers, who worked irregularly for very low wages, and large numbers of domestic servants, most of whom were women.

The Experiences of Women

In 1800, women were largely defined by family and household roles. They remained legally inferior and economically dependent. Women struggled to change their status throughout the nineteenth century.

THE HOUSING VENTURE OF OCTAVIA HILL

Octavia Hill was a practical-minded British housing reformer who believed that workers and their families were entitled to happy homes. At the same time, she was convinced that the poor needed guidance and encouragement, not charity. In this selection, she describes her housing venture.

OCTAVIA HILL, *HOMES OF THE LONDON POOR*

About four years ago I was put in possession of three houses in one of the worst courts of Marylebone. Six other houses were bought subsequently. All were crowded with inmates.

The first thing to be done was to put them in decent tenantable order. The set last purchased was a row of cottages facing a bit of desolate ground, occupied with wretched, dilapidated cowsheds, manure heaps, old timber, and rubbish of every description. The houses were in a most deplorable condition—the plaster was dropping from the walls; on one staircase a pail was placed to catch the rain that fell through the roof. All the staircases were perfectly dark; the banisters were gone, having been burnt as firewood by tenants. The grates, with large holes in them, were falling forward into the rooms. The washhouse, full of lumber belonging to the landlord, was locked up; thus the inhabitants had to wash clothes, as well as to cook, eat and sleep in their small rooms. The dustbin [trash bin], standing in the front part of the houses, was accessible to the whole neighbourhood, and boys often dragged from it quantities of unseemly objects and spread them over the court. The state of the drainage was in keeping with everything else. The pavement of the backyard was all broken up, and great puddles stood in it, so that the damp crept up the outer walls. . . .

As soon as I entered into possession, each family had an opportunity of doing better: those who would not pay, or who led clearly immoral lives, were ejected. The rooms they vacated were cleansed; the tenants who showed signs of improvement moved into them, and thus, in turn, an opportunity was obtained for having each room distempered and papered. The drains were put in order, a large slate cistern was fixed, the washhouse was cleared of its lumber, and thrown open on stated days to each tenant in turn. The roof, the plaster, the woodwork was repaired; the staircase walls were distempered; new grates were fixed; the layers of paper and rag (black with age) were torn from the windows, and glass was put in; out of 192 panes only eight were found unbroken. The yard and footpath were paved.

The rooms, as a rule, were re-let at the same prices at which they had been let before; but tenants with large families were counselled to take two rooms, and for these much less was charged than if let singly: this plan I continue to pursue. Incoming tenants are not allowed to take a decidedly insufficient quantity of room, and no subletting is permitted. . . .

The pecuniary result has been very satisfactory. Five per cent has been paid on all the capital invested. A fund for the repayment of capital is accumulating. A liberal allowance has been made for repairs. . . .

My tenants are mostly of a class far below that of mechanics. They are, indeed, of the very poor. And yet, although the gifts they have received have been next to nothing, none of the families who have passed under my care during the whole four years have continued in what is called "distress," except such as have been unwilling to exert themselves. Those who will not exert the necessary self-control cannot avail themselves of the means of livelihood held out to them. But, for those who are willing, some small assistance in the form of work has, from time to time, been provided—not much, but sufficient to keep them from want or despair.

MARRIAGE AND THE FAMILY

Many women in the nineteenth century aspired to the ideal of femininity popularized by writers and poets. Alfred Lord Tennyson's poem *The Princess* expressed it well:

> *Man for the field and woman for the hearth:*
> *Man for the sword and for the needle she:*
> *Man with the head and woman with the heart:*
> *Man to command and woman to obey;*
> *All else confusion.*

This traditional characterization of the sexes, based on gender-defined social roles, was virtually elevated to the status of universal male and female attributes in the nineteenth century. As the chief family wage earners, men worked outside the home for pay, while women were left with the care of the family, for which they were paid nothing.

For most women throughout most of the nineteenth century, marriage was viewed as the only honorable and available career. While the middle class glorified the ideal of domesticity, for most women, marriage was a matter of economic necessity. The lack of meaningful work and the lower wages paid to women for their work made it difficult for single women to earn a living. Most women chose to marry.

The most significant development in the modern family was the decline in the number of offspring born to the average woman. While some historians attribute increased birth control to more widespread use of coitus interruptus, or male withdrawal before ejaculation, others have emphasized female control of family size through abortion and even infanticide or abandonment. That a change in attitude occurred was apparent in the development of a movement to increase awareness of birth control methods. Europe's first birth control clinic opened in Amsterdam in 1882.

with the French over conflicting colonial ambitions in North Africa. The Triple Alliance of 1882—Germany, Austria-Hungary, and Italy—committed the three powers to a defensive alliance against France. At the same time, Bismarck maintained a separate treaty with Russia.

When Emperor William II cashiered Bismarck in 1890 and took over direction of Germany's foreign policy, he embarked on an activist foreign policy dedicated to enhancing German power by finding, as he put it, Germany's rightful "place in the sun." One of his changes in Bismarck's foreign policy was to drop the treaty with Russia, which he viewed as being at odds with Germany's alliance with Austria. The ending of the alliance brought France and Russia together, and in 1894, the two powers concluded a military alliance. During the next ten years, German policies abroad caused the British to draw closer to France. By 1907, an alliance of Great Britain, France, and Russia—known as the Triple Entente—stood opposed to the Triple Alliance of Germany, Austria-Hungary, and Italy. Europe became divided into two opposing camps that became more and more inflexible and unwilling to compromise. A series of crises in the Balkans between 1908 and 1913 set the stage for World War I.

CRISIS IN THE BALKANS

Over the course of the nineteenth century, the Balkan provinces of the Ottoman Empire had gradually gained their freedom, although the rivalry in the region between Austria and Russia complicated the process. By 1878, Greece, Serbia, and Romania had become independent states. Although freed from Ottoman rule, Montenegro was placed under an Austrian protectorate, while Bulgaria achieved autonomous status under Russian protection. Bosnia and Herzegovina were placed under Austrian protection; Austria could occupy but not annex them.

Nevertheless, in 1908, Austria did annex the two Slavic-speaking territories. Serbia was outraged because the annexation dashed the Serbs' hopes of creating a large Serbian kingdom that would unite most of the southern Slavs. The Russians, as protectors of their fellow Slavs, supported the Serbs and opposed the Austrian action. Backed by the Russians, the Serbs prepared for war against Austria. At this point, William II intervened and demanded that the Russians accept Austria's annexation of

lived. By 1907, the tsar had curtailed the power of the Duma, and he fell back on the army and bureaucracy to rule Russia.

International Rivalries and the Winds of War

Bismarck had realized in 1871 that the emergence of a unified Germany as the most powerful state on the Continent (see Map 19.2) had upset the balance of power established at Vienna in 1815. Fearful of a possible anti-German alliance between France, Russia, and possibly even Austria, Bismarck made a defensive alliance with Austria in 1879. Three years later, this German-Austrian alliance was enlarged with the entrance of Italy, angry

The Balkans in 1913

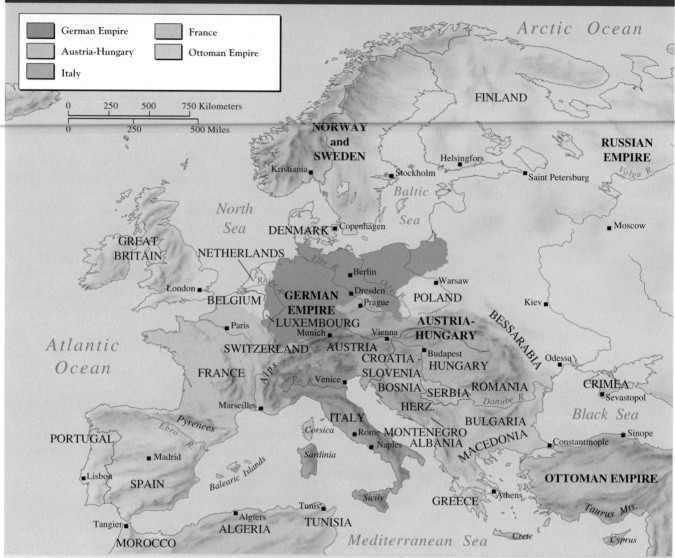

MAP 19.2 Europe in 1871. German unification in 1871 upset the balance of power established at Vienna in 1815 and eventually led to a realignment of European alliances. By 1907, Europe was divided into two opposing camps: the Triple Entente of Great Britain, Russia, and France and the Triple Alliance of Germany, Austria-Hungary, and Italy. ➤ *How was Germany affected by the formation of the Triple Entente?*

German Empire
Austria-Hungary
Italy
France
Ottoman Empire

Bosnia and Herzegovina or face war with Germany. Weakened from their defeat in the Russo-Japanese War in 1904–1905, the Russians backed down but vowed revenge. Two wars between the Balkan states in 1912–1913 further embittered the inhabitants of the region and generated more tensions among the great powers.

Serbia's desire to create a large Serbian kingdom remained unfulfilled. In their frustration, Serbian nationalists blamed the Austrians. Austria-Hungary was convinced that Serbia was a mortal threat to its empire and must at some point be crushed. As Serbia's chief supporters, the Russians were determined not to back down again in the event of a confrontation with Austria or Germany in the Balkans. The allies of Austria-Hungary and Russia were also determined to be more supportive of their

respective allies in another crisis. By the beginning of 1914, two armed camps viewed each other with suspicion.

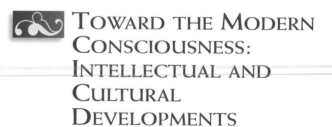

Toward the Modern Consciousness: Intellectual and Cultural Developments

Before 1914, many people in the Western world continued to believe in the values and ideals that had been generated by the Scientific Revolution and the Enlightenment. The idea that human beings could improve themselves and achieve a better society seemed to be proved by a rising standard of living, urban comforts, and mass education. It was easy to think that the human mind could make sense of the universe. Between 1870 and 1914, radically new ideas challenged these optimistic views and opened the way to a modern consciousness.

A New Physics

Science was one of the chief pillars underlying the optimistic and rationalistic view of the world that many Westerners shared in the nineteenth century. Supposedly based on hard facts and cold reason, science offered a certainty of belief in the orderliness of nature. The new physics dramatically altered that perspective.

Throughout much of the nineteenth century, Westerners adhered to the mechanical conception of the universe postulated by the classical physics of Isaac Newton. In this perspective, the universe was viewed as a giant machine in which time, space, and matter were objective realities that existed independently of the observers. Matter was thought to be composed of indivisible and solid material bodies called atoms.

Albert Einstein (1879–1955), a German-born patent officer working in Switzerland, questioned this view of the universe. In 1905, Einstein published his special theory of relativity, which stated that space and time are not absolute but relative to the observer. Neither space nor time had an existence independent of human experience. As Einstein later explained simply to a journalist: "It was formerly believed that if all material things disappeared out of the universe, time and space would be left. According to the relativity theory, however, time and space disappear together with the things."[5] Einstein concluded that matter was nothing but another form of energy. His epochal formula $E = mc^2$—stating that each particle of matter is equivalent to its mass times the square of the velocity of light—was the key theory explaining the vast energies contained within the atom. It led to the atomic age and to uncertainty. To some, a relative universe—unlike Newton's universe—seemed a universe without certainty.

Sigmund Freud and the Emergence of Psychoanalysis

At the turn of the twentieth century, Viennese physician Sigmund Freud (1856–1939) advanced a series of theories that undermined optimism about the rational nature of the human mind. Freud's thought, like the new physics, added to the uncertainties of the age. His major ideas were published in 1900 in *The Interpretation of Dreams*.

According to Freud, human behavior was strongly determined by the unconscious, by past experiences and internal forces of which people were largely oblivious. For Freud, human behavior was no longer truly rational but rather, instinctive or irrational. He argued that painful and unsettling experiences were blotted from conscious awareness but still continued to influence behavior since they had become part of the unconscious (see the box on p. 430). Repression began in childhood. Freud devised a method, known as psychoanalysis, by which a psychotherapist and patient could probe deeply into the memory in order to retrace the chain of repression all the way back to its childhood origins. By making the conscious mind aware of the unconscious and its repressed contents, the patient's psychic conflict was resolved.

The Impact of Darwin: Social Darwinism and Racism

In the second half of the nineteenth century, scientific theories were sometimes wrongly applied to meet other ends. For example, the ideas of Charles Darwin were applied to human society in a radical way by rabid nationalists and racists. In their pursuit of national greatness, extreme nationalists insisted that nations, too, were engaged in a "struggle for existence" in which only the fittest survived.

Perhaps nowhere was the combination of extreme nationalism and racism more evident or more dangerous than in Germany. One of the chief propagandists of German racism was Houston Stewart Chamberlain (1855–1927), a Briton who became a German citizen. According to Chamberlain, modern-day Germans were the only pure successors of the Aryans, who were portrayed as the true and original founders of Western culture. The Aryan race, under German leadership, must be prepared to fight for Western civilization and save it from the destructive assaults of such lower races as Jews, Negroes, and Orientals. Chamberlain singled out the Jews as the racial enemy who wanted to destroy the Aryan race.

ANTI-SEMITISM

Anti-Semitism had a long history in European civilization, but in the nineteenth century, as a result of the ideals of the Enlightenment and the French Revolution, Jews were increasingly granted legal equality in many European countries. Many Jews now left the ghetto and became assimilated into the cultures around them. Many became successful as bankers, lawyers, scientists, scholars, journalists, and stage performers.

These achievements represent only one side of the picture, however. In Germany and Austria during the 1880s and 1890s, conservatives founded right-wing anti-Jewish parties that used anti-Semitism to win the votes of traditional lower-middle-class groups who felt threatened by the new economic forces of the times. However, the worst treatment of Jews at the turn of the century occurred in eastern Europe, where 72 percent of the entire world Jewish population lived. Russian Jews were forced to live in certain regions of the country, and persecutions and pogroms were widespread. Hundreds of thousands of Jews decided to emigrate to escape the persecution.

Many Jews went to the United States, although some moved to Palestine, which soon became the focus of a Jewish

FREUD AND THE CONCEPT OF REPRESSION

Freud's psychoanalytical theories resulted from his attempt to understand the world of the unconscious. This excerpt is taken from a lecture given in 1909 in which Freud describes how he arrived at his theory of the role of repression. Although Freud valued science and reason, his theories of the unconscious produced a new image of the human being as governed less by reason than by irrational forces.

SIGMUND FREUD, *FIVE LECTURES ON PSYCHOANALYSIS*

I did not abandon it [the technique of encouraging patients to reveal forgotten experiences], however, before the observations I made during my use of it afforded me decisive evidence. I found confirmation of the fact that the forgotten memories were not lost. They were in the patient's possession and were ready to emerge in association to what was still known by him; but there was some force that prevented them from becoming conscious and compelled them to remain unconscious. The existence of this force could be assumed with certainty, since one became aware of an effort corresponding to it if, in opposition to it, one tried to introduce the unconscious memories into the patient's consciousness. The force which was maintaining the pathological condition became apparent in the form of resistance on the part of the patient.

It was on this idea of resistance, then, that I based my view of the course of psychical events in hysteria. In order to effect a recovery, it had proved necessary to remove these resistances. Starting out from the mechanism of cure, it now became possible to construct quite definite ideas of the origin of the illness. The same forces which, in the form of resistance, were now offering opposition to the forgotten material's being made conscious, must formerly have brought about the forgetting and must have pushed the pathogenic experiences in question out of consciousness. I gave the name of "repression" to this hypothetical process, and I considered that it was proved by the undeniable existence of resistance.

The further question could then be raised as to what these forces were and what the determinants were of the repression in which we now recognized the pathogenic mechanism of hysteria. A comparative study of the pathogenic situations which we had come to know through the cathartic procedure made it possible to answer this question. All these experiences had involved the emergence of a wishful impulse which was in sharp contrast to the subject's other wishes and which proved incompatible with the ethical and aesthetic standards of his personality. There had been a short conflict, and the end of this internal struggle was that the idea which had appeared before consciousness as the vehicle of this irreconcilable wish fell a victim to repression, was pushed out of consciousness with all its attached memories, and was forgotten. Thus the incompatibility of the wish in question with the patient's ego was the motive for the repression; the subject's ethical and other standards were the repressing forces. An acceptance of the incompatible wishful impulse or a prolongation of the conflict would have produced a high degree of unpleasure; this unpleasure was avoided by means of repression, which was thus revealed as one of the devices serving to protect the mental personality.

---

nationalist movement called Zionism. For many Jews, Palestine, the land of ancient Israel, had long been the land of their dreams. Settlement in Palestine was difficult, however, because it was then part of the Ottoman Empire, which was opposed to Jewish immigration. Despite the problems, however, the First Zionist Congress, which met in Switzerland in 1897, proclaimed as its aim the creation of a "home in Palestine secured by public law" for the Jewish people. In 1900, around a thousand Jews migrated to Palestine, and the trickle rose to about three thousand a year between 1904 and 1914, keeping the Zionist dream alive.

The Culture of Modernity

The revolution in physics and psychology was paralleled by a revolution in literature and the arts. Before 1914, writers and artists were rebelling against the traditional literary and artistic styles that had dominated European cultural life since the Renaissance. The changes that they produced have since been called Modernism.

At the beginning of the twentieth century, a group of writers known as the Symbolists caused a literary revolution. Primarily interested in writing poetry and strongly influenced by the ideas of Freud, the Symbolists believed that an objective knowledge of the world was impossible. The external world was not real but only a collection of symbols that reflected the true reality of the individual human mind.

The period from 1870 to 1914 was one of the most fertile in the history of art. By the late nineteenth century, artists were seeking new forms of expression. The preamble to modern painting can be found in Impressionism, a movement that originated in France in the 1870s when a group of artists rejected the studios and museums and went out into the countryside to paint nature directly. Camille Pissarro (1830–1903), one of Impressionism's founders, expressed what they sought: "Don't proceed according to rules and principles, but paint what you observe and feel. Paint generously and unhesitatingly, for it is best not to lose the first impression."[6]

An important Impressionist painter was Berthe Morisot (1841–1895), who believed that women had a special vision, which was, as she said, "more delicate than that of men." She made use of lighter colors and flowing brush strokes. Near the end of her life, she lamented the refusal of men to take her work seriously: "I don't think there has ever been a man

during the age of imperialism, as well as the complex union of moral concern and vaulting ambition that motivated their actions on the world stage.

Through their efforts, Western colonialism spread throughout much of the non-Western world during the nineteenth and early twentieth centuries. Spurred by the demands of the Industrial Revolution, a few powerful Western states—notably, Great Britain, France, Germany, Russia, and the United States—competed avariciously for consumer markets and raw materials for their expanding economies. By the end of the nineteenth century, virtually all of the traditional societies in Asia and Africa were under direct or indirect colonial rule. As the new century began, the Western imprint on Asian and African societies, for better or for worse, appeared to be a permanent feature of the political and cultural landscape. •

THE SPREAD OF COLONIAL RULE

In the nineteenth century, a new phase of Western expansion into Asia and Africa began. Whereas European aims in the East before 1800 could be summed up in Vasco da Gama's famous phrase "Christians and spices," now a new relationship took shape as European nations began to view Asian and African societies as sources of industrial raw materials and as markets for Western manufactured goods. No longer were Western gold and silver exchanged for cloves, pepper, tea, silk, and porcelain. Now the prodigious output of European factories was sent to Africa and Asia in return for oil, tin, rubber, and the other resources needed to fuel the Western industrial machine.

The reason for this change, of course, was the Industrial Revolution. Now industrializing countries in the West needed vital raw materials that were not available at home, as well as a reliable market for the goods produced in their factories. The latter factor became increasingly crucial as producers began to discover that their home markets could not always absorb domestic output, and thus they had to export their manufactures to make a profit.

As Western economic expansion into Asia and Africa gathered strength during the nineteenth century, it became fashionable to call the process imperialism. Although the term *imperialism* has many meanings, in this instance it referred to the efforts of capitalist states in the West to seize markets, cheap raw materials, and lucrative avenues for investment in the countries beyond Western civilization. In this interpretation, the primary motives behind the Western expansion were economic. Promoters of this view maintained that modern imperialism was a direct consequence of the modern industrial economy.

As in the earlier phase of Western expansion, however, the issue was not simply an economic one. Economic concerns were inevitably tinged with political overtones and with questions of national grandeur and moral purpose as well. In the minds of nineteenth-century Europeans, economic wealth, national status, and political power went hand in hand with the possession of a colonial empire. To global strategists, colonies brought tangible benefits in the world of balance-of-power politics as well as economic profits, and many nations became involved in the pursuit of colonies as much to gain advantage over their rivals as to acquire territory for its own sake.

The relationship between colonialism and national greatness was expressed directly by Cecil Rhodes, the most famous empire builder of his day. "My ruling purpose," he remarked, "is the extension of the British Empire."[2] The British Empire, on which, as the saying went, "the sun never set," was the envy of its rivals and was viewed as the primary source of British global dominance during the second half of the nineteenth century.

With the change in European motives for colonization came a corresponding shift in tactics. Earlier, when their economic interests were more limited, European states had generally been satisfied to deal with existing independent states rather than attempting to establish direct control over vast territories. There had been exceptions, but for the most part, the Western presence in Asia and Africa had been limited to controlling the regional trade network and establishing a few footholds where the foreigners could carry on trade and missionary activity.

After 1800, the demands of industrialization in Europe created a new set of dynamics. Maintaining access to industrial raw materials such as oil and rubber and setting up reliable markets for European manufactured products required more extensive control over colonial territories. As competition for colonies increased, the colonial powers sought to solidify their hold over their territories to protect them from attack by their rivals. During the last two decades of the nineteenth century, the quest for colonies became a scramble as all the major European states, now joined by the United States and Japan, engaged in a global land grab. In many cases, economic interests were secondary to security concerns or the requirements of national prestige. In Africa, for example, the British engaged in a struggle with their rivals to protect their interests in the Suez Canal and the Red Sea.

By 1900, almost all the societies of Africa and Asia were either under full colonial rule or, as in the case of China and the Ottoman Empire, at a point of virtual collapse. Only a handful of states, such as Japan in East Asia, Thailand in

Southeast Asia, Afghanistan and Iran in the Middle East, and mountainous Ethiopia in East Africa, managed to escape internal disintegration or subjection to colonial rule. For the most part, the exceptions were the result of good fortune rather than design. Thailand escaped subjugation primarily because officials in London and Paris found it more convenient to transform the country into a buffer state than to fight over it. Ethiopia and Afghanistan survived due to their remote location and mountainous terrain. Only Japan managed to avoid the common fate through a concerted strategy of political and economic reform.

"Opportunity in the Orient": The Colonial Takeover in Southeast Asia

In 1800, only two societies in Southeast Asia were under effective colonial rule: the Spanish Philippines and the Dutch East Indies. During the nineteenth century, however, European interest in Southeast Asia increased rapidly, and by 1900, virtually the entire area was under colonial rule (see Map 20.1). The process began after the Napoleonic Wars, when the British, by agreement with the Dutch, abandoned their claims to territorial possessions in the East Indies in return for a

Singapore and Malaya

Strait of Malacca

MALAYA

Singapore

SUMATRA

0 — 400 Kilometers
0 — 300 Miles

free hand in the Malay peninsula. In 1819, the colonial administrator Stamford Raffles founded a new British colony on the island of Singapore at the tip of the peninsula. Singapore became a major stopping point for traffic en route to and from China and other commercial centers in the region.

During the next few decades, the pace of European penetration into Southeast Asia accelerated as the British established control over Burma, arousing fears in France that its British rival might soon establish a monopoly of trade in South China. In 1857, the French government decided to force the Vietnamese to accept French protection. A naval attack launched a year later was not a total success, but the French eventually forced the Nguyen dynasty in Vietnam to cede territories in the Mekong River delta. A generation later, French rule was extended over the remainder of the country. By 1900, French seizure of neighboring Cambodia and Laos had led to the creation of the French-ruled Indochinese Union.

After the French conquest of Indochina, Thailand was the only remaining independent state on the Southeast Asian mainland. Under the astute leadership of two remarkable rulers, King Mongkut and his son, King Chulalongkorn, the Thai attempted to introduce Western learning and maintain relations with the major European powers without undermining internal stability or inviting an imperialist attack. In 1896, the British and the French agreed to preserve Thailand as an independent buffer zone between their possessions in Southeast Asia.

The final piece in the colonial edifice in Southeast Asia was put in place in 1898, when U.S. naval forces under Commodore George Dewey defeated the Spanish fleet in Manila Bay. President William McKinley agonized

➤ **THE ESPLANADE.** After occupying the island of Singapore early in the nineteenth century, the British turned what was once a pirate lair located at the entrance to the Strait of Malacca into one of the most important commercial seaports in Asia. By the end of the century, Singapore was home to a rich mixture of peoples, both European and Asian. This painting by a turn-of-the-century British artist graphically displays the multiracial character of the colony as strollers, rickshaw drivers, and lamplighters share space along the Esplanade, in Singapore harbor.

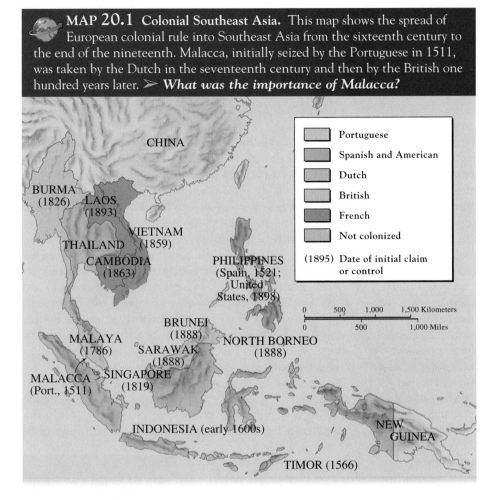

MAP 20.1 Colonial Southeast Asia. This map shows the spread of European colonial rule into Southeast Asia from the sixteenth century to the end of the nineteenth. Malacca, initially seized by the Portuguese in 1511, was taken by the Dutch in the seventeenth century and then by the British one hundred years later. ➤ *What was the importance of Malacca?*

CHINA

BURMA (1826)

LAOS (1893)

VIETNAM (1859)

THAILAND

CAMBODIA (1863)

PHILIPPINES (Spain, 1521; United States, 1898)

Portuguese

Spanish and American

Dutch

British

French

Not colonized

(1895) Date of initial claim or control

0   500   1,000   1,500 Kilometers
0   500   1,000 Miles

BRUNEI (1888)

MALAYA (1786)

SARAWAK (1888)

NORTH BORNEO (1888)

MALACCA (Port., 1511)

SINGAPORE (1819)

INDONESIA (early 1600s)

NEW GUINEA

TIMOR (1566)

over the fate of the Philippines but ultimately decided that the moral thing to do was to turn the islands into an American colony to prevent them from falling into the hands of the Japanese. In fact, the Americans (like the Spanish before them) found the islands convenient as a jumping-off point for the China trade (see Chapter 21). The mixture of moral idealism and the desire for profit was reflected in a speech given in the Senate in January 1900 by Senator Albert Beveridge of Indiana:

> Mr. President, the times call for candor. The Philippines are ours forever, "territory belonging to the United States," as the Constitution calls them. And just beyond the Philippines are China's illimitable markets. We will not retreat from either. . . . We will not renounce our part in the mission of our race, trustee, under God, of the civilization of the world. And we will move forward to our work, not howling out regrets like slaves whipped to their burdens, but with gratitude for a task worthy of our strength, and thanksgiving to Almighty God that He has marked us as His chosen people, henceforth to lead in the regeneration of the world.[3]

Not all Filipinos agreed with Senator Beveridge's portrayal of the situation. Under the leadership of Emilio Aguinaldo, guerrilla forces fought bitterly against U.S. troops to establish their independence from both Spain and the United States. But America's first war against guerrilla forces in Asia was a success, and the bulk of the resistance collapsed in 1901. President McKinley had his stepping-stone to the rich markets of China.

Empire Building in Africa

Up to the beginning of the nineteenth century, the relatively limited nature of European economic interests in Africa had provided little temptation for the penetration of the interior or the political takeover of the coastal areas. The slave trade, the main source of European profit during the eighteenth century, could be carried on by using African rulers and merchants as intermediaries. Disease, political instability, the lack of transportation, and the generally unhealthy climate all deterred the Europeans from more extensive efforts in Africa.

THE GROWING EUROPEAN PRESENCE IN WEST AFRICA

As the new century dawned, the slave trade itself was in a state of decline. One reason was the growing sense of outrage among humanitarians in several European countries over the purchase, sale, and exploitation of human beings. Dutch merchants effectively ceased trafficking in slaves in 1795, and the Danes stopped in 1803. A few years later, the slave trade was declared illegal in both Great Britain and the United States. The British began to apply pressure on other nations to follow suit, and most did so after the end of the Napoleonic Wars in 1815, leaving only Portugal and Spain as practitioners of the trade south of the equator. In the meantime, the demand for slaves began to decline in the Western Hemisphere. When slavery was abolished in the United States in 1863 and in Cuba and Brazil seventeen years later, the slave trade across the Atlantic was effectively brought to an end.

As the slave trade in the Atlantic declined during the first half of the nineteenth century, European interest in what was sometimes called "legitimate trade" in natural resources increased. Exports of peanuts, timber, hides, and palm oil from West Africa increased substantially during the first decades of the century, while imports of textile goods and other manufactured products rose.

Stimulated by growing commercial interests in the area, European governments began to push for a more permanent presence along the coast. During the first decades of the nineteenth century, the British established settlements along the Gold Coast and in Sierra Leone, where they set up agricultural plantations for freed slaves who had returned from the Western Hemisphere or had been liberated by British ships while en route to the Americas. A similar haven for ex-slaves was developed with the assistance of the United States in Liberia. The French occupied the area around the Senegal River near Cape Verde, where they attempted to develop peanut plantations.

The growing European presence in West Africa led to the emergence of a new class of Africans educated in Western culture and often employed by Europeans. Many became Christians, and some studied in European or American universities. At the same time, the European presence inevitably led to increasing tensions with African governments in the area. Most African states, especially those with a fairly high degree of political integration, were able to maintain their independence from this creeping European encroachment, called "informal empire" by some historians, but the prospects for the future were ominous. When local groups attempted to organize to protect their interests, the British stepped in and annexed the coastal states as the British colony of Gold Coast in 1874. At about the same time, the British extended an informal protectorate over warring ethnic groups in the Niger delta (see Map 20.2).

IMPERIALIST SHADOW OVER THE NILE

A similar process was under way in the Nile valley. There had long been interest in shortening the trade route to the East by digging a canal across the low, swampy isthmus separating the Mediterranean from the Red Sea. At the end of the eighteenth century, Napoleon planned a military takeover of Egypt to cement French power in the eastern Mediterranean and open a faster route to India.

Napoleon's plan proved abortive. French troops landed in Egypt in 1798 and destroyed the ramshackle Mamluk regime in Cairo, but the British counterattacked, destroying the French fleet and eventually forcing the French to evacuate in disorder. The British restored the Mamluks to power, but in 1805, Muhammad Ali, an Ottoman army officer of either Turkish or Albanian extraction, seized control.

During the next three decades, Muhammad Ali introduced a series of reforms to bring Egypt into the modern world. He modernized the army, set up a public educational system (supplementing the traditional religious education provided in Muslim schools), and sponsored the creation of a small industrial sector producing refined sugar, textiles, munitions, and even ships. Muhammad Ali also extended Egyptian authority southward into the Sudan and across the Sinai peninsula into Arabia, Syria, and northern Iraq and even briefly threatened to seize Istanbul itself. To prevent the possible collapse of the Ottoman Empire, the British and the French recognized Muhammad Ali as the hereditary pasha (later to be known as the *khedive*) of Egypt under the loose authority of the Ottoman government.

The growing economic importance of the Nile valley, along with the development of steam navigation, made the heretofore visionary plans for a Suez canal more urgent. In 1854, the French entrepreneur Ferdinand de Lesseps signed a contract to begin construction of the canal, and it was completed in 1869. The project brought little immediate benefit to Egypt, however. The construction not only cost thousands of lives but also left the Egyptian government deep in debt, forcing it to depend increasingly on foreign financial support. When an army revolt against growing foreign influence broke out in 1881, the British stepped in to protect their investment (they had bought Egypt's canal company shares in 1875) and establish an informal protectorate that would last until World War I.

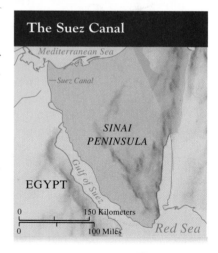

The Suez Canal

Rising discontent in the Sudan added to Egypt's growing internal problems. In 1881, the Muslim cleric Muhammad Ahmad, known as the Mahdi (in Arabic, the "rightly guided one"), led a religious revolt that brought much of the upper Nile under his control. The famous British general Charles Gordon led a military force to Khartoum to restore Egyptian authority, but his besieged army was captured in 1885 by the Mahdi's troops, thirty-six hours before

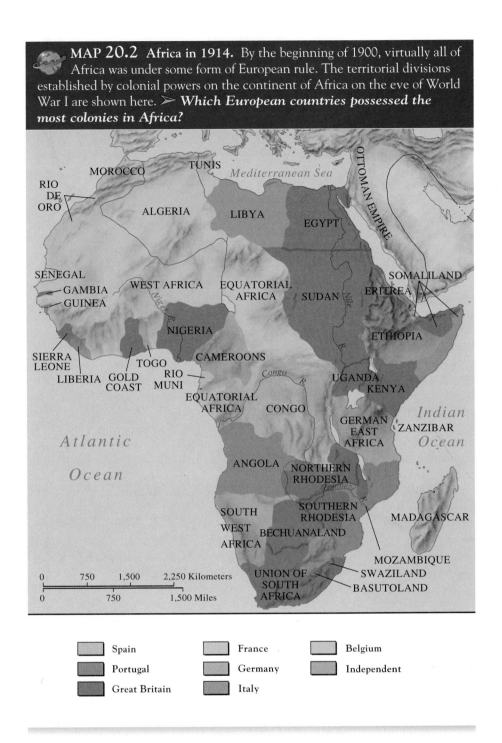

Spain

France

Belgium

Portugal

Germany

Independent

Great Britain

Italy

a British rescue mission reached Khartoum. Gordon himself died in the battle, which became one of the most dramatic news stories of the last quarter of the century.

The weakening of Turkish rule in the Nile valley had a parallel farther to the west, where local viceroys in Tripoli, Tunis, and Algiers had begun to establish their autonomy. In 1830, the French, on the pretext of protecting European shipping in the Mediterranean from pirates, seized the area surrounding Algiers and integrated it into the French Empire. In 1881, the French imposed a protectorate on neighboring Tunisia. Only Tripoli and Cyrenaica

(the Ottoman provinces that comprise modern Libya) remained under Turkish rule until the Italians took them in 1911–1912.

ARAB MERCHANTS AND EUROPEAN MISSIONARIES IN EAST AFRICA

As always, events in East Africa followed their own distinctive pattern of development. Whereas the Atlantic slave trade was in decline, demand for slaves was increasing on the other side of the continent due to the growth of plantation agriculture in the region and on the islands off the coast. The French introduced sugar to the island of Réunion early in the century, and plantations of cloves (introduced from the Moluccas in the eighteenth century) were established under Omani Arab ownership on the island of Zanzibar. Zanzibar itself became the major shipping port along the entire east coast during the early nineteenth century, and the sultan of Oman, who had reasserted Arab suzerainty over the region in the aftermath of the collapse of Portuguese authority, established his capital at Zanzibar in 1840.

The tenacity of the slave trade in East Africa—Zanzibar had now become the largest slave market in Africa—was undoubtedly a major reason for the rise of Western interest and Christian missionary activity in the region during the middle of the century. The most renowned missionary was the Scottish doctor David Livingstone, who arrived in Africa in 1841. Because Livingstone spent much of his time exploring the interior of the continent, discovering Victoria Falls in the process, he was occasionally criticized for being more explorer than missionary. But Livingstone was convinced that it was his divinely appointed task to bring Christianity to the far reaches of the continent, and his passionate opposition to slavery did far more to win public support for the abolitionist cause than did the efforts of any other figure of his generation. Public outcries provoked the British to redouble their efforts to bring the slave trade in East Africa to an end, and in 1873, the slave market at Zanzibar was finally closed as the result of pressure from London. Shortly before, Livingstone had died of illness in Central Africa, but some of his followers brought his body to the coast for burial.

BANTUS, BOERS, AND BRITISH IN THE SOUTH

Nowhere in Africa did the European presence grow more rapidly than in the south. During the eighteenth century, the Boers, Afrikaans-speaking farmers descended from the original Dutch settlers of the Cape Colony, began to migrate eastward. After the British seized control of the cape from the Dutch during the Napoleonic Wars, the Boers' eastward migration intensified, culminating in the Great Trek of the mid-1830s. In part, the Boers' departure was provoked by the different attitude of the British to the native population. Slavery was abolished in the British Empire in 1834, and the British government was generally more sympathetic to the rights of the local African population than were the Afrikaners, many of whom believed that white superiority was ordained by God and fled from British rule to control their own destiny. Eventually the Boers formed their own independent republics—the Orange Free State and the South African Republic (usually called the Transvaal; see Map 20.3).

Although the Boer occupation of the eastern territory was initially facilitated by internecine warfare among the

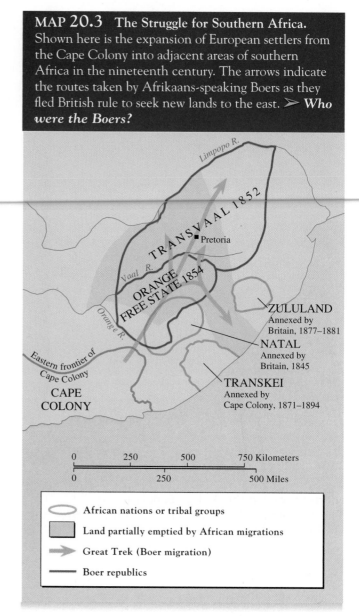

MAP 20.3 The Struggle for Southern Africa. Shown here is the expansion of European settlers from the Cape Colony into adjacent areas of southern Africa in the nineteenth century. The arrows indicate the routes taken by Afrikaans-speaking Boers as they fled British rule to seek new lands to the east. ➤ **Who were the Boers?**

local inhabitants of the region, the new settlers met some resistance. In the early nineteenth century, the Zulus, a Bantu people led by a talented ruler named Shaka, engaged in a series of wars with the Europeans that ended only when Shaka was overthrown. Ultimately most of the black Africans in the Boer republics were confined to reservations.

THE SCRAMBLE FOR AFRICA

At the beginning of the 1880s, most of Africa was still independent. European rule was limited to the fringes of the continent, such as Algeria, the Gold Coast, and South Africa. Other areas like Egypt, lower Nigeria, Senegal, and Mozambique were under various forms of loose protectorate. But the pace of European penetration was accelerating, and the constraints that had limited European rapaciousness were fast disappearing.

The scramble began in the mid-1880s, when several European states, including Belgium, France, Germany, Great Britain, and Portugal, engaged in a feeding frenzy to seize a piece of African territory before the carcass had been picked clean. By 1900, virtually all of the continent had been placed under some form of European rule. The British had consolidated their authority over the Nile valley and seized additional territories in East Africa (see Map 20.2 on p. 439). The French retaliated by advancing eastward from Senegal into the central Sahara. They also occupied the island of Madagascar and other territories in West and Central Africa. In between, the Germans claimed the hinterland opposite Zanzibar, as well as coastal strips in West and Southwest Africa north of the cape, and King Leopold II of Belgium claimed the Congo. Eventually Italy entered the contest and seized modern Libya and some of the Somali coast.

What had happened to spark the sudden imperialist hysteria that brought an end to African independence? Clearly, the level of trade between Europe and Africa was not sufficient to justify the risks and the expense of conquest. More important than economic interests were the intensified rivalries among the European states that led them to engage in imperialist takeovers out of fear that if they did not, another state might do so, leaving them at a disadvantage. In the most famous example, the British solidified their control over the entire Nile valley to protect the Suez Canal from seizure by the French.

Another consideration might be called the "missionary factor," as European missionary interests lobbied with their governments for colonial takeovers to facilitate their efforts to convert the African population to Christianity. The concept of social Darwinism and the "white man's burden" persuaded many that it was in the interests of the African people, as well as their conquerors, to be introduced more rapidly to the benefits of Western civilization (see the box on p. 442). Even David Livingstone had become convinced that missionary work and economic development had to go hand in hand, pleading to his fellow Europeans to introduce the "three Cs" (Christianity, commerce, and civilization) to the continent. How much easier such a task would be if African peoples were under benevolent European rule!

There were more prosaic reasons as well. Advances in Western technology and European superiority in firearms made it easier than ever for a small European force to defeat superior numbers. Furthermore, life expectancy for Europeans living in Africa had improved. With the discovery that quinine (extracted from the bark of the cinchona tree) could provide partial immunity from the ravages of malaria, the mortality rate for Europeans living in Africa dropped dramatically in the 1840s. By the end of the century, European residents in tropical Africa faced only slightly higher risks of death by disease than individuals living in Europe.

Under these circumstances, King Leopold of Belgium used missionary activities as an excuse to claim vast ter-

IMPERIALISM IN AFRICA

Dutch abolish slave trade in Africa	1795
Napoleonic invasion of Egypt	1798
Slave trade declared illegal in Great Britain	1808
Boers' Great Trek in southern Africa	1830s
French seize Algeria	1830
Sultan of Oman establishes capital at Zanzibar	1840
David Livingstone arrives in Africa	1841
Slavery abolished in the United States	1863
Completion of Suez Canal	1869
Zanzibar slave market closed	1873
British establish Gold Coast colony	1874
British establish informal protectorate over Egypt	1881
Berlin Conference on Africa	1884
Charles Gordon killed at Khartoum	1885
Confrontation at Fashoda	1898
Boer War	1899–1902
Union of South Africa established	1910

ritories in the Congo River basin (Belgium, he said, as "a small country, with a small people," needed a colony to enhance its image).[4] This set off a desperate race among European nations to stake claims throughout sub-Saharan Africa. Leopold ended up with the territories south of the Congo River, while France occupied areas to the north (Leopold bequeathed the Congo to Belgium on his death). Meanwhile, on the eastern side of the continent, Germany annexed the colony of Tanganyika. To avert the possibility of violent clashes among the great powers, the German chancellor, Otto von Bismarck, convened a conference in Berlin in 1884 to set ground rules for future annexations of African territory by European nations. Like the famous Open Door Notes fifteen years later (see Chapter 21), the conference combined high-minded resolutions with a hardheaded recognition of practical interests. The delegates called for free commerce in the Congo and along the Niger River as well as for further efforts to end the slave trade. At the same time, the participants recognized the inevitability of the imperialist dynamic, agreeing only that future annexations of African territory should not be given international recognition until effective occupation had been demonstrated. No African delegates were present.

The Berlin Conference had been convened to avert war and reduce tensions among European nations competing for the spoils of Africa. During the next few years, African

WHITE MAN'S BURDEN,
BLACK MAN'S SORROW

*O*ne of the justifications for modern imperialism was the notion that the allegedly "more advanced" white peoples had the moral responsibility to raise ignorant native peoples to a higher level of civilization. Few captured this notion better than the British poet Rudyard Kipling (1865–1936) in his famous poem The White Man's Burden. His appeal, directed to the United States, became one of the most famous set of verses in the English-speaking world.

That sense of moral responsibility, however, was often misplaced, or even worse, laced with hypocrisy. All too often, the consequences of imperial rule were detrimental to everyone living under colonial authority. Few observers described the destructive effects of Western imperialism on the African people as well as Edward Morel, a British journalist whose book The Black Man's Burden pointed out some of the more harmful aspects of colonialism in the Belgian Congo.

RUDYARD KIPLING, *THE WHITE MAN'S BURDEN*

Take up the White Man's burden—
Send forth the best ye breed—
Go bind your sons to exile
To serve your captives' need;
To wait in heavy harness,
On fluttered folk and wild—
Your new-caught sullen peoples,
Half-devil and half-child.

Take up the White Man's burden—
In patience to abide,
To veil the threat of terror
And check the show of pride;
By open speech and simple,
An hundred times made plain
To seek another's profit,
And work another's gain.

Take up the White Man's burden—
The savage wars of peace—
Fill full the mouth of Famine
And bid the sickness cease;
And when your goal is nearest
The end for others sought,
Watch Sloth and heathen Folly
Bring all your hopes to nought.

EDMUND MOREL, *THE BLACK MAN'S BURDEN*

It is [the Africans] who carry the "Black man's burden." They have not withered away before the white man's occupation. Indeed . . . Africa has ultimately absorbed within itself every Caucasian and, for that matter, every Semitic invader, too. In hewing out for himself a fixed abode in Africa, the white man has massacred the African in heaps. The African has survived, and it is well for the white settlers that he has. . . .

What the partial occupation of his soil by the white man has failed to do; what the mapping out of European political "spheres of influence" has failed to do; what the Maxim and the rifle, the slave gang, labour in the bowels of the earth and the lash, have failed to do; what imported measles, smallpox and syphilis have failed to do; whatever the overseas slave trade failed to do; the power of modern capitalistic exploitation, assisted by modern engines of destruction, may yet succeed in accomplishing.

For from the evils of the latter, scientifically applied and enforced, there is no escape for the African. Its destructive effects are not spasmodic; they are permanent. In its permanence resides its fatal consequences. It kills not the body merely, but the soul. It breaks the spirit. It attacks the African at every turn, from every point of vantage. It wrecks his polity, uproots him from the land, invades his family life, destroys his natural pursuits and occupations, claims his whole time, enslaves him in his own home.

---

territories were annexed without provoking a major confrontation between the Western powers, but in the late 1890s, Britain and France reached the brink of conflict at Fashoda, a small town on the Nile River in the Sudan. The French had been advancing eastward across the Sahara with the transparent objective of controlling the regions around the upper Nile. In 1898, British and Egyptian troops seized the Sudan from successors of the Mahdi and then marched southward to head off the French. After a tense face-off at Fashoda, the French government backed down, and British authority over the area was secured.

Ironically, the only major clash between Europeans over Africa took place in southern Africa, where competition among the powers was almost nonexistent. The discovery of gold and diamonds in the Boer republic of the Transvaal was the source of the problem. Clashes between the Afrikaner population and foreign (mainly British) miners and developers led to an attempt by Cecil Rhodes, prime minister of the Cape Colony and a prominent entrepreneur in the area, to subvert the Transvaal and bring it under British rule. In 1899, the so-called Boer War broke out between Britain and the Transvaal, which was backed by its fellow republic, the Orange Free State. Guerrilla resistance by the Boers was fierce, but the vastly superior forces of the British were able to prevail by 1902. To compensate the defeated Afrikaner population for the loss of independence, the British government agreed that only whites would vote in the now essentially self-governing colony. The Boers were placated, but the brutalities committed during the war (the British introduced an institution later to be known as the concentration camp) created bitterness on both sides that continued to fester through future decades.

 ## THE COLONIAL SYSTEM

Now that they had control of most of the world, what did the colonial powers do with it? As we have seen, their primary objective was to exploit the natural resources of the subject areas and to open up markets for manufactured goods and capital investment from the mother country. In some cases, that goal could be realized in cooperation with local political elites, whose loyalty could be earned, or purchased, by economic rewards or by confirming them in their positions of authority and status in a new colonial setting. Sometimes, however, this policy of indirect rule was not feasible because local leaders refused to cooperate with their colonial masters or even actively resisted the foreign conquest. In such cases, the local elites were removed from power and replaced with a new set of officials recruited from the mother country.

In general, the societies most likely to actively resist colonial conquest were those with a long tradition of national cohesion and independence, such as China, Burma, and Vietnam in Asia and the African Muslim states in northern Nigeria and Morocco. In those areas, the colonial powers tended to dispense with local collaborators and govern directly. In parts of Africa, the Indian subcontinent, and the Malay peninsula, where the local authorities, for whatever reason, were willing to collaborate with the imperialist powers, indirect rule was more common.

The Philosophy of Colonialism

To justify their rule, the colonial powers appealed in part to the time-honored maxim of "might makes right." By the end of the nineteenth century, that attitude received pseudoscientific validity from the concept of social Darwinism, which maintained that only societies that moved aggressively to adapt to changing circumstances would

REVERE THE CONQUERING HEROES. European colonial officials were quick to place themselves at the top of the political and social hierarchy in their conquered territories. Here British officials accept the submission of the Ashanti king and queen, according to African custom, in 1896.

Mansell/Time Life Pictures/Getty Images

survive and prosper in a world governed by the Darwinian law of "survival of the fittest."

Some people, however, were uncomfortable with such a brutal view of the law of nature and sought a moral justification that appeared to benefit the victim. Here again, as we have seen, the concept of social Darwinism pointed the way. By bringing the benefits of Western democracy, capitalism, and Christianity to the feudalistic and tradition-ridden societies of Africa and Asia, the colonial powers were enabling primitive peoples to adapt to the challenges of the modern world. Buttressed by such comforting theories, sensitive Western minds could ignore the brutal aspects of colonialism and persuade themselves that in the long run, the results would be beneficial for both sides. Few were as adept at describing the "civilizing mission" of colonialism as the French administrator and twice governor-general of French Indochina Albert Sarraut. While admitting that colonialism was originally an "act of force" undertaken for commercial profit, he insisted that by redistributing the wealth of the earth, the colonial process would result in a better life for all: "Is it just, is it legitimate that such [an uneven distribution of resources] should be indefinitely prolonged? . . . No! . . . Humanity is distributed throughout the globe. No race, no people has the right or power to isolate itself egotistically from the movements and necessities of universal life."[5]

But what about the possibility that historically and culturally the societies of Asia and Africa were fundamentally different from those of the West and could not, or would not, be persuaded to transform themselves along Western lines? In that case, a policy of cultural transformation could not be expected to succeed and could even lead to disaster.

In fact, colonial theorists never decided this issue one way or the other. The French, who were most inclined to philosophize about the problem, adopted the terms *assimilation* (which implied an effort to transform colonial societies in the Western image) and *association* (implying collaboration with local elites while leaving local traditions alone) to describe the two alternatives and then proceeded to vacillate between them. French policy in Indochina, for example, began as one of association but switched to assimilation under pressure from those who felt that colonial powers owed a debt to their subject peoples. But assimilation (which in any case was never accepted as feasible or desirable by many colonial officials) aroused resentment among the local population, many of whom opposed the destruction of their native traditions. In the end, the French abandoned the attempt to justify their presence and fell back on a policy of ruling by force of arms.

Other colonial powers had little interest in the issue. The British, whether out of a sense of pragmatism or of racial superiority, refused to entertain the possibility of assimilation and treated their subject peoples as culturally and racially distinct.

BLENDING EAST AND WEST. After establishing colonies throughout the continents of Africa and Asia, the British began to erect monumental buildings to demonstrate their power and authority. They built stately mansions, sumptuous hotels, opulent government buildings, and especially grandiose railroad stations, railroads being the greatest capitalist enterprise in the colonies. In an effort to incorporate indigenous styles in their colonial architecture, the British often combined arched colonnades with domed and canopied turrets such as those that appear on this railroad station, erected in 1911 in Kuala Lumpur, on the Malay peninsula.

Colonialism in Action

In practice, colonialism in India, Southeast Asia, and Africa exhibited many similarities but also some differences. Some of these variations can be traced to political or social differences among the colonial powers themselves. The French, for example, often tried to impose a centralized administrative system on their colonies that mirrored the system in use in France, while the British sometimes attempted to transform local aristocrats into the equivalent of the landed gentry at home in Britain. Other differences stemmed from conditions in the colonies themselves.

INDIA UNDER THE BRITISH RAJ

By 1800, the once glorious empire of the Mughals had been reduced by British military power to a shadow of its former greatness. During the next few decades, the British sought to consolidate their control over the Indian subcontinent, expanding from their base areas along the coast into the interior. Some territories were taken over directly, first by the

Courtesy of William J. Duiker

➤ GATEWAY TO INDIA?   Built in the Roman imperial style by the British to commemorate the visit to India of King George V and Queen Mary in 1911, the Gateway of India was erected at the water's edge in the harbor of Bombay, India's greatest port city. For thousands of British citizens arriving in India, the Gateway of India was the first view of their new home and a symbol of the power and majesty of the British raj. Only a few dozen yards away was the luxurious Taj Mahal Hotel. Constructed in the popular Anglo-Indian style, it was built to house European visitors upon their arrival to India.

East India Company and later by the British crown; others were ruled indirectly through their local maharajas and rajas.

Not all of the effects of British rule were bad. British governance over the subcontinent brought order and stability to a society that had been rent by civil war. By the early nineteenth century, British control had been consolidated and led to a relatively honest and efficient government that in many respects operated to the benefit of the average Indian. One of the benefits of the period was the heightened attention given to education. Through the efforts of the British administrator Thomas Babington Macaulay, a new school system was established to train the children of Indian elites, and the British civil service examination was introduced (see the box on p. 446). The instruction of young girls also expanded, with the primary purpose of making them better wives and mothers for the educated male population. The first Indian woman accepted to a Madras medical college, for example, was in 1875.

British rule also brought an end to some of the more inhumane aspects of Indian tradition. The practice of *sati* was outlawed, and widows were legally permitted to remarry. The British also attempted to put an end to the endemic brigandage (known as *thuggee*, which gave rise to the English word *thug*) that had plagued travelers in India since time immemorial. Railroads, the telegraph, and the postal service were introduced to India shortly after they appeared in Great Britain itself. Work began on the main highway from Calcutta to Delhi in 1839 (see Map 20.4), and the first rail network was opened in 1853.

But the Indian people paid a high price for the peace and stability brought by the British raj (from the Indian *raja,* or prince). Perhaps the most flagrant cost was economic. While British entrepreneurs and a small percentage of the Indian population attached to the imperial system reaped financial benefits from British rule, it brought hardship to millions of others in both the cities and the rural areas. The introduction of British textiles put thousands of Bengali women out of work and severely damaged the local textile industry.

In rural areas, the British introduced the *zamindar* system (see Chapter 15) in the misguided expectation that it would both facilitate the collection of agricultural taxes and create a new landed gentry, who could, as in Britain, become the conservative foundation of imperial rule. But the local gentry took advantage of this new authority to increase taxes and force the less fortunate peasants to become tenants or lose their land entirely. British officials also made few efforts during the nineteenth century to introduce democratic institutions or values to the Indian people. As one senior political figure remarked in Parliament in 1898, democratic institutions "can no more be

INDIAN IN BLOOD, ENGLISH IN TASTE AND INTELLECT

Thomas Babington Macaulay (1800–1859) was named a member of the Supreme Council of India in the early 1830s. In that capacity, he was responsible for drawing up a new educational policy for British subjects in the area. In his Minute on Education, he considered the claims of English and various local languages to become the vehicle for educational training and decided in favor of the former. It is better, he argued, to teach Indian elites about Western civilization so as "to form a class who may be interpreters between us and the millions whom we govern; a class of persons, Indian in blood and color, but English in taste, in opinions, in morals, and in intellect." Later Macaulay became a prominent historian. The debate over the relative benefits of English and the various Indian languages continues today.

THOMAS BABINGTON MACAULAY, MINUTE ON EDUCATION

We have a fund to be employed as government shall direct for the intellectual improvement of the people of this country. The simple question is, what is the most useful way of employing it?

All parties seem to be agreed on one point, that the dialects commonly spoken among the natives of this part of India contain neither literary or scientific information, and are, moreover so poor and rude that, until they are enriched from some other quarter, it will not be easy to translate any valuable work into them. . . .

What, then, shall the language [of education] be? One half of the Committee maintain that it should be the English. The other half strongly recommend the Arabic and Sanskrit. The whole question seems to me to be, which language is the best worth knowing?

I have no knowledge of either Sanskrit or Arabic—but I have done what I could to form a correct estimate of their value. I have read translations of the most celebrated Arabic and Sanskrit works. I have conversed both here and at home with men distinguished by their proficiency in the Eastern tongues. I am quite ready to take the Oriental learning at the valuation of the Orientalists themselves. I have never found one among them who could deny that a single shelf of a good European library was worth the whole native literature of India and Arabia. . . .

It is, I believe, no exaggeration to say, that all the historical information which has been collected from all the books written in the Sanskrit language is less valuable than what may be found in the most paltry abridgments used at preparatory schools in England. In every branch of physical or moral philosophy the relative position of the two nations is nearly the same.

---

carried to India by Englishmen . . . than they can carry ice in their luggage."[6]

British colonialism was also remiss in bringing the benefits of modern science and technology to India. Some limited forms of industrialization took place, notably in the manufacturing of textiles and jute (used in making rope). The first textile mill opened in 1856. Seventy years later, there were eighty mills in the city of Bombay alone. Nevertheless, the lack of local capital and the advantages given to British imports prevented the emergence of other vital new commercial and manufacturing operations.

Foreign rule also had a psychological effect on the Indian people. Although many British colonial officials sincerely tried to improve the lot of the people under their charge, British arrogance and contempt for native tradition cut deeply into the pride of many Indians, especially those of high caste, who were accustomed to a position of superior status in India. Educated Indians trained in the Anglo-Indian school system for a career in the civil service, as well as Eurasians born to mixed marriages, often imitated the behavior and dress of their rulers, speaking English, eating Western food, and taking up European leisure activities, but many rightfully wondered where their true cultural loyalties lay.

COLONIAL REGIMES IN SOUTHEAST ASIA

In Southeast Asia, economic profit was the immediate and primary aim of colonial enterprise. For that purpose, colonial powers tried wherever possible to work with local elites to facilitate the exploitation of natural resources. Indirect rule reduced the cost of training European administrators and had a less corrosive impact on the local culture. In the Dutch East Indies, for example, officials of the Dutch East India Company (VOC) entrusted local administration to the indigenous landed aristocracy, who maintained law and order and collected taxes in return for a payment from the VOC (see the box on p. 448). The British followed a similar practice in Malaya. While establishing direct rule over the crucial commercial centers of Singapore and Malacca, the British allowed local Muslim rulers to maintain princely power in the interior of the peninsula.

Indirect rule, however convenient and inexpensive, was not always feasible. In some instances, local resistance to the colonial conquest made such a policy impossible. In Burma, the staunch opposition of the monarchy and other traditionalist forces caused the British to abolish the monarchy and administer the country directly through

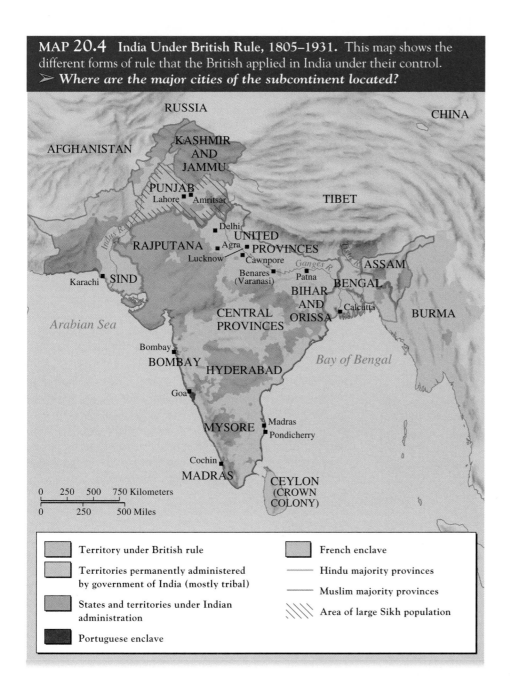

MAP 20.4 India Under British Rule, 1805–1931. This map shows the different forms of rule that the British applied in India under their control.
➢ *Where are the major cities of the subcontinent located?*

Legend:
- Territory under British rule
- Territories permanently administered by government of India (mostly tribal)
- States and territories under Indian administration
- Portuguese enclave
- French enclave
- Hindu majority provinces
- Muslim majority provinces
- Area of large Sikh population

their colonial government in India. In Indochina, the French used both direct and indirect means. They imposed direct rule on the southern provinces in the Mekong delta but governed the north as a protectorate, with the emperor retaining titular authority from his palace in Huê. The French adopted a similar policy in Cambodia and Laos, where local rulers were left in charge with French advisers to counsel them.

Whatever method was used, colonial regimes in Southeast Asia, as elsewhere, were slow to create democratic institutions. The first legislative councils and assemblies were composed almost exclusively of European residents in the colony. The first representatives from the indigenous population were wealthy and conservative in their political views. When Southeast Asians complained, colonial officials gradually and reluctantly began to broaden the franchise. Albert Sarraut advised patience in awaiting the full benefits of colonial policy: "I will treat you like my younger brothers, but do not forget that I am the older brother. I will slowly give you the dignity of humanity."[7]

Colonial officials were also slow to adopt educational reforms. Although the introduction of Western education was one of the justifications of colonialism, colonial officials soon discovered that educating native elites could backfire. Often there were few jobs for highly trained lawyers, engineers, and architects in colonial societies, leading to the threat of an indigestible mass of unemployed

The Effects of Dutch Colonialism in Java

Eduard Douwes Dekker was a Dutch colonial official who served in the East Indies for nearly twenty years. In 1860, he published a critique of the Dutch colonial system that had an impact in the Netherlands similar to that of Harriet Beecher Stowe's Uncle Tom's Cabin *in the United States. In the following excerpt from his book* Max Havelaar, or Coffee Auctions of the Dutch Trading Company, *Douwes Dekker described the system as it was applied on the island of Java, in the Indonesian archipelago.*

EDUARD DOUWES DEKKER, MAX HAVELAAR

The Javanese is by nature a husbandman; the ground whereon he is born, which gives much for little labor, allures him to it, and, above all things, he devotes his whole heart and soul to the cultivating of his rice fields, in which he is very clever. He grows up in the midst of his sawahs [rice fields] . . . ; when still very young, he accompanies his father to the field, where he helps him in his labor with plow and spade, in constructing dams and drains to irrigate his fields; he counts his years by harvests; he estimates time by the color of the blades in his field; he is at home amongst the companions who cut paddy with him; he chooses his wife amongst the girls of the dessah [village], who every evening tread the rice with joyous songs. The possession of a few buffaloes for plowing is the ideal of his dreams. The cultivation of rice is in Java what the vintage is in the Rhine provinces and in the south of France. But there came foreigners from the West, who made themselves masters of the country. They wished to profit by the fertility of the soil, and ordered the native to devote a part of his time and labor to the cultivation of other things which should produce higher profits in the markets of Europe. To persuade the lower orders to do so, they had only to follow a very simple policy. The Javanese obeys his chiefs; to win the chiefs, it was only necessary to give them a part of the gain,—and success was complete.

To be convinced of the success of that policy we need only consider the immense quantity of Javanese products sold in Holland; and we shall also be convinced of its injustice, for, if anybody should ask if the husbandman himself gets a reward in proportion to that quantity, then I must give a negative answer. The Government compels him to cultivate certain products on his ground; it punishes him if he sells what he has produced to any purchaser but itself; and it fixes the price actually paid. The expenses of transport to Europe through a privileged trading company are high; the money paid to the chiefs for encouragement increases the prime cost; and because the entire trade *must* produce profit, that profit cannot be got in any other way than by paying the Javanese just enough to keep him from starving, which would lessen the producing power of the nation.

---

intellectuals who would take out their frustrations on the colonial regime. As one French official noted in voicing his opposition to increasing the number of schools in Vietnam, educating the natives meant not "one coolie less, but one rebel more."

Colonial powers were equally reluctant to take up the "white man's burden" in the area of economic development. As we have seen, their primary goals were to secure a source of cheap raw materials and to maintain markets for manufactured goods. Such objectives would be undermined by the emergence of advanced industrial economies. So colonial policy concentrated on the export of raw materials—teakwood from Burma; rubber and tin from Malaya; spices, tea and coffee, and palm oil from the East Indies; and sugar and copra from the Philippines.

In some Southeast Asian colonial societies, a measure of industrial development did take place to meet the needs of the European population and local elites. Major manufacturing cities like Rangoon in lower Burma, Batavia on the island of Java, and Saigon in French Indochina grew rapidly. Although the local middle class benefited from the increased economic activity, most large industrial and commercial establishments were owned and managed by Europeans or, in some cases, by Indian or Chinese merchants.

Despite the growth of an urban economy, the vast majority of people in the colonial societies continued to farm the land. Many continued to live by subsistence agriculture, but the colonial policy of emphasizing cash crops for export also led to the creation of a form of plantation agriculture in which peasants were recruited to work as wage laborers on rubber and tea plantations owned by Europeans. To maintain a competitive edge, the plantation owners kept the wages of their workers at poverty level. Many plantation workers were "shanghaied" (the English term originated from the practice of recruiting laborers, often from the docks and streets of Shanghai, by unscrupulous means such as the use of force, alcohol, or drugs) to work on plantations, where conditions were often so inhumane that thousands died. High taxes, enacted by colonial governments to pay for administrative costs or improvements in the local infrastructure, were a heavy burden for poor peasants.

The situation was made even more difficult by the steady growth of the population. Peasants in Asia had always had large families on the assumption that a high proportion of their children would die in infancy. But improved sanitation and medical treatment resulted in lower rates of infant mortality and a staggering increase in population. The population of the island of Java, for example, increased from about a million in the precolonial era to about 40 million at the end of the nineteenth century. Under these conditions, the rural areas could no longer support the growing populations, and many young people fled to the cities to seek jobs in factories or shops. The migratory pattern gave rise to squatter settlements in the suburbs of the major cities.

As in India, colonial rule did bring some benefits to Southeast Asia. It led to the beginnings of a modern eco-nomic infrastructure and to what is sometimes called a "modernizing elite" dedicated to the creation of an advanced industrialized society. The development of an export market helped create an entrepreneurial class in rural areas. This happened, for example, on the outer islands of the Dutch East Indies (such as Borneo and Sumatra), where small growers of rubber trees, palm trees for oil, coffee, tea, and spices began to share in the profits of the colonial enterprise.

COLONIALISM IN AFRICA

Having seized Africa in what could almost be described as a fit of hysteria, the European powers had to decide what to do with it. With economic concerns relatively limited except for isolated areas like the gold mines in the Transvaal

Cultural Influences: East and West

When Europeans moved into Asia in the nineteenth century, some Asians began to imitate European customs for prestige or social advancement. Seen at left, for example, is a young Vietnamese during the 1920s dressed in Western sports clothes, learning to lift weights. Sometimes, however, the cultural influence went the other way. At right an English nabob, as European residents in India were often called, apes the manner of an Indian aristocrat, complete with the harem and hookah, the Indian water pipe. The paintings on the wall, however, are in the European style.

and copper deposits in the Belgian Congo, interest in Africa declined, and most European governments settled down to govern their new territories with the least effort and expense possible. In many cases, this meant a form of indirect rule similar to what the British used in the princely states in India. The British with their tradition of decentralized government at home were especially prone to adopt this approach.

In the minds of British administrators, the stated goal of indirect rule was to preserve African political traditions. The desire to limit cost and inconvenience was one reason for this approach, but it may also have been due to the conviction that Africans were inherently inferior to the white race and thus incapable of adopting European customs and institutions. In any event, indirect rule entailed relying to the greatest extent possible on existing political elites and institutions. Initially, in some areas, the British simply asked a local ruler to formally accept British authority and to fly the Union Jack over official buildings. Sometimes it was the Africans who did the bidding, as in the case of the African leaders in Cameroons who wrote to Queen Victoria:

> We *wish* to have your laws in our towns. We want to have every *fashion* altered; also we will do according to your Consul's *word*. Plenty wars here in our country. Plenty murder and plenty idol worshippers. Perhaps these *lines* of our writing will *look* to you as an *idle* tale.
>
> We have *spoken* to the English consul plenty times about having an English *government* here. We never have answer from you, so we wish to write you *ourselves*.[8]

Nigeria offers a typical example of British indirect rule. British officials maintained the central administration, but local authority was assigned to native chiefs, with British district officers serving as intermediaries with the central administration. Where a local aristocracy did not exist, the British assigned administrative responsibility to clan heads from communities in the vicinity. The local authorities were expected to maintain law and order and to collect taxes from the native population. As a general rule, indigenous customs were left undisturbed, although the institution of slavery was abolished. A dual legal system was instituted that applied African laws to Africans and European laws to foreigners.

One advantage of such an administrative system was that it did not severely disrupt local customs and institutions. Nevertheless, it had several undesirable consequences. In the first place, it was essentially a fraud, since all major decisions were made by the British administrators while the native authorities served primarily as the means of enforcing decisions. Moreover, indirect rule served to perpetuate the autocratic system often in use prior to colonial takeover.

The situation was somewhat different in East Africa, especially in Kenya, which had a relatively large European population attracted by the temperate climate in the central highlands. The local government had encouraged white settlers to migrate to the area as a means of promoting economic development and encouraging financial self-sufficiency. To attract Europeans, fertile farmlands in the central highlands were reserved for European settlement, while, as in South Africa, specified reserve lands were set aside for Africans. The presence of a substantial European minority (although, in fact, they represented only about one percent of the entire population) had an impact on Kenya's political development. The white settlers actively sought self-government and dominion status similar to that granted to such former British possessions as Canada and Australia. The British government, however, was not willing to run the risk of provoking racial tensions with the African majority and agreed only to establish separate government organs for the European and African populations.

The British used a different system in southern Africa, where there was a high percentage of European settlers. The situation was further complicated by the division between English-speaking and Afrikaner elements within the European population. In 1910, the British agreed to the creation of the independent Union of South Africa, which combined the old Cape Colony and Natal with the Boer republics. The new union adopted a representative government, but only for the European population, while the African reserves of Basutoland (now Lesotho), Bechuanaland (now Botswana), and Swaziland were subordinated directly to the crown. The union was now free to manage its own domestic affairs and possessed considerable autonomy in foreign relations. Formal British rule was also extended to the remaining lands south of the Zambezi River, which were eventually divided into the territories of Northern and Southern Rhodesia. Southern Rhodesia attracted many British immigrants, and in 1922, after a popular referendum, it became a crown colony (see the box on p. 451).

Most other European nations governed their African possessions through a form of direct rule. The prototype was the French system, which reflected the centralized administrative system introduced in France itself by Napoleon. As in the British colonies, at the top of the pyramid was a French official, usually known as the governor-general, who was appointed from Paris and governed with the aid of a bureaucracy in the capital city. At the provincial level, French commissioners were assigned to deal with local administrators, but the latter were required to be conversant in French and could be transferred to a new position at the needs of the central government.

Moreover, the French ideal was to assimilate their African subjects into French culture rather than preserving their native traditions. Africans were eligible to run for office and to serve in the French National Assembly, and a few were appointed to high positions in the colonial administration. Such policies reflected the relative absence of racist attitudes in French society, as well as the conviction among the French of the superiority of Gallic culture and their revolutionary belief in the universality of human nature.

THE NDEBELE REBELLION

s British forces advanced northward from the Cape Colony toward the Zambezi River in the 1890s, they overran the Ndebele people, who occupied rich lands in the region near the site of the ruins of Great Zimbabwe. Angered by British brutality, Ndebele warriors revolted in 1896 to throw off their oppressors. Despite the great superiority in numbers of the Ndebele, British units possessed the feared Maxim gun, which mowed down African attackers by the hundreds. Faced with defeat, the Ndebele king, Lobengula, fled into the hills and committed suicide. In the following account, a survivor describes the conflict.

NDANSI KUMALO, A PERSONAL ACCOUNT

We surrendered to the white people and were told to go back to our homes and live our usual lives and attend to our crops. But the white men sent native police who did abominable things; they were cruel and assaulted a lot of our people and helped themselves to our cattle and goats. . . . They interfered with our wives and molested them. . . . We thought it best to fight and die rather than bear it. . . .

We knew that we had very little chance because their weapons were so much superior to ours. But we meant to fight to the last, feeling that even if we could not beat them we might at least kill a few of them and so have some sort of revenge. . . .

I remember a fight in the Matoppos when we charged the white men. There were some hundreds of us; the white men also were many. We charged them at close quarters: we thought we had a good chance to kill them but the Maxims were too much for us. . . . Many of our people were killed in this fight. . . .

We were still fighting when we heard that [Cecil] Rhodes was coming and wanted to make peace with us. It was best to come to terms he said, and not go shedding blood like this on both sides. . . . So peace was made. Many of our people had been killed, and now we began to die of starvation; and then came the rinderpest and the cattle that were still left to us perished. We could not help thinking that all these dreadful things were brought by the white people.

The establishment of colonial rule often had the effect of reducing the rights and the status of women in Africa. African women had traditionally benefited from the prestige of matrilineal systems and were empowered by their traditional role as the primary agricultural producer in their community. Under colonialism, European settlers not only took the best land for themselves but also, in introducing new agricultural techniques, tended to deal exclusively with males, encouraging the latter to develop lucrative cash crops, while women were restricted to traditional farming methods. Whereas African men applied chemical fertilizer to the fields, women used manure. While men began to use bicycles, and eventually trucks, to transport goods, women still carried their goods on their heads, a practice that continues today.

THE EMERGENCE OF ANTICOLONIALISM

Thus far we have looked at the colonial experience primarily from the point of view of the colonial powers. Equally important is the way the subject peoples reacted to the experience. From the perspective of nearly half a century, it seems clear that their primary response was to turn to nationalism.

As we have seen, nationalism refers to a state of mind rising out of an awareness of being part of a community that possesses common institutions, traditions, language, and customs. Few nations in the world today meet such criteria. Most modern states contain a variety of ethnic, religious, and linguistic communities, each with its own sense of cultural and national identity. Should Canada, for example, which includes peoples of French, English, and Native American heritage, be considered a nation? Another question is how nationalism differs from other forms of tribal, religious, or linguistic affiliation. Should every group that resists assimilation into a larger cultural unity be called nationalist?

Such questions complicate the study of nationalism even in Europe and North America and make agreement on a definition elusive. They create even greater dilemmas in discussing Asia and Africa, where most societies are deeply divided by ethnic, linguistic, and religious differences and the very term *nationalism* is a foreign phenomenon imported from the West. Prior to the colonial era, most traditional societies in Africa and Asia were formed on the basis of religious beliefs, tribal loyalties, or devotion to hereditary monarchies.

The advent of European colonialism brought the consciousness of modern nationhood to many of the societies of Asia and Africa. The creation of European colonies with defined borders and a powerful central government led to the weakening of tribal and village ties and a significant reorientation in the individual's sense of political identity. The introduction of Western ideas of citizenship and representative government produced a new sense of participation in the affairs of government. At the same time, the appearance of a new elite class based not on hereditary privilege or religious sanction but on alleged racial or cultural superiority aroused a shared sense of resentment among the subject peoples who felt a common commitment to the creation of an independent society. By the first quarter of the twentieth century, political movements dedicated to the overthrow of colonial rule had arisen throughout much of the non-Western world.

Traditional Resistance: A Precursor to Nationalism

The beginnings of modern nationalism can be found in the initial resistance by the indigenous peoples to the colonial conquest. Although, strictly speaking, such resistance was not "nationalist" because it was essentially motivated by the desire to defend traditional institutions, it did reflect a primitive concept of nationhood in that it aimed at protecting the homeland from the invader; later patriotic groups have often hailed early resistance movements as the precursors of twentieth-century nationalist movements. Thus traditional resistance to colonial conquest may logically be viewed as the first stage in the development of modern nationalism.

Such resistance took various forms. For the most part, it was led by the existing ruling class. In the Ashanti kingdom in Africa and in Burma and Vietnam in Southeast Asia, resistance to Western domination was initially directed by the imperial courts. In some cases, traditionalists continued to oppose foreign conquest even after resistance had collapsed at the center. After the decrepit monarchy in Vietnam had bowed to French pressure, a number of civilian and military officials set up an organization called Can Vuong (literally "save the king") and continued their resistance without imperial sanction.

The first stirrings of nationalism in India took place in the early nineteenth century with the search for a renewed sense of cultural identity. In 1828, Ram Mohan Roy, a brahmin from Bengal, founded the Brahmo Samaj (Society of Brahma). Roy probably had no intention of promoting Indian national independence but created the new organization as a means of helping his fellow religionists defend the Hindu religion against verbal attacks by their British acquaintances.

Sometimes traditional resistance to Western penetration went beyond elite circles. Most commonly, it appeared in the form of peasant revolts. Rural rebellions were not uncommon in traditional Asian societies as a means of expressing peasant discontent with high taxes, official corruption, rising rural debt, and famine in the countryside. Under colonialism, rural conditions often deteriorated as population density increased and peasants were driven off the land to make way for plantation agriculture. Angry peasants then vented their frustration at the foreign invaders. For example, in Burma, the Buddhist monk Saya San led a peasant uprising against the British many years after they had completed their takeover.

Sometimes the resentment had a religious basis, as in the Sudan, where the revolt led by the Mahdi had strong Islamic overtones, although it was initially provoked by Turkish misrule in Egypt. More significant than Roy's Brahmo Samaj in its impact on British policy was the famous Sepoy Rebellion of 1857 in India. The sepoys (derived from *sipahi*, a Turkish word meaning horseman or soldier) were native troops hired by the East India Company to protect British interests in the region. Unrest within Indian units of the colonial army had been common since early in the century, when it had been sparked by economic issues, religious sensitivities, or nascent anticolonial sentiment. In 1857, tension erupted when the British adopted the new Enfield rifle for use by sepoy infantrymen. The new weapon was a muzzle loader that used paper cartridges covered with animal fat and lard; because the cartridge had to be bitten off, it broke strictures against high-class Hindus' eating animal products and Muslim prohibitions against eating pork. Protests among sepoy units in northern India turned into a full-scale mutiny, supported by uprisings in rural districts in various parts of the country. But the revolt lacked clear goals, and rivalries between Hindus and Muslims and discord among the leaders within each community prevented coordination of operations. Although Indian troops often fought bravely and outnumbered the British six to one, they were poorly organ-

⟫ VIETNAMESE PRISONERS IN STOCKS. Whereas some Vietnamese took up Western ways, others resisted the foreign incursion but were vigorously suppressed by the French. In this photograph from 1907, Vietnamese prisoners who had plotted against the French are held in stocks in preparation for trial.

© Sipahioglu/Gamma Presse

ized, and the British forces (supplemented in many cases by sepoy troops) suppressed the rebellion. Still, the revolt frightened the British, who introduced a number of reforms and suppressed the final remnants of the Mughal dynasty, which had supported the mutiny.

Like the Sepoy Rebellion, traditional resistance movements usually met with little success. Peasants armed with pikes and spears were no match for Western armies possessing the most terrifying weapons then known to human society. In a few cases, such as the revolt of the Mahdi at Khartoum, the natives were able to defeat the invaders temporarily. But such successes were rare, and the late nineteenth century witnessed the seemingly inexorable march of the Western powers, armed with the Gatling gun (the first rapid-fire weapon and the precursor of the modern machine gun), to mastery of the globe.

CONCLUSION

By the first quarter of the twentieth century, virtually all of Africa and a good part of South and Southeast Asia were under some form of colonial rule. With the advent of the age of imperialism, a global economy was finally established, and the domination of Western civilization over those of Africa and Asia appeared to be complete.

Defenders of colonialism argue that the system was a necessary if painful stage in the evolution of human societies. Although its immediate consequences were admittedly sometimes unfortunate, Western imperialism was ultimately beneficial to colonial powers and subjects alike, since it created the conditions for global economic development and the universal application of democratic institutions. Critics, however, charge that the Western colonial powers were driven by an insatiable lust for profits. They dismiss the Western civilizing mission as a fig leaf to cover naked greed and reject the notion that imperialism played a salutary role in hastening the adjustment of traditional societies to the demands of industrial civilization. In the blunt words of two Western critics of imperialism: "Why is Africa (or for that matter Latin America and much of Asia) so poor? . . . The answer is very brief: we have made it poor."[9]

Between these two irreconcilable views, where does the truth lie? This chapter has contended that neither extreme position is justified. The sources of imperialism lie not simply in the demands of industrial capitalism but in the search for security, national greatness, and even such psychological factors as the spirit of discovery and the drive to excel. Though some regard the concept of the "white man's burden" as a hypocritical gesture to moral sensitivities, others see it as a meaningful reality justifying a lifelong commitment to the colonialist enterprise. Although the "civilizing urge" of missionaries and officials may have been tinged with self-interest, it was nevertheless often sincerely motivated. At the same time, the introduction of new technology has had a long-term beneficial impact on the colonial world, much as had been the case with the Arab Empire and the Mongol invasions in early centuries.

Still, the critics have a point. Although colonialism did introduce the peoples of Asia and Africa to new technology and the expanding economic marketplace, it was unnecessarily brutal in its application and all too often failed to realize the exalted claims and objectives of its promoters. Existing economic networks—often potentially valuable as a foundation for later economic development—were ruthlessly swept aside in the interests of providing markets for Western manufactured goods. Potential sources of native industrialization were nipped in the bud to avoid competition for factories in Amsterdam, London, Pittsburgh, or Manchester. Training in Western democratic ideals and practices was ignored out of fear that the recipients might use them as weapons against the ruling authorities.

The fundamental weakness of colonialism, then, was that it was ultimately based on the self-interests of the citizens of the colonial powers. Where those interests collided with the needs of the colonial peoples, those of the former always triumphed. The ultimate result was to deprive the colonial peoples of the right to make their own choices about their own destiny.

In one area of Asia, the spreading tide of imperialism did not result in the establishment of formal Western colonial control. In East Asia, the traditional societies of China and Japan were buffeted by the winds of Western expansionism during the nineteenth century but successfully resisted foreign conquest. In the next chapter, we will see how they managed to retain their independence while attempting to cope with the demands of a changing world.

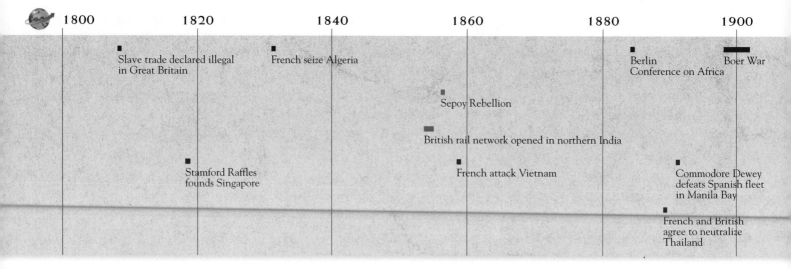

Slave trade declared illegal in Great Britain

French seize Algeria

Berlin Conference on Africa

Boer War

Sepoy Rebellion

British rail network opened in northern India

Stamford Raffles founds Singapore

French attack Vietnam

Commodore Dewey defeats Spanish fleet in Manila Bay

French and British agree to neutralize Thailand

CHAPTER NOTES

1. J. G. Lockhart and C. M. Woodhouse, *Cecil Rhodes: The Colossus of Southern Africa* (New York, 1963), pp. 69–70.
2. Quoted in Henry Braunschwig, *French Colonialism, 1871–1914* (London, 1961), p. 80.
3. Quoted in Ruhl Bartlett, ed., *The Record of American Diplomacy: Documents and Readings in the History of American Foreign Relations* (New York, 1952), p. 385.
4. Thomas Pakenham, *The Scramble for Africa* (New York, 1991), p. 13.
5. Quoted in Georges Garros, *Forceries Humaines* (Paris, 1926), p. 21.
6. Cited in review by Benjamin Schwartz of David Cannadine's *Ornamentalism: How the British Saw Their Empire* (Oxford, 2000), in *Atlantic Monthly*, November 2001, p. 135.
7. Sarraut's comment is quoted in Louis Roubaud, *Vietnam: La Tragédie Indochinoise* (Paris, 1926), p. 80.
8. Quoted in Pakenham, *The Scramble for Africa*, p. 182, citing a letter to Queen Victoria dated August 7, 1879.
9. Peter C. W. Gutkind and Immanuel Wallerstein, eds., *The Political Economy of Contemporary Africa* (Beverly Hills, Calif., 1976), p. 14.

SUGGESTED READING

There are a number of good works on the subject of imperialism and colonialism. For a recent study that directly focuses on the question of whether colonialism was beneficial to subject peoples, see D. K. Fieldhouse, *The West and the Third World: Trade, Colonialism, Dependence, and Development* (Oxford, 1999). Also see W. Baumgart, *Imperialism: The Idea and Reality of British and French Colonial Expansion, 1880–1914* (Oxford, 1982), and H. M. Wright, ed., *The "New Imperialism": Analysis of Late-Nineteenth-Century Expansion* (New York, 1976). On technology, see D. R. Headrick, *The Tentacles of Progress: Technology Transfer in the Age of Imperialism, 1850–1940* (Oxford, 1988).

On the imperialist age in Africa, above all see R. Robinson and J. Gallagher, *Africa and the Victorians: The Official Mind of Imperialism* (London, 1961). Also see B. Davidson, *Modern Africa: A Social and Political History* (London, 1989); T. Pakenham, *The Scramble for Africa* (New York, 1991); and T. Pakenham, *The Boer War* (London, 1979). On southern Africa, see J. Guy, *The Destruction of the Zulu Kingdom* (London, 1979), and D. Nenoon and B. Nyeko, *Southern Africa Since 1800* (London, 1984). Also useful is R. O. Collins,

ed., *Historical Problems of Imperial Africa* (Princeton, N.J., 1994).

For an overview of the British takeover and administration of India, see S. Wolpert, *A New History of India* (New York, 1989). C. A. Bayly, *Indian Society and the Making of the British Empire* (Cambridge, 1988), is a scholarly analysis of the impact of British conquest on the Indian economy. For a comparative approach, see R. Murphey, *The Outsiders: The Western Experience in China and India* (Ann Arbor, Mich., 1977). In a provocative work, *Ornamentalism: How the British Saw Their Empire* (Oxford, 2000), D. Cannadine argues that it was class, and not race, that motivated British policy in the subcontinent.

General studies of the colonial period in Southeast Asia are rare because most authors focus on specific areas. For some stimulating essays on a variety of aspects of the topic, see *Continuity and Change in Southeast Asia: Collected Journal Articles of Harry J. Benda* (New Haven, Conn., 1972). The role of religion is examined in F. von der Mehden, *Religion and Nationalism in Southeast Asia* (Madison, Wis., 1963). On nationalist movements, see also R. Emerson's classic *From*

Empire to Nation (Boston, 1960). For a view of the region from the inside, see D. J. Steinberg et al., eds., *In Search of Southeast Asia* (New York, 1986). On the French conquest of Indochina, see M. O. Osborne, *The French Presence in Cochin China and Cambodia* (Ithaca, N.Y., 1969).

For an introduction to the effects of colonialism on women in Africa and Asia, see S. Hughes and B. Hughes, *Women in World History*, vol. 2 (Armonk, N.Y., 1997). Also consult the classic by E. Boserup, *Women's Role in Economic Development* (London, 1970), and see J. Taylor, *The Social World of Batavia* (Madison, Wis., 1983).

INFOTRAC COLLEGE EDITION

Visit the source collections at infotrac.thomsonlearning.com and use the Search function with the following key terms.

Boer War

Imperialism

Nationalism

WORLD HISTORY RESOURCES

Visit the *Essential World History* Companion Web Site for resources specific to this textbook:

http://history.wadsworth.com/duikeressentials02/

The CD in the back of this book and the World History Resource Center at **http://history.wadsworth.com/world/** offer a variety of tools to help you succeed in this course, including access to quizzes; images; documents; interactive simulations, maps, and timelines; movie explorations; and a wealth of other sources.

National Maritime Museum, London

Chapter 21

SHADOWS OVER THE PACIFIC: EAST ASIA UNDER CHALLENGE

CHAPTER OUTLINE

- THE DECLINE OF THE MANCHUS
- CHINESE SOCIETY IN TRANSITION
- A RICH COUNTRY AND A STRONG STATE: THE RISE OF MODERN JAPAN
- CONCLUSION

FOCUS QUESTIONS

- Why did the Qing dynasty decline and ultimately collapse, and what role did the Western powers play in this process?
- What role did Sun Yat-sen play in the collapse of the Qing dynasty, and what were his goals for China?
- What political, economic, and social reforms were instituted by Meiji reformers in Japan?
- To what degree was the Meiji Restoration a "revolution," and to what degree did it succeed in transforming Japan?
- ➤ How did China and Japan respond to Western pressures in the nineteenth century, and what implications did their different responses have for each nation's history?

The British emissary Lord Macartney had arrived in Beijing in 1793 with a caravan loaded with six hundred cases of gifts for the emperor. Flags and banners provided by the Chinese proclaimed in Chinese characters that the visitor was an "ambassador bearing tribute from the country of England." But the tribute was in vain, for Macartney's request for an increase in trade between the two countries was flatly rejected, and he left Beijing in October with nothing to show for his efforts. Not until half a century later would the Qing dynasty—at the point of a gun—agree to the British demand for an expansion of commercial ties.

Historians have often viewed the failure of the Macartney mission as a reflection of the disdain of Chinese rulers toward their counterparts in other countries and their serene confidence in the superiority of Chinese civilization in a world inhabited by barbarians. But in retrospect, it is clear that China's concern was justified. At the beginning of the nineteenth century, the country faced a growing challenge from the escalating power and ambitions of the West. Backed by European guns, Western merchants and missionaries pressed insistently for the right to carry out their activities in China and Japan. Despite their initial reluctance, the Chinese and Japanese governments were eventually forced to open their doors to the foreigners, whose presence escalated rapidly during the final years of the century.

Unlike other Asian societies, both Japan and China were able to maintain their national independence against the Western onslaught. In other respects, however, the results in Japan and China were strikingly different. Japan responded quickly to the challenge by adopting Western institutions and customs and eventually becoming a significant competitor for the spoils of empire. In contrast, China grappled unsuccessfully with the problem, which eventually undermined the foundations of the Qing dynasty and brought it to an unceremonious end. •

THE DECLINE OF THE MANCHUS

In 1800, the Qing (Ch'ing) or Manchu dynasty was at the height of its power. China had experienced a long period of peace and prosperity under the rule of two great emperors, Kangxi and Qianlong. Its borders were secure, and its culture and intellectual achievements were the envy of the world. Its rulers, hidden behind the walls of the Forbidden City in Beijing, had every reason to describe their patrimony as the "Central Kingdom." But a little over a century later, humiliated and harassed by the black ships and big guns of the Western powers, the Qing dynasty, the last in a series that had endured for more than two thousand years, collapsed in the dust.

Historians once assumed that the primary reason for the rapid decline and fall of the Manchu dynasty was the intense pressure applied to a proud but somewhat complacent traditional society by the modern West. Now, however, most historians believe that internal changes played a role in the dynasty's collapse and point out that at least some of the problems suffered by the Manchus during the nineteenth century were self-inflicted.

Both explanations have some validity. Like so many of its predecessors, after an extended period of growth, the Qing dynasty began to suffer from the familiar dynastic ills of official corruption, peasant unrest, and incompetence at court. Such weaknesses were probably exacerbated by the rapid growth in population. The long era of peace and stability, the introduction of new crops from the Americas, and the cultivation of new, fast-ripening strains of rice enabled the Chinese population to double between 1550 and 1800. The population continued to grow, reaching the unprecedented level of 400 million by the end of the nineteenth century. Even without the irritating presence of the Western powers, the Manchus were probably destined to repeat the fate of their imperial predecessors. The ships, guns, and ideas of the foreigners simply highlighted the growing weakness of the Manchu dynasty and likely hastened its demise. In doing so, Western imperialism still exerted an indelible impact on the history of modern China—but as a contributing, not a causal, factor.

Opium and Rebellion

By 1800, Westerners had been in contact with China for more than two hundred years, but after an initial period of flourishing relations, Western traders had been limited to a small commercial outlet at Canton. This arrangement was not acceptable to the British, however. Not only did they chafe at being restricted to a tiny enclave, but the growing British appetite for Chinese tea created a severe balance-of-payments problem. The British tried negotiations, dispatching Lord Macartney to Beijing in 1793 and another mission, led by Lord Amherst, in 1816. But both missions foundered on the rock of protocol and managed only to worsen the already strained relations between the two countries. The British solution was opium. A product more addictive than tea, opium was grown in northeastern India and then shipped to China. Now, as imports increased, popular demand for the product in southern China became insatiable despite an official prohibition on its use. Soon bullion was flowing out of the Chinese imperial treasury into the pockets of British merchants.

The Chinese became concerned and tried to negotiate. In 1839, Lin Zexu (Lin Tse-hsu, 1785–1850), a Chinese official appointed by the court to curtail the opium trade, appealed to Queen Victoria on both moral and practical grounds and threatened to prohibit the sale of rhubarb (widely used as a laxative in nineteenth-century Europe) to Great Britain if she did not respond. But moral principles, then as now, paled before the lure of commercial profits, and the British continued to promote the opium trade, arguing that if the Chinese did not want the opium, they did not have to buy it. Lin Zexu attacked on three fronts, imposing penalties on smokers, arresting dealers, and seizing supplies from importers as they attempted to smuggle the drug into China. The last tactic caused his downfall. When he blockaded the foreign factory area in Canton to force traders to hand over their remaining chests of opium, the British government, claiming that it could not permit British subjects "to be exposed to insult and injustice," launched a naval expedition to punish the

THE OPIUM WAR. The Opium War, waged between China and Great Britain between 1839 and 1842, was China's first conflict with a European power. Lacking modern military technology, the Chinese suffered a humiliating defeat. In this painting, heavily armed British steamships destroy unwieldy Chinese junks along the Chinese coast. China's humiliation at sea was a legacy of its rulers' lack of interest in maritime matters since the middle of the fifteenth century, when Chinese junks were among the most advanced sailing ships in the world.

Manchus and force the court to open China to foreign trade.[1]

The Opium War (1839–1842) lasted three years and demonstrated the superiority of British firepower and military tactics (including the use of a shallow-draft steamboat that effectively harassed Chinese coastal defenses). British warships destroyed Chinese coastal and river forts and seized the offshore island of Chusan, not far from the mouth of the Yangtze River. When a British fleet sailed virtually unopposed up the Yangtze to Nanjing and cut off the supply of "tribute grain" from southern to northern China, the Qing finally agreed to British terms. In the Treaty of Nanjing in 1842, the Chinese agreed to open five coastal ports to British trade, limit tariffs on imported British goods, grant extraterritorial rights to British citizens in China, and pay a substantial indemnity to cover the costs of the war. China also agreed to cede the island of Hong Kong (dismissed by a senior British official as a "barren rock") to Great Britain. Nothing was said in the treaty about the opium trade, which continued unabated until it was brought under control through Chinese government efforts in the early twentieth century.

Although the Opium War has traditionally been considered the beginning of modern Chinese history, it is unlikely that many Chinese at the time would have seen it that way. This was not the first time that a ruling dynasty had been forced to make concessions to foreigners, and the opening of five coastal ports to the British hardly constituted a serious threat to the security of the empire. Although a few concerned Chinese argued that the court should learn more about European civilization, others contended that China had nothing to learn from the barbarians and that borrowing foreign ways would undercut the purity of Confucian civilization.

For the time being, the Manchus attempted to deal with the problem in the traditional way of playing the foreigners off against each other. Concessions granted to the British were offered to other Western nations, including the United States, and soon thriving foreign concession areas were operating in treaty ports along the southern Chinese coast from Canton to Shanghai.

In the meantime, the Qing court's failure to deal with pressing internal economic problems led to a major peasant revolt that shook the foundations of the empire. On the surface, the Taiping (T'ai p'ing) Rebellion owed something to the Western incursion; the leader of the uprising, Hong Xiuquan (Hung Hsiu-ch'uan), a failed examination candidate, was a Christian convert who viewed himself as a younger brother of Jesus and hoped to establish what he referred to as a "Heavenly Kingdom of Supreme Peace" in China. But there were many local causes as well. The rapid increase in population forced millions of peasants to eke out a living as sharecroppers or landless laborers. Official corruption and incompetence led to the whipsaw of increased taxes and a decline in government services; even the Grand Canal was allowed to silt up, hindering the shipment of grain. In 1853, the rebels seized the old Ming capital of Nanjing, but that proved to be the rebellion's high-water mark. Plagued by factionalism, the rebellion gradually lost momentum until it was finally suppressed in 1864.

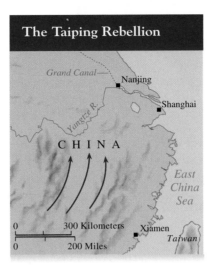

The Taiping Rebellion

One reason for the dynasty's failure to deal effectively with the internal unrest was its continuing difficulties with the Western imperialists. In 1856, the British and the French, still smarting from trade restrictions and limitations on their missionary activities, launched a new series of attacks against China and seized Beijing in 1860. As punishment, British troops destroyed the imperial summer palace just outside the city. In the ensuing Treaty of Tianjin (Tientsin), the Qing agreed to humiliating new concessions: the legalization of the opium trade, the opening of additional ports to foreign trade, and the cession of the peninsula of Kowloon (opposite the island of Hong Kong) to the British (see Map 21.1). Additional territories in the north were ceded to Russia.

The Climax of Imperialism in China

By the late 1870s, the old dynasty was well on the road to internal disintegration. In fending off the Taiping Rebellion, the Manchus had been compelled to rely for support on armed forces under regional command. After quelling the revolt, many of these regional commanders refused to disband their units and, with the support of the local gentry, continued to collect local taxes for their own use. The dreaded pattern of imperial breakdown, so familiar in Chinese history, was beginning to appear once again.

In its weakened state, the court finally began to listen to the appeals of reform-minded officials, who called for a new policy of "self-strengthening," in which Western technology would be adopted while Confucian principles and institutions were maintained intact. This policy, popularly known by its slogan "East for Essence, West for Practical Use," remained the guiding standard for Chinese foreign and domestic policy for nearly a quarter of a century. Some even called for reforms in education and in China's hallowed political institutions (see the box on p. 460). Pointing to the power and prosperity of Great Britain, the journalist Wang Tao (Wang T'ao, 1828–1897) remarked, "The real strength of England . . . lies in the fact that there is a sympathetic understanding between the governing and the governed, a close relationship between the ruler and the people. . . . My observation is that the

daily domestic political life of England actually embodies the traditional ideals of our ancient Golden Age."[2] Such democratic ideas were too radical for most reformers, however. One of the leading court officials of the day, Zhang Zhidong (Chang Chih-tung), countered:

The doctrine of people's rights will bring us not a single benefit but a hundred evils. Are we going to establish a parliament? . . . Even supposing the confused and clamorous people are assembled in one house, for every one of them who is clear-sighted, there will be a hundred others whose vision is beclouded; they will converse at random and talk as if in a dream—what use will it be?[3]

For the time being, Zhang Zhidong's arguments won the day. During the last quarter of the century, the Manchus attempted to modernize their military establishment and build up an industrial base without disturbing the essential elements of traditional Chinese civilization. Railroads, weapons arsenals, and shipyards were built, but the value system remained essentially unchanged.

In the end, the results spoke for themselves. During the last two decades of the nineteenth century, the European penetration of China, both political and military, intensified. Rapacious imperialists began to bite off the outer edges of the Qing Empire (see Map 21.2). The Gobi Desert north of the Great Wall, Central Asia, and Tibet, all inhabited by

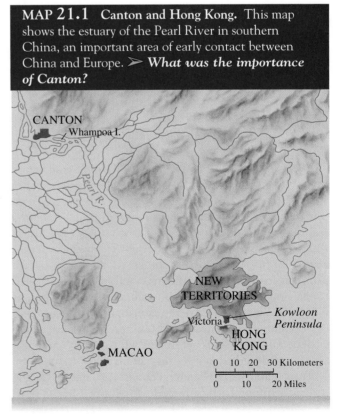

MAP 21.1 Canton and Hong Kong. This map shows the estuary of the Pearl River in southern China, an important area of early contact between China and Europe. ➢ *What was the importance of Canton?*

AN APPEAL FOR CHANGE IN CHINA

*A*fter the humiliating defeat at the hands of the British in the Opium War, a few Chinese intellectuals began to argue that China must change its ways in order to survive. Among such reformist thinkers was the journalist and author Wang Tao. After a trip to Europe in the late 1860s, Wang returned to China convinced of the technological superiority of the West and the need for his country to adopt reforms to enable it to compete effectively in a changing world. He had only limited success in persuading his contemporaries of the need for dramatic change. Many Chinese were undoubtedly reluctant to believe his claim that China was not the Middle Kingdom or "all under Heaven" but only one nation among many in a rapidly changing world.

WANG TAO ON REFORM

I know that within a hundred years China will adopt all Western methods and excel in them. For though both are vessels, a sailboat differs in speed from a steamship; though both are vehicles, a horse-drawn carriage cannot cover the same distance as a locomotive train. Among weapons, the power of the bow and arrow, sword and spear, cannot be compared with that of firearms; and of firearms, the old types do not have the same effect as the new. Although it be the same piece of work, there is a difference in the ease with which it can be done by machine and by human labor. When new methods do not exist, people will not think of changes; but when there are new instruments, to copy them is certainly possible. Even if the Westerners should give no guidance, the Chinese must surely exert themselves to the utmost of their ingenuity and resources on these things.

Alas! People all understand the past, but they are ignorant of the future. Only scholars whose thoughts run deep and far can grasp the trends. As the mind of Heaven changes above, so do human affairs below. Heaven opens the minds of the Westerners and bestows upon them intelligence and wisdom. Their techniques and skills develop without bound. They sail eastward and gather in China. This constitutes an unprecedented situation in history, and a tremendous change in the world. The foreign nations come from afar with their superior techniques, contemptuous of us in our deficiencies. They show off their prowess and indulge in insults and oppression; they also fight among themselves. Under these circumstances, how can we not think of making changes? . . .

If China does not make any change at this time, how can she be on a par with the great nations of Europe, and compare with them in power and strength? Nevertheless, the path of reform is beset with difficulties. What the Western countries have today are regarded as of no worth by those who arrogantly refuse to pay attention. Their argument is that we should use our own laws to govern the empire, for that is the Way of our sages. They do not know that the Way of the sages is valued only because it can make proper accommodations according to the times. If Confucius lived today, we may be certain that he would not cling to antiquity and oppose making changes. . . .

But how is this to be done? First, the method of recruiting civil servants should be changed. The examination essays, coming down to the present, have gone from bad to worse and should be discarded. And yet we are still using them to select civil servants.

Second, the method of training soldiers should be changed. Now our army units and naval forces have only names registered on books, but no actual persons enrolled. The authorities consider our troops unreliable and so they recruit militia who, however, can be assembled but cannot be disbanded. . . . The arms of the Manchu banners and the ships of the naval forces should all be changed. . . . If they continue to hold on to their old ways and make no plans for change, it may be called "using untrained people to fight," which is no different from driving them to their deaths.

---

non-Chinese peoples and never fully assimilated into the Chinese Empire, were gradually lost. In the north and northwest, the main beneficiary was Russia, which took advantage of the dynasty's weakness to force the cession of territories north of the Amur River in Siberia. In Tibet, competition between Russia and Great Britain prevented either power from seizing the territory outright but at the same time enabled Tibetan authorities to revive local autonomy never recognized by the Chinese. In the south, British and French advances in mainland Southeast Asia removed Burma and Vietnam from their traditional vassal relationship to the Manchu court. Even more ominous were the foreign spheres of influence in the Chinese heartland, where local commanders were willing to sell exclusive commercial, railroad-building, or mining privileges.

The breakup of the Manchu dynasty accelerated at the end of the nineteenth century. In 1894, the Qing went to war with Japan over Japanese incursions into the Korean peninsula, which threatened China's long-held suzerainty over the area (see "Joining the Imperialist Club" later in this chapter). To the surprise of many observers, the Chinese were roundly defeated, confirming to some critics the devastating failure of the policy of self-strengthening by halfway measures. The disintegration of China accelerated in 1897, when Germany, a new entry in the race for spoils in East Asia, used the pretext of the murder of two German missionaries by Chinese rioters to demand the cession of territories in the Shandong (Shantung) peninsula. The approval of the demand by the imperial court set off a scramble for territory by other interested powers (see Map 21.3). Russia now demanded the Liaodong peninsula with its ice-free port at Port Arthur, and Great Britain weighed in with a request for a coaling station in northern China.

MAP 21.2 **The Qing Empire.** Shown here is the Qing Empire at the height of its power in the late eighteenth century, together with its shrunken boundaries at the moment of dissolution in 1911. ➤ *Where are China's tributary states on the map?*

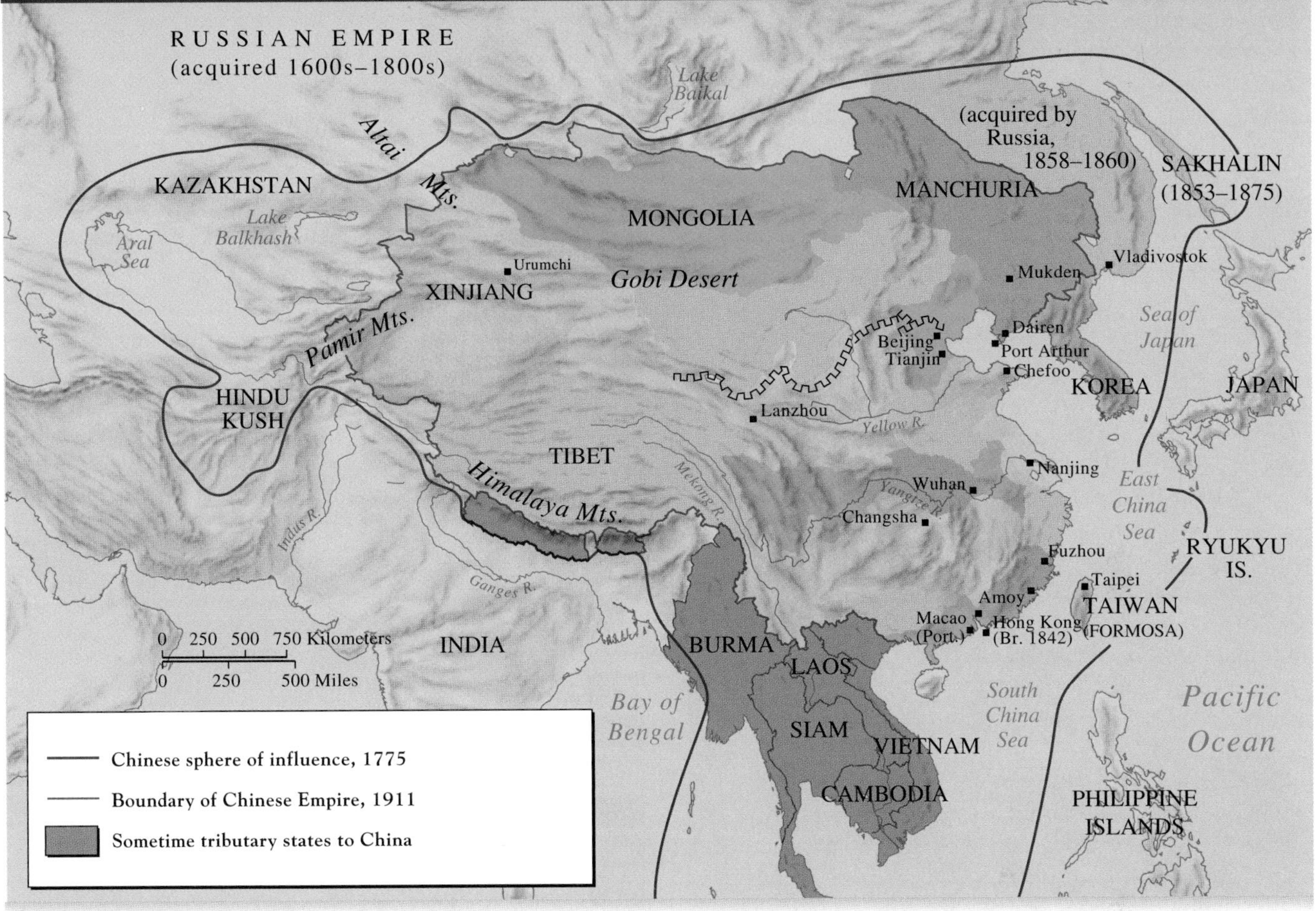

The government responded to the challenge with yet another effort at reform. In the spring of 1898, an outspoken advocate of change, the progressive Confucian scholar Kang Youwei (K'ang Yu-wei), won the support of the young Guangxu (Kuang Hsu) emperor for a comprehensive reform program patterned after recent measures in Japan. Without change, Kang argued, China would perish. During the next several weeks, the emperor issued edicts calling for major political, administrative, and educational reforms. Not surprisingly, Kang's proposals were opposed by many conservatives, who saw little advantage and much risk in copying the West. More important, the new program was opposed by the emperor's aunt, the Empress Dowager Cixi (Tz'u Hsi), the real power at court. Cixi had begun her political career as a concubine to an earlier emperor. After his death, she became a dominant force at court and in 1878 placed her infant nephew, the future Guangxu emperor, on the throne. For two decades, she ruled in his name as regent. With the aid of conservatives in the army, she arrested and executed several of the reformers and had the emperor incarcerated in the palace. With Cixi's palace coup, the so-called One Hundred Days of reform came to an end.

OPENING THE DOOR TO CHINA

During the next two years, foreign pressure on the dynasty intensified. With encouragement from the British, who hoped to avert a total collapse of the Manchu Empire, U.S. Secretary of State John Hay presented the other imperialist powers with a proposal to ensure equal economic access to the China market for all states. Hay also suggested that all powers join together to guarantee the territorial and administrative integrity of the Chinese Empire. Though probably motivated more by the United States' preference for open markets than by a benevolent wish to protect China, the Open Door policy did have the practical effect of reducing the imperialist hysteria over access to the China market. The "gentlemen's agreement" about the Open Door (it was not a treaty, merely a pious and nonbinding expression of intent) served to deflate fears in Britain, France, Germany, and Russia that other powers would take advantage of China's weakness to dominate the China market.

In the long run, then, the Open Door was a positive step that brought a measure of sanity to imperialist behavior in East Asia. Unfortunately, it came too late to stop the

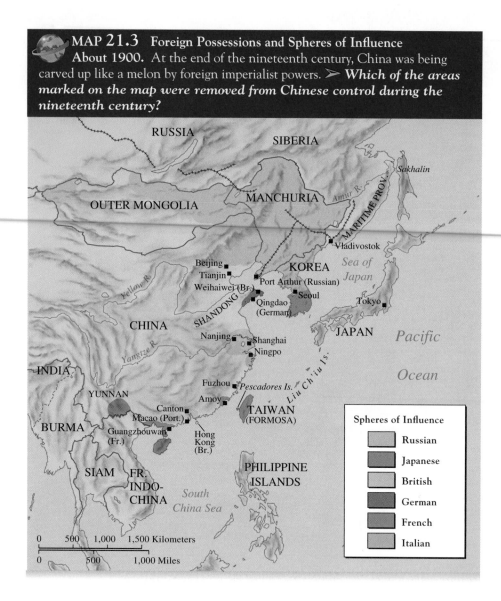

MAP 21.3 Foreign Possessions and Spheres of Influence About 1900.
At the end of the nineteenth century, China was being carved up like a melon by foreign imperialist powers. ➤ *Which of the areas marked on the map were removed from Chinese control during the nineteenth century?*

Spheres of Influence

- Russian
- Japanese
- British
- German
- French
- Italian

domestic explosion known as the Boxer Rebellion. The Boxers, so-called because of the physical exercises they performed, were members of a secret society operating primarily in rural areas in northern China. Provoked by a damaging drought and high unemployment caused in part by foreign economic activity (the introduction of railroads and steamships, for example, undercut the livelihood of barge workers on the rivers and canals), the Boxers attacked foreign residents and besieged the foreign legation quarter in Beijing until the foreigners were rescued by an international expeditionary force in the late summer of 1900. As punishment, the foreign troops destroyed a number of temples in the capital suburbs, and the Chinese government was compelled to pay a heavy indemnity to the foreign governments involved in suppressing the uprising.

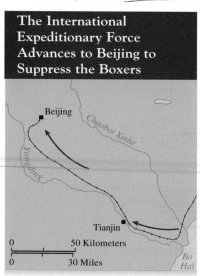

The International Expeditionary Force Advances to Beijing to Suppress the Boxers

The Collapse of the Old Order

During the next few years, the old dynasty tried desperately to reform itself. The empress dowager, who had long resisted change, now embraced a number of reforms. The venerable civil service examination system was replaced by a new educational system based on the Western model. In 1905, a commission was formed to study constitutional changes; over the next few years, legislative assemblies were established at the provincial level, and elections for a national assembly were held in 1910.

Such moves helped shore up the dynasty temporarily, but history shows that the most dangerous period for

for long hours in the coal mines and textile mills, often under horrendous conditions. Reportedly, coal miners employed on a small island in Nagasaki harbor worked naked in temperatures up to 130 degrees Fahrenheit. If they tried to escape, they were shot.

BUILDING A MODERN SOCIAL STRUCTURE

By the late Tokugawa era, the rigidly hierarchical social order was showing signs of disintegration. Rich merchants were buying their way into the ranks of the samurai, and Japanese of all classes were beginning to abandon their rice fields and move into the growing cities. Nevertheless, community and hierarchy still formed the basis of Japanese society. The lives of all Japanese were determined by their membership in various social organizations—the family, the village, and their social class. Membership in a particular social class determined a person's occupation and social relationships with others. Women in particular were constrained by the "three obediences" imposed on their sex: child to father, wife to husband, and widow to son. Husbands could easily obtain a divorce, but wives could not (one regulation allegedly decreed that a husband could divorce his spouse if she drank too much tea or talked too much). Marriages were arranged, and the average age at marriage for females was sixteen years. Females did not share inheritance rights with males, and few received any education outside the family.

The Meiji reformers destroyed much of the traditional social system in Japan. With the abolition of hereditary rights in 1871, the legal restrictions of the past were brought to an end with a single stroke. Special privileges for the aristocracy were abolished, as were the legal restrictions on the *eta*, the traditional slave class (numbering about 400,000 in the 1870s). Another key focus of the reformers was the army. The Sat-Cho reformers had been struck by the weakness of the Japanese forces in clashes with Western powers and embarked on a major program to create a military force that could compete in the modern world. The old feudal army based on the traditional warrior class was abolished, and an imperial army based on universal conscription was formed in 1871.

Education also underwent major changes. The Meiji leaders recognized the need for universal education including technical subjects, and after a few years of experimenting, they adopted the American model of a three-tiered system culminating in a series of universities and specialized institutes. In the meantime, they sent bright students to study abroad and brought foreign scholars to Japan to teach in the new schools, where much of the content was inspired by Western models. In another break with tradition, women for the first time were given an opportunity to get an education.

Western influence was evident elsewhere as well. Western fashions became the rage in elite circles, and the ministers of the first Meiji government were known as the "dancing cabinet" because of their addiction to Western-style ballroom dancing. Young people, increasingly exposed to Western culture and values, began to imitate the clothing styles, eating habits, and social practices of their European and American counterparts. They even took up American sports when baseball was introduced.

The self-proclaimed transformation of Japan into a "modern society," however, by no means detached the country entirely from its traditional moorings. Although an educational order in 1872 increased the percentage of Japanese women exposed to public education, conservatives soon began to impose restrictions and bring about a return to more traditional social relationships. Traditional values were given a firm legal basis in the Constitution of 1890, which restricted the franchise to males and defined individual liberties as "subject to the limitations imposed by law," and by the Civil Code of 1898, which deemphasized individual rights and essentially placed women within the context of their role in the family.

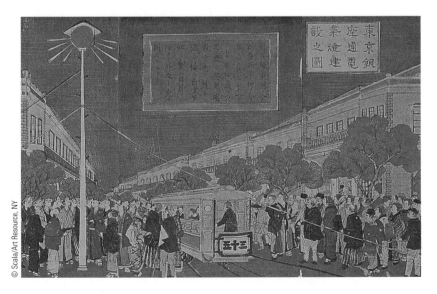

⋙ THE GINZA IN DOWNTOWN TOKYO. This 1877 woodblock print shows the Ginza (a major commercial thoroughfare) in downtown Tokyo, with modern brick buildings, rickshaws, and a horse-drawn streetcar. The centerpiece and focus of public attention is a new electric streetlight.

By the end of the nineteenth century, however, changes were under way as women began to play a crucial role in their nation's effort to modernize. Urged by their parents to augment the family income, as well as by the government to fulfill their patriotic duty, young girls were sent en masse to work in textile mills. From 1894 to 1912, women represented 60 percent of the Japanese labor force. Thanks to them, by 1914, Japan was the world's leading exporter of silk and dominated cotton manufacturing. If it had not been for the export revenues earned from textile exports, Japan might not have been able to develop its heavy industry and military prowess without an infusion of foreign capital.

Japanese women received few rewards, however, for their contribution to the nation. In 1900, new regulations prohibited women from joining political organizations or attending public meetings. Beginning in 1905, a group of independent-minded women petitioned the Japanese parliament to rescind this restriction, but it was not repealed until 1922.

Joining the Imperialist Club

Traditionally, Japan had not been an expansionist country. Now, however, the Japanese did not just imitate the domestic policies of their Western mentors; they also emulated the Western approach to foreign affairs. This is perhaps not surprising. The Japanese regarded themselves as particularly vulnerable in the world economic arena. Their territory was small, lacking in resources, and densely populated, and they had no natural outlet for expansion. To observant Japanese, the lessons of history were clear. Western nations had amassed wealth and power not only because of their democratic systems and high level of education but also because of their colonies.

The Japanese began their program of territorial expansion close to home (see Map 21.4). In 1874, after a brief conflict with China, Japan was able to claim suzerainty over the Ryukyu Islands, long tributary to the Chinese Empire. Two years later, Japanese naval pressure forced Korea to open three ports to Japanese commerce.

During the early decades of the nineteenth century, Korea had followed Japan's example and attempted to isolate itself from outside contact except for periodic tribute missions to China. Christian missionaries, mostly Chinese or French, were vigorously persecuted. But Korea's problems were basically internal. In the early 1860s, a peasant revolt, inspired in part by the Taiping Rebellion in China, caused considerable devastation before being crushed in 1864. In succeeding years, the Yi dynasty sought to strengthen the country by returning to traditional values and fending off outside intrusion, but rural poverty and official corruption remained rampant. A U.S. fleet, following the example of Commodore Perry in Japan, sought to open the country in 1871 but was driven off with considerable loss of life.

Korea's most persistent suitor, however, was Japan, which was determined to bring an end to Korea's dependency status with China and modernize it along Japanese lines. In 1876, the two countries signed an agreement opening three treaty ports to Japanese commerce in return for Japanese recognition of Korean independence. During the 1880s, Sino-Japanese rivalry over Korea intensified. When a new peasant rebellion broke out in Korea in 1894, China and Japan intervened on opposite sides. During the war, the Japanese navy destroyed the Chinese fleet and seized the Manchurian city of Port Arthur. In the Treaty of Shimonoseki, the Chinese were forced to recognize the independence of Korea and cede Taiwan and the Liaodong peninsula with its strategic naval base at Port Arthur to Japan.

Shortly thereafter, under pressure from the European powers, the Japanese returned the Liaodong peninsula to China, but in the early twentieth century, they went back on the offensive. Rivalry with Russia over influence in Korea led to increasingly strained relations between the two countries. In 1904, Japan launched a surprise attack on the Russian naval base at Port Arthur, which Russia had taken from China in 1898. The Japanese armed forces were weaker, but Russia faced difficult logistical problems along its new Trans-Siberian Railway and severe political instability at home. In 1905, after Japanese warships sank almost the entire Russian fleet off the coast of Korea, the Russians agreed to a humiliating peace, ceding the strategically located Liaodong peninsula back to Japan, as well as southern Sakhalin and the Kurile Islands. Russia also agreed to abandon its political and economic influence in Korea and southern Manchuria, which now came increasingly under Japanese control. The Japanese victory stunned the world, including the colonial peoples of Southeast Asia, who now began to realize that the white race was not necessarily invincible.

During the next few years, the Japanese consolidated their position in northeastern Asia, annexing Korea in 1908 as an integral part of Japan. When the Koreans protested the seizure, Japanese reprisals resulted in thousands of deaths. The United States was the first nation to recognize the annexation in return for Tokyo's declaration of respect for U.S. authority in the Philippines. In 1908, the United States recognized Japanese interests in the region in return for Japanese acceptance of the principles of the Open Door. But mutual suspicion between the two countries was growing, sparked in part by U.S. efforts to restrict immigration from all Asian countries.

Japanese Culture in Transition

The wave of Western technology and ideas that entered Japan in the second half of the nineteenth century greatly altered the shape of traditional Japanese culture. Literature in particular was affected as European models eclipsed

MAP 21.4 Japanese Overseas Expansion During the Meiji Era. Beginning in the late nineteenth century, Japan ventured beyond its home islands and became an imperialist power. The extent of Japanese colonial expansion through World War I is shown here. ➤ *Which parts of imperial China were now under Japanese influence?*

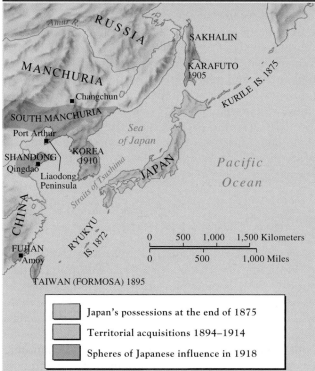

Japan's possessions at the end of 1875

Territorial acquisitions 1894–1914

Spheres of Japanese influence in 1918

Chronology

JAPAN AND KOREA IN THE ERA OF IMPERIALISM

Commodore Perry arrives in Tokyo Bay	1853
Townsend Harris Treaty	1858
Fall of Tokugawa shogunate	1868
U.S. fleet fails to open Korea	1871
Feudal titles abolished	1871
Imperial army formed	1871
Meiji Constitution adopted	1890
Imperial Rescript on Education	1890
Treaty of Shimonoseki awards Taiwan to Japan	1895
Russo-Japanese War	1904–1905
Korea annexed	1908

the repetitive and frivolous tales of the Tokugawa era. Dazzled by this "new" literature, Japanese authors began translating and imitating the imported models. Experimenting with Western verse, Japanese poets were at first influenced primarily by the British but eventually adopted such French styles as Symbolism, Dadaism, and Surrealism, although some traditional poetry was still composed.

As the Japanese invited technicians, engineers, architects, and artists from Europe and the United States to teach their "modern" skills to a generation of eager students, the Meiji era became a time of massive consumption of Western artistic techniques and styles. Japanese architects and artists created huge buildings of steel and reinforced concrete adorned with Greek columns and cupolas, oil paintings reflecting the European concern with depth perception and shading, and bronze sculptures of secular subjects.

Cultural exchange also went the other way as Japanese arts and crafts, porcelains, textiles, fans, folding screens, and woodblock prints became the vogue in Europe and North America. Japanese art influenced Western painters such as Vincent van Gogh, Edgar Degas, and James Whistler, who experimented with flatter compositional perspectives and unusual poses. Japanese gardens, with their exquisite attention to the positioning of rocks and falling water, also became especially popular.

After the initial period of mass absorption of Western art, a national reaction occurred at the end of the nineteenth century as many artists returned to pre-Meiji techniques. In 1889, the Tokyo School of Fine Arts (today the Tokyo National University of Fine Arts and Music) was founded to promote traditional Japanese art. Over the next several decades, Japanese art underwent a dynamic resurgence, reflecting the nation's emergence as a prosperous and powerful state. While some Japanese artists attempted to synthesize native and foreign techniques, others returned to past artistic traditions for inspiration.

The Meiji Restoration: A Revolution from Above

Japan's transformation from a feudal, agrarian society to an industrializing, technologically advanced society in little more than half a century has frequently been described by outside observers (if not by the Japanese themselves) in almost miraculous terms. Some historians have questioned this characterization, pointing out that the achievements of the Meiji leaders were spotty. In *Japan's Emergence as a Modern State*, the Canadian historian E. H. Norman lamented that the Meiji Restoration was an "incomplete revolution" because it had not ended the economic and social inequities of feudal society or enabled the common people to participate fully in the governing process. Although the *genro* were enlightened in many respects, they were also despotic and elitist, and the distribution of wealth remained as unequal as it had been under the old system.[5]

These criticisms are persuasive, although they could also be applied to most other societies going through the early stages of industrialization. In any event, from an economic perspective, the Meiji Restoration was certainly one of the great success stories of modern times. Not only did the Meiji leaders put Japan firmly on the path to economic and political development, but they also managed to remove the unequal treaty provisions that had been imposed at mid-century. Japanese achievements are especially impressive when compared with the difficulties experienced by China, which was not only unable to realize significant changes in its traditional society but had not even reached a consensus on the need for doing so. Japan's achievements more closely resemble those of Europe, but whereas the West needed a century and a half to achieve a significant level of industrial development, the Japanese realized it in forty years.

One of the distinctive features of Japan's transition from a traditional to a modern society during the Meiji era was that it took place for the most part without violence or the kind of social or political revolution that occurred in so many other countries. The Meiji Restoration, which began the process, has been called a "revolution from above," a comprehensive restructuring of Japanese society by its own ruling group.

The differences between the Japanese response to the West and that of China and many other nations in the region have sparked considerable debate among students of comparative history, and a number of explanations have been offered. Some have argued that Japan's success was partly due to good fortune. Lacking abundant natural resources, it was exposed to less pressure from the West than many of its neighbors. That argument is problematic, however, and would probably not have been accepted by Japanese observers at the time. Nor does it explain why nations under considerably less pressure, such as Laos and Nepal, did not advance even more quickly. All in all, the luck hypothesis is not very persuasive.

Some explanations have already been suggested in this book. Japan's unique geographical position in Asia was certainly a factor. China, a continental nation with a heterogeneous ethnic composition, was distinguished from its neighbors by its Confucian culture. By contrast, Japan was an island nation, ethnically and linguistically homogeneous, and had never been conquered. Unlike the Chinese or many other peoples in the region, the Japanese had little to fear from cultural change in terms of its effect on their national identity. If Confucian culture, with all its accouterments, was what defined the Chinese gentleman, his Japanese counterpart, in the familiar image, could discard his sword and kimono and don a modern military uniform or a Western business suit and still feel comfortable in both worlds.

The final product was an amalgam of old and new, native and foreign, forming a new civilization that was still uniquely Japanese. There were some undesirable consequences, however. Because Meiji politics was essentially despotic, Japanese leaders were able to fuse key traditional elements such as the warrior ethic and the concept of feudal loyalty with the dynamics of modern industrial capitalism to create a state totally dedicated to the possession of material wealth and national power. This combination of *kokutai* and capitalism was highly effective but explosive in its international manifestation. Like modern Germany, which also entered the industrial age directly from feudalism, Japan eventually engaged in a policy of repression at home and expansion abroad in order to achieve its national objectives. In Japan, as in Germany, it took defeat in war to disconnect the drive for national development from the feudal ethic and bring about the transformation to a pluralistic society dedicated to living in peace and cooperation with its neighbors.

CONCLUSION

Few areas of the world resisted the Western incursion as stubbornly and effectively as East Asia. Although military, political, and economic pressure by the European powers was relatively intense during this era, two of the main states in the area were able to retain their independence, while the third—Korea—was temporarily absorbed by one of its larger neighbors. Why the Chinese and the Japanese were able to prevent a total political and military takeover by foreign powers is an interesting question. One key reason was that both had a long history as well-defined states with a strong sense of national community and territorial cohesion. Although China had frequently been conquered, it had retained its sense of unique culture and identity. Geography, too, was in its favor. As a continental nation, China was able to survive partly because of its sheer size. Japan possessed the advantage of an island location.

Even more striking, however, is the different way in which the two states attempted to deal with the challenge. While the Japanese chose to face the problem in a pragmatic manner, borrowing foreign ideas and institutions that appeared to be of value and at the same time not in conflict with traditional attitudes and customs, China agonized over the issue for half a century while conservative elements fought a desperate battle to retain a maximum of the traditional heritage intact.

This chapter has discussed some of the possible reasons for those differences. In retrospect, it is difficult to avoid the conclusion that the Japanese approach was the more effective one. Whereas the Meiji leaders were able to set in motion an orderly transition from a traditional to an advanced society, in China the old system collapsed in disorder, leaving chaotic conditions that were still not rectified a generation later. China would pay a heavy price for its failure to respond coherently to the challenge.

But the Japanese "revolution from above" was by no means an unalloyed success. Ambitious efforts by Japanese leaders to carve out a share in the spoils of empire led to escalating conflict with China as well as with rival Western powers and in the early 1940s to global war. We will deal with that issue in Chapter 24. Meanwhile, in Europe, a combination of old rivalries and the effects of the Industrial Revolution were leading to a bitter regional conflict that eventually engulfed the entire world.

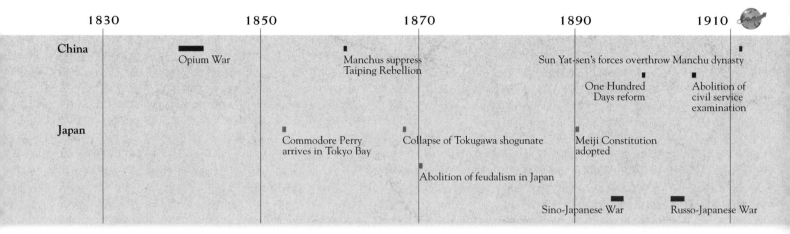

| | 1830 | 1850 | 1870 | 1890 | 1910 |

China

Opium War

Manchus suppress Taiping Rebellion

Sun Yat-sen's forces overthrow Manchu dynasty

One Hundred Days reform

Abolition of civil service examination

Japan

Commodore Perry arrives in Tokyo Bay

Collapse of Tokugawa shogunate

Meiji Constitution adopted

Abolition of feudalism in Japan

Sino-Japanese War

Russo-Japanese War

CHAPTER NOTES

1. Hosea Ballou Morse, *The International Relations of the Chinese Empire* (London, 1910–1918), vol. 2, p. 622.
2. Quoted in Ssu-yu Teng and John K. Fairbank, eds., *China's Response to the West: A Documentary Survey, 1839–1923* (New York, 1970), p. 140.
3. Ibid., p. 167.

4. John K. Fairbank, Albert M. Craig, and Edwin O. Reischauer, *East Asia: Tradition and Transformation* (Boston, 1973), p. 514.
5. Quoted in John W. Dower, ed., *The Origins of the Modern Japanese State: Selected Writings of E. H. Norman* (New York, 1975), p. 13.

SUGGESTED READING

For a general overview of this period of East Asian history, see C. Schirokauer, *Modern China and Japan: A Brief History* (New York, 1982), and J. K. Fairbank, A. M. Craig, and E. O. Reischauer, *East Asia: Tradition and Transformation* (Boston, 1973). See also J. D. Spence's highly stimulating *Search for Modern China* (New York, 1990); *The Cambridge History of China*, vols. 10–11 (Cambridge, 1978–1980), dealing with the Qing period; and *The Cambridge History of Japan*, vols. 5–6 (Cambridge, 1988).

On the Western intrusion into China during the nineteenth century, see the classic work by J. K. Fairbank, *Trade and Diplomacy on the China Coast* (Cambridge, 1953), and F. Wakeman Jr., *Strangers at the Gate: Social Disorder in South China, 1839–1861* (Berkeley, Calif., 1966). On the Opium War, see A. Waley, *The Opium War Through Chinese Eyes* (London, 1958), and P. W. Fay, *The Opium War, 1840–1842* (Chapel Hill, N.C., 1975). On the Taiping Rebellion, see F. Michael and C. Chung-li, *The Taiping Rebellion: History and Documents*, 3 vols. (Seattle, 1966–1971), and J. D. Spence, *God's Chinese Son: The Taiping Heavenly Kingdom of Hong Xiuquan* (New York, 1996).

There are a number of important works on the final decades of the Chinese Empire. For a general overview, see F. Wakeman Jr., *The Fall of Imperial China* (New York, 1975). For economic developments, see A. Feuerwerker's classic *China's Early Industrialization: Sheng Hsuan-huai and Mandarin Enterprise* (Cambridge, 1958). China's response to the Western challenge is chronicled in S. Teng and J. K. Fairbank, eds., *China's Response to the West: A Documentary Survey, 1839–1923* (New York, 1970).

On the 1911 revolution, see M. C. Wright, ed., *China in Revolution: The First Phase, 1900–1913* (New Haven, Conn., 1968). Sun Yat-sen's career is explored in M. C. Bergère, *Sun Yat-sen*, trans. J. Lloyd (Stanford, Calif., 2000). On the Boxer Rebellion, the definitive study is J. Esherick, *The Origins of the Boxer Uprising* (Berkeley, Calif., 1987). Also see D. Preston, *The Boxer Rebellion: The Dramatic Story of China's War on Foreigners That Shook the World in the Summer of 1900* (Berkeley, Calif., 2001).

For a survey of modern Japanese history, see J. Hunter, *The Emergence of Modern Japan: An Introductory History Since 1853* (London,

1989). See also J. W. Dower, ed., *The Origins of the Modern Japanese State: Selected Writings of E. H. Norman* (New York, 1975).

The Meiji period is discussed in W. G. Beasley, *The Meiji Restoration* (Stanford, Calif., 1972). An earlier and more controversial view is E. H. Norman, *Japan's Emergence as a Modern State: Political and Economic Problems of the Meiji Period* (New York, 1940). See also C. Gluck, *Japan's Modern Myths: Ideology in the Late Meiji Period* (Princeton, N.J., 1985); C. Totman, *The Collapse of the Tokugawa Bakufu, 1862–1868* (Honolulu, 1980); and M. B. Jansen, ed., *The Emergence of Meiji Japan* (Cambridge, 1995).

On the economy, see R. Smethurst, *Agricultural Development and Tenancy Disputes in Japan, 1870–1940* (Princeton, N.J., 1986), and G. C. Allen, *A Short Economic History of Japan, 1867–1937* (London, 1972). Social developments are examined in R. Dore, ed., *Aspects of Social Change in Modern Japan* (Princeton, N.J., 1967). The rise of the modern Japanese army is chronicled in R. F. Hack-ett, *Yamagata Aritomo and the Rise of Meiji Japan* (Cambridge, 1971). For the best introduction to Japanese art, consult P. Mason, *History of Japanese Art* (New York, 1993). See also J. S. Baker's concise *Japanese Art* (London, 1984).

On Japan's emergence as an imperialist power, see A. Iriye, *Pacific Estrangement: Japanese and American Expansion, 1897–1911* (Cambridge, 1972); M. R. Peattie and R. Myers, *The Japanese Colonial Empire, 1895–1945* (Princeton, N.J., 1984); and M. B. Jansen, *Japan and Its World: Two Centuries of Change* (Princeton, N.J., 1980).

For a brief introduction to the women of this era in China and Japan, see S. Hughes and B. Hughes, *Women in World History* (Armonk, N.Y., 1997). For a more detailed account, consult O. Kazuko, *Chinese Women in a Century of Revolution, 1850–1950,* ed. J. A. Fogel (Stanford, Calif., 1989), and O. Kazuko, *Japanese Women: New Feminist Perspectives on the Past, Present, and Future,* ed. K. Fujimura-Fanselow and A. Kameda (New York, 1995).

INFOTRAC COLLEGE EDITION

Visit the source collections at infotrac.thomsonlearning.com and use the Search function with the following key terms.

China history

Japan history

Meiji

Qing

Sun Yat-sen

WORLD HISTORY RESOURCES

Visit the *Essential World History* Companion Web Site for resources specific to this textbook:

http://history.wadsworth.com/duikeressentials02/

The CD in the back of this book and the World History Resource Center at **http://history.wadsworth.com/world/** offer a variety of tools to help you succeed in this course, including access to quizzes; images; documents; interactive simulations, maps, and timelines; movie explorations; and a wealth of other sources.

© Bettmann/CORBIS

CHAPTER OUTLINE

- THE ROAD TO WORLD WAR I
- THE GREAT WAR
- WAR AND REVOLUTION
- THE FUTILE SEARCH FOR STABILITY
- IN PURSUIT OF A NEW REALITY: CULTURAL AND
  INTELLECTUAL TRENDS
- CONCLUSION

FOCUS QUESTIONS

- What were the long-range and the immediate causes of World
  War I, and why did the course of the war turn out to be so different
  from what the belligerents had expected?

- How did World War I affect the belligerents' governmental and
  political institutions, economic affairs, and social life?

- What were the main events of the Russian Revolution of 1917, and
  why did the Bolsheviks prevail in the civil war and gain control of
  Russia?

- What were the objectives of the chief participants at the Paris
  Peace Conference of 1919, and how closely did the final settlement mirror their objectives?

- What crises did Europe and the United States face in the interwar
  years, and how did the cultural and intellectual trends of that
  period reflect those crises as well as the experience of World War I?

- What was the relationship between World War I and the Russian
  Revolution?

THE BEGINNING OF THE TWENTIETH-CENTURY CRISIS: WAR AND REVOLUTION

O n July 1, 1916, British and French infantry forces attacked German defensive
lines along a 25-mile front near the Somme River in France. Each soldier carried
almost 70 pounds of equipment, making it "impossible to move much quicker than a
slow walk." German machine guns soon opened fire: "We were able to see our comrades move forward in an attempt to cross No-Man's Land, only to be mown down
like meadow grass," recalled one British soldier. "I felt sick at the sight of this carnage
and remember weeping." In one day, more than 21,000 British soldiers died. After six
months of fighting, the British had advanced 5 miles; one million British, French,

and German soldiers had been killed or wounded.

World War I (1914–1918) was the defining event of the twentieth century. Overwhelmed by the size of its battles, the extent of its casualties, and its impact on all facets of life, contemporaries referred to it simply as the "Great War." The Great War was all the more disturbing to Europeans because it came after a period that many believed to have been an age of progress. Material prosperity and a fervid belief in scientific and technological advancement had convinced many people that the world stood on the verge of creating the utopia that humans had dreamed of for centuries. The historian Arnold Toynbee expressed what the pre–World War I era had meant to his generation:

> [We had expected] that life throughout the world would become more rational, more humane, and more democratic and that, slowly, but surely, political democracy would produce greater social justice. We had also expected that the progress of science and technology would make mankind richer, and that this increasing wealth would gradually spread from a minority to a majority. We had expected that all this would happen peacefully. In fact we thought that mankind's course was set for an earthly paradise.[1]

After 1918, it was no longer possible to maintain naive illusions about the progress of Western civilization. As World War I was followed by revolutionary upheavals, the mass murder machines of totalitarian regimes, and the destructiveness of World War II, it became all too apparent that instead of a utopia, Western civilization had become a nightmare. World War I and the revolutions it spawned can properly be seen as the first stage in the crisis of the twentieth century. ●

 # THE ROAD TO WORLD WAR I

On June 28, 1914, the heir to the Austrian throne, Archduke Francis Ferdinand, was assassinated in the Bosnian city of Sarajevo. Although this event precipitated the confrontation between Austria and Serbia that led to World War I, underlying forces had been propelling Europeans toward armed conflict for a long time.

Nationalism and Internal Dissent

The system of nation-states that had emerged in Europe in the second half of the nineteenth century (see Map 22.1) had led to severe competition. Rivalries over colonies and trade intensified during an era of frenzied imperialist expansion, while the division of Europe's great powers into two loose alliances (Germany, Austria, and Italy on one side and France, Great Britain, and Russia on the other) only added to the tensions. The series of crises that tested these alliances in the 1900s and early 1910s had left European states embittered, eager for revenge, and willing to go to war to preserve the power of their national states.

The growth of nationalism in the nineteenth century had yet another serious consequence. Not all ethnic groups had achieved the goal of nationhood. Slavic minorities in the Balkans and the multinational Habsburg Empire, for example, still dreamed of creating their own national states. So did the Irish in the British Empire and the Poles in the Russian Empire.

National aspirations, however, were not the only source of internal strife at the beginning of the twentieth century. Socialist labor movements had grown more powerful and were increasingly inclined to use strikes, even violent ones, to achieve their goals. Some conservative leaders, alarmed at the increase in labor strife and class division, even feared that European nations were on the verge of revolution. Did these statesmen opt for war in 1914 because they believed that "prosecuting an active foreign policy," as some Austrian leaders expressed it, would smother "internal troubles"? Some historians have argued that the desire to suppress internal disorder may have encouraged some leaders to take the plunge into war in 1914.

Militarism

The growth of large mass armies after 1900 not only heightened the existing tensions in Europe but also made it inevitable that if war did come, it would be highly destructive. Conscription had been established as a regular practice in most Western countries before 1914 (the United States and Britain were major exceptions). European military machines had doubled in size between 1890 and 1914. The Russian army was the largest, with 1.3 million men, and the French and Germans were not far behind, with 900,000 each. The British, Italian, and Austrian armies numbered between 250,000 and 500,000 soldiers.

Militarism, however, involved more than just large armies. As armies grew, so did the influence of military leaders, who drew up vast and complex plans for quickly mobilizing millions of men and enormous quantities of supplies in the event of war. Fearful that changes in these plans would cause chaos in the armed forces, military leaders insisted that their plans could not be altered. In the

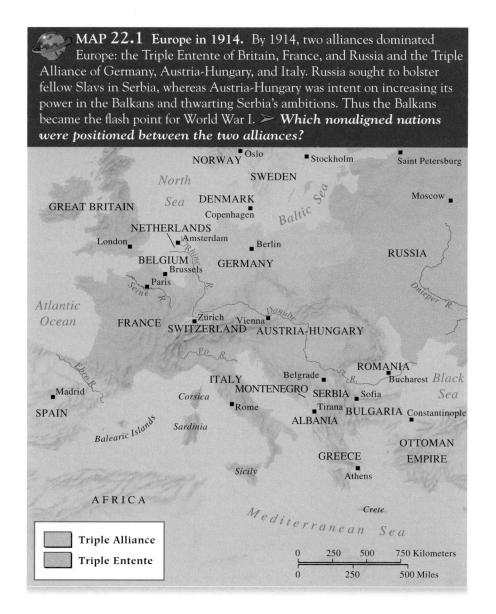

MAP 22.1 Europe in 1914. By 1914, two alliances dominated Europe: the Triple Entente of Britain, France, and Russia and the Triple Alliance of Germany, Austria-Hungary, and Italy. Russia sought to bolster fellow Slavs in Serbia, whereas Austria-Hungary was intent on increasing its power in the Balkans and thwarting Serbia's ambitions. Thus the Balkans became the flash point for World War I. ➢ *Which nonaligned nations were positioned between the two alliances?*

crises during the summer of 1914, the generals' lack of flexibility forced European political leaders to make decisions for military instead of political reasons.

The Outbreak of War: Summer 1914

Militarism, nationalism, and the desire to stifle internal dissent may all have played a role in the coming of World War I, but the decisions made by European leaders in the summer of 1914 directly precipitated the conflict. It was another crisis in the Balkans that forced this predicament on European statesmen.

As we have seen, states in southeastern Europe had struggled to free themselves of Ottoman rule in the course of the nineteenth and early twentieth centuries. But the rivalry between Austria-Hungary and Russia for domination of these new states created serious tensions in the region. By 1914, Serbia, supported by Russia, was determined to create a large, independent Slavic state in the

Balkans, while Austria-Hungary, which had its own Slavic minorities to contend with, was equally set on preventing that possibility. Many Europeans perceived the inherent dangers in this explosive situation. The British ambassador to Vienna wrote in 1913:

> Serbia will some day set Europe by the ears, and bring about a universal war on the Continent. . . . I cannot tell you how exasperated people are getting here at the continual worry which that little country causes to Austria under encouragement from Russia. . . . It will be lucky if Europe succeeds in avoiding war as a result of the present crisis. The next time a Serbian crisis arises . . . , I feel sure that Austria-Hungary will refuse to admit of any Russian interference in the dispute and that she will proceed to settle her differences with her little neighbor by herself.[2]

It was against this backdrop of mutual distrust and hatred that the events of the summer of 1914 were played out.

The assassination of the Austrian Archduke Francis Ferdinand and his wife, Sophia, on June 28, 1914, was carried out by a Bosnian activist who worked for the Black Hand, a Serbian terrorist organization dedicated to the creation of a pan-Slavic kingdom. The Austrian government saw an opportunity to "render Serbia innocuous once and for all by a display of force," as the Austrian foreign minister put it. Fearful of Russian intervention on Serbia's behalf, Austrian leaders sought the backing of their German allies. Emperor William II and his chancellor gave their assurance that Austria-Hungary could rely on Germany's "full support," even if "matters went to the length of a war between Austria-Hungary and Russia."

Strengthened by German support, Austrian leaders issued an ultimatum to Serbia on July 23 in which they made such extreme demands that Serbia had little choice but to reject some of them in order to preserve its sovereignty. Austria then declared war on Serbia on July 28. But Russia was determined to support Serbia's cause, and on July 28, Tsar Nicholas II ordered partial mobilization of the Russian army against Austria. The Russian general staff informed the tsar that their mobilization plans were based on a war against both Germany and Austria simultaneously. They could not execute partial mobilization without creating chaos in the army. Consequently the Russian government ordered full mobilization of the Russian army on July 29, knowing that the Germans would consider this an act of war against them. Germany reacted quickly. It issued an ultimatum that Russia must halt its mobilization within twelve hours. When the Russians ignored it, Germany declared war on Russia on August 1.

At this stage of the conflict, German war plans determined whether or not France would become involved in the war. Under the guidance of General Alfred von Schlieffen, chief of staff from 1891 to 1905, the German general staff had devised a military plan based on the assumption of a two-front war with France and Russia, because the two powers had formed a military alliance in 1894. The Schlieffen Plan called for a small holding action against Russia while most of the German army would make a rapid invasion of France before Russia could become effective in the east or before the British could cross the English Channel to help France. This meant invading France by advancing faster along the level coastal area through neutral Belgium rather than the rougher terrain to the southeast. After the planned quick defeat of the French, the German army expected to redeploy to the east against Russia. Under the Schlieffen Plan, Germany could not mobilize its troops solely against Russia and therefore declared war on France on August 3 after it had issued an ultimatum to Belgium on August 2 demanding the right of German troops to pass through Belgian territory. On August 4, Great Britain declared war on Germany, officially over this violation of Belgian neutrality but in fact over the British desire to maintain its world power. As one British diplomat argued, if Germany and Austria would win the war, "what would be the position of a friendless England?" By August 4, all the great powers of Europe were at war.

THE GREAT WAR

Before 1914, many political leaders had become convinced that war involved so many political and economic risks that it was not worth fighting. Others had believed that "rational" diplomats could control any situation and prevent the outbreak of war. At the beginning of August 1914, both of these prewar illusions were shattered, but the new illusions that replaced them soon proved equally foolish.

1914–1915: Illusions and Stalemate

Europeans went to war in 1914 with great enthusiasm (see the box on p. 481). Government propaganda had been successful in stirring up national antagonisms before the war. Now in August 1914, the urgent pleas of governments for defense against aggressors fell on receptive ears in every belligerent nation. A new set of illusions also fed the enthusiasm for war. Almost everyone in August 1914 believed that the war would be over in a few weeks. People were reminded that all European wars since 1815 had, in fact, ended in a matter of weeks, conveniently overlooking the U.S. Civil War (1861–1865), which was the real prototype for World War I. Both the soldiers who exuberantly boarded the trains for the war front in August 1914 and the jubilant citizens who bombarded them with flowers when they departed believed that the warriors would be home by Christmas.

German hopes for a quick end to the war rested on a military gamble. The Schlieffen Plan had called for the German army to make a vast encircling movement through Belgium into northern France that would sweep around Paris and encircle most of the French army (see Map 22.2). But the German advance was halted only 20 miles from Paris at the first Battle of the Marne (September 6–10). The war quickly turned into a stalemate as neither the Germans nor the French could dislodge each other from the trenches they had begun to dig for shelter.

In contrast to the Western Front, the war in the east was marked by much

The Schlieffen Plan

nia on May 7, 1915, when over a hundred Americans lost their lives, forced the German government to suspend unrestricted submarine warfare in September 1915.

In January 1917, however, eager to break the deadlock in the war, the Germans decided on another military gamble by returning to unrestricted submarine warfare. German naval officers convinced Emperor William II that the use of unrestricted submarine warfare could starve the British into submission within five months, certainly before the Americans could act. The return to unrestricted submarine warfare brought the United States into the war on April 6, 1917. Although U.S. troops did not arrive in large numbers in Europe until the following year, the entry of the United States into the war gave the Allied Powers a psychological boost when they needed it.

The year 1917 had not been a good year for them. Allied offensives on the Western Front were disastrously defeated. The Italian armies were smashed in October, and in November, the Bolshevik Revolution in Russia (see "The Russian Revolution" later in this chapter) led to Russia's withdrawal from the war, leaving Germany free to concentrate entirely on the Western Front. The cause of the Central Powers looked favorable, although war weariness in the Ottoman Empire, Bulgaria, Austria-Hungary, and Germany was beginning to take its toll. The home front was rapidly becoming a cause for as much concern as the war front.

The Home Front: The Impact of Total War

The prolongation of World War I affected the lives of all citizens, however remote they might be from the battlefields. The need to organize masses of men and matériel for years of combat (Germany alone had 5.5 million men in active units in 1916) led to increased centralization of government powers, economic regimentation, and manipulation of public opinion to keep the war effort going.

Because the war was expected to be short, little thought had been given to long-term wartime needs. Governments had to respond quickly, however, when the war machines failed to achieve their knockout blows and made ever-greater demands for men and matériel. To meet these needs, governments expanded their powers. Countries drafted tens of millions of young men for that elusive breakthrough to victory.

Throughout Europe, wartime governments also expanded their powers over their economies. Free-market capitalistic systems were temporarily shelved as governments experimented with price, wage, and rent controls, rationed food supplies and materials, and nationalized transportation systems and industries. Under total war mobilization, the distinction between soldiers at war and civilians at home was narrowed. In the view of political leaders, all citizens constituted a national army.

As the Great War dragged on and casualties grew worse, the patriotic enthusiasm that had marked the early days of the conflict waned. By 1916, there were numerous signs that civilian morale was beginning to crack under the pressure of total war. Governments fought the growing opposition to the war. Authoritarian regimes, such as those of Germany, Russia, and Austria-Hungary, had always relied on force to subdue their populations, but under the pressures of the war, even parliamentary regimes resorted to an expansion of police powers to stifle internal dissent. The British Parliament, for example, passed the Defence of the Realm Act (DORA), which allowed the public authorities to arrest dissenters and charge them as traitors. Newspapers were censored, and sometimes their publication was even suspended.

Wartime governments made active use of propaganda to arouse enthusiasm for the war. At first, public officials needed to do little to achieve this goal. The British and

⇒ **BRITISH RECRUITING POSTER.** As the conflict persisted month after month, governments resorted to active propaganda campaigns to generate enthusiasm for the war. In this British recruiting poster, the government tried to pressure men into volunteering for military service. By 1916, the British were forced to adopt compulsory military service.

French, for example, exaggerated German atrocities in Belgium and found that their citizens were only too willing to believe these accounts. But as the war progressed and morale sagged, governments were forced to devise new techniques for stimulating declining enthusiasm.

World War I opened up new roles for women. Because so many men went off to fight at the front, women were called on to take over jobs and responsibilities that had not been available to them before. Overall the number of women employed in Britain who held new jobs or replaced men rose by 1,345,000. Women were also now employed in jobs that had been considered beyond the "capacity of women." These included such occupations as chimney sweeps, truck drivers, farm laborers, and factory workers in heavy industry. Thirty-eight percent of the workers in the Krupp Armaments works in Germany in 1918 were women. Nevertheless, despite the noticeable increase in women's wages that resulted from government regulations, women's industrial wages still never equaled men's wages at any time during the war.

Even worse, women had achieved little real security about their place in the workforce. Both men and women seemed to expect that many of the new jobs for women were only temporary, an expectation quite evident in the British poem "War Girls," written in 1916:

> There's the girl who clips your ticket for the train,
> And the girl who speeds the lift from floor to floor,
> There's the girl who does a milk-round in the rain,
> And the girl who calls for orders at your door.
> Strong, sensible, and fit,
> They're out to show their grit,
> And tackle jobs with energy and knack.
> No longer caged and penned up,
> They're going to keep their end up
> Till the khaki soldier boys come marching back.[4]

At the end of the war, governments moved quickly to remove women from the jobs they had been encouraged to take earlier, and wages for women who remained employed were lowered. The work benefits for women from World War I seemed to be overturned as demobilized men returned to the job market.

Nevertheless, in some countries, the role played by women in the wartime economies did have a positive impact on the women's movement for political emancipation. The most obvious gain was the right to vote, granted to women in Britain in January 1918 and in Germany and Austria immediately after the war. Contemporary media, however, tended to focus on the more noticeable yet in some ways more superficial social emancipation of upper- and middle-class women. In ever-larger numbers, these young women took jobs, had their own apartments, and showed their new independence by smoking in public, wearing shorter dresses, and adopting radical new hairstyles.

 ## WAR AND REVOLUTION

By 1917, total war was creating serious domestic turmoil in all of the European belligerent states. Only one, however, experienced the kind of complete collapse that others were predicting might happen throughout Europe. Out of Russia's collapse came the Russian Revolution.

The Russian Revolution

Tsar Nicholas II was an autocratic ruler who relied on the army and the bureaucracy to prop up his regime. Russia was unprepared both technologically and militarily for the total war of World War I. Competent military leadership was lacking, and Russian industry was unable to produce the weapons needed for the army. Many soldiers were sent to the front without rifles and told to pick one up from a dead comrade. Ill-led and ill-armed, Russian armies suffered incredible losses. Between 1914 and 1916, two million soldiers had been killed and another four to six million had been wounded or captured. By 1917, the Russian will to fight had vanished.

In the meantime, Tsar Nicholas II was increasingly insulated from events by his German-born wife, Alexandra, a well-educated woman who had fallen under the influence of Rasputin, a Siberian peasant who belonged to a religious sect that indulged in sexual orgies. Rasputin's influence made him an important power behind the throne, and he did not hesitate to interfere in government affairs. As the leadership at the top stumbled its way through a series of military and economic disasters, the middle class, aristocrats, peasants, soldiers, and workers grew more and more disenchanted with the tsarist regime. Even aristocrats who supported the monarchy felt the need to do something to reverse the deteriorating situation. For a start, they assassinated Rasputin in December 1916. By then, it was too late to save the monarchy.

At the beginning of March 1917, a series of strikes led by working-class women broke out in the capital city of Petrograd (formerly Saint Petersburg). A few weeks earlier, the government had introduced bread rationing in the capital city after the price of bread had skyrocketed. Many of the women who stood in the lines waiting for bread were also factory workers who had put in twelve-hour days. The Russian government had become aware of the volatile situation in the capital from a police report: "Mothers of families, exhausted by endless standing in line at stores, distraught over their half-starving and sick children, are today perhaps closer to revolution than [the liberal opposition leaders] and of course they are a great deal more dangerous because they are the combustible material for which only a single spark is needed to burst into flame."[5] On March 8, about ten thousand women marched through Petrograd demanding "peace and bread." Soon the women were joined by other workers, and together they called for a general strike that succeeded in shutting down all the factories in the city on March 10. Nicholas ordered his troops to disperse the crowds by shooting them if necessary, but large numbers of the soldiers soon joined the demonstrators. The Duma (legislature), which the tsar had tried to dissolve, met anyway and on March 12 declared that it was assuming governmental responsibility. It established a provisional government on March 15; the tsar abdicated the same day.

The Provisional Government, headed by Alexander Kerensky, decided to carry on the war to preserve Russia's honor—a major blunder because it satisfied neither the workers nor the peasants, who wanted more than anything an end to the war. The Provisional Government also faced another authority, the soviets, or councils of workers' and soldiers' deputies. The soviet of Petrograd had been formed in March 1917; at the same time, soviets sprang up spontaneously in army units, factory towns, and rural areas. The soviets represented the more radical interests of the lower classes and were largely composed of socialists of various kinds. One group—the Bolsheviks—came to play a crucial role.

LENIN AND THE BOLSHEVIK SEIZURE OF POWER

The Bolsheviks were a small faction of Marxist social democrats who had come under the leadership of Vladimir Ulianov, known to the world as V. I. Lenin (1870–1924). Under Lenin's direction, the Bolsheviks became a party that believed that only a violent revolution could destroy the capitalist system and that a "vanguard" of activists must form a small party of well-disciplined professional revolutionaries to accomplish the task. Between 1900 and 1917, Lenin spent most of his time in exile in Switzerland. When the Provisional Government was set up in March 1917, he believed

that an opportunity for the Bolsheviks to seize power had come. A month later, with the connivance of the German High Command, who hoped to create disorder in Russia, Lenin was shipped to Russia in a "sealed train" by way of Finland.

Lenin believed that the Bolsheviks must work toward gaining control of the soviets of soldiers, workers, and peasants and then use them to overthrow the Provisional Government. At the same time, the Bolsheviks sought mass support through promises geared to the needs of the people: an end to the war, redistribution of all land to the peasants, the transfer of factories and industries from capitalists to committees of workers, and the relegation of government power from the Provisional Government to the soviets. Three simple slogans summed up the Bolshevik program: "Peace, Land, Bread," "Worker Control of Production," and "All Power to the Soviets."

By the end of October, the Bolsheviks had achieved a slight majority in the Petrograd and Moscow soviets. The number of party members had also grown from 50,000 to 240,000. With Leon Trotsky (1877–1940), a fervid revolutionary, as chairman of the Petrograd soviet, Lenin and the Bolsheviks were in a position to seize power in the name of the soviets. During the night of November 6, pro-soviet and pro-Bolshevik forces took control of Petrograd. The Provisional Government quickly collapsed with little bloodshed. The following night, the All-Russian Congress of Soviets, representing local soviets from all over the country, affirmed the transfer of power. At the second session, the night of November 8, Lenin announced the new Soviet government, the Council of People's Commissars, with himself as its head (see the box on p. 488).

⤜ **LENIN ADDRESSES A CROWD.** V. I. Lenin was the driving force behind the success of the Bolsheviks in seizing power in Russia and creating the Union of Soviet Socialist Republics. Here Lenin is seen addressing a rally in Moscow in 1917.

© Brown Brothers

TEN DAYS THAT SHOOK THE WORLD:
LENIN AND THE BOLSHEVIK SEIZURE OF POWER

John Reed was an American journalist who helped found the American Communist Labor Party. Accused of sedition, he fled the United States and went to Russia. In Ten Days That Shook the World, *Reed left an impassioned eyewitness account of the Russian Revolution. It is apparent from his comments that Reed considered Lenin the indispensable hero of the Bolshevik success.*

JOHN REED, *TEN DAYS THAT SHOOK THE WORLD*

It was just 8:40 when a thundering wave of cheers announced the entrance of the presidium, with Lenin—great Lenin—among them. A short, stocky figure, with a big head set down in his shoulders, bald and bulging. Little eyes, a snubbish nose, wide, generous mouth, and heavy chin; clean-shaven now, but already beginning to bristle with the well-known beard of his past and future. Dressed in shabby clothes, his trousers much too long for him. Unimpressive, to be the idol of a mob, loved and revered as perhaps few leaders in history have been. A strange popular leader—a leader purely by virtue of intellect; colorless, humorless, uncompromising and detached; without picturesque idiosyncrasies—but with the power of explaining profound ideas in simple terms, of analyzing a concrete situation. And combined with shrewdness, the greatest intellectual audacity. . . .

Now Lenin, gripping the edge of the reading stand, letting his little winking eyes travel over the crowd as he stood there waiting, apparently oblivious to the long-rolling ovation, which lasted several minutes. When it finished, he said simply, "We shall now proceed to construct the Socialist order!" Again that overwhelming human roar.

"The first thing is the adoption of practical measures to realize peace. . . . We shall offer peace to the peoples of all the belligerent countries upon the basis of the Soviet terms—no annexations, no indemnities, and the right of self-determination of peoples. At the same time, according to our promise, we shall publish and repudiate the secret treaties. . . . The question of War and Peace is so clear that I think that I may, without preamble, read the project of a Proclamation to the Peoples of All the Belligerent Countries. . . ."

His great mouth, seeming to smile, opened wide as he spoke; his voice was hoarse—not unpleasantly so, but as if it had hardened that way after years and years of speaking—and went on monotonously, with the effect of being able to go forever. . . . For emphasis he bent forward slightly. No gestures. And before him, a thousand simple faces looking up in intent adoration.

[Reed then reproduces the full text of the Proclamation.]

When the grave thunder of applause had died away, Lenin spoke again: "We propose to the Congress to ratify this declaration. . . . This proposal of peace will meet with resistance on the part of the imperialist governments—we don't fool ourselves on that score. But we hope that revolution will soon break out in all the belligerent countries; that is why we address ourselves especially to the workers of France, England, and Germany. . . .

"The revolution of November 6th and 7th," he ended, "has opened the era of the Social Revolution. . . . The labor movement, in the name of peace and Socialism, shall win, and fulfill its destiny. . . ."

There was something quiet and powerful in all this, which stirred the souls of men. It was understandable why people believed when Lenin spoke.

But the Bolsheviks, soon renamed the Communists, still faced enormous obstacles. For one thing, Lenin had promised peace, and that, he realized, was not an easy promise to fulfill because of the humiliating losses of Russian territory that it would entail. There was no real choice, however. On March 3, 1918, Lenin signed the Treaty of Brest-Litovsk with Germany and gave up eastern Poland, the Ukraine, Finland, and the Baltic provinces. He had promised peace to the Russian people; but real peace did not come, for the country soon sank into civil war.

CIVIL WAR

There was great opposition to the new communist regime, not only from groups loyal to the tsar but also from bourgeois and aristocratic liberals and anti-Leninist socialists. In addition, thousands of Allied troops were eventually sent to different parts of Russia.

Between 1918 and 1921, the Communist (Red) Army was forced to fight on many fronts. The first serious threat to the Communists came from Siberia, where a White (anticommunist) force attacked westward and advanced almost to the Volga River. Attacks also came from the Ukrainians in the southwest and from the Baltic regions. In mid-1919, White forces swept through the Ukraine and advanced almost to Moscow before being pushed back. By 1920, the major White forces had been defeated, and the Ukraine had been retaken. The next year, the communist regime regained control over the independent nationalist governments in the Caucasus: Georgia, Russian Armenia, and Azerbaijan.

How had Lenin and the Bolsheviks triumphed over what seemed at one time to be overwhelming forces? For one thing, the Red Army became a well-disciplined fighting force, largely due to the organizational genius of Leon Trotsky. As commissar of war, Trotsky reinstated the draft and insisted on rigid discipline; soldiers who deserted or refused to obey orders were summarily executed.

Furthermore, the disunity of the anticommunist forces seriously weakened the efforts of the Whites. Political differences created distrust among the Whites and prevented them from cooperating effectively. It was difficult enough to achieve military cooperation; political differences made it virtually impossible.

The lack of a common goal on the part of the Whites was paralleled by a single-minded sense of purpose on the part of the Communists. Inspired by their vision of a new socialist order, the Communists had the advantage of possessing the determination that comes from revolutionary fervor and revolutionary convictions. The Communists also succeeded in translating their revolutionary faith into practical instruments of power. A policy of "war communism," for example, was used to ensure regular supplies for the Red Army. "War communism" included the nationalization of banks and most industries, the forcible requisition of grain from peasants, and the centralization of state power under Bolshevik control. Another Bolshevik instrument was "revolutionary terror." A new Red secret police—known as the Cheka—instituted the Red Terror, aimed at nothing less than the destruction of all who opposed the new regime.

Finally, the intervention of foreign armies enabled the Communists to appeal to the powerful force of Russian patriotism. Appalled by the takeover of power in Russia by the radical Communists, the Allied Powers intervened. At one point, over 100,000 foreign troops—mostly Japanese, British, American, and French—were stationed on Russian soil. This intervention by the Allies enabled the communist government to appeal to patriotic Russians to fight the attempts of foreigners to control their country.

By 1921, the Communists were in control of Russia. In the course of the civil war, the communist regime had also transformed Russia into a bureaucratically centralized state dominated by a single party. It was also a state that was largely hostile to the Allied Powers that had sought to assist the Communists' enemies in the civil war.

The Last Year of the War

For Germany, the withdrawal of the Russians in March 1918 offered renewed hope for a favorable end to the war. The victory over Russia persuaded Erich von Ludendorff, who guided German military operations, and most German leaders to make one final military gamble—a grand offensive in the west to break the military stalemate. The German attack was launched in March and lasted into July, but an Allied counterattack, supported by the arrival of 140,000 fresh American troops, defeated the Germans at the Second Battle of the Marne on July 18. Ludendorff's gamble had failed. With the arrival of two million more American troops on the Continent, Allied forces began making a steady advance toward Germany.

Chronology

THE RUSSIAN REVOLUTION

1917

March of women in Petrograd	March 8
General strike in Petrograd	March 10
Establishment of Provisional Government	March 12
Abdication of Tsar Nicholas II	March 15
Arrival of Lenin in Russia	April 3
Bolshevik majority in Petrograd soviet	October
Bolshevik overthrow of Provisional Government	November 6–7

1918

Treaty of Brest-Litovsk	March 3
Civil war	1918–1921

On September 29, 1918, General Ludendorff informed German leaders that the war was lost and demanded that the government sue for peace at once. When German officials discovered, however, that the Allies were unwilling to make peace with the autocratic imperial government, reforms were instituted to create a liberal government. In addition, popular demonstrations broke out throughout Germany. William II capitulated to public pressure and abdicated on November 9, and the Socialists under Friedrich Ebert announced the establishment of a republic. Two days later, on November 11, 1918, the new German government agreed to an armistice. The war was over.

The Peace Settlement

In January 1919, the delegations of twenty-seven victorious Allied nations gathered in Paris to conclude a final settlement of the Great War. Over a period of years, the reasons for fighting World War I had been transformed from selfish national interests to idealistic principles. No one expressed the latter better than U.S. president Woodrow Wilson. Wilson's proposals for a truly just and lasting peace included "open covenants of peace, openly arrived at" instead of secret diplomacy; the reduction of national armaments to a "point consistent with domestic safety"; and the self-determination of people so that "all well-defined national aspirations shall be accorded the utmost satisfaction." As the spokesman for a new world order based on democracy and international cooperation, Wilson was enthusiastically cheered by many Europeans when he arrived in Europe for the peace conference.

Wilson soon found, however, that more practical motives guided other states at the Paris Peace Conference. The secret treaties and agreements that had been made

Chronology

WORLD WAR I

1914

Battle of Tannenberg	August 26–30
First Battle of the Marne	September 6–10
Battle of Masurian Lakes	September 15

1915

Battle of Gallipoli begins	April 25
Italy declares war on Austria-Hungary	May 23

1916

Battle of Verdun	February 21–December 18

1917

Germany returns to unrestricted submarine warfare	January
United States enters the war	April 6

1918

Last German offensive	March 21–July 18
Second Battle of the Marne	July 18
Allied counteroffensive	July 18–November 10
Armistice between Allies and Germany	November 11

before the war could not be totally ignored, even if they did conflict with the principle of self-determination enunciated by Wilson. National interests also complicated the deliberations of the Paris Peace Conference. David Lloyd George, prime minister of Great Britain, had won a decisive electoral victory in December 1918 on a platform of making the Germans pay for this dreadful war.

France's approach to peace was primarily determined by considerations of national security. To Georges Clemenceau, the feisty premier of France who had led his country to victory, the French people had borne the brunt of German aggression. They deserved revenge and security against future German aggression.

The most important decisions at the Paris Peace Conference were made by Wilson, Clemenceau, and Lloyd George. Italy was considered one of the so-called Big Four powers but played a much less important role than the other three countries. Germany, of course, was not invited to attend, and Russia could not because of its civil war.

In view of the many conflicting demands at the peace conference, it was inevitable that the victorious powers would quarrel. Wilson was determined to create a "league of nations" to prevent future wars. Clemenceau and Lloyd

George were equally determined to punish Germany. In the end, only compromise made it possible to achieve a peace settlement. Wilson's wish that the creation of an international peacekeeping organization be the first order of business was granted, and already on January 25, 1919, the conference adopted the principle of the League of Nations. In return, Wilson agreed to make compromises on territorial arrangements to guarantee the establishment of the League, believing that a functioning League could later rectify bad arrangements.

THE TREATY OF VERSAILLES

The final peace settlement consisted of five separate treaties with the defeated nations—Germany, Austria, Hungary, Bulgaria, and Turkey. The Treaty of Versailles with Germany, signed on June 28, 1919, was by far the most important one. The Germans considered it a harsh peace and were particularly unhappy with Article 231, the so-called War Guilt Clause, which declared Germany (and Austria) responsible for starting the war and ordered Germany to pay reparations for all the damage to which the Allied governments and their people were subjected as a result of the war.

The military and territorial provisions of the treaty also rankled Germans. Germany had to lower its army to 100,000 men, reduce its navy, and eliminate its air force. German territorial losses included the return of Alsace and Lorraine to France and sections of Prussia to the new Polish state (see Map 22.3). German land west and as far as 30 miles east of the Rhine was established as a demilitarized zone and stripped of all armaments or fortifications to serve as a barrier to any future German military moves westward against France. Outraged by the "dictated peace," the new German government complained but accepted the treaty.

THE OTHER PEACE TREATIES

The separate peace treaties made with the other Central Powers extensively redrew the map of eastern Europe. Many of these changes merely ratified what the war had already accomplished. Both the German and Russian Empires lost considerable territory in eastern Europe, and the Austro-Hungarian Empire disappeared altogether. New nation-states emerged from the lands of these three empires: Finland, Latvia, Estonia, Lithuania, Poland, Czechoslovakia, Austria, and Hungary. Territorial rearrangements were also made in the Balkans. Romania acquired additional lands from Russia, Hungary, and Bulgaria. Serbia formed the nucleus of a new southern Slavic state, called Yugoslavia, which combined Serbs, Croats, and Slovenes.

Although the Paris Peace Conference was supposedly guided by the principle of self-determination, the mixtures of peoples in eastern Europe made it impossible to draw boundaries along neat ethnic lines. As a result of compromises, virtually every eastern European state was left with a minorities problem that could lead to future conflicts. Ger-

MAP 22.3 Territorial Changes in Europe and the Middle East After World War I. The victorious Allies met in Paris to determine the shape and nature of postwar Europe. At the urging of U.S. president Woodrow Wilson, many nationalist aspirations of former imperial subjects were realized with the creation of several new countries from the prewar territory of Austria-Hungary, Germany, Russia, and the Ottoman Empire. ➢ *What new countries emerged in Europe and the Middle East?*

Lost immediately after World War I
- By Russia
- By Germany
- By Ottoman Empire
- By Bulgaria
- By Austria-Hungary

mans in Poland; Hungarians, Poles, and Germans in Czechoslovakia; Hungarians in Romania; and the combination of Serbs, Croats, Slovenes, Macedonians, and Albanians in Yugoslavia all became sources of later conflict.

Yet another centuries-old empire, the Ottoman Empire, was dismembered by the peace settlement after the war. To gain Arab support against the Ottoman Turks during the war, the Western Allies had promised to recognize the independence of Arab states in the Middle Eastern lands of the Ottoman Empire. But the imperialist habits of Western nations died hard. After the war, France was given control of Lebanon and Syria, while Britain received Iraq and Palestine. Officially, both acquisitions were called "mandates," a system whereby a nation officially administered a territory on behalf of the League of Nations. The system of mandates could not hide the fact that the principle of national self-determination at the Paris Peace Conference was largely for Europeans.

THE FUTILE SEARCH FOR STABILITY

The peace settlement at the end of World War I had tried to fulfill the nineteenth-century dream of nationalism by creating new boundaries and new states. From its inception, however, this peace settlement had left nations unhappy and only too eager to revise it.

Uneasy Peace, Uncertain Security

President Woodrow Wilson had recognized that the peace treaties contained unwise provisions that could serve as new causes for conflicts, and he had placed many of his hopes for the future in the League of Nations. The League, however, was not particularly effective in maintaining the peace. The failure of the United States to join the League in a backlash of isolationist sentiment undermined its effectiveness from the beginning. Moreover, the League could use only economic sanctions to halt aggression.

France's search for security between 1919 and 1924 was founded primarily on a strict enforcement of the Treaty of Versailles. This tough policy toward Germany began with the issue of reparations, the payments that the Germans were supposed to make to compensate for war damage. In April 1921, the Allied Reparations Commission settled on a sum of 132 billion marks ($33 billion) for German reparations, payable in annual installments of 2.5 billion (gold) marks. The new German republic made its first payment in 1921, but by the following year, facing financial problems, the German government announced that it was unable to pay more. Outraged, the French government sent troops to occupy the Ruhr valley, Germany's chief industrial and mining center. Because the Germans would not pay reparations, the French would collect reparations in kind by operating and using the Ruhr mines and factories.

Both Germany and France suffered from the French occupation of the Ruhr. The German government adopted a policy of passive resistance to French occupation that was largely financed by printing more paper money. This only intensified the inflationary pressures that had already begun in Germany by the end of the war. The German mark became worthless, and economic disaster fueled political upheavals. All the nations, including France, were happy to cooperate with the American suggestion for a new conference of experts to reassess the reparations problem.

In August 1924, an international commission produced a new plan for reparations. The Dawes Plan, named after the American banker who chaired the commission, reduced reparations and stabilized Germany's payments on the basis of its ability to pay. The Dawes Plan also granted an initial $200 million loan for German recovery, which opened the door to heavy American investments in Europe that helped create a new era of European prosperity between 1924 and 1929.

With prosperity came a new age of European diplomacy. A spirit of cooperation was fostered by the foreign ministers of Germany and France, Gustav Stresemann and Aristide Briand, who concluded the Treaty of Locarno in 1925. This guaranteed Germany's new western borders with France and Belgium. Although Germany's new eastern borders with Poland were conspicuously absent from the agreement, the Locarno pact was viewed by many as the beginning of a new era of European peace.

The spirit of Locarno was based on little real substance, however. Germany lacked the military power to alter its western borders even if it wanted to. And the issue of disarmament soon proved that even the spirit of Locarno could not bring nations to cut back on their weapons. The League of Nations had suggested the "reduction of national armaments to the lowest point consistent with national safety." Germany, of course, had been disarmed with the expectation that other states would do likewise. Numerous disarmament conferences, however, failed to achieve anything substantial as states were unwilling to trust their security to anyone but their own military forces.

The Great Depression

Almost as devastating as the two world wars in the first half of the twentieth century was the economic collapse that ravaged the world in the 1930s. Two events set the stage for the Great Depression: a downturn in domestic economic activities and an international financial crisis precipitated by the collapse of the American stock market in 1929.

Already in the mid-1920s, prices for agricultural goods were beginning to decline rapidly due to overproduction of basic commodities, such as wheat. In addition to domestic economic troubles, much of the European prosperity between 1924 and 1929 had been built on American bank loans to Germany. Already in 1928 and 1929, American investors had begun to pull money out of Germany in order to invest in the booming New York stock market. The crash of the U.S. stock market in October 1929 led panicky American investors to withdraw even more of their funds from Germany and other European markets. The withdrawal of funds seriously weakened the banks of Germany and other central European states. By 1931, trade was slowing down, industrialists were cutting back production, and unemployment was increasing as the effects of international bank failures had a devastating impact on domestic economies.

Economic depression was by no means a new phenomenon in European history, but the depth of the economic downturn after 1929 fully justifies the label Great Depression. During 1932, the worst year of the depression, one British worker in four was unemployed; in Germany, six million people, 40 percent of the labor force, were out of work. The unemployed and homeless filled the streets of the cities of the advanced industrial countries (see the box on p. 493).

Governments seemed powerless to deal with the crisis. The classical liberal remedy for depression, a deflationary policy of balanced budgets, which involved cutting costs by lowering wages and raising tariffs to exclude other countries' goods from home markets, only served to worsen the economic crisis and cause even greater mass discontent. This in turn led to serious political repercussions. Increased government activity in the economy was one reaction. Another effect was a renewed interest in Marxist doctrines. Hadn't Marx predicted that capitalism would destroy itself through overproduction? Communism took on new popularity, especially with workers and intellectuals. Finally, the Great Depression increased the attractiveness of facile dictatorial solutions, especially from a

THE GREAT DEPRESSION: UNEMPLOYED AND HOMELESS IN GERMANY

In 1932, Germany had six million unemployed workers, many of them wandering aimlessly about the country, begging for food and seeking shelter in city lodging for the homeless. The Great Depression was an important factor in the rise to power of Adolf Hitler and the Nazis. This selection presents a description of the unemployed homeless in 1932.

HEINRICH HAUSER, "WITH GERMANY'S UNEMPLOYED"

An almost unbroken chain of homeless men extends the whole length of the great Hamburg-Berlin highway. . . . All the highways in Germany over which I have traveled this year presented the same aspect. . . .

Most of the hikers paid no attention to me. They walked separately or in small groups, with their eyes on the ground. And they had the queer, stumbling gait of barefooted people, for their shoes were slung over their shoulders. Some of them were guild members. . . . Far more numerous were those whom one could assign to no special profession or craft—unskilled young people, for the most part, who had been unable to find a place for themselves in any city or town in Germany, and who had never had a job and never expected to have one. There was something else that had never been seen before—whole families that had piled all their goods into baby carriages and wheelbarrows that they were pushing along as they plodded forward in dumb despair. It was a whole nation on the march.

I saw them—and this was the strongest impression that the year 1932 left with me—I saw them, gathered into groups of fifty or a hundred men, attacking fields of potatoes. I saw them digging up the potatoes and throwing them into sacks while the farmer who owned the field watched them in despair and the local policeman looked on gloomily from the distance. I saw them staggering toward the lights of the city as night fell, with their sacks on their backs. What did it remind me of? Of the War, of the worst periods of starvation in 1917 and 1918, but even then people paid for the potatoes. . . .

I saw that the individual can know what is happening only by personal experience. I know what it is to be a tramp. I know what cold and hunger are. . . . But there are two things that I have only recently experienced—begging and spending the night in a municipal lodging house.

I entered the huge Berlin municipal lodging house in a northern quarter of the city. . . .

Distribution of spoons, distribution of enameled-ware bowls with the words "Property of the City of Berlin" written on their sides. Then the meal itself. A big kettle is carried in. Men with yellow smocks have brought it in, and men with yellow smocks ladle out the food. These men, too, are homeless and they have been expressly picked by the establishment and given free food and lodging and a little pocket money in exchange for their work about the house. . . .

Now the men are standing in a long row, dressed in their plain nightshirts that reach to the ground, and the noise of their shuffling feet is like the noise of big wild animals walking up and down the stone floor of their cages before feeding time. The men lean far over the kettle so that the warm steam from the food envelops them, and they hold out their bowls as if begging and whisper to the attendant, "Give me a real helping. Give me a little more." A piece of bread is handed out with every bowl.

My next recollection is sitting at table in another room on a crowded bench that is like a seat in a fourth-class railway carriage. Hundreds of hungry mouths make an enormous noise eating their food. The men sit bent over their food like animals who feel that someone is going to take it away from them. They hold their bowl with their left arm partway around it, so that nobody can take it away, and they also protect it with their other elbow and with their head and mouth, while they move the spoon as fast as they can between their mouth and the bowl.

---

new movement known as fascism. Everywhere, democracy seemed on the defensive in the 1930s.

The Democratic States

After World War I, Great Britain went through a period of serious economic difficulties. During the war, Britain had lost many of the markets for its industrial products, especially to the United States and Japan. The postwar decline of such staple industries as coal, steel, and textiles led to a rise in unemployment, which reached the two million mark in 1921. But Britain soon rebounded and from 1925 to 1929 experienced an era of renewed prosperity, even though unemployment remained at the startling level of 10 percent.

By 1929, Britain faced the growing effects of the Great Depression. A national government, dominated by the Conservatives, claimed credit for bringing Britain out of the worst stages of the depression, primarily by using the traditional policies of balanced budgets and protective tariffs. British politicians had largely ignored the new ideas of a Cambridge economist, John Maynard Keynes (1883–1946), who published his *General Theory of Employment, Interest, and Money* in 1936. He condemned the traditional view that in a free economy, depressions should be left to work themselves out. Keynes argued instead that unemployment stemmed not from overproduction but from a decline in demand and that demand could be increased by putting people back to work building highways and public

THE GREAT DEPRESSION: BREAD LINES IN PARIS. The Great Depression devastated the European economy and had serious political repercussions. Because of its more balanced economy, France did not feel the effects of the depression as quickly as other European countries. By 1931, however, even France was experiencing lines of unemployed people at free-food centers.

structures, even if governments had to go into debt to pay for these works, a concept known as deficit spending.

After the defeat of Germany, France had become the strongest power on the European continent. Its greatest need was to rebuild the devastated areas of northern and eastern France. However, no French government seemed capable of solving France's financial problems between 1921 and 1926. Like other European countries, though, France did experience a period of relative prosperity between 1926 and 1929.

Because it had a more balanced economy than other nations, France did not begin to feel the full effects of the Great Depression until 1932. Economic instability soon had political repercussions. During a nineteen-month period in 1932 and 1933, six different cabinets were formed as France faced political chaos. Finally, in June 1936, a coalition of leftist parties—Communists, Socialists, and Radicals—formed a new government, the Popular Front.

Although the Popular Front initiated a program for workers that consisted of the right of collective bargaining, a forty-hour workweek, two-week paid vacations, and minimum wages, its policies failed to solve the problems of the depression. By 1938, the French were experiencing a serious decline of confidence in their political system.

After the imperial Germany of William II had come to an end in 1918 with Germany's defeat in World War I, a German democratic state known as the Weimar Republic was established. From its beginnings, the Weimar Republic was plagued by a series of problems. The republic had no truly outstanding political leaders, and in 1925, Paul von Hindenburg, a World War I military hero, was elected president at the age of seventy-seven. Hindenburg was a traditional military man, monarchist in sentiment, who at heart was not in favor of the republic he had been elected to serve.

The Weimar Republic also faced serious economic difficulties. Germany experienced runaway inflation in 1922 and 1923; widows, orphans, the retired elderly, army officers, teachers, civil servants, and others who lived on fixed incomes all watched their monthly stipends become worthless and their lifetime savings disappear. Their economic losses increasingly pushed the middle class to the rightist parties that were hostile to the republic. To make matters worse, after a period of prosperity from 1924 to 1929, Germany faced the Great Depression. Unemployment increased to 3 million in March 1930 and 4.4 million by December of the same year. The depression paved the way for the rise of extremist parties.

After Germany, no Western nation was more affected by the Great Depression than the United States. By 1932, U.S. industrial production fell to 50 percent of what it had been in 1929. By 1933, there were fifteen million unemployed. Under these circumstances, the Democrat Franklin Delano Roosevelt (1882–1945) was able to win a landslide electoral victory in 1932. He and his advisers pursued a policy of active government intervention in the economy that came to be known as the New Deal. Economic intervention included a stepped-up program of public works, such as the Works Progress Administration (WPA), which was established in 1935 and employed between two and three million people who worked at building bridges, roads, post offices, and airports. In 1935, the Social Security Act created a system of old-age pensions and unemployment insurance.

The New Deal provided some social reform measures that perhaps averted the possibility of social revolution in the United States. It did not, however, solve the unemployment problems of the Great Depression. In May 1937, during what was considered a period of full recovery, American unemployment still stood at seven million.

Only World War II and the subsequent growth of the armaments industry brought American workers back to full employment.

Socialism in Soviet Russia

The civil war in Russia had taken an enormous toll of life. Lenin had pursued a policy of "war communism," but once the war was over, peasants began to sabotage the program by hoarding food. Added to this problem was drought, which caused a famine between 1920 and 1922 that claimed as many as five million lives. Industrial collapse paralleled the agricultural disaster. By 1921, industrial output was only 20 percent of its 1913 levels. Russia was exhausted. A peasant banner proclaimed, "Down with Lenin and horseflesh, Bring back the Tsar and pork." As Leon Trotsky said, "The country, and the government with it, were at the very edge of the abyss."[6]

In March 1921, Lenin pulled Russia back from the abyss by adopting his New Economic Policy (NEP), a modified version of the old capitalist system. Peasants were now allowed to sell their produce openly. Retail stores as well as small industries that employed fewer than twenty employees could now operate under private ownership, although heavy industry, banking, and mines remained in the hands of the government.

In 1922, Lenin and the Communists formally created a new state called the Union of Soviet Socialist Republics, known as the USSR by its initials or the Soviet Union by its shortened form. Already by that year, a revived market and a good harvest had brought the famine to an end; Soviet agricultural production climbed to 75 percent of its prewar level. Overall the NEP had saved the nation from complete economic disaster even though Lenin and other leading Communists intended it to be only a temporary, tactical retreat from the goals of communism.

Lenin's death in 1924 inaugurated a struggle for power among the seven members of the Politburo, the institution that had become the leading organ of the party. The Politburo was divided over the future direction of Soviet Russia. The Left, led by Leon Trotsky, wanted to end the NEP, launch Russia on the path of rapid industrialization, and spread the revolution abroad. Another group in the Politburo, called the Right, rejected the cause of world revolution and wanted instead to concentrate on constructing a socialist state in Russia. This group also favored a continuation of Lenin's NEP.

These ideological divisions were underscored by an intense personal rivalry between Leon Trotsky and Joseph Stalin. In 1924, Trotsky held the post of commissar of war and was the leading spokesman for the Left in the Politburo. Joseph Stalin (1879–1953) was content to hold the dull bureaucratic job of party general secretary while other Politburo members held party positions that enabled them to display their brilliant oratorical abilities. But Stalin was a good

organizer (his fellow Bolsheviks called him "Comrade Index-Card") and used his post as party general secretary to gain complete control of the Communist Party. Trotsky was expelled from the party in 1927. By 1929, Stalin had succeeded in eliminating the Bolsheviks of the revolutionary era from the Politburo and establishing a dictatorship.

In Pursuit of a New Reality: Cultural and Intellectual Trends

Four years of devastating war left many Europeans with a profound sense of despair and a conviction that something was dreadfully wrong with Western values. The Great Depression only added to the despair lingering from World War I.

Political and economic uncertainties were paralleled by social innovations. The Great War had served to break down many traditional middle-class attitudes, especially toward sexuality. In the 1920s, women's physical appearance changed dramatically. Short skirts, short hair, the use of cosmetics that were once thought to be the preserve of prostitutes, and the new practice of suntanning gave women a new image. This change in physical appearance, which stressed more exposure of a woman's body, was also accompanied by frank discussions of sexual matters. In 1926, the Dutch physician Theodor van de Velde published *Ideal Marriage: Its Physiology and Technique*, which became an international best-seller. Van de Velde described female and male anatomy and glorified sexual pleasure in marriage.

Nightmares and New Visions

Uncertainty also pervaded the cultural and intellectual achievements of the interwar years. Postwar artistic trends were largely a working out of the implications of prewar developments. Abstract painting, for example, became ever more popular. In addition, prewar fascination with the absurd and the unconscious content of the mind seemed even more appropriate after the nightmare landscapes of World War I battlefronts. This gave rise to both the Dada movement and Surrealism.

Dadaism enshrined the purposelessness of life; revolted by the insanity of life, the Dadaists tried to give it expression by creating "anti-art." The 1918 Berlin Dada Manifesto maintained that "Dada is the international expression of our times, the great rebellion of artistic movements." In the hands of Hannah Höch (1889–1978), however, Dada became an instrument to comment on women's roles in the new mass culture.

Perhaps more important as an artistic movement was Surrealism, which sought a reality beyond the material, sensible world and found it in the world of the unconscious through the portrayal of fantasies, dreams, or nightmares.

Erich Lessing/Art Resource, NY. © 2002 Artist's Rights Society (ARS), New York/VG Bild-Kunst, Bonn

➤ HANNAH HÖCH, *CUT WITH THE KITCHEN KNIFE DADA THROUGH THE LAST WEIMAR BEER BELLY CULTURAL EPOCH OF GERMANY*. Hannah Höch, a prominent figure in the postwar Dada movement, used photomontage to create images that reflected on women's issues. In *Cut with the Kitchen Knife*, she combined pictures of German political leaders with sports stars, Dada artists, and scenes from urban life. One major theme emerged: the confrontation between the anti-Dada world of German political leaders and the Dada world of revolutionary ideals. Höch associated women with Dada and the new world.

The Spaniard Salvador Dalí (1904–1989) became the high priest of Surrealism and in his mature phase became a master of representational Surrealism. Dalí portrayed recognizable objects entirely divorced from their normal context. By placing objects into unrecognizable relationships, Dalí created a disturbing world in which the irrational had become tangible.

Probing the Unconscious

Interest in the unconscious, evident in Surrealism, was also apparent in the development of new literary techniques that emerged in the 1920s. One of its most apparent manifestations was in a "stream of consciousness" technique in which the writer presented an interior monologue or a report of the innermost thoughts of each character. The most famous example of this genre was written by the

Irish exile James Joyce (1882–1941). His *Ulysses,* published in 1922, told the story of one day in the life of ordinary people in Dublin by following the flow of their inner dialogue.

The German writer Hermann Hesse (1877–1962) dealt with the unconscious in a different fashion. His novels reflected the influence of new psychological theories and Eastern religions and focused on, among other things, the spiritual loneliness of modern human beings in a mechanized urban society. Hesse's novels made a large impact on German youth in the 1920s. He won the Nobel Prize for literature in 1946.

For much of the Western world, the best way to find (or escape) reality was in the field of mass entertainment. The 1930s was the heyday of the Hollywood studio system, which in the single year of 1937 turned out nearly six hundred feature films. Supplementing the movies were cheap paperbacks and radio, which brought sports, soap operas, and popular music to the depression-weary masses.

The increased size of audiences and the ability of radio and cinema, unlike the printed word, to provide an immediate mass experience added new dimensions to mass culture. Favorite film actors and actresses became stars, whose lives then became subject to public adoration and scrutiny. Sensuous actresses such as Marlene Dietrich, whose appearance in the early sound film *The Blue Angel* catapulted her to fame, popularized new images of women's sexuality.

☙ CONCLUSION

World War I shattered the liberal, rational society of late nineteenth- and early twentieth-century Europe. The incredible destruction and the death of almost ten million people undermined the whole idea of progress. New propaganda techniques had manipulated entire populations into sustaining their involvement in a meaningless slaughter.

World War I was a total war that involved a mobilization of resources and populations and increased government centralization of power over the lives of its citizens. Civil liberties, such as freedom of the press, speech, assembly, and movement, were circumscribed in the name of national security. The war made the practice of strong central authority a way of life.

The turmoil wrought by the Great War seemed to lead to even greater insecurity. Revolutions dismembered old empires and created new states that fostered unexpected problems. Expectations that Europe and the world would return to normalcy were soon dashed by the failure to achieve a lasting peace, economic collapse, and the rise of authoritarian governments that not only restricted individual freedoms but also sought even greater control over the lives of their subjects in order to guide them to achieve the goals of their totalitarian regimes.

Finally, World War I ended European hegemony over world affairs. By demolishing their own civilization on the battlegrounds of Europe, Europeans inadvertently encouraged the subject peoples of their vast colonial empires to initiate movements for national independence. In the next chapter, we examine some of those movements.

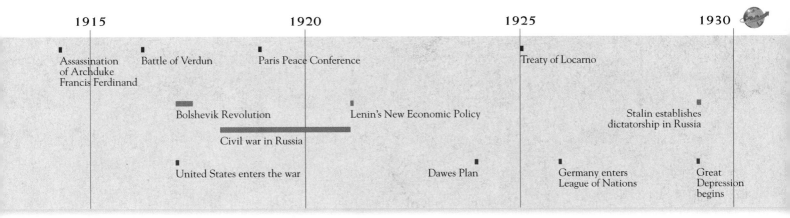

1915

Assassination of Archduke Francis Ferdinand

Battle of Verdun

Bolshevik Revolution

Civil war in Russia

United States enters the war

1920

Paris Peace Conference

Lenin's New Economic Policy

Dawes Plan

1925

Treaty of Locarno

Germany enters League of Nations

1930

Stalin establishes dictatorship in Russia

Great Depression begins

CHAPTER NOTES

1. Arnold Toynbee, *Surviving the Future* (New York, 1971), pp. 106–107.
2. Quoted in Joachim Remak, "1914—The Third Balkan War: Origins Reconsidered," *Journal of Modern History*, 43 (1971): 364–365.
3. Quoted in J. M. Winter, *The Experience of World War I* (New York, 1989), p. 142.
4. Quoted in Catherine W. Reilly, ed., *Scars upon My Heart: Women's Poetry and Verse of the First World War* (London, 1981), p. 90.
5. Quoted in William M. Mandel, *Soviet Women* (Garden City, N.Y., 1975), p. 43.
6. Quoted in Irving Howe, ed., *The Basic Writings of Trotsky* (London, 1963), p. 162.

SUGGESTED READING

The historical literature on the causes of World War I is enormous. A good starting point is the work by J. Joll, *The Origins of the First World War*, 2d ed. (London, 1992). The belief that Germany was primarily responsible for the war was argued vigorously by the German scholar F. Fischer in *Germany's Aims in the First World War* (New York, 1967), *World Power or Decline: The Controversy over Germany's Aims in World War I* (New York, 1974), and *War of Illusions: German Policies from 1911 to 1914* (New York, 1975). On the role of militarism, see D. Hermann, *The Arming of Europe and the Making of the First World War* (New York, 1997).

Two good accounts of World War I are M. Gilbert, *The First World War* (New York, 1994), and the lavishly illustrated book by J. M. Winter, *The Experience of World War I* (New York, 1989). See also the brief work by N. Heyman, *World War I* (Westport, Conn., 1997). There is an excellent collection of articles in H. Strachan, *The Oxford Illustrated History of the First World War* (New York, 1998). The nature of trench warfare is examined in T. Ashworth, *Trench Warfare, 1914–1918: The Live-and-Let-Live System* (London, 1980). On the role of women in World War I, see G. Braybon, *Women Workers in the First World War: The British Experience* (London, 1981), and G. Braybon and P. Summerfield, *Women's Experiences in Two World Wars* (London, 1987).

The role of war aims in the shaping of the peace settlement is examined in V. H. Rothwell, *British War Aims and Peace Diplomacy, 1914–1918* (Oxford, 1971), and D. R. Stevenson, *French War Aims Against Germany, 1914–1919* (New York, 1982).

A good introduction to the Russian Revolution can be found in R. A. Wade, *The Russian Revolution, 1917* (Cambridge, 2000), and S. Fitzpatrick, *The Russian Revolution, 1917–1932*, 2d ed. (New York, 1994). See also R. Pipes, *The Russian Revolution* (New York, 1990). On Lenin, see R. W. Clark, *Lenin* (New York, 1988), and the valuable work by A. B. Ulam, *The Bolsheviks* (New York, 1965). A comprehensive study of the Russian civil war is W. B. Lincoln, *Red Victory: A History of the Russian Civil War* (New York, 1989).

World War I and the Russian Revolution are also well covered in a good general survey, R. Paxton, *Europe in the Twentieth Century*, 2d ed. (San Diego, Calif., 1985).

For a general introduction to the interwar period, see R. J. Sontag, *A Broken World, 1919–39* (New York, 1971). On European security issues after the Paris Peace Conference, see S. Marks, *The Illusion of Peace: Europe's International Relations, 1918–1933* (New York, 1976). The Locarno agreements are examined in J. Jacobson, *Locarno Diplomacy* (Princeton, N.J., 1972). The best study on the problem of reparations is M. Trachtenberg, *Reparations in World Politics* (New York, 1980), which paints a positive view of French policies. The "return to normalcy" after the war is analyzed in C. S. Maier, *Recasting Bourgeois Europe: Stabilization in France, Germany, and Italy in the Decade After World War I* (Princeton, N.J., 1975). On the Great Depression, see C. P. Kindleberger, *The World in Depression, 1929–39*, rev. ed. (Berkeley, Calif., 1986). On Weimar Germany, see P. Bookbinder, *Weimar Germany* (New York, 1996), and R. Henig, *The Weimar Republic, 1919–1933* (New York, 1998), a brief study.

INFOTRAC COLLEGE EDITION

Visit the source collections at infotrac.thomsonlearning.com and use the Search function with the following key terms.

Bolshevik

Great Depression

Russia Revolution

Versailles Treaty

World War, 1914–1918

WORLD HISTORY RESOURCES

Visit the *Essential World History* Companion Web Site for resources specific to this textbook:

http://history.wadsworth.com/duikeressentials02/

The CD in the back of this book and the World History Resource Center at **http://history.wadsworth.com/world/** offer a variety of tools to help you succeed in this course, including access to quizzes; images; documents; interactive simulations, maps, and timelines; movie explorations; and a wealth of other sources.

Chapter 23

NATIONALISM, REVOLUTION, AND DICTATORSHIP: AFRICA, ASIA, AND LATIN AMERICA FROM 1919 TO 1939

FOCUS QUESTIONS

- What forms did the independence movements in India and the Middle East take, and what problems did each movement face?
- What forms did modernization take in Turkey, Iran, and Japan in the interwar years?
- What problems did China face between 1919 and 1939, and what solutions did the Nationalists and the Communists propose to solve these problems?
- What problems did the nations of Latin America face in the interwar years, and how did they respond to these problems?
- ➤ What developments contributed to the rise of nationalism after 1919, and what role did nationalism play in the Middle East, Asia, and Latin America?

*I*n the spring of 1913, the Bolshevik leader Vladimir Lenin wrote an article in the Communist Party newspaper *Pravda* on the awakening of Asia. "Was it so long ago," he asked his readers, "that China was considered typical of the lands that had been standing still for centuries? Today China is a land of seething political activity, the scene of a virile social movement and of a democratic upsurge." Similar conditions, he added, were spreading the democratic revolution to other parts of Asia—to Turkey, Persia, and China. Ferment was on the rise even in British India.[1]

A year later, the Great War erupted, and Lenin, like millions of others, turned his eyes to events in Europe. In February 1917, riots in the streets of Petrograd (the renamed Saint Petersburg) marked the onset of the Russian Revolution. By the end of the year, the Bolsheviks were in power in Moscow. For the next few years, Lenin and his colleagues were preoccupied with consolidating their control over the vast territories of the old tsarist Russian Empire. But he had not forgotten his earlier prediction that the colonial world was on the verge of revolt. Now, with the infant Soviet state virtually surrounded by its capitalist enemies, Lenin argued that the oppressed masses of Asia and Africa were potential allies in the bitter struggle against the brutal yoke of world imperialism. For the next two decades, the leaders in Moscow periodically turned their attention to China and other parts of Asia in an effort to ride what they hoped would be a mounting wave of revolt against foreign domination. •

 ## THE RISE OF NATIONALISM

Although the West had emerged from World War I relatively intact, its political and social foundations and its self-confidence had been severely undermined. Within Europe, doubts about the future viability of Western civilization were widespread, especially among the intellectual elite. In Asia and Africa, a rising tide of unrest against Western political domination began to emerge throughout the colonial and semicolonial world. That unrest took a variety of forms but was most notably displayed in increasing worker activism, rural protest, and a rising sense of national fervor among anticolonialist intellectuals. In areas of Asia, Africa, and Latin America where independent states had successfully resisted the Western onslaught, the discontent fostered by the war and later by the Great Depression led to a loss of confidence in democratic institutions and the rise of political dictatorships.

Modern Nationalism

The first stage of resistance to the West in Asia and Africa had met with humiliation and failure and must have confirmed many Westerners' conviction that colonial peoples lacked both the strength and the know-how to create modern states and govern their own destinies. In fact, the process was just beginning. The next phase—the rise of modern nationalism—began to take shape at the beginning of the twentieth century and was the product of the convergence of several factors. The primary source of anticolonialist sentiment was a new urban middle class of westernized intellectuals. In many cases, these merchants, petty functionaries, clerks, students, and professionals had been educated in Western-style schools. A few had spent time in the West. Many spoke Western languages, wore Western clothes, and worked in occupations connected with the colonial regime. Some, like Mahatma Gandhi in India, José Rizal in the Philippines, and Kwame Nkrumah in the Gold Coast, even wrote in the languages of their colonial masters.

The results were paradoxical. On the one hand, this "new class" admired Western culture and sometimes harbored a deep sense of contempt for traditional ways. On the other hand, many strongly resented the foreigners and their arrogant contempt for colonial peoples. They also resented the gap between ideal and reality, theory and practice, in colonial policy. Although Western political thought exalted democracy, equality, and individual freedom, such values were rarely practiced in the colonies.

Equality in economic opportunity and social life was also noticeably lacking. Normally the middle classes did not suffer in the same manner as impoverished peasants or menial workers on sugar or rubber plantations, but they, too, had complaints. They were usually relegated to menial jobs in the government or business and were paid lower salaries than Europeans in similar occupations. The superiority of the Europeans was expressed in a variety of ways, including "whites only" clubs and the use of the familiar form of the language (normally used by adults to children) when addressing the natives.

Under these conditions, many in the new urban educated class were very ambivalent toward their colonial masters and the civilization that they represented. Out of this mixture of hopes and resentments emerged the first stirrings of modern nationalism in Asia and Africa. During the first quarter of the century, in colonial and semicolonial societies from the Suez Canal to the shores of the Pacific Ocean, educated native peoples began to organize political parties and movements seeking reforms or the end of foreign rule and the restoration of independence.

INDEPENDENCE OR MODERNIZATION? THE NATIONALIST QUANDARY

Building a new nation, however, requires more than a shared sense of grievances against the foreign invader. A host of other issues also had to be resolved. Soon patriots throughout the colonial world were engaged in a lively and sometimes acrimonious debate over such questions as whether independence or modernization should be their primary objective. The answer depended in part on how the colonial regime was perceived. If it was viewed as a source of needed reforms in a traditional society, a gradualist approach made sense. But if it was seen primarily as an impediment to change, the first priority was to bring it to an end. The vast majority of patriotic individuals were convinced that to survive, their societies must adopt much of the Western way of life; yet many were equally determined that the local culture would not, and should not, become a carbon copy of the West. What was the national identity, after all, if it did not incorporate some elements from the traditional way of life and provide ideological symbols that the common people could understand and would rally around? Though aware that they needed to enlist the mass of the population in the common struggle, most urban intellectuals had difficulty communicating with the teeming population in the countryside who did not understand such complicated and unfamiliar concepts as democracy and nationhood. As one French colonial official remarked in some surprise to a Vietnamese reformist, "Why, Monsieur, you are more French than I am!"

Gandhi and the Indian National Congress

Nowhere in the colonial world were these issues debated more vigorously than in India. In the latter half of the nineteenth century, a stronger sense of national consciousness began to arise, provoked by the conservative policies and racial arrogance of the British colonial authorities.

The first Indian nationalists were almost invariably upper-class and educated. Many of them were from urban areas such as Bombay, Madras, and Calcutta. Some were trained in law and were members of the civil service. At first, many tended to prefer reform to revolution and believed that India needed modernization before it could handle the problems of independence. Such reformists did have some effect. In the 1880s, the government introduced a measure of self-government for the first time. All too often, however, such efforts were sabotaged by local British officials.

The slow pace of reform convinced many Indian nationalists that relying on British benevolence was futile. In 1885, a small group of Indians, with some British participation, met in Bombay to form the Indian National Congress (INC). They hoped to speak for all India, but most were high-caste English-trained Hindus. Like their reformist predecessors, members of the INC did not demand immediate independence and accepted the need for reforms to end traditional abuses like child marriage and *sati*. At the same time, they called for an Indian share in the governing process and more spending on economic development and less on military campaigns along the frontier. The British responded with a few concessions, but change was glacially slow.

The INC also had difficulty reconciling religious differences within its ranks. The stated goal of the INC was to seek self-determination for all Indians regardless of class or religious affiliation, but many of its leaders were Hindu and inevitably reflected Hindu concerns. In the first decade of the twentieth century, the separate Muslim League was created to represent the interests of the millions of Muslims in Indian society.

In 1915, a young Hindu lawyer returned from South Africa to become active in the INC. He transformed the movement and galvanized India's struggle for independence and identity. Mohandas Gandhi was born in 1869 in Gujarat, in western India, the son of a government minister. In the late nineteenth century, he studied in London and became a lawyer. In 1893, he went to South Africa to work in a law firm serving Indian émigrés working as laborers there. He soon became aware of the racial prejudice and exploitation experienced by Indians living in the territory and tried to organize them to protect their interests.

On his return to India, Gandhi immediately became active in the independence movement, setting up a movement based on nonviolent resistance (the Hindi term was *satyagraha*, "hold fast to the truth") to try to force the British to improve the lot of the poor and grant independence to India. His goal was twofold: to convert the British to his views while simultaneously strengthening the unity and sense of self-respect of his compatriots. When the British attempted to suppress dissent, he called on his followers to refuse to obey British regulations. He began to manufacture his own clothes (Gandhi now dressed in a simple *dhoti* made of coarse homespun cotton) and adopted the spinning wheel as a symbol of Indian resistance to imports of British textiles.

Gandhi, now increasingly known as India's "Great Soul" (*Mahatma*), organized mass protests to achieve his aims, but in 1919, they got out of hand and led to violence and British reprisals. British troops killed hundreds of unarmed protesters in the enclosed square in the city of Amritsar in northwestern India. When the protests spread, Gandhi was horrified at the violence and briefly retreated from active politics. Nevertheless, he was arrested for his role in the protests and spent several years in prison.

Gandhi combined his anticolonial activities with an appeal to the spiritual instincts of all Indians. Though he had been born and raised a Hindu, his universalist approach to the idea of God transcended individual religion, although it was shaped by the historical themes of Hindu belief. At a speech given in London in September 1931, he expressed his view of the nature of God as "an indefinable mysterious power that pervades everything . . . , an unseen power which makes itself felt and yet defies all proof."[2]

While Gandhi was in prison, the political situation continued to evolve. In 1921, the British passed the Government of India Act, transforming the heretofore advisory Legislative Council into a bicameral parliament, two-thirds of whose members would be elected. Similar bodies were created at the provincial level. In a stroke, five million Indians were enfranchised. But such reforms were no longer enough for many members of the INC, who wanted to push aggressively for full independence. The British exacerbated the situation by increasing the salt tax and prohibiting the Indian people from manufacturing or harvesting their own salt. Gandhi, now released from prison, returned to his earlier policy of civil disobedience by openly joining several dozen supporters in a 200-mile walk to the sea, where he picked up a lump of salt and urged Indians to ignore the law. Gandhi and many other members of the INC were arrested.

Indian women were active in the movement. Women accounted for about twenty thousand, or nearly 10 percent, of all those arrested and jailed for taking part in demonstrations during the interwar period. Women marched, picketed foreign shops, and promoted the spinning and wearing of homemade cloth. By the 1930s, women's associations were actively involved in promoting a number of reforms, including women's education, the introduction of birth control devices, the abolition of child

NEHRU AND GANDHI. Mahatma Gandhi (on the right), India's "Great Soul," became the emotional leader of India's struggle for independence from British colonial rule. Unlike many other nationalist leaders, Gandhi rejected the materialistic culture of the West and urged his followers to return to the native traditions of the Indian village. To illustrate his point, Gandhi dressed in the simple Indian *dhoti* rather than in the Western fashion favored by many of his colleagues. With Gandhi, Jawaharlal Nehru (on the left) was a leading figure in the Indian struggle for independence. Unlike Gandhi, however, his goal was to transform India into a modern industrial society. After independence, he became the nation's prime minister until his death in 1964.

AP/Wide World Photos

marriage, and universal suffrage. In 1929, the Sarda Act raised the minimum age of marriage to fourteen.

In the 1930s, a new figure entered the movement in the person of Jawaharlal Nehru (1889–1964), son of an earlier INC leader. Educated in the law in Great Britain and a *brahmin* by birth, Nehru personified the new Anglo-Indian politician: secular, rational, upper-class, and intellectual. In fact, he appeared to be everything that Gandhi was not. With his emergence, the independence movement embarked on two paths, religious and secular, native and Western, traditional and modern. The dual character of the INC leadership may well have strengthened the movement by bringing together the two primary impulses behind the desire for independence: elite nationalism and the primal force of Indian traditionalism. But it portended trouble for the nation's new leadership in defining India's future path in the contemporary world. In the meantime, Muslim discontent with Hindu dominance over the INC was increasing. In 1940, the Muslim League called for the creation of a separate Muslim state of Pakistan ("land of the pure") in the northwest (see the box on p. 503). As communal strife between Hindus and Muslims increased, many Indians came to realize with sorrow (and some British colonialists with satisfaction) that British rule was all that stood between peace and civil war.

The Nationalist Revolt in the Middle East

In the Middle East, as in Europe, World War I hastened the collapse of old empires. The Ottoman Empire, which had dominated the eastern Mediterranean since the seizure of Constantinople in 1453, had been growing steadily weaker since the end of the eighteenth century, troubled by rising governmental corruption, a decline in the effectiveness of the sultans, and the loss of considerable territory in the Balkans and southwestern Russia. In North Africa, Ottoman authority, tenuous at best, had disintegrated in the nineteenth century, enabling the French to seize Algeria and Tunisia and the British to establish a protectorate over the Nile River valley.

MUSTAPHA KEMAL AND THE MODERNIZATION OF TURKEY

Reformist elements in Istanbul, to be sure, had tried from time to time to resist the trend, but military defeats continued: Greece declared its independence, and Ottoman power declined steadily in the Middle East. A rising sense of nationality among Serbs, Armenians, and other minority peoples threatened the internal stability and cohesion of the empire. In the 1870s, a new generation of Ottoman reformers seized power in Istanbul and pushed through a constitution aimed at forming a legislative assembly that would represent all the peoples in the state. But the sultan they placed on the throne suspended the new charter and attempted to rule by traditional authoritarian means.

By the end of the nineteenth century, the defunct 1876 constitution had become a symbol of change for reformist elements, now grouped together under the common name Young Turks. They found support in the Ottoman army and administration and among Turks living in exile. In 1908, the Young Turks forced the sultan to restore the constitution, and he was removed from power the following year.

A CALL FOR A MUSLIM STATE

*M*ohammed Iqbal, a well-known Muslim poet in colonial India, was also a prominent advocate of the creation of a separate state for Muslims in South Asia. In this passage from an address he presented to the All-India Muslim League in December 1930, he explained the rationale for his proposal.

MOHAMMED IQBAL, SPEECH TO THE ALL-INDIA MUSLIM LEAGUE

It cannot be denied that Islam, regarded as an ethical ideal plus a certain kind of polity—by which expression I mean a social structure regulated by a legal system and animated by a specific ethical ideal—has been the chief formative factor in the life history of the Muslims of India. It has furnished those basic emotions and loyalties which gradually unify scattered individuals and groups and finally transform them into a well-defined people. Indeed it is no exaggeration to say that India is perhaps the only country in the world where Islam, as a people-building force, has worked at its best. In India, as elsewhere, the structure of Islam as a society is almost entirely due to the working of Islam as a culture inspired by a specific ethical ideal. What I mean to say is that Muslim society, with its remarkable homogeneity and inner unity, has grown to be what it is under the pressure of the laws and institutions associated with the culture of Islam.

Communalism in its higher aspect, then, is indispensable to the formation of a harmonious whole in a country like India. The units of Indian society are not territorial as in European countries. India is a continent of human groups belonging to different religions. Their behavior is not at all determined by a common race consciousness. Even the Hindus do not form a homogeneous group. The principle of European democracy cannot be applied to India without recognizing the fact of communal groups. The Muslim demand for the creation of a Muslim India within India is, therefore, perfectly justified.

The idea need not alarm the Hindus or the British. India is the greatest Muslim country in the world. The life of Islam, as a cultural force, in this country very largely depends on its centralization in a specified territory. This centralization of the most living portion of the Muslims of India, whose military and police service has, notwithstanding unfair treatment from the British, made the British rule possible in this country, will eventually solve the problem of India as well as of Asia. It will intensify their sense of responsibility and deepen their patriotic feeling. Thus possessing full opportunity of development within the body politic of India, the northwest India Muslims will prove the best defenders of India against a foreign invasion, be the invasion one of ideas or of bayonets. . . .

I therefore demand the formation of a consolidated Muslim State in the best interests of India and Islam. For India it means security and peace resulting from an internal balance of power; for Islam an opportunity to rid itself of the stamp that Arabian imperialism was forced to give it, to mobilize its law, its education, its culture, and to bring them into closer contact with its own original spirit and with the spirit of modern times.

But the Young Turks had appeared at a moment of crisis for the empire. Internal rebellions, combined with Austrian annexations of Ottoman territories in the Balkans, undermined support for the new government and provoked the army to step in. With most minorities from the old empire now removed from Istanbul's authority, many ethnic Turks began to embrace a new concept of a Turkish state based on all those of Turkish nationality.

The final blow to the old empire came in World War I, when the Ottoman government allied with Germany in the hope of driving the British from Egypt and restoring Ottoman rule over the Nile valley. In response, the British declared an official protectorate over Egypt and, aided by the efforts of the dashing if eccentric British adventurer T. E. Lawrence (popularly known as Lawrence of Arabia), sought to undermine Ottoman rule in the Arabian peninsula by encouraging Arab nationalists there. In 1916, the local governor of Mecca declared Arabia independent from Ottoman rule, while British troops, advancing from Egypt, seized Palestine. In October 1918, having suffered more than 300,000 casualties during the war, the Ottoman Empire negotiated an armistice with the Allied Powers.

During the next few years, the tottering empire began to fall apart as the British and the French made plans to divide up Ottoman territories in the Middle East and the Greeks won Allied approval to seize the western parts of the Anatolian peninsula for their dream of re-creating the substance of the old Byzantine Empire. The impending collapse energized key elements in Turkey under the leadership of a war hero, Colonel Mustapha Kemal (1881–1938), who had commanded Turkish forces in their defense of the Dardanelles against a British invasion during World War I. Now he resigned from the army and convoked a national congress that called for the creation of an elected government and the preservation of the remaining territories of the old empire in a new republic of Turkey. Establishing his new capital at Ankara, Kemal's forces drove the Greeks from the Anatolian peninsula and persuaded the British to agree to a new treaty. In 1923, the last of the Ottoman sultans fled the country, which was now declared a Turkish republic. The Ottoman Empire had come to an end.

During the next few years, President Mustapha Kemal (now popularly known as Atatürk, or "Father Turk") attempted to transform Turkey into a modern secular republic. The trappings of a democratic system were put in place, centered on an elected Grand National Assembly, but the president was relatively intolerant of opposition and harshly suppressed critics of his rule. Turkish nationalism was emphasized, and the Turkish language, now written in the Roman alphabet, was shorn of many of its Arabic elements. Popular education was emphasized, old aristocratic titles like *pasha* and *bey* were abolished, and all Turkish citizens were given family names in the European style.

Atatürk also took steps to modernize the economy, overseeing the establishment of a light industrial sector producing textiles, glass, paper, and cement and instituting a five-year plan on the Soviet model to provide for state direction over the economy. Atatürk was no admirer of Soviet communism, however, and the Turkish economy can be better described as a form of state capitalism. He also encouraged the modernization of the agricultural sector through the establishment of training institutions and model farms, but such reforms had relatively little effect on the nation's predominantly conservative peasantry.

Perhaps the most significant aspect of Atatürk's reform program was his attempt to break the power of the Islamic clerics and transform Turkey into a secular state. The caliphate was formally abolished in 1924, and *Shari'a* (Islamic law) was replaced by a revised version of the Swiss law code. The fez (the brimless cap worn by Turkish Muslims) was abolished as a form of headdress, and women were discouraged from wearing the veil in the traditional Islamic custom. Women received the right to vote in 1934 and were legally guaranteed equal rights with men in all aspects of marriage and inheritance. Education and the professions were now open to citizens of both sexes, and some women even began to participate in politics. All citizens were given the right to convert to another religion at will.

The legacy of Mustapha Kemal Atatürk was enormous. Although not all of his reforms were widely accepted in practice, especially by devout Muslims, most of the changes he introduced were retained after his death in 1938. In virtually every respect, the Turkish republic was the product of his determined efforts to create a modern Turkish nation.

MODERNIZATION IN IRAN

In the meantime, a similar process was under way in Persia. Under the Qajar dynasty (1794–1925), the country had not been very successful in resisting Russian advances in the Caucasus or resolving its domestic problems. To secure themselves from foreign influence, the shahs moved the capital from Tabriz to Tehran, in a mountainous area just south of the Caspian Sea. During the mid-nineteenth century, one modernizing shah attempted to introduce political and economic reforms but was impeded by resistance from tribal and religious—predominantly Shi'ite—forces. To buttress its rule, the dynasty turned increasingly to Russia and Great Britain to protect itself from its own people.

Eventually the growing foreign presence led to the rise of a native Persian nationalist movement. Supported actively by Shi'ite religious leaders, opposition to the regime rose steadily among both peasants and merchants in the cities, and in 1906, popular pressures forced the reigning shah to grant a constitution on the Western model.

As in the Ottoman Empire and Manchu China, however, the modernizers had moved too soon, before their power base was secure. With the support of the Russians and the British, the shah was able to regain control, while the two foreign powers began to divide the country into separate spheres of influence. One reason for the growing foreign presence in Persia was the discovery of oil reserves in the southern part of the country in 1908. Within a few years, oil exports increased rapidly, with the bulk of the profits going into the pockets of British investors.

In 1921, an officer in the Persian army by the name of Reza Khan (1878–1944) led a mutiny that seized power in Tehran. The new ruler's original intention had been to establish a republic; but resistance from traditional forces impeded his efforts, and in 1925, the new Pahlavi dynasty, with Reza Khan as shah, replaced the now defunct Qajar dynasty. During the next few years, Reza Khan attempted to follow the example of Atatürk in Turkey, introducing a number of reforms to strengthen the central government, modernize the civilian and military bureaucracy, and establish a modern economic infrastructure. He also officially changed the name of the nation to Iran.

Iran Under the Pahlavi Dynasty

Unlike Atatürk, Reza Khan did not attempt to destroy the power of Islamic beliefs, but he did encourage the establishment of a Western-style educational system and forbade women to wear the veil in public. Women continued to be exploited, however; it was their intensive labor in the carpet industry that provided major export earnings—second only to oil—in the interwar period. To strengthen the sense of Persian nationalism and reduce the power of Islam, Reza Khan attempted to popularize the symbols and beliefs of pre-Islamic times. Like his Qajar predecessors, however, he was hindered by strong foreign influence. When the Soviet Union and Great Britain decided to send troops into the country during World War II, he resigned in protest and died three years later.

THE RISE OF ARAB NATIONALISM AND THE PROBLEM OF PALESTINE

Unrest against Ottoman rule had existed in the Arabian peninsula since the eighteenth century, when the Wahhabi revolt attempted to drive out the outside influences and cleanse Islam of corrupt practices that had developed in past centuries. The revolt was eventually suppressed, but Wahhabi influence persisted.

World War I offered an opportunity for the Arabs to throw off the shackles of Ottoman rule—but what would replace them? The Arabs were not a nation but an idea, and disagreement over what constitutes an Arab plagued generations of political leaders who sought unsuccessfully to knit together the disparate peoples of the region into a single Arab nation.

When the Arab leaders in Mecca declared their independence from Ottoman rule in 1916, they had hoped for British support, but they were to be sorely disappointed. At the close of the war, the British and French agreed to create a number of mandates in the area under the general supervision of the League of Nations. Iraq and Trans-Jordan were assigned to the British; Syria and Lebanon (the two areas were separated so that Christian peoples in Lebanon could be placed under Christian administration) were given to the French.

The land of Palestine—once the home of the Jews but now inhabited primarily by Muslim Palestinians—became a separate mandate. According to the Balfour Declaration, issued by the British foreign secretary, Lord Balfour, in November 1917, Palestine was to be a national home for the Jews. The declaration was ambiguous on the legal status of the territory and promised that the decision would not undermine the rights of the non-Jewish peoples currently living in the area. But Arab nationalists were incensed. How could a national home for the Jewish people be established in a territory where 90 percent of the population was Muslim?

In the early 1920s, a leader of the Wahhabi movement, Ibn Saud (1880–1953), united Arab tribes in the northern part of the Arabian peninsula and drove out the remnants of Ottoman rule. Ibn Saud was a descendant of the family that had led the Wahhabi revolt in the eighteenth century. Devout and gifted, he won broad support among Arab tribal peoples and established the kingdom of Saudi Arabia throughout much of the peninsula in 1932.

At first, his new kingdom, consisting essentially of the vast wastes of central Arabia, was desperately poor. But during the 1930s, American companies began to explore for oil, and in 1938, Standard Oil made a successful strike at Dhahran, on the Persian Gulf. Soon an Arabian-American oil conglomerate, popularly called Aramco, was established, and the isolated kingdom was suddenly inundated by Western oilmen and untold wealth.

In the meantime, Jewish settlers began to arrive in Palestine in response to the promises made in the Balfour Declaration. As tensions between the new arrivals and existing Muslim residents began to escalate, the British tried to restrict Jewish immigration into the territory and rejected the concept of a separate state. They also created a separate emirate of Trans-Jordan out of the eastern section of Palestine. After World War II, it would

Chronology

THE MIDDLE EAST BETWEEN THE WARS

Balfour Declaration on Palestine	1917
Reza Khan seizes power in Persia	1921
End of Ottoman Empire and establishment of a republic in Turkey	1923
Rule of Mustapha Kemal Atatürk in Turkey	1923–1938
Beginning of Pahlavi dynasty in Iran	1925
Establishment of kingdom of Saudi Arabia	1932

become the independent kingdom of Jordan. The stage was set for the conflicts that would take place in the region after World War II.

Nationalism and Revolution in Asia and Africa

Before the Russian Revolution, to most intellectuals in Asia and Africa, "westernization" referred to the capitalist democratic civilization of western Europe and the United States, not the doctrine of social revolution developed by Karl Marx. Until 1917, Marxism was regarded as a utopian idea rather than a concrete system of government. Moreover, to many intellectuals, Marxism appeared to have little relevance to conditions in Asia and Africa. Marxist doctrine, after all, declared that a communist society would arise only from the ashes of an advanced capitalism that had already passed through an industrial revolution. From the perspective of Marxist historical analysis, most societies in Asia and Africa were still at the feudal stage of development; they lacked the economic conditions and political awareness to achieve a socialist revolution that would bring the working class to power. Finally, the Marxist view of nationalism and religion had little appeal to many patriotic intellectuals in the non-Western world. Marx believed that nationhood and religion were essentially false ideas that diverted the attention of the oppressed masses from the critical issues of class struggle. Instead Marx stressed an "internationalist" outlook based on class consciousness and the eventual creation of a classless society with no artificial divisions based on culture, nation, or religion.

The situation began to change after the Russian Revolution in 1917. The rise to power of Lenin's Bolsheviks demonstrated that a revolutionary party espousing Marxist principles could overturn a corrupt, outdated system and launch a new experiment dedicated to ending human inequality and achieving a paradise on earth. In 1920,

‬ שׁמרוּ אֶת השׁערים

CORBIS

➤ EUROPEAN JEWISH REFUGEES.
After the Balfour Declaration (1917)
promised a Jewish homeland in
Palestine, increasing numbers of
European Jews emigrated to Palestine.
Their goal was to build a new life in a
Jewish land. Like the refugees aboard
this ship, they celebrated as they
reached their new homeland. The sign
reads "Keep the gates open"—a refer-
ence to British efforts to slow the pace
of Jewish immigration in response to
protests by Muslim residents.

Lenin proposed a new revolutionary strategy designed to
relate Marxist doctrine and practice to non-Western societies. His reasons were not entirely altruistic. Soviet Russia, surrounded by capitalist powers, desperately needed
allies in its struggle to survive in a hostile world. To Lenin,
the anticolonial movements emerging in North Africa,
Asia, and the Middle East after World War I were natural
allies of the beleaguered new regime in Moscow. Lenin was
convinced that only the ability of the imperialist powers to
find markets, raw materials, and sources of capital investment in the non-Western world kept capitalism alive. If
the tentacles of capitalist influence in Asia and Africa
could be severed, imperialism would weaken and collapse.

Establishing such an alliance was not easy, however.
Most nationalist leaders in colonial countries belonged to
the urban middle class, and many abhorred the idea of a
comprehensive revolution to create a totally egalitarian
society. In addition, many still adhered to traditional religious beliefs and were opposed to the atheistic principles
of classical Marxism.

Since it was unrealistic to expect bourgeois nationalist
support for social revolution, Lenin sought a compromise
by which communist parties could be organized among the
working classes in the preindustrial societies of Asia and
Africa. These parties would then forge informal alliances
with existing middle-class parties to struggle against the
traditional ruling class and Western imperialism. Such an
alliance, of course, could not be permanent because many
bourgeois nationalists in Asia and Africa would reject an
egalitarian, classless society. Once the imperialists had been
overthrown, therefore, the communist parties would turn
against their erstwhile nationalist partners to seize power
on their own and carry out the socialist revolution.

Lenin's strategy became a major element in Soviet foreign
policy in the 1920s. Soviet agents fanned out across the world
to carry Marxism beyond the boundaries of industrial Europe.
The primary instrument of this effort was the Communist
International, or Comintern for short. Formed in 1919 at

Lenin's prodding, the Comintern was a worldwide organization of communist parties dedicated to the advancement of
world revolution. At its headquarters in Moscow, agents from
around the world were trained in the precepts of world communism and then sent back to their countries to form Marxist parties and promote the cause of social revolution. By
the end of the 1920s, almost every colonial or semicolonial
society in Asia had a party based on Marxist principles. The
Soviets had less success in the Middle East, where Marxist
ideology appealed mainly to minorities such as Jews and
Armenians in the cities, and in black Africa, where Soviet
strategists in any case did not feel conditions were sufficiently
advanced for the creation of communist organizations.

According to Marxist doctrine, the rank and file of communist parties should be urban factory workers alienated from
capitalist society by inhuman working conditions. In practice, many of the leaders even in European communist parties tended to be urban intellectuals or members of the lower
middle class. That phenomenon was even more true in the
non-Western world, where most early Marxists were rootless
intellectuals. Some were probably drawn into the movement
for patriotic reasons and saw Marxist doctrine as a new, more
effective means of modernizing their societies and removing the colonial exploiters (see the box on page 507). Others were attracted by the message of egalitarian communism
and the utopian dream of a classless society. For those who
had lost their faith in traditional religion, communism often
served as a new secular ideology, dealing not with the hereafter but with the here and now or, indeed, with a remote
future when the state would wither away and the "classless
society" would replace the lost truth of traditional faiths.

Of course, the new doctrine's appeal was not the same
in all non-Western societies. In Confucian societies such
as China and Vietnam, where traditional belief systems had
been badly discredited by their failure to counter the Western challenge, communism had an immediate impact and
rapidly became a major factor in the anticolonial movement.
In Buddhist and Muslim societies, where traditional religion

THE PATH OF LIBERATION

In 1919, the Vietnamese revolutionary Ho Chi Minh (1890–1969) was living in exile in France, where he first became acquainted with the new revolutionary experiment in Bolshevik Russia. He became a leader of the Vietnamese communist movement. In the following passage, written in 1960, he reminisces about his reasons for becoming a Communist. The Second International mentioned in the text was an organization created in 1889 by moderate socialists who pursued their goal by parliamentary means. Lenin created the Third International, or Comintern, in 1919 to promote violent revolution.

HO CHI MINH, "THE PATH WHICH LED ME TO LENINISM"

After World War I, I made my living in Paris, now as a retoucher at a photographer's, now as a painter of "Chinese antiquities" (made in France!). I would distribute leaflets denouncing the crimes committed by the French colonialists in Vietnam.

At that time, I supported the October Revolution only instinctively, not yet grasping all its historic importance. I loved and admired Lenin because he was a great patriot who liberated his compatriots; until then, I had read none of his books.

The reason for my joining the French Socialist Party was that these "ladies and gentlemen"—as I called my comrades at that moment—had shown their sympathy toward me, toward the struggle of the oppressed peoples. But I understood neither what was a party, a trade union, nor what was Socialism nor Communism.

Heated discussions were then taking place in the branches of the Socialist Party, about the question whether the Socialist Party should remain in the Second International, should a Second-and-a-Half International be founded, or should the Socialist Party join Lenin's Third International? I attended the meetings regularly, twice or three times a week, and attentively listened to the discussion. First, I could not understand thoroughly. Why were the discussions so heated? Either with the Second, Second-and-a-Half, or Third International, the revolution could be waged. What was the use of arguing then? As for the First International, what had become of it?

What I wanted most to know—and this precisely was not debated in the meetings—was: which International sides with the peoples of colonial countries?

I raised this question—the most important in my opinion—in a meeting. Some comrades answered: It is the Third, not the Second International. And a comrade gave me Lenin's "Thesis on the national and colonial questions," published by *l'Humanité*, to read.

There were political terms difficult to understand in this thesis. But by dint of reading it again and again, finally I could grasp the main part of it. What emotion, enthusiasm, clear-sightedness, and confidence it instilled in me! I was overjoyed to tears. Though sitting alone in my room, I shouted aloud as if addressing large crowds: "Dear martyrs, compatriots! This is what we need, this is the path to our liberation!"

After that, I had entire confidence in Lenin, in the Third International.

---

remained strong and actually became a cohesive factor in the resistance movement, communism had less success. To maximize their appeal and minimize potential conflict with traditional ideas, communist parties frequently attempted to adapt Marxist doctrine to indigenous values and institutions. In the Middle East, for example, the Ba'ath Party in Syria adopted a hybrid socialism combining Marxism with Arab nationalism. In Africa, radical intellectuals talked vaguely of a uniquely "African road to socialism."

The degree to which these parties were successful in establishing alliances with nationalist parties and building a solid base of support among the mass of the population also varied from place to place. In some instances, the Communists were briefly able to establish a cooperative relationship with the bourgeois parties. The most famous example was the alliance between the Chinese Communist Party and Sun Yat-sen's Nationalist Party (discussed in the next section). These efforts were abandoned in 1928 when the Comintern, reacting to Chiang Kai-shek's betrayal of the alliance with the Chinese Communist Party, declared that communist parties should restrict their recruiting efforts to the most revolutionary elements in society—notably, the urban intellectuals and the working class. Harassed by colo-

nial authorities and saddled with strategic directions from Moscow that often had little relevance to local conditions, communist parties in most colonial societies had little success in the 1930s and failed to build a secure base of support among the mass of the population.

REVOLUTION IN CHINA

Overall, revolutionary Marxism had its greatest impact in China, where a group of young radicals founded the Chinese Communist Party (CCP) in 1921. The rise of the CCP was a consequence of the failed revolution of 1911. When political forces are too weak or too divided to consolidate their power during a period of instability, the military usually steps in to fill the vacuum. In China, Sun Yat-sen and his colleagues had accepted General Yuan Shikai (Yuan Shih-k'ai) as president of the new Chinese republic in 1911 because they lacked the military force to compete with his control over the army. But some had misgivings about Yuan's intentions. As one remarked in a letter to a friend, "We don't know whether he will be a George Washington or a Napoleon."

As it turned out, he was neither. Understanding little of the new ideas sweeping into China from the West, Yuan ruled in a traditional manner, reviving Confucian rituals and institutions and eventually trying to found a new imperial dynasty. Yuan's dictatorial inclinations rapidly led to clashes with Sun's party, now renamed the *Guomindang* (*Kuomintang*), or Nationalist Party. When Yuan dissolved the new parliament, the Nationalists launched a rebellion. When it failed, Sun Yat-sen fled to Japan.

Yuan was strong enough to brush off the challenge from the revolutionary forces but not to turn back the clock of history. He died in 1916 and was succeeded by one of his military subordinates. For the next several years, China slipped into semianarchy as the power of the central government disintegrated and military warlords seized power in the provinces.

Mr. Science and Mr. Democracy: The New Culture Movement

In the meantime, discontent with existing conditions continued to rise in various sectors of Chinese society. The most vocal protests came from radical intellectuals, who opposed Yuan Shikai's conservative rule but were now convinced that political change could not take place until the Chinese people were more familiar with trends in the outside world. Braving the displeasure of Yuan and his successors, progressive intellectuals at Peking University launched the New Culture Movement, aimed at abolishing the remnants of the old system and introducing Western values and institutions into China. Using the classrooms of China's most prestigious university as well as the pages of newly established progressive magazines and newspapers, the intellectuals introduced a bewildering mix of new ideas, from the philosophy of Friedrich Nietzsche to the feminist plays of Henrik Ibsen. As such ideas flooded into China, they stirred up a new generation of educated Chinese youth, who chanted "Down with Confucius and sons" and talked of a new era dominated by "Mr. Sai" (Mr. Science) and "Mr. De" (Mr. Democracy). No one was a greater defender of free thought and speech than the chancellor of Peking University, Cai Yuanpei (Ts'ai Yüan-p'ei): "Regardless of what school of thought a person may adhere to, so long as that person's ideas are justified and conform to reason and have not been passed by through the process of natural selection, although there may be controversy, such ideas have a right to be presented."[3] Not surprisingly, such views earned the distrust of conservative military officers, one of whom threatened to lob artillery shells into Peking University to destroy the poisonous new ideas and their advocates.

Discontent among intellectuals, however, was soon joined by the rising chorus of public protest against Japan's efforts to expand its influence on the mainland. During the first decade of the twentieth century, Japan had taken advantage of the Qing's decline to extend its domination over Manchuria and Korea (see Chapter 21). In 1915, the Japanese government insisted that Yuan Shikai accept a series of twenty-one demands that would have given Japan a virtual protectorate over the Chinese government and economy. Yuan was able to fend off the most far-reaching Japanese demands by arousing popular outrage in China, but at the Paris Peace Conference four years later, Japan received Germany's sphere of influence in Shandong Province as a reward for its support of the Allied cause in World War I. On hearing that the Chinese government had accepted the decision, on May 4, 1919, patriotic students, supported by other sectors of the urban population, demonstrated in Beijing and other major cities of the country. Although this May Fourth Movement did not lead to the restoration of Shandong, it did alert a substantial part of the politically literate population to the threat to national survival and the incompetence of the warlord government.

By 1920, central authority had almost ceased to exist in China. Two competing political forces now began to emerge from the chaos. One was Sun Yat-sen's Nationalist Party. From Canton, Sun sought international assistance to carry out his national revolution. The other was the CCP. Following Lenin's strategy, Comintern agents soon advised the new party to link up with the more experienced Nationalists. Sun Yat-sen needed the expertise and the diplomatic support that the Soviet Union could provide because his anti-imperialist rhetoric had alienated many Western powers. In 1923, the two parties formed an alliance to oppose the warlords and drive the imperialist powers out of China.

For three years, with the assistance of a Comintern mission in Canton, the two parties submerged their mutual suspicions and mobilized and trained a revolutionary army to march north and seize control over China. The so-called Northern Expedition began in the summer of 1926 (see Map 23.1). By the following spring, revolutionary forces were in control of all Chinese territory south of the Yangtze River, including the major river ports of Wuhan and Shanghai. But tensions between the two parties now surfaced. Sun Yat-sen had died of cancer in 1925 and was succeeded as head of the Nationalist Party by his military subordinate, Chiang Kai-shek. Chiang feigned support for the alliance with the Communists but actually planned to destroy them. In April 1927, he struck against the Communists and their supporters in Shanghai, killing thousands. After the massacre, most of the Communist leaders went into hiding in the city, where they attempted to revive the movement in its traditional base among the urban working class. Some party members, however, led by the young Communist organizer Mao Zedong (Mao Tse-tung), fled to the hilly areas south of the Yangtze River.

Unlike most CCP leaders, Mao was convinced that the Chinese revolution must be based on the impoverished peasants in the countryside. The son of a prosperous peasant, Mao served as an agitator in rural villages in his native province of Hunan during the Northern Expedition in the fall of 1926. At that time, he wrote a famous report to the party leadership suggesting that the CCP support peasant

STUDENT DEMONSTRATIONS IN BEIJING. The massive popular demonstrations in Tiananmen Square in downtown Beijing in 1989 were not the first of their kind in China. On May 4, 1919, students gathered at the same spot to protest against the Japanese takeover of the Shandong peninsula after World War I. The event triggered the famous May Fourth Movement, which highlighted the demand of progressive forces in China for political and social reforms.

demands for a land revolution (see the box on p. 510). But his superiors refused, fearing that such radical policies would destroy the alliance with the Nationalists.

The Nanjing Republic

In 1928, Chiang Kai-shek founded a new Chinese republic at Nanjing, and over the next three years, he sought to reunify China by a combination of military operations and inducements to various northern warlords to join his movement. He also attempted to put an end to the Communists, rooting them out of their urban base in Shanghai and their rural redoubt in the rugged hills of Jiangxi (Kiangsi) Province. He succeeded in the latter task in 1931, when most party leaders were forced to flee Shanghai for Mao's base in southern China. Three years later, using their superior military strength, Chiang's troops surrounded the Communist base in Jiangxi, inducing Mao's young People's Liberation Army (PLA) to abandon its guerrilla lair and embark on the famous Long March, an arduous journey of thousands of miles on foot through mountains, marshes, and deserts to the small provincial town of Yan'an (Yenan) 200 miles north of the city of Xian in the dusty hills of northern China (see Map 23.1).

Meanwhile, Chiang was trying to build a new nation. When the Nanjing republic was established in 1928, Chiang publicly declared his commitment to Sun Yat-sen's Three People's Principles. In a program announced in 1918, Sun had written about the all-important second stage of "political tutelage":

China . . . needs a republican government just as a boy needs school. As a schoolboy must have good teachers and helpful friends, so the Chinese people, being for the first time under republican rule, must

have a farsighted revolutionary government for their training. This calls for the period of political tutelage, which is a necessary transitional stage from monarchy to republicanism. Without this, disorder will be unavoidable.[4]

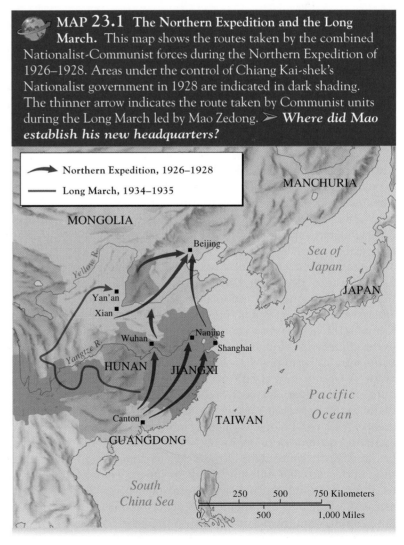

MAP 23.1 The Northern Expedition and the Long March. This map shows the routes taken by the combined Nationalist-Communist forces during the Northern Expedition of 1926–1928. Areas under the control of Chiang Kai-shek's Nationalist government in 1928 are indicated in dark shading. The thinner arrow indicates the route taken by Communist units during the Long March led by Mao Zedong. ➤ *Where did Mao establish his new headquarters?*

Northern Expedition, 1926–1928
Long March, 1934–1935

MANCHURIA
MONGOLIA
Yellow R.
Beijing
Sea of Japan
JAPAN
Yan'an
Xian
Wuhan
Nanjing
Shanghai
Yangtze R.
HUNAN
JIANGXI
Pacific Ocean
Canton
TAIWAN
GUANGDONG
South China Sea

0   250   500   750 Kilometers
0   500   1,000 Miles

A CALL FOR REVOLT

In the fall of 1926, Nationalist and Communist forces moved north from Canton on their Northern Expedition in an effort to defeat the warlords. The young Communist Mao Zedong accompanied revolutionary troops into his home province of Hunan, where he submitted a report to the CCP Central Committee calling for a massive peasant revolt against the ruling order. The report shows his confidence that peasants could play an active role in the Chinese revolution despite the skepticism of many of his colleagues.

MAO ZEDONG, "THE PEASANT MOVEMENT IN HUNAN"

During my recent visit to Hunan I made a firsthand investigation of conditions. . . . In a very short time, . . . several hundred million peasants will rise like a mighty storm, . . . a force so swift and violent that no power, however great, will be able to hold it back. They will smash all the trammels that bind them and rush forward along the road to liberation. They will sweep all the imperialists, warlords, corrupt officials, local tyrants, and evil gentry into their graves. Every revolutionary party and every revolutionary comrade will be put to the test, to be accepted or rejected as they decide. There are three alternatives. To march at their head and lead them? To trail behind them, gesticulating and criticizing? Or to stand in their way and oppose them? Every Chinese is free to choose, but events will force you to make the choice quickly.

The main targets of attack by the peasants are the local tyrants, the evil gentry and the lawless landlords, but in passing they also hit out against patriarchal ideas and institutions, against the corrupt officials in the cities and against bad practices and customs in the rural areas. . . . As a result, the privileges which the feudal landlords enjoyed for thousands of years are being shattered to pieces. . . . With the collapse of the power of the landlords, the peasant associations have now become the sole organs of authority, and the popular slogan "All power to the peasant associations" has become a reality.

The peasants' revolt disturbed the gentry's sweet dreams. When the news from the countryside reached the cities, it caused immediate uproar among the gentry. . . . From the middle social strata upwards to the Kuomintang right-wingers, there was not a single person who did not sum up the whole business in the phrase, "It's terrible!" . . . Even quite progressive people said, "Though terrible, it is inevitable in a revolution." In short, nobody could altogether deny the word "terrible." But . . . the fact is that the great peasant masses have risen to fulfill their historic mission. . . . What the peasants are doing is absolutely right; what they are doing is fine! "It's fine!" is the theory of the peasants and of all other revolutionaries. Every revolutionary comrade should know that the national revolution requires a great change in the countryside. The Revolution of 1911 did not bring about this change, hence its failure. This change is now taking place, and it is an important factor for the completion of the revolution. Every revolutionary comrade must support it, or he will be taking the stand of counterrevolution.

In keeping with Sun's program, Chiang announced a period of political indoctrination to prepare the Chinese people for a final stage of constitutional government. In the meantime, the Nationalists would use their dictatorial power to carry out a land reform program and modernize the urban industrial sector.

But it would take more than paper plans to create a new China. Years of neglect and civil war had severely frayed the political, economic, and social fabric of the nation. There were faint signs of an impending industrial revolution in the major urban centers, but most of the people in the countryside, drained by warlord exactions and civil strife, were still grindingly poor and overwhelmingly illiterate. A westernized middle class had begun to emerge in the cities and formed much of the natural constituency of the Nanjing government. But this new westernized elite, preoccupied with bourgeois values of individual advancement and material accumulation, had few links with the peasants in the countryside or the rickshaw drivers "running in this world of suffering," in the poignant words of a Chinese poet. In an expressive phrase, some critics dismissed Chiang and his chief followers as "banana Chinese"—yellow on the outside, white on the inside.

Chiang was aware of the difficulty of introducing exotic foreign ideas into a society still culturally conservative. While building a modern industrial sector, he attempted to synthesize modern Western ideas with traditional Confucian values of hard work, obedience, and moral integrity. In the officially promoted New Life Movement, sponsored by his Wellesley-educated wife, Mei-ling Soong, Chiang sought to propagate traditional Confucian social ethics such as integrity, propriety, and righteousness, while rejecting what he considered the excessive individualism and material greed of Western capitalism.

Unfortunately for Chiang, Confucian ideas—at least in their institutional form—had been widely discredited by the failure of the traditional system to solve China's growing problems. With only a tenuous hold over the Chinese provinces, a growing Japanese threat in the north, and a world suffering from the Great Depression, Chiang made little progress with his program. Chiang repressed all opposition and censored free expression, thereby alienating many intellectuals and political moderates. A land reform program was enacted in 1930 but had little effect.

Chiang Kai-shek's government had little more success in promoting industrial development. During the decade of precarious peace following the Northern Expedition, industrial growth averaged only about one percent annually. Much of the national wealth was in the hands of senior officials and close subordinates of the ruling elite. Military expenses consumed half the budget, and distressingly little was devoted to social and economic development.

The new government, then, had little success in dealing with China's deep-seated economic and social problems. The deadly combination of internal disintegration

and foreign pressure now began to coincide with the virtual collapse of the global economic order during the Great Depression and the rise of militant political forces in Japan determined to extend Japanese influence and power in an unstable Asia. These forces and the turmoil they unleashed will be examined in the next chapter.

"Down with Confucius and Sons": Economic, Social, and Cultural Change in Republican China

The transformation of the old order that had commenced at the end of the Qing era continued into the period of the early Chinese republic. The industrial sector continued to grow, albeit slowly. Although about 75 percent of all industrial production was still craft-produced in the early 1930s, mechanization was gradually beginning to replace manual labor in a number of traditional industries, notably in the manufacture of textile goods. Traditional Chinese exports, such as silk and tea, were hard-hit by the Great Depression, however, and manufacturing suffered a decline

Communist Leaders in China and the Soviet Union

In 1934, Mao Zedong led his bedraggled forces on the famous Long March from southern China to a new location at Yan'an, in the hills just south of the Gobi Desert. In the photo at the left Chairman Mao (on the left) and Zhu De, one of his generals, pose outside the Chinese Communist Party's new headquarters. By this time, Mao had become the leader of the communist movement, although the Communists did not take complete control of China until 1949. Joseph Stalin had become leader of the Communist Party in the Soviet Union in 1928 and within a year had established a powerful dictatorship over the entire country. In the picture at the right, from 1933, Stalin is signing what is supposedly a death warrant. As the terror increased in the late 1930s, Stalin signed such lists every day.

© Earl Leaf/Rapho

David King Collection, London

during the 1930s. It is difficult to gauge conditions in the countryside during the early republican era, but there is no doubt that farmers were often victimized by high taxes imposed by local warlords and the endemic political and social conflict.

Social changes followed shifts in the economy and the political culture. By 1915, the assault on the old system and values by educated youth was intense. The main focus of the attack was the Confucian concept of the family—in particular, filial piety and the subordination of women. Young people demanded the right to choose their own mates and their own careers. Women demanded rights and opportunities equal to those enjoyed by men. More broadly, progressives called for an end to the concept of duty to the community and praised the Western individualist ethos. The popular short story writer Lu Xun (Lu Hsun) criticized the Confucian concept of family as a "man-eating" system that degraded humanity. In a famous short story titled "Diary of a Madman," the protagonist remarks:

> I remember when I was four or five years old, sitting in the cool of the hall, my brother told me that if a man's parents were ill, he should cut off a piece of his flesh and boil it for them if he wanted to be considered a good son. I have only just realized that I have been living all these years in a place where for four thousand years they have been eating human flesh.[5]

Such criticisms did have some beneficial results. During the early republic, the tyranny of the old family system began to decline, at least in urban areas, under the impact of economic changes and the urgings of the New Culture intellectuals. Women began to escape their cloistered existence and seek education and employment alongside their male contemporaries. Free choice in marriage and a more relaxed attitude toward sex became commonplace among affluent families in the cities, where the teenage children of westernized elites aped the clothing, social habits, and even the musical tastes of their contemporaries in Europe and the United States.

But as a rule, the new individualism and women's rights did not penetrate to the villages, where traditional attitudes and customs held sway. Arranged marriages continued to be the rule rather than the exception, and concubinage remained common. According to a survey taken in the 1930s, well over two-thirds of the marriages even among urban couples had been arranged by their parents (see the box on p. 513).

Nowhere was the struggle between traditional and modern more visible than in the field of culture. Beginning with the New Culture era, radical reformists criticized traditional culture as the symbol and instrument of feudal oppression that must be entirely eradicated before a new China could stand with dignity in the modern world. During the 1920s and 1930s, Western literature and art became highly popular, especially among the urban middle class. Traditional culture continued to prevail among more conservative elements, and some intellectuals argued for a new art that would synthesize the best of Chinese and foreign culture. But the most creative artists were interested in imitating foreign trends, while traditionalists were more concerned with preservation.

Literature in particular was influenced by foreign ideas as Western genres like the novel and the short story attracted a growing audience. Although most Chinese novels written after World War I dealt with Chinese subjects, they reflected the Western tendency toward social realism and often dealt with the new westernized middle class (Mao Dun's *Midnight,* for example, describes the changing mores of Shanghai's urban elites) or the disintegration of the traditional Confucian family (Ba Jin's famous novel *Family* is an example). Most of China's modern authors displayed a clear contempt for the past.

JAPAN BETWEEN THE WARS

During the first two decades of the twentieth century, Japan made remarkable progress toward the creation of an advanced society on the Western model. The political system based on the Meiji Constitution of 1890 began to evolve along Western pluralistic lines, and a multiparty system took shape. The economic and social reforms launched during the Meiji era led to increasing prosperity and the development of a modern industrial and commercial sector.

Experiment in Democracy

During the first quarter of the twentieth century, Japanese political parties expanded their popular following and became increasingly competitive. Individual pressure groups began to appear in Japanese society, along with an independent press and a bill of rights. The influence of the old ruling oligarchy, the *genro,* had not yet been significantly challenged, however, nor had that of its ideological foundation.

These fragile democratic institutions were able to survive throughout the 1920s. During that period, the military budget was reduced, and a suffrage bill enacted in 1925 granted the vote to all Japanese males, thus continuing the process of democratization begun earlier in the century. Women remained disenfranchised; but women's associations gained increasing visibility during the 1920s, and many women were active in the labor movement and in campaigning for various social reforms.

But the era was also marked by growing social turmoil, and two opposing forces within the system were gearing up to challenge the prevailing wisdom. On the left, a Marxist labor movement began to take shape in the early

AN ARRANGED MARRIAGE

*U*nder Western influence, Chinese social customs changed dramatically for many urban elites in the interwar years. A vocal women's movement, inspired in part by translations of Henrik Ibsen's play A Doll's House, campaigned aggressively for universal suffrage and an end to sexual discrimination. Some progressives called for free choice in marriage and divorce and even for free love. By the 1930s, the government had taken some steps to free women from patriarchal marriage constraints and realize sexual equality. But life was generally unaffected in the villages, where traditional patterns held sway. This often created severe tensions between older and younger generations, as this passage by the popular twentieth-century novelist Ba Jin shows.

BA JIN, *FAMILY*

Brought up with loving care, after studying with a private tutor for a number of years, Chueh-hsin entered middle school. One of the school's best students, he graduated four years later at the top of his class. He was very interested in physics and chemistry and hoped to study abroad, in Germany. His mind was full of beautiful dreams. At that time he was the envy of his classmates.

In his fourth year at middle school, he lost his mother. His father later married again, this time to a younger woman who had been his mother's cousin. Chueh-hsin was aware of his loss, for he knew full well that nothing could replace the love of a mother. But her death left no irreparable wound in his heart; he was able to console himself with rosy dreams of his future. Moreover, he had someone who understood him and could comfort him—his pretty cousin Mei, "mei" for "plum blossom."

But then, one day, his dreams were shattered, cruelly and bitterly shattered. The evening he returned home carrying his diploma, the plaudits of his teachers and friends still ringing in his ears, his father called him into his room and said:

"Now that you've graduated, I want to arrange your marriage. Your grandfather is looking forward to having a great-grandson, and I, too, would like to be able to hold a grandson in my arms. You're old enough to be married; I won't feel easy until I fulfill my obligation to find you a wife. Although I didn't accumulate much money in my years away from home as an official, still I've put by enough for us to get along on. My health isn't what it used to be; I'm thinking of spending my time at home and having you help me run the household affairs. All the more reason you'll be needing a wife. I've already arranged a match with the Li family. The thirteenth of next month is a good day. We'll announce the engagement then. You can be married within the year. . . ."

Chueh-hsin did not utter a word of protest, nor did such a thought ever occur to him. He merely nodded to indicate his compliance with his father's wishes. But after he returned to his own room, and shut the door, he threw himself down on his bed, covered his head with the quilt and wept. He wept for his broken dreams.

He was deeply in love with Mei, but now his father had chosen another, a girl he had never seen, and said that he must marry within the year. What's more, his hopes of continuing his studies had burst like a bubble. It was a terrible shock to Chueh-hsin. His future was finished, his beautiful dreams shattered.

He cried his disappointment and bitterness. But the door was closed and Chueh-hsin's head was beneath the bedding. No one knew. He did not fight back, he never thought of resisting. He only bemoaned his fate. But he accepted it. He complied with his father's will without a trace of resentment. But in his heart he wept for himself, wept for the girl he adored—Mei, his "plum blossom."

1920s in response to growing economic difficulties. On the right, ultranationalist groups called for a rejection of Western models of development and a more militant approach to realizing national objectives.

This cultural conflict between old and new, native and foreign, was reflected in literature. Japanese self-confidence had been somewhat restored after the victories over China and Russia, and this resurgence sparked a great age of creativity in the early twentieth century. Now more adept at handling European literary forms, Japanese writers blended Western psychology with Japanese sensibility in exquisite novels reeking with nostalgia for the old Japan. A well-known example is Junichiro Tanizaki's *Some Prefer Nettles*, published in 1928, which delicately juxtaposes the positive aspects of both traditional and modern Japan. By the 1930s, however, military censorship increasingly inhibited free literary expression. Many authors contin-

ued to write privately, producing works that reflected the gloom of the era. This attitude is perhaps best exemplified by Shiga Naoya's novel *A Dark Night's Journey*, written during the early 1930s and capturing a sense of the approaching global catastrophe. It is regarded as the masterpiece of modern Japanese literature.

A Zaibatsu Economy

Japan also continued to make impressive progress in economic development. Spurred by rising domestic demand as well as continued government investment in the economy, the production of raw materials tripled between 1900 and 1930, and industrial production increased more than twelvefold. Much of the increase went into exports, and Western manufacturers began to complain about increasing competition from the Japanese.

As often happens, rapid industrialization was accompanied by some hardship and rising social tensions. In the Meiji model, various manufacturing processes were concentrated in a single enterprise, the *zaibatsu*, or financial clique. Some of these firms were existing merchant companies that had the capital and the foresight to move into new areas of opportunity. Others were formed by enterprising samurai, who used their status and experience in management to good account in a new environment. Whatever their origins, these firms gradually developed, often with official encouragement, into large conglomerates that controlled a major segment of the Japanese economy. By 1937, the four largest *zaibatsu* (Mitsui, Mitsubishi, Sumitomo, and Yasuda) controlled 21 percent of the banking industry, 26 percent of mining, 35 percent of shipbuilding, 38 percent of commercial shipping, and more than 60 percent of paper manufacturing and insurance.

This concentration of power and wealth in a few major industrial combines created problems in Japanese society. In the first place, it resulted in the emergence of a dual economy: on the one hand, a modern industry characterized by up-to-date methods and massive government subsidies, and on the other, a traditional manufacturing sector characterized by conservative methods and small-scale production techniques.

Concentration of wealth also led to growing economic inequalities. As we have seen, economic growth had been achieved at the expense of the peasants, many of whom fled to the cities to escape rural poverty. That labor surplus benefited the industrial sector, but the urban proletariat was still poorly paid and ill-housed. A rapid increase in population (the total population of the Japanese islands increased from an estimated 43 million in 1900 to 73 million in 1940) led to food shortages and the threat of rising unemployment. In the meantime, those left on the farm continued to suffer. As late as the beginning of World War II, an estimated one-half of all Japanese farmers were tenants.

Shidehara Diplomacy

A final problem for Japanese leaders in the post-Meiji era was the familiar dilemma of finding sources of raw materials and foreign markets for the nation's manufactured goods. Until World War I, Japan had dealt with the problem by seizing territories such as Taiwan, Korea, and southern Manchuria and transforming them into colonies or protectorates of the growing Japanese empire. That policy had begun to arouse the concern, and in some cases the hostility, of the Western nations. China was also becoming apprehensive; as we have seen, Japanese demands for Shandong Province at the Paris Peace Conference in 1919 aroused massive protests in major Chinese cities.

The United States was especially concerned about Japanese aggressiveness. Although the United States had been less active than some European states in pursuing colonies in the Pacific, it had a strong interest in keeping the area open for U.S. commercial activities. In 1922, in Washington, D.C., the United States convened a major conference of nations with interests in the Pacific to discuss problems of regional security. The Washington Conference led to agreements on several issues, but the major accomplishment was a nine-power treaty recognizing the territorial integrity of China and the Open Door. The other participants induced Japan to accept these provisions by accepting its special position in Manchuria.

During the remainder of the 1920s, Japanese governments attempted to play by the rules laid down at the Washington Conference. Known as Shidehara diplomacy, after the foreign minister (and later prime minister) who attempted to carry it out, this policy sought to use diplomatic and economic means to realize Japanese interests in Asia. But this approach came under severe pressure as Japanese industrialists began to move into new areas, such as heavy industry, chemicals, mining, and the manufacturing of appliances and automobiles. Because such industries desperately needed resources not found in abundance locally, the Japanese government came under increasing pressure to find new sources abroad.

In the early 1930s, with the onset of the Great Depression and growing tensions in the international arena, nationalist forces rose to dominance in the government. While party leaders during the 1920s had attempted to realize Japanese aspirations within the existing global political and economic framework, the dominant elements in the government in the 1930s, a mixture of military officers and ultranationalist politicians, were convinced that the diplomacy of the 1920s had failed; they advocated a more aggressive approach to protecting national interests in a brutal and competitive world.

NATIONALISM AND DICTATORSHIP IN LATIN AMERICA

Although the nations of Latin America played little role in World War I, that conflict nevertheless exerted an impact on the region, especially on its economy. By the end of the 1920s, the region was also strongly influenced by another event of global proportions—the Great Depression.

The Economy and the United States

At the beginning of the twentieth century, virtually all of Latin America, except for the three Guianas, British Honduras, and some of the Caribbean islands, had achieved independence (see Map 23.2). The economy of the region was based largely on the export of foodstuffs and raw materials. Some countries relied on exports of only one or two products. Argentina, for example, exported

MAP 23.2 Latin America in the First Half of the Twentieth Century.
Shown here are the boundaries dividing the countries of Latin America after the
independence movements of the nineteenth century. ➤ *Which areas
remained under European rule?*

MEXICO
BRITISH HONDURAS
HONDURAS
NICARAGUA
COSTA RICA
PANAMA
EL SALVADOR
GUATEMALA

Caribbean Sea

BRITISH GUIANA
DUTCH GUIANA
FRENCH GUIANA

Caracas
VENEZUELA

Bogotá
COLOMBIA

Quito
ECUADOR

North Atlantic Ocean

PERU
Lima

BRAZIL

La Paz
BOLIVIA

PARAGUAY

Rio de Janeiro

South Pacific Ocean

CHILE

Asunción

ARGENTINA

URUGUAY

Santiago

Buenos Aires
Montevideo

South Atlantic Ocean

0   500   1,000   1,500 Kilometers
0   500   1,000 Miles

Falkland Islands (U.K.)

South Georgia Island (U.K.)

primarily beef and wheat; Chile, nitrates and copper; Brazil and the Caribbean nations, sugar; and the Central American states, bananas. A few reaped large profits from these exports, but for the majority of the population, the returns were meager.

World War I led to a decline in European investment in Latin America and a rise in the U.S. role in the local economies. By the late 1920s, the United States had replaced Great Britain as the foremost source of investment in Latin America. Unlike the British, however, U.S.

investors put their funds directly into production enterprises, causing large segments of the area's export industries to fall into American hands. A number of Central American states, for example, were popularly labeled "banana republics" because of the power and influence of the U.S.-owned United Fruit Company. American firms also dominated the copper mining industry in Chile and Peru and the oil industry in Mexico, Peru, and Bolivia.

Increasing economic power reinforced the traditionally high level of U.S. political influence in Latin America. This influence was especially evident in Central America and the Caribbean, regions that many Americans considered their backyard and thus vital to U.S. national security. The growing U.S. presence in the region provoked hostility among some Latin Americans, who viewed the United States as an aggressive imperialist power. Some charged that Washington worked to keep ruthless dictators, such as Juan Vicente Gómez of Venezuela and Fulgencio Batista of Cuba, in power in order to preserve U.S. economic influence; sometimes the United States even intervened militarily. In a bid to improve relations with Latin American countries, President Franklin D. Roosevelt in 1935 promulgated the Good Neighbor policy, which rejected the use of U.S. military force in the region.

Because so many Latin American nations depended for their livelihood on the export of raw materials and food products, the Great Depression of the 1930s was a disaster for the region. The total value of Latin American exports in 1930 was almost 50 percent below the figure for the previous five years. Spurred by the decline in foreign revenues, Latin American governments began to encourage the development of new industries. In some cases—the steel industry in Chile and Brazil, the oil industry in Argentina and Mexico—government investment made up for the absence of local sources of capital.

The Move to Authoritarianism

During the late nineteenth century, most governments in Latin America had been increasingly dominated by landed or military elites, who controlled the mass of the population—mostly impoverished peasants—by the blatant use of military force. This trend toward authoritarianism increased during the 1930s as domestic instability caused by the effects of the Great Depression led to the creation of military dictatorships throughout the region. This trend was especially evident in Argentina, Brazil, and Mexico—three countries that together possessed more than half of the land and wealth of Latin America.

The political domination of the country by an elite minority often had disastrous effects. The government of Argentina, controlled by landowners who had benefited from the export of beef and wheat, was slow to recognize the growing importance of establishing a local industrial base. In 1916, Hipólito Irigoyen (1852–1933), head of the Radical Party, was elected president on a program to improve conditions for the middle and lower classes. Little was achieved, however, as the party became increasingly corrupt and drew closer to the large landowners. In 1930, the army overthrew Irigoyen's government and reestablished the power of the landed class. But their efforts to return to the previous export economy and suppress the growing influence of labor unions failed.

Brazil followed a similar path. In 1889, the army overthrew the Brazilian monarchy, installed by Portugal years

Chronology

LATIN AMERICA BETWEEN THE WARS

Hipólito Irigoyen becomes president of Argentina	1916
Argentinian military overthrows Irigoyen	1930
Rule of Getúlio Vargas in Brazil	1930–1945
Presidency of Lázaro Cárdenas in Mexico	1934–1940
Beginning of Good Neighbor policy	1935

before, and established a republic. But it was dominated by landed elites, many of whom had grown wealthy through their ownership of coffee plantations. By 1900, three-quarters of the world's coffee was grown in Brazil. As in Argentina, the ruling oligarchy ignored the importance of establishing an urban industrial base. When the Great Depression ravaged profits from coffee exports, a wealthy rancher, Getúlio Vargas (1883–1954), seized power and ruled the country as president from 1930 to 1945. At first, Vargas sought to appease workers by declaring an eight-hour workday and a minimum wage, but, influenced by the apparent success of fascist regimes in Europe, he ruled by increasingly autocratic means and relied on a police force that used torture to silence his opponents. His industrial policy was relatively enlightened, however, and by the end of World War II, Brazil had become Latin America's major industrial power. In 1945, the army, fearing that Vargas might prolong his power illegally after calling for new elections, forced him to resign.

Mexico, in the years after World War I, was not an authoritarian state, but neither was it democratic. The Mexican Revolution at the beginning of the twentieth century had been the first significant effort in Latin American history to overturn the system of large estates and improve the living standards of the masses (see Chapter 19). Out of the political revolution emerged a relatively stable political order. The revolution, however, was democratic in form only, as the official political party, known as the Institutional Revolutionary Party (PRI), controlled the levers of power throughout society. Every six years, PRI bosses chose the party's presidential candidate, who was then dutifully elected by the people.

The situation began to change with the election of Lázaro Cárdenas (1895–1970) as president in 1934. Cárdenas won wide popularity with the peasants by ordering the redistribution of 44 million acres of land controlled by landed elites. He also won popular support by adopting a stronger stand against the United States, seizing control over the oil industry, which had hitherto been dominated

 **RIVERA'S MURAL ART.** Diego Rivera was an important figure in the development of Mexico's mural art in the 1920s and 1930s. One of Rivera's goals—to portray Mexico's past and native traditions—is evident in this mural, which conveys the complexity and variety of Aztec civilization. When the Spanish arrived, they were amazed at the variety of foods and merchandise for sale in the marketplace in Tenochtitlán (present-day Mexico City).

by major U.S. oil companies. Alluding to the Good Neighbor policy, President Roosevelt refused to intervene, and eventually Mexico agreed to compensate U.S. oil companies for their lost property. It then set up PEMEX, a state-administered organization, to run the oil industry.

Latin American Culture

During the early twentieth century, modern European artistic and literary movements began to penetrate Latin America. In major cities, such as Buenos Aires and São Paulo, wealthy elites supported avant-garde trends, but other artists returned from abroad to adapt modern techniques to their native roots.

For many artists and writers, their work provided a means of promoting the emergence of a new national essence. An example was the Mexican muralist Diego Rivera (1886–1957). Rivera had studied in Europe, where he was influenced by fresco painting in Italy. After his return to Mexico, where the government provided financial support for the painting of murals on public buildings, he began to produce a monumental style of mural art that served two purposes: to illustrate the national past by portraying Aztec legends as well as Mexican festivals and folk customs and to promote a political message in favor of realizing the social goals of the Mexican Revolution. Rivera's murals can be found in such diverse locations as the Ministry of Education and the Social Security Hospital in Mexico City and the chapel of the Agricultural School at Chapingo.

CONCLUSION

The turmoil brought about by World War I not only resulted in the destruction of several of the major Western empires and a redrawing of the map of Europe but also opened the door to political and social upheavals elsewhere in the world. In the Middle East, the decline and fall of the Ottoman Empire led to the creation of the secular republic of Turkey. The state of Saudi Arabia emerged in the Arabian peninsula, and Palestine became a source of tension between newly arrived Jewish settlers and longtime Muslim residents.

Other parts of Asia and Africa also witnessed the rise of movements for national independence. In Africa, these movements were spearheaded by native leaders educated in Europe or the United States. In India, Gandhi and his campaign of civil disobedience played a crucial role in his country's bid to be free of British rule. Communist movements also began to emerge in Asian societies as radical elements sought new methods of bringing about the overthrow of Western imperialism. Japan continued to follow its own path to modernization, which, although successful from an economic point of view, took a menacing turn during the 1930s.

Between 1919 and 1939, China experienced a dramatic struggle to establish a modern nation. Two dynamic political organizations—the Nationalists and the Communists—competed for legitimacy as the rightful heirs of the old order. At first, they formed an alliance in an effort to defeat their common adversaries, but cooperation ultimately turned to conflict. The Nationalists under Chiang Kai-shek emerged supreme, but Chiang found it difficult to control the remnants of the warlord regime in China, while the Great Depression undermined his efforts to build an industrial nation.

During the interwar years, the nations of Latin America faced severe economic problems because of their dependence on exports. Increasing U.S. investments in Latin America contributed to growing hostility against the powerful neighbor to the north. The Great Depression forced the region to begin developing new industries, but it also led to the rise of authoritarian governments, some of them modeled after the fascist regimes of Italy and Germany.

By demolishing the remnants of their old civilization on the battlefields of World War I, Europeans had inadvertently encouraged the subject peoples of their vast colonial empires to begin their own movements for national independence. The process was by no means completed in the two decades following the Treaty of Versailles, but the bonds of imperial rule had been severely strained. Once Europeans began to weaken themselves in the even more destructive conflict of World War II, the hopes of African and Asian peoples for national independence and freedom could at last be realized. It is to that devastating world conflict that we now turn.

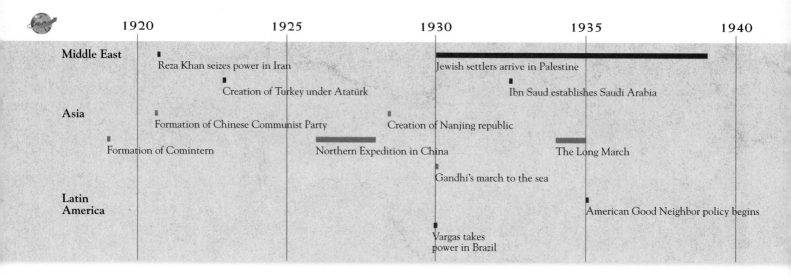

	1920	1925	1930	1935	1940
Middle East	Reza Khan seizes power in Iran	Creation of Turkey under Atatürk	Jewish settlers arrive in Palestine	Ibn Saud establishes Saudi Arabia	
Asia	Formation of Chinese Communist Party / Formation of Comintern	Northern Expedition in China	Creation of Nanjing republic / Gandhi's march to the sea	The Long March	
Latin America			Vargas takes power in Brazil	American Good Neighbor policy begins	

CHAPTER NOTES

1. Vladimir I. Lenin, "The Awakening of Asia," in *The Awakening of Asia: Selected Essays* (New York, 1963–1968), p. 22.
2. Speech by Mahatma Gandhi, delivered in London in September 1931 during his visit for the first Roundtable Conference.
3. Ts'ai Yuan-p'ei, "Ta Lin Ch'in-nan Han," in *Ts'ai Yuan-p'ei Hsien-sheng Ch'uan-chi* [Collected Works of Mr. Ts'ai Yuan-p'ei] (Taipei, 1968), pp. 1057–1058.
4. Quoted in William Theodore de Bary et al., eds., *Sources of Chinese Tradition* (New York, 1963), p. 783.
5. Lu Xun, "Diary of a Madman," in *Selected Works of Lu Hsun* (Peking, 1957), vol. 1, p. 20.

another war in Europe. World War II in Europe was Hitler's war. Other countries may have contributed by not resisting Hitler earlier, but Nazi Germany's actions alone made World War II inevitable.

It became far more than just Hitler's war, however. World War II was really two conflicts: one provoked by the ambitions of Germany in Europe, the other by the ambitions of Japan in Asia. By 1941, with the United States involved in both wars, the two had merged into a single global conflict.

Although World War I had been described as a total war, World War II was even more so and was fought on a scale unique in history. Almost everyone in the warring countries was involved in one way or another—as soldiers; as workers in wartime industries; as ordinary citizens subject to invading armies, military occupation, or bombing raids; as refugees; or as victims of mass extermination. The world had never witnessed such widespread human-made death and destruction. •

RETREAT FROM DEMOCRACY: DICTATORIAL REGIMES

The rise of dictatorial regimes in the 1930s had a great deal to do with the coming of World War II. By 1939, only two major states in Europe, France and Great Britain, remained democratic. Italy and Germany had succumbed to the political movement called fascism, and Soviet Russia under Stalin moved toward repressive totalitarianism. A host of other European states and Latin American countries adopted authoritarian structures of different kinds, while a militarist regime in Japan moved that country down the path of war.

The dictatorial regimes between the wars assumed both old and new forms. Dictatorship was not new, but the modern totalitarian state was. The totalitarian regimes, best exemplified by Stalinist Russia and Nazi Germany, greatly extended the functions and power of the central state. The new "total states" expected the active loyalty and commitment of citizens to the regime's goals, whether they be war, a socialist society, or a thousand-year Reich. They used modern mass propaganda techniques and high-speed communications to conquer the minds and hearts of their subjects. The total state sought to control not only the economic, political, and social aspects of life but the intellectual and cultural aspects as well.

The modern totalitarian state was to be led by a single leader and a single party. It ruthlessly rejected the liberal ideal of limited government power and constitutional guarantees of individual freedoms. Indeed, individual freedom was to be subordinated to the collective will of the masses, organized and determined for them by the leader or leaders. Modern technology also gave total states unprecedented police controls to enforce their wishes on their subjects.

The Birth of Fascism

In the early 1920s, Benito Mussolini burst on the Italian scene with the first fascist movement in Europe. In 1919, Mussolini (1883–1945) established a new political group, the *Fascio di Combattimento* (League of Combat), which won support from middle-class industrialists fearful of working-class agitation and large landowners who objected to agricultural strikes. The movement gained momentum as Mussolini's nationalist rhetoric and the middle-class fear of socialism, communist revolution, and disorder made the Fascists seem more and more attractive. On October 29, 1922, after Mussolini and the Fascists threatened to march on Rome if they were not given power, King Victor Emmanuel (1900–1946) capitulated and made Mussolini prime minister of Italy.

By 1926, Mussolini had established the institutional framework for a fascist dictatorship. The prime minister was made "head of government" with the power to legislate by decree. The police were empowered to arrest and confine anybody for both nonpolitical and political crimes without due process of law. The government was given the power to dissolve political and cultural associations. In 1926, all antifascist parties were outlawed, and a secret police force, known as the OVRA, was also established. By the end of the year, Mussolini ruled Italy as *Il Duce*, the leader.

Mussolini conceived of the fascist state as totalitarian: "Fascism is totalitarian, and the Fascist State, the synthesis and unity of all values, interprets, develops and gives strength to the whole life of the people."[1] Mussolini did try to create a police state, but it was not very effective. Likewise the Italian Fascists' attempt to exercise control over all forms of mass media, including newspapers, radio, and cinema, in order to use propaganda as an instrument to integrate the masses into the state, failed to achieve its major goals. Most commonly, fascist propaganda was disseminated through simple slogans, such as "Mussolini is always right," plastered on walls all over Italy.

The Fascists portrayed the family as the pillar of the state and women as the basic foundation of the family. "Woman into the home" became the fascist slogan. Women were to be homemakers and baby producers, "their natural and fundamental mission in life," according

MUSSOLINI, THE IRON DUCE. One of Mussolini's favorite images of himself was that of the Iron *Duce*—the strong leader who is always right. Consequently he was often seen in military-style uniforms and military poses. This photograph shows Mussolini in one of his numerous uniforms with his Black Shirt body-guards giving the Fascist salute.

to Mussolini, for population growth was viewed as an indicator of national strength. Employment outside the home was an impediment distracting from conception: "It forms an independence and consequent physical and moral habits contrary to child bearing."[2]

Despite the instruments of repression, the use of propaganda, and the creation of numerous fascist organizations, Mussolini never achieved the degree of totalitarian control attained in Hitler's Germany or Stalin's Soviet Union. Mussolini and the Fascist Party did not completely destroy the old power structure. The Italian Fascists promised much but actually delivered considerably less, and they were soon overshadowed by a much more powerful fascist movement to the north.

Hitler and Nazi Germany

In 1923, a small rightist party led by an obscure Austrian rabble-rouser named Adolf Hitler (1889–1945) attempted to seize power in southern Germany in the notorious Beer Hall Putsch. Although the effort failed, the attempted putsch brought Hitler and the Nazis to national prominence.

HITLER'S RISE TO POWER, 1919–1933

At the end of World War I, after four years of service on the Western Front, Hitler went to Munich and decided to enter politics. In 1919, he joined the obscure German Worker's Party, one of a number of right-wing extreme nationalist parties. By the summer of 1921, Hitler had assumed control of the party, which he renamed the National Socialist German Workers' Party, or Nazi Party

for short. In two years, membership reached 55,000, including 15,000 in the party militia, the SA (for *Sturmabteilung,* or Storm Troops).

The overconfident Hitler staged an armed uprising against the government in Munich in November 1923, the Beer Hall Putsch. The putsch was quickly crushed, and Hitler was sentenced to prison. During his brief stay in jail, he wrote *Mein Kampf* (*My Struggle*), an autobiographical account of his movement and its underlying ideology—extreme German nationalism, virulent anti-Semitism, and anticommunism linked together by a social Darwinian theory of struggle that stresses the right of superior nations to *Lebensraum* (living space) through expansion and the right of superior individuals to secure authoritarian leadership over the masses.

During his imprisonment, Hitler also came to the realization that the Nazis would have to come to power by constitutional means, not by overthrowing the Weimar Republic. This implied the formation of a mass political party that would actively compete for votes with the other political parties. After his release from prison, Hitler reorganized the Nazi Party and expanded it to all parts of Germany. By 1929, the Nazis had a national party organization.

Three years later, the Nazi Party had 800,000 members and had become the largest party in the Reichstag. No doubt Germany's economic difficulties were a crucial factor in the Nazi rise to power. Unemployment rose dramatically, from 4.35 million in 1931 to 6 million by the winter of 1932. Hitler, in particular, claimed to stand above all differences and promised to create a new Germany free of class differences and party infighting. His appeal to national pride, national honor, and traditional

JAPAN'S JUSTIFICATION FOR EXPANSION

Advocates of Japanese expansion justified their proposals by claiming both economic necessity and moral imperatives. Note the familiar combination of motives in this passage written by an extremist military leader in the late 1930s.

HASHIMOTO KINGORO, THE NEED FOR EMIGRATION AND EXPANSION

We have already said that there are only three ways left to Japan to escape from the pressure of surplus population. We are like a great crowd of people packed into a small and narrow room, and there are only three doors through which we might escape, namely emigration, advance into world markets, and expansion of territory. The first door, emigration, has been barred to us by the anti-Japanese immigration policies of other countries. The second door, advance into world markets, is being pushed shut by tariff barriers and the abrogation of commercial treaties. What should Japan do when two of the three doors have been closed against her?

It is quite natural that Japan should rush upon the last remaining door.

It may sound dangerous when we speak of territorial expansion, but the territorial expansion of which we speak does not in any sense of the word involve the occupation of the possessions of other countries, the planting of the Japanese flag thereon, and the declaration of their annexation to Japan. It is just that since the Powers have suppressed the circulation of Japanese materials and merchandise abroad, we are looking for some place overseas where Japanese capital, Japanese skills and Japanese labor can have free play, free from the oppression of the white race.

We would be satisfied with just this much. What moral right do the world powers who have themselves closed to us the two doors of emigration and advance into world markets have to criticize Japan's attempt to rush out of the third and last door?

If they do not approve of this, they should open the door which they have closed against us and permit the free movement overseas of Japanese emigrants and merchandise. . . .

At the time of the Manchurian incident, the entire world joined in criticism of Japan. They said that Japan was an untrustworthy nation. They said that she had recklessly brought cannon and machine guns into Manchuria, which was the territory of another country, flown airplanes over it, and finally occupied it. But the military action taken by Japan was not in the least a selfish one. Moreover, we do not recall ever having taken so much as an inch of territory belonging to another nation. The result of this incident was the establishment of the splendid new nation of Manchuria. The Powers are still discussing whether or not to recognize this new nation, but regardless of whether or not other nations recognize her, the Manchurian empire has already been established, and now, seven years after its creation, the empire is further consolidating its foundations with the aid of its friend, Japan.

And if it is still protested that our actions in Manchuria were excessively violent, we may wish to ask the white race just which country it was that sent warships and troops to India, South Africa, and Australia and slaughtered innocent natives, bound their hands and feet with iron chains, lashed their backs with iron whips, proclaimed these territories as their own, and still continues to hold them to this very day.

---

in December, but Chiang Kai-shek refused to capitulate and moved his government upriver to Hankow and then, when the Japanese seized that city, to Chungking, in remote Szechuan Province. Japanese strategists had hoped to force Chiang to agree to join a Japanese-dominated "new order" in East Asia, comprising Japan, Manchuria, and China. This was part of a larger plan to seize Soviet Siberia, with its rich resources, and create a new "Monroe Doctrine for Asia," with Japan guiding its Asian neighbors on the path to development and prosperity. After all, who better to instruct Asian societies on the path to modernization than the one Asian country that had already achieved it (see the box above)?

During the late 1930s, Japan had begun to cooperate with Nazi Germany on the assumption that the two countries would ultimately launch a joint attack on the Soviet Union and divide up its resources between them. But when Berlin suddenly surprised the world by signing a nonaggression pact with Moscow in August 1939, Japanese strategists were compelled to reevaluate their long-term objectives. Japan was not strong enough to defeat the USSR alone and so began to shift its eyes southward, to the vast resources of Southeast Asia—the oil of the Dutch East Indies, the rubber and tin of Malaya, and the rice of Burma and Indochina.

A move southward, of course, would risk war with the European colonial powers and the United States. Japan's attack on China in the summer of 1937 had already aroused strong criticism abroad, particularly in the United States. When Japan demanded the right to occupy airfields and exploit economic resources in French Indochina in the summer of 1940, Washington warned Tokyo that it would apply economic sanctions unless Japan withdrew from the area and returned to its borders of 1931.

In Tokyo, the American threat of retaliation was viewed as a threat to Japan's long-term objectives. It badly needed

A JAPANESE VICTORY IN CHINA. After consolidating its authority over Manchuria, Japan began to expand into northern China. Direct hostilities between Japanese and Chinese forces began in 1937. By 1939, Japan had conquered most of eastern China. This photograph shows victorious Japanese soldiers amid the ruins of the railway station in Hankow, which became China's temporary capital after the fall of Nanjing.

liquid fuel and scrap iron from the United States. Should they be cut off, Japan would have to find them elsewhere. Japan was thus caught in a dilemma. To obtain guaranteed access to natural resources that would be necessary to fuel the Japanese military machine, Japan must risk a cutoff of its current source of raw materials that would be needed in case of a conflict. After much debate, Japan decided to launch a surprise attack on American and European colonies in Southeast Asia in the hope of a quick victory and the eviction of the United States from the region.

WORLD WAR II

Hitler stunned Europe with the speed and efficiency of the German *Blitzkrieg*, or "lightning war." Armored columns or panzer divisions (a panzer division was a strike force of about three hundred tanks and accompanying forces and supplies) supported by airplanes broke quickly through Polish lines and encircled the bewildered Polish troops. Conventional infantry units then moved in to hold the newly conquered territory. Within four weeks, Poland had surrendered. On September 28, 1939, Germany and the Soviet Union officially divided Poland between them.

Europe at War

After a winter of waiting, Hitler resumed the war on April 9, 1940, with another *Blitzkrieg* against Denmark and Norway (see Map 24.1). One month later, on May 10, the Germans launched their attack on the Netherlands, Bel-

gium, and France. The main assault through Luxembourg and the Ardennes forest, completely unexpected by the French and British forces, enabled German panzer divisions to break through the weak French defensive positions there and race across northern France, splitting the Allied armies and trapping French troops and the entire British army on the beaches of Dunkirk. Only by heroic efforts did the British succeed in achieving a gigantic evacuation of 330,000 Allied troops. The French capitulated on June 22. German armies occupied about three-fifths of France while the French hero of World War I, Marshal Henri Pétain, established an authoritarian regime (known as Vichy France) over the remainder. Germany was now in control of western and central Europe, but Britain had still not been defeated.

As Hitler realized, an amphibious invasion of Britain would be possible only if Germany gained control of the air. At the beginning of August 1940, the *Luftwaffe* (the German air force) launched a major offensive against British air and naval bases, harbors, communication centers, and war industries. The British fought back doggedly, supported by an effective radar system that gave them early warning of German attacks. Nevertheless the British air force suffered critical losses by the end of August and was probably saved by Hitler's change of strategy. In September, in retaliation for a British attack on Berlin, Hitler ordered a shift from military targets to massive bombing of British cities to break British morale. The British rebuilt their air strength quickly and were soon inflicting major losses on *Luftwaffe* bombers. By the end of September, Germany had to postpone the invasion of Britain.

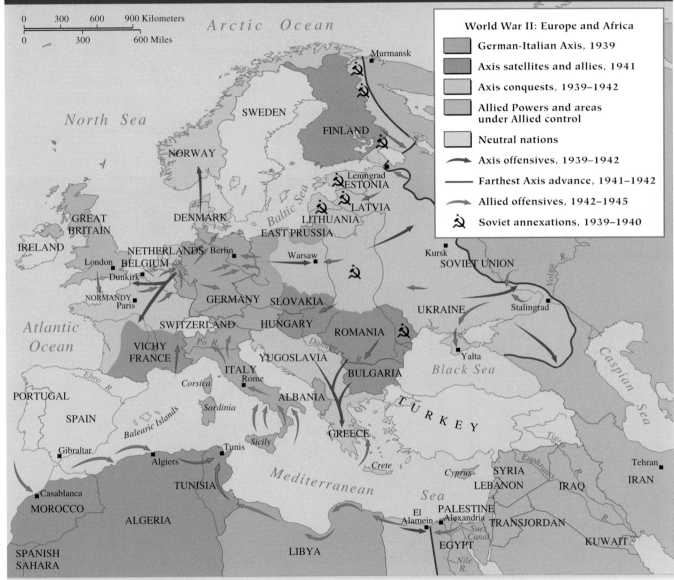

MAP 24.1 World War II in Europe and North Africa. With its fast and effective military, Germany quickly overwhelmed much of western Europe. However, Hitler overestimated his country's capabilities and underestimated those of his foes. By late 1942, his invasion of the Soviet Union was failing, and the United States had become a major factor in the war. The Allies successfully invaded Italy in 1943 and France in 1944. ➤ **Which countries were neutral, and how did geography help make their neutrality an option?**

World War II: Europe and Africa

- German-Italian Axis, 1939
- Axis satellites and allies, 1941
- Axis conquests, 1939–1942
- Allied Powers and areas under Allied control
- Neutral nations
- Axis offensives, 1939–1942
- Farthest Axis advance, 1941–1942
- Allied offensives, 1942–1945
- Soviet annexations, 1939–1940

Although he had no desire for a two-front war, Hitler became convinced that Britain was remaining in the war only because it expected Russian support. If Russia were smashed, Britain's last hope would be eliminated. Although the invasion of the Soviet Union was scheduled for spring 1941, the attack was delayed because of problems in the Balkans. Hitler had already obtained the political cooperation of Hungary, Bulgaria, and Romania, but Mussolini's disastrous invasion of Greece in October 1940 exposed Hitler's southern flank to British air bases in Greece. To secure his Balkan flank, German troops seized both Yugoslavia and Greece in April. Now reassured, Hitler turned to the east and invaded the Soviet Union on June 22, 1941.

The massive attack stretched out along a 1,800-mile front. German troops advanced rapidly, capturing two million Soviet soldiers. By November, one German army group had swept through the Ukraine, while a second was besieging Leningrad; a third approached within 25 miles of Moscow, the Soviet capital. An early Soviet winter and unexpected Soviet resistance, however, brought a halt to the German advance. For the first time in the war, German armies had been stopped. A Soviet counterattack in December 1941 came as an ominous ending to the year for the Germans. By that time, another of Hitler's decisions—the declaration of war on the United States—turned another European conflict into a global war.

Japan at War

On December 7, 1941, Japanese aircraft attacked the U.S. naval base at Pearl Harbor in the Hawaiian Islands. The same day, other units launched additional assaults on the Philippines and began advancing toward the British colony of Malaya (see Map 24.2). Shortly after this, Japanese forces invaded the Dutch East Indies and occupied a number of islands in the Pacific Ocean. By the spring of 1942, almost all of Southeast Asia and much of the western Pacific had fallen to the Japanese. Japan declared the establishment of the Greater East Asia Co-Prosperity Sphere, encompassing the entire region under Japanese tutelage, and announced its intention to liberate the colonial areas of Southeast Asia from Western colonial rule. For the moment, however, Japan needed the resources of the region for its war machine and placed the countries under its own rule on a wartime basis.

Japanese leaders had hoped that their lightning strike at American bases would destroy the U.S. Pacific fleet and persuade President Roosevelt to accept Japanese domination of the Pacific. But Japan had miscalculated. The

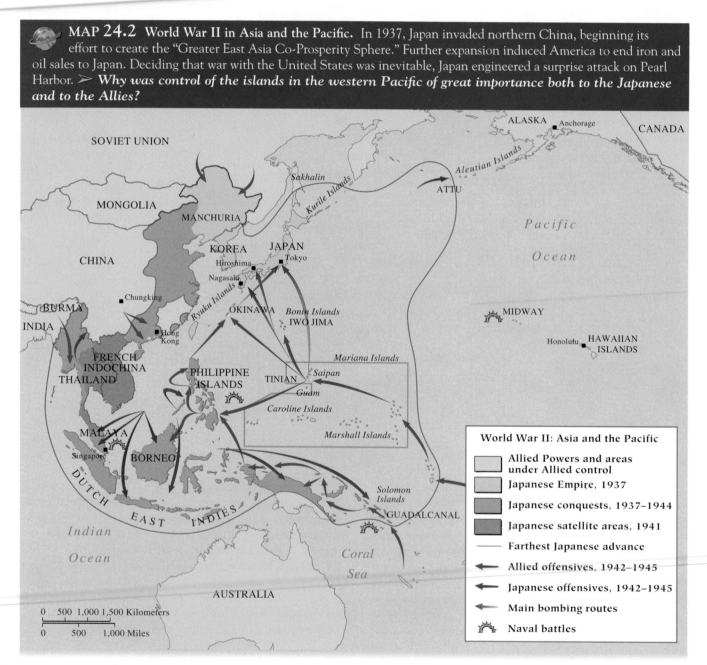

MAP 24.2 World War II in Asia and the Pacific. In 1937, Japan invaded northern China, beginning its effort to create the "Greater East Asia Co-Prosperity Sphere." Further expansion induced America to end iron and oil sales to Japan. Deciding that war with the United States was inevitable, Japan engineered a surprise attack on Pearl Harbor. ➤ *Why was control of the islands in the western Pacific of great importance both to the Japanese and to the Allies?*

World War II: Asia and the Pacific

Allied Powers and areas under Allied control
Japanese Empire, 1937
Japanese conquests, 1937–1944
Japanese satellite areas, 1941
Farthest Japanese advance
Allied offensives, 1942–1945
Japanese offensives, 1942–1945
Main bombing routes
Naval battles

attack on Pearl Harbor galvanized American opinion and won broad support for Roosevelt's war policy. The United States now joined with European nations and Nationalist China in a combined effort to defeat Japan and end its hegemony in the Pacific. Believing the American involvement in the Pacific would render the United States ineffective in the European theater of war, Hitler declared war on the United States four days after Pearl Harbor.

The Turning Point of the War, 1942–1943

The entry of the United States into the war created a coalition (the Grand Alliance) that ultimately defeated the Axis Powers (Germany, Italy, and Japan). To overcome mutual suspicions, the three major Allies, Britain, the United States, and the Soviet Union, agreed to stress military operations while ignoring political differences. At the beginning of 1943, the Allies also agreed to fight until the Axis Powers surrendered unconditionally, which had the effect of cementing the Grand Alliance by making it nearly impossible for Hitler to divide his foes.

Defeat, however, was far from Hitler's mind at the beginning of 1942. As Japanese forces advanced into the Pacific after crippling the American naval fleet at Pearl Harbor, Hitler continued the war in Europe against Britain and the Soviet Union. Until the fall of 1942, it appeared that the Germans might still prevail on the battlefield. Reinforcements in North Africa enabled the Afrika Korps under General Erwin Rommel to break through the British defenses in Egypt and advance toward Alexandria. In the spring of 1942, a renewed German offensive in Russia led to the capture of the entire Crimea. But by the fall of 1942, the war had turned against the Germans.

In North Africa, British forces had stopped Rommel's troops at El Alamein in the summer of 1942 and then forced them back across the desert. In November 1942, British and American forces invaded French North Africa and forced the German and Italian troops to surrender in May 1943. On the Eastern Front, the turning point of the war occurred at Stalingrad. After the capture of the Crimea, Hitler decided that Stalingrad, a major industrial center on the Volga, should be taken next. Between November 1942 and February 1943, German troops were stopped, then encircled, and finally forced to surrender on February 2, 1943 (see the box on p. 532). The entire German Sixth Army of 300,000 men was lost. By February 1943, German forces in the Soviet Union were back to their positions of June 1942.

The tide of battle in the Far East also turned dramatically in 1942. In the Battle of the Coral Sea on May 7–8, 1942, American naval forces stopped the Japanese advance. On June 4, at the Battle of Midway Island, American planes destroyed all four of the attacking Japanese aircraft carriers and established American naval superiority in the Pacific. By the fall of 1942, Allied forces were begin-

ning to gather for offensive operations: into South China from Burma, through the East Indies by a process of "island hopping" by troops commanded by U.S. general Douglas MacArthur, and across the Pacific with a combination of U.S. army, marine, and navy attacks on Japanese-held islands. After a series of bitter engagements in the waters of the Solomon Islands from August to November 1942, Japanese fortunes began to fade.

The Last Years of the War

By the beginning of 1943, the tide of battle had turned against Germany, Italy, and Japan. After the Axis forces had surrendered in Tunisia on May 13, 1943, the Allies crossed the Mediterranean and carried the war to Italy. After taking Sicily, Allied troops began the invasion of mainland Italy in September. In the meantime, after the ouster and arrest of Benito Mussolini, a new Italian government offered to surrender to Allied forces. But Mussolini was liberated by the Germans in a daring raid and then set up as the head of a puppet German state in northern Italy while German troops moved in and occupied much of Italy. The new defensive lines established by the Germans in the hills south of Rome were so effective that the Allied advance up the Italian peninsula was a painstaking affair accompanied by heavy casualties. Rome did not fall to the Allies until June 4, 1944. By that time, the Italian war had assumed a secondary role anyway as the Allies opened their long-awaited "second front" in western Europe.

Under the direction of the American general Dwight D. Eisenhower (1890–1969), the Allies landed five assault divisions on the beaches of Normandy on June 6 in history's greatest naval invasion. An initially indecisive German response enabled the Allied forces to establish a beachhead. Within three months, they had landed two million men and a half-million vehicles that pushed inland and broke through German defensive lines.

After the breakout, Allied troops moved south and east and liberated Paris by the end of August. By March 1945, they had crossed the Rhine River and advanced deep into Germany. At the end of April 1945, Allied armies in northern Germany moved toward the Elbe River, where they finally linked up with the Soviets. The Soviets had come a long way since the Battle of Stalingrad in 1943. In the summer of 1943, German forces were soundly defeated by the Soviets at the Battle of Kursk (July 5–12), the greatest tank battle of World War II. Soviet forces now began a relentless advance westward. The Soviets had reoccupied the Ukraine by the end of 1943 and lifted the siege of Leningrad and moved into the Baltic States by the beginning of 1944. Advancing along a northern front, Soviet troops occupied Warsaw in January 1945 and entered Berlin in April. Meanwhile Soviet troops along a southern front swept through Hungary, Romania, and Bulgaria.

A GERMAN SOLDIER AT STALINGRAD

The Soviet victory at Stalingrad was a major turning point in World War II. This excerpt comes from the diary of a German soldier who fought and died in the Battle of Stalingrad. His dreams of victory and a return home with medals are soon dashed by the realities of Soviet resistance.

DIARY OF A GERMAN SOLDIER

Today, after we'd had a bath, the company commander told us that if our future operations are as successful, we'll soon reach the Volga, take Stalingrad, and then the war will inevitably soon be over. Perhaps we'll be home by Christmas.

July 29. The company commander says the Russian troops are completely broken, and cannot hold out any longer. To reach the Volga and take Stalingrad is not so difficult for us. The Führer knows where the Russians' weak point is. Victory is not far away. . . .

August 10. The Führer's orders were read out to us. He expects victory of us. We are all convinced that they can't stop us.

August 12. This morning outstanding soldiers were presented with decorations. . . . Will I really go back to Elsa without a decoration? I believe that for Stalingrad the Führer will decorate even me. . . .

September 4. We are being sent northward along the front toward Stalingrad. We marched all night and by dawn had reached Voroponovo Station. We can already see the smoking town. It's a happy thought that the end of the war is getting nearer. That's what everyone is saying. . . .

September 8. Two days of nonstop fighting. The Russians are defending themselves with insane stubbornness. Our regiment has lost many men. . . .

September 16. Our battalion, plus tanks, is attacking the [grain storage] elevator, from which smoke is pouring—the grain in it is burning; the Russians seem to have set light to

it themselves. Barbarism. The battalion is suffering heavy losses. . . .

October 10. The Russians are so close to us that our planes cannot bomb them. We are preparing for a decisive attack. The Führer has ordered the whole of Stalingrad to be taken as rapidly as possible. . . .

October 22. Our regiment has failed to break into the factory. We have lost many men; every time you move you have to jump over bodies. . . .

November 10. A letter from Elsa today. Everyone expects us home for Christmas. In Germany everyone believes we already hold Stalingrad. How wrong they are. If they could only see what Stalingrad has done to our army. . . .

November 21. The Russians have gone over to the offensive along the whole front. Fierce fighting is going on. So, there it is—the Volga, victory, and soon home to our families! We shall obviously be seeing them next in the other world.

November 29. We are encircled. It was announced this morning that the Führer has said: "The army can trust me to do everything necessary to ensure supplies and rapidly break the encirclement."

December 3. We are on hunger rations and waiting for the rescue that the Führer promised. . . .

December 14. Everybody is racked with hunger. Frozen potatoes are the best meal, but to get them out of the ice-covered ground under fire from Russian bullets is not so easy. . . .

December 26. The horses have already been eaten. I would eat a cat; they say its meat is also tasty. The soldiers look like corpses or lunatics, looking for something to put in their mouths. They no longer take cover from Russian shells; they haven't the strength to walk, run away, and hide. A curse on this war!

In January 1945, Adolf Hitler had moved into a bunker 55 feet under Berlin to direct the final stages of the war. In his final political testament, Hitler, consistent to the end in his rabid anti-Semitism, blamed the Jews for the war. Hitler committed suicide on April 30, two days after Mussolini had been shot by partisan Italian forces. On May 7, German commanders surrendered. The war in Europe was over.

The war in Asia continued. Beginning in 1943, American forces had gone on the offensive and advanced their way, slowly at times, across the Pacific. American forces took an increasing toll of enemy resources, especially at sea and in the air. As Allied military power drew inexorably closer to the main Japanese islands in the first months of 1945, President Harry Truman, who had succeeded to the presidency on the death of Franklin Roosevelt in April,

decided to use atomic weapons to bring the war to an end without the necessity of an Allied invasion of the Japanese homeland. The first bomb was dropped on the city of Hiroshima on August 6. Three days later, a second bomb was dropped on Nagasaki. Japan surrendered unconditionally on August 14. World War II, in which seventeen million soldiers died in battle and perhaps eighteen million civilians perished as well, was finally over.

THE NEW ORDER

The initial victories of the Germans and the Japanese had given them the opportunity to restructure society in Europe and Asia. Both followed policies of ruthless domination of their subject peoples.

Chronology

THE COURSE OF WORLD WAR II

Germany and the Soviet Union divide Poland	September 28, 1939
Blitzkrieg against Denmark and Norway	April 1940
Blitzkrieg against Belgium, Netherlands, France	May 1940
France surrenders	June 22, 1940
Battle of Britain	Fall 1940
Nazi seizure of Yugoslavia and Greece	April 1941
Germany invades the Soviet Union	June 22, 1941
Japanese attack on Pearl Harbor	December 7, 1941
Battle of the Coral Sea	May 7–8, 1942
Battle of Midway Island	June 4, 1942
Allied invasion of North Africa	November 1942
German surrender at Stalingrad	February 2, 1943
Axis forces surrender in North Africa	May 1943
Battle of Kursk	July 5–12, 1943
Invasion of mainland Italy	September 1943
Allied invasion of France	June 6, 1944
Hitler commits suicide	April 30, 1945
Surrender of Germany	May 7, 1945
Atomic bomb dropped on Hiroshima	August 6, 1945
Japan surrenders	August 14, 1945

The New Order in Europe

In 1942, the Nazi empire stretched across continental Europe from the English Channel in the west to the outskirts of Moscow in the east. Nazi-occupied Europe was largely organized in one of two ways. Some areas, such as western Poland, were directly annexed by Nazi Germany and made into German provinces. Most of occupied Europe was administered by German military or civilian officials, combined with different degrees of indirect control from collaborationist regimes.

Because the conquered lands in the east contained the living space for German expansion and were, in Nazi eyes, populated by racially inferior Slavic peoples, Nazi administration there was considerably more ruthless. Soon after the conquest of Poland, Heinrich Himmler, the leader of the SS, was put in charge of German resettlement plans in the east. Himmler's task was to evacuate the inferior Slavic peoples and replace them with Germans, a policy first applied to the new German provinces created from the lands of western Poland. One million Poles were uprooted and dumped in southern Poland. Hundreds of thousands of ethnic Germans (descendants of Germans who had migrated years earlier from Germany to different parts of southern and eastern Europe) were encouraged to colonize the designated areas in Poland. By 1942, two million ethnic Germans had been settled in Poland.

Labor shortages in Germany led to a policy of ruthless mobilization of foreign labor for Germany. In 1942, a special office was created to recruit labor for German farms and industries. By the summer of 1944, seven million foreign workers were laboring in Germany and constituted 20 percent of Germany's labor force. At the same time, another seven million workers were supplying forced labor in their own countries on farms, in industries, and even in military camps. The brutality of Germany's recruitment policies often led more and more people to resist the Nazi occupation forces.

The Holocaust

No aspect of the Nazi new order was more terrifying than the deliberate attempt to exterminate the Jews of Europe. Racial struggle was a key element in Hitler's ideology and meant to him a clearly defined conflict of opposites: the Aryans, creators of human cultural development, against the Jews, parasites who were trying to destroy the Aryans. Himmler and the SS organization closely shared Hitler's racial ideology. The SS was given responsibility for what the Nazis called their "final solution" to the "Jewish problem"—annihilation of the Jews. After the defeat of Poland, the SS ordered special strike forces (*Einsatzgruppen*) to round up all Polish Jews and concentrate them in ghettos established in a number of Polish cities.

In June 1941, the *Einsatzgruppen* were given new responsibilities as mobile killing units. These SS death squads followed the regular army's advance into Russia. Their job was to round up Jews in their villages, execute them, and bury them in mass graves, often giant pits dug by the victims themselves before they were shot. Such constant killing produced morale problems among the SS executioners. During a visit to Minsk in the Soviet Union, SS leader Heinrich Himmler tried to build morale by pointing out that he "would not like it if Germans did such a thing gladly. But their conscience was in no way impaired, for they were soldiers who had to carry out every order unconditionally. He alone had responsibility before God and Hitler for everything that was happening."[6]

➤ **THE HOLOCAUST: ACTIVITIES OF THE EINSATZGRUPPEN.** The mobile killing units known as the *Einsatzgruppen* were active during the first phase of mass killings of the Holocaust. This picture shows the execution of a Jew by a member of one of these SS killing squads. Onlookers include members of the German army, the German Labor Service, and even Hitler Youth. When it became apparent that this method of killing was inefficient, it was replaced by the death camps.

Although it has been estimated that as many as one million Jews were killed by the *Einsatzgruppen*, this approach to solving the Jewish problem was soon perceived as inadequate. Instead the Nazis opted for the systematic annihilation of the European Jewish population in specially built death camps. The plan was basically simple. Jews from countries occupied by Germany (or sympathetic to Germany) would be rounded up, packed like cattle into freight trains, and shipped to Poland, where six extermination centers were built to dispose of them. The largest and most famous was Auschwitz-Birkenau. Medical technicians chose Zyklon B (the commercial name for hydrogen cyanide) as the most effective gas for quickly killing large numbers of people in gas chambers designed to look like "shower rooms" to facilitate the cooperation of the victims. After gassing, the corpses would be burned in specially built crematoria.

By the spring of 1942, the death camps were in operation; by the summer, Jews were also being shipped from France, Belgium, and the Netherlands. Even as the Allies were making significant advances in 1944, Jews were being shipped from Greece and Hungary. A harrowing experience awaited the Jews when they arrived at one of the six death camps. Rudolf Höss, commandant at Auschwitz-Birkenau, described it:

> We had two SS doctors on duty at Auschwitz to examine the incoming transports of prisoners. The prisoners would be marched by one of the doctors who would make spot decisions as they walked by. Those who were fit for work were sent into the camp. Others were sent immediately to the extermination plants. Children of tender years were invariably exterminated since by reason of their youth they were unable to work. . . . At Auschwitz we endeavored to fool the victims into thinking that they were to go through a delousing process. Of course, frequently they realized our true intentions and we sometimes had riots and difficulties due to that fact.[7]

About 30 percent of the arrivals at Auschwitz were sent to a labor camp; the remainder went to the gas chambers (see the box on p. 535). After they had been gassed, the bodies were burned in the crematoria. The victims' goods and even their bodies were used for economic gain. Female hair was cut off, collected, and turned into cloth or used to stuff mattresses. The Germans killed between five and six million Jews, more than three million of them in the death camps. Virtually 90 percent of the Jewish population of Poland, the Baltic countries, and Germany were exterminated.

The Nazis were also responsible for another Holocaust, the death by shooting, starvation, or overwork of at least another nine to ten million people. Because the Nazis considered the Gypsies of Europe a race containing alien blood (like the Jews), they were systematically rounded up for extermination. About 40 percent of Europe's one million Gypsies were killed in the death camps. The leading elements of the "subhuman" Slavic peoples—the clergy, intelligentsia, civil leaders, judges, and lawyers—were arrested and deliberately killed. Probably an additional four million Poles, Ukrainians, and Byelorussians lost their lives as slave laborers for Nazi Germany. Finally, at least three million Soviet prisoners of war, and probably more, were killed in captivity.

The New Order in Asia

Once Japan's takeover was completed, Japanese war policy in the occupied areas in Asia became essentially defensive, as Japan hoped to use its new possessions to meet its needs for raw materials, such as tin, oil, and rubber, as well as to serve as an outlet for Japanese manufactured goods. To provide a structure for the arrangement, Japanese leaders set up the Greater East Asia Co-Prosperity Sphere as a self-sufficient community designed to provide mutual benefits to the occupied areas and the home country.

THE HOLOCAUST: THE CAMP COMMANDANT AND THE CAMP VICTIMS

The systematic annihilation of millions of men, women, and children in extermination camps makes the Holocaust one of the most horrifying events in history. The first document is taken from an account by Rudolf Höss, commandant of the extermination camp at Auschwitz-Birkenau. In the second document, a French doctor explains what happened at one of the crematoria described by Höss.

COMMANDANT HÖSS DESCRIBES THE EQUIPMENT

The two large crematoria, Nos. I and II, were built during the winter of 1942–43. . . . They each . . . could cremate c. 2,000 corpses within twenty-four hours. . . . Crematoria I and II both had underground undressing and gassing rooms which could be completely ventilated. The corpses were brought up to the ovens on the floor above by lift. The gas chambers could hold c. 3,000 people.

The firm of Topf had calculated that the two smaller crematoria, III and IV, would each be able to cremate 1,500 corpses within twenty-four hours. However, owing to the wartime shortage of materials, the builders were obliged to economize, and so the undressing rooms and gassing rooms were built above ground and the ovens were of a less solid construction.

A FRENCH DOCTOR DESCRIBES THE VICTIMS

It is mid-day, when a long line of women, children, and old people enter the yard. The senior official in charge . . . climbs on a bench to tell them that they are going to have a bath and that afterward they will get a drink of hot coffee. They all undress in the yard. . . . The doors are opened and an indescribable jostling begins. The first people to enter the gas chamber begin to draw back. They sense the death which awaits them. The SS men put an end to this pushing and shoving with blows from their rifle butts beating the heads of the horrified women who are desperately hugging their children. The massive oak double doors are shut. For two endless minutes one can hear banging on the walls and screams which are no longer human. And then— not a sound. Five minutes later the doors are opened. The corpses, squashed together and distorted, fall out like a waterfall. . . . The bodies, which are still warm, pass through the hands of the hairdresser, who cuts their hair, and the dentist, who pulls out their gold teeth. . . . One more transport has just been processed through No. IV crematorium.

The Japanese conquest of Southeast Asia had been accomplished under the slogan "Asia for the Asians." Japanese officials in occupied territories quickly promised that independent governments would be established under Japanese tutelage. Such governments were eventually established in Burma, the Dutch East Indies, Vietnam, and the Philippines.

In fact, however, real power rested with Japanese military authorities in each territory, and the local Japanese military command was directly subordinated to the army general staff in Tokyo. The economic resources of the colonies were exploited for the benefit of the Japanese war machine, while natives were recruited to serve in local military units or were conscripted to work on public works projects. In some cases, the people living in the occupied areas were subjected to severe hardships. In Indochina, for example, forced acquisitions of rice by the local Japanese authorities for shipment abroad led to the starvation of over a million Vietnamese in 1944 and 1945.

At first, many Southeast Asian nationalists took Japanese promises at face value and agreed to cooperate with their new masters. But as the exploitative nature of Japanese occupation policies became clear, sentiment turned against the new order. Japanese officials sometimes unwittingly provoked such attitudes by their arrogance and contempt for local customs.

Like German soldiers in occupied Europe, Japanese military forces often had little respect for the lives of their subject peoples. In their conquest of Nanjing, China, in 1937, Japanese soldiers had spent several days killing, raping, and looting. Almost 800,000 Koreans were sent overseas, most of them as forced laborers, to Japan. Tens of thousands of Korean women were forced to be "comfort women" (prostitutes) for Japanese troops. In construction projects to help their war effort, the Japanese also made extensive use of labor forces composed of both prisoners of war and local peoples. In building the Burma-Thailand railway in 1943, for example, the Japanese used 61,000 Australian, British, and Dutch prisoners of war and almost 300,000 workers from Burma, Malaya, Thailand, and the Dutch East Indies. An inadequate diet and appalling work conditions in an unhealthy climate led to the death of 12,000 Allied prisoners of war and 90,000 native workers by the time the railway was completed.

THE HOME FRONT

World War II was even more of a total war than World War I. Fighting was much more widespread and covered most of the world. The number of civilians killed was far higher.

The Mobilization of Peoples: Three Examples

The initial defeats of the Soviet Union led to drastic emergency mobilization measures that affected the civilian population. Leningrad, for example, experienced nine hundred days of siege, during which its inhabitants became so desperate for food that they ate dogs, cats, and mice. As the German army made its rapid advance into Soviet territory, the factories in the western part of the Soviet Union were dismantled and shipped to the interior—to the Urals, western Siberia, and the Volga regions. Machines were set down on the bare earth, and walls went up around them as workers began their work.

Stalin called the widespread military and industrial mobilization of the nation a "battle of machines," and the Soviets won, producing 78,000 tanks and 98,000 artillery pieces. In 1943, fully 55 percent of Soviet national income went for war materials, compared to 15 percent in 1940.

Soviet women played a major role in the war effort. Women and girls were enlisted for work in industries, mines, and railroads. Overall the number of women working in industry increased almost 60 percent. Soviet women were also expected to dig antitank ditches and work as air raid wardens. In addition, the Soviet Union was the only country in World War II to use women as combatants. Soviet women functioned as snipers and as crews in bomber squadrons.

In August 1914, Germans had enthusiastically cheered their soldiers marching off to war; in September 1939, the streets were quiet. Many Germans were apathetic or, even worse for the Nazi regime, had a foreboding of disaster. Hitler was very aware of the importance of the home front. He believed that the collapse of the home front in World War I had caused Germany's defeat. To avoid a repetition of that experience, he adopted economic policies that may indeed have cost Germany the war.

To maintain the morale of the home front during the first two years of the war, Hitler refused to cut consumer goods production or increase the production of armaments. After German defeats on the Russian front and the American entry into the war, however, the situation changed. Early in 1942, Hitler finally ordered a massive increase in armaments production and the size of the army. Hitler's architect, Albert Speer, was made minister for armaments and munitions in 1942. By eliminating waste and rationalizing procedures, Speer was able to triple the production of armaments between 1942 and 1943, despite the intense Allied air raids. Speer's urgent plea for a total mobilization of resources for the war effort went unheeded, however. Hitler, fearful of civilian morale problems that would undermine the home front, refused any dramatic cuts in the production of consumer goods. A total mobilization of the economy was not implemented until 1944, but by that time, it was too late.

The war produced a reversal in Nazi attitudes toward women. Nazi resistance to female employment declined as the war progressed and more and more men were called up for military service. Nazi magazines now proclaimed, "We see the woman as the eternal mother of our people, but also as the working and fighting comrade of the man."[8] But the number of women working in industry, agriculture, commerce, and domestic service increased only slightly. The total number of employed women in September 1944 was 14.9 million, compared to 14.6 million in May 1939. Many women, especially those of the middle class, resisted regular employment, particularly in factories.

Wartime Japan was a highly mobilized society. To guarantee its control over all national resources, the government set up a planning board to control prices, wages, the utilization of labor, and the allocation of resources. Traditional habits of obedience and hierarchy, buttressed by the concept of imperial divinity, were emphasized to encourage citizens to sacrifice their resources, and sometimes their lives, for the national cause. The system culminated in the final years of the war, when young Japanese were encouraged to volunteer en masse to serve as pilots in the suicide missions (known as *kamikaze*, "divine wind") against U.S. battleships.

Women's rights too were to be sacrificed to the greater national cause. Already by 1937, Japanese women were being exhorted to fulfill their patriotic duty by bearing more children and by espousing the slogans of the Greater Japanese Women's Association. However, Japan was extremely reluctant to mobilize women on behalf of Japan's war effort. General Hideki Tojo, prime minister from 1941 to 1944, opposed female employment, arguing that "the weakening of the family system would be the weakening of the nation. . . . We are able to do our duties only because we have wives and mothers at home."[9] Female employment increased during the war, but only in areas where women traditionally worked, such as the textile industry and farming. Instead of using women to meet labor shortages, the Japanese government brought in Korean and Chinese laborers.

The Frontline Civilians: The Bombing of Cities

Bombing was used in World War II against a variety of targets, including military targets, enemy troops, and civilian populations. The bombing of civilians made World War II as devastating for civilians as for frontline soldiers. A small number of bombing raids in the last year of World War I had given rise to the argument that public outcry over the bombing of civilian populations would be an effective way to coerce governments into making peace. Consequently European air forces began to develop long-range bombers in the 1930s.

The first sustained use of civilian bombing contradicted the theory. Beginning in early September, the German *Luftwaffe* subjected London and many other British cities and towns to nightly air raids, making the Blitz (as the British called the German air raids) a national experience. Londoners took the first heavy blows, and it was their maintenance of morale that set the standard for the rest of the British population.

The British failed to learn from their own experience, however; Prime Minister Winston Churchill and his advisers believed that destroying German communities would break civilian morale and bring victory. Major bombing raids began in 1942. On May 31, 1942, Cologne became the first German city to be subjected to an attack by a thousand bombers. Bombing raids added an element of terror to circumstances already made difficult by growing shortages of food, clothing, and fuel. Germans especially feared incendiary bombs, which ignited firestorms that swept destructive paths through the cities. The ferocious bombing of Dresden from February 13 to 15, 1945, set off a firestorm that may have killed as many as 100,000 inhabitants and refugees.

Germany suffered enormously from the Allied bombing raids. Millions of buildings were destroyed, and possibly half a million civilians died from the raids. Nevertheless it is highly unlikely that Allied bombing sapped the morale of the German people. Instead Germans, whether pro-Nazi or anti-Nazi, fought on stubbornly, often driven simply by a desire to live. Nor did the bombing destroy Germany's industrial capacity. The Allied strategic bombing survey revealed that the production of war materials actually increased between 1942 and 1944.

In Japan, the bombing of civilians reached a horrendous new level with the use of the first atomic bomb. Attacks on Japanese cities by the new American B-29 Superfortresses, the biggest bombers of the war, had begun on November 24, 1944. By the summer of 1945, many of Japan's industries had been destroyed, along with one-fourth of its dwellings. After the Japanese government decreed the mobilization of all people between the ages of thirteen and sixty into the so-called People's Volunteer Corps, President Truman and his advisers decided that Japanese fanaticism might mean a million American casualties, and Truman decided to drop the newly developed atomic bomb on Hiroshima and

The Bombing of Civilians—East and West

World War II was the most destructive war in world history, not only for frontline soldiers but for civilians at home as well. The most devastating bombing of civilians came near the end of World War II when the United States dropped atomic bombs on the Japanese cities of Hiroshima and Nagasaki. At the left is a view of Hiroshima after the bombing that shows the incredible devastation produced by the atomic bomb. The picture at the right shows a street in Clydebank, near Glasgow in Scotland, the day after the city was bombed by the Germans in March 1941. Only seven of the city's twelve thousand houses were left undamaged; 35,000 of the 47,000 inhabitants became homeless overnight.

© J.R. Eyerman/Time Life Pictures/Getty Images

The Herald and Evening Times Picture Library, © SMG Newspapers Ltd.

Nagasaki. The destruction was incredible. Of 76,000 buildings near the hypocenter of the explosion in Hiroshima, 70,000 were flattened, and 140,000 of the city's 400,000 inhabitants had died by the end of 1945. Over the next five years, another 50,000 perished from the effects of radiation. The dropping of the atomic bomb on Hiroshima on August 6, 1945, announced the dawn of the nuclear age.

AFTERMATH: THE COLD WAR

The total victory of the Allies in World War II was followed not by a real peace but by yet another period of conflict, known as the Cold War, that dominated world politics for the next fifty years.

The Conferences at Tehran, Yalta, and Potsdam

Stalin, Roosevelt, and Churchill, the leaders of the Big Three of the Grand Alliance, met at Tehran, the capital of Iran, in November 1943 to decide the future course of the war. Stalin and Roosevelt argued successfully for an American-British invasion of the Continent through France, which they scheduled for the spring of 1944. This meant that Soviet and British-American forces would meet in defeated Germany along a north-south dividing line and that Soviet forces would liberate eastern Europe. The Allies also agreed to a partition of postwar Germany.

By the time of the conference at Yalta in southern Russia in February 1945, the defeat of Germany was a foregone conclusion. The Western powers now faced the reality of eleven million Red Army soldiers taking possession of large portions of Europe. Stalin, deeply suspicious of the Western powers, desired a buffer to protect the Soviet Union from possible future Western aggression but at the same time was eager to obtain important resources and strategic military positions. Roosevelt by this time was moving toward the idea of self-determination for Europe. The Grand Alliance approved the "Declaration on Liberated Europe." This was a pledge to assist liberated European nations in the creation of "democratic institutions of their own choice." Liberated countries were to hold free elections to determine their political systems.

At Yalta, Roosevelt sought Russian military help against Japan. Development of the atomic bomb was not yet assured, and American military planners feared the possible loss of as many as one million men in invading the Japanese home islands. Roosevelt therefore agreed to Stalin's price for military assistance against Japan: possession of Sakhalin and the Kurile Islands, as well as railroad rights in Manchuria.

The creation of the United Nations was a major American concern at Yalta. Roosevelt hoped to ensure the participation of the Big Three in a postwar international organization before difficult issues divided them into hostile camps. After a number of compromises, both Churchill and Stalin accepted Roosevelt's plans for a United Nations organization and set the first meeting for San Francisco in April 1945.

The issues of Germany and eastern Europe were treated less decisively. The Big Three reaffirmed that Germany must surrender unconditionally and created four occupation zones (see Map 24.3). A compromise was also worked out in regard to Poland. Stalin agreed to free elections in the future to determine a new government. But the issue of free elections in eastern Europe caused a serious rift between the Soviets and the Americans. The principle was that eastern European governments would be freely elected, but they were also supposed to be pro-Russian. This attempt to reconcile two irreconcilable goals was doomed to failure, as soon became evident at the next conference of the Big Three.

The Potsdam conference of July 1945 began under a cloud of mistrust. Roosevelt had died on April 12 and had been succeeded as president by Harry Truman. At Potsdam, Truman demanded free elections throughout eastern Europe. Stalin responded, "A freely elected government in any of these East European countries would be anti-Soviet, and that we cannot allow."[10] After a bitterly fought and devastating war, Stalin sought absolute military security. To him, it could be gained only by the presence of communist states in eastern Europe. Free elections might result in governments hostile to the Soviets. By the middle of 1945, only an invasion by Western forces could undo developments in eastern Europe, and few people favored such a policy.

As the war slowly receded into the past, the reality of conflicting ideologies reappeared. Many in the West interpreted Soviet policy as part of a worldwide communist conspiracy. The Soviets, for their part, viewed Western—especially American—policy as nothing less than global capitalist expansionism or, in Leninist terms, economic imperialism. In March 1946, in a speech to an American audience, former British prime minister Winston Churchill, declared that "an iron curtain" had "descended across the continent," dividing Germany and Europe into two hostile camps. Stalin branded Churchill's speech a "call to war with the Soviet Union." Only months after the world's most devastating conflict had ended, the world seemed once again bitterly divided.

CONCLUSION

World War II was the most devastating total war in human history. Germany, Italy, and Japan had been utterly defeated. Perhaps as many as forty million people—com-

MAP 24.3 **Territorial Changes in Europe After World War II.** In the last months of World War II, the Red Army occupied much of eastern Europe. Stalin sought pro-Soviet satellite states in the region as a buffer against future invasions from western Europe, whereas Britain and the United States wanted democratically elected governments. Soviet military control of the territory settled the question. ➤ *Which country gained the greatest territory at the expense of Germany?*

batants and civilians—had been killed in only six years. In Asia and Europe, cities had been reduced to rubble, and millions of people faced starvation as once fertile lands stood neglected or wasted.

What were the underlying causes of the war? One direct cause was the effort by two rising powers, Germany and Japan, to make up for their relatively late arrival on the scene to carve out global empires. Key elements in both countries had resented the agreements reached after the end of World War I, which divided the world in a manner favorable to their rivals, and hoped to overturn them at the earliest opportunity. In Germany and Japan, the legacy of a past marked by a strong military tradition still wielded

strong influence over the political system and the mindset of the entire population. It is no surprise that under the impact of the Great Depression, which had severe effects in both countries, militant forces determined to enhance national wealth and power soon overwhelmed fragile democratic institutions.

Whatever the causes of World War II, the consequences were soon evident. European hegemony over the world was at an end, and two new superpowers had emerged on the fringes of Western civilization to take its place. Even before the last battles had been fought, the United States and the Soviet Union had arrived at different visions of the postwar world, and their differences soon led to the new and potentially even more devastating conflict known as the Cold War. And even though Europeans seemed merely pawns in the struggle between the two superpowers, they managed to stage a remarkable recovery of their own civilization. In Asia, defeated Japan made a miraculous economic recovery, while the era of European domination finally came to an end.

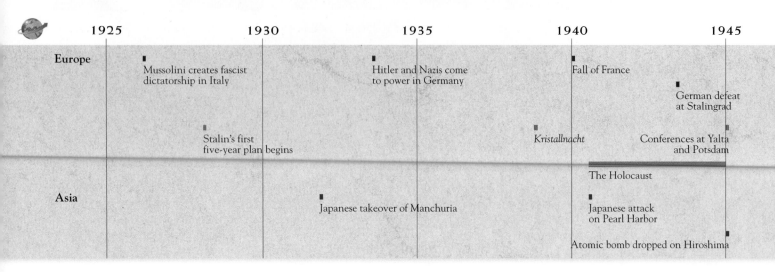

	1925	1930	1935	1940	1945

Europe

Mussolini creates fascist dictatorship in Italy

Hitler and Nazis come to power in Germany

Fall of France

German defeat at Stalingrad

Stalin's first five-year plan begins

Kristallnacht

Conferences at Yalta and Potsdam

The Holocaust

Asia

Japanese takeover of Manchuria

Japanese attack on Pearl Harbor

Atomic bomb dropped on Hiroshima

CHAPTER NOTES

1. Benito Mussolini, "The Doctrine of Fascism," in Adrian Lyttleton, ed., *Italian Fascisms* (London, 1973), p. 42.
2. Quoted in Alexander De Grand, "Women Under Italian Fascism," *Historical Journal*, 19 (1976), pp. 958–959.
3. Quoted in Jackson J. Spielvogel, *Hitler and Nazi Germany: A History*, 4th ed. (Englewood Cliffs, N.J., 2001), pp. 58–59.
4. Quoted in Joachim Fest, *Hitler*, trans. Richard Winston and Clara Winston (New York, 1974), p. 418.
5. *Documents on German Foreign Policy* (London, 1956), ser. D, vol. 7, p. 204.
6. Quoted in Raul Hilberg, *The Destruction of the European Jews*, rev. ed. (New York, 1985), vol. 1, pp. 332–333.
7. *Nazi Conspiracy and Aggression* (Washington, D.C., 1946), vol. 6, p. 789.
8. Quoted in Claudia Koonz, "Mothers in the Fatherland: Women in Nazi Germany," in Renate Bridenthal and Claudia Koonz, eds., *Becoming Visible: Women in European History* (Boston, 1977), p. 466.
9. Quoted in John Campbell, *The Experience of World War II* (New York, 1989), p. 143.
10. Quoted in Norman Graebner, *Cold War Diplomacy, 1945–1960* (Princeton, N.J., 1962), p. 117.

SUGGESTED READING

For a general interpretation of fascism, see S. G. Payne, *A History of Fascism* (Madison, Wis., 1996). The best biography of Mussolini is R. J. B. Bosworth, *Mussolini* (London, 2002). Two brief but excellent surveys of Fascist Italy are A. Cassels, *Fascist Italy*, 2d ed. (Arlington Heights, Ill., 1985), and J. Whittam, *Fascist Italy* (New York, 1995).

Two succinct but sound surveys of Nazi Germany are J. J. Spielvogel, *Hitler and Nazi Germany: A History*, 4th ed. (Englewood Cliffs, N.J., 2001), and J. Dülffer, *Nazi Germany, 1933–1945* (New York, 1996). The best biographies of Hitler are A. Bullock, *Hitler: A Study in Tyranny* (New York, 1964); J. Fest, *Hitler*, trans. R. Winston and C. Winston (New York, 1974); and I. Kershaw, *Hitler, 1889–1936: Hubris* (New York, 1999), and *Hitler, 1936–1945: Nemesis* (New York, 2000). Two works that examine the enormous literature on Hitler are J. Lukacs, *The Hitler of History* (New York, 1997), and R. Rosenbaum, *Explaining Hitler* (New York, 1998). On women, see C. Koonz, *Mothers in the Fatherland: Women, the Family, and Nazi Politics* (New York, 1987). On Nazi anti-Jewish policies between 1933 and 1939, see S. Friedlander, *Nazi Germany and the Jews*, vol. 1, *The Years of Persecution, 1933–1939* (New York, 1997).

The collectivization of agriculture in the Soviet Union is examined in S. Fitzpatrick, *Stalin's Peasants: Resistance and Survival in the Russian Village After Collectivization* (New York, 1995). Industrialization is covered in H. Kuromiya, *Stalin's Industrial Revolution: Politics and Workers, 1928–1932* (New York, 1988). On Stalin, see R. Tucker, *Stalin in Power: The Revolution from Above, 1928–1941* (New York, 1990).

A basic study of Germany's foreign policy from 1933 to 1939 can be found in G. Weinberg, *The Foreign Policy of Hitler's Germany: Diplomatic Revolution in Europe, 1933–1936* (Chicago, 1970), and *The Foreign Policy of Hitler's Germany: Starting World War II, 1937–1939* (Chicago, 1980). Japan's march to war is examined in A. Iriye, *The Origins of the Second World War in Asia and the Pacific* (London, 1987).

General works on World War II include M. K. Dziewanowski, *War at Any Price: World War II in Europe, 1939–1945*, 2d ed. (Englewood Cliffs, N.J., 1991); G. Weinberg, *A World at Arms: A Global History of World War II* (Cambridge, 1994); and J. Campbell, *The Experience of World War II* (New York, 1989).

Among the best studies of the Holocaust are R. Hilberg, *The Destruction of the European Jews*, rev. ed., 3 vols. (New York, 1985), and L. Yahil, *The Holocaust* (New York, 1990). For a brief study, see J. Fischel, *The Holocaust* (Westport, Conn., 1998).

On the home front in Germany, see M. Kitchen, *Nazi Germany at War* (New York, 1995). The Soviet Union during the war is examined in M. Harrison, *Soviet Planning in Peace and War, 1938–1945* (Cambridge, 1985). The Japanese home front is examined in T. R. H. Havens, *The Valley of Darkness: The Japanese People and World War Two* (New York, 1978).

On the emergence of the Cold War, see W. Loth, *The Division of the World, 1941–1955* (New York, 1988). On the wartime summit conferences, see H. Feis, *Churchill, Roosevelt, Stalin: The War They Waged and the Peace They Sought*, 2d ed. (Princeton, N.J., 1967).

![icon] INFOTRAC COLLEGE EDITION

Visit the source collections at infotrac.thomsonlearning.com and use the Search function with the following key terms.

Hitler	Totalitarianism
Holocaust	Weimar Republic
Nazi or Nazism	World War, 1939–1945

WORLD HISTORY RESOURCES

Visit the *Essential World History* Companion Web Site for resources specific to this textbook:

http://history.wadsworth.com/duikeressentials02/

The CD in the back of this book and the World History Resource Center at **http://history.wadsworth.com/world/** offer a variety of tools to help you succeed in this course, including access to quizzes; images; documents; interactive simulations, maps, and timelines; movie explorations; and a wealth of other sources.

MODERN PATTERNS OF WORLD HISTORY (1800–1945)

At the outset of Part IV, we remarked that two of the most significant developments during the nineteenth and early twentieth centuries were the Industrial Revolution and the onset of the era of imperialism. Of these two factors, the first was clearly the more important, for it created the conditions for the latter. It was, of course, the major industrial powers—Great Britain, France, and later Germany, Japan, and the United States—that took the lead in building large colonialist empires.

The advent of the industrial age had a number of lasting consequences for the world at large. On the one hand, the material wealth of the nations that successfully passed through the process increased significantly. In many cases, the creation of advanced industrial societies strengthened democratic institutions and led to a higher standard of living for the majority of the population. It also helped reduce class barriers and bring about the emancipation of women from many of the legal and social restrictions that had characterized the previous era. The spread of technology and trade outside of Europe created the basis for a new international economic order based on the global exchange of goods.

On the other hand, as we have seen, not all the consequences of the Industrial Revolution were beneficial. In the industrializing societies themselves, rapid economic change often led to widening disparities in the distribution of wealth and, with the decline in pervasiveness of religious belief, a sense of rootlessness and alienation among much of the population. While some societies were able to manage these problems with some degree of success, others experienced a breakdown of social values and widespread political instability. In imperial Russia, internal tensions became too much for the traditional landholding elites, leading to social revolution and imposition of the Soviet state. In other cases, such as Germany, deepseated ethnic and class antagonisms remained under the surface until conditions of economic depression led to the rise of militant fascist regimes.

A second development that had a major impact on the era was the rise of nationalism. Like the Industrial Revolution, the idea of nationalism originated in eighteenth-century Europe, where it was a product of the secularization of the age and the experiences of the French revolutionary and Napoleonic eras. Although the concept provided the basis for a new sense of community and the rise of the modern nation-state, it also gave birth to ethnic tensions and hatred that resulted in bitter disputes and civil strife and contributed to the competition that eventually erupted into world war.

Finally, industrialization and the rise of national consciousness transformed the nature of war itself. New weapons of mass destruction created the potential for a new kind of warfare that reached beyond the battlefield into the very heartland of the enemy's territory, while the concept of nationalism transformed war from the sport of kings to a matter of national honor and commitment. Since the French Revolution, when the revolutionary government in Paris had mobilized the entire country by mass conscription to fight against the forces that opposed the Revolution, governments had relied on mass conscription to defend the national cause while their engines of destruction reached far into enemy territory to destroy the industrial base and undermine the will to fight. This trend was amply demonstrated in the two world wars of the twentieth century.

In the end, then, industrial power and the driving force of nationalism, the very factors that had created the conditions for European global dominance, contained the seeds for the decline of that dominance. These seeds germinated during the 1930s, when the Great Depression sharpened international competition and mutual antagonisms, and then sprouted in the ensuing conflict, which for the first time spanned the entire globe. By the time World War II came to an end, the once powerful countries of Europe were exhausted, leaving the door ajar for the emergence of two new global superpowers, the United States and the Soviet Union, which dominated the postwar political scene. Although the new superpowers were both products of modern European civilization, they were physically and politically separate from it, and their intense competition, which marked the postwar period, threatened to transform the old map of Europe into a battleground for a new ideological conflict.

If in Europe the dominant fact of the era was the Industrial Revolution, in the rest of the world it was undoubtedly Western imperialism. Between the end of the Napoleonic wars and the end of the nineteenth century, European powers, or their rivals in Japan and the United States, achieved political mastery over virtually the entire remainder of the world.

What was the overall economic effect of imperialism on the subject peoples? For most of the population in colonial areas, Western domination was rarely beneficial and often destructive. Although a limited number of merchants, large landowners, and traditional hereditary elites undoubtedly prospered under the umbrella of the expanding imperialist economic order, the majority of colonial peoples, urban and rural alike, probably suffered considerable hardship as a result of the policies adopted by their foreign rulers.

Some historians point out, however, that for all the inequities of the colonial system, there was a positive side to the experience as well. The expansion of markets and the beginnings of a modern transportation and communications network, while bringing few immediate benefits to the colonial peoples, offered considerable promise for future economic growth. At the same time, the introduction of new ways of looking at human freedom and the relationship between the individual and society set the stage for a reevaluation of such ideas after the restoration of independence following World War II.

Perhaps the Western concept that had the most immediate impact was that of nationalism. The concept of nationalism often served a useful role in many countries in Asia and Africa, where it provided colonial peoples with a sense of common purpose that later proved vital in knitting together the coherent elements in their societies to oppose colonial regimes and create the conditions for future independent states.

Another idea that gained currency in colonial areas was democracy. As a rule, colonial regimes did not make a serious attempt to introduce democratic institutions to their subject populations; understandably, they feared that such institutions would undermine colonial authority. Nevertheless, Western notions of representative government and individual freedom had their advocates in

PATHS TO MODERNIZATION

Why some societies were able to embark on the road to industrialization and others were not has long been a matter of scholarly debate. Some observers have found the answer in the cultural characteristics of individual societies, such as the Protestant work ethic in parts of Europe or the tradition of social discipline and class hierarchy in Japan. Others have placed more emphasis on practical considerations, such as the lack of an urban market for agricultural goods in China (which reduced the landowners' incentives to introduce mechanized farming) or the absence of a foreign threat in Japan (which provided increased opportunities for local investment). To historian Peter Stearns, the availability of capital, natural resources, a network of trade relations, and navigable rivers all helped stimulate industrial growth in nineteenth-century England.

Whatever the truth of such speculations, it is clear that there has been more than one road to industrialization. In his highly respected work on the subject titled *Social Origins of Dictatorship and Democracy*, sociologist Barrington Moore found at least three paths to economic modernization: the bourgeois capitalist route followed in Great Britain, France, and the United States; the "revolution from above" approach adopted in Germany and Meiji Japan; and the Marxist-Leninist strategy used in the Soviet Union. The first approach, fostered by an independent urban mercantile class, led to the emergence of democratic societies on the capitalist model. The second, carried out by traditional elites in the absence of a strong independent bourgeois class, led ultimately to fascist and militarist regimes; the third, guided by the Communist Party in the almost total absence of an urban middle class, led to the creation of an advanced industrial society based on a totalitarian political system.

Which approach is the most effective? The bourgeois capitalist model appears to have had the most success in promoting economic growth based on the preservation of human rights, but often such results have been achieved at the cost of vast inequalities in the distribution of wealth within individual societies.

OLD CHINA, NEW CHINA. This illustration, used on a People's Republic of China calendar in 1960, was made by using traditional Chinese techniques of landscape painting. However, the drawing shows a modern industrial landscape instead of a tranquil pastoral scene. The three junks at the right are the only reminder of traditional China.

Courtesy of William J. Duiker

IMPERIALISM AND THE GLOBAL ENVIRONMENT

Beginning in the 1870s, European states engaged in an intense scramble for overseas territory. This "new imperialism" led Europeans to carve up Asia and Africa and create colonial empires. Within these empires, European states exercised complete political control over the indigenous societies and redrew political boundaries to meet their needs. In Africa, for example, in drawing the boundaries that separated one colony from another (boundaries that often became the boundaries of the modern countries of Africa), Europeans paid no attention to the political divisions of the indigenous tribes. Europeans often divided tribes between colonies or made two tribes that were hostile to each other members of the same colony.

In similar fashion, Europeans paid little or no heed to the economic needs of their colonial subjects but instead set up the economies of their empires to meet their own needs in the new world market. In the process, Europeans often dramatically altered the global environment, a transformation that was made visible in a variety of ways. Westerners built railways and ports, erected telegraph lines, drilled for oil, and dug mines for gold, tin, iron ore, and copper. All of these projects transformed and often scarred the natural landscape.

Landscapes, however, were even more dramatically altered by Europe's demand for cash food crops. Throughout vast regions of Africa and Asia, tropical forests were felled to make way for plantations that cultivated crops that could be exported for sale. In Ceylon and India, the British cut down vast tropical forests to plant row upon row of tea bushes. The Dutch did the same in the East Indies, where they planted cinchona trees imported from Peru. Quinine, derived from the tree's bark, dramatically reduced the death rate for malaria and made it possible for Europeans to live more securely in the tropical regions of Africa and Asia. In Southeast Asia, the French replaced extensive forests with sugar and coffee plantations. Native workers, who were usually paid pitiful wages by their European overseers, provided the labor for all of these vast plantations.

European states greatly profited from this transformed environment. In *Agriculture in the Tropics: An Elementary Treatise*, written in 1909, the British botanist John Christopher Willis expressed his thoughts on this European policy:

Whether planting in the tropics will always continue to be under European management is another question, but the northern powers will not permit that the rich and as yet comparatively undeveloped countries of the tropics should be entirely wasted by being devoted merely to the supply of the food and clothing wants of their own people, when they can also supply the wants of the colder zones in so many indispensable products.

In Willis's eyes, the imperialist transformation of the environments of Asia and Africa to serve European needs was entirely justified.

▶ **PICKING TEA LEAVES IN CEYLON.** Shown here in this 1900 photograph are women picking tea leaves for shipment abroad on a plantation in Ceylon (now Sri Lanka). The British cut down enormous stands of tropical forests in Ceylon and India to grow tea to satisfy demand back home.

© Popperfoto

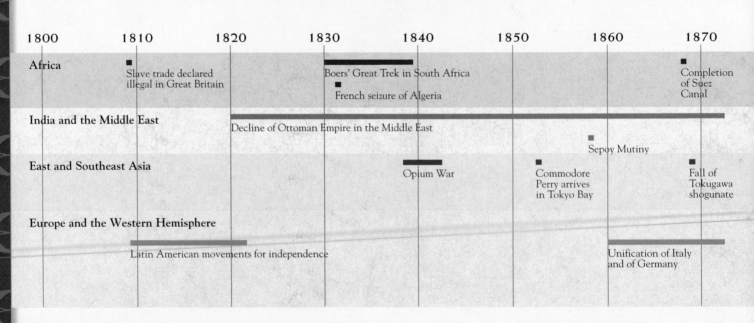

	1800	1810	1820	1830	1840	1850	1860	1870
Africa		Slave trade declared illegal in Great Britain		Boers' Great Trek in South Africa / French seizure of Algeria				Completion of Suez Canal
India and the Middle East			Decline of Ottoman Empire in the Middle East				Sepoy Mutiny	
East and Southeast Asia					Opium War	Commodore Perry arrives in Tokyo Bay		Fall of Tokugawa shogunate
Europe and the Western Hemisphere		Latin American movements for independence						Unification of Italy and of Germany

India, Vietnam, China, and Japan well before the end of the nineteenth century. Later, countless Asians and Africans were exposed to such ideas in schools set up by the colonial regime or in the course of travel to Europe or the United States. Most of the nationalist parties founded in colonial territories espoused democratic principles and attempted to apply them when they took power after the restoration of independence.

Finally, the colonial experience offered new ways of looking at the relationship between men and women. Although colonial rule was by no means uniformly beneficial to the position of women in African and Asian societies, growing awareness of the struggle by women in the West to seek sexual equality offered their counterparts in the colonial territories a weapon to fight against the long-standing barriers of custom and legal discrimination.

How are we to draw up a final balance sheet on the era of Western imperialism? To its defenders, it was a necessary stage in the evolution of the human race, a flawed but essentially humanitarian effort to provide the backward peoples of Africa and Asia with a boost up the ladder of evolution. To its critics, it was a tragedy of major proportions. The insatiable drive of the advanced economic powers for access to raw materials and markets resulted in the widespread destruction of traditional cultures and created an exploitative environment that transformed the vast majority of colonial peoples into a permanent underclass while restricting the benefits of modern technology to a privileged few. Sophisticated, age-old societies that should have been left to respond to the technological revolution in their own way were subjected to foreign rule and squeezed dry of precious national resources under the guise of the "civilizing mission."

In this debate, the critics surely have the better argument. All in all, the colonial experience was brutal, and its benefits accrued almost entirely to citizens of the ruling power. The argument that the Western societies had a "white man's burden" to civilize the world was all too often a hypocritical gesture to salve the guilty feelings of those who recognized imperialism for what it was—a savage act of rape.

But although the experience was a painful one, human societies were able to survive it and to earn a second chance to make better use of the stunning promise of the industrial era. How they have fared in that effort will be the subject of the final section of this book.

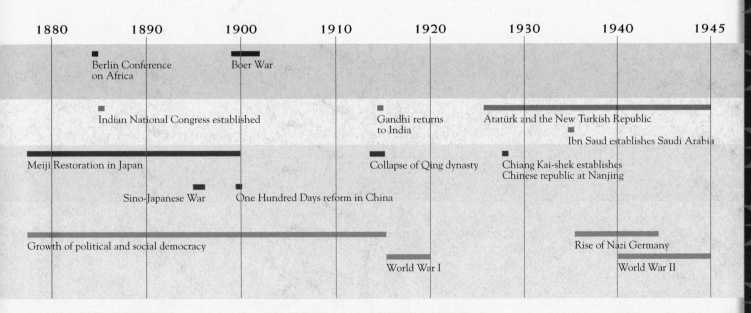

1880   1890   1900   1910   1920   1930   1940   1945

Berlin Conference on Africa

Boer War

Indian National Congress established

Gandhi returns to India

Atatürk and the New Turkish Republic

Ibn Saud establishes Saudi Arabia

Meiji Restoration in Japan

Collapse of Qing dynasty

Chiang Kai-shek establishes Chinese republic at Nanjing

Sino-Japanese War

One Hundred Days reform in China

Growth of political and social democracy

Rise of Nazi Germany

World War I

World War II

TOWARD A GLOBAL CIVILIZATION? THE WORLD SINCE 1945

When U.S. president Franklin Roosevelt and British prime minister Winston Churchill met off the coast of Newfoundland in August 1941 to discuss their common objectives in a postwar world, they appeared to recognize that imperialist rivalry had been the crucial factor leading to the outbreak of the two world wars. The Atlantic Charter stated that the two countries hoped to realize equality of economic opportunity, abandonment of force, and friendly collaboration among the peoples of the world, as well as the right of nations to choose their own form of government.

In a number of respects, the wartime allies achieved their aims for the peace. The rapacious efforts of Germany and Japan to dominate the world were thwarted, and the intense rivalry that had characterized relations among the Western powers came to an end. Outside of Europe, the colonial system was gradually dismantled, and the peoples of Asia and Africa were granted self-determination in the form of independent states. But even before the final defeat of Japan, tension had begun to build in Europe between the Soviet Union and the Western powers. By the end of the 1940s, that tension had spread throughout the world, and the Cold War had begun.

In the meantime, the end of colonial empires did not bring to the peoples of Asia and Africa a new world of political stability, peaceful cooperation, and material prosperity. Economic difficulties, a product of their own inexperience and the continued Western domination of the global economy, led to internal factionalism, military rule, and sometimes regional conflict. Competition between the capitalist and socialist power blocs—led by the United States and the Soviet Union, respectively—compounded the problem. In the late 1980s, however, the Soviet Empire began to come apart, and in December 1991, the Soviet Union itself became a memory as onetime Soviet republics now split into independent states, bringing an end to the ideological Cold War. In the meantime, a number of nations in Asia have apparently entered the lists of the

Courtesy of William J. Duiker

advanced industrial countries and have embarked on the road to political democracy. Half a century after the end of World War II, some of the dreams embodied in the Atlantic Charter appear to be reaching fruition.

But challenges remain, and many of them appear intimidating. The breakup of the Soviet empire has led to the emergence of squabbling nationalities throughout eastern Europe, while in other parts of the world, including the Middle East, Africa, and Northern Ireland, age-old rivalries and ethnic and religious suspicions continue to be sources of bitter conflict. A global economic slowdown brought recession to the advanced nations and severe political and economic difficulties to many societies in the rest of the world. In the meantime, the effects of untrammeled industrial development are coming home to roost in the form of growing environmental pollution. The combined effects of ethnic and religious differences and intense competition for markets continue to strain efforts to achieve global cooperation in solving the common problems of humanity.

© David King Collection, London

Chapter 25

In the Grip of the Cold War: The Breakdown of the Yalta System

CHAPTER OUTLINE

- THE COLLAPSE OF THE GRAND ALLIANCE
- COLD WAR IN ASIA
- FROM CONFRONTATION TO COEXISTENCE
- AN ERA OF EQUIVALENCE
- CONCLUSION

FOCUS QUESTIONS

- Why were the United States and the Soviet Union suspicious of each other after World War II, and what events between 1945 and 1949 heightened the tensions between the two nations?
- How have historians answered the question of whether the United States or the Soviet Union bears the primary responsibility for the Cold War, and what evidence can be presented on each side of the issue?
- How and why did Mao Zedong and the Communists come to power in China, and what were the implications of their triumph for the Cold War?
- What were the major developments in the Cold War between 1950 and 1989?
- ➤ How and why did the Cold War change from a European confrontation to a conflict of global significance?

"Our meeting here in the Crimea has reaffirmed our common determination to maintain and strengthen in the peace to come that unity of purpose and of action which has made victory possible and certain for the United Nations in this war. We believe that this is a sacred obligation which our Governments owe to our peoples and to all the peoples of the world."[1]

With these ringing words, drafted at the Yalta Conference in February 1945, U.S. President Franklin D. Roosevelt, Soviet leader Joseph Stalin, and British Prime Minister Winston Churchill affirmed their common hope that the Grand Alliance that had been victorious in World War II could be sustained into the postwar era. Only through continuing and growing cooperation and understanding among the three Allies, the statement asserted, could a secure and lasting peace be realized that, in the words of the Atlantic Charter, would "afford assurance that all the men in all the lands may live out their lives in freedom from fear and want."

Roosevelt hoped that the decisions reached at Yalta would provide the basis for a stable peace in the postwar era. Allied occupation forces—American, British, and French in the west and Soviet in the east—were to bring about the end of Axis administration and to organize the free election of democratic governments throughout Europe. To foster mutual trust and an end to the suspicions that had marked relations between the capitalist world and the Soviet Union prior to the war, Roosevelt tried to reassure Stalin that Moscow's legitimate territorial aspirations and genuine security needs would be adequately met in a durable peace settlement.

However, this was not to be. Within months after the German surrender, the mutual trust among the Allies—if it had ever truly existed—rapidly disintegrated, and the dream of a stable peace was replaced by the specter of a potential nuclear holocaust. As the Cold War between Moscow and Washington intensified, Europe was divided into two armed camps, while the two superpowers, glaring at each other across a deep ideological divide, held the survival of the entire world in their hands. •

THE COLLAPSE OF THE GRAND ALLIANCE

The problem started in Europe. At the end of the war, Soviet military forces occupied all of Eastern Europe and the Balkans (except Greece, Albania, and Yugoslavia), while U.S. and other Allied forces completed their occupation of the western part of the Continent. Roosevelt had assumed that free elections administered by "democratic and peace-loving forces" would lead to democratic governments responsive to the local population. But it soon became clear that the Soviet Union and the United States interpreted the Yalta agreement differently. When Soviet occupation authorities began forming a new Polish government, Stalin refused to accept the Polish government-in-exile—headquartered in London during the war, it was composed primarily of landed aristocrats, who harbored a deep distrust of the Soviet Union—and instead created a government composed of Communists who had spent the war in Moscow. Roosevelt complained to Stalin but eventually agreed to a compromise whereby two members of the London government were included in a new communist regime. A week later, Roosevelt was dead of a cerebral hemorrhage.

Similar developments took place in all of the states occupied by Soviet troops. Coalitions of all political parties (except fascist or right-wing parties) were formed to run the government, but within a year or two, the communist parties in these coalitions had assumed the lion's share of power. The next step was the creation of one-party communist governments. Between 1945 and 1947, communist governments became firmly entrenched in East Germany, Bulgaria, Romania, Poland, and Hungary. In Czechoslovakia, with its strong tradition of democratic institutions, the Communists did not achieve their goals until 1948. After the elections of 1946, the Communist Party shared control of the government with the non-Communist parties. When it appeared that the latter might win new elections early in 1948, the Communists seized control of the government on February 25. All other parties were dissolved, and the Communist leader Klement Gottwald became the new president of Czechoslovakia.

Yugoslavia was a notable exception to the pattern of growing Soviet dominance in Eastern Europe. The Communist Party there had led resistance to the Nazis during the war and easily took over power when the war ended. Josip Broz, known as Tito (1892–1980), the leader of the communist resistance movement, appeared to be a loyal Stalinist. After the war, however, he moved to establish an independent communist state. Stalin hoped to take control of Yugoslavia, but Tito refused to capitulate to Stalin's demands and gained the support of the people (and some sympathy in the West) by portraying the struggle as one of Yugoslav national freedom. In 1958, the Yugoslav party congress asserted that Yugoslav Communists did not see themselves as deviating from communism, only from Stalinism. They considered their more decentralized system, in which workers managed themselves and local communes exercised some political power, closer to the Marxist-Leninist ideal.

To Stalin (who had once boasted "I will shake my little finger, and there will be no more Tito"), the creation of pliant pro-Soviet regimes throughout Eastern Europe may simply have represented his interpretation of the Yalta peace agreement and a reward for sacrifices suffered during the war, satisfying Moscow's aspirations for a buffer zone against the capitalist West. If the Soviet leader had any intention of promoting future communist revolutions in Western Europe—and there is some indication that he did—such developments would have to await the appearance of a new capitalist crisis a decade or more into the future. As Stalin undoubtedly recalled, Lenin had always maintained that revolutions come in waves.

The Truman Doctrine and the Marshall Plan

To the United States, however, the Soviet takeover of Eastern Europe represented an ominous development that threatened Roosevelt's vision of a durable peace. Public suspicion of Soviet intentions grew rapidly, especially among the millions of Americans who still had relatives living in Eastern Europe. Winston Churchill was quick to put such fears into words. In a highly publicized speech at Westminster College in Fulton, Missouri, in March 1946, the former British prime minister declared that an "iron curtain" had "descended across the Continent," dividing Germany and Europe itself into two hostile camps. Stalin responded by branding Churchill's speech a "call to war with the Soviet Union." But he need not have worried. Although public opinion in the United States placed increasing pressure on Roosevelt's successor, Harry S Truman (1884–1972), to devise an effective strategy to counter Soviet advances abroad, the American people were in no mood for another war.

A civil war in Greece created another potential arena for confrontation between the superpowers and an opportunity for the Truman administration to take a stand. Communist guerrilla forces supported by Tito's Yugoslavia had taken up arms against the pro-Western government in Athens. Great Britain had initially assumed primary responsibility for promoting postwar reconstruction in the eastern Mediterranean, but in 1947, continuing economic problems caused the British to withdraw from the active role they had been playing in both Greece and Turkey. President Truman, alarmed by British weakness and the possibility of Soviet expansion into the eastern Mediterranean, responded with the Truman Doctrine (see the box on p. 551), which said in essence that the United States would provide money to countries that claimed they were threatened by communist expansion. If the Soviets were not stopped in Greece, the Truman argument ran, then the United States would have to face the spread of communism throughout the free world. As Dean Acheson, the U.S. secretary of state, explained, "Like apples in a barrel infected by disease, the corruption of Greece would infect Iran and all the East . . . likewise Africa . . . Italy . . . France. . . . Not since Rome and Carthage has there been such a polarization of power on this earth."[2]

The U.S. suspicion that Moscow was actively supporting the insurgent movement in Greece turned out to be unfounded. Stalin was apparently unhappy with Tito's promoting the conflict, not only because he suspected that the latter was attempting to create his own sphere of influence in the Balkans but also because it risked provoking a direct confrontation between the United States and the Soviet Union.

The proclamation of the Truman Doctrine was followed in June 1947 by the European Recovery Program, better known as the Marshall Plan, which provided $13 billion for the economic recovery of war-torn Europe. Underlying the program was the belief that communist aggression fed off economic turmoil. General George C. Marshall noted in a speech at Harvard University, "Our policy is not directed against any country or doctrine but against hunger, poverty, desperation, and chaos."[3]

From the Soviet perspective, the Marshall Plan was capitalist imperialism, a thinly veiled attempt to buy the

A CALL TO ARMS. In March 1946, former British prime minister Winston Churchill gave a speech before a college audience in Fulton, Missouri, that electrified the world. Soviet occupation of the countries of Eastern Europe, he declared, had divided the Continent into two conflicting halves, separated by an "iron curtain." Churchill's speech has often been described as the opening salvo in the Cold War, and Moscow responded by labeling the speech "reactionary" and "unconvincing." In the photo, Churchill, with President Harry S Truman behind him, prepares to give his address.

© CORBIS

THE TRUMAN DOCTRINE

y 1947, the battle lines in the Cold War had been clearly drawn. This excerpt is taken from a speech by President Harry Truman to the U.S. Congress in which he justified his request for aid to Greece and Turkey. Truman expressed the urgent need to contain the expansion of communism. Compare this statement with that of Soviet leader Leonid Brezhnev cited in the box in Chapter 26.

TRUMAN'S SPEECH TO CONGRESS, MARCH 12, 1947

The peoples of a number of countries of the world have recently had totalitarian regimes forced upon them against their will. The Government of the United States has made frequent protests against coercion and intimidation, in violation of the Yalta agreement, in Poland, Rumania, and Bulgaria. I must also state that in a number of other countries there have been similar developments.

At the present moment in world history nearly every nation must choose between alternative ways of life. The choice is too often not a free one.

One way of life is based upon the will of the majority, and is distinguished by free institutions, representative government, free elections, guarantees of individual liberty, freedom of speech and religion, and freedom from political oppression.

The second way of life is based upon the will of a minority forcibly imposed upon the majority. It relies upon terror and oppression, a controlled press and radio, fixed elections, and the suppression of personal freedoms.

I believe that it must be the policy of the United States to support free peoples who are resisting attempted subjugation by armed minorities or by outside pressures.

I believe that we must assist free people to work out their own destinies in their own way.

I believe that our help should be primarily through economic and financial aid, which is essential to economic stability and orderly political processes. . . . I therefore ask the Congress for assistance to Greece and Turkey in the amount of $400,000,000.

---

support of the smaller European countries "in return for the relinquishing . . . of their economic and later also their political independence."[4] A Soviet spokesperson described the United States as the "main force in the imperialist camp," whose ultimate goal was "the strengthening of imperialism, preparation for a new imperialist war, a struggle against socialism and democracy, and the support of reactionary and antidemocratic, pro-fascist regimes and movements." Although the Marshall Plan was open to the Soviet Union and its Eastern European satellite states, they refused to participate. The Soviets were in no position to compete financially with the United States, however, and could do little to counter the Marshall Plan except tighten their control in Eastern Europe.

Europe Divided

By 1947, the split in Europe between East and West had become a fact of life. At the end of World War II, the United States had favored a quick end to its commitments in Europe. But American fears of Soviet aims caused the United States to play an increasingly important role in European affairs. In an article in *Foreign Affairs* in July 1947, George Kennan, a well-known U.S. diplomat with much knowledge of Soviet affairs, advocated a policy of containment against further aggressive Soviet moves. Kennan favored the "adroit and vigilant application of counter-force at a series of constantly shifting geographical and political points, corresponding to the shifts and maneuvers of Soviet policy." When the Soviets blockaded Berlin in 1948, containment of the Soviet Union became formal U.S. policy.

The fate of Germany had become a source of heated contention between East and West. Aside from denazification and the partitioning of Germany (and Berlin) into four occupied zones, the Allied Powers had agreed on little with regard to the conquered nation. Even denazification proceeded differently in the various zones of occupation. The Americans and British proceeded methodically—the British had tried two million cases by 1948—while the Soviets (and French) went after major criminals and allowed lesser officials to go free. The Soviet Union, hardest hit by the war, took reparations from Germany in the form of booty. The technology-starved Soviets dismantled and removed to Russia 380 factories from the western zones of Berlin before transferring their control to the Western powers. By the summer of 1946, two hundred chemical, paper, and textile factories in the East German zone had likewise been shipped to the Soviet Union. At the same time, the German Communist Party was reestablished, under the control of Walter Ulbricht (1893–1973), and was soon in charge of the political reconstruction of the Soviet zone in eastern Germany.

Although the foreign ministers of the four occupying powers kept meeting in an attempt to arrive at a final peace treaty with Germany, they moved further and further apart. At the same time, the British, French, and Americans gradually began to merge their zones economically and by February 1948 were making plans for unification of these sectors and the formation of a national government. In an effort to secure all of Berlin and to halt the creation of a West German government, the Soviet Union imposed a blockade of West Berlin that prevented

Divided Berlin During the Cold War

FRENCH ZONE

BRITISH ZONE

SOVIET ZONE

U.S. ZONE

GERMAN DEMOCRATIC REPUBLIC

all traffic from entering the city's western zones through Soviet-controlled territory in East Germany.

The Western powers faced a dilemma. Direct military confrontation seemed dangerous, and no one wished to risk World War III. Therefore an attempt to break through the blockade with tanks and trucks was ruled out. The solution was to deliver supplies for the city's inhabitants by plane. At its peak, the Berlin Airlift flew 13,000 tons of supplies daily into Berlin. The Soviets, also not wanting war, did not interfere and finally lifted the blockade in May 1949. The blockade of Berlin had severely increased tensions between the United States and the Soviet Union and brought the separation of Germany into two states. The Federal Republic of Germany was formally created from the three western zones in September 1949, and a month later, the separate German Democratic Republic (GDR) was established in East Germany. Berlin remained a divided city and the source of much contention between East and West.

The search for security in the new world of the Cold War also led to the formation of military alliances. The North Atlantic Treaty Organization (NATO) was formed in April 1949 when Belgium, Luxembourg, the Netherlands, France, Britain, Italy, Denmark, Norway, Portugal, and Iceland signed a treaty with the United States and

➤• A CITY DIVIDED. In 1948, U.S. planes airlifted supplies into Berlin to break the blockade that Soviet troops had imposed to isolate the city. Shown here is "Checkpoint Charlie," located at the boundary between the U.S. and Soviet zones of Berlin, just as Soviet roadblocks are about to be removed. The banner at the entrance to the Soviet sector reads, ironically, "The sector of freedom greets the fighters for freedom and right of the western sectors."

Canada. All the powers agreed to provide mutual assistance if any one of them was attacked. A few years later, West Germany and Turkey joined NATO.

The Eastern European states soon followed suit. In 1949, they formed the Council for Mutual Economic Assistance (COMECON) for economic cooperation. Then, in 1955, Albania, Bulgaria, Czechoslovakia, East Germany, Hungary, Poland, Romania, and the Soviet Union organized a formal military alliance, the Warsaw Pact. Once again, Europe was tragically divided into hostile alliance systems (see Map 25.1).

There has been considerable historical debate over who bears responsibility for starting the Cold War. In the 1950s, most scholars in the West assumed that the bulk of the blame must fall on the shoulders of Stalin, whose determination to impose Soviet rule on Eastern Europe snuffed out hopes for freedom and self-determination there and aroused justifiable fears of communist expansion in the West. During the next decade, however, revisionist historians—influenced in part by aggressive U.S. policies in Southeast Asia—began to argue that the fault lay primarily with Washington, where Truman and his anticommunist

MAP 25.1 The New European Alliance Systems During the Cold War. This map shows postwar Europe as it was divided during the Cold War into two contending power blocs, the NATO alliance and the Warsaw Pact. Major military and naval bases are indicated by symbols on the map. ➤ *Where on the map was the so-called Iron Curtain?*

United States/NATO

- Missile bases: NATO
- Troops: U.S.
- Nuclear bombers: U.S.
- Naval port: U.S.
- Fleet: U.S.
- Nuclear missile submarine: U.S.

Soviet Union/Warsaw Pact

- Missile bases: Warsaw Pact
- Troops: Soviet
- Nuclear bombers: Soviet
- Naval port: Soviet
- Fleet: Soviet
- Nuclear missile submarine: Soviet

- NATO member
- Non-NATO ally✦
- NATO member until 1969
- Warsaw Pact member
- Unrest/revolt in Eastern Europe

advisers abandoned the precepts of Yalta and sought to encircle the Soviet Union with a tier of pliant U.S. client states.

In retrospect, both the United States and the Soviet Union took some unwise steps at the end of World War II. However, both nations were working within a framework conditioned by the past. The rivalry between the two superpowers ultimately stemmed from their different historical perspectives and their irreconcilable political ambitions. Intense competition for political and military supremacy had long been a regular feature of Western civilization. The United States and the Soviet Union were the heirs of that European tradition of power politics, and it should not surprise us that two such different systems would seek to extend their way of life to the rest of the world. Because of its need to secure its western border, the Soviet Union was not prepared to give up the advantages it had gained in Eastern Europe from Germany's defeat. But neither were Western leaders prepared to accept without protest the establishment of a system of Soviet satellites that not only threatened the security of Western Europe but also deeply offended Western sensibilities because of its blatant disregard of the Western concept of human rights.

This does not necessarily mean that both sides bear equal responsibility for starting the Cold War. Some revisionist historians have claimed that the U.S. doctrine of containment was a provocative action that aroused Stalin's suspicions and drove Moscow into a position of hostility toward the West. This charge lacks credibility. As information from the Soviet archives and other sources has become available, it is increasingly clear that Stalin's suspicions of the West were rooted in his Marxist-Leninist worldview and long predated Washington's enunciation of the doctrine of containment. As his foreign minister, Vyacheslav Molotov, once remarked, Soviet policy was inherently aggressive and would be triggered whenever the opportunity offered itself. Although Stalin apparently had no master plan to advance Soviet power into Western Europe, he was probably prepared to make every effort to do so once the next revolutionary wave arrived. Western leaders were fully justified in reacting to this possibility by strengthening their own lines of defense. On the other hand, a case can be made that in deciding to respond to the Soviet challenge in a primarily military manner, Western leaders overreacted to the situation and virtually guaranteed that the Cold War would be transformed into an arms race that could conceivably result in a new and uniquely destructive war.

COLD WAR IN ASIA

The Cold War was somewhat slower to make its appearance in Asia. At Yalta, Stalin formally agreed to enter the Pacific War against Japan three months after the close of the conflict with Germany. As a reward for Soviet participation in the struggle against Japan, Roosevelt promised that Moscow would be granted "preeminent interests" in Manchuria (interests reminiscent of those possessed by imperial Russia prior to its defeat at the hands of Japan in 1904–1905) and the establishment of a Soviet naval base at Port Arthur. In return, Stalin promised to sign a treaty of alliance with the Republic of China, thus implicitly committing the Soviet Union not to provide the Chinese Communists with support in a possible future civil war. Although many observers would later question Stalin's sincerity in making such a commitment to the vocally anticommunist Chiang Kai-shek, in Moscow the decision probably had a logic of its own. Stalin had no particular liking for the independent-minded Mao Zedong and indeed did not anticipate a Communist victory in any civil war in China. Only an agreement with Chiang could provide the Soviet Union with a strategically vital economic and political presence in northern China.

Despite these commitments, the Allied agreements soon broke down, and East Asia was sucked into the vortex of the Cold War by the end of the 1940s. The root of the problem lay in the underlying weakness of the Chiang regime, which threatened to create a political vacuum in East Asia that both Moscow and Washington would be tempted to fill.

The Chinese Civil War

As World War II came to an end in the Pacific, relations between the government of Chiang Kai-shek in China and its powerful U.S. ally had become frayed. Although Roosevelt had hoped that republican China would be the keystone of his plan for peace and stability in Asia after the war, U.S. officials became disillusioned with the corruption of Chiang's government and his unwillingness to risk his forces against the Japanese (he hoped to save them for use against the Communists after the war in the Pacific ended), and China was no longer the focus of Washington's close attention as the war came to a close. Nevertheless, U.S. military and economic aid to China had been substantial, and at war's end, the new Truman administration still hoped that it could rely on Chiang to support U.S. postwar goals in the region.

While Chiang Kai-shek wrestled with Japanese aggression and problems of national development, the Communists were building up their strength in northern China. To enlarge their political base, they carried out a "mass line" policy (from the masses to the masses), reducing land rents and confiscating the lands of wealthy landlords. By the end of World War II, twenty to thirty million Chinese were living under the administration of the Communists, and their People's Liberation Army (PLA) included nearly one million troops.

As the war came to an end, world attention began to focus on the prospects for renewed civil strife in China.

Members of a U.S. liaison team stationed in Yan'an were impressed by the performance of the Communists, and some recommended that the United States should support them or at least remain neutral in a possible conflict between Communists and Nationalists for control of China. The Truman administration, though skeptical of Chiang's ability to forge a strong and prosperous country, was increasingly concerned about the spread of communism in Europe and tried to find a peaceful solution through the formation of a coalition government of all parties in China.

The effort failed. By 1946, full-scale war between the Nationalist government, now reinstalled in Nanjing, and the Communists resumed. Now Chiang Kai-shek's errors came home to roost. In the countryside, millions of peasants, attracted to the Communists by promises of land and social justice, flocked to serve in Mao Zedong's PLA. In the cities, middle-class Chinese, who were normally hostile to communism, were alienated by Chiang's brutal suppression of all dissent and his government's inability to slow the ruinous rate of inflation or solve the economic problems it caused. With morale dropping in the cities, Chiang's troops began to defect to the Communists. Sometimes whole divi-

⟫ **A PLEDGE OF ETERNAL FRIENDSHIP.** After the Communist victory in the Chinese civil war, Chairman Mao Zedong traveled to Moscow, where in 1950 he negotiated a treaty of friendship and cooperation with the Soviet Union. Here Joseph Stalin and his eventual successor, Georgy Malenkov, observe as Chinese Foreign Minister Zhou Enlai signs the treaty. Behind the pledges of friendship, a long tradition of mutual distrust divided the two countries, which almost went to war over border disputes in the late 1970s.

© David King Collection, London

sions, officers as well as ordinary soldiers, changed sides. By 1948, the PLA was advancing south out of Manchuria and had encircled Beijing. Communist troops took the old imperial capital, crossed the Yangtze the following spring, and occupied the commercial hub of Shanghai. During the next few months, Chiang's government and two million of his followers fled to Taiwan, which the Japanese had returned to Chinese control after World War II.

The Truman administration reacted to the spread of communist power in China with acute discomfort. Washington had no desire to see a communist government on the mainland, but it had little confidence in Chiang Kai-shek's ability to realize Roosevelt's dream of a strong, united, and prosperous China. In December 1945, President Truman sent General George C. Marshall to China in a last-ditch effort to bring about a peaceful settlement, but anticommunist elements in the Republic of China resisted U.S. efforts to create a coalition government with the Chinese Communist Party (CCP). During the next two years, the United States gave limited military support to Chiang's regime but refused to commit U.S. power to guarantee its survival. The administration's hands-off policy deeply angered many members of Congress, who charged that the White House was "soft on communism" and declared further that Roosevelt had betrayed Chiang Kai-shek at Yalta by granting privileges in Manchuria to the Soviet Union. In their view, Soviet troops had hindered the dispatch of Chiang's forces to the area and provided the PLA with weapons to use against its rivals.

In later years, sources in both Moscow and Beijing suggested that the Soviet Union gave little assistance to the CCP in its struggle against the Nanjing regime. In fact, Stalin periodically advised Mao against undertaking the effort. Although Communist forces undoubtedly received some assistance from Soviet occupation troops in Manchuria, their victory ultimately stemmed from conditions inside China, not from the intervention of outside powers. So indeed argued the Truman administration in 1949, when it issued a white paper that placed most of the blame for the debacle at the feet of Chiang Kai-shek's regime (see the box on p. 556).

Many Americans, however, did not agree. With the Communist victory, Asia became a theater of the Cold War and an integral element of American politics. During the spring of 1950, under pressure from Congress and public opinion to define U.S. interests in Asia, the Truman administration adopted a new national security policy that implied that the United States would take whatever steps were necessary to stem the further expansion of communism in the region.

The Korean War

Communist leaders in China, from their new capital of Beijing, hoped that their accession to power in 1949 would bring about an era of peace in the region and permit their

"IT'S NOT OUR FAULT"

In 1949, with China about to fall under the control of the Communists, President Harry S Truman instructed the State Department to prepare a white paper explaining why the U.S. policy of seeking to avoid a Communist victory in China had failed. The authors of the paper concluded that responsibility lay at the door of Nationalist Chinese leader Chiang Kaishek and that there was nothing the United States could have done to alter the result. Most China observers today would accept that assessment, but it did little at the time to deflect criticism of the administration for selling out the interests of our ally in China.

U.S. STATE DEPARTMENT WHITE PAPER ON CHINA, 1949

When peace came the United States was confronted with three possible alternatives in China: (1) it could have pulled out lock, stock, and barrel; (2) it could have intervened militarily on a major scale to assist the Nationalists to destroy the Communists; (3) it could, while assisting the Nationalists to assert their authority over as much of China as possible, endeavor to avoid a civil war by working for a compromise between the two sides.

The first alternative would, and I believe American public opinion at the time so felt, have represented an abandonment of our international responsibilities and of our traditional policy of friendship for China before we had made a determined effort to be of assistance. The second alternative policy, while it may look attractive theoretically, in retrospect, was wholly impracticable. The Nationalists had been unable to destroy the Communists during the ten years before the war. Now after the war the Nationalists were, as indicated above, weakened, demoralized, and unpopular. They had quickly dissipated their popular support and prestige in the areas liberated from the Japanese by the conduct of their civil and military officials. The Communists on the other hand were much stronger than they had ever been and were in control of most of North China. Because of the ineffectiveness of the Nationalist forces, which was later to be tragically demonstrated, the Communists probably could have been dislodged only by American arms. It is obvious that the American people would not have sanctioned such a colossal commitment of our armies in 1945 or later. We therefore came to the third alternative policy whereunder we faced the facts of the situation and attempted to assist in working out a *modus vivendi* which would avert civil war but nevertheless preserve and even increase the influence of the National Government. . . .

The distrust of the leaders of both the Nationalist and Communist Parties for each other proved too deep-seated to permit final agreement, notwithstanding temporary truces and apparently promising negotiations. The Nationalists, furthermore, embarked in 1946 on an overambitious military campaign in the face of warnings by General Marshall that it not only would fail but would plunge China into economic chaos and eventually destroy the National Government. . . .

The unfortunate but inescapable fact is that the ominous result of the civil war in China was beyond the control of the government of the United States. Nothing that this country did or could have done within the reasonable limits of its capabilities could have changed that result; nothing that was left undone by this country has contributed to it. It was the product of internal Chinese forces, forces which this country tried to influence but could not. A decision was arrived at within China, if only a decision by default.

---

new government to concentrate on domestic goals. But the desire for peace was tempered by their determination to erase a century of humiliation at the hands of imperialist powers and to restore the traditional outer frontiers of the empire. In addition to recovering territories that had been part of the Manchu Empire, such as Manchuria, Taiwan, and Tibet, the Chinese leaders also hoped to restore Chinese influence in former tributary areas such as Korea and Vietnam.

It soon became clear that these two goals were not always compatible. Negotiations with the Soviet Union led to Soviet recognition of Chinese sovereignty over Manchuria and Xinjiang (the desolate lands north of Tibet that were known as Chinese Turkestan because many of the peoples in the area were of Turkish origin), although the Soviets retained a measure of economic influence in both areas. Chinese troops occupied Tibet in 1950 and brought it under Chinese administration for the first time in more than a century. But in Korea and Taiwan, China's efforts to re-create the imperial buffer zone provoked new conflicts with foreign powers.

The problem of Taiwan was a consequence of the Cold War. As the civil war in China came to an end, the Truman administration appeared determined to avoid entanglement in China's internal affairs and indicated that it would not seek to prevent a Communist takeover of the island, now occupied by Chiang Kai-shek's Republic of China. But as tensions between the United States and the new Chinese government escalated during the winter of 1949–1950, influential figures in the United States began to argue that Taiwan was crucial to U.S. defense strategy in the Pacific.

The outbreak of war in Korea also helped bring the Cold War to East Asia. After the Sino-Japanese War in

1894–1895, Korea, long a Chinese tributary, had fallen increasingly under the rival influences of Japan and Russia. After the Japanese defeated the Russians in 1905, Korea became an integral part of the Japanese Empire and remained so until 1945. The removal of Korea from Japanese control had been one of the stated objectives of the Allies in World War II, and on the eve of Japanese surrender in August 1945, the Soviet Union and the United States agreed to divide the country into two separate occupation zones at the 38th parallel. They originally planned to hold national elections after the restoration of peace to reunify Korea under an independent government. But as U.S.–Soviet relations deteriorated, two separate governments emerged in Korea, a communist one in the north and an anticommunist one in the south.

Tensions between the two governments ran high along the dividing line, and on June 25, 1950, with the apparent approval of Stalin, North Korean troops invaded the south. The Truman administration immediately ordered U.S. naval and air forces to support South Korea, and the United Nations Security Council (with the Soviet delegate absent to protest the refusal of the UN to assign China's seat to the new government in Beijing) passed a resolution calling on member nations to jointly resist the invasion. By September, UN forces under the command of U.S. General Douglas MacArthur marched northward across the 38th parallel with the aim of unifying Korea under a single, noncommunist government.

President Truman worried that by approaching the Chinese border at the Yalu River, the UN troops could trigger Chinese intervention, but MacArthur assured him that China would not respond. In November, however, Chinese "volunteer" forces intervened in force on the side of North Korea and drove the UN troops southward in disarray. A static defense line was eventually established near the original dividing line at the 38th parallel (see Map 25.2), although the war continued.

To many Americans, the Chinese intervention in Korea was clear evidence that China intended to promote communism throughout Asia, and recent evidence suggests that Mao was convinced that a revolutionary wave was on the rise in Asia. In fact, however, China's decision to enter the war was probably motivated in large part by the fear that hostile U.S. forces might be stationed on the Chinese frontier and perhaps even launch an attack across the border. MacArthur intensified such fears by calling publicly for air attacks on Manchurian cities in preparation for an attack on Communist China. In any case, the outbreak of the Korean War was particularly unfortunate for China. Immediately after the invasion, President Truman dispatched the U.S. Seventh Fleet to the Taiwan Strait to prevent a possible Chinese invasion of Taiwan. Even more unfortunate, the invasion hardened Western attitudes against the new Chinese government and led to China's isolation from the major capitalist powers for

MAP 25.2 The Korean Peninsula. In January 1950, North Korean forces crossed the 38th parallel in a sudden invasion of the south. Shown here is the cease-fire line that brought an end to the war in 1953. Major railroad lines are also shown. ➤ *What is the importance of the Yalu River?*

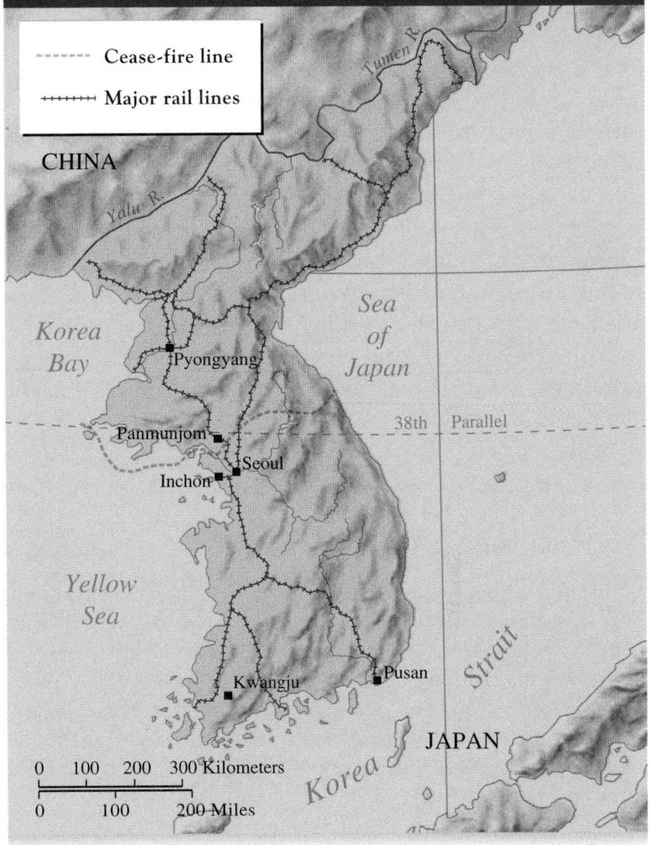

two decades. As a result, China was cut off from all forms of economic and technological assistance and was forced to rely almost entirely on the Soviet Union, with which it had signed a pact of friendship and cooperation in early 1950.

Conflict in Indochina

During the mid-1950s, China sought to build contacts with the nonsocialist world. A cease-fire agreement brought the Korean War to an end in July 1953, and China signaled its desire to live in peaceful coexistence with other independent countries in the region. But a relatively minor conflict now began to intensify on China's southern flank, in French Indochina. The struggle had begun after World War II, when Ho Chi Minh's Indochinese Communist Party, at the head of a multiparty nationalist alliance called the Vietminh Front, seized power in northern and central Vietnam after the surrender of imperial Japan. After abortive negotiations between Ho's government and the returning French, war broke out in December 1946. French forces occupied the cities and the densely populated lowlands, while the Vietminh took refuge in the mountains.

For three years, the Vietminh gradually increased in size and effectiveness. What had begun as an anticolonial struggle by Ho's Vietminh Front against the French after World War II became entangled in the Cold War in the early 1950s, when both the United States and the new communist government in China began to intervene in the conflict to promote their own national security objectives. China began to provide military assistance to the Vietminh to protect its own borders from hostile forces. The Americans supported the French but pressured the French government to prepare for an eventual transition to noncommunist governments in Vietnam, Laos, and Cambodia.

At the Geneva Conference in 1954, with the French public tired of fighting the "dirty war" in Indochina, the French agreed to a peace settlement with the Vietminh. Vietnam was temporarily divided into a northern communist half (known as the Democratic Republic of Vietnam) and a noncommunist southern half based in Saigon (eventually to be known as the Republic of Vietnam). Elections were to be held in two years to create a unified government. Cambodia and Laos were both declared independent under neutral governments.

China had played an active role in bringing about the settlement and clearly hoped that it would reduce tensions in the area, but subsequent efforts to improve relations between China and the United States foundered on the issue of Taiwan. In the fall of 1954, the United States signed a mutual security treaty with the Republic of China guaranteeing U.S. military support in case of an invasion of Taiwan. When Beijing demanded U.S. withdrawal from Taiwan as the price for improved relations, diplomatic talks between the two countries collapsed.

The Vietnamese and the French

Unlike many peoples in Southeast Asia, the Vietnamese had to fight for their independence after World War II because of the French determination to hold on to their colonial empire in the region. That fight was led by the talented communist leader Ho Chi Minh. In the photograph on the left, Ho (at the left), assisted by his chief strategist, Vo Nguyen Giap (at the far right), plans an attack on French positions at Dienbienphu. The results of that battle are evident in the photo at the right, which shows French forces surrendering to the Vietnamese on May 7, 1954. The French now faced total defeat in Vietnam. As General Giap said, "A poor feudal nation had beaten a great colonial power. . . . It meant a lot; not just to us but to people all over the world."

FROM CONFRONTATION TO COEXISTENCE

The decade of the 1950s opened with the world teetering on the edge of a nuclear holocaust. The Soviet Union had detonated its first nuclear device in 1949, and the two blocs—capitalist and socialist—viewed each other across an ideological divide that grew increasingly bitter with each passing year. Yet as the decade drew to a close, a measure of sanity crept into the Cold War, and the leaders of the major world powers began to seek ways to coexist in a peaceful and stable world (see Map 25.3).

Khrushchev and the Era of Peaceful Coexistence

The first clear sign of change occurred after Stalin's death in early 1953. His successor, Georgy Malenkov (1902–1988), openly hoped to improve relations with the Western powers in order to reduce defense expenditures and shift government spending to growing consumer needs. Nikita Khrushchev (1894–1971), who replaced Malenkov in 1955, continued his predecessor's efforts to reduce tensions with the West and improve the living standards of the Soviet people.

In an adroit public relations touch, Khrushchev promoted an appeal for a policy of "peaceful coexistence" with the West. In 1955, he surprisingly agreed to negotiate an end to the postwar occupation of Austria by the victorious allies and allow the creation of a neutral country with strong cultural and economic ties with the West. He also called for a reduction in defense expenditures and reduced the size of the Soviet armed forces.

At first, Washington was suspicious of Khrushchev's motives, especially after the Soviet crackdown in Hungary in the fall of 1956 (see Chapter 26). A new crisis over Berlin added to the tension. The Soviet Union had launched its first intercontinental ballistic missile (ICBM) in August 1957, arousing U.S. fears of a missile gap between the United States and the Soviet Union. Khrushchev attempted to take advantage of the U.S.

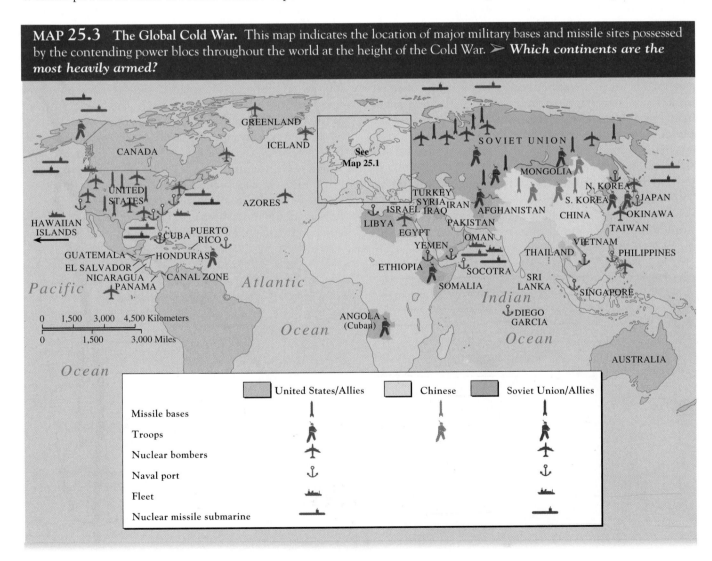

MAP 25.3 **The Global Cold War.** This map indicates the location of major military bases and missile sites possessed by the contending power blocs throughout the world at the height of the Cold War. ➢ *Which continents are the most heavily armed?*

frenzy over missiles to solve the problem of West Berlin, which had remained a "Western island" of prosperity inside the relatively poverty-stricken state of East Germany. Many East Germans sought to escape to West Germany by fleeing through West Berlin, a serious blot on the credibility of the GDR and a potential source of instability in East-West relations. In November 1958, Khrushchev announced that unless the West removed its forces from West Berlin within six months, he would turn over control of the access routes to the East Germans. Unwilling to accept an ultimatum that would have abandoned West Berlin to the Communists, President Dwight D. Eisenhower and the West stood firm, and Khrushchev eventually backed down.

Despite such periodic crises in East-West relations, there were tantalizing signs that an era of true peaceful coexistence between the two power blocs could be achieved. In the late 1950s, the United States and the Soviet Union initiated a cultural exchange program. While the Leningrad Ballet appeared at theaters in the United States, Benny Goodman and the film *West Side Story* played in Moscow. In 1958, Khrushchev visited the United States and had a brief but friendly encounter with President Eisenhower at the presidential retreat in northern Maryland.

Yet Khrushchev could rarely avoid the temptation to gain an advantage over the United States in the competition for influence throughout the world, and this resulted in an unstable relationship between the two superpowers. Moscow also took every opportunity to promote its interests in the Third World, as the unaligned countries of Asia, Africa, and Latin America were now popularly called. Unlike Stalin, Khrushchev viewed the dismantling of colonial regimes in the area as a potential advantage for the Soviet Union and sought especially to exploit the deep suspicions of the United States in Latin America. To improve Soviet influence in such areas, Khrushchev established alliances with key Third World leaders such as Sukarno in Indonesia, Gamel Abdul Nasser in Egypt, Jawaharlal Nehru in India, and Fidel Castro in Cuba. In January 1961, just as John F. Kennedy assumed the U.S. presidency, Khrushchev unnerved the new president at an informal summit meeting in Vienna by declaring that the Soviet Union would provide active support to national liberation movements throughout the world. There were rising fears in Washington of Soviet meddling in such sensitive trouble spots as Southeast Asia, Central Africa, and the Caribbean.

The Cuban Missile Crisis

The Cold War confrontation between the United States and the Soviet Union reached frightening levels during the Cuban Missile Crisis. In 1959, a left-wing revolutionary named Fidel Castro (b. 1927) overthrew the Cuban dictator Fulgencio Batista and established a Soviet-supported totalitarian regime. After the utter failure of a U.S.-supported attempt to overthrow Castro's regime in 1961 (known as the "Bay of Pigs" incident), the Soviet Union decided to place nuclear missiles in Cuba in 1962. The United States was not prepared to allow nuclear weapons within striking distance of the American mainland, even though it had placed some of its own nuclear weapons in Turkey, within range of the Soviet Union. Khrushchev was quick to point out that "your rockets are in Turkey. You are worried by Cuba . . . because it is 90 miles from the American coast. But Turkey is next to us."[5] When U.S. intelligence discovered that a Soviet fleet carrying missiles was indeed heading to Cuba, President Kennedy decided to blockade Cuba and prevent the fleet from reaching its destination. This approach to the problem had the benefit of delaying confrontation and giving

AP/Wide World Photos

➤ **THE KITCHEN DEBATE.** During the late 1950s, the United States and the Soviet Union sought to defuse Cold War tensions by encouraging cultural exchanges between the two countries. On one occasion, U.S. vice president Richard M. Nixon visited Moscow in conjunction with the arrival of an exhibit to introduce U.S. culture and society to the Soviet people. Here Nixon lectures Soviet Communist Party chief Nikita Khrushchev on the technology of the U.S. kitchen. To Nixon's left is future Soviet president Leonid Brezhnev.

the two sides time to find a peaceful solution. Khrushchev agreed to turn back the fleet if Kennedy pledged not to invade Cuba. In a conciliatory letter to Kennedy, Khrushchev wrote:

> We and you ought not to pull on the ends of the rope in which you have tied the knot of war, because the more the two of us pull, the tighter that knot will be tied. And a moment may come when that knot will be tied too tight that even he who tied it will not have the strength to untie it. . . . Let us not only relax the forces pulling on the ends of the rope; let us take measures to untie that knot. We are ready for this.[6]

The intense feeling that the world might have been annihilated in a few days had a profound influence on both sides. A hotline between Moscow and Washington was installed in 1963 to expedite communications between the two superpowers in time of crisis. In the same year, the two powers agreed to ban nuclear tests in the atmosphere, a step that served to lessen the tensions between the two nations.

The Sino-Soviet Dispute

Nikita Khrushchev had launched his slogan of peaceful coexistence as a means of improving relations with the capitalist powers; ironically, one result of the campaign was to undermine Moscow's ties with its close ally China. During Stalin's lifetime, Beijing had accepted the Soviet Union as the acknowledged leader of the socialist camp. After Stalin's death, however, relations began to deteriorate. Part of the reason may have been Mao Zedong's contention that he, as the most experienced Marxist leader, should now be acknowledged as the most authoritative voice within the socialist community. But another determining factor was that just as Soviet policies were moving toward moderation, China's were becoming more radical.

Several other issues were involved, including territorial disputes and China's unhappiness with limited Soviet economic assistance. But the key sources of disagreement involved ideology and the Cold War. Chinese leaders were convinced that the successes of the Soviet space program confirmed that the socialists were now technologically superior to the capitalists (the East wind, trumpeted the Chinese official press, had now triumphed over the West wind), and they urged Khrushchev to go on the offensive to promote world revolution. Specifically, China wanted Soviet assistance in retaking Taiwan from Chiang Kai-shek. But Khrushchev was trying to improve relations with the West and rejected Chinese demands for support against Taiwan.

By the end of the 1950s, the Soviet Union had begun to remove its advisers from China, and in 1961, the dispute broke into the open. Increasingly isolated, China voiced its hostility to what Mao described as the "urban industrialized countries" (which included the Soviet Union) and portrayed itself as the leader of the "rural underdeveloped countries" of Asia, Africa, and Latin America in a global struggle against imperialist oppression. In effect, China had applied Mao Zedong's famous concept of people's war in an international framework.

The Second Indochina War

China's radicalism was intensified in the early 1960s by the outbreak of renewed war in Indochina. The Eisenhower administration had opposed the peace settlement at Geneva in 1954, which divided Vietnam temporarily into two separate regroupment zones, specifically because the provision for future national elections opened up the possibility that the entire country would come under communist rule. But Eisenhower had been unwilling to introduce U.S. military forces to continue the conflict without the full support of the British and the French, who preferred to seek a negotiated settlement. In the end, Washington promised not to break the provisions of the agreement but refused to commit itself to the results.

During the next several months, the United States began to provide aid to a new government in South Vietnam. Under the leadership of the anticommunist politician Ngo Dinh Diem, the South Vietnamese government began to root out dissidents. With the tacit approval of the United States, Diem refused to hold the national elections called for by the Geneva Accords. It was widely anticipated, even in Washington, that the Communists would win such elections. In 1959, Ho Chi Minh, despairing of the peaceful unification of the country under communist rule, returned to a policy of revolutionary war in the south.

By 1963, South Vietnam was on the verge of collapse. Diem's autocratic methods and inattention to severe economic inequality had alienated much of the population, and revolutionary forces, popularly known as the Viet Cong (Vietnamese Communists), expanded their influence throughout much of the country. In the fall of 1963, with the approval of the Kennedy administration, senior military officers overthrew the Diem regime. But factionalism kept the new military leadership from reinvigorating the struggle against the insurgent forces, and the situation in South Vietnam grew worse. By early 1965, the Viet Cong, whose ranks were now swelled by military units infiltrating from North Vietnam, were on the verge of seizing control of the entire country. In March, President Lyndon Johnson decided to send U.S. combat troops to South Vietnam to prevent a total defeat of the anticommunist government in Saigon (see the box on p. 512).

Chinese leaders observed the gradual escalation of the conflict in South Vietnam with mixed feelings. They were undoubtedly pleased to have a firm communist ally—one that had in many ways followed the path of Mao

COMBATING THE AMERICANS

In December 1960, the National Front for the Liberation of South Vietnam, or NLF, was born. Composed of political and social leaders opposed to the anticommunist government of Ngo Dinh Diem in South Vietnam, it operated under the direction of the Vietnam Workers' Party in North Vietnam and served as the formal representative of revolutionary forces in the south throughout the remainder of the Vietnam War. In the spring of 1965, when U.S. president Lyndon Johnson began to dispatch U.S. combat troops to Vietnam to prevent a communist victory there, the NLF issued the following declaration.

STATEMENT OF THE NATIONAL LIBERATION FRONT OF SOUTH VIETNAM

American imperialist aggression against South Vietnam and interference in its internal affairs have now continued for more than ten years. More American troops and supplies, including missile units, Marines, B-57 strategic bombers, and mercenaries from South Korea, Taiwan, the Philippines, Australia, Malaysia, etc., have been brought to South Vietnam. . . .

The Saigon puppet regime, paid servant of the United States, is guilty of the most heinous crimes. These despicable traitors, these boot-lickers of American imperialism, have brought the enemy into our country. They have brought to South Vietnam armed forces of the United States and its satellites to kill our compatriots, occupy and ravage our sacred soil and enslave our people.

The Vietnamese, the peoples of all Indo-China and Southeast Asia, supporters of peace and justice in every part of the world, have raised their voice in angry protest against this criminal unprovoked aggression of the United States imperialists.

In the present extremely grave situation, the South Vietnam National Liberation Front considers it necessary to proclaim anew its firm and unswerving determination to resist the U.S. imperialists and fight for the salvation of our country. . . . [It] will continue to rely chiefly on its own forces and potentialities, but it is prepared to accept any assistance, moral and material, including arms and other military equipment, from all the socialist countries, from nationalist countries, from international organizations, and from the peace-loving peoples of the world.

Zedong—just beyond their southern frontier. Yet they were concerned that renewed bloodshed in South Vietnam might enmesh China in a new conflict with the United States. Nor did they welcome the specter of a powerful and ambitious united Vietnam, which might wish to extend its influence throughout mainland Southeast Asia, an area that Beijing considered its own backyard.

Chinese leaders therefore tiptoed delicately through the minefield of the Indochina conflict. As the war escalated in 1964 and 1965, Beijing publicly announced that the Chinese people fully supported their comrades seeking national liberation but privately assured Washington that China would not directly enter the conflict unless U.S. forces threatened its southern border. Beijing also refused to cooperate fully with Moscow in shipping Soviet goods to North Vietnam through Chinese territory (see the box on p. 563).

Despite its dismay at the lack of full support from China, the communist government in North Vietnam responded to U.S. escalation by infiltrating more of its own regular force troops into the south, and by 1968, the war had reached a stalemate. The Communists were not strong enough to overthrow the government in Saigon, whose weakness was shielded by the presence of half a million U.S. troops, but President Johnson was reluctant to engage in all-out war on North Vietnam for fear of provoking a global nuclear conflict. In the fall, after the Communist-led Tet offensive aroused intense antiwar protests in the United States, peace negotiations began in Paris.

Richard Nixon came into the White House in 1969 on a pledge to bring an honorable end to the Vietnam War. With U.S. public opinion sharply divided on the issue, he began to withdraw U.S. troops while continuing to hold peace talks in Paris. But the centerpiece of his strategy was to improve relations with China and thus undercut Chinese support for the North Vietnamese war effort. During the 1960s, relations between Moscow and Beijing had reached a point of extreme tension, and thousands of troops were stationed on both sides of their long common frontier. To intimidate their communist rivals, Soviet sources hinted that they might launch a preemptive strike to destroy Chinese nuclear facilities in Xinjiang. Sensing an opportunity to split the two onetime allies, Nixon sent his emissary Henry Kissinger on a secret trip to China. Responding to assurances that the United States was determined to withdraw from Indochina and hoped to improve relations with the mainland regime, Chinese leaders invited President Nixon to visit China in early 1972.

Incensed at the apparent betrayal by their close allies, North Vietnamese leaders decided to seek a peaceful settlement of the war in the south. In January 1973, a peace treaty was signed in Paris calling for the removal of all U.S. forces from South Vietnam. In return, the Communists agreed to seek a political settlement of their differences with the Saigon regime. But negotiations between north and south over the political settlement soon broke down,

A MANUAL FOR REVOLUTIONARIES

In the 1920s, Mao Zedong formulated his theory of people's war, which held that in preindustrial societies, revolution could be more readily fomented in the countryside than in the cities. Forty years later, Lin Biao, Mao's colleague and the minister of defense, placed the concept in an international framework, arguing that the rural nations of the world (led, of course, by China) would defeat the industrialized "urban" nations (represented by the United States and the Soviet Union). This is an excerpt from the article in which Lin Biao presented his thesis. His message was also intended as a signal to North Vietnamese leaders not to escalate the conflict in South Vietnam to a point that might involve a direct confrontation with the United States.

LIN BIAO, "LONG LIVE THE VICTORY OF PEOPLE'S WAR"

Many countries and peoples in Asia, Africa, and Latin America are now being subjected to aggression and enslavement on a serious scale by the imperialists headed by the United States and their lackeys. The basic political and economic conditions in many of these countries have many similarities to those that prevailed in old China. As in China, the peasant question is extremely important in these regions. The peasants constitute the main force of the national-democratic revolution against the imperialists and their lackeys. In committing aggression against these countries, the imperialists usually begin by seizing the big cities and the main lines of communication. But they are unable to bring the vast countryside completely under their control. The countryside, and the countryside alone, can provide the broad areas in which the revolutionaries can maneuver freely. The countryside, and the countryside alone, can provide the revolutionary basis from which the revolutionaries can go forward to final victory. Precisely for

this reason, Mao Tse-tung's theory of establishing revolutionary base areas in the rural districts and encircling the cities from the countryside is attracting more and more attention among the people in these regions.

Taking the entire globe, if North America and Western Europe can be called "the cities of the world," then Asia, Africa, and Latin America constitute "the rural areas of the world." Since World War II, the proletarian revolutionary movement has for various reasons been temporarily held back in the North American and West European capitalist countries, while the people's revolutionary movement in Asia, Africa, and Latin America has been growing vigorously. In a sense, the contemporary world revolution also presents a picture of the encirclement of cities by the rural areas. In the final analysis, the whole cause of world revolution hinges on the revolutionary struggles of the Asian, African, and Latin American peoples, who make up the overwhelming majority of the world's population. The socialist countries should regard it as their internationalist duty to support the people's revolutionary struggles in Asia, Africa, and Latin America. . . .

Ours is the epoch in which world capitalism and imperialism are heading for their doom and communism is marching to victory. Comrade Mao Tse-tung's theory of people's war is not only a product of the Chinese revolution, but has also the characteristic of our epoch. The new experience gained in the people's revolutionary struggles in various countries since World War II has provided continuous evidence that Mao Tse-tung's thought is a common asset of the revolutionary people of the whole world. This is the great international significance of the thought of Mao Tse-tung.

---

and in early 1975, the Communists resumed the offensive. At the end of April, under a massive assault by North Vietnamese military forces, the South Vietnamese government surrendered. A year later, the country was unified under communist rule.

The communist victory in Vietnam was a severe humiliation for the United States, but its strategic impact was limited because of the new relationship with China. During the next decade, Sino-American relations continued to improve. In 1979, diplomatic ties were established between the two countries under an arrangement whereby the United States renounced its mutual security treaty with the Republic of China in return for a pledge from China to seek reunification with Taiwan by peaceful means. By the end of the 1970s, China and the United States had forged a "strategic relationship" in which they would cooperate against the common threat of Soviet hegemony in Asia.

 ## AN ERA OF EQUIVALENCE

When the Johnson administration sent U.S. combat troops to South Vietnam in 1965, Washington's main concern was with Beijing, not Moscow. By the mid-1960s, U.S. officials viewed the Soviet Union as an essentially conservative power, more concerned with protecting its vast empire than with expanding its borders. In fact, U.S. policy makers periodically sought Soviet assistance in seeking a peaceful settlement of the Vietnam War. So long as Khrushchev was in power, they found a receptive ear in Moscow. Khrushchev was firmly dedicated to promoting peaceful coexistence (at least on his terms) and sternly advised the North Vietnamese against a resumption of revolutionary war in South Vietnam.

After October 1964, when Khrushchev was replaced by a new leadership headed by party chief Leonid Brezhnev

(1906–1982) and Prime Minister Alexei Kosygin (1904–1980), Soviet attitudes about Vietnam became more ambivalent. On the one hand, the new Soviet leaders had no desire to see the Vietnam conflict poison relations between the great powers. On the other hand, Moscow was eager to demonstrate its support for the North Vietnamese to deflect Chinese charges that the Soviet Union had betrayed the interests of the oppressed peoples of the world. As a result, Soviet officials publicly voiced sympathy for the U.S. predicament in Vietnam but put no pressure on their allies to bring an end to the war. Indeed, the Soviet Union became Hanoi's main supplier of advanced military equipment in the final years of the war.

Still, under Brezhnev and Kosygin, the Soviet Union continued to pursue peaceful coexistence with the West and adopted a generally cautious posture in foreign affairs. By the early 1970s, a new age in Soviet-American relations had emerged, often referred to by the French term détente, meaning a reduction of tensions between the two sides. One symbol of the new relationship was the Antiballistic Missile (ABM) Treaty, often called SALT I (for Strategic Arms Limitation Talks), signed in 1972, in which the two nations agreed to limit the size of their ABM systems.

Washington's objective in pursuing the treaty was to make it unlikely that either superpower could win a nuclear exchange by launching a preemptive strike against the other. U.S. officials believed that a policy of "equivalence," in which there was a roughly equal power balance on each side, was the best way to avoid a nuclear confrontation. Détente was pursued in other ways as well. When President Nixon took office in 1969, he sought to increase trade and cultural contacts with the Soviet Union. His purpose was to set up a series of "linkages" in U.S.-Soviet relations that would persuade Moscow of the economic and social benefits of maintaining good relations with the West.

A symbol of that new relationship was the Helsinki Agreement. Signed in 1975 by the United States, Canada, and all European nations on both sides of the Iron Curtain, these accords recognized all borders in Europe that had been established since the end of World War II, thereby formally acknowledging for the first time the Soviet sphere of influence in Eastern Europe. The Helsinki Agreement also committed the signatories to recognize and protect the human rights of their citizens, a clear effort by the Western states to improve the performance of the Soviet Union and its allies in that arena.

An End to Détente?

Protection of human rights became one of the major foreign policy goals of the next U.S. president, Jimmy Carter (b. 1924). Ironically, just at the point when U.S. involvement in Vietnam came to an end and relations with China

began to improve, U.S.-Soviet relations began to sour, for several reasons. Some Americans had become increasingly concerned about aggressive new tendencies in Soviet foreign policy. The first indication came in Africa. Soviet influence was on the rise in Somalia, across the Red Sea in South Yemen, and later in neighboring Ethiopia. In Angola, once a colony of Portugal, an insurgent movement supported by Cuban troops came to power. In 1979, Soviet troops were sent across the border into Afghanistan to protect a newly installed Marxist regime facing internal resistance from fundamentalist Muslims. Some observers suspected that the ultimate objective of the Soviet advance into hitherto neutral Afghanistan was to extend Soviet power into the oil fields of the Persian Gulf. To deter such a possibility, the White House promulgated the Carter Doctrine, which stated that the United States would use its military power, if necessary, to safeguard Western access to the oil reserves in the Middle East. In fact, sources in Moscow later disclosed that the Soviet advance had little to do with the oil of the Persian Gulf but was an effort to increase Soviet influence in a region increasingly beset by Islamic fervor. Soviet officials feared that Islamic activism could spread to the Muslim populations in the Soviet republics in Central Asia and were confident that the United States was too distracted by the "Vietnam syndrome" (the public fear of U.S. involvement in another Vietnam-type conflict) to respond.

Another reason for the growing suspicion of the Soviet Union in the United States was that some U.S. defense analysts began to charge that the Soviet Union had rejected the policy of equivalence and was seeking strategic superiority in nuclear weapons. Accordingly, they argued for a substantial increase in U.S. defense spending. Such charges, combined with evidence of Soviet efforts in Africa and the Middle East and reports of the persecution of Jews and dissidents in the Soviet Union, helped undermine public support for détente in the United States. These changing attitudes were reflected in the failure of the Carter administration to obtain congressional approval of a new arms limitation agreement (SALT II), signed with the Soviet Union in 1979.

Countering the Evil Empire

The early years of the administration of President Ronald Reagan (b. 1911) witnessed a return to the harsh rhetoric, if not all of the harsh practices, of the Cold War. President Reagan's anticommunist credentials were well known. In a speech given shortly after his election in 1980, he referred to the Soviet Union as an "evil empire" and frequently voiced his suspicion of its motives in foreign affairs. In an effort to eliminate perceived Soviet advantages in strategic weaponry, the White House began a military buildup that stimulated a renewed arms race. In 1982, the Reagan administration introduced the nuclear-tipped

Chronology

THE COLD WAR TO 1980

Truman Doctrine	1947
Formation of NATO	1949
Soviet Union explodes first nuclear device	1949
Communists come to power in China	1949
Nationalist government retreats to Taiwan	1949
Korean War	1950–1953
Geneva Conference ends Indochina War	July 21, 1954
Warsaw Pact created	1955
Khrushchev calls for peaceful coexistence	1956
Sino-Soviet dispute breaks into the open	1961
Cuban Missile Crisis	1962
SALT I treaty signed	1972
Nixon's visit to China	1972
Fall of South Vietnam	1975
Soviet invasion of Afghanistan	1979

cruise missile, whose ability to fly at low altitudes made it difficult to detect by enemy radar. Reagan also became an ardent exponent of the Strategic Defense Initiative (SDI), nicknamed "Star Wars." Its purposes were to create a space shield that could destroy incoming missiles and to force Moscow into an arms race that it could not hope to win.

The Reagan administration also adopted a more activist, if not confrontational, stance in the Third World. That attitude was most directly demonstrated in Central America, where the revolutionary Sandinista regime had been established in Nicaragua after the overthrow of the Somoza dictatorship in 1979. Charging that the Sandinista regime was supporting a guerrilla insurgency movement in nearby El Salvador, the Reagan administration began to provide material aid to the government in El Salvador while simultaneously supporting an anticommunist guerrilla movement (called the Contras) in Nicaragua. Though the administration insisted that it was countering the spread of communism in the Western Hemisphere, its Central American policy aroused considerable controversy in Congress, where some members charged that growing U.S. involvement could lead to a repeat of the nation's bitter experience in Vietnam.

The Reagan administration also took the offensive in other areas. By providing military support to the anti-Soviet insurgents in Afghanistan, the White House helped maintain a Vietnam-like war in Afghanistan that would embed the Soviet Union in its own quagmire. Like the Vietnam War, the conflict in Afghanistan resulted in heavy casualties and demonstrated that the influence of a superpower was limited in the face of strong nationalist, guerrilla-type opposition.

CONCLUSION

At the end of World War II, a new conflict erupted in Europe as the new superpowers, the United States and the Soviet Union, began to compete for political domination. This ideological division soon spread to the rest of the world as the United States fought in Korea and Vietnam to prevent the spread of communism, promoted by the new Maoist government in China, while the Soviet Union used its influence to prop up pro-Soviet regimes in Asia, Africa, and Latin America.

Thus what had begun as a confrontation across the great divide of the Iron Curtain in Europe eventually took on global significance. As a result, both Moscow and Washington became entangled in areas that in themselves had little importance in terms of national security interests. To make matters worse, U.S. policy makers all too often applied the lessons of World War II (the so-called Munich syndrome, according to which efforts to appease an aggressor only encourage his appetite for conquest) to crisis points in the Third World, where conditions were not remotely comparable.

By the 1980s, however, there were tantalizing signs of a thaw in the Cold War. China and the United States, each hoping to gain leverage with Moscow, had agreed to establish diplomatic relations. Freed from its concerns over Beijing's open support of revolutions in the Third World, the United States decided to withdraw from South Vietnam, and the war there came to an end without involving the great powers in a dangerous confrontation. Although Washington and Moscow continued to compete for advantage all over the world, both sides gradually came to realize that the struggle for domination could best be carried out in the political and economic arenas rather than on the battlefield.

Central America

MEXICO

0 — 300 Kilometers
0 — 200 Miles

GUATEMALA
BELIZE
Caribbean Sea
HONDURAS
EL SALVADOR
NICARAGUA
Pacific Ocean
COSTA RICA

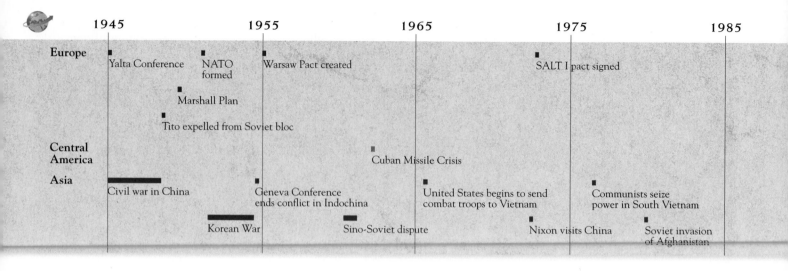

	1945	1955	1965	1975	1985

Europe
- Yalta Conference
- NATO formed
- Warsaw Pact created
- Marshall Plan
- Tito expelled from Soviet bloc
- SALT I pact signed

Central America
- Cuban Missile Crisis

Asia
- Civil war in China
- Geneva Conference ends conflict in Indochina
- United States begins to send combat troops to Vietnam
- Communists seize power in South Vietnam
- Korean War
- Sino-Soviet dispute
- Nixon visits China
- Soviet invasion of Afghanistan

CHAPTER NOTES

1. *Department of State Bulletin* 12 (February 11, 1945), pp. 213–216.
2. Quoted in Joseph M. Jones, *The Fifteen Weeks (February 21–June 5, 1947)*, 2d ed. (New York, 1964), pp. 140–141.
3. Quoted in Walter Laqueur, *Europe in Our Time* (New York, 1992), p. 111.
4. Quoted in Wilfried Loth, *The Division of the World, 1941–1955* (New York, 1988), pp. 160–161.
5. Quoted in Peter Lane, *Europe Since 1945: An Introduction* (Totowa, N.J., 1985), p. 248.
6. Quoted in Robert F. Kennedy, *Thirteen Days: A Memoir of the Cuban Missile Crisis* (New York, 1969), pp. 89–90.

SUGGESTED READING

There is a detailed literature on the Cold War. Two general accounts are R. B. Levering, *The Cold War, 1945–1972* (Arlington Heights, Ill., 1982), and B. A. Weisberger, *Cold War, Cold Peace: The United States and Russia Since 1945* (New York, 1984). Two works that maintain that the Soviet Union was chiefly responsible for the Cold War are H. Feis, *From Trust to Terror: The Onset of the Cold War, 1945–1950* (New York, 1970), and A. B. Ulam, *The Rivals: America and Russia Since World War II* (New York, 1971). Revisionist studies on the Cold War have emphasized U.S. responsibility for the Cold War, especially its global aspects. These works include J. Kolko and G. Kolko, *The Limits of Power: The World and United States Foreign Policy, 1945–1954* (New York, 1972); W. La Feber, *America, Russia and the Cold War, 1945–1966*, 2d ed. (New York, 1972); and M. Sherwin, *A World Destroyed: The Atomic Bomb and the Grand Alliance* (New York, 1975). For a critique of the revisionist studies, see R. L. Maddox, *The New Left and the Origins of the Cold War* (Princeton, N.J., 1973). R. Garthoff, *Détente and Confrontation: American-Soviet Relations from Nixon to Reagan* (Washington, D.C., 1985), provides a detailed analysis of U.S.-Soviet relations in the 1970s and 1980s. For a highly competent retrospective analysis of the Cold War era, see J. L. Gaddis, *We Now Know: Rethinking Cold War History* (Oxford, 1997).

A number of studies of the early stages of the Cold War have been based on documents unavailable until the late 1980s or early 1990s. See, for example, O. A. Westad, *Cold War and Revolution: Soviet-American Rivalry and the Origins of the Chinese Civil War* (New York, 1993); D. A. Mayers, *Cracking the Monolith: U.S. Policy Against the Sino-Soviet Alliance, 1949–1955* (Baton Rouge, 1986); and Chen Jian, *China's Road to the Korean War: The Making of the Sino-American Confrontation* (New York, 1994). S. Goncharov, J. W. Lewis, and Xue Litai, *Uncertain Partners: Stalin, Mao, and the Korean War* (Stanford, Calif., 1993), provides a fascinating view of the war from several perspectives.

For important studies of Soviet foreign policy, see A. B. Ulam, *Expansion and Coexistence: Soviet Foreign Policy, 1917–1973*, 2d ed. (New York, 1974), and *Dangerous Relations: The Soviet Union in World Politics, 1970–1982* (New York, 1983). The effects of the Cold War on Germany are examined in J. H. Backer, *The Decision to Divide Germany: American Foreign Policy in Transition* (Durham, N.C., 1978). On atomic diplomacy in the Cold War, see G. F. Herken, *The Winning Weapon: The Atomic Bomb in the Cold War, 1945–1950* (New York, 1981). For a good introduction to the arms race, see E. M. Bottome, *The Balance of Terror: A Guide to the Arms Race*, rev. ed. (Boston, 1986).

There are several surveys of Chinese foreign policy since the Communists' rise to power. On the revolutionary period, see P. Van Ness, *Revolution and Chinese Foreign Policy* (Berkeley, Calif., 1971), and J. Gittings, *The World and China* (New York, 1974). On Sino-

U.S. relations, see H. Harding, *A Fragile Relationship: The United States and China Since 1972* (Washington, D.C., 1992), and W. Burr, ed., *The Kissinger Transcripts: The Top-Secret Talks with Beijing and Moscow* (New York, 1998). On Chinese policy in Korea, see the classic by A. S. Whiting, *China Crosses the Yalu* (Stanford, Calif., 1960). On Sino-Vietnamese relations, see Ang Cheng Guan, *Vietnamese Communists' Relations with China and the Second Indochina Conflict* (Jefferson, N.C., 1997).

INFOTRAC
COLLEGE EDITION

Visit the source collections at infotrac.thomsonlearning.com and use the Search function with the following key terms.

Cold War

Korean War

Soviet Union relations with the United States

Vietnamese conflict

WORLD HISTORY
RESOURCES

Visit the *Essential World History* Companion Web Site for resources specific to this textbook:

http://history.wadsworth.com/duikeressentials02/

The CD in the back of this book and the World History Resource Center at **http://history.wadsworth.com/world/** offer a variety of tools to help you succeed in this course, including access to quizzes; images; documents; interactive simulations, maps, and timelines; movie explorations; and a wealth of other sources.

Chapter 26

BRAVE NEW WORLD: COMMUNISM ON TRIAL

CHAPTER OUTLINE

- THE POSTWAR SOVIET UNION
- FERMENT IN EASTERN EUROPE
- CULTURE AND SOCIETY IN THE SOVIET BLOC
- THE DISINTEGRATION OF THE SOVIET EMPIRE
- THE EAST IS RED: CHINA UNDER COMMUNISM
- "SERVE THE PEOPLE": CHINESE SOCIETY AND CULTURE UNDER COMMUNISM
- CONCLUSION

FOCUS QUESTIONS

- What were the chief characteristics of Soviet political, economic, and social life prior to Mikhail Gorbachev, and what reforms did he introduce?
- What were the main developments in Eastern Europe between 1945 and 1989?
- What were Mao Zedong's goals for China, and what policies did he institute to try to achieve them?
- What have been the major political, economic, and social developments in China since Mao's death in 1976?
- ➤ Why has communism survived in China but not in Eastern Europe and Russia, and what impact has it had on Chinese life and culture?

According to Karl Marx, capitalism is a system that involves the exploitation of man by man; under socialism, it is the other way around. That wry joke was typical of popular humor in post–World War II Moscow, where the dreams of a future utopia had faded in the grim reality of life in the Soviet Union.

Nevertheless, the communist monopoly on power seemed secure, as did Moscow's hold over its client states in Eastern Europe. In fact, for three decades after the end of World War II, the Soviet Empire appeared to be a permanent feature of the international landscape. But by the early 1980s, it became clear that there were cracks in the Kremlin wall. The Soviet economy was stagnant, the minority nationalities were restive, and Eastern European leaders were increasingly emboldened to test the waters of the global capitalist marketplace. In the United States, the newly elected president, Ronald Reagan, boldly predicted the imminent collapse of the "evil empire."

Within a period of less than three years (1989–1991), the Soviet Union ceased to exist as a nation. Russia and other former Soviet republics declared their separate independence, communist regimes in Eastern Europe were toppled, and the long-standing division of postwar Europe came to an end. Although communist parties survived the demise of the system and showed signs of renewed vigor in some countries in the region, their monopoly is gone, and they must now compete with other parties for power.

The fate of communism in China has been quite different. Despite some turbulence, communism has survived in China, even as that nation takes giant strides toward becoming an economic superpower. Yet as China's leaders struggle to bring the nation into the twenty-first century, many of the essential principles of Marxist-Leninist dogma have been tacitly abandoned. •

THE POSTWAR SOVIET UNION

World War II had left the Soviet Union as one of the world's two superpowers and its leader, Joseph Stalin, in a position of strength. He and his Soviet colleagues were now in control of a vast empire that included Eastern Europe, much of the Balkans, and new territory gained from Japan in East Asia.

From Stalin to Khrushchev

World War II devastated the Soviet Union. Twenty million citizens lost their lives, and cities such as Kiev, Kharkov, and Leningrad suffered enormous physical destruction. As the lands that had been occupied by the German forces were liberated, the Soviet government turned its attention to restoring their economic structures. Nevertheless, in 1945, agricultural production was only 60 percent and steel output only 50 percent of prewar levels. The Soviet people faced incredibly difficult conditions: they worked longer hours; they ate less; they were ill-housed and poorly clothed.

In the immediate postwar years, the Soviet Union removed goods and materials from occupied Germany and extorted valuable raw materials from its satellite states in Eastern Europe. More important, however, to create a new industrial base, Stalin returned to the method he had used in the 1930s—the extraction of development capital from Soviet labor. Working hard for little pay and for precious few consumer goods, Soviet laborers were expected to produce goods for export with little in return for themselves. The incoming capital from abroad could then be used to purchase machinery and Western technology. The loss of millions of men in the war meant that much of this tremendous workload fell upon Soviet women, who performed almost 40 percent of the heavy manual labor.

The pace of economic recovery in the Soviet Union was impressive. By 1947, industrial production had attained 1939 levels. New power plants, canals, and giant factories were built, and industrial enterprises and oil fields were established in Siberia and Soviet Central Asia.

Although Stalin's economic recovery policy was successful in promoting growth in heavy industry, primarily for the benefit of the military, consumer goods remained scarce. Heavy industry grew at a rate three times that of personal consumption. Moreover, the housing shortage was acute, with living conditions especially difficult in the overcrowded cities.

When World War II ended in 1945, Stalin had been in power for more than fifteen years. Political terror enforced by several hundred thousand secret police ensured that he would remain in power. By the late 1940s, there were an estimated nine million Soviet citizens in Siberian concentration camps.

Increasingly distrustful of competitors, Stalin exercised sole authority and pitted his subordinates against each other. His morbid suspicions extended to even his closest colleagues. Stalin's colleagues became completely cowed. As he remarked mockingly on one occasion, "When I die, the imperialists will strangle all of you like a litter of kittens."[1]

Stalin died in 1953 and, after some bitter infighting within the party leadership, was succeeded by Georgy Malenkov, a veteran administrator and ambitious member of the Politburo (the party's governing body). But Malenkov's reform goals did not necessarily appeal to key groups, including the army, the Communist Party, the managerial elite, and the security services (now known as the Committee on Government Security, or KGB). In 1953, Malenkov was removed from his position, and power shifted to his rival, the new party general secretary, Nikita Khrushchev.

Once in power, Khrushchev moved vigorously to boost the performance of the Soviet economy and revitalize Soviet society. In an attempt to release the stranglehold of the central bureaucracy over the national economy, he abolished dozens of government ministries and split up

KHRUSHCHEV DENOUNCES STALIN

Three years after Stalin's death, the new Soviet premier, Nikita Khrushchev, addressed the Twentieth Congress of the Communist Party and denounced the former Soviet dictator for his crimes. This denunciation was the beginning of a policy of destalinization.

KHRUSHCHEV ADDRESSES THE TWENTIETH PARTY CONGRESS, FEBRUARY 1956

Comrades, . . . quite a lot has been said about the cult of the individual and about its harmful consequences. . . . The cult of the person of Stalin . . . became at a certain specific stage the source of a whole series of exceedingly serious and grave perversions of Party principles, of Party democracy, of revolutionary legality.

Stalin absolutely did not tolerate collegiality in leadership and in work and . . . practiced brutal violence, not only toward everything which opposed him, but also toward that which seemed to his capricious and despotic character, contrary to his concepts.

Stalin abandoned the method of ideological struggle for that of administrative violence, mass repressions and terror. . . . Arbitrary behavior by one person encouraged and permitted arbitrariness in others. Mass arrests and deportations of many thousands of people, execution without trial and without normal investigation created conditions of insecurity, fear, and even desperation.

Stalin showed in a whole series of cases his intolerance, his brutality, and his abuse of power. . . . He often chose the path of repression and annihilation, not only against actual enemies, but also against individuals who had not committed any crimes against the Party and the Soviet government. . . .

Many Party, Soviet, and economic activists who were branded in 1937–8 as "enemies" were actually never enemies, spies, wreckers, and so on, but were always honest communists; they were only so stigmatized, and often, no longer able to bear barbaric tortures, they charged themselves (at the order of the investigative judges-falsifiers) with all kinds of grave and unlikely crimes.

This was the result of the abuse of power by Stalin, who began to use mass terror against the Party cadres. . . . Stalin put the Party and the NKVD [the Soviet police agency] up to the use of mass terror when the exploiting classes had been liquidated in our country and when there were no serious reasons for the use of extraordinary mass terror. The terror was directed . . . against the honest workers of the Party and the Soviet state. . . .

Stalin was a very distrustful man, sickly, suspicious. . . . Everywhere and in everything he saw "enemies," "two-facers," and "spies." Possessing unlimited power, he indulged in great willfulness and choked a person morally and physically. A situation was created where one could not express one's own will. When Stalin said that one or another would be arrested, it was necessary to accept on faith that he was an "enemy of the people." What proofs were offered? The confession of the arrested. . . How is it possible that a person confesses to crimes that he had not committed? Only in one way—because of application of physical methods of pressuring him, tortures, bringing him to a state of unconsciousness, deprivation of his judgment, taking away of his human dignity.

---

the party and government apparatus. Khrushchev also attempted to rejuvenate the stagnant agricultural sector. He attempted to spur production by increasing profit incentives and opened "virgin lands" in Soviet Kazakhstan to bring thousands of acres of new land under cultivation.

An innovator by nature, Khrushchev had to overcome the inherently conservative instincts of the Soviet bureaucracy, as well as those of the mass of the Soviet population. His plan to remove the "dead hand" of the state, however laudable in intent, alienated much of the Soviet official class, and his effort to split the party angered those who saw it as the central force in the Soviet system. Khrushchev's agricultural schemes inspired similar opposition. His effort to persuade Russians to eat more corn (an idea he had apparently picked up during a visit to the United States) earned him the mocking nickname "Cornman." The industrial growth rate, which had soared in the early 1950s, now declined dramatically, from 13 percent in 1953 to 7.5 percent in 1964.

Khrushchev was probably best known for his policy of destalinization. Khrushchev had risen in the party hierarchy as a Stalin protégé, but he had been deeply disturbed by his mentor's excesses and, once in a position of authority, moved to excise the Stalinist legacy from Soviet society. The campaign began at the Twentieth National Congress of the Communist Party in February 1956, when Khrushchev gave a long speech in private criticizing some of Stalin's major shortcomings. The speech had apparently not been intended for public distribution, but it was quickly leaked to the Western press and created a sensation throughout the world (see the box above). Under Khrushchev's instructions, thousands of prisoners were released from concentration camps.

Khrushchev's personality, however, did not endear him to higher Soviet officials, who frowned at his tendency to crack jokes and play the clown. Foreign policy failures further damaged Khrushchev's reputation among his colleagues (see Chapter 25). While he was away on vacation in 1964, a special meeting of the Soviet Politburo voted him out of office (because of "deteriorating health") and forced him into retirement.

The Brezhnev Years (1964–1982)

The ouster of Nikita Khrushchev in October 1964 vividly demonstrated the challenges that would be encountered by any leader sufficiently bold to try to reform the Soviet system. Leonid Brezhnev (1906–1982), the new party chief, was undoubtedly aware of these realities of Soviet politics, and his long tenure in power was marked, above all, by the desire to avoid changes that might provoke instability, either at home or abroad. Brezhnev was himself a product of the Soviet system. He had entered the ranks of the party leadership under Stalin, and although he was not a particularly avid believer in party ideology, he was no partisan of reform.

Still, Brezhnev sought stability in the domestic arena. He and his prime minister, Alexei Kosygin, undertook what might be described as a program of "de-Khrushchevization," returning the responsibility for long-term planning to the central ministries and reuniting the Communist Party apparatus. Despite some cautious attempts to stimulate the stagnant farm sector, there was no effort to revise the basic collective system. In the industrial sector, the regime launched a series of reforms designed to give factory managers (themselves employees of the state) more responsibility for setting prices, wages, and production quotas. These "Kosygin reforms" had little effect, however, because they were stubbornly resisted by the bureaucracy.

A CONTROLLED SOCIETY

Brezhnev also initiated a significant retreat from Khrushchev's policy of destalinization. Criticism of the "Great Leader" had angered conservatives both within the party hierarchy and among the public at large, many of whom still revered Stalin as a hero and a defender of Russia against Nazi Germany. Early in Brezhnev's reign, Stalin's reputation began to revive. Although his alleged shortcomings were not totally ignored, he was now described in the official press as "an outstanding party leader" who had been primarily responsible for the successes achieved by the Soviet Union.

The regime also adopted a more restrictive policy toward dissidents in Soviet society. Critics of the Soviet system, such as the physicist Andrei Sakharov, were harassed and arrested or, like the famous writer Alexander Solzhenitsyn, forced to leave the country. Free expression was also restricted. The media were controlled by the state and presented only what the state wanted people to hear. The government made strenuous efforts to prevent the Soviet people from exposure to harmful foreign ideas, especially modern art, literature, and contemporary Western rock music. When the Summer Olympic Games were held in Moscow in 1980, Soviet newspapers advised citizens to keep their children indoors to keep them from being polluted with "bourgeois" ideas passed on by foreign visitors.

A STAGNANT ECONOMY

Soviet leaders also failed to achieve their objective of revitalizing the national economy. Whereas growth rates during the early Khrushchev era had been impressive (prompting Khrushchev during one visit to the United States in the 1950s to chortle, "We will bury you"), under Brezhnev industrial growth declined to an annual rate of less than 4 percent in the early 1970s and less than 3 percent in the period from 1975 to 1980. Successes in the agricultural sector were equally meager.

One of the primary problems with the Soviet economy was the absence of incentives. Salary structures offered little reward for hard labor and extraordinary achievement. Pay differentials operated in a much narrower range than in most Western societies, and there was little danger of being dismissed. According to the Soviet constitution, every Soviet citizen was guaranteed an opportunity to work.

There were, of course, some exceptions to this general rule. Athletic achievement was highly prized, and a gymnast of Olympic stature would receive great rewards in the form of prestige and lifestyle. Senior officials did not receive high salaries but were provided with countless perquisites, such as access to foreign goods, official automobiles with a chauffeur, and entry into prestigious institutions of higher learning for their children.

PROBLEMS OF GERONTOCRACY

Brezhnev died in November 1982 and was succeeded by Yuri Andropov (1914–1984), a party veteran and head of the Soviet secret services. During his brief tenure as party chief, Andropov was a vocal advocate of reform, but when he died after only a few months in office, little had been done to change the system. He was succeeded, in turn, by a mediocre party stalwart, the elderly Konstantin Chernenko (1911–1985). With the Soviet system in crisis, Moscow seemed stuck in a time warp.

 FERMENT IN EASTERN EUROPE

The key to security along the western frontier of the Soviet Union was the string of Eastern European satellite states that had been assembled in the aftermath of World War II (see Map 26.1). Once communist power had been assured, a series of "little Stalins" put into power by Moscow instituted Soviet-type five-year plans that emphasized heavy industry rather than consumer goods, the collectivization of agriculture, and the nationalization of industry. They also appropriated the political tactics that Stalin had perfected in the Soviet Union, eliminating all noncommunist parties and establishing the classical

Courtesy of William J. Duiker

⇒ HOW TO SHOP IN MOSCOW. Because of the policy of state control over the Soviet economy, the availability of goods was a consequence not of market factors but of decisions made by government bureaucrats. As a result, needed goods were often in short supply. When Soviet citizens heard that a shipment of a particular product had arrived at a state store, they queued up to buy it. Here shoppers during the mid-1980s line up in front of a state-run store selling dinnerware in Moscow.

institutions of repression—the secret police and military forces. Dissidents were tracked down and thrown into prison, and "national Communists" who resisted total subservience to the Soviet Union were charged with treason in mass show trials and executed.

Despite these repressive efforts, discontent became increasingly evident in several Eastern European countries. For the vast majority of peoples in Eastern Europe, the imposition of the so-called people's democracies (a term invented by Moscow to define a society in the early stage of socialist transition) resulted in economic hardship and severe threats to the most basic political liberties.

In Poland, public demonstrations against an increase in food prices in 1956 escalated into widespread protests against the regime's economic policies, restrictions on the freedom of Catholics to practice their religion, and the continued presence of Soviet troops (as called for by the Warsaw Pact) on Polish soil. In a desperate effort to defuse the unrest, the party leader stepped down and was replaced by Wladyslaw Gomulka (1905–1982), a popular figure. When Gomulka took steps to ease the crisis, Khrushchev flew to Warsaw to warn him against adopting policies that could undermine the political dominance of the party and weaken security links with the Soviet Union. Ultimately

Poland agreed to remain in the Warsaw Pact and to maintain the sanctity of party rule; in return, Gomulka was authorized to adopt domestic reforms, such as easing restrictions on religious practice and ending the policy of forced collectivization in rural areas.

The developments in Poland sent shock waves throughout the region. The impact was strongest in neighboring Hungary, where in late October 1956, student-led popular riots broke out in the capital of Budapest and soon spread to other towns and villages throughout the country. The local party leader was forced to resign and was replaced by Imre Nagy (1896–1958), a "national Communist" who attempted to satisfy popular demands without arousing the anger of Moscow. On November 1, Nagy promised free elections, which, given the mood of the country, would probably have brought an end to communist rule. After a brief moment of uncertainty, Moscow decided on firm action. Soviet troops, recently withdrawn at Nagy's request, returned to Budapest and installed a new government under the more pliant party leader János Kádár (1912–1989).

Czechoslovakia did not share in the thaw of the mid-1950s and remained under the rule of Antonin Novotny (1904–1975), who had been placed in power by Stalin

MAP 26.1 **Eastern Europe and the Soviet Union.** After World War II, the boundaries of Eastern Europe were redrawn as a result of Allied agreements reached at the Tehran and Yalta conferences. This map shows the new boundaries that were established throughout the region, placing Soviet power at the center of Europe. ➤ *How had the boundaries changed from the prewar era?*

himself. By the late 1960s, however, Novotny's policies had led to widespread popular alienation, and in 1968, with the support of intellectuals and reformist party members, Alexander Dubček was elected first secretary of the Communist Party. He immediately attempted to create what was popularly called "socialism with a human face," relaxing restrictions on freedom of speech and the press and the right to travel abroad. Economic reforms were announced, and party control over all aspects of society was reduced. A period of euphoria erupted that came to be known as the "Prague Spring."

It proved to be short-lived. Encouraged by Dubček's actions, some Czechs called for more far-reaching reforms, including neutrality and withdrawal from the Soviet bloc. To forestall the spread of this "spring fever," the Soviet Red Army, supported by troops from other Warsaw Pact states, invaded Czechoslovakia in August 1968 and crushed the reform movement. Gustav Husak (1913–1991), a com-

mitted Stalinist, replaced Dubček and restored the old order (see the box on p. 574).

Elsewhere in Eastern Europe, Stalinist policies continued to hold sway. The ruling communist government in East Germany, led by Walter Ulbricht, consolidated its position in the early 1950s and became a faithful Soviet satellite. After a 1953 workers' revolt was crushed by Soviet tanks, a steady flight of East Germans to West Germany ensued, primarily through the city of Berlin. This exodus of mostly skilled laborers ("Soon only party chief Ulbricht will be left," remarked one Soviet observer sardonically) created economic problems and in 1961 led the East German government to erect a wall separating East Berlin from West Berlin. In 1971, Ulbricht was succeeded by Erich Honecker (1912–1994), a party hard-liner who was deeply committed to the ideological battle against détente. Propaganda increased, and the use of the Stasi, the secret police, became a hallmark of Honecker's virtual

THE BREZHNEV DOCTRINE

In the summer of 1968, when the new Communist Party leaders in Czechoslovakia were seriously considering proposals for reforming the totalitarian system there, the Warsaw Pact nations met under the leadership of Soviet party chief Leonid Brezhnev to assess the threat to the socialist camp. Shortly after, military forces of several Soviet bloc nations entered Czechoslovakia and imposed a new government subservient to Moscow. The move was justified by the spirit of "proletarian internationalism" and was widely viewed as a warning to China and other socialist states not to stray too far from Marxist-Leninist orthodoxy, as interpreted by the Soviet Union.

A LETTER TO THE CENTRAL COMMITTEE OF THE COMMUNIST PARTY OF CZECHOSLOVAKIA

Dear comrades!

On behalf of the Central Committees of the Communist and Workers' Parties of Bulgaria, Hungary, the German Democratic Republic, Poland, and the Soviet Union, we address ourselves to you with this letter, prompted by a feeling of sincere friendship based on the principles of Marxism-Leninism and proletarian internationalism and by the concern of our common affairs for strengthening the positions of socialism and the security of the socialist community of nations.

The development of events in your country evokes in us deep anxiety. It is our firm conviction that the offensive of the reactionary forces, backed by imperialists, against your Party and the foundations of the social system in the Czechoslovak Socialist Republic, threatens to push your country off the road of socialism and that consequently it jeopardizes the interests of the entire socialist system. . . .

We neither had nor have any intention of interfering in such affairs as are strictly the internal business of your Party and your state, nor of violating the principles of respect, independence, and equality in the relations among the Communist Parties and socialist countries. . . .

At the same time we cannot agree to have hostile forces push your country from the road of socialism and create a threat of severing Czechoslovakia from the socialist community. . . . This is the common cause of our countries, which have joined in the Warsaw Treaty to ensure independence, peace, and security in Europe, and to set up an insurmountable barrier against the intrigues of the imperialist forces, against aggression and revenge. . . . We shall never agree to have imperialism, using peaceful or non-peaceful methods, making a gap from the inside or from the outside in the socialist system, and changing in imperialism's favor the correlation of forces in Europe. . . .

That is why we believe that a decisive rebuff of the anti-communist forces, and decisive efforts for the preservation of the socialist system in Czechoslovakia are not only your task but ours as well. . . .

We express the conviction that the Communist Party of Czechoslovakia, conscious of its responsibility, will take the necessary steps to block the path of reaction. In this struggle you can count on the solidarity and all-round assistance of the fraternal socialist countries.

Warsaw, July 15, 1968

---

dictatorship. Honecker ruled unchallenged for the next eighteen years.

 CULTURE AND SOCIETY IN THE SOVIET BLOC

In his occasional musings about the future communist utopia, Karl Marx had predicted that a new, classless society would replace the exploitative and hierarchical systems of feudalism and capitalism. In their free time, workers would produce a new, advanced culture, proletarian in character and egalitarian in content.

The reality in the post–World War II Soviet Union and Eastern Europe was somewhat different. Under Stalin, a series of government decrees made all forms of literary and scientific expression dependent on the state. All Soviet culture was expected to follow the party line. Historians, philosophers, and social scientists all grew accustomed to quoting Marx, Lenin, and, above all, Stalin as their chief authorities. Novels and plays, too, were supposed to portray communist heroes and their efforts to create a better society. No criticism of existing social conditions was permitted. Some areas of intellectual activity were virtually abolished; the science of genetics disappeared, and few movies were made during Stalin's final years.

Stalin's death brought a modest respite from cultural repression. Writers and artists banned during the Stalin years were again allowed to publish. Still, Soviet authorities, including Khrushchev, were reluctant to allow cultural freedom to move far beyond official Soviet ideology.

These restrictions, however, did not prevent the emergence of some significant Soviet literature, although authors paid a heavy price if they alienated the Soviet authorities. Boris Pasternak (1890–1960), who began his literary career as a poet, won the Nobel Prize in 1958 for his celebrated novel *Doctor Zhivago*, written between 1945 and 1956 and published in Italy in 1957. But the Soviet government condemned Pasternak's anti-Soviet tendencies, banned the novel, and would not allow him to accept the prize. The author had alienated the authorities by describing a society scarred by the excesses of Bolshevik revolutionary zeal.

Alexander Solzhenitsyn (b. 1918) created an even greater furor than Pasternak. Solzhenitsyn had spent eight years in forced labor camps for criticizing Stalin, and his *One Day in the Life of Ivan Denisovich,* which won him the Nobel Prize in 1970, was an account of life in those camps. Khrushchev allowed the book's publication as part of his destalinization campaign. Solzhenitsyn then wrote *The Gulag Archipelago,* a detailed indictment of the whole system of Soviet oppression. Soviet authorities expelled Solzhenitsyn from the Soviet Union in 1973.

In the Eastern European satellites, cultural freedom varied considerably from country to country. In Poland, intellectuals had access to Western publications as well as greater freedom to travel to the West. Hungarian and Yugoslav Communists, too, tolerated a certain level of intellectual activity that was not liked but at least not prohibited. Elsewhere intellectuals were forced to conform to the regime's demands. After the Soviet invasion of Czechoslovakia in 1968, Czech Communists pursued a policy of strict cultural control.

According to Marxist doctrine, state control of industry and the elimination of private property were supposed to lead to a classless society. Although that ideal was never achieved, it did have important social consequences. The desire to create a classless society, for example, led to noticeable changes in education. In some countries, laws mandated quota systems based on class. Education became crucial in preparing for new jobs in the communist system and led to higher enrollments in both secondary schools and universities.

Still, the new managers of society, regardless of class background, realized the importance of higher education and used their power to gain special privileges for their children. By 1971, 60 percent of the children of white-collar workers attended university, and even though blue-collar families constituted 60 percent of the population, only 36 percent of their children attended institutions of higher learning.

Ideals of equality did not include women. Men dominated the leadership positions of the communist parties. Women did have greater opportunities in the workforce and even in the professions, however. In the Soviet Union, women comprised 51 percent of the labor force in 1980; by the mid-1980s, they constituted 50 percent of the engineers, 80 percent of the doctors, and 75 percent of the teachers and teachers' aides. But many of these were low-paying jobs; most female doctors, for example, worked in primary care and were paid less than skilled machinists. The chief administrators in hospitals and schools were still men.

Moreover, although women made up nearly half of the workforce, they were never freed of their traditional roles in the home. Most women confronted what came to be known as the "double shift." After working eight hours in their jobs, they came home to face the housework and care of the children. They might spend two hours a day in long lines at a number of stores waiting to buy food and clothes. Because of the housing situation, they were forced to use kitchens that were shared by a number of families.

Nearly three-quarters of a century after the Bolshevik Revolution, then, the Marxist dream of an advanced, egalitarian society was as far away as ever. Although in some respects, conditions in the socialist camp were a distinct improvement over those before World War II, many problems and inequities were as intransigent as ever.

⇒ **STALINIST HEROIC: AN EXAMPLE OF SOCIALIST REALISM.** Under Stalin and his successors, art was assigned the task of indoctrinating the Soviet population on the public virtues, such as hard work, loyalty to the state, and patriotism. Grandiose statuary erected to commemorate the heroic efforts of the Red Army during World War II appeared in every Soviet city. Here is an example in Minsk, today the capital of Belarus. The current president of Belarus, Alexander Lukashenko, still proclaims his allegiance to the principles of communism.

Courtesy of William J. Duiker

THE DISINTEGRATION OF THE SOVIET EMPIRE

On the death of Konstantin Chernenko in 1985, party leaders selected the talented and vigorous Soviet official Mikhail Gorbachev to succeed him. The new Soviet leader had shown early signs of promise. Born into a peasant family in 1931, Gorbachev combined farmwork with school and received the Order of the Red Banner for his agricultural efforts. This award and his good school record enabled him to study law at the University of Moscow. After receiving his law degree in 1955, he returned to his native southern Russia, where he eventually became first secretary of the Communist Party in the city of Stavropol. In 1978, he was made a member of the party's Central Committee in Moscow. Two years later, he became a full member of the ruling Politburo and secretary of the Central Committee.

During the early 1980s, Gorbachev began to realize the immensity of Soviet problems and the crucial need for massive reform to transform the system. During a visit to Canada in 1983, he discovered to his astonishment that Canadian farmers worked hard on their own initiative.

"We'll never have this for fifty years," he reportedly remarked.[2] On his return to Moscow, he set in motion a series of committees to evaluate the situation and recommend measures to improve the system.

The Gorbachev Era

With his election as party general secretary in 1985, Gorbachev seemed intent on taking earlier reforms to their logical conclusions. The cornerstone of his program was *perestroika*, or "restructuring." At first, it meant only a reordering of economic policy, as Gorbachev called for the beginning of a market economy with limited free enterprise and some private property. But Gorbachev soon perceived that in the Soviet system, the economic sphere was intimately tied to the social and political spheres. Any efforts to reform the economy without political or social reform would be doomed to failure. One of the most important instruments of *perestroika* was *glasnost*, or "openness." Soviet citizens and officials were encouraged to discuss openly the strengths and weaknesses of the Soviet Union. The arts also benefited from the new policy as previously banned works were now published and motion pictures were allowed to depict negative aspects of Soviet life. Music based on Western styles, such as jazz and rock, could now be performed openly.

Political reforms were equally revolutionary. In June 1987, the principle of two-candidate elections was introduced; previously, voters had been presented with only one candidate. At the Communist Party conference in 1988, Gorbachev called for the creation of a new Soviet parliament, the Congress of People's Deputies, whose members were to be chosen in competitive elections. It convened in 1989, the first such meeting in the nation since 1918. Early in 1990, Gorbachev legalized the formation of other political parties and struck out Article 6 of the Soviet Constitution, which guaranteed the "leading role" of the Communist Party. Hitherto, the position of first secretary of the party was the most important post in the Soviet Union, but as the Communist Party became less closely associated with the state, the powers of this office diminished. Gorbachev attempted to consolidate his power by creating a new state presidency and in March 1990 became the Soviet Union's first president.

One of Gorbachev's most serious problems stemmed from the character of the Soviet Union. The Union of Soviet Socialist Republics was a truly multiethnic country, containing 92 nationalities and 112 recognized languages. Previously the iron hand of the Communist Party, centered in Moscow, had kept a lid on the centuries-old ethnic tensions that had periodically erupted throughout the history of this region. As Gorbachev released this iron grip, ethnic groups throughout the Soviet Union began to call for sovereignty of the republics and independence from Russian-based rule centered in Moscow. Such movements sprang up first in Georgia in late 1988

 AN AFGHAN WAR MEMORIAL. Moscow's failed war in Afghanistan in the 1980s cost the lives of an estimated 27,000 Soviet soldiers. Reportedly, at least half the troops lost in the war came from Belarus, once a Soviet republic and now an independent state under a dictatorial regime. A war memorial to commemorate those who died in the war was recently built in Minsk, the capital of Belarus. The bridegroom in this wedding party is from Syria, which accentuates the multiethnic composition of contemporary Eastern Europe.

and then in Latvia, Estonia, Moldavia, Uzbekistan, Azerbaijan, and Lithuania.

In December 1989, the Communist Party of Lithuania declared itself independent of the Communist Party of the Soviet Union. Despite pleas from Gorbachev, who supported self-determination but not secession, other Soviet republics eventually followed suit. Ukraine voted for independence on December 1, 1991. A week later, the leaders of Russia, Ukraine, and Belarus announced that the Soviet Union had "ceased to exist" and would be replaced by a "commonwealth of independent states." Gorbachev resigned on December 25, 1991, and turned over his responsibilities as commander in chief to Boris Yeltsin (b. 1931), the president of Russia. By the end of 1991, one of the largest empires in world history had come to an end, and a new era had begun in its lands (see Map 26.2).

Courtesy of William J. Duiker

The New Russia: From Empire to Nation

Yeltsin, a onetime engineer from Sverdlovsk who had been dismissed from the Politburo in 1987 for radicalism, was committed to introducing a free market economy as quickly as possible. But former Communist Party members and their allies in the Congress of People's Deputies were opposed to many of Yeltsin's economic reforms and tried to place new limits on his powers. Yeltsin fought back. After winning a vote of confidence on April 25, 1993, Yeltsin pushed ahead with plans for a new Russian constitution that would abolish the Congress of People's Deputies, create a two-chamber parliament, and establish a strong presidency.

A hard-line parliamentary minority resisted and even took the offensive, urging supporters to take over government offices and the central television station. On October 4, Yeltsin responded by ordering military forces to storm the parliament building and arrest hard-line opponents. Yeltsin then used his victory to consolidate his power.

During the mid-1990s, Yeltsin was able to maintain a precarious grip on power while seeking to implement reforms that would place Russia on a firm course toward a pluralistic political system and a market economy. But the new postcommunist Russia remained as fragile as ever. Burgeoning economic inequality and rampant corruption aroused widespread criticism and shook the confidence of the Russian people in the superiority of the capitalist system over the one that existed under communist rule. A nagging war in the Caucasus—where the people of Chechnya have resolutely sought national independence from Russia—drained the government budget and exposed the decrepit state of the once vaunted Red Army. In presidential elections held in 1996, Yeltsin was reelected, but the rising popularity of a revived Communist Party and the growing strength of nationalist elements, combined with Yeltsin's precarious health, raised serious questions about the future of the country.

At the end of 1999, Yeltsin suddenly resigned his office and was replaced by Vladimir Putin, a former member of the KGB. Putin vowed to bring an end to the rampant corruption and inexperience that permeated Russian political culture and to strengthen the role of the central government in managing the affairs of state.

He also sought to bring the breakaway state of Chechnya back under Russian authority and to assume a more assertive role in international affairs. The new president took advantage of growing public anger at Western plans to expand the NATO alliance into Eastern Europe, as well as aggressive actions by NATO countries against Serbia in the Balkans (see Chapter 27), to restore Russia's position as an influential force in the world. To assuage national pride, he entered negotiations with such former republics of the old Soviet Union as Belarus and Ukraine to tighten forms of mutual political and economic cooperation.

What had happened to derail Yeltsin's plan to transform Soviet society? To some critics, Yeltsin tried to achieve too much too fast. Between 1991 and 1995, state firms that had previously provided about 80 percent of all industrial production and employment had been privatized, while the price of goods (previously subject to government regulation) was opened up to market forces. There were other problems as well. With the harsh official and ideological constraints of the Soviet system suddenly removed, corruption became rampant, and the government often appeared inept in coping with the complexities of a market economy. Few Russians seemed to grasp the realities of modern capitalism and understandably reacted to the inevitable transition pains from the old system by placing all the blame at the foot of the new one. The fact is, Yeltsin had attempted to change the structure of the Soviet system without due regard to the necessity of changing the mentality of the people as well.

Eastern Europe: From Satellites to Sovereign Nations

The disintegration of the Soviet Union had an immediate impact on its neighbors to the west. First to respond, as in 1956, was Poland, where popular protests at high food prices had erupted in the early 1980s, leading to the rise of an independent labor movement called Solidarity. Led by Lech Walesa (b. 1943), Solidarity rapidly became an influential force for change and a threat to the government's monopoly of power. In 1988, the communist government bowed to the inevitable and permitted free national elections to take place, resulting in the election of Walesa as president of Poland in December 1990. When Moscow

Chronology

THE SOVIET BLOC AND ITS DEMISE

Death of Joseph Stalin	1953
Rise of Nikita Khrushchev	1955
Destalinization speech	1956
Removal of Khrushchev	1964
The Brezhnev era	1964–1982
Rule of Andropov and Chernenko	1982–1985
Gorbachev comes to power in Soviet Union	1985
Collapse of communist governments in Eastern Europe	1989
Disintegration of Soviet Union	1991
Presidency of Boris Yeltsin in Russia	1991–1999
Vladimir Putin elected president of Russia	2000

MAP 26.2 Eastern Europe and the Former Soviet Union. After the disintegration of the Soviet Union in 1991, several onetime Soviet republics declared their independence. This map shows the new configuration of the states that emerged in the 1990s, including the boundaries after the dissolution of Czechoslovakia and Yugoslavia.
➤ *What new nations have appeared since the end of the Cold War?*

took no action to reverse the verdict in Warsaw, Poland entered the postcommunist era.

In Hungary, as in Poland, the process of transition had begun many years previously. After crushing the Hungarian revolution of 1956, the communist government of János Kádár had tried to assuage popular opinion by enacting a series of far-reaching economic reforms (labeled "communism with a capitalist face-lift"). But as the 1980s progressed, the economy sagged, and in 1989, the regime permitted the formation of opposition political parties, leading eventually to the formation of a noncommunist coalition government in elections held in March 1990.

The transition in Czechoslovakia was more abrupt. After Soviet troops crushed the Prague Spring in 1968, hard-line Communists under Gustav Husak followed a policy of massive repression to maintain their power. In 1977, dissident intellectuals formed an organization called Charter 77 as a vehicle for protest against violations of human rights. Dissident activities increased during the

1980s, and when massive demonstrations broke out in several major cities in 1989, President Husak's government, lacking any real popular support, collapsed. At the end of December, he was replaced by Václav Havel, a dissident playwright who had been a leading figure in Charter 77.

But the most dramatic events took place in East Germany, where a persistent economic slump and the ongoing oppressiveness of the regime of Erich Honecker led to a flight of refugees and mass demonstrations against the regime in the summer and fall of 1989. Capitulating to popular pressure, the communist government opened its entire border with the West. The Berlin Wall, the most tangible symbol of the Cold War, became the site of a massive celebration, and most of it was dismantled by joyful Germans from both sides of the border. In March 1990, free elections led to the formation of a noncommunist government that rapidly carried out a program of political and economic reunification with West Germany (see Chapter 27).

THE EAST IS RED: CHINA UNDER COMMUNISM

In the fall of 1949, China was at peace for the first time in twelve years. The newly victorious Communist Party, under the leadership of its chairman, Mao Zedong, turned its attention to consolidating its power base and healing the wounds of war. Its long-term goal was to construct a socialist society, but its leaders realized that popular support for the revolution was based on the party's platform of honest government, land reform, social justice, and peace rather than on the utopian goal of a classless society. Accordingly, the new regime adopted a moderate program of political and economic recovery known as New Democracy.

New Democracy

With New Democracy—patterned roughly after Lenin's New Economic Policy in Soviet Russia in the 1920s (see Chapter 22)—the new Chinese leadership tacitly recognized that time and extensive indoctrination would be needed to convince the Chinese people of the superiority of socialism. In the meantime, the party would rely on capitalist profit incentives to spur productivity. Manufacturing and commercial firms were permitted to remain under private ownership, although with stringent government regulations. To win the support of the poorer peasants, who made up the majority of the population, a land redistribution program was adopted, but the collectivization of agriculture was postponed (see the box on p. 580).

In a number of key respects, New Democracy was a success. About two-thirds of the peasant households in the country received land and thus had reason to be grateful to the new regime. Spurred by official tolerance for capitalist activities and the end of internal conflict, the national economy began to rebound, although agricultural production still lagged behind both official targets and the growing population, which was increasing at an annual rate of more than 2 percent.

The Transition to Socialism

In 1953, party leaders launched the nation's first five-year plan (patterned after similar Soviet plans), which called for substantial increases in industrial output. Lenin had believed that mechanization would induce Russian peasants to join collective farms, which, because of their greater size and efficiency, could better afford to purchase expensive farm machinery. But the difficulty of providing tractors and reapers for millions of rural villages eventually convinced Mao that it would take years, if not decades, for China's infant industrial base to meet the needs of a modernizing agricultural sector. He therefore decided to begin collectivization immediately, in the hope that collective farms would increase food production and release land, labor, and capital for the industrial sector. Accordingly, beginning in 1955, virtually all private farmland was collectivized (although peasant families were allowed to retain small private plots), and most businesses and industries were nationalized.

Collectivization was achieved without provoking the massive peasant unrest that had taken place in the Soviet Union during the 1930s, but the hoped-for production increases did not materialize; in 1958, at Mao's insistent urging, party leaders approved a more radical program known as the Great Leap Forward. Existing rural collectives, normally the size of a traditional village, were combined into vast "people's communes," each containing more than thirty thousand people. These communes were to be responsible for all administrative and economic tasks at the local level. The party's official slogan promised "Hard work for a few years, happiness for a thousand."[3]

The communes were a disaster. Administrative bottlenecks, bad weather, and peasant resistance to the new system (which, among other things, attempted to eliminate work incentives and destroy the traditional family as the basic unit of Chinese society) combined to drive food production downward, and over the next few years, as many as fifteen million people may have died of starvation. In 1960, the experiment was essentially abandoned. Although the commune structure was retained, ownership and management were returned to the collective level. Mao was severely criticized by some of his more pragmatic colleagues.

The Great Proletarian Cultural Revolution

But Mao was not yet ready to abandon either his power or his dream of a totally egalitarian society. In 1966, he returned to the attack, mobilizing discontented youth and disgruntled party members into revolutionary units known as Red Guards, who were urged to take to the streets to cleanse Chinese society—from local schools and factories to government ministries in Beijing—of impure elements who (in Mao's mind, at least) were guilty of "taking the capitalist road." Supported by his wife, Jiang Qing, and other radical party figures, Mao launched China on a new forced march toward communism.

The so-called Great Proletarian Cultural Revolution lasted for ten years, from 1966 to 1976. Some Western observers interpreted it as a simple power struggle between Mao Zedong and some of his key rivals such as Liu Shaoqi (Liu Shao-ch'i), Mao's designated successor, and Deng Xiaoping (Teng Hsiao-p'ing), the party's general secretary. Both were removed from their positions, and Liu later died, allegedly of torture, in a Chinese prison. But real policy disagreements were involved. Mao and his supporters feared that capitalist values and the remnants of "feudalist" Confucian ideas would undermine ideological fervor and betray the revolutionary cause. He was convinced that only an atmosphere of "uninterrupted revolution" could

LAND REFORM IN ACTION

One of the great achievements of the new communist regime in China was the land reform program, which resulted in the distribution of farmland to almost two-thirds of the rural population. The program consequently won the gratitude of millions of Chinese. But it also had a dark side as local land reform tribunals routinely convicted "wicked landlords" of crimes against the people and then put them to death. The following passage, written by a foreign observer, describes the process in one village.

REVOLUTION IN A CHINESE VILLAGE

T'ien-ming [a Party cadre] called all the active young cadres and the militiamen of Long Bow [village] together and announced to them the policy of the county government, which was to confront all enemy collaborators and their backers at public meetings, expose their crimes, and turn them over to the county authorities for punishment. He proposed that they start with Kuo Te-yu, the puppet village head. Having moved the group to anger with a description of Te-yu's crimes, T'ien-ming reviewed the painful life led by the poor peasants during the occupation and recalled how hard they had all worked and how as soon as they harvested all the grain the puppet officials, backed by army bayonets, took what they wanted, turned over huge quantities to the Japanese devils, forced the peasants to haul it away, and flogged those who refused.

As the silent crowd contracted toward the spot where the accused man stood, T'ien-ming stepped forward. . . . "This is our chance. Remember how we were oppressed. The traitors seized our property. They beat us and kicked us. . . .

"Let us speak out the bitter memories. Let us see that the blood debt is repaid. . . ."

He paused for a moment. The peasants were listening to every word but gave no sign as to how they felt. . . .

"Come now, who has evidence against this man?"

Again there was silence.

Kuei-ts'ai, the new vice-chairman of the village, found it intolerable. He jumped up [and] struck Kuo Te-yu on the jaw with the back of his hand. "Tell the meeting how much you stole," he demanded.

The blow jarred the ragged crowd. It was as if an electric spark had tensed every muscle. Not in living memory had any peasant ever struck an official. . . .

The people in the square waited fascinated as if watching a play. They did not realize that in order for the plot to unfold they themselves had to mount the stage and speak out what was on their minds.

That evening T'ien-ming and Kuei-ts'ai called together the small groups of poor peasants from various parts of the village and sought to learn what it was that was really holding them back. *They soon found the root of the trouble was fear* of the old established political forces, and their military backers. The old reluctance to move against the power of the gentry, the fear of ultimate defeat and terrible reprisal that had been seared into the consciousness of so many generations, lay like a cloud over the peasants' minds and hearts.

Emboldened by T'ien-ming's words, other peasants began to speak out. They recalled what Te-yu had done to them personally. Several vowed to speak up and accuse him the next morning. After the meeting broke up, the passage of time worked its own leaven. In many a hovel and tumbledown house talk continued well past midnight. Some people were so excited they did not sleep at all. . . .

On the following day the meeting was livelier by far. It began with a sharp argument as to who would make the first accusation, and T'ien-ming found it difficult to keep order. Before Te-yu had a chance to reply to any questions, a crowd of young men, among whom were several militiamen, surged forward ready to beat him.

---

enable the Chinese to overcome the lethargy of the past and achieve the final stage of utopian communism.

Mao's opponents argued for a more pragmatic strategy that gave priority to nation building over the ultimate communist goal of spiritual transformation. (Deng Xiaoping reportedly once remarked, "Black cat, white cat, what does it matter so long as it catches the mice?"). But with Mao's supporters now in power, the party carried out vast economic and educational reforms that virtually eliminated any remaining profit incentives, established a new school system that emphasized "Mao Zedong thought," and stressed practical education at the elementary level at the expense of specialized training in science and the humanities in the universities. School learning was discouraged as a legacy of capitalism, and Mao's famous Little Red Book (officially, *Quotations of Chairman Mao Zedong*, a slim volume of Maoist aphorisms to encourage good

behavior and revolutionary zeal) was hailed as the most important source of knowledge in all areas.

The radicals' efforts to destroy all vestiges of traditional society were reminiscent of the Reign of Terror in revolutionary France, when the Jacobins sought to destroy organized religion and even created a new revolutionary calendar. Red Guards rampaged through the country, attempting to eradicate the "four olds" (old thought, old culture, old customs, and old habits). They destroyed temples and religious sculptures; they tore down street signs and replaced them with new ones carrying revolutionary names. At one point, the city of Shanghai even ordered that the significance of colors in stoplights be changed so that red (the revolutionary color) would indicate that traffic could move.

But a mood of revolutionary ferment and enthusiasm is difficult to sustain. Key groups, including bureaucrats, urban professionals, and many military officers, did not share Mao's belief in the benefits of "uninterrupted revolution" and constant turmoil. Inevitably, the sense of anarchy and uncertainty caused popular support for the movement to erode, and when the end came in 1976, the vast majority of the population may well have welcomed its demise.

From Mao to Deng

Mao Zedong died in September 1976 at the age of eighty-three. After a short but bitter succession struggle, the pragmatists led by Deng Xiaoping seized power from the radicals and formally brought the Cultural Revolution to an end. The egalitarian policies of the previous decade were reversed, and a new program emphasizing economic modernization was introduced.

Under the leadership of Deng Xiaoping, who placed his supporters in key positions throughout the party and the government, attention focused on what were called the "Four Modernizations": industry, agriculture, technology, and national defense. Many of the restrictions against private activities and profit incentives were eliminated, and

⇒ **HAIL THE GREAT HELMSMAN!** During the Great Proletarian Cultural Revolution, Chinese art was restricted to topics that promoted revolution and the thoughts of Chairman Mao Zedong. All the knowledge that the true revolutionary required was to be found in Mao's Little Red Book, a collection of his sayings on proper revolutionary behavior. In this painting, Chairman Mao stands among his admirers, who wave copies of the book as a symbol of their total devotion to him and his vision of a future China.

people were encouraged to work hard to benefit themselves and Chinese society. The familiar slogan "Serve the people" was replaced by a new one repugnant to the tenets of Mao Zedong thought: "Create wealth for the people."

By adopting this pragmatic approach in the years after 1976, China made great strides in ending its chronic problems of poverty and underdevelopment. Per capita income roughly doubled during the 1980s; housing, education, and sanitation improved; and both agricultural and industrial output skyrocketed.

But critics, both Chinese and foreign, complained that Deng Xiaoping's program had failed to achieve a "fifth modernization": democracy. In the late 1970s, ordinary citizens pasted "big character posters" criticizing the abuses of the past on the so-called Democracy Wall near Tiananmen Square in downtown Beijing. Yet it soon became clear that the new leaders would not tolerate any direct criticism of the Communist Party or of Marxist-Leninist ideology. Dissidents were suppressed, and some were sentenced to long prison terms.

Incident at Tiananmen Square

As long as economic conditions for the majority of Chinese were improving, the government was able to isolate dissidents from other elements in society. But in the late 1980s, an overheated economy led to rising inflation and growing discontent among salaried workers, especially in the cities. At the same time, corruption, nepotism, and favored treatment for senior officials and party members were provoking increasing criticism. In May 1989, student protesters carried placards demanding "Science and Democracy," an end to official corruption, and the resignation of China's aging party leadership. These demands received widespread support from the urban population (although notably less in rural areas) and led to massive demonstrations in Tiananmen Square.

Deng Xiaoping and other aging party leaders turned to the army to protect their base of power and suppress what they described as "counterrevolutionary elements." Deng was undoubtedly counting on the fact that many Chinese, particularly in rural areas, feared a recurrence of the disorder of the Cultural Revolution and craved economic prosperity more than political reform. In the months following the confrontation, the government issued new regulations requiring courses on Marxist-Leninist ideology in the schools, suppressed dissidents within the intellectual community, and made it clear that while economic reforms would continue, the CCP's monopoly of power would not be allowed to decay. Harsh punishments were imposed on those accused of undermining the communist system and supporting its enemies abroad.

A New Era?

In the 1990s, the government began to nurture urban support by reducing the rate of inflation and guaranteeing the availability of consumer goods in great demand among the rising middle class. Under Deng Xiaoping's successor, Jiang

Zemin, who occupied the positions of both party chief and president of China, the government promoted rapid economic growth while cracking down harshly on political dissent. That policy paid dividends in bringing about a perceptible decline in alienation among the population in the cities. Industrial production continued to increase rapidly, leading to predictions that China would become one of the economic superpowers of the twenty-first century. But discontent in rural areas began to increase, as lagging farm income, high taxes, and official corruption sparked resentment in the countryside.

Whether the current leadership will be able to prevent further erosion of the party's power and prestige is unclear. In the short term, such efforts may succeed in slowing the process of change because many Chinese are understandably fearful of punishment and concerned for their careers. And high economic growth rates can sometimes cover a multitude of problems as many will opt to chase the fruits of materialism rather than the less tangible benefits of individual freedom. But in the long run, the party leadership must resolve the contradiction between political authoritarianism and economic prosperity.

There is also growing unrest among China's national minorities: in Xinjiang (see Map 26.3), where restless Muslim peoples observe with curiosity the emergence of independent Islamic states in Central Asia, and in Tibet, where the official policy of quelling separatism has led to the violent suppression of Tibetan culture and an influx of thousands of ethnic Chinese immigrants.

"SERVE THE PEOPLE": CHINESE SOCIETY AND CULTURE UNDER COMMUNISM

Enormous changes have taken place in Chinese society since the end of the Cultural Revolution. Yet beneath the surface are hints of the survival of elements of the old China. Despite all the efforts of Mao Zedong and his colleagues, China under communism remains a society that in many respects is in thrall to its past.

Economics in Command

Deng Xiaoping recognized the need to restore credibility to a system on the verge of breakdown and hoped that rapid economic growth would satisfy the Chinese people and prevent them from demanding political reforms. China's new leaders clearly placed economic performance over ideological purity. To stimulate the stagnant industrial sector, which had been under state control since the end of the New Democracy era, they reduced bureaucratic controls over state industries and allowed local managers to have more say over prices, salaries, and quality control. Productivity was encouraged by permitting bonuses for extra effort, a policy that had been discouraged during the Cultural Revolution. The regime also tolerated the emer-

Student Rebellions in France and China

University students played an important role in revolutionary upheavals in the late 1960s in France and in the late 1980s in Eastern Europe and China. The discontent of university students in France exploded in the late 1960s in a series of student revolts. At the left is a scene from a student revolt in 1968. The photograph shows the barricades that students erected by overturning cars on a Parisian street on the morning of May 11 during the height of the revolt. The demonstrations that erupted in Tiananmen Square in the spring of 1989 spread rapidly to other parts of China. Seen at the right is a group of students from a high school who are marching to the city of Guilin to display their own determination to take part in the reform of Chinese society.

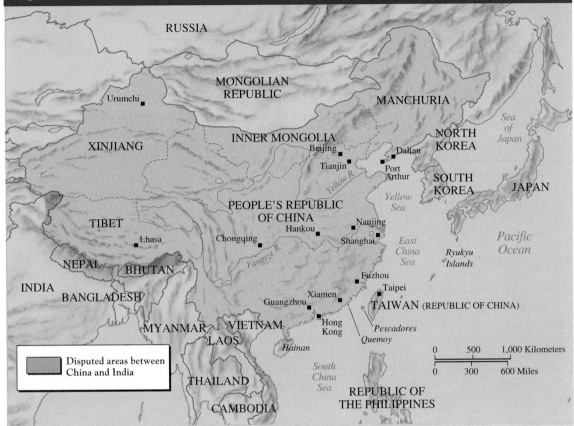

MAP 26.3 The People's Republic of China. This map shows China's current boundaries. Major regions are indicated in capital letters. Areas in dispute are shown by darker shading. ➤ *In which regions are there movements against Chinese rule?*

gence of a small private sector. Unemployed youth were encouraged to set up restaurants, bicycle or radio repair shops, and handicraft shops on their own initiative.

Finally, the regime opened up the country to foreign investment and technology. The Maoist policy of self-reliance was abandoned, and China openly sought the advice of foreign experts and the money of foreign capitalists. Special economic zones were established in urban centers near the coast, where lucrative concessions were offered to encourage foreign firms to build factories. The tourist industry was encouraged, and students were sent abroad to study.

The new leaders especially stressed educational reform. The system adopted during the Cultural Revolution, emphasizing practical education and ideology at the expense of higher education and modern science, was rapidly abandoned, and a new system based generally on the Western model was instituted. Admission to higher education was based on success in merit examinations, and courses on science and mathematics received high priority.

No economic reform program could succeed unless it included the countryside. Three decades of socialism had done little to increase food production or to lay the basis for a modern agricultural sector. China, with a population now numbering one billion, could still barely feed itself.

Peasants had little incentive to work and few opportunities to increase production through mechanization, the use of fertilizer, or better irrigation.

Under Deng Xiaoping, agricultural policy made a rapid about-face. Under the new "rural responsibility system," collectives leased land to peasant families, who paid a quota in the form of rent to the collective. Anything produced on the land above that payment could be sold on the private market or consumed. To soak up excess labor in the villages, the government encouraged the formation of so-called sideline industries, a modern equivalent of the traditional cottage industries in premodern China. Peasants raised fish or shrimp, made consumer goods, and even assembled living room furniture and appliances for sale to their newly affluent compatriots. The reform program had a striking effect on rural production. Grain production increased rapidly, and farm income doubled during the 1980s.

The overall effects of the modernization program were impressive. The standard of living improved for the majority of the population. Whereas a decade earlier, the average Chinese had struggled to earn enough to buy a bicycle, radio, watch, or washing machine, by the late 1980s, many were beginning to purchase videocassette recorders, refrigerators,

Chronology

CHINA UNDER COMMUNIST RULE

New Democracy	1949–1955
Era of collectivization	1955–1958
Great Leap Forward	1958–1960
Great Proletarian Cultural Revolution	1966–1976
Death of Mao Zedong	1976
Era of Deng Xiaoping	1978–1997
Tiananmen Square incident	1989
Jiang Zemin appointed president of China	1993

and color television sets. Yet the rapid growth of the economy created its own problems: inflationary pressures, greed, envy, increased corruption, and—most dangerous of all for the regime—rising expectations. Young people in particular resented restrictions on employment and opportunities to study abroad. Disillusionment ran high, especially in the cities, where lavish living by officials and rising prices for goods aroused widespread alienation and cynicism.

During the 1990s, growth rates in the industrial sector continued to be high as domestic capital became increasingly available to compete with the growing presence of foreign enterprises. The government finally recognized the need to close down inefficient state enterprises, and by the end of the decade, the private sector, with official encouragement, accounted for over 10 percent of the gross domestic product. A stock market opened, and China's prowess in the international marketplace improved dramatically.

As a result of these developments, China now possesses a large and increasingly affluent middle class. The domestic market for consumer goods has burgeoned in recent years, as indicated by the fact that over 80 percent of all urban Chinese possess a color TV, a refrigerator, and a washing machine. One-third own their own homes, and nearly as many have an air conditioner.

But rapid economic change never comes without cost. The closing of state-run factories has led to the dismissal of millions of workers each year, and the private sector, although growing at over 20 percent annually, is unable to absorb them all. Discontent has been growing in the countryside as well, where a grain surplus has cut into farm incomes. Millions of rural Chinese have left for the big cities, where many of them are unable to find steady employment and are forced to live in squalid conditions in crowded tenements or in the sprawling suburbs.

Another factor hindering China's rush to economic advancement is the impact on the environment. With the rising population, fertile land is in increasingly short supply (China, with twice the population, now has only

➤ **NANJING ROAD: A CONSUMER'S PARADISE.** Shanghai has exploded into China's most affluent city, its forest of shimmering skyscrapers testifying to the phenomenal expansion of the Chinese economy in recent years. Nanjing Road, seen here, is one long avenue of towering banks, office buildings, hotels, and luxurious department stores. Along with these competing Chinese commercial signs, the ubiquitous American enterprises, such as Kentucky Fried Chicken, Pepsi-Cola, and McDonald's, vie for the attention of the fashionably dressed Shanghainese as they shop for the latest styles.

Courtesy of William J. Duiker

two-thirds as much irrigable land as it had in 1950). Soil erosion is a major problem, especially in the north, where the desert is encroaching on farmlands. Water is also a problem. A massive dam project now under way in the Yangtze River valley has sparked protests from environmentalists, as well as from local peoples forced to migrate from the area. The rate of air pollution is ten times the level in the United States, contributing to growing health concerns.

Social Changes

At the root of Marxist-Leninist ideology is the idea of building a new citizen free from the prejudices, ignorance, and superstition of the "feudal" era and the capitalist desire for self-gratification. This new citizen would be characterized not only by a sense of racial and sexual equality but also by the selfless desire to contribute his or her utmost for the good of all.

The new government wasted no time in taking steps to bring a definitive end to the old system in China. Women were permitted to vote and encouraged to become active in the political process. At the local level, an increasing number of women became active in the CCP and in collective organizations. In 1950, a new marriage law guaranteed women equal rights with men. Most important, perhaps, it permitted women for the first time to initiate divorce proceedings against their husbands. Within a year, nearly one million divorces had been granted.

The regime also undertook to destroy the influence of the traditional family system. To the Communists, loyalty to the family undercut loyalty to the state and to the dictatorship of the proletariat. The attack began during the Great Leap Forward, when children were encouraged to report to the authorities any comments by their parents that criticized the system. Such practices continued during the Cultural Revolution, when children were expected to tell on their parents, students on their teachers, and employees on their superiors.

The post-Mao era brought a decisive shift away from revolutionary utopianism and a return to the pragmatic approach to nation building. For most people, it meant improved living conditions and a qualified return to family traditions. For the first time, millions of Chinese saw the prospect of a house or an urban flat with a washing machine, television set, and indoor plumbing. Young people whose parents had given them patriotic names such as Build the Country, Protect Mao Zedong, and Assist Korea began to choose more elegant and cosmopolitan names for their own children.

The new attitudes were also reflected in physical appearance. For a generation after the civil war, clothing had been restricted to the traditional baggy "Mao suit" in olive drab or dark blue, but by the 1980s, young people craved such fashionable Western items as designer jeans, trendy sneakers, and sweat suits (or reasonable facsimiles). Cosmetic surgery to create a more buxom figure or a more Western facial look became increasingly common among affluent young women in the cities.

Religious practices and beliefs also changed. As the government became more tolerant, some Chinese began returning to the traditional Buddhist faith or to folk religions, and Buddhist and Taoist temples were once again crowded with worshipers. Despite official efforts to suppress its more evangelical forms, Christianity became increasingly popular; many viewed it as a symbol of success and cosmopolitanism.

As with all social changes, China's reintegration into the outside world has had consequences. Arranged marriages, nepotism, and mistreatment of females (for example, many parents in rural areas reportedly have killed female infants in the hope of having a son) have come back, although such behavior likely had survived under the cloak of revolutionary purity for a generation. Materialistic attitudes are highly prevalent among young people, along with a corresponding cynicism about politics and the CCP. Expensive weddings are now increasingly common, and bribery and favoritism are all too frequent. Crime of all types, including an apparently growing incidence of prostitution and sex crimes against women, appears to be on the rise. To discourage sexual abuse, the government now seeks to provide free legal services for women living in rural areas.

There is also a price to pay for the trend toward privatization. Under the Maoist system, the elderly and the sick were provided with retirement benefits and health care by the state or by the collective organizations. Under current conditions, with the latter no longer playing such a social role and more workers operating in the private sector, the safety net has been removed. The government recently attempted to fill the gap by enacting a social security law, but because of lack of funds, eligibility is limited primarily to individuals in the urban sector of the economy. Those living in the countryside—who still represent 60 percent of the population—are essentially left to their own devices.

China's Changing Culture

The rise to power of the Communists in 1949 added a new dimension to the debate over the future of culture in China. The new leaders rejected the Western attitude of "art for art's sake" and, like their Soviet counterparts, viewed culture as an important instrument of indoctrination. The standard would no longer be aesthetic quality or the personal preference of the artist but "art for life's sake," whereby culture would serve the interests of socialism.

At first, the new emphasis on socialist realism did not entirely extinguish the influence of traditional culture. Mao and his colleagues tolerated—and even encouraged—efforts by artists to synthesize traditional ideas with socialist concepts and Western techniques. During the Cultural Revolution, however, all forms of traditional culture came to be viewed as reactionary. Socialist realism became the only acceptable standard in literature, art, and music. All forms of traditional expression were forbidden.

Nowhere were the dilemmas of the new order more challenging than in literature. In the heady afterglow of

GLASS CEILING, CHINESE STYLE

Ding Ling was the most prominent woman writer in China during the twentieth century. Born in 1904, she joined the Chinese Communist Party during the early 1930s and settled in Yan'an, where she authored her most famous novel, The Sun Shines over the Sangan River, *which praised the land reform program. After the Communist victory in 1949, however, she was criticized for individualism and her outspoken views, and was sentenced to hard labor during the Cultural Revolution. She died in 1981. In this short story written in the 1940s, she voices her frustration through the experience of Lu Ping, who has been informed by the party that she must abandon her college career to become a nurse in a small rural hospital.*

DING LING, "IN THE HOSPITAL"

She argued, saying that she didn't have the right disposition for such work, and that she would do anything else, no matter how significant or insignificant. She even dropped a few tears, but these arguments weren't enough to shake the chief's determination. She couldn't overturn this decision, so she had no choice but to obey.

The party branch secretary came to talk to her and the section leader wouldn't leave the subject alone. Their tactics irritated her. She knew the rationale behind all this. They simply wanted her to cut herself off from the bright future which she had been dreaming of for the past year and to return to her old life again. She knew she could never become a great doctor and was nothing more than

an ordinary midwife. Whether she was there or not made no difference at all. She was full of illusions about her ability to break out of the confines of her life. But now that the iron collar of "party" and "needs of the party" was locked about her neck, could she disobey party orders? Could she ignore this iron collar which she had cast upon herself?

The realities of life frightened her. She wondered why many people had walked by her that night, yet not a single one of them had helped her. And she thought about the fact that the director of the hospital would endanger patients, doctors, and nurses just to save a little money. She looked back on her daily life. Of what use was it to the revolution? Since the revolution was for the whole of mankind, why were even the closest of comrades so devoid of love? She was wavering. She asked herself: "Is it that I am vacillating in my attitude toward the revolution?" The neurasthenia which she had had of old gripped her once again. Night after night she could not sleep.

People in the party branch were criticizing her. They capped her with labels like "petty-bourgeois consciousness," "audacious and liberal intellectualism," and many other dangerous doctrines; in short, they said that her party spirit was weak. The director of the hospital called her in for a talk.

Even patients were cool and distant toward her, saying she was a romantic. Yes, she should struggle! But whom should she struggle against? Against everyone?

---

the Communist victory, many progressive writers supported the new regime and enthusiastically embraced Mao's exhortation to create a new Chinese literature for the edification of the masses. But in the harsher climate of the 1960s, many writers were criticized by the party for their excessive individualism and admiration for Western culture. Such writers either toed the new line and suppressed their doubts or were jailed and silenced (see the box above).

After Mao's death, Chinese culture was finally released from the shackles of socialist realism. In painting, where for a decade, the only acceptable standard for excellence was praise for the party and its policies, the new permissiveness led to a revival of interest in both traditional and Western forms. Some painters imitated trends from abroad, experimenting with a wide range of previously prohibited art styles, including Cubism and abstract painting.

The limits of freedom of expression were most apparent in literature. During the early 1980s, party leaders encouraged Chinese writers to express their views on the mistakes of the past, and a new "literature of the wounded" began to describe the brutal and arbitrary character of the Cultural Revolution. One of the most prominent writers was Bai Hua, whose script for the film *Bitter Love* described

the life of a young Chinese painter who joined the revolutionary movement during the 1940s but was destroyed during the Cultural Revolution when his work was condemned as counterrevolutionary. Driven from his home for posting a portrait of a third-century B.C.E. defender of human freedom on a Beijing wall, the artist dies in a snowy field, where his corpse and a semicircle made by his footprints form a giant question mark.

In criticizing the excesses of the Cultural Revolution, Bai Hua was only responding to Deng Xiaoping's appeal for intellectuals to speak out, but he was soon criticized for failing to point out the essentially beneficial role of the CCP in recent Chinese history. His film was withdrawn from circulation in 1981. Bai Hua was compelled to recant his errors and to state that the great ideas of Mao Zedong on art and literature were "still of universal guiding significance today."[4]

As the attack on Bai Hua illustrates, many party leaders remained suspicious of the impact that "decadent" bourgeois culture could have on the socialist foundations of Chinese society. Conservatives were especially incensed by the tendency of many writers to dwell on the shortcomings of the socialist system and to come uncomfortably close to direct criticism of the role of the CCP.

CONCLUSION

For four decades after the end of World War II, the world's two superpowers competed for global hegemony. What began as a dispute on the future shape of Eastern Europe spread rapidly to Asia and ultimately penetrated virtually every part of the earth. The Cold War became the dominant feature on the international scene and determined the internal politics of many countries around the world as well.

By the early 1980s, some of the tension had gone out of the conflict as it appeared that both Moscow and Washington had learned to tolerate the other's existence. Skeptical minds even suspected that both countries drew benefits from their mutual rivalry and saw it as an advantage in carrying on their relations with friends and allies. Few suspected that the Cold War, which had long seemed a permanent feature of world politics, was about to come to an end.

What brought about the collapse of the Soviet Empire? Some observers argue that the ambitious defense policies adopted by the Reagan administration forced Moscow into an arms race it could not afford, which ultimately led to a collapse of the Soviet economy. Others suggest that Soviet problems were more deep-rooted and would have ended in the disintegration of the Soviet Union even without outside stimulation. Both arguments have some validity, but the latter is surely closer to the mark.

Why has communism survived in China, albeit in a substantially altered form, when it failed in Eastern Europe and the Soviet Union? One of the primary factors is probably cultural. Although Marxism originated in Europe, many of its main precepts, such as the primacy of the community over the individual and the denial of the concept of private property, run counter to trends in Western civilization. By contrast, Marxism found a more receptive climate in China and other countries in the region influenced by Confucian tradition. In its political culture, the communist system exhibits many of the same characteristics as traditional Confucianism—a single truth, an elite governing class, and an emphasis on obedience to the community and its governing representatives. On the surface, China today bears a number of uncanny similarities to the China of the past.

Whether or not communism survives in China—or revives in some form in the lands of the former Soviet Union—the Cold War is not likely to return in its old form, and for that we can be thankful, because it not only kept the earth on the knife edge of a great power conflict but also distracted world leaders from turning their attention to the deeper problems that afflict all of humankind. Still, it is now clear that the end of the Cold War was not necessarily a harbinger of a new era of peace and prosperity. To the contrary, it has opened a new stage of history that will be marked by increased global instability and severe challenges in the areas of environmental pollution, technological change, and population growth. These issues will be addressed in more detail in our final chapters.

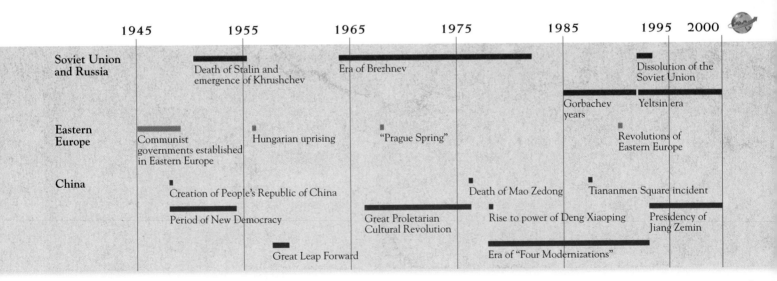

CHAPTER NOTES

1. Vladislav Zubok and Constantin Pleshakov, *Inside the Kremlin's Cold War: From Stalin to Khrushchev* (Cambridge, Mass., 1996), p. 166.
2. Hedrick Smith, *The New Russians* (New York, 1990), p. 74.
3. Quoted in Stanley Karnow, *Mao and China: Inside China's Cultural Revolution* (New York, 1972), p. 95.
4. Quoted in Jonathan Spence, *Chinese Roundabout: Essays in History and Culture* (New York, 1992), p. 285.

SUGGESTED READING

For a general view of modern Russia, see M. Malia, *Russia Under Western Eyes* (Cambridge, Mass., 1999). On the Khrushchev years, see E. Crankshaw, *Khrushchev: A Career* (New York, 1966). For the final years of the Soviet era, see S. F. Cohen, *Rethinking the Soviet Experience* (New York, 1985); M. Lewin, *The Gorbachev Phenomenon* (Berkeley, Calif., 1988); G. Hosking, *The Awakening of the Soviet Union* (London, 1990); and S. White, *Gorbachev and After* (Cambridge, 1991). For an inquiry into the reasons for the Soviet collapse, see R. Conquest, *Reflections on a Ravaged Century* (New York, 1999), and R. Strayer, *Why Did the Soviet Union Collapse? Understanding Historical Change* (New York, 1998). On economic conditions in post-Soviet Russia, see J. Blasi, M. Kroumova, and D. Kruse, *Kremlin Capitalism: The Privatization of the Russian Economy* (Ithaca, N.Y., 1997).

For a general study of the Soviet satellites in Eastern Europe, see S. Fischer-Galati, *Eastern Europe in the 1980s* (London, 1981). Also see M. Glenny, *The Balkans* (New York, 1999). On East Germany, see C. B. Scharf, *Politics and Change in East Germany* (Boulder, Colo., 1984). Additional studies on the recent history of these countries include T. G. Ash, *The Polish Revolution: Solidarity* (New York, 1984); B. Kovrig, *Communism in Hungary from Kun to Kádár* (Stanford, Calif., 1979); T. G. Ash, *The Magic Lantern: The Revolution of '89 Witnessed in Warsaw, Budapest, Berlin, and Prague* (New York, 1990); M. Shafir, *Romania: Politics, Economics and Society* (London, 1985); E. Biberaj, *Albania: A Socialist Maverick* (Boulder, Colo., 1990); and S. Ramet, *Nationalism and Federalism in Yugoslavia* (Bloomington, Ind., 1992).

A number of useful surveys deal with China after World War II. The most comprehensive treatment of the communist period is M. Meisner, *Mao's China and After: A History of the People's Republic* (New York, 1986). For shorter accounts of the period, see J. Grasso et al., *Modernization and Revolution in China* (Armonk, N.Y., 1991), and C. Dietrich, *People's China: A Brief History* (New York, 1986).

The Cultural Revolution is treated dramatically in S. Karnow, *Mao and China: Inside China's Cultural Revolution* (New York, 1972). For individual accounts of the impact of the revolution on people's lives, see the celebrated book by Nien Cheng, *Life and Death in Shanghai* (New York, 1986), and Liang Heng and J. Shapiro, *After the Revolution* (New York, 1986).

For the early post-Mao period, see O. Schell, *To Get Rich Is Glorious* (New York, 1986), and the sequel, *Discos and Democracy: China in the Throes of Reform* (New York, 1988). The 1989 demonstrations and their aftermath are chronicled in L. Feigon's eyewitness account, *China Rising: The Meaning of Tiananmen* (Chicago, 1990), and D. Morrison, *Massacre in Beijing* (New York, 1989). For commentary by Chinese dissidents, see Liu Binyan, *China's Crisis, China's Hope* (Cambridge, 1990), and Fang Lizhi, *Bringing Down the Great Wall: Writings on Science, Culture, and Democracy in China* (New York, 1991). Recent events are analyzed in J. Fewsmith, *China Since Tiananmen: The Politics of Transition* (Cambridge, 2001).

For a comprehensive introduction to twentieth-century Chinese literature, consult E. Widmer and D. Der-Wei Wang, eds., *From May Fourth to June Fourth: Fiction and Film in Twentieth-Century China* (Cambridge, Mass., 1993), and J. Lau and H. Goldblatt, *The Columbia Anthology of Modern Chinese Literature* (New York, 1995). To witness daily life in the mid-1980s, see Z. Xinxin and S. Ye, *Chinese Lives: An Oral History of Contemporary China* (New York, 1987). An excellent survey of Chinese women writers is found in M. S. Duke, ed., *Modern Chinese Women Writers: Critical Appraisals* (Armonk, N.Y., 1989).

For a discussion of the women's movement in China during this period, see J. Stacey, *Patriarchy and Socialist Revolution in China* (Berkeley, Calif., 1983), and M. Wolf, *Revolution Postponed: Women in Contemporary China* (Stamford, Conn., 1985). To follow the first-hand account of a Chinese woman revolutionary, read Y. Daiyun and C. Wakeman, *To the Storm: The Odyssey of a Revolutionary Chinese Woman* (Berkeley, Calif., 1985).

INFOTRAC COLLEGE EDITION

Visit the source collections at infotrac.thomsonlearning.com and use the Search function with the following key terms.

Gorbachev	Perestroika
Khrushchev	Stalin
Mao Zedong	

WORLD HISTORY RESOURCES

Visit the *Essential World History* Companion Web Site for resources specific to this textbook:

http://history.wadsworth.com/duikeressentials02/

The CD in the back of this book and the World History Resource Center at **http://history.wadsworth.com/world/** offer a variety of tools to help you succeed in this course, including access to quizzes; images; documents; interactive simulations, maps, and timelines; movie explorations; and a wealth of other sources.

CHAPTER OUTLINE

- RECOVERY AND RENEWAL IN EUROPE
- EMERGENCE OF THE SUPERPOWER: THE UNITED STATES
- THE DEVELOPMENT OF CANADA
- LATIN AMERICA SINCE 1945
- SOCIETY AND CULTURE IN THE WESTERN WORLD
- CONCLUSION

FOCUS QUESTIONS

- What problems have the nations of Western Europe faced since 1945, and what steps have they taken to try to solve these problems?
- What political, social, and economic changes have the United States and Canada experienced since 1945?
- What problems have the nations of Latin America faced since 1945, and what role has Marxist ideology played in their efforts to solve these problems?
- What major social developments have occurred in Western Europe and North America since 1945?
- What major cultural and intellectual developments have occurred in Western Europe and North America since 1945?
- ➤ What are the similarities and differences between the feminist movement of the nineteenth century and the post–World War II feminist movement?

EUROPE AND THE WESTERN HEMISPHERE SINCE 1945

he end of World War II in Europe had been met with great joy. One visitor in Moscow reported, "I looked out of the window [at 2 A.M.], almost everywhere there were lights in the windows—people were staying awake. Everyone embraced everyone else, someone sobbed aloud." But after the victory parades and celebrations, Europeans awoke to a devastating realization: their civilization was in ruins. Almost forty million people (both soldiers and civilians) had been killed over the last six years. Massive air raids and artillery bombardments had reduced many of the great cities of Europe to heaps of rubble. An American general described Berlin: "Wherever we looked, we saw desolation. It was like a city of the dead.

Suffering and shock were visible in every face. Dead bodies still remained in canals and lakes and were being dug out from under bomb debris." Many Europeans were homeless.

Between 1945 and 1970, Europe not only recovered from the devastating effects of World War II but also experienced an economic resurgence that seemed nothing less than miraculous. Economic growth and virtually full employment continued so long that the first postwar recession, in 1973, came as a shock to Western Europe. It was short-lived, however, and economic growth returned. After the collapse of communist governments in the revolutions of 1989, a number of Eastern European states sought to create market economies and join the military and economic unions first formed by Western European states.

The most significant factor after 1945 was the emergence of the United States as the world's richest and most powerful nation. American prosperity reached new heights in the two decades after World War II, but a series of economic and social problems—including racial division and staggering budget deficits—have given the nation plenty of internal matters to grapple with over the past half century.

To the south of the United States lay the vast world of Latin America, with its own unique heritage. Although some Latin Americans in the nineteenth century had looked to the United States as a model for their own development, in the twentieth century, many attacked the United States for its military and economic domination of Central and South America. At the same time, many Latin American countries struggled with economic and political instability.

In the transformation from Cold War to post–Cold War realities, other changes also shaped the Western world. New artistic and intellectual currents, the growth of science and technology, new threats from terrorists, environmental problems, the surge of women's liberation—all of these reflect a vibrant, ever-changing, and yet challenging new world. ●

RECOVERY AND RENEWAL IN EUROPE

All the nations of Europe faced similar problems at the end of World War II. Above all, they needed to rebuild their shattered economies. Within a few years after the defeat of Germany and Italy, an incredible economic revival brought renewed growth to Western Europe.

Western Europe: The Triumph of Democracy

With the economic aid of the Marshall Plan, the countries of Western Europe recovered relatively rapidly from the devastation of World War II. Between the early 1950s and late 1970s, industrial production surpassed all previous records, and Western Europe experienced virtually full employment.

FRANCE: FROM DE GAULLE TO NEW UNCERTAINTIES

The history of France for nearly a quarter century after the war was dominated by one man—Charles de Gaulle (1890–1970). The creation of the Fourth Republic, with a return to a parliamentary system based on parties that de Gaulle considered weak, led him to withdraw for a while from politics. However, in 1958, frightened by the bitter divisions within France caused by the Algerian crisis (see Chapter 28), the panic-stricken leaders of the Fourth Republic offered to let de Gaulle take over the government and revise the constitution.

In 1958, de Gaulle drafted a constitution for the Fifth Republic that greatly enhanced the power of the office of president, who now had the right to choose the prime minister, dissolve parliament, and supervise both defense and foreign policy. As the new president, de Gaulle sought to return France to a position of great power. With that goal in mind, de Gaulle invested heavily in the nuclear arms race. France exploded its first nuclear bomb in 1960. Despite his successes, de Gaulle did not really achieve his ambitious goals; in truth, France was too small for such global ambitions.

During de Gaulle's presidency, the French gross national product experienced an annual increase of 5.5 percent, faster than that of the United States. France became a major industrial producer and exporter, particularly in such areas as automobiles and armaments. But problems remained. The expansion of traditional industries, such as coal, steel, and railroads, which had all been nationalized, led to large government deficits. The cost of living increased faster than in the rest of Europe. Increased dissatisfaction led in May 1968 to a series of student protests, followed by a general strike by the labor unions. Tired and discouraged by the turn of events, de Gaulle resigned from office in April 1969 and died within a year.

The worsening of France's economic situation in the 1970s brought a shift to the left politically. By 1981, the Socialists had become the dominant party in the National Assembly, and the Socialist leader, François Mitterrand (1916–1995), was elected president. Mitterrand passed a number of measures to aid workers: an increased minimum wage, expanded social benefits, a mandatory fifth week of paid vacation for salaried workers, and a thirty-nine-hour workweek. The victory of the Socialists led them to enact some of their more radical reforms: the government nationalized the steel industry, major banks, the space and electronics industries, and important insurance firms.

The Socialist policies, however, largely failed, and within three years, a decline in support for the Socialists caused the Mitterrand government to return some of the economy to private enterprise. But France's economic decline continued. In 1993, French unemployment stood at 10.6 percent, and in the elections in March of that year, the Socialists won only 28 percent of the vote; a coalition of conservative parties won 80 percent of the seats. The move to the right was strengthened when the conservative mayor of Paris, Jacques Chirac, was elected president in May 1995.

FROM WEST GERMANY TO GERMANY

Under the pressures of the Cold War, the three western zones of Germany were unified as the Federal Republic of Germany in 1949. Konrad Adenauer (1876–1967), the leader of the Christian Democratic Union (CDU), served as chancellor from 1949 to 1963 and became the Federal Republic's "founding hero." Adenauer sought respect for Germany by cooperating with the United States and the other Western European nations.

Adenauer's chancellorship is largely associated with the resurrection of the West German economy, often referred to as the "economic miracle." It was largely guided by the minister of finance, Ludwig Erhard. Although West Germany had only 52 percent of the territory of prewar Germany, by 1955 the West German gross national product exceeded that of prewar Germany. Real wages doubled between 1950 and 1965. Unemployment fell from 8 percent in 1950 to 0.4 percent in 1965.

After the Adenauer era, German voters moved politically from the center-right of the Christian Democrats to center-left politics; in 1969, the Social Democrats became the leading party. The first Social Democratic chancellor was Willy Brandt (1913–1992), who was especially successful with his "opening toward the east" (known as Ostpolitik), for which he received the Nobel Peace Prize in 1972. On March 19, 1971, Brandt worked out the details of a treaty with East Germany (the former Russian zone) that led to greater cultural, personal, and economic contacts between West and East Germany.

In 1982, the Christian Democratic Union of Helmut Kohl (b. 1930) formed a new center-right government.

Kohl was a clever politician who benefited greatly from an economic boom in the mid-1980s and the 1989 revolution in East Germany, which led to the reunification of the two Germanies, making the new Germany, with its 79 million people, the leading power in Europe. Reunification brought immediate political dividends to the Christian Democrats, but all too soon, the realization set in that the revitalization of eastern Germany would take far more money than was originally thought. Kohl's government was soon forced to face the politically undesirable task of raising taxes substantially. Moreover, the virtual collapse of the economy in eastern Germany led to extremely high unemployment and severe discontent. One response was a return to power for the Social Democrats under the leadership of Gerhard Schroeder (b. 1944) as a result of elections in 1998.

THE DECLINE OF GREAT BRITAIN

The end of World War II left Britain with massive economic problems. In elections held immediately after the war, the Labour Party overwhelmingly defeated Churchill's Conservatives. Labour had promised far-reaching reforms, particularly in the area of social welfare, and in a country with a tremendous shortage of consumer goods and housing, its platform was quite appealing. The new Labour government under Clement Attlee (1883–1967) proceeded to turn Britain into a modern welfare state.

The process began with the nationalization of the Bank of England, the coal and steel industries, public transportation, and public utilities, such as electricity and gas. In 1946, the new government established a comprehensive social security program and nationalized medical insurance, thereby enabling the state to subsidize the unemployed, the sick, and the aged. A health act established a system of socialized medicine that forced doctors and dentists to work with state hospitals, although private practice could be maintained. The British welfare state became the norm for most European nations after the war.

Continuing economic problems, however, brought the Conservatives back into power from 1951 to 1964. Although they favored private enterprise, the Conservatives accepted the welfare state. Although the British economy had recovered from the war, its slow rate of recovery masked a long-term economic decline. As a result of World War II, Britain had lost much of its prewar revenues from abroad but was left with a burden of debt from its many international commitments. At the same time, as the influence of the United States and the Soviet Union continued to rise, Britain's ability to play the role of a world power declined substantially. Between 1964 and 1979, Conservatives and Labour alternated in power, but neither party was able to deal with Britain's ailing economy.

MARGARET THATCHER:
ENTERING A MAN'S WORLD

In this excerpt from her autobiography, Margaret Thatcher describes how she was interviewed by Conservative Party officials when they first considered her as a possible candidate for Parliament. Thatcher ran for Parliament for the first time in 1950; she lost but increased the Conservative vote total in the district by 50 percent over the previous election.

MARGARET THATCHER, THE PATH TO POWER

And, as always with me, there was politics. I immediately joined the Conservative Association and threw myself into the usual round of Party activities. In particular, I thoroughly enjoyed what was called the "'39–'45" discussion group, where Conservatives of the war generation met to exchange views and argue about the political topics of the day. . . . After one of the debates, I found myself engaged in one of those speculative conversations which young people have about their future prospects. An Oxford friend, John Grant, said he supposed that one day I would like to be a Member of Parliament. "Well, yes," I replied, "but there's not much hope of that. The chances of my being selected are just nil at the moment." I might have added that with no private income of my own there was no way I could have afforded to be an MP on the salary then available. I had not even tried to get on the Party's list of approved candidates.

Later in the day, John Grant happened to be sitting next to the Chairman of the Dartford Conservative Association, John Miller. The Association was in search of a candidate. I learned afterwards that the conversation went something like this: "I understand that you're still looking for a candidate at Dartford?". . .

"That's right. Any suggestions?"

"Well, there's a young woman, Margaret Roberts, that you might look at. She's very good."

"Oh, but Dartford is a real industrial stronghold. I don't think a woman would do at all."

"Well, you know best of course. But why not just look at her?"

And they did. I was invited to have lunch with John Miller and his wife, Phee, and the Dartford Woman's Chairman, Mrs. Fletcher, on the Saturday on Llandudno Pier. Presumably, and in spite of any reservations about the suitability of a woman candidate for their seat, they liked what they saw. I certainly got on well with them. . . .

I did not hear from Dartford until December, when I was asked to attend an interview at Palace Chambers, Bridge Street. . . . I found myself short-listed, and was asked to go to Dartford itself for a further interview. . . . As one of five would-be candidates, I had to give a fifteen-minute speech and answer questions for a further ten minutes.

It was the questions which were more likely to cause me trouble. There was a good deal of suspicion of woman candidates, particularly in what was regarded as a tough industrial seat like Dartford. This was quite definitely a man's world into which not just angels feared to tread. . . .

The most reliable sign that a political occasion has gone well is that you have enjoyed it. I enjoyed that evening at Dartford, and the outcome justified my confidence. I was selected.

In 1979, the Conservatives returned to power under Margaret Thatcher (b. 1925), who became the first woman prime minister in British history (see the box above). Thatcher pledged to lower taxes, reduce government bureaucracy, limit social welfare, restrict union power, and end inflation. The "Iron Lady," as she was called, did break the power of the labor unions. Although she did not eliminate the basic components of the social welfare system, she did use austerity measures to control inflation. "Thatcherism," as her economic policy was termed, improved the British economic situation, but at a price. The south of England, for example, prospered, but the old industrial areas of the Midlands and north declined and were beset by high unemployment, poverty, and even violence.

Margaret Thatcher dominated British politics in the 1980s. But in 1990, Labour's fortunes revived when Thatcher's government attempted to replace local property taxes with a flat-rate tax payable by every adult. Many British subjects argued that this was nothing more than a poll tax that would allow the rich to get away with paying the same rate as the poor. In 1990, Thatcher's popularity plummeted, and a revolt within her own party forced her to resign as prime minister. She was replaced by John Major (b. 1943), but his government failed to capture the imagination of most Britons. In new elections on May 1, 1997, the Labour Party won a landslide victory. The new prime minister, Tony Blair (b. 1953), was a moderate whose youthful energy immediately injected new vigor into British politics. Blair was one of the major leaders in forming an international coalition against terrorism after the terrorist attack on the United States on September 11, 2001. Two years later, his support of the U.S. war in Iraq caused his popularity to plummet.

Western Europe: The Move Toward Unity

As we have seen, the divisions created by the Cold War led the nations of Western Europe to seek military security by forming the North Atlantic Treaty Organization in 1949. The destructiveness of two world wars, however,

© Mark Stewart/Camera Press, London

MARGARET THATCHER. Great Britain's first female prime minister and also its longest-lasting, Margaret Thatcher was a strong leader who dominated British politics in the 1980s. This picture of Thatcher was taken at the Chelsea Flower Show in May 1990. Six months later, a revolt within her own party caused her to resign as prime minister.

caused many thoughtful Europeans to consider the need for some additional form of unity.

In 1957, France, West Germany, the Benelux countries (Belgium, the Netherlands, and Luxembourg), and Italy signed the Treaty of Rome, which created the European Economic Community (EEC), also known as the Common Market. The EEC eliminated customs barriers for the six member nations and created a large free-trade area protected from the rest of the world by a common external tariff. All the member nations benefited economically. In 1973, Great Britain, Ireland, and Denmark gained membership in what now was called the European Community (EC). Three additional members—Spain, Portugal, and Greece—were added in 1986, and Austria, Finland, and Sweden later joined.

The European Community was primarily an economic union. By 1992, it comprised 344 million people and constituted the world's largest single trading entity, transacting almost one-fourth of the world's commerce. In the 1980s and 1990s, the EC moved toward even greater economic integration. The Treaty on European Union, which went into effect on January 1, 1994, turned the European Community into the European Union, a true economic and monetary union of all EC members. One of its first goals was achieved in 1999 with the introduction of a common currency, the euro (see Map 27.1). On January 1, 2002, eleven of the EC nations abandoned their currency in favor of the euro.

Eastern Europe After Communism

The fall of communist governments in Eastern Europe during the revolutions of 1989 brought a wave of euphoria to Europe. The new structures meant an end to a postwar European order that had been imposed on unwilling peoples by the victorious forces of the Soviet Union (see Chapter 26). In 1989 and 1990, new governments throughout Eastern Europe worked diligently to scrap the remnants of the old system and introduce the democratic procedures and market systems they believed would revitalize their scarred lands. But this process proved to be neither simple nor easy. Nevertheless, by the beginning of the twenty-first century, many of these states, especially Poland and the Czech Republic, were making a successful transition to both free markets and democracy.

The revival of the post–Cold War Eastern European states was evident in their desire to join both NATO and the European Union, the two major Cold War institutions of Western European unity. In 1997, Poland, the Czech Republic, and Hungary became full members of NATO.

MAP 27.1 **Europe, 2000.** After the collapse of the communist order in Eastern Europe and the Soviet Union, a new order and a number of new states appeared in Central and Eastern Europe. At the same time, the European Union expanded and included fifteen states by 2000. ➤ *What new countries emerged from the breakup of the Soviet Union?*

In October 2002, the European Union's executive commission declared that ten nations—including Hungary, Poland, the Czech Republic, Slovenia, Estonia, Latvia, and Lithuania—would be invited to join the EU in 2004.

THE DISINTEGRATION OF YUGOSLAVIA

From its beginning in 1919, Yugoslavia had been an artificial creation. After World War II, the dictatorial Marshal Tito had managed to hold together the six republics and two autonomous provinces that constituted Yugoslavia. After his death in 1980, no strong leader emerged, and at the end of the 1980s, Yugoslavia was caught up in the reform movements sweeping through Eastern Europe.

After negotiations among the six republics failed, Slovenia and Croatia declared their independence in June 1991. This action was opposed by Slobodan Milosěvić, the leader of the province of Serbia. He asserted that these republics could only be independent if new border arrangements were made to accommodate the Serb minorities in those republics who did not want to live outside the boundaries of Serbia. Serbian forces attacked both new states and although unsuccessful against Slovenia, captured one-third of Croatia's territory.

The recognition of Slovenia, Croatia, and Bosnia-Herzegovina by many European states and the United States early in 1992 did not stop the Serbs from turning their guns on Bosnia. By mid-1993, Serbian forces had acquired 70 percent of Bosnian territory. The Serbian policy of "ethnic cleansing"—killing or forcibly removing Bosnian Muslims from their lands—revived memories of Nazi atrocities in World War II. As the fighting spread, European nations and the United States began to intervene to stop the bloodshed, and in the fall of 1995, a fragile cease-fire agreement was reached. An international peacekeeping force was stationed in the area to maintain tranquillity.

Peace in Bosnia, however, did not bring peace to Yugoslavia. A new war erupted in 1999 over Kosovo, which had been made an autonomous province within Yugoslavia by Tito in 1974. Kosovo's inhabitants were mainly ethnic Albanians. But the province was also home to a large Serbian minority. In 1989, Yugoslav president Milošěvić stripped Kosovo of its autonomous status. Four years later, some groups of ethnic Albanians founded the Kosovo Liberation Army (KLA) and began a campaign against Serbian rule in Kosovo. When Serb forces began to massacre ethnic Albanians in an effort to crush the KLA, the United States and its NATO allies began a bombing campaign that forced Milošěvić to stop. In the fall elections of 2000, Milošěvić himself was ousted from power and later put on trial by an international tribunal for war crimes against humanity for his ethnic cleansing policies throughout Yugoslavia's disintegration.

EMERGENCE OF THE SUPERPOWER: THE UNITED STATES

At the end of World War II, the United States emerged as one of the world's two superpowers. As its Cold War confrontation with the Soviet Union intensified, the United States directed much of its energy toward combating the spread of communism throughout the world. With the collapse of the Soviet Union at the beginning of the 1990s, the United States became the world's foremost military power.

American Politics and Society Through the Vietnam Era

Between 1945 and 1970, Franklin Roosevelt's New Deal gave rise to a distinct pattern that signified a basic transformation in American society. This pattern included a dramatic increase in the role and power of the federal government, the rise of organized labor as a significant force in the economy and politics, a commitment to the welfare state, and a grudging acceptance of minority problems. The New Deal in American politics was bolstered by the election of Democratic presidents—Harry S Truman in 1948, John F. Kennedy in 1960, and Lyndon B. Johnson in 1964. Even the election of a Republican president, Dwight D. Eisenhower, in 1952 and 1956 did not significantly alter the fundamental direction of the New Deal.

The economic boom after World War II fueled confidence in the American way of life. A shortage of consumer goods during the war left Americans with both surplus income and the desire to purchase these goods after the war. Then, too, the development of organized labor enabled more and more workers to get the wage increases that spurred the growth of the domestic market. Between 1945 and 1973, real wages grew an average of 3 percent a year, the most prolonged advance in U.S. history.

Starting in the 1960s, problems that had been glossed over earlier came to the fore. The decade began on a youthful and optimistic note when John F. Kennedy (1917–1963), age forty-three, became the youngest elected president in the history of the United States and the first born in the twentieth century. His own administration, cut short by an assassin's bullet on November 22, 1963, focused primarily on foreign affairs. Kennedy's successor, Lyndon B. Johnson (1908–1973), who won a new term as president in a landslide in 1964, used his stunning mandate to pursue the growth of the welfare state, first begun in the New Deal. Johnson's programs included health care for the elderly and the War on Poverty, to be fought with food stamps and the Job Corps.

Johnson's other domestic passion was achieving equal rights for black Americans. In August 1963, the eloquent Rev. Martin Luther King Jr. (1929–1968) led the March on Washington for Jobs and Freedom to dramatize blacks' desire for freedom. This march and King's impassioned plea for racial equality had an electrifying effect on the American people. President Johnson pursued the cause of civil rights. As a result of his initiative, Congress enacted the Civil Rights Act of 1964, which created the machinery to end segregation and discrimination in the workplace and all public accommodations. The Voting Rights Act the following year eliminated obstacles to black participation in elections in southern states. But laws alone could not guarantee the Great Society that Johnson envisioned, and soon the administration faced bitter social unrest.

In the North and the West, blacks had had voting rights for many years, but local patterns of segregation resulted in considerably higher unemployment rates for blacks (and Hispanics) than for whites and left blacks segregated in huge urban ghettos. In the summer of 1965, race riots erupted in the Watts district of Los Angeles that led to thirty-four deaths and the destruction of over one thousand buildings. After King was assassinated in 1968, more than one hundred cities erupted in rioting, including Washington, D.C., the nation's capital. The riots led to a "white backlash" and a severe racial division of America.

Antiwar protests also divided the American people after President Johnson committed American troops to a costly war in Vietnam (see Chapter 25). The killing of four student protesters at Kent State University in 1970 by the Ohio National Guard shocked both activists and ordinary Americans, and thereafter the vehemence of the antiwar movement began to subside. But the combination of antiwar demonstrations and riots in the cities caused many people to call for "law and order," an appeal used by Richard Nixon (1913–1994), the Republican presidential candidate in 1968. With Nixon's election in 1968, a shift to the right in American politics had begun.

The Shift Rightward After 1973

Nixon eventually ended American involvement in Vietnam by gradually withdrawing American troops. Politically, he pursued a "southern strategy," carefully calculating that "law and order" issues and a slowdown in racial desegregation would appeal to southern whites. The Republican strategy, however, also gained support among white Democrats in northern cities, where court-mandated busing to achieve racial integration had provoked a white backlash.

As president, Nixon was paranoid about conspiracies and resorted to subversive methods of gaining political intelligence on his political opponents. Nixon's zeal led to the Watergate scandal—a botched attempt to bug the Democratic National Headquarters and the ensuing coverup. Although Nixon repeatedly denied involvement in the affair, secret tapes he made of his own conversations in the White House revealed otherwise. On August 9, 1974, Nixon resigned in disgrace, an act that saved him from almost certain impeachment and conviction.

After Watergate, American domestic politics focused on economic issues. Gerald Ford (b. 1913) became president when Nixon resigned, only to lose in the 1976 election to the former governor of Georgia, Jimmy Carter (b. 1924), who campaigned as an outsider against the Washington establishment. By 1980, the Carter administration faced two devastating problems. High inflation and a decline in average weekly earnings were causing a perceptible drop in American living standards. At the same time, a crisis abroad had erupted when fifty-three Americans were taken hostage by the Iranian government of Ayatollah Khomeini and held for nearly fifteen months. Carter's inability to gain the release of the American hostages led to perceptions at home that he was a weak president. His overwhelming loss to Ronald Reagan (b. 1911) in the election of 1980 brought forward the chief exponent of right-wing Republican policies.

The Reagan Revolution, as it has been called, sent U.S. policy in a number of new directions. Reversing decades of changes, Reagan cut back on the welfare state by decreasing spending on food stamps, school lunch programs, and job programs. At the same time, his administration fostered the largest peacetime military buildup in American history. Total federal spending rose from $631 billion in 1981 to over $1 trillion by 1986. But instead of raising taxes to pay for the new expenditures, Reagan convinced Congress that massive tax cuts would supposedly stimulate rapid economic growth and produce new revenues. The administration's spending policies produced record government deficits, which loomed as an obstacle to long-term growth. In the 1970s, the total deficit was $420 billion; Reagan's budget deficits were three times that amount.

The inability of Reagan's successor, George H. W. Bush (b. 1924), to deal with the deficit problem, coupled with an economic downturn, led to the election of a Democrat, Bill Clinton, in November 1992. The new president was a southerner who claimed to be a new Democrat—one who favored a number of the Republican policies of the 1980s. This was a clear indication that the rightward drift in American politics was by no means ended by this Democratic victory.

President Clinton's political fortunes were aided considerably by a lengthy economic revival. A steady reduction in the annual government budget deficit strengthened confidence in the performance of the national economy. Much of Clinton's second term, however, was overshadowed by charges of misconduct stemming from the president's affair with Monica Lewinsky, a White House intern. After a bitter partisan struggle, the U.S. Senate acquitted the president on two articles of impeachment brought by the House of Representatives. But Clinton's problems helped the Republican candidate, George W. Bush, to win the presidential election in 2000. Although Bush lost the popular vote to Al Gore, he narrowly won the electoral vote after a highly controversial victory in the state of Florida.

The first three years of Bush's administration were largely occupied with the war on terrorism. The Office of Homeland Security was established to help protect the United States from terrorist acts. At the same time, Bush pushed tax cuts through Congress that mainly favored the wealthy and helped produce record budget deficits reminiscent of the Reagan years. Environmentalists were especially disturbed by the Bush administration's efforts to weaken environmental laws and regulations to benefit American corporations.

THE DEVELOPMENT OF CANADA

For twenty-five years after World War II, Canada realized extraordinary economic prosperity as it set out on a new path of industrial development, including electronic, aircraft, nuclear, and chemical engineering industries. Much of the Canadian growth, however, was financed by capital from the United States, which resulted in American ownership of Canadian businesses. While many Canadians welcomed the economic growth, others feared American economic domination of Canada.

After 1945, the Liberal Party continued to dominate Canadian politics. Under Lester Pearson (1897–1972), the Liberals created Canada's welfare state by enacting a national social security system (the Canada Pension Plan) and a national health insurance program. The most prominent Liberal government, however, was that of Pierre Trudeau (1919–2000), who came to power in 1968.

Trudeau's government pushed a vigorous program of industrialization, but inflation and Trudeau's efforts to impose the will of the federal government on the powerful provincial governments alienated voters and weakened his government. Economic recession in the early 1980s brought Brian Mulroney (b. 1939), leader of the Progressive Conservative Party, to power in 1984. Mulroney's government sought greater privatization of Canada's state-run corporations and negotiated a free-trade agreement with the United States. Bitterly assaulted by many Canadians, the agreement cost Mulroney's government much of its popularity.

Mulroney's government was also unable to settle the ongoing crisis over the French-speaking province of Quebec. In the late 1960s, the Parti Québécois, headed by René Lévesque, campaigned on a platform of Quebec's secession from the Canadian confederation. To pursue their dream of separation, some underground separatist groups even used terrorist bombings and kidnapped two prominent government officials. In 1976, the Parti Québécois won Quebec's provincial elections and in 1980 called for a referendum that would enable the provincial government to negotiate Quebec's independence from the rest of Canada. Voters in Quebec rejected the plan, however, and debate over Quebec's status continues to divide Canada.

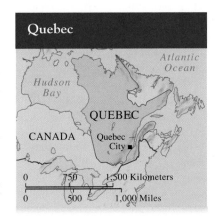

LATIN AMERICA SINCE 1945

The Great Depression of the 1930s had caused a political instability in many Latin American countries that led to military coups and militaristic regimes (see Chapter 23). But the Great Depression also led Latin America to move from a traditional to a modern economic structure. Since the nineteenth century, Latin Americans had exported raw materials, especially minerals and foodstuffs, while buying the manufactured goods of the industrialized countries in Europe and the United States. As a result of the Great Depression, however, exports were cut in half, and the revenues available to buy manufactured goods declined. This encouraged many Latin American countries to develop industries to produce goods that were formerly imported. Due to a shortage of capital in the private sector, governments often invested in the new industries, thus leading, for example, to government-run steel industries in Chile and Brazil and oil industries in Argentina and Mexico.

By the 1960s, however, Latin American countries still found themselves dependent on the United States, Europe,

and now Japan, especially for the advanced technology needed for modern industries. Because of the great poverty in many Latin American countries, domestic markets were limited in size, and many Latin American countries often failed to find markets abroad for their products. These failures led to instability and a new reliance on military regimes, especially to curb the power of the new industrial middle class and working classes, which had increased in size and power as a result of industrialization. In the 1960s, repressive military regimes in Chile, Brazil, and Argentina abolished political parties and often returned to export-import economies financed by foreigners.

In the 1970s, Latin American regimes grew even more dependent on maintaining their failing economies by borrowing from abroad, especially from banks in Europe and the United States. Between 1970 and 1982, debt to foreigners increased from $27 billion to $315.3 billion. By 1982, a number of governments announced that they could no longer pay interest on their debts to foreign banks, and their economies began to crumble.

In the 1980s, the debt crisis was paralleled by a movement toward democracy. Many people realized that military power without popular consent was incapable of providing a strong state. Then, too, there was a swelling of popular support for basic rights and free and fair elections. The movement toward democracy was the most noticeable trend of the 1980s and early 1990s in Latin America. In the mid-1980s, democratic regimes were everywhere except Cuba, some of the Central American states, Chile, and Paraguay.

The United States has also played an important role in Latin America since 1945. Beginning in the 1920s, the United States replaced Britain as the foremost investor in Latin America. Unlike the British, however, American investors put funds directly into production enterprises, so that large segments of Latin America's export industries fell into American hands. The American-owned United Fruit Company turned a number of Central American nations into "banana republics," while American companies gained control of the copper-mining industry in Chile and Peru and the oil industry in Mexico, Peru, and Bolivia. The control of these industries by American investors reinforced a growing nationalist consciousness against America as a neo-imperialist power.

But the United States had also tried to pursue a new relationship with Latin America. In 1948, the nations of the Western Hemisphere formed the Organization of American States (OAS), which was intended to eliminate unilateral action by one state within the internal or external affairs of any other state. But as the Cold War between the United States and the Soviet Union intensified, American policy makers grew anxious about

CASTRO'S REVOLUTIONARY IDEALS

On July 26, 1953, Fidel Castro and a small group of supporters launched an ill-fated attack on the Moncada Barracks in Santiago de Cuba. Castro was arrested and put on trial. This excerpt is taken from his defense speech, in which he discussed the goals of the revolutionaries.

FIDEL CASTRO, "HISTORY WILL ABSOLVE ME"

I stated that the second consideration on which we based our chances for success was one of social order because we were assured of the people's support. When we speak of the people we do not mean the comfortable ones, the conservative elements of the nation, who welcome any regime of oppression, any dictatorship, and despotism, prostrating themselves before the master of the moment until they grind their foreheads into the ground. When we speak of struggle, the people means the vast unredeemed masses, to whom all make promises and whom all deceive; we mean the people who yearn for a better, more dignified, and more just nation. . . .

In the brief of this cause there must be recorded the five revolutionary laws that would have been proclaimed immediately after the capture of the Moncada barracks and would have been broadcast to the nation by radio. . . .

The First Revolutionary Law would have returned power to the people and proclaimed the Constitution of 1940 the supreme Law of the land, until such time as the people should decide to modify or change it. . . .

The Second Revolutionary Law would have granted property, not mortgageable and not transferable, to all planters, subplanters, lessees, partners, and squatters who hold parcels of five or less "caballerias" [about 33 acres] of land, and the state would indemnify the former owners on the basis of the rental which they would have received for these parcels over a period of ten years.

The Third Revolutionary Law would have granted workers and employees the right to share 30 percent of the profits of all the large industrial, mercantile, and mining enterprises, including the sugar mills. . . .

The Fourth Revolutionary Law would have granted all planters the right to share 55 percent of the sugar production and a minimum quota of forty thousand "arrobas" [25 pounds] for all small planters who have been established for three or more years.

The Fifth Revolutionary Law would have ordered the confiscation of all holdings and ill-gotten gains of those who had committed frauds during previous regimes, as well as the holdings and ill-gotten gains of all their legatees and heirs.

---

the possibility of communist regimes arising in Central America and the Caribbean and returned to a policy of unilateral action when they believed that Soviet agents were attempting to establish communist governments. Especially after the success of Castro in Cuba (see the next section), the desire of the United States to prevent "another Cuba" largely determined American policy toward Latin America until the collapse of the Cold War in the 1990s. The United States provided massive military aid to anticommunist regimes, regardless of their nature.

The Threat of Marxist Revolutions: The Example of Cuba

A dictatorship, headed by Fulgencio Batista (1901–1973) and closely tied economically to American investors, had ruled Cuba since 1934. A strong opposition movement to Batista's government developed, led by Fidel Castro (b. 1926) and assisted by Ernesto Ché Guevara (1928–1967), an Argentinean who believed in the need for revolutionary upheaval to change Latin America. Castro maintained that only armed force could overthrow Batista, but when their initial assaults on Batista's regime brought little success, Castro's forces, based in the Sierra Maestra, went over to guerrilla warfare (see the box above). As the rebels gained more support, Batista's regime responded with such

brutality that he alienated his own supporters. The dictator fled in December 1958, and Castro's revolutionaries seized Havana on January 1, 1959.

Relations between Cuba and the United States quickly deteriorated when the Soviet Union early in 1960 agreed to buy Cuban sugar and provide $100 million in credits. In October 1960, the United States declared a trade embargo of Cuba, thus driving Castro closer to the Soviet Union.

On January 3, 1961, the United States broke diplomatic relations with Cuba. The new American president, John F. Kennedy, supported a coup attempt against Castro's government, but the landing of fourteen hundred CIA-assisted Cuban exiles in Cuba at the Bay of Pigs on April 17, 1961, turned into a total military disaster. The Soviets were now encouraged to make an even greater commitment to Cuban independence by placing nuclear missiles in the country, an act that led to a showdown with the United States. As its part of the bargain to defuse the crisis, the United States agreed not to invade Cuba.

In Cuba, Castro's socialist revolution proceeded, with mixed results. The Cuban revolution did secure some social gains for its people, especially in health care and education. The regime provided free medical services for all citizens, and the country's health improved noticeably. Illiteracy was wiped out by developing new schools and establishing teacher-training institutes that tripled the number of teachers within ten years.

Eschewing rapid industrialization, Castro encouraged agricultural diversification. But the Cuban economy continued to rely on the production and sale of sugar. Economic problems forced the Castro regime to depend on Soviet subsidies and the purchase of Cuban sugar by Soviet bloc countries. After the collapse of these communist regimes in 1989, Cuba lost their support. Although economic conditions in Cuba have steadily declined, Castro manages to remain in power.

Nationalism and the Military: The Example of Argentina

The military became the power brokers of many twentieth-century Latin American nations. Fearful of the forces unleashed by the development of industry, the military intervened in Argentinean politics in 1930 and propped up the cattle and wheat oligarchy that had controlled the reins of power since the beginning of the twentieth century. An organization of restless military officers overthrew the civilian oligarchy in June 1943. But the new military regime was unsure of how to deal with working classes. One member, Juan Perón (1895–1974), used his position as labor secretary in the military government to curry favor with the workers. In 1944, Perón became vice president of the military government and made sure that people knew he was responsible for social welfare measures. But as Perón grew more popular, other army officers grew fearful of his power and arrested him. An uprising by workers forced the officers to back down, and in 1946, Perón was elected president.

Perón pursued a policy of increased industrialization in order to please his chief supporters—labor and the urban middle class. At the same time, he sought to free Argentina from foreign investors. The government bought the railways; took over the banking, insurance, shipping, and communications industries; and assumed regulation of imports and exports. But Perón's regime was also authoritarian. His wife, Eva Perón, founded women's organizations to support the government while Perón organized fascist gangs, modeled after Hitler's Brown Shirts, who used violence to overawe his opponents. But growing corruption in the Perón government and the alienation of more and more people by the regime's excesses encouraged the military to overthrow the Argentinean leader in September 1955. Perón went into exile in Spain.

Overwhelmed by problems, however, military leaders decided to allow Juan Perón to come back from exile in Spain. Reelected as president in September 1973, Perón died one year later. In 1976, the military installed a new regime and used the occasion to kill more than six thousand leftists. But economic problems remained, and the regime tried to divert people's attention by invading the Falkland Islands in April 1982. Great Britain, which had controlled the islands since the nineteenth century, decisively defeated the Argentinean forces. The loss discredited the military and opened the door to civilian rule. In 1983, Raúl Alfonsín (b. 1927) was elected president and sought to reestablish democratic practices. In elections in 1989, the Peronist Carlos Saúl Menem (b. 1930) won. This peaceful transfer of power gave hope that Argentina was moving on a democratic path. Reelected in 1995, President Menem pushed to control inflation.

JUAN AND EVA PERÓN.   Elected president of Argentina in 1946, Juan Perón soon established an authoritarian regime that nationalized some of Argentina's basic industries and organized fascist gangs to overwhelm its opponents. He is shown here with his wife, Eva, during the inauguration ceremonies initiating his second term as president in 1952.

The Mexican Way

During the 1950s and 1960s, Mexico's ruling party (known as the Institutional Revolutionary Party, or PRI) focused on a balanced program of industrial policy. Fifteen years of steady economic growth combined with low inflation and real gains in wages for more and more people made those years seem a golden age in Mexico's economic development. At the end of the 1960s, students began to protest Mexico's one-party system. On October 2, 1968, a demonstration of university students in Tlatelolco Square in Mexico City was met by police, who opened fire, killing hundreds of students. Leaders of the PRI became concerned about the need for change in the system.

The next two presidents, Luis Echeverría (1970–1976) and José López Portillo (1976–1982), introduced political reforms. Rules for the registration of political parties were eased, thus making their growth more likely, and greater freedom of debate in the press and at universities was introduced. But economic problems continued to trouble Mexico. In the late 1970s, vast new reserves of oil were discovered in Mexico, making the government even more dependent on oil revenues. When world oil prices dropped in the mid-1980s, Mexico was no longer able to make payments on its foreign debt, which had reached $80 billion in 1982.

The debt crisis and rising unemployment increased dissatisfaction with the government, which was especially evident in the 1988 election, when the PRI's choice for president, Carlos Salina, who would be expected to win in a landslide, won by only a 50.3 percent majority. Increasing dissatisfaction with the government's economic policies finally led to the unthinkable: in 2000, Vicente Fox defeated the PRI candidate for the presidency.

SOCIETY AND CULTURE IN THE WESTERN WORLD

Socially, culturally, and intellectually, the Western world during the second half of the twentieth century has been marked by much diversity.

The Emergence of a New Society

During the postwar era, such products of new technologies as computers, television, jet planes, contraceptive devices, and new surgical techniques all dramatically altered the nature of human life. The rapid changes in postwar society were fueled by scientific advances and rapid economic growth. Called a technocratic society by some observers and the consumer society by others, postwar Western society was marked by a fluid social structure and new movements for change.

Especially noticeable in European society after 1945 were the changes in the middle class. Such traditional middle-class groups as businesspeople and professionals in law, medicine, and the universities were greatly augmented by a new group of managers and technicians as large companies and government agencies employed increasing numbers of white-collar supervisory and administrative personnel. Changes also occurred among the traditional lower classes. Especially notable was the dramatic shift of people from rural to urban areas. The number of people in agriculture declined drastically; by the 1950s, the number of farmers in most parts of Europe was less than half of what it was at the end of the war. Nor did the size of the industrial working class expand. In West Germany, industrial workers made up 48 percent of the labor force throughout the 1950s and 1960s. Thereafter the number of industrial workers began to dwindle as the number of white-collar service employees increased. At the same time, a substantial increase in real wages enabled the working classes to aspire to the consumption patterns of the middle class. Buying on the installment plan became widespread in the 1950s and gave workers a chance to imitate the middle class by buying such products as televisions, washing machines, refrigerators, vacuum cleaners, record players, and automobiles.

Rising incomes, combined with shorter working hours, created an even greater market for mass leisure activities. Between 1900 and 1980, the workweek was reduced from sixty hours to around forty hours, and the number of paid holidays increased. All aspects of popular culture—music, sports, media—became commercialized and opened opportunities for leisure activities.

Social change was also evident in both educational patterns and student attitudes. Before World War II, higher education had largely remained the preserve of Europe's wealthier classes. After the war, European states began to foster greater equality of opportunity in higher education by eliminating fees, and universities experienced an influx of students from the middle and lower classes. Enrollments grew dramatically; in France, 4.5 percent of young people went to a university in 1950. By 1965, the figure had increased to 14.5 percent.

But there were problems. Overcrowded classrooms, professors who paid little attention to students, administrators who acted in an authoritarian fashion, and an education that to many seemed irrelevant to the realities of the modern age led to an outburst of student revolts in the late 1960s. In part, these were an extension of the anti–Vietnam War protests in American universities in the mid-1960s. Perhaps the most famous student revolt occurred in France in 1968. It erupted at the University of Nanterre outside Paris but soon spread to the Sorbonne, the main campus of the University of Paris. French students demanded a greater voice in the administration of the university, took over buildings, and then expanded the scale of their protests by inviting workers to support them. Half of France's workforce went on strike in May 1968. After the Gaullist government instituted a hefty wage hike, the workers returned to work and the police repressed the remaining student protesters.

There were several reasons for the student radicalism. Some students were genuinely motivated by the desire to reform the university. Others were protesting the Vietnam War, which they viewed as a product of Western imperialism. They also attacked other aspects of Western society, such as its materialism, and expressed concern about becoming cogs in the large and impersonal bureaucratic mechanisms of the modern world.

The Permissive Society

Some critics referred to the new society of postwar Europe as the "permissive society." Sweden took the lead in the propagation of the so-called sexual revolution of the 1960s, and the rest of Europe and the United States soon followed. Sex education in the schools and the decriminalization of homosexuality were but two aspects of Sweden's liberal approach. The introduction of the birth control pill, which became widely available by the mid-1960s, gave people more freedom in sexual behavior. Meanwhile sexually explicit movies, plays, and books broke new ground in the treatment of once-hidden subjects. Cities like Amsterdam, which allowed open prostitution and the public sale of hard-core pornography, attracted thousands of curious tourists.

The new standards were evident in the breakdown of the traditional family. Divorce rates increased dramatically, especially in the 1960s, while premarital and extramarital sexual experiences also rose substantially. A survey in the Netherlands in 1968 revealed that 78 percent of men and 86 percent of women had participated in extramarital sex.

The 1960s also saw the emergence of the drug culture. Marijuana, though illegal, was widely used by college and university students. For young people more interested in higher levels of consciousness, Timothy Leary, who had done research at Harvard on the psychedelic (perception-altering) effects of lysergic acid diethylamide (LSD), became the high priest of hallucinogenic experiences.

New attitudes toward sex and the use of drugs were only two manifestations of a growing youth movement in the 1960s that questioned authority and fostered rebellion against the older generation. Spurred on by opposition to the Vietnam War and a growing political consciousness, the youth rebellion became a youth protest movement by the second half of the 1960s (see the box on p. 602).

Women in the Postwar World

Despite their enormous contributions to the war effort, women at the end of World War II were removed from the workforce to provide jobs for the soldiers returning home. After the horrors of war, people seemed willing for a while to return to traditional family practices. Female participation in the workforce declined, and birthrates began to rise, creating a "baby boom." This increase in the birthrate, however, did not last, and the size of families began to decline by the mid-1960s. Largely responsible for this decline was the widespread practice of birth control. The condom, invented in the nineteenth century, was already in wide use, but the development in the 1960s of oral contraceptives, known as birth control pills or simply "the pill," provided a convenient and reliable means of birth control that quickly spread to all Western countries.

↠ A "LOVE-IN." In the 1960s, a number of outdoor public festivals for young people combined music, drugs, and sex. Flamboyant dress, facial painting, free-form dancing, and drugs were vital ingredients in creating an atmosphere dedicated to "love and peace." Shown here is a "love-in" that was held on the grounds of an English country estate in the "Summer of Love," 1967.

© Popperfoto

"THE TIMES THEY ARE A-CHANGIN'":
THE MUSIC OF YOUTHFUL PROTEST

*I*n the 1960s, the lyrics of rock music reflected the rebellious mood of many young people. Bob Dylan (b. 1941), a well-known recording artist, expressed the feelings of the younger generation. His song "The Times They Are A-Changin'," released in 1964, has been called an "anthem for the protest movement."

BOB DYLAN, "THE TIMES THEY ARE A-CHANGIN'"

Come gather 'round people
Wherever you roam
And admit that the waters
Around you have grown
And accept it that soon
You'll be drenched to the bone
If your time to you
Is worth savin'
Then you better start swimmin'
Or you'll sink like a stone
For the times they are a-changin'

Come writers and critics
Who prophesize with your pen
And keep your eyes wide
The chance won't come again
And don't speak too soon
For the wheel's still in spin
And there's no tellin' who
That it's namin'
For the loser now
Will be later to win
For the times they are a-changin'

Come senators, congressmen
Please heed the call

Don't stand in the doorway
Don't block up the hall
For he that gets hurt
Will be he who has stalled
There's a battle outside
And it is ragin'
It'll soon shake your windows
And rattle your walls
For the times they are a-changin'

Come mothers and fathers
Throughout the land
And don't criticize
What you can't understand
Your sons and your daughters
Are beyond your command
Your old road
Is rapidly agin'
Please get out of the new one
If you can't lend your hand
For the times they are a-changin'

The line it is drawn
The curse it is cast
The slow one now
Will later be fast
As the present now
Will later be past
The order is
Rapidly fadin'
And the first one now
Will later be last
For the times they are a-changin'

The trend toward smaller families contributed to changes in women's employment in both Europe and the United States, primarily because women now needed to devote far fewer years to rearing children. That led to a large increase in the number of married women in the workforce. At the beginning of the twentieth century, even working-class wives tended to stay at home if they could afford to do so. In the postwar period, this was no longer the case. In the United States, for example, in 1900, married women made up about 15 percent of the female labor force; by 1970, their number had increased to 62 percent.

But the increased number of women in the workforce did not change some old patterns. Working-class women in particular still earned salaries lower than those of men for equal work. In the 1960s, women earned only 60 per-

cent of men's wages in Britain, 50 percent in France, and 63 percent in West Germany. In addition, women still tended to enter traditionally female jobs. Many European women also still faced the double burden of earning income on the one hand and raising a family and maintaining the household on the other. Such inequalities led increasing numbers of women to rebel.

THE FEMINIST MOVEMENT:
THE SEARCH FOR LIBERATION

Women's wartime participation helped them achieve one of the major aims of the nineteenth-century feminist movement—the right to vote. After World War I, many governments acknowledged the contributions of women to the war effort by granting them suffrage. Sweden, Great

Britain, Germany, Poland, Hungary, Austria, and Czechoslovakia did so in 1918, followed by the United States in 1920. Women in France and Italy did not obtain the right to vote until 1945. After World War II, little was heard of feminist concerns, but by the 1960s, women began to assert their rights again and speak as feminists. Along with the student upheavals of the late 1960s came renewed interest in feminism, or the women's liberation movement, as it was now called.

Of great importance to the emergence of the postwar women's liberation movement was the work of Simone de Beauvoir (1908–1986), who supported herself as a teacher and later as a novelist and writer. De Beauvoir believed that she lived a "liberated" life for a twentieth-century European woman, but for all her freedom, she still came to perceive that as a woman, she faced limits that men did not. In 1949, she published her highly influential work *The Second Sex*, in which she argued that as a result of male-dominated societies, women had been defined by their differences from men and consequently received second-class status: "What particularly signalizes the situation of woman is that she—a free autonomous being like all human creatures—nevertheless finds herself in a world where men compel her to assume the status of the Other."[1] De Beauvoir took an active role in the French women's movement of the 1970s, and her book was a major influence on both sides of the Atlantic.

TRANSFORMATION IN WOMEN'S LIVES

To ensure natural replacement of a country's population, women need to produce an average of 2.1 children each. Many European countries fell far short of this mark; their populations stopped growing in the 1960s, and the trend has continued ever since. By the 1990s, among the nations of the European Union, the average number of children per mother was 1.4. Spain's rate, 1.15 in 2002, was among the lowest in the world.

At the same time, the number of women in the workforce has continued to rise. In Britain, for example, women accounted for 32 percent of the labor force in 1970 but 44 percent in 1990. Moreover, women have entered new employment areas. Greater access to universities and professional schools enabled women to take jobs in law, medicine, government, business, and education. In the Soviet Union, for example, about 70 percent of doctors and teachers were women. Nevertheless, economic inequality still often prevailed; women received lower wages than men for comparable work and received fewer promotions to management positions.

Feminists in the women's liberation movement came to believe that women themselves must transform the fundamental conditions of their lives. Women sought and gained a measure of control over their own bodies by seeking to legalize both contraception and abortion. In the 1960s and 1970s, hundreds of thousands of European women worked to repeal laws that outlawed contraception and abortion and began to meet with success. Even in Catholic countries, where the church remained opposed to abortion, legislation allowing contraception and abortion was passed in the 1970s and 1980s.

As more women became activists, they also became involved in new issues. Some women began to try to affect the political environment by allying with the antinuclear movement. In 1981, a group of women protested American nuclear missiles in Britain by chaining themselves to the fence of an American military base. Thousands more joined in creating a peace camp around the military compound. Enthusiasm ran high; one participant said, "I'll never forget that feeling; it'll live with me for ever. . . . As we walked round, and we clasped hands . . . It was for women; it was for peace; it was for the world."[2]

Some women joined the ecological movement. As one German writer who was concerned with environmental issues said, it is women "who must give birth to children, willingly or unwillingly, in this polluted world of ours." Especially prominent was the number of women members in the Green Party in Germany (see "The Environment and the Green Movements" later in this chapter).

Women in the West have also reached out to work with women from the rest of the world in international conferences to change the conditions of their lives. Between 1975 and 1995, the United Nations held conferences on women's issues in Mexico City, Copenhagen, Nairobi, and Beijing. These meetings made clear the differences between women from Western and non-Western countries. Whereas women from Western countries spoke about political, economic, cultural, and sexual rights, women from developing countries in Latin America, Africa, and Asia focused their attention on bringing an end to the violence, hunger, and disease that haunt their lives.

The Growth of Terrorism

Acts of terror by opponents of governments became a frightening aspect of modern Western society. During the late 1970s and early 1980s, small bands of terrorists used assassination, indiscriminate killing of civilians, the taking of hostages, and the hijacking of airplanes to draw attention to their demands or to destabilize governments in the hope of achieving their political goals. Terrorist acts garnered considerable media attention. When Palestinian terrorists kidnapped and killed eleven Israeli athletes at the Munich Olympic Games in 1972, hundreds of millions of people watched the drama unfold on television.

Motivations for terrorist acts varied considerably. Left- and right-wing terrorist groups flourished in the late 1970s and early 1980s, but terrorist acts also stemmed from militant nationalists who wished to create separatist states. Most prominent was the Irish Republican Army (IRA), which resorted to vicious attacks against the ruling government and innocent civilians in Northern Ireland.

Although left- and right-wing terrorist activities declined in Europe in the 1980s, international terrorism remained rather commonplace. Angered over the loss of their territory to Israel, some militant Palestinians responded with a policy of terrorist attacks against Israel's supporters. Palestinian terrorists operated throughout European countries, attacking both Europeans and American tourists; Palestinian terrorists massacred vacationers at airports in Rome and Vienna in 1985. State-sponsored terrorism was often an integral part of international terrorism. Militant governments, especially in Iran, Libya, and Syria, assisted terrorist organizations that made attacks on Europeans and Americans. On December 21, 1988, Pan American flight 103 from Frankfurt to New York exploded over Lockerbie, Scotland, killing all 259 passengers and crew members. A massive investigation finally revealed that the bomb responsible for the explosion had been planted by two Libyan terrorists.

TERRORIST ATTACK ON THE UNITED STATES

One of the most destructive acts of terrorism occurred on September 11, 2001, in the United States. Four groups of terrorists hijacked four commercial jet airplanes after takeoff from Boston, Newark, and Washington, D.C. The hijackers flew two of the airplanes directly into the towers of the World Trade Center in New York City, causing these buildings, as well as a number of surrounding buildings, to collapse. A third hijacked plane slammed into the Pentagon near Washington, D.C. The fourth plane, apparently headed for Washington, crashed instead in an isolated area of Pennsylvania. In total, more than three thousand people were killed, including everyone aboard the four airliners.

These coordinated acts of terror were carried out by hijackers connected to an international terrorist organization known as al-Qaeda, run by Osama bin Laden. A native of Saudi Arabia of Yemeni extraction, bin Laden used an inherited fortune to set up terrorist training camps in Afghanistan, under the protection of the nation's militant fundamentalist Islamic rulers known as the Taliban.

U.S. president George W. Bush vowed to wage a lengthy and thorough war on terrorism and worked to create a coalition of nations to assist in ridding the world of al-Qaeda and other terrorist groups. Within weeks of the attack on America, United States and NATO air forces began bombing Taliban-controlled command centers, airfields, and al-Qaeda hiding places in Afghanistan. On the ground, Afghan forces, assisted by U.S. special forces, pushed the Taliban out and gained control of the country by the end of November (see Chapter 28).

International Terrorism

International terrorism became commonplace by the beginning of the twenty-first century. At the left is a picture of a hijacked U.S. airliner about to hit one of the twin towers of the World Trade Center while smoke billows from the site of the first attack. This devastating attack on September 11, 2001, was carried out by the international terrorist group known as al-Qaeda. Seen at the right is a scene from another terrorist attack on October 12, 2002, in two nightclubs in Bali, a popular resort island of Indonesia. Almost two hundred people, including Indonesians, Australians, Canadians, French, Britons, and others were killed, with more than one hundred wounded. Both U.S. and Indonesian intelligence officials blamed al-Qaeda terrorist groups for the bombing incident.

The Environment and the Green Movements

Beginning in the 1970s, environmentalism became an important item on the European political agenda. By that time, serious ecological problems had become all too apparent. Air pollution, produced by nitrogen oxide and sulfur dioxide emissions from road vehicles, power plants, and industrial factories, was causing respiratory illnesses and having corrosive effects on buildings and monuments. Many rivers, lakes, and seas had become so polluted that they posed serious health risks. Dying forests and disappearing wildlife alarmed more and more people. The opening of Eastern Europe after the revolutions of 1989 brought to the world's attention the incredible environmental destruction of that region caused by unfettered industrial pollution.

Environmental concerns forced the major political parties in Europe to advocate new regulations for the protection of the environment. A disastrous accident at the Soviet nuclear power plant at Chernobyl, Ukraine, in 1986 made Europeans even more aware of potential environmental hazards, and 1987 was touted as the "year of the environment."

Growing ecological awareness also gave rise to "green" movements and "green" parties throughout Europe in the 1970s. Most visible was the Green Party in Germany, which was officially organized in 1979 and by 1987 had elected forty-two delegates to the West German parliament. Green parties also competed successfully in Sweden, Austria, and Switzerland.

Trends in Art and Literature

For the most part, the United States dominated the art world, much as it did the world of popular culture. American art, often vibrantly colored and filled with activity, reflected the energy and exuberance of postwar America. After 1945, New York City became the artistic center of the Western world.

Abstractionism, especially Abstract Expressionism, took over the artistic mainstream. American exuberance in Abstract Expressionism is evident in the enormous canvases of Jackson Pollock (1912–1956). In such works as *Lavender Mist* (1950), paint seems to explode, assaulting the viewer with emotion and movement. Pollock's swirling forms and seemingly chaotic patterns broke all conventions of form and structure. His drip paintings, with their total abstraction, were extremely influential with other artists, although the public was initially quite hostile to his work.

In the 1980s, styles emerged that some have referred to as Postmodern. Though still ill defined, Postmodernism has tended to move away from the futuristic or "cutting edge" qualities of Modernism. Instead it has favored "using tradition," whether that includes more styles of painting or elevating traditional craftsmanship to the level of fine art.

The most significant new trend in postwar literature has been called the "Theater of the Absurd." Its most famous proponent was the Irishman Samuel Beckett (1906–1990), who lived in France. In Beckett's *Waiting for Godot* (1952), the action on the stage is transparently unrealistic. Two men wait around for the appearance of someone, with whom they may or may not have an appointment. During the course of the play, nothing seems to be happening. The audience is never told if the action in front of them is real or imagined. Suspense is maintained not by having the audience wonder "What is going to happen next?" but simply "What is happening now?"

The Theater of the Absurd reflected its time. The postwar period was one of disillusionment with fixed ideological beliefs in politics or religion. The same disillusionment that inspired the existentialism of writers Albert Camus (1913–1960) and Jean-Paul Sartre (1905–1980), with its

➤➤ JACKSON POLLOCK AT WORK.   One of the best-known practitioners of Abstract Expressionism, which remained at the center of the artistic mainstream after World War II, was the American Jackson Pollock, who achieved his ideal of total abstraction in his drip paintings. He is shown here at work at his Long Island studio. Pollock found it easier to cover his large canvases with exploding patterns of color when he put them on the ground.

© Hans Namuth/Photo Researchers Inc.

sense of the world's meaninglessness, underscored the bleak worldview of absurdist drama and literature. The beginning point of the existentialism of Sartre and Camus was the absence of God in the universe. While the death of God was tragic, it meant that humans had no preordained destiny and were utterly alone in the universe with no future and no hope. As Camus expressed it:

> A world that can be explained even with bad reasons is a familiar world. But, on the other hand, in a universe suddenly divested of illusions and lights, man feels an alien, a stranger. His exile is without remedy since he is deprived of the memory of a lost home or the hope of a promised land. This divorce between man and his life, the actor and his setting, is properly the feeling of absurdity.[3]

According to Camus, then, the world was absurd and without meaning; humans, too, are without meaning and purpose. Reduced to despair and depression, humans have but one ground of hope—themselves.

Postmodernism was also evident in literature. One center of Postmodernism was in Central and Eastern Europe, especially in the work of Milan Kundera (b. 1929) of Czechoslovakia. Kundera blended fantasy with realism, using fantasy to examine moral issues while remaining optimistic about the human condition. Indeed, in his first novel, *The Unbearable Lightness of Being*, published in 1984, Kundera does not despair because of the political repression that he so aptly describes in his native Czechoslovakia but allows his characters to use love as a way to a better life. The human spirit can be lessened but not destroyed.

Advances in Science and Technology

Many of the scientific and technological achievements since World War II have revolutionized people's lives. During World War II, university scientists were recruited to work for their governments and develop new weapons and practical instruments of war. British physicists played a crucial role in the development of an improved radar system in 1940 that helped defeat the German air force in the Battle of Britain. German scientists created self-propelled rockets as well as jet airplanes to keep Hitler's hopes alive for a miraculous turnaround in the war. The computer, too, was a wartime creation. The British mathematician Alan Turing designed a primitive computer to assist British intelligence in breaking the secret codes of German ciphering machines. The most famous product of wartime scientific research was the atomic bomb, created by a team of American and European scientists under the guidance of the physicist J. Robert Oppenheimer. Although most wartime devices were created for destructive purposes, they could easily be adapted for peacetime uses.

The computer may yet prove to be the most revolutionary of all the technological inventions of the twentieth century. Early computers, which required thousands of vacuum tubes to function, were large and took up considerable space. The development of the transistor and then the silicon chip permitted a revolutionary new approach to computers. The 1971 invention of the microprocessor, a machine that combines the equivalent of thousands of transistors on a single, tiny silicon chip, opened the road for the development of the personal computer. By the 1990s, the personal computer had become a regular fixture in businesses, schools, and homes. The Internet—the world's largest computer network—provides millions of people around the world with quick access to immense quantities of information, as well as rapid communication and commercial transactions. By 2000, an estimated half billion people were using the Internet.

Despite the marvels produced by science and technology, some people came to question their underlying assumption—that scientific knowledge gave human beings the ability to manipulate the environment for their benefit. They maintained that some technological advances had far-reaching side effects that were damaging to the environment. Chemical fertilizers, for example, once touted for producing larger crops, wreaked havoc with the ecological balance of streams, rivers, and woodlands. *Small Is Beautiful*, written by the British economist E. F. Schumacher (1911–1977), was a fundamental critique of the dangers of the new science and technology (see the box on p. 607).

The Explosion of Popular Culture

Popular culture in the twentieth century, especially since World War II, has played an important role in helping Western people define themselves. It also reflects the economic system that supports it, for this system manufactures, distributes, and sells the images that people consume as popular culture. Modern popular culture is therefore inextricably tied to the mass consumer society in which it has emerged.

The United States has been the most influential force in shaping popular culture in the West and, to a lesser degree, the entire world. Through movies, music, advertising, and television, the United States has spread its particular form of consumerism and the American dream to millions around the world. In 1923, the *New York Morning Post* noted that "the film is to America what the flag was once to Britain. By its means Uncle Sam may hope some day . . . to Americanize the world."[4] That day has already come.

Motion pictures were the primary vehicle for the diffusion of American popular culture in the years immediately following World War I and continued to find ever wider markets as the century rolled on. Television, developed in the 1930s, did not become readily available until the late 1940s, but by 1954, there were 32 million sets in

SMALL IS BEAUTIFUL: THE LIMITS OF MODERN TECHNOLOGY

Although science and technology have produced an amazing array of achievements in the postwar world, some voices have been raised in criticism of their sometimes destructive aspects. In 1975, in his book Small Is Beautiful, *the British economist E. F. Schumacher examined the effects modern industrial technology has had on the earth's resources.*

E. F. SCHUMACHER, *SMALL IS BEAUTIFUL*

Is it not evident that our current methods of production are already eating into the very substance of industrial man? To many people this is not at all evident. Now that we have solved the problem of production, they say, have we ever had it so good? Are we not better fed, better clothed, and better housed than ever before—and better educated? Of course we are: most, but by no means all, of us: in the rich countries. But this is not what I mean by "substance." The substance of [humankind] cannot be measured by Gross National Product. Perhaps it cannot be measured at all, except for certain symptoms of loss. However, this is not the place to go into the statistics of these symptoms, such as crime, drug addiction, vandalism, mental breakdown, rebellion, and so forth. Statistics never prove anything.

I started by saying that one of the most fateful errors of our age is the belief that the problem of production has been solved. This illusion, I suggested, is mainly due to our inability to recognize that the modern industrial system, with all its intellectual sophistication, consumes the very basis on which it has been erected. To use the language of the economist, it lives on irreplaceable capital which it cheerfully treats as income. I specified three categories of such capital: fossil fuels, the tolerance margins of nature, and the human substance. Even if some readers should refuse to accept all three parts of my argument, I suggest that any one of them suffices to make my case.

And what is my case? Simply that our most important task is to get off our present collision course. And who is there to tackle such a task? I think every one of us. . . . To talk about the future is useful only if it leads to action *now*. And what can we do *now*, while we are still in the position of "never having had it so good"? To say the least . . . we must thoroughly understand the problem and begin to see the possibility of evolving a new lifestyle, with new methods of production and new patterns of consumption: a lifestyle designed for permanence. To give only three preliminary examples: in agriculture and horticulture, we can interest ourselves in the perfection of production methods which are biologically sound, build up soil fertility, and produce health, beauty, and permanence. Productivity will then look after itself. In industry, we can interest ourselves in the evolution of small-scale technology, relatively nonviolent technology, "technology with a human face," so that people have a chance to enjoy themselves while they are working, instead of working solely for their pay packet and hoping, usually forlornly, for enjoyment solely during their leisure time.

---

the United States as television became the centerpiece of middle-class life. In the 1960s, as television spread around the world, American networks unloaded their products on Europe and the Third World at extraordinarily low prices.

The United States has also dominated popular music since the end of World War II. Jazz, blues, rhythm and blues, rap, and rock and roll have been by far the most popular music forms in the Western world—and much of the non-Western world—during this time. All of them originated in the United States, and all are rooted in African American musical innovations. These forms later spread to the rest of the world, inspiring local artists, who then transformed the music in their own ways.

In the postwar years, sports have become a major product of both popular culture and the leisure industry. The development of satellite television and various electronic breakthroughs helped make sports a global phenomenon. Olympic games could now be broadcast across the world from anywhere in the world. Sports became a cheap form of entertainment, as fans did not have to leave their homes to enjoy athletic competitions. As sports television revenues escalated, many sports came to receive the bulk of their yearly revenue from television contracts.

 ## CONCLUSION

Western Europe became a new community in the 1950s and 1960s as a remarkable economic recovery fostered a new optimism. Western European states became accustomed to political democracy, and with the development of the European Community, many of them began to move toward economic unity. But nagging economic problems, new ethnic divisions, environmental degradation, and the inability to work together to stop a civil war in their own backyard have all indicated that what had been seen as a glorious new path for Europe in the 1950s and 1960s had become laden with pitfalls in the 1990s and early 2000s.

In the Western Hemisphere, the two North American countries—the United States and Canada—built prosperous economies and relatively stable communities in the 1950s, but there too, new problems, including ethnic, racial, and linguistic differences as well as persistent economic difficulties, dampened the optimism of the earlier decade. While some Latin American nations shared in the economic growth of the 1950s and 1960s, it was not matched by any real political stability. Only in the 1980s did democratic governments begin to replace oppressive military regimes.

Western societies after 1945 were also participants in an era of rapidly changing international relationships. While Latin American countries struggled to find a new relationship with the colossus to the north, European states reluctantly let go of their colonial empires. Between 1947 and 1962, virtually every colony achieved independence and statehood. Decolonization was a difficult and even bitter process, but as we shall see in the next chapters, it created a new world as the non-Western states ended the long ascendancy of the Western nations.

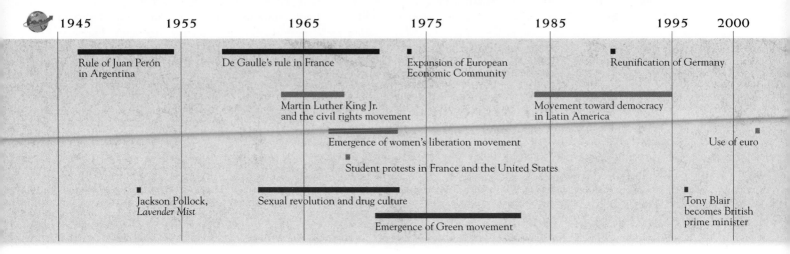

| 1945 | 1955 | 1965 | 1975 | 1985 | 1995 | 2000 |

Rule of Juan Perón in Argentina

De Gaulle's rule in France

Expansion of European Economic Community

Reunification of Germany

Martin Luther King Jr. and the civil rights movement

Movement toward democracy in Latin America

Emergence of women's liberation movement

Use of euro

Student protests in France and the United States

Jackson Pollock, *Lavender Mist*

Sexual revolution and drug culture

Tony Blair becomes British prime minister

Emergence of Green movement

CHAPTER NOTES

1. Simone de Beauvoir, *The Second Sex*, trans. H. M. Parshley (New York, 1961), p. xxviii.
2. Quoted in Renate Bridenthal, "Women in the New Europe," in Renate Bridenthal, Susan Mosher Stuard, and Merry E. Wiesner, eds., *Becoming Visible: Women in European History*, 3d ed. (Boston, 1998), pp. 564–565.
3. Quoted in Henry Grosshans, *The Search for Modern Europe* (Boston, 1970), p. 421.
4. Quoted in Richard Maltby, ed., *Passing Parade: A History of Popular Culture in the Twentieth Century* (New York, 1989), p. 11.

SUGGESTED READING

For a survey of postwar European history, see W. Laqueur, *Europe in Our Time* (New York, 1992), and W. I. Hitchcock, *The Struggle for Europe, 1945–2002* (New York, 2003). The rebuilding of postwar Europe is examined in D. W. Ellwood, *Rebuilding Europe: Western Europe, America, and Postwar Reconstruction* (London, 1992). On the building of common institutions in Western Europe, see S. Henig, *The Uniting of Europe: From Discord to Concord* (London, 1997). For a survey of West Germany, see H. A. Turner, *Germany from Partition to Reunification* (New Haven, Conn., 1992). France under de Gaulle is examined in A. Shennan, *De Gaulle* (New York, 1993), and D. J. Mahoney, *De Gaulle: Statesmanship, Grandeur, and Modern Democracy* (Westport, Conn., 1996). On Britain, see K. O. Morgan, *The People's Peace: British History, 1945–1990* (Oxford, 1992). On the recent history of these countries, see E. J. Evans, *Thatcher and Thatcherism* (New York, 1997); S. Baumann-Reynolds, *François Mitterrand* (Westport, Conn., 1995); and K. Jarausch, *The Rush to German Unity* (New York, 1994).

For a general survey of American history, see S. Thernstrom, *A History of the American People*, 2d ed. (San Diego, Calif., 1989).

D. J. Garrow, *Martin Luther King Jr. and the Southern Christian Leadership Conference* (New York, 1986), discusses the emergence of the civil rights movement. On the postwar social transformations in America, see W. Nugent, *Structures of American Social History* (Bloomington, Ind., 1981). On the turbulent decade of the 1960s, see W. O'Neill, *Coming Apart: An Informal History of America in the 1960s* (Chicago, 1971). On Nixon and Watergate, see J. Anthony Lukas, *Nightmare: The Underside of the Nixon Years* (New York, 1976). On Canadian history, see R. Bothwell, I. Drummond, and J. English, *Canada Since 1945* (Toronto, 1981).

For general surveys of Latin American history, see E. B. Burns, *Latin America: A Concise Interpretive Survey*, 4th ed. (Englewood Cliffs, N.J., 1986), and E. Williamson, *The Penguin History of Latin America* (London, 1992). The twentieth century is the focus of T. E. Skidmore and P. H. Smith, *Modern Latin America*, 3d ed. (New York, 1992). On the role of the military, see A. Rouquié, *The Military and the State in Latin America* (Berkeley, Calif., 1987). Works on the countries examined in this chapter include L. A. Pérez, *Cuba: Between Reform and Revolution* (New York, 1988); J. A. Page, *Perón:*

A Biography (New York, 1983); D. Rock, *Argentina, 1516–1987: From Spanish Colonization to Alfonsín,* 2d ed. (Berkeley, Calif., 1987); and M. C. Meyer and W. L. Sherman, *The Course of Mexican History,* 4th ed. (New York, 1991).

The student revolts of the late 1960s are put into a broader context in D. Caute, *The Year of the Barricades: A Journey Through 1968* (New York, 1988). On the women's liberation movement, see D. Bouchier, *The Feminist Challenge: The Movement for Women's Liberation in Britain and the United States* (New York, 1983); T. Keefe, *Simone de Beauvoir* (New York, 1998); and C. Duchen, *Women's Rights and Women's Lives in France, 1944–1968* (New York, 1994). More general works that include much information on the contemporary period are B. G. Smith, *Changing Lives: Women in European History Since 1700* (Lexington, Mass., 1989), and F. Thebuad,

ed., *A History of Women in the West,* vol. 5, *Toward a Cultural Identity in the Twentieth Century* (Cambridge, Mass., 1994). On terrorism, see W. Laqueur, *Terrorism,* 2d ed. (New York, 1988). On the development of the green parties, see M. O'Neill, *Green Parties and Political Change in Contemporary Europe* (Aldershot, England, 1997).

For a general view of postwar thought, see R. N. Stromberg, *European Intellectual History Since 1789,* 5th ed. (Englewood Cliffs, N.J., 1990). On contemporary art, see R. Lambert, *Cambridge Introduction to the History of Art: The Twentieth Century* (Cambridge, 1981). A physicist's view of science is contained in J. Ziman, *The Force of Knowledge: The Scientific Dimension of Society* (Cambridge, 1976). There is an excellent survey of twentieth-century popular culture in R. Maltby, ed., *Passing Parade: A History of Popular Culture in the Twentieth Century* (New York, 1989).

INFOTRAC COLLEGE EDITION

Visit the source collections at infotrac.thomsonlearning.com and use the Search function with the following key terms.

Europe Communism

Green parties

Feminism

Single European market

Germany reunification

WORLD HISTORY RESOURCES

Visit the *Essential World History* Companion Web Site for resources specific to this textbook:

http://history.wadsworth.com/duikeressentials02/

The CD in the back of this book and the World History Resource Center at **http://history.wadsworth.com/world/** offer a variety of tools to help you succeed in this course, including access to quizzes; images; documents; interactive simulations, maps, and timelines; movie explorations; and a wealth of other sources.

Courtesy of William J. Duiker

CHALLENGES OF NATION BUILDING IN AFRICA AND THE MIDDLE EAST

FOCUS QUESTIONS

• What role has nationalism played in Africa and the Middle East since World War II, and how have other forces in each area exerted counteracting effects?

• How have dreams clashed with realities in the independent nations of Africa, and how have the resulting tensions affected African culture?

• How has the role of women changed in African and Middle Eastern society since 1945?

• What political and economic problems have Middle Eastern nations faced since 1945, and how have they attempted to solve these problems?

➤ What impact did colonialism have on Africa and the Middle East, and how does its legacy continue to affect developments in these areas?

*A*lthough many Europeans complacently assumed that colonialism was a necessary evil in the process of introducing civilization to the backward peoples of Africa and Asia, some African intellectuals argued that the Western drive for economic profit and political hegemony was a plague that threatened ultimately to destroy civilization. It was the obligation of Africans to use their own humanistic and spiritual qualities to help save the human race. In *Whither Bound Africa*, written in 1946, the Ghanaian official Michael Francis Dei-Anang scathingly unmasked the pretensions of Western superiority:

Forward! To what?
The Slums, where man is dumped upon man,
Where penury
And misery
Have made their hapless homes,
And all is dark and drear?

. . . .

Forward! To what?
To the reeking round
Of medieval crimes,
Where the greedy hawks
of Aryan stock
Prey with bombs and guns
On men of lesser breed?
Forward to CIVILIZATION.[1]

To Africans like Dei-Anang, the new Africa that emerged from imperialist rule had a duty to seek new ways of resolving the problems of humanity. •

 ## UHURU: THE STRUGGLE FOR INDEPENDENCE

In the three decades following the end of World War II, the peoples of Africa were gradually liberated from the formal trappings of European colonialism.

The Colonial Legacy

As in Asia, colonial rule had a mixed impact on the societies and peoples of Africa. The Western presence brought a number of short-term and long-term benefits to Africa, such as improved transportation and communication facilities, and in a few areas laid the foundation for a modern industrial and commercial sector. Improved sanitation and medical care increased life expectancy. The introduction of selective elements of Western political systems after World War II laid the basis for the gradual creation of democratic societies.

Yet the benefits of westernization were distributed very unequally, and the vast majority of Africans found their lives little improved, if at all. Only South Africa and French-held Algeria, for example, developed modern industrial sectors, extensive railroad networks, and modern communications systems. In both countries, European settlers were numerous, most investment capital for industrial ventures was European, and whites constituted almost the entire professional and managerial class. Members of the native population were generally restricted to unskilled or semiskilled jobs at wages less than one-fifth those enjoyed by Europeans.

Many colonies concentrated on export crops—peanuts in Senegal and Gambia, cotton in Egypt and Uganda, coffee in Kenya, palm oil and cocoa products in the Gold Coast. Here the benefits of development were somewhat more widespread. In some cases, the crops were grown on plantations, which were usually owned by Europeans. But plantation agriculture was not always suitable in Africa, and much farming was done by free or tenant farmers. In some areas, where landownership was traditionally vested in the community, the land was owned and leased by the corporate village. The vast majority of the profits from the exports, however, accrued to Europeans or to merchants from other foreign countries, such as India and the Arab emirates. The vast majority of Africans continued to be subsistence farmers growing food for their own consumption.

The Rise of Nationalism

Political organizations for African rights did not arise until after World War I, and then only in a few areas, such as British-ruled Kenya and the Gold Coast. After World War II, following the example of independence movements elsewhere, groups organized political parties with independence as their objective. In the Gold Coast, Kwame Nkrumah (1909–1972) led the Convention People's Party, the first formal political party in black Africa. In the late 1940s, Jomo Kenyatta (1894–1978) founded the Kenya African National Union (KANU), which focused on economic issues but had an implied political agenda as well.

For the most part, these political activities were basically nonviolent and were led by Western-educated African intellectuals. Their constituents were primarily urban professionals, merchants, and members of labor unions. But the demand for independence was not entirely restricted to the cities. In Kenya, for example, the widely publicized Mau Mau movement among the Kikuyu people used terrorism as an essential element of its program to achieve *uhuru* (Swahili for "freedom") from the British. Although most of the violence was directed against other Africans, the specter of Mau Mau terrorism alarmed the European population and convinced the British government in 1959 to promise eventual independence.

In areas such as South Africa and Algeria, where the political system was dominated by European settlers, the transition to independence was more complicated. In South Africa, political activity by local Africans began with the formation of the African National Congress (ANC) in 1912. Initially the ANC was dominated by Western-oriented intellectuals and had little mass support. Its goal was to achieve economic and political reforms, including full equality for educated Africans, within the framework of the existing system. But the ANC's efforts met with little success, while conservative white parties managed to stiffen the segregation laws. In response, the ANC became increasingly radicalized, and by the 1950s, the prospects for a violent confrontation were growing.

In Algeria, resistance to French rule by Berbers and Arabs in rural areas had never ceased. After World War II, urban agitation intensified, leading to a widespread rebellion against colonial rule in the mid-1950s. At first, the French government tried to maintain its authority in Algeria. But when Charles de Gaulle became president in 1958, he reversed French policy, and Algeria became independent under President Ahmad Ben Bella (b. 1918) in 1962. The armed struggle in Algeria hastened the transition to statehood in its neighbors as well. Tunisia won its independence in 1956 after some urban agitation and rural unrest but retained close ties with Paris. The French

attempted to suppress the nationalist movement in Morocco by sending Sultan Muhammad V into exile, but the effort failed; in 1956, he returned as the ruler of the independent state of Morocco.

Most black African nations achieved their independence in the late 1950s and 1960s, beginning with the Gold Coast, now renamed Ghana, in 1957 (see Map 28.1). Nigeria, the Belgian Congo (renamed Zaire and then the Democratic Republic of the Congo), Kenya, Tanganyika (later, when joined with Zanzibar, renamed Tanzania), and several other countries soon followed. Most of the French colonies agreed to accept independence within the framework of de Gaulle's French Community. By the late 1960s, only parts of southern Africa and the Portuguese possessions of Mozambique and Angola remained under European rule.

Independence came later to Africa than to most of Asia. Several factors help explain the delay. For one thing, colonialism was established in Africa somewhat later than

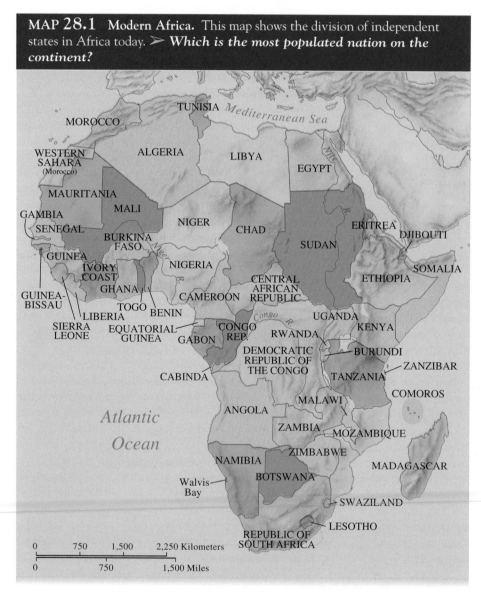

MAP 28.1   Modern Africa. This map shows the division of independent states in Africa today. ➤ *Which is the most populated nation on the continent?*

in most areas of Asia, and the inevitable reaction from the local population was consequently delayed. Furthermore, with the exception of a few areas in West Africa and along the Mediterranean, coherent states with a strong sense of cultural, ethnic, and linguistic unity did not exist in most of Africa. Most traditional states, such as Ashanti in West Africa, Songhai in the southern Sahara, and Bakongo in the Congo basin, were collections of heterogeneous peoples with little sense of national or cultural identity. It is hardly surprising that when opposition to colonial rule emerged, unity was difficult to achieve.

THE ERA OF INDEPENDENCE

The newly independent African states faced intimidating challenges. Although Western political institutions, values, and technology had been introduced, at least in the cities, the exposure to European civilization had been superficial at best for most Africans and tragic for many. At the outset of independence, most African societies were still primarily agrarian and traditional, and their modern sectors depended mainly on imports from the West.

Pan-Africanism and Nationalism: The Destiny of Africa

Like the leaders of the new states in South and Southeast Asia, most African leaders came from the urban middle class. They had studied in either Europe or the United States and spoke and read European languages. Although most were profoundly critical of colonial policies, they appeared to accept the relevance of the Western model to Africa and gave at least lip service to Western democratic values.

Their views on economics were somewhat more diverse. Some, like Jomo Kenyatta of Kenya and General Mobutu Sese Seko (1930–1998) of Zaire, were advocates of Western-style capitalism. Others, like Julius Nyerere (b. 1922) of Tanzania, Kwame Nkrumah of Ghana, and Sékou Touré (1922–1984) of Guinea, preferred an "African form of socialism," which bore slight resemblance to the Marxist-Leninist socialism practiced in the Soviet Union. According to its advocates, it was descended from traditional communal practices in precolonial Africa.

Like the leaders of other developing countries, the new political leaders in Africa were highly nationalistic and generally accepted the colonial boundaries. But as we have seen, these boundaries were artificial creations of the colonial powers. Virtually all of the new states included widely diverse ethnic, linguistic, and territorial groups. Zaire, for example, was composed of more than two hundred territorial groups speaking seventy-five different languages.

A number of leaders—including Nkrumah of Ghana, Touré of Guinea, and Kenyatta of Kenya—were enticed by the dream of pan-Africanism, a concept of continental unity that transcended national boundaries. Nkrumah in particular hoped a pan-African union could be established that would unite all of the new countries of the continent in a broader community. His dream achieved concrete manifestation in the Organization of African Unity (OAU), which was founded in 1963.

Pan-Africanism originated among African intellectuals during the first half of the twentieth century. A basic element was the conviction that there was a distinctive "African personality" that owed nothing to Western materialism and provided a common sense of destiny for all black African peoples. Whereas Western civilization prized rational thought and material achievement, African culture emphasized emotional expression and a common sense of humanity.

Dream and Reality: Political and Economic Conditions in Contemporary Africa

The program of the OAU called for an Africa based on freedom, equality, justice, and dignity and on the unity, solidarity, and territorial integrity of African states. It did not take long for reality to set in. Vast disparities in education and income made it hard to establish democracy in much of Africa. Expectations that independence would lead to stable political structures based on "one person, one vote" were soon disappointed as the initial phase of pluralistic governments gave way to a series of military regimes and one-party states. Between 1957 and 1982, more than seventy leaders of African countries were overthrown by violence, and the pace has increased in recent years.

Hopes that independence would inaugurate an era of economic prosperity and equality were similarly dashed. Part of the problem could be (and was) ascribed to the lingering effects of colonialism. Most new countries in Africa were dependent on the export of a single crop or natural resource. When prices fluctuated or dropped, these countries were at the mercy of the vagaries of the international market. In several cases, the resources were still controlled by foreigners, leading to the charge that colonialism had been succeeded by "neocolonialism," in which Western domination was maintained by economic rather than by political or military means. To make matters worse, most African states had to import technology and manufactured goods from the West, and the prices of those goods rose more rapidly than those of the export products.

The new states also contributed to their own problems. Scarce national resources were squandered on military equipment or expensive consumer goods rather than on building up their infrastructure to provide the foundation for an industrial economy. Corruption, a painful reality throughout the modern world, became almost a way of life in Africa as bribery became necessary to obtain even the most basic services (see the box on p. 614).

STEALING THE NATION'S RICHES

After 1965, African novelists transferred their anger from the foreign oppressor to their own national leaders, deploring their greed, corruption, and inhumanity. One of the most pessimistic expressions of this betrayal of newly independent Africa is found in The Beautiful Ones Are Not Yet Born, *a novel published by the Ghanaian author Ayi Kwei Armah in 1968. The author decried the government of Kwame Nkrumah and was unimpressed with the rumors of a military coup, which, he predicted, would simply replace the present regime with a new despot and his entourage of "fat men."*

AYI KWEI ARMAH, *THE BEAUTIFUL ONES ARE NOT YET BORN*

The net had been made in the special Ghanaian way that allowed the really big corrupt people to pass through it. A net to catch only the small, dispensable fellows, trying in their anguished blindness to leap and to attain the gleam and the comfort the only way these things could be done. And the big ones floated free, like all the slogans. End bribery and corruption. Build Socialism. Equality. Shit. A man would just have to make up his mind that there was never going to be anything but despair, and there would be no way of escaping it. . . .

In the life of the nation itself, maybe nothing really new would happen. New men would take into their hands the power to steal the nation's riches and to use it for their own satisfaction. That, of course, was to be expected. New people would use the country's power to get rid of men and women who talked a language that did not flatter them. There would be nothing different in that. That would only be a continuation of the Ghanaian way of life. But here was the real change. The individual man of power now shivering, his head filled with the fear of the vengeance of those he had wronged. For him everything was going to change. And for those like him who had grown greasy and fat singing the praises of their chief, for those who had been getting themselves ready for the enjoyment of hoped-for favors, there would be long days of pain ahead. The flatterers with their new white Mercedes cars would have to find ways of burying old words. For those who had come directly against the old power, there would be much happiness. But for the nation itself there would only be a change of embezzlers and a change of the hunters and the hunted. A pitiful shrinking of the world from those days Teacher still looked back to, when the single mind was filled with the hopes of a whole people. A pitiful shrinking, to days when all the powerful could think of was to use the power of a whole people to fill their own paunches. Endless days, same days, stretching into the future with no end anywhere in sight.

Finally, population growth, which more than anything else has hindered economic growth in the new nations of Asia and Africa, became a serious problem and crippled efforts to create modern economies. By the mid-1980s, annual population growth averaged nearly 3 percent throughout Africa, the highest rate of any continent. Drought conditions and the inexorable spread of the Sahara (usually known as desertification, a condition caused partly by overcultivation of the land) have led to widespread hunger and starvation, first in West African countries such as Niger and Mali and then in Ethiopia, Somalia, and the Sudan.

In recent years, the spread of HIV and AIDS in Africa has reached epidemic proportions. According to one recent report, over 75 percent of all the AIDS cases reported around the world are on the continent of Africa. Some observers estimate that without measures to curtail the effects of the disease, it will have a significant impact on several African countries by reducing population growth, which is presently predicted to increase throughout the continent by at least 300 million in the next fifteen years.

Poverty is endemic in Africa, particularly among the three-quarters of the population still living off the land. Urban areas have grown tremendously, but as in much of Asia, most are surrounded by massive squatter settlements of rural peoples who had fled to the cities in search of a better life. The expansion of the cities has overwhelmed fragile transportation and sanitation systems and led to rising pollution and perpetual traffic jams, while millions are forced to live without running water and electricity. Meanwhile, the fortunate few (all too often government officials on the take) live the high life and emulate the consumerism of the West (in a particularly expressive phrase, the rich in many East African countries are known as *wabenzi*, or Mercedes-Benz people).

THE SEARCH FOR SOLUTIONS

Concern over the dangers of economic inequality inspired a number of African leaders—including Nkrumah in Ghana, Nyerere in Tanzania, and Samora Michel of Mozambique—to restrict foreign investment and nationalize the major industries and utilities while promoting social ideals and values. Nyerere was the most consistent, promoting the ideals of socialism and self-reliance through his Arusha Declaration of 1967. Taking advantage of his powerful political influence, Nyerere placed limitations on income and established village collectives to avoid the corrosive effects of economic inequality and government corruption. Sympathetic foreign countries provided considerable economic aid to assist the experiment, and many observers noted that levels of corruption, political instability, and ethnic strife were lower in Tanzania than in many other African countries. Unfortunately, cor-

KEEPING THE CAMEL OUT OF THE TENT

"*Almighty God created sexual desire in ten parts; then he gave nine parts to women and one to men.*" So pronounced Ali, Muhammad's son-in-law, as he explained why women are held morally responsible as the instigators of sexual intercourse. Consequently, over the centuries, Islamic women have been secluded, veiled, and in many cases genitally mutilated in order to safeguard male virtue. Women are forbidden to look directly at, speak to, or touch a man prior to marriage. Even today, they are often sequestered at home or limited to strictly segregated areas away from all male contact. Women normally pray at home or in an enclosed antechamber of the mosque so their physical presence will not disturb men's spiritual concentration.

Especially limiting today are the laws governing women's behavior in Saudi Arabia. Schooling for girls has never been compulsory because fathers believe that "educating women is like allowing the nose of the camel into the tent; eventually the beast will edge in and take up all the room inside." The country did not establish its first girls' school until 1956. The following description of Saudi women is from Nine Parts Desire: The Hidden World of Islamic Women, by the journalist Geraldine Brooks.

GERALDINE BROOKS, *NINE PARTS DESIRE*

Women were first admitted to university in Saudi Arabia in 1962, and all women's colleges remain strictly segregated. Lecture rooms come equipped with closed-circuit TVs and telephones, so women students can listen to a male professor and question him by phone, without having to contaminate themselves by being seen by him. When the first dozen women graduated from university in 1973, they were devastated to find that their names hadn't been printed on the commencement program. The old tradition, that it dishonors women to mention them, was depriving them of recognition they believed they'd earned. The women and their families protested, so a separate program was printed and a segregated graduation ceremony was held for the students' female relatives. . . .

But while the opening of women's universities widened access to higher learning for women, it also made the educational experience much shallower. Before 1962, many progressive Saudi families had sent their daughters abroad for education. They had returned to the kingdom not only with a degree but with experience of the outside world. . . . Now a whole generation of Saudi women have completed their education entirely within the country. . . .

Lack of opportunity for education abroad means that Saudi women are trapped in the confines of an education system that still lags men's. Subjects such as geology and petroleum engineering—tickets to influential jobs in Saudi Arabia's oil economy—remain closed to women. . . . Few women's colleges have their own libraries, and libraries shared with men's schools are either entirely off limits to women or open to them only one day per week. . . .

But women and men sit the same degree examinations. Professors quietly acknowledge the women's scores routinely outstrip the men's. "It's no surprise," said one woman professor. "Look at their lives. The boys have their cars, they can spend the evenings cruising the streets with their friends, sitting in cafés, buying black-market alcohol and drinking all night. What do the girls have? Four walls and their books. For them, education is everything."

---

authors translated Western works into Arabic and Persian and began to experiment with new literary forms.

Iran has produced one of the most prominent national literatures in the contemporary Middle East. Since World War II, Iranian literature has been hampered somewhat by political considerations, since it has been expected to serve first the Pahlavi monarchy and then the Islamic republic. Nevertheless, Iranian writers are among the most prolific in the region and often write in prose, which has finally been accepted as the equal of poetry.

Despite the male-oriented character of Iranian society, many of the new writers have been women. Since the revolution, the veil (*chador*) has become the central metaphor in Iranian women's writing. Those who favor the veil praise it as the last bastion of defense against Western cultural imperialism. Behind the veil, the Islamic woman can breathe freely, unpolluted by foreign exploitation and moral corruption. Other Iranian women, however, consider the veil a "mobile prison" or an oppressive anachronism from the Dark Ages. As one writer, Sousan Azadi, expressed it, "As I pulled the chador over me, I felt a heaviness descending over me. I was hidden and in hiding. There was nothing visible left of Sousan Azadi."[4] Whether or not they accept the veil, women writers are a vital part of contemporary Iranian literature.

Like Iran, Egypt in the twentieth century has experienced a flowering of literature accelerated by the establishment of the Egyptian republic in the early 1950s. The most illustrious contemporary Egyptian writer is Naguib Mahfouz, who won the Nobel Prize for literature in 1988. His *Cairo Trilogy* (1952) chronicles three generations of a merchant family in Cairo during the tumultuous years between the world wars. Mahfouz is particularly adept at blending panoramic historical events with the intimate lives of ordinary human beings. Unlike many other modern writers, his message is essentially optimistic and reflects his hope that religion and science can work together for the overall betterment of humankind.

Like literature, the art of the modern Middle East has been profoundly influenced by its exposure to Western culture. At first, artists tended to imitate Western models, but later they began to experiment with national styles, returning to earlier forms for inspiration. Some emulated the writers in returning to the village to depict peasants and shepherds, but others followed international trends and attempted to express the alienation and disillusionment that characterize so much of modern life.

 ## CONCLUSION

The Middle East, like the continent of Africa, is one of the most unstable regions in the world today. In part, this turbulence is due to the continued interference of outsiders attracted by the massive oil reserves under the parched wastes of the Arabian peninsula and in the vicinity of the Persian Gulf. Oil is indeed both a blessing and a curse to the peoples of the region.

Another factor contributing to the volatility of the Middle East is the tug-of-war between the sense of ethnic identity in the form of nationalism and the intense longing to be part of a broader Islamic community, a dream that dates back to the time of the prophet Muhammad. The desire to create that community—a vision threatened by the presence of the alien state of Israel—inspired Gamal Abdul Nasser in the 1950s and Ayatollah Khomeini in the 1970s and 1980s and probably has motivated many of the actions of Saddam Hussein and Osama bin Laden.

A final reason for the turmoil currently affecting the Middle East is the intense debate over the role of religion in civil society. Although efforts in various Muslim countries to return to an allegedly purer form of Islam appear harsh and even repugnant to many observers, it is important to note that Muslim societies are not alone in deploring the sense of moral decline that is now allegedly taking place in societies throughout the world. Nor are they alone in advocating a restoration of traditional religious values as a means of reversing the trend. Not infrequently, members of such groups turn to violence as a means of making their point.

Whatever the reasons, it is clear that a deep-seated sense of anger is surging through much of the Islamic world today, an anger that transcends specific issues like the situation in Iraq or the Arab-Israeli dispute. Although economic privation and political oppression are undoubtedly important factors, the roots of Muslim resentment, as historian Bernard Lewis has pointed out, lie in a historical sense of humiliation at the hands of a Western colonialism that first emerged centuries ago, when the Arab hegemony in the Mediterranean region was replaced by European domination, and culminated early in the twentieth century, when much of the Middle East was occupied by Western colonial regimes. Today the world is reaping the harvest of that long-cultivated bitterness, and the consequences cannot be foreseen.

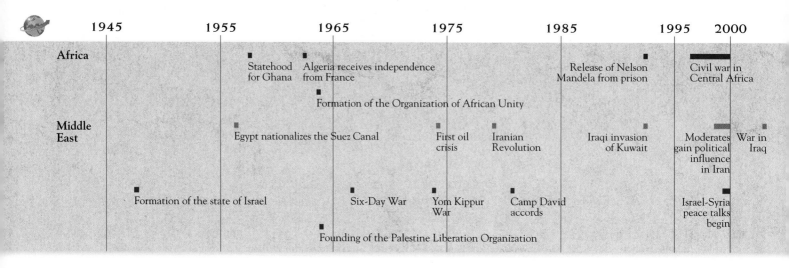

CHAPTER NOTES

1. Quoted in G.-C. M. Mutiso, *Socio-Political Thought in African Literature* (New York, 1974), p. 117.
2. Kenneth Little, *African Women in Towns: An Aspect of Africa's Social Revolution* (Cambridge, 1973), p. 6.
3. Quoted in Roy R. Andersen, Robert F. Seibert, and Jon G. Wagner, *Politics and Change in the Middle East: Sources of Conflict and Accommodation*, 4th ed. (Englewood Cliffs, N.J., 1982), p. 51.
4. Sousan Azadi, with Angela Ferrante, *Out of Iran* (London, 1987), p. 223, quoted in *Stories by Iranian Women Since the Revolution*, ed. S. Sullivan (Austin, Tex., 1991), p. 13

SUGGESTED READING

For a general survey of contemporary African history, see R. Oliver, *The African Experience* (New York, 1992), which contains interesting essays on a variety of themes, and K. Shillington, *History of Africa* (New York, 1989), which takes a chronological and geographical approach and includes excellent maps and illustrations.

Two excellent treatments by preeminent historians of the African continent are B. Davidson, *Africa in History: Themes and Outlines*, rev. ed. (New York, 1991), and P. Curtin et al., *African History* (London, 1995).

On nationalist movements, see P. Gifford and W. R. Louis, eds., *The Transfer of Power in Africa* (New Haven, Conn., 1982), and J. D. Hargreaves, *Decolonisation in Africa* (London, 1988). For an African perspective, see D. Birmingham, *Kwame Nkrumah: The Father of African Nationalism* (Athens, Ohio, 1998). For a poignant analysis of the hidden costs of nation building, see N. F. Mostert, *The Epic of South Africa's Creation and the Tragedy of the Xhosa People* (London, 1992). Also see A. Mazrui and M. Tidy, *Nationalism and New States in Africa* (Portsmouth, N.H., 1984), and S. Decalo, *Coups and Army Rule in Africa* (New Haven, Conn., 1990).

For a survey of economic conditions in Africa, see *Sub-Saharan Africa: From Crisis to Sustainable Growth* (Washington, D.C., 1989), issued by the World Bank. Also see A. O'Connor, *The African City* (London, 1983), and J. Illiffe, *The African Poor* (Cambridge, 1983).

For a survey of African literature, see L. S. Klein, ed., *African Literatures in the Twentieth Century: A Guide* (New York, 1986), and D. Wright, *New Directions in African Fiction* (New York, 1997). On art, see M. B. Visona et al., *A History of Art in Africa* (New York, 2000).

For interesting analyses of women's issues in the Africa of this time frame, see C. Robertson and I. Berger, eds., *Women and Class in Africa* (New York, 1986); S. B. Stichter and J. L. Parpart, eds., *Patriarchy and Class: African Women in the Home and the Workforce* (Boulder, Colo., 1988); and I. Berger and E. F. White, *Women in Sub-Saharan Africa* (Bloomington, Ind., 1999).

Finally, for contrasting views on the reasons for Africa's current difficulties, see J. Marah, *The African People in the Global Village:* *An Introduction to Pan-African Studies* (Lanham, Md., 1998), and G. Ayittey, *Africa in Chaos* (New York, 1998).

Good general surveys of the modern Middle East include A. Goldschmidt Jr., *A Concise History of the Middle East* (Boulder, Colo., 1991), and G. E. Perry, *The Middle East: Fourteen Islamic Centuries* (Elizabeth City, N.J., 1992).

On Israel and the Palestinian question, see B. Reich, *Israel: Land of Tradition and Conflict* (Boulder, Colo., 1985), and C. C. O'Brien, *The Siege: The Saga of Israel and Zionism* (New York, 1986). On the struggle for Jerusalem, see B. Wasserstein, *Divided Jerusalem: The Struggle for the Holy City* (New Haven, Conn., 2000).

On the Iranian Revolution, see S. Bakash, *The Reign of the Ayatollahs* (New York, 1984), and B. Rubin, *Iran Since the Revolution* (Boulder, Colo., 1985). The Iran-Iraq War is discussed in C. Davies, ed., *After the War: Iran, Iraq and the Arab Gulf* (Chichester, England, 1990), and S. C. Pelletiere, *The Iran-Iraq War: Chaos in a Vacuum* (New York, 1992).

On the politics of the Middle East, see R. R. Anderson, R. F. Seibert, and J. G. Wagner, *Politics and Change in the Middle East: Sources of Conflict and Accommodation* (Englewood Cliffs, N.J., 1993). For expert analysis on the current situation in the region, see B. Lewis, *What Went Wrong? Western Impact and Middle Eastern Response* (Oxford, 2001), and P. L. Bergen, *Holy War, Inc.: Inside the Secret World of Osama bin Laden* (New York, 2001).

Two excellent surveys of women in Islam from pre-Islamic society to the present are L. Ahmed, *Women and Gender in Islam: Historical Roots of a Modern Debate* (New Haven, Conn., 1993), and G. Nashat and J. E. Tucker, *Women in the Middle East and North Africa* (Bloomington, Ind., 1999).

For a scholarly but accessible overview of Arabic literature, see M. M. Badawi, *A Short History of Modern Arab Literature* (Oxford, 1993). For Iranian literature, see M. Southgate, *Modern Persian Short Stories* (Washington, D.C., 1980), and S. Sullivan and F. Milani, *Stories by Iranian Women Since the Revolution* (Austin, Tex., 1991).

InfoTrac College Edition

Visit the source collections at infotrac.thomsonlearning.com and use the Search function with the following key terms.

Africa

Developing countries

Israel history

Nelson Mandela

Palestine

World History Resources

Visit the *Essential World History* Companion Web Site for resources specific to this textbook:

http://history.wadsworth.com/duikeressentials02/

The CD in the back of this book and the World History Resource Center at **http://history.wadsworth.com/world/** offer a variety of tools to help you succeed in this course, including access to quizzes; images; documents; interactive simulations, maps, and timelines; movie explorations; and a wealth of other sources.

Chapter 29

TOWARD THE PACIFIC CENTURY?

CHAPTER OUTLINE
- SOUTH ASIA
- SOUTHEAST ASIA
- EAST ASIA
- CONCLUSION

FOCUS QUESTIONS
- How did Mahatma Gandhi's and Jawaharlal Nehru's goals for India differ, and what role have each leader's views played in shaping modern India?
- What problems has India faced since independence, and how have its leaders attempted to solve these problems?
- What problems have the nations of Southeast Asia faced since 1945, and how have they attempted to solve these problems?
- How did the Allied occupation after World War II change Japan's political and economic institutions, and what remained unchanged?
- What have been the major developments in South Korea, Taiwan, Singapore, and Hong Kong since World War II?
- ➢ What factors have contributed to the economic success achieved by Japan and the "little tigers" in recent years? Are there some less beneficial consequences?

irst-time visitors to the Malaysian capital of Kuala Lumpur are astonished to observe a pair of twin towers thrusting up above the surrounding buildings into the clouds. The Petronas Towers rise 1,483 feet from ground level, leading to claims by Malaysian officials that they are the world's tallest buildings, at least for the time being.

More than an architectural achievement, the towers announced the emergence of Southeast Asia as a major player on the international scene. It is probably no accident that the foundations were laid on the site of the Selangor Cricket Club, symbol of colonial hegemony in Southeast Asia. "These towers," commented one local official, "will do wonders for Asia's self-esteem and confidence, which I think is very important, and which I think at this moment are at the point of takeoff."[1]

Slightly more than a year after that remark, Malaysia and several of its neighbors were mired in a financial crisis that threatened to derail their rapid advance to economic affluence and severely undermined the "self-esteem" that the Petronas Towers were meant to symbolize. That ironic reality serves as a warning to the region's leaders that the road to industrialized status is often strewn with hidden obstacles. At the moment, the buildings serve less as a symbol of the opening of a "Pacific century" than as a testament to the danger of hubris and a potential target for a future terrorist attack. •

 SOUTH ASIA

In 1947, nearly two centuries of British colonial rule came to an end when two new independent nations, India and Pakistan, came into being.

The End of the British Raj

During the 1930s, the nationalist movement in India was severely shaken by factional disagreements between Hindus and Muslims. The outbreak of World War II subdued these sectarian clashes, but they erupted again after the war ended in 1945. Battles between Hindus and Muslims broke out in several cities, and Mohammed Ali Jinnah, leader of the Muslim League, demanded the creation of a separate state for each. Meanwhile, the Labour Party, which had long been critical of the British colonial legacy on both moral and economic grounds, had come to power in Britain, and the new prime minister, Clement Attlee, announced that power would be transferred to "responsible Indian hands" by June 1948.

But the imminence of independence did not dampen communal strife. As riots escalated, the British reluctantly accepted the inevitability of partition and declared that on August 15, 1947, two independent nations—Hindu India and Muslim Pakistan—would be established. Pakistan would be divided between the main area of Muslim habitation in the Indus River valley in the west and a separate territory in east Bengal 2,000 miles to the east. Although Mahatma Gandhi warned that partition would provoke "an orgy of blood,"[2] he was increasingly regarded as a figure of the past, and his views were ignored.

The British instructed the rulers in the princely states to choose which state they would join by August 15, but problems arose in predominantly Hindu Hyderabad, where the nawab (viceroy) was a Muslim, and mountainous Kashmir, where a Hindu prince ruled over a Muslim population. After independence was declared, the flight of millions of Hindus and Muslims across the borders led to violence and the death of more than a million people. One of the casualties was Gandhi, who was assassinated on January 30, 1948, as he was going to morning prayer. The assassin, a Hindu militant, was apparently motivated by Gandhi's opposition to a Hindu India.

Independent India

With independence, the Indian National Congress, now renamed the Congress Party, moved from opposition to the responsibility of power under Jawaharlal Nehru, the new prime minister. The prospect must have been intimidating. The vast majority of India's 400 million people were poor and illiterate. The new nation encompassed a bewildering number of ethnic groups and fourteen major languages. Although Congress Party leaders spoke bravely of building a new nation, Indian society still bore the scars of past wars and divisions.

The government's first problem was to resolve disputes left over from the transition period. The rulers of Hyderabad and Kashmir had both followed their own preferences rather than the wishes of their subject populations. Nehru was determined to include both states within India. In 1948, Indian troops invaded Hyderabad and annexed the area. India was also able to seize most of Kashmir, but at the cost of creating an intractable problem that has poisoned relations with Pakistan down to the present day.

AN EXPERIMENT IN DEMOCRATIC SOCIALISM

Under Nehru's leadership, India adopted a political system on the British model, with a figurehead president and a parliamentary form of government. A number of political parties operated legally, but the Congress Party, with its enormous prestige and charismatic leadership, was dominant at both the central and the local levels.

Nehru had been influenced by British socialism and patterned his economic policy roughly after the program of the British Labour Party. The state took over ownership of the major industries and resources, transportation, and utilities, while private enterprise was permitted at the local and retail levels. Farmland remained in private hands, but rural cooperatives were officially encouraged.

In other respects, Nehru was a devotee of Western materialism. He was convinced that to succeed, India must industrialize. In advocating industrialization, Nehru departed sharply from Gandhi, who believed that materialism was morally corrupting and that only simplicity and nonviolence (as represented by the traditional Indian village and the symbolic spinning wheel) could save India, and the world itself, from self-destruction (see the box on p. 634).

TWO VISIONS FOR INDIA

Although Jawaharlal Nehru and Mohandas Gandhi agreed on their desire for an independent India, their visions of the future of their homeland were dramatically different. Nehru favored industrialization to build material prosperity, whereas Gandhi praised the simple virtues of manual labor. The first excerpt is from a speech by Nehru; the second is from a letter written by Gandhi to Nehru.

NEHRU'S SOCIALIST CREED

I am convinced that the only key to the solution of the world's problems and of India's problems lies in socialism, and when I use this word I do so not in a vague humanitarian way but in the scientific economic sense. . . . I see no way of ending the poverty, the vast unemployment, the degradation and the subjection of the Indian people except through socialism. That involves vast and revolutionary changes in our political and social structure, the ending of vested interests in land and industry, as well as the feudal and autocratic Indian states system. That means the ending of private property, except in a restricted sense, and the replacement of the present profit system by a higher ideal of cooperative service. . . . In short, it means a new civilization, radically different from the present capitalist order. Some glimpse we can have of this new civilization in the territories of the U.S.S.R. Much has happened there which has pained me greatly and with which I disagree, but I look upon that great and fascinating unfolding of a new order and a new civilization as the most promising feature of our dismal age.

A LETTER TO JAWAHARLAL NEHRU

I believe that if India, and through India the world, is to achieve real freedom, then sooner or later we shall have to go and live in the villages—in huts, not in palaces. Millions of people can never live in cities and palaces in comfort and peace. Nor can they do so by killing one another, that is, by resorting to violence and untruth. . . . We can have the vision of . . . truth and nonviolence only in the simplicity of the villages. That simplicity resides in the spinning wheel and what is implied by the spinning wheel. . . .

You will not be able to understand me if you think that I am talking about the villages of today. My ideal village still exists only in my imagination. . . . In this village of my dreams the villager will not be dull—he will be all awareness. He will not live like an animal in filth and darkness. Men and women will live in freedom, prepared to face the whole world. There will be no plague, no cholera, and no smallpox. Nobody will be allowed to be idle or to wallow in luxury. Everyone will have to do body labor. Granting all this, I can still envisage a number of things that will have to be organized on a large scale. Perhaps there will even be railways and also post and telegraph offices. I do not know what things there will be or will not be. Nor am I bothered about it. If I can make sure of the essential thing, other things will follow in due course. But if I give up the essential thing, I give up everything.

The primary themes of Nehru's foreign policy were anticolonialism and antiracism. Under his guidance, India took a neutral stance in the Cold War and sought to provide leadership to all newly independent nations in Asia, Africa, and Latin America. India's neutrality put it at odds with the United States, which during the 1950s was trying to mobilize all nations against what it viewed as the menace of international communism.

Relations with Pakistan continued to be troubled. India refused to consider Pakistan's claim to Kashmir, even though the majority of the population there was Muslim. Tension between the two countries persisted, erupting into war in 1965. In 1971, when riots against the Pakistani government broke out in East Pakistan, India intervened on the side of East Pakistan, which declared its independence as the new nation of Bangladesh (see Map 29.1).

THE POST-NEHRU ERA

Nehru's death in 1964 aroused concern that Indian democracy was dependent on the Nehru mystique. When his successor, a Congress Party veteran, died in 1966, party leaders selected Nehru's daughter, Indira Gandhi (no relation to Mahatma Gandhi), as the new prime minister.

Gandhi was inexperienced in politics, but she quickly showed the steely determination of her father.

Like Nehru, Gandhi embraced democratic socialism and a policy of neutrality in foreign affairs, but she was more activist than her father. To combat rural poverty, she nationalized banks, provided loans to peasants on easy terms, built low-cost housing, distributed land to the landless, and introduced electoral reforms to enfranchise the poor.

Gandhi was especially worried by India's growing population and in an effort to curb the growth rate, adopted a policy of enforced sterilization. This policy proved unpopular, however, and, along with growing official corruption and Gandhi's authoritarian tactics, led to her defeat in the general election of 1975, the first time the Congress Party had failed to win a majority at the national level.

A minority government of procapitalist parties was formed, but within two years, Gandhi was back in power. She now faced a new challenge, however, in the rise of religious strife. The most dangerous situation was in the Punjab, where militant Sikhs were demanding autonomy or even independence from India. Gandhi did not shrink from a confrontation and attacked Sikh rebels hiding in their Golden Temple in the city of Amritsar. The incident aroused widespread anger among the Sikh community, and

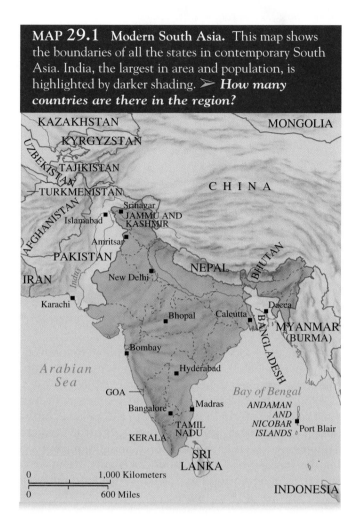

MAP 29.1 Modern South Asia. This map shows the boundaries of all the states in contemporary South Asia. India, the largest in area and population, is highlighted by darker shading. ➤ *How many countries are there in the region?*

KAZAKHSTAN
KYRGYZSTAN
UZBEKISTAN
TAJIKISTAN
TURKMENISTAN
MONGOLIA
CHINA
AFGHANISTAN
Srinagar
JAMMU AND KASHMIR
Islamabad
Amritsar
PAKISTAN
NEPAL
BHUTAN
IRAN
Indus
New Delhi
Karachi
Dacca
Bhopal
Calcutta
BANGLADESH
MYANMAR (BURMA)
Bombay
Arabian Sea
Hyderabad
GOA
Bay of Bengal
Bangalore
Madras
ANDAMAN AND NICOBAR ISLANDS
Port Blair
KERALA
TAMIL NADU
SRI LANKA
INDONESIA

0   1,000 Kilometers
0   600 Miles

in 1984, Sikh members of Gandhi's personal bodyguard assassinated her.

By now, Congress Party politicians were convinced that the party could not remain in power without a member of the Nehru family at the helm. Gandhi's son Rajiv, a commercial airline pilot with little interest in politics, was persuaded to replace his mother as prime minister. Rajiv lacked the strong ideological and political convictions of his mother and grandfather and allowed a greater role for private enterprise. But his government was criticized for cronyism, inefficiency, and corruption.

Rajiv Gandhi also sought to play a role in regional affairs, mediating a dispute between the government in Sri Lanka and Tamil rebels (known as the "Elam tigers") who were ethnically related to the majority population in southern India. The decision cost him his life: while campaigning for reelection in 1991, he was assassinated by a member of the Tiger organization. India faced the future without a member of the Nehru family as prime minister.

During the early 1990s, the Congress Party remained the leading party, but the powerful hold it once had on the Indian electorate was gone. New parties, such as the militantly Hindu Bharata Janata Party (BJP), actively vied with the Congress Party for control of the central and state govern-

ments. Growing political instability at the center was accompanied by rising tensions between Hindus and Muslims.

When a coalition government formed under Congress Party leadership collapsed, the BJP, under Prime Minister A. B. Vajpayee, ascended to power and played on Hindu sensibilities to build its political base. Rajiv Gandhi's Italian-born wife, Sonia, has taken over the leadership of the Congress Party to improve its political fortunes.

The Land of the Pure: Pakistan Since Independence

When Pakistan achieved independence in August 1947, it was, unlike its neighbor India, in all respects a new nation, based on religious conviction rather than historical or ethnic tradition. The unique state comprised two separate territories 2,000 miles apart. West Pakistan, including the Indus River basin and the West Punjab, was perennially short of water and was populated by dry-crop farmers and peoples of the steppe. East Pakistan was made up of the marshy deltas of the Ganges and Brahmaputra Rivers. Densely populated with rice farmers, it was the home of the artistic and intellectual Bengalis.

Even though the new state was an essentially Muslim society, its first years were marked by intense internal conflicts over religious, linguistic, and regional issues. Mohammed Ali Jinnah's vision of a democratic state that would ensure freedom of religion and equal treatment for all was opposed by those who advocated a state based on Islamic principles. Even more dangerous was the division between east and west. Many in East Pakistan felt that the government, based in the west, ignored their needs, and in March 1971, East Pakistan declared its independence as the new nation of Bangladesh.

The breakup of the union between East and West Pakistan undermined the fragile authority of the military regime that had ruled Pakistan since 1958 and led to its replacement by a civilian government under Zulfikar Ali Bhutto. But now religious tensions came to the fore, despite a new constitution that made a number of key concessions to conservative Muslims. In 1977, a new military government under General Zia Ul Ha'q came to power with a commitment to make Pakistan a truly Islamic state. Islamic law became the basis for social behavior as well as for the legal system. Laws governing the consumption of alcohol and the role of women were tightened in accordance with strict Muslim beliefs. But after Zia was killed in a plane crash, Pakistanis elected Benazir Bhutto, the daughter of Zulfikar Ali Bhutto and a supporter of secularism who had been educated in the United States. She too was removed from power by a military regime, in 1990, on charges of incompetence and corruption. Reelected in 1993, she attempted to crack down on opposition forces but was removed once again amid renewed charges of official corruption. Her successor soon came under fire for the same reason and in 1999 was ousted by a military coup led by General Pervaiz Musharraf, who promised to restore political stability and honest government. His situation was complicated by renewed tensions with India over Kashmir and a series of violent clashes between Muslims and Hindus in India.

Poverty and Pluralism in South Asia

The leaders of the new states that emerged in South Asia after World War II faced a number of problems. The peoples of South Asia were still overwhelmingly poor and illiterate, while the sectarian, ethnic, and cultural divisions that had plagued Indian society for centuries had not dissipated.

THE POLITICS OF COMMUNALISM

Perhaps the most sincere effort to create democratic institutions was in India, where the new constitution called for social justice, liberty, equality of status and opportunity, and fraternity. All citizens were guaranteed protection from discrimination on the grounds of religious belief, race, caste, sex, or place of birth.

In theory, then, India became a full-fledged democracy on the British parliamentary model. In actuality, a number of distinctive characteristics made the system less than fully democratic in the Western sense but may also have enabled it to survive. As we have seen, India became in essence a one-party state. By leading the independence movement, the Congress Party had amassed massive public support, which enabled it to retain its preeminent position in Indian politics for three decades. After Nehru's death in 1964, however, problems emerged that had been disguised by his adept maneuvering. Part of the problem was the familiar one of a party too long in power. Party officials became complacent and all too easily fell prey to the temptations of corruption and pork-barrel politics.

Another problem was communalism. Beneath the surface unity of the new republic lay age-old ethnic, linguistic, and religious divisions. Because of India's vast size and complex history, no national language had ever emerged. Hindi was the most prevalent, but it was the native language of less than one-third of the population. During the colonial period, English had served as the official language of government, but it was spoken only by the educated elite and represented an affront to national pride. Eventually India recognized fourteen official tongues, making the parliament sometimes sound like the Tower of Babel.

Divisiveness increased after Nehru's death, and under his successors, official corruption grew. Only the lack of appeal of its rivals and the Nehru family charisma carried on by his daughter Indira Gandhi kept the party in power. But she was unable to prevent the progressive disintegration of the party's power base at the state level, where regional or ideological parties won the allegiance of voters by exploiting ethnic or social revolutionary themes.

Chronology

SOUTH ASIA

India and Pakistan become independent	1947
Assassination of Mahatma Gandhi	1948
Death of Jawaharlal Nehru	1964
Indo-Pakistani War	1965
Indira Gandhi elected prime minister	1966
Bangladesh declares its independence	1971
Assassination of Indira Gandhi	1984
Rajiv Gandhi assassinated	1991
Military coup overthrows civilian government in Pakistan	1999

During the 1980s, religious tensions began to intensify. As we have seen, Gandhi's uncompromising approach to Sikh separatism led to her assassination in 1984. In 1992, at Ayodhya, in northern India, Hindu militants destroyed a mosque allegedly built on the site of King Rama's birthplace, where a Hindu temple had once existed, and erected a temporary temple at the site, provoking clashes between Hindus and Muslims throughout the country. In protest, rioters in neighboring Pakistan destroyed a number of Hindu shrines in that country.

In recent years, communal divisions have intensified, as militant Hindu groups agitate for a state that caters to the Hindu majority, now numbering more than 700 million people. In the spring of 2002, violence between Hindus and Muslims flared up again over plans by Hindu activists to build a permanent temple to Rama at the site of the destroyed mosque at Ayodhya.

THE ECONOMY

Nehru's answer to the social and economic inequality that had long afflicted the subcontinent was socialism. He instituted a series of five-year plans, which led to the creation of a relatively large and reasonably efficient industrial sector, centered on steel, vehicles, and textiles. Industrial production almost tripled between 1950 and 1965, and per capita income rose by 50 percent between 1950 and 1980, although it was still less than $300 (in U.S. dollars). By the 1970s, however, industrial growth had slowed. The lack of modern infrastructure was a problem, as was the rising price of oil, most of which had to be imported.

India's major economic weakness, however, was in agriculture. At independence, mechanization was almost unknown, fertilizer was rarely used, and most farms were small and uneconomical because of the Hindu tradition of dividing the land equally among all male children. As a result, the vast majority of the Indian people lived in conditions of abject poverty. Landless laborers outnumbered landowners by almost two to one. The government attempted to relieve the problem by redistributing land to the poor, limiting the size of landholdings, and encouraging farmers to form voluntary cooperatives. But all three programs ran into widespread opposition.

Another problem was overpopulation. Even before independence, the country had had difficulty supporting its people. In the 1950s and 1960s, the population grew by more than 2 percent annually, twice the nineteenth-century rate. Beginning in the 1960s, the Indian government sought to curb population growth. Indira Gandhi instituted a program combining monetary rewards and compulsory sterilization. Males who had fathered too many children were sometimes forced to undergo a vasectomy. Popular resistance undermined the program, however, and the goals were scaled back in the 1970s. As a result, India has made little progress in holding down its burgeoning population, now estimated at more than one billion. Nevertheless, as a result of media popularization and better government programs, the trend today, even in poor rural villages, is toward smaller families. The average number of children a woman bears has been reduced from six in 1950 to three today.

After the death of Indira Gandhi in 1984, her son Rajiv proved more receptive to foreign investment and a greater role for the private sector in the economy. India began to export more manufactured goods, including computer software. The pace of change has accelerated under Rajiv Gandhi's successors, who have continued to transfer state-run industries to private hands. These policies have stimulated the growth of a prosperous new middle class, now estimated at more than 100 million. Consumerism has soared, and sales of television sets, automobiles, videocassette recorders, and telephones have increased dramatically. Equally important, Western imports are being replaced by new products manufactured in India with Indian brand names.

As in the industrialized countries of the West, economic growth has been accompanied by environmental damage. Water and air pollution has led to illness and death for many people, and an environmental movement has emerged. Some critics, reflecting the traditional anti-imperialist attitude of Indian intellectuals, blame Western capitalist corporations for the problem, as in the highly publicized case of leakage from a foreign-owned chemical plant at Bhopal. Much of the problem, however, comes from state-owned factories erected with Soviet aid. And not all the environmental damage can be ascribed to industrialization. The Ganges River is so polluted by human overuse that it is risky for Hindu believers to bathe in it.

Moreover, many Indians have not benefited from the new prosperity. Nearly one-third of the population lives below the national poverty line. Millions continue to live in urban slums, such as the famous "City of Joy" in Cal-

FETCHING WATER AT THE VILLAGE WELL. The scarcity of water will surely become one of the planet's most crucial problems in the twenty-first century. It will affect all nations, developed and developing, rich and poor. Although many Indians live with an inadequate water supply, these women are fortunate to have a well in their village. More typical is the image of the Indian woman, dressed in a colorful sari, children encircling her as she heads to her distant home on foot, carrying a heavy pail of water on her head.

cutta, and most farm families remain desperately poor. Despite the socialist rhetoric of India's leaders, the inequality of wealth in India is as pronounced as it is in capitalist nations in the West.

CASTE, CLASS, AND GENDER

Although the constitution of 1950 guaranteed equal treatment and opportunity for all, regardless of caste, and prohibited discrimination based on untouchability, prejudice is hard to eliminate. Untouchability persists, particularly in the villages, where *harijans*, now called *dalits*, still perform menial tasks and are often denied fundamental human rights.

After independence, India's leaders also sought to equalize treatment of the sexes. The constitution expressly forbade discrimination based on sex and called for equal pay for equal work. Laws prohibited child marriage, *sati*, and the payment of a dowry by the bride's family. Women were encouraged to attend school and enter the labor market.

Such laws, along with the dynamics of economic and social change, have had a major impact on the lives of many Indian women. Middle-class women in urban areas are much more likely to seek employment outside the home, and many hold managerial and professional positions. Some Indian women, however, choose to play a dual role—a modern one in their work and in the marketplace and a more submissive, traditional one at home (see the box on p. 638).

A CRITIQUE OF WESTERN FEMINISM

*O*rganized efforts to protect the rights of women have been under way in India since the 1970s, when the Progressive Organization for Women (POW) instituted a campaign against sexual harassment and other forms of discrimination against women in Indian society. Like many of their counterparts in other parts of Asia and Africa, however, many activists for women's rights in India are critical of Western feminism, charging that it is irrelevant to their own realities. Although Indian feminists feel a bond with their sisters all over the world, they insist on resolving Indian problems with Indian solutions. The author of this editorial is Madhu Kishwar, founder and editor of a women's journal in New Delhi.

FINDING INDIAN SOLUTIONS TO WOMEN'S PROBLEMS

Western feminism, exported to India and many other Third World countries in recent decades, has brought with it serious problems.

As products of a more homogenized culture, most Western feminists assume women's aspirations the world over must be quite similar. Yet a person's idea of a good life and her aspirations are closely related to what is valued in her particular society. This applies to feminism itself. An offshoot of individualism and liberalism, it posits that each individual is responsible primarily to herself. . . .

In societies like India, most of us find it difficult to tune in to this extreme individualism. For instance, most Indian women are unwilling to assert rights in a way that estranges them not just from their family but also from their larger community. . . .

This isn't slavery to social opinion. Rather, many of us believe life is a poor thing if our own dear ones don't honor and celebrate our rights, if our freedom cuts us off from others. In our culture, both men and women are taught to value the interests of our families more than our self-interest. . . .

Cultural issues aside, my most fundamental reservation regarding feminism is that it has strengthened the tendency among India's Western-educated elites to adopt the statist authoritarian route to social reform. The characteristic feminist response to most social issues affecting women—in the workplace, in the media, in the home—is to demand more and more stringent laws. . . .

But dearly held and deeply cherished cultural norms cannot be changed simply by applying the instruments of state repression through legal punishment. Social reform is too complex and important a matter to be left to the police and courts. The best of laws will tend to fail if social opinion is contrary to them. Therefore, the statist route of using laws as a substitute for creating a new social consensus about women's rights tends to be counterproductive.

Like other aspects of life, the role of women has changed much less in rural areas. In the early 1960s, many villagers still practiced the institution of *purdah*. Female children are still much less likely to receive an education. The overall literacy rate in India today is less than 40 percent, but it is undoubtedly much lower among women. Laws relating to dowry, child marriage, and inheritance are routinely ignored in the countryside. There have been a few highly publicized cases of *sati*, although undoubtedly more women die of mistreatment at the hands of their husband or of other members of his family.

South Asian Art and Literature Since Independence

Recent decades have witnessed a prodigious outpouring of literature in India. Because of the vast quantity of works published (India is currently the third-largest publisher of English-language books in the world), only a few of the most prominent fiction writers can be mentioned here. Anita Desai (b. 1937) was one of the first prominent female writers in contemporary India. Her writing focuses on the struggle of Indian women to achieve a degree of independence. In her first novel, *Cry, the Peacock,* the heroine finally seeks liberation by murdering her husband, preferring freedom at any cost to remaining a captive of traditional society.

The most controversial writer in India today is Salman Rushdie (b. 1947). In *Midnight's Children,* published in 1980, the author linked his protagonist, born on the night of independence, to the history of modern India, its achievements and its frustrations. Rushdie's later novels have tackled such problems as religious intolerance, political tyranny, social injustice, and greed and corruption. His attack on Islamic fundamentalism in *The Satanic Verses* (1988) won plaudits from literary critics but provoked widespread criticism among Muslims, including a death sentence by Ayatollah Khomeini in Iran.

Like Chinese and Japanese artists, Indian artists have agonized over how best to paint with a modern yet indigenous mode of expression. During the colonial period, Indian art went in several directions at once. One school of painters favored traditional themes; another experimented with a colorful primitivism founded on folk art. Many Indian artists painted representational social art extolling the suffering and silent dignity of India's impoverished millions. After 1960, however, most Indian artists adopted abstract art as their medium. Surrealism in particular, with its emphasis on spontaneity and the unconscious, appeared closer to the Hindu tradition of favoring intuition over reason. Yet Indian artists are still struggling to find the ideal way to be both modern and Indian.

⟩ **YOUNG HINDU BRIDE IN GOLD BANGLES.** Awaiting the marriage ceremony, a young bride sits with the female relatives of her family at the Meenakshi Hindu temple, one of the largest in southern India. Although child marriage is illegal, Indian girls are still married at a young age. With the marital union arranged by the parents, this young bride has perhaps never met the groom. Bedecked in gold jewelry and rich silks—part of her dowry—she nervously awaits the priest's blessing before she moves to her husband's home. There she will begin a life of servitude to her in-laws' family.

SOUTHEAST ASIA

As we have seen (see Chapter 24), Japanese wartime occupation had a great impact on attitudes among the peoples of Southeast Asia. It demonstrated the vulnerability of colonial rule in the region and showed that an Asian power could defeat Europeans. The Allied governments themselves also contributed—sometimes unwittingly—to rising aspirations for independence by promising self-determination for all peoples at the end of the war.

Some followed through on their promise. In July 1946, the United States granted total independence to the Philippines. The Americans maintained a military presence on the islands, however, and U.S. citizens retained economic and commercial interests in the new country.

The British, too, were willing to bring an end to a century of imperialism in the region. In 1948, the Union of Burma received its independence. Malaya's turn came in 1957, after a communist guerrilla movement had been suppressed.

The French and the Dutch, however, both regarded their colonies in the region as economic necessities as well as symbols of national grandeur and refused to turn them over to nationalist movements at the end of the war. The Dutch attempted to suppress a rebellion in the East Indies led by Sukarno, leader of the Indonesian Nationalist Party. But the United States, which feared a communist victory there, pressured the Dutch to grant independence to Sukarno and his noncommunist forces, and in 1950, the Dutch finally agreed to recognize the new Republic of Indonesia.

The situation was somewhat different in Vietnam, where the Communists seized power throughout most of the country. After the French refused to recognize

the new government and reimposed their rule, war broke out in December 1946. At the time, it was only an anticolonial war, but it would soon become much more (see Chapter 25).

The Era of Independent States

Many of the leaders of the newly independent states in Southeast Asia (see Map 29.2) admired Western political institutions and hoped to adapt them to their own countries. New constitutions were patterned on Western democratic models, and multiparty political systems quickly sprang into operation.

THE SEARCH FOR A NEW POLITICAL CULTURE

By the 1960s, most of these budding experiments in pluralist democracy had been abandoned or were under serious threat. Some had been replaced by military or one-party autocratic regimes. In Burma, a moderate government based on the British parliamentary system and dedicated to Buddhism and nonviolent Marxism had given way to a military government. In Thailand, too, the military now ruled. In the Philippines, President Ferdinand Marcos discarded democratic restraints and established his own centralized control. In South Vietnam, Ngo Dinh Diem and his successors paid lip service to the Western democratic model but ruled by authoritarian means.

One problem faced by most of these states was that independence had not brought material prosperity or ended economic inequality and the domination of the local economies by foreign interests. Most economies in the region were still characterized by tiny industrial

sectors; they lacked technology, educational resources, and capital investment.

The presence of widespread ethnic, linguistic, cultural, and economic differences also made the transition to Western-style democracy difficult. In Malaya, for example, the majority Malays—most of whom were farmers—feared economic and political domination by the local Chinese minority, who were much more experienced in industry and commerce. In 1961, the Federation of Malaya, whose ruling party was dominated by Malays, integrated former British possessions on the island of Borneo into the new Union of Malaysia in a move to increase the non-Chinese proportion of the country's population.

The most publicized example of a failed experiment in democracy was in Indonesia. In 1950, the new leaders drew up a constitution creating a parliamentary system under a titular presidency. Sukarno was elected the first president. A spellbinding orator, Sukarno played a major role in creating a sense of national identity among the disparate peoples of the Indonesian archipelago.

In the late 1950s, Sukarno, exasperated at the incessant maneuvering among devout Muslims, Communists, and the army, dissolved the constitution and attempted to rule on his own through what he called "guided democracy." As he described it, guided democracy was closer to Indonesian traditions and superior to the Western variety. Highly suspicious of the West, Sukarno nationalized foreign-owned enterprises and sought economic aid from China and the Soviet Union while relying for domestic support on the Indonesian Communist Party.

The army and conservative Muslims resented Sukarno's increasing reliance on the Communists, and the Muslims were further upset by his refusal to consider a state based on Islamic principles. In 1965, military officers launched a coup d'état that provoked a mass popular uprising, which resulted in the slaughter of several hundred thousand suspected Communists, many of whom were overseas Chinese, long distrusted by the Muslim majority. In 1967, a military government under General Suharto was installed.

The new government made no pretensions of reverting to democratic rule, but it did restore good relations with the West and sought foreign investment to repair the country's ravaged economy. But it also found it difficult to placate Muslim demands for an Islamic state.

The one country in Southeast Asia that explicitly rejected the Western model was North Vietnam. Its leaders opted for the Stalinist pattern of national development, based on Communist Party rule and socialist forms of ownership. In 1958, stimulated by the success of collectivization in neighboring China, the government launched a three-year plan to lay the foundation for a socialist society. Collective farms were established, and all industry and commerce above the family level were nationalized.

RECENT TRENDS TOWARD DEMOCRACY

In recent years, some Southeast Asian societies have shown signs of evolving toward more democratic forms. In the Philippines, the dictatorial Marcos regime was overthrown by a massive public uprising in 1986 and replaced by a democratically elected government under President Corazon Aquino, the widow of a popular politician assassinated a few years earlier. Aquino was unable to resolve many of the country's chronic economic and social difficulties, however, and political stability remains elusive; one of her successors, ex-actor Joseph Estrada, was forced to resign on the charge of corruption. At the same time, Muslims in the southern island of Mindanao have mounted a terrorist campaign in their effort to obtain autonomy or independence.

In other nations, the results have also been mixed. Although Malaysia is a practicing democracy, tensions persist between Malays and Chinese as well as between secular and orthodox Muslims who seek to create an Islamic state. In neighboring Thailand, the military has found it expedient to hold national elections for civilian governments, but the danger of a military takeover is never far beneath the surface.

In Indonesia, difficult economic conditions caused by the financial crisis of 1997 (see the next section), combined with popular anger against the Suharto government (several members of his family had reportedly used their positions to amass considerable wealth), led to violent street riots and demands for his resignation. Forced to step down in the spring of 1998, Suharto was replaced by his deputy, B. J. Habibie, who called for the establishment of a national assembly to select a new government based on popular aspirations. The assembly selected a moderate Muslim leader as president, but he was charged with corruption and incompetence and was replaced in 2001 by his vice president, Sukarno's daughter Megawati Sukarnoputri.

In Vietnam, the trend in recent years has been toward a greater popular role in the governing process. Elections for the unicameral parliament are more open than in the

SOUTHEAST ASIA

Philippines become independent	1946
Beginning of Franco-Vietminh War	1946
Burma becomes independent	1948
Recognition of the Republic of Indonesia	1950
Malaya becomes independent	1957
Beginning of Sukarno's "guided democracy" in Indonesia	1959
Military seizes power in Indonesia	1965
Foundation of ASEAN	1967
Vietnamese invade Cambodia	1978
Corazon Aquino elected president in the Philippines	1986
United Nations forces arrive in Cambodia	1991
Islamic and student protests in Indonesia	1996–1997
Suharto steps down as president of Indonesia	1998

past. The government remains suspicious of Western-style democracy, however, and represses any opposition to the Communist Party's guiding role over the state.

Only in Burma (now renamed Myanmar), where the military has been in complete control since the early 1960s, have the forces of greater popular participation been virtually silenced. Even there, however, the power of the ruling regime of General Ne Win has been vocally challenged by Aung San Suu Kyi, the admired daughter of one of the heroes of the country's struggle for national liberation after World War II.

INCREASING PROSPERITY AND FINANCIAL CRISIS

The trend toward more representative systems of government has been due in part to increasing prosperity and the growth of an affluent and educated middle class. Although Indonesia, Burma, and the three Indochinese states are still overwhelmingly agrarian, Malaysia and Thailand have been undergoing relatively rapid economic development.

In the late summer of 1997, however, these economic gains were threatened, and popular faith in the ultimate benefits of globalization was shaken as a financial crisis swept through the region. The crisis was triggered by a number of problems, including growing budget deficits caused by excessive government expenditures on ambitious development projects, and irresponsible lending and investment practices by financial institutions. An underlying cause of these problems was the prevalence of backroom deals between politicians and business leaders that temporarily enriched both groups at the cost of eventual economic dislocation.

As local currencies plummeted in value, the International Monetary Fund agreed to provide assistance, but only on the condition that the governments concerned allow market forces to operate more freely, even at the price of bankruptcies and the loss of jobs. In the early 2000s, although there were signs that some political leaders recognized the serious nature of their problems and were willing to take steps to resolve them, the political cost of such changes remained uncertain.

Regional Conflict and Cooperation: The Rise of ASEAN

In addition to their continuing internal challenges, Southeast Asian states have been hampered by serious tensions among themselves. Some of these tensions were a consequence of historical rivalries and territorial disputes that had been submerged during the long era of colonial rule. Cambodia, for example, has bickered with both of its neighbors, Thailand and Vietnam, over mutual frontiers drawn up originally by the French for their own convenience.

After the reunification of Vietnam under communist rule in 1975, the lingering border dispute between Cambodia and Vietnam erupted again. In April 1975, a brutal revolutionary regime under the leadership of the Khmer Rouge dictator Pol Pot came to power in Cambodia and proceeded to carry out the massacre of more than one million Cambodians. Then, claiming that vast territories in the Mekong delta had been seized from Cambodia by the Vietnamese in previous centuries, the Khmer Rouge regime launched attacks across the common border. In response, Vietnamese forces invaded Cambodia in December 1978 and installed a pro-Hanoi regime in Phnom Penh. Fearful of Vietnam's increasing power in the region, China launched a brief attack on Vietnam to demonstrate its displeasure.

The outbreak of war among the erstwhile communist allies aroused the concern of other countries in the neighborhood. In 1967, several noncommunist countries had established the Association of Southeast Asian Nations (ASEAN). Composed of Indonesia, Malaysia, Thailand, Singapore, and the Philippines, ASEAN at first concentrated on cooperative social and economic endeavors, but after the end of the Vietnam War, it cooperated with other states in an effort to force the Vietnamese to withdraw from Cambodia. In 1991, the Vietnamese finally withdrew, and a new government was formed in Phnom Penh.

The growth of ASEAN from a weak collection of diverse states into a stronger organization whose members cooperate militarily and politically has helped provide the nations of Southeast Asia with a more cohesive voice to represent their interests on the world stage. That Vietnam was admitted into ASEAN in 1996 should provide both Hanoi and its neighbors with greater leverage in dealing with China—their powerful neighbor to the north.

Daily Life: Town and Country in Contemporary Southeast Asia

The urban-rural dichotomy observed in India also is found in Southeast Asia, where the cities resemble those in the West while the countryside often appears little changed from

Courtesy of William J. Duiker

HOLOCAUST IN CAMBODIA. When the Khmer Rouge seized power in Cambodia in April 1975, they immediately emptied the capital of Phnom Penh and systematically began to eliminate opposition elements throughout the country. Thousands were tortured in the infamous Tuol Sleng prison and then marched out to the countryside, where they were massacred. Their bodies were thrown into massive pits. The succeeding government disinterred the remains, which are now displayed at an outdoor museum on the site.

precolonial days. In cities such as Bangkok, Manila, and Jakarta, broad boulevards lined with skyscrapers alternate with muddy lanes passing through neighborhoods packed with wooden shacks topped by thatch or rusty tin roofs. Nevertheless, in recent decades, millions of Southeast Asians have fled to these urban slums. Although most available jobs are menial, the pay is better than in the villages.

The urban migrants change not only their physical surroundings but their attitudes and values as well. Sometimes the move leads to a decline in traditional beliefs. Nevertheless, Buddhist, Muslim, and Confucian beliefs remain strong, even in cosmopolitan cities such as Bangkok, Jakarta, and Singapore. This preference for the traditional also shows up in lifestyle. Native dress—or an eclectic blend of Asian and Western dress—is still common. Traditional music, art, theater, and dance remain popular, although Western rock music has become fashionable among the young, and Indonesian filmmakers complain that Western films are beginning to dominate the market.

One of the most significant changes that has taken place in Southeast Asia in recent decades is in the role of women in society. In general, women in the region have historically faced fewer restrictions on their activities and enjoyed a higher status than women elsewhere in Asia. Nevertheless, they were not the equal of men in every respect. With independence, Southeast Asian women gained new rights. Virtually all of the constitutions adopted by the newly independent states granted women full legal and political rights, including the right to work.

Today women have increased opportunities for education and have entered careers previously reserved for men. Women have become more active in politics, and as we have seen, some have served as heads of state.

Yet women are not truly equal to men in any country in Southeast Asia. In Vietnam, women are legally equal to men, yet until recently no women had served in the Communist Party's ruling Politburo. In Thailand, Malaysia, and Indonesia, women rarely hold senior positions in government service or in the boardrooms of major corporations.

A Region in Flux

Today the Western image of a Southeast Asia mired in the Vietnam conflict and the tensions of the Cold War has become a memory. In ASEAN, the states in the region have created the framework for a regional organization that can serve their common political, economic, technological, and security interests. A few members of ASEAN are already on the road to advanced development.

To be sure, there are continuing signs of trouble. The recent financial crisis has aroused serious political unrest in Indonesia and has the potential to create similar problems elsewhere. There are disquieting signs that al-Qaeda has established a presence in the region. Myanmar remains isolated and appears mired in a state of chronic underdevelopment and brutal military rule. The three states of Indochina remain potentially unstable and have not yet been fully integrated into the region as a whole.

Exchange of Foods: East and West

McDonald's fast-food chain has become a prime symbol of U.S. cultural influence throughout the world. Popular with young people, it is often the target of attacks from those who criticize the impact that American values have had on traditional cultures, from Europe to East Asia. Some especially focus on the health problems that will arise from the typical American junk-food diet. At the left, we see a giant statue of Ronald McDonald welcoming young Indonesians to a restaurant in the capital city of Jakarta. At the same time, Eastern foods and eating styles have also made an enormous impact on the Western world, where they are appreciated by some for their nutritional value and health benefits, as well as for their exotic flavors. Seen at the right is a Chinese restaurant in the city of Amsterdam.

EAST ASIA

In August 1945, Japan was in ruins, its cities destroyed, its vast Asian empire in ashes, its land occupied by a foreign army. Half a century later, Japan had emerged as the second-greatest industrial power in the world, democratic in form and content and a source of stability throughout the region. Japan's achievement spawned a number of Asian imitators.

The Japanese Miracle: The Transformation of Modern Japan

For five years after the end of the war in the Pacific, Japan was governed by an Allied administration under the command of U.S. general Douglas MacArthur. As commander of the occupation administration, MacArthur was responsible for demilitarizing Japanese society, destroying the Japanese war machine, trying Japanese civilian and military officials charged with war crimes, and laying the foundations of postwar Japanese society.

One of the sturdy pillars of Japanese militarism had been the giant business cartels, known as *zaibatsu*. Allied policy was designed to break up the *zaibatsu* into smaller units in the belief that corporate concentration not only hindered competition but was inherently undemocratic and conducive to political authoritarianism. Occupation planners also intended to promote the formation of independent labor unions in order to lessen the power of the state over the economy and provide a mouthpiece for downtrodden Japanese workers. Economic inequality in rural areas was to be reduced by a comprehensive land reform program that would turn the land over to those who farmed it. Finally, the educational system was to be remodeled along American lines so that it would turn out independent individuals rather than automatons subject to manipulation by the state.

The Allied program was an ambitious and even audacious plan to remake Japanese society and has been justly praised for its clear-sighted vision and altruistic motives. Parts of the program, such as the constitution, the land reforms, and the educational system, succeeded brilliantly. But as other concerns began to intervene, changes or compromises were made that were not always successful. In particular, with the rise of Cold War sentiment in the United States in the late 1940s, the goal of decentralizing the Japanese economy gave way to the desire to make Japan a key partner in the effort to defend East Asia against international communism. Convinced of the need to promote economic recovery in Japan, U.S. policy makers began to show more tolerance for the *zaibatsu*. Concerned at growing radicalism within the new labor movement, U.S. occupation authorities placed less emphasis on the independence of the labor unions.

The Cold War also affected U.S. foreign relations with Japan. On September 8, 1951, the United States and other former belligerent nations signed a peace treaty restoring Japanese independence. In turn, Japan renounced any claim to such former colonies or territories as Taiwan, Korea, and southern Sakhalin and the Kurile Islands (see Map 29.3). On the same day, Japan and the United States signed a defensive alliance and agreed that the latter could maintain military bases on the Japanese islands. Japan was now formally independent but in a new dependency relationship with the United States. A provision in the new constitution renounced war as an instrument of national policy and prohibited the raising of an army.

POLITICS AND GOVERNMENT

The Allied occupation administrators started with the conviction that Japanese expansionism was directly linked to the institutional and ideological foundations of the Meiji constitution. Accordingly, they set out to change Japanese politics into something closer to the pluralistic model used in most Western nations. Yet a number of characteristics of the postwar Japanese political system reflected the tenacity of the traditional political culture. Although Japan had a multiparty system with two major parties, the Liberal Democrats and the Socialists, in practice there was a "government party" and a permanent opposition—the Liberal Democrats were not voted out of office for thirty years.

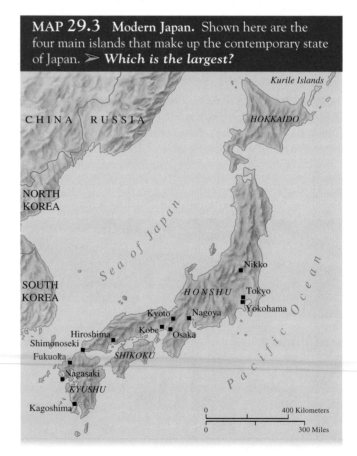

MAP 29.3 Modern Japan. Shown here are the four main islands that make up the contemporary state of Japan. ➢ *Which is the largest?*

That tradition changed suddenly in 1993, when the ruling Liberal Democrats, shaken by persistent reports of corruption and cronyism between politicians and business interests, failed to win a majority of seats in parliamentary elections. The new coalition government, however, quickly split into feuding factions, and in 1995, the Liberal Democrats returned to power. Successive prime ministers proved unable to carry out promised reforms, and in 2001, Junichiro Koizumi, an ex-minister of health and welfare, was elected prime minister. He too promised far-reaching reforms to make the political system more responsive to the challenges facing the country—so far, he has had little success.

These challenges include not only curbing persistent political corruption but also reducing the government's involvement in the economy. Since the Meiji period, the government has played an active role in mediating management-labor disputes, establishing price and wage policies, and subsidizing vital industries and enterprises producing goods for export. This government intervention in the economy was once cited as a key reason for the efficiency of Japanese industry and the emergence of the country as an industrial giant.

The issue of Japan's behavior during World War II has been especially sensitive. During the 1990s, critics at home and abroad charged that textbooks printed under the guidance of the Ministry of Education did not adequately discuss the atrocities committed by the Japanese government and armed forces during World War II. The government expressed remorse, but only in the context of the aggressive actions of all colonial powers during the imperialist era.

THE ECONOMY

Nowhere are the changes in postwar Japan so visible as in the economic sector, where Japan developed into a major industrial and technological power in the space of a century, surpassing such advanced Western societies as Germany, France, and Great Britain.

Although this "Japanese miracle" has often been described as beginning after the war as a result of the Allied reforms, Japanese economic growth in fact began much earlier, with the Meiji reforms, which helped transform Japan from an autocratic society based on semifeudal institutions into an advanced capitalist democracy.

As noted, the officials of the Allied occupation identified the Meiji economic system with centralized power and the rise of Japanese militarism. But with the rise of Cold War tensions, the policy of breaking up the *zaibatsu* was scaled back. Looser ties between companies were still allowed, and a new type of informal relationship, sometimes called the *keiretsu*, or "interlocking arrangement," began to take shape. Through such arrangements among suppliers, wholesalers, retailers, and financial institutions, the *zaibatsu* system was reconstituted under a new name.

The occupation administration had more success with its program to reform the agricultural system. Half of the population still lived on farms, and half of all farmers were still tenants. Under the land reform program, all lands owned by absentee landlords and all cultivated landholdings over an established maximum were sold on easy credit terms to the tenants. The program created a strong class of yeoman farmers, and tenants declined to about 10 percent of the rural population.

During the next fifty years, Japan re-created the stunning results of the Meiji era. In 1950, the Japanese gross domestic product was about one-third that of Great Britain or France. Today it is larger than both put together and well over half that of the United States. Japan is the greatest exporting nation in the world, and its per capita income equals or surpasses that of most advanced Western states.

In recent years, the Japanese economy has run into serious difficulties, raising the question as to whether the vaunted Japanese model is as appealing as many observers earlier declared. A rise in the value of the yen hurt exports and burst the bubble of investment by Japanese banks that had taken place under the umbrella of government protection. Lacking a domestic market equivalent in size to the United States, in the 1990s the Japanese economy slipped into a recession that continues today.

These economic difficulties have placed heavy pressure on some of the vaunted features of the Japanese economy. The tradition of lifetime employment created a bloated white-collar workforce and has made downsizing difficult. Today job security is on the decline as increasing numbers of workers are being laid off. A disproportionate burden has fallen on women, who lack seniority and continue to suffer from various forms of discrimination in the workplace.

A final change is that slowly but inexorably, the Japanese market is beginning to open up to international competition. Greater exposure to foreign competition may improve the performance of Japanese manufacturers. In recent years, Japanese consumers have become increasingly critical of the quality of some domestic products, provoking one cabinet minister to complain about "sloppiness and complacency" among Japanese firms. One apparent reason for the country's recent quality problems is the cost-cutting measures adopted by Japanese companies to meet the challenges from abroad.

A SOCIETY IN TRANSITION

During the occupation, Allied planners set out to change social characteristics that they believed had contributed to Japanese aggressiveness before and during World War II. The new educational system removed all references to filial piety, patriotism, and loyalty to the emperor while emphasizing the individualistic values of Western civilization. The new constitution and a revised civil code eliminated remaining legal restrictions on women's rights to obtain a divorce, hold a job, or change their domicile. Women were guaranteed the right to vote and were encouraged to enter politics.

GROWING UP IN JAPAN

Japanese schoolchildren are exposed to a much more regimented environment than U.S. children experience. Most Japanese schoolchildren, for example, wear black-and-white uniforms to school. These regulations are examples of rules adopted by middle school systems in various parts of Japan. The Ministry of Education in Tokyo concluded that these regulations were excessive, but they are probably typical.

SCHOOL REGULATIONS, JAPANESE-STYLE

1. Boys' hair should not touch the eyebrows, the ears, or the top of the collar.
2. No one should have a permanent wave, or dye his or her hair. Girls should not wear ribbons or accessories in their hair. Hair dryers should not be used.
3. School uniform skirts should be ____ centimeters above the ground, no more and no less (differs by school and region).
4. Keep your uniform clean and pressed at all times. Girls' middy blouses should have two buttons on the back collar. Boys' pant cuffs should be of the prescribed width. No more than 12 eyelets should be on shoes. The number of buttons on a shirt and tucks in a shirt are also prescribed.
5. Wear your school badge at all times. It should be positioned exactly.
6. Going to school in the morning, wear your book bag strap on the right shoulder; in the afternoon on the way home, wear it on the left shoulder. Your book case thickness, filled and unfilled, is also prescribed.
7. Girls should wear only regulation white underpants of 100% cotton.
8. When you raise your hand to be called on, your arm should extend forward and up at the angle prescribed in your handbook.
9. Your own route to and from school is marked in your student rule handbook; carefully observe which side of each street you are to use on the way to and from school.
10. After school you are to go directly home, unless your parent has written a note permitting you to go to another location. Permission will not be granted by the school unless this other location is a suitable one. You must not go to coffee shops. You must be home by ____ o'clock.
11. It is not permitted to drive or ride a motorcycle, or to have a license to drive one.
12. Before and after school, no matter where you are, you represent our school, so you should behave in ways we can all be proud of.

Such efforts to remake Japanese behavior through legislation were only partially successful. During the past sixty years, Japan has unquestionably become a more individualistic and egalitarian society. At the same time, many of the distinctive characteristics of traditional Japanese society have persisted to the present day, although in somewhat altered form. The emphasis on loyalty to the group and community relationships, for example, is reflected in the strength of corporate loyalties in contemporary Japan.

Emphasis on the work ethic also remains strong. The tradition of hard work is taught at a young age. The Japanese school year runs for 240 days a year, compared to 180 days in the United States, and work assignments outside class tend to be more extensive. The results are impressive: Japanese schoolchildren consistently earn higher scores on achievement tests than children in other advanced countries. At the same time, this devotion to success has often been accompanied by bullying by teachers and what Americans might consider an oppressive sense of conformity (see the box above).

By all accounts, independent thinking is on the increase in Japan. In some cases, it leads to antisocial behavior, such as crime or membership in a teenage gang. Usually it is expressed in more indirect ways, such as the recent fashion among young people of dyeing their hair brown (known in Japanese as "tea hair"). Because the practice is banned in many schools and generally frowned upon by the older generation (one police chief dumped a pitcher of beer on a student with brown hair whom he noticed in a bar), many young Japanese dye their hair as a gesture of independence. When seeking employment or getting married, however, they often return their hair to its natural color.

One of the more tenacious legacies of the past in Japanese society is sexual inequality. Although women are now legally protected against discrimination in employment, very few have reached senior levels in business, education, or politics. Women now constitute nearly 50 percent of the workforce; but most are in retail or service occupations, and their average salary is only about half that of men. There is a feminist movement in Japan, but it has none of the vigor and mass support of its counterpart in the United States.

RELIGION AND CULTURE

When Japan was opened to the West in the nineteenth century, many Japanese became convinced of the superiority of foreign ideas and institutions and were especially interested in Western religion and culture. Although Christian converts were few, numbering less than one percent of the population, the influence of Christianity was out of proportion to the size of the community.

Today Japan includes almost 1.5 million Christians, along with 93 million Buddhists. Many Japanese also follow Shinto, no longer identified with reverence for the emperor

➤ **COOL OTAKU FASHION TEENS.**
Fashion-conscious teenagers have
become Japan's most dedicated consumers. With the economy in the
doldrums and real estate costs soaring,
many young people live with their
families well into their twenties, using
the money saved to purchase the latest
styles in clothing. Avid readers of fashion magazines, these *otaku* ("obsessed")
teenagers—heirs of Japan's long affluence—pay exorbitant prices for hip-
hop outfits, platform shoes, and
layered dresses.

and the state. As in the West, increasing urbanization has led to a decline in the practice of organized religion, although evangelical sects have proliferated in recent years. The largest and best-known sect is Soka Gakkai, a lay Buddhist organization that has attracted millions of followers and formed its own political party, the Komeito. Zen Buddhism retains its popularity, and some business-people seek to use Zen techniques to learn how to focus on willpower as a means of outwitting a competitor.

Western literature, art, and music have also had a major impact on Japanese society. After World War II, many of the writers who had been active before the war resurfaced, but now their writing reflected demoralization. Many were attracted to existentialism, and some turned to hedonism and nihilism. For these disillusioned authors, defeat was compounded by fear of the Americanization of postwar Japan. One of the best examples of this attitude was the novelist Yukio Mishima, who led a crusade to stem the tide of what he described as America's "universal and uniform 'Coca-Colonization' " of the world in general and Japan in partic-ular.[3] Mishima's ritual suicide in 1970 was the subject of widespread speculation and transformed him into a cult figure.

One of Japan's most serious-minded contemporary authors is Kenzaburo Oe (b. 1935). His work, rewarded with a Nobel Prize for literature in 1994, presents Japan's ongoing quest for modern identity and purpose. His char-acters reflect the spiritual anguish precipitated by the collapse of the imperial Japanese tradition and the subse-quent adoption of Western culture—a trend that Oe con-tends has culminated in unabashed materialism, cultural decline, and a moral void. Yet unlike Mishima, Oe does not wish to reinstill the imperial traditions of the past but rather, seeks to regain spiritual meaning by retrieving the sense of communality and innocence found in rural Japan.

Other aspects of Japanese culture have also been influenced by Western ideas. Western music is very popu-lar in Japan, and scores of Japanese classical musicians have succeeded in the West. Even rap music has gained a foothold among Japanese youth, although without the association with sex, drugs, and violence that it has

in the United States. As one singer remarked, "We've been very fortunate, and we don't want to bother our Moms and Dads. So we don't sing songs that would disturb parents."[4]

The Little Tigers

The success of postwar Japan in meeting the challenge from the capitalist West soon caught the eye of other Asian nations. By the 1980s, several smaller states in the region—known collectively as the "little tigers"—had suc-cessively followed the Japanese example.

SOUTH KOREA: A PENINSULA DIVIDED

In 1953, the Korean peninsula was exhausted from three years of bitter fraternal war, a conflict that took the lives of an estimated four million Koreans on both sides of the 38th parallel. Although a cease-fire was signed at Pan-munjom in July 1953, it was a fragile peace that left two heavily armed and mutually hostile countries facing each other suspiciously.

North of the truce line was the People's Republic of Korea (PRK), a police state under the dictatorial rule of the communist leader Kim Il Sung (1912–1994). To the south was the Republic of Korea, under the equally auto-cratic President Syngman Rhee (1875–1965), a fierce anti-communist who had led the resistance to the northern invasion. After several years of harsh rule in the Republic of Korea, marked by government corruption, fraudulent elections, and police brutality, demonstrations broke out in the capital city of Seoul in the spring of 1960 and forced Rhee into retirement.

In 1961, a coup d'état in South Korea placed General Chung Hee Park (1917–1979) in power. The new regime promulgated a new constitution, and in 1963, Park was elected president of a civilian government. He set out to foster recovery of the economy from decades of foreign occupation and civil war. Because the private sector had been relatively weak under Japanese rule, the government played an active role in the process by instituting a series of five-year plans that targeted specific industries for development, promoted exports, and funded infrastructure development.

The program was a solid success. Benefiting from the Confucian principles of thrift, respect for education, and hard work, as well as from Japanese capital and technology, Korea gradually emerged as a major industrial power in East Asia. The largest corporations—including Samsung, Daewoo, and Hyundai—were transformed into massive conglomerates called *chaebol*, the Korean equivalent of the *zaibatsu* of prewar Japan. Korean businesses began to compete actively with the Japanese for export markets in Asia and throughout the world.

But like many other countries in the region, South Korea was slow to develop democratic principles. Although his government functioned with the trappings of democracy, Park continued to rule by autocratic means and suppressed all forms of dissidence. In 1979, Park was assassinated. But after a brief interregnum of democratic rule, in 1980 a new military government under General Chun Doo Hwan seized power. The new regime was as authoritarian as its predecessors; but opposition to autocratic rule had now spread to much of the urban population, and national elections were finally held in 1989. A series of civilian rulers promised to make Korea "a freer and more mature democracy."

But the nation faced serious problems. A growing trade deficit, combined with a declining growth rate, led to increased unemployment and bankruptcy. After the Asian financial crisis emerged in 1997, economic conditions worsened, leading to the election of a longtime opposition figure, Kim Dae Jung, to the presidency. The new leader promised drastic reforms, but his regime too has been charged with corruption and incompetence; and relations with North Korea, now on the verge of becoming a nuclear power, remain tense.

TAIWAN: THE OTHER CHINA

After retreating to Taiwan following their defeat by the Communists, Chiang Kai-shek's government, which continued to refer to itself as the Republic of China (ROC), contended that it remained the legitimate representative of the Chinese people and would eventually return in triumph to the mainland.

The Nationalists had much more success on Taiwan than they had achieved on the mainland. In the relatively secure environment provided by a security treaty with the United States, signed in 1954, the ROC was able to concentrate on economic growth without worrying about a Communist invasion.

The government moved rapidly to create a solid agricultural base. A land reform program led to the reduction of rents, and landholdings over 3 acres were purchased by the government and resold to the tenants at reasonable prices. At the same time, local manufacturing and commerce were strongly encouraged. By the 1970s, Taiwan had become one of the most dynamic industrial economies in East Asia.

In contrast to the communist regime in the People's Republic of China (PRC), the ROC actively maintained Chinese tradition, promoting respect for Confucius and the ethical principles of the past, such as hard work, frugality, and filial piety. Although there was some corruption in both the government and the private sector, income differentials between the wealthy and the poor were generally less than elsewhere in the region, and the overall standard of living increased substantially. Health and sanitation improved, literacy rates were quite high, and an active family planning program reduced the rate of population growth.

After the death of Chiang Kai-shek in 1975, the ROC slowly began to move toward a more representative form of government, including elections and legal opposition parties. A national election in 1992 resulted in a bare majority for the Nationalists over strong opposition from the Democratic Progressive Party (DPP). But political liberalization had its dangers; some members of the DPP began to agitate for an independent Republic of Taiwan, a possibility that aroused concern within the Nationalist government in Taipei and frenzied hostility in the PRC. The election of DPP leader Chen Shuibian as ROC president in March 2000 angered Beijing, which threatened to invade Taiwan should the island continue to delay unification with the mainland.

The United States continues to provide defensive military assistance to the Taiwanese armed forces and has made it clear that it supports self-determination for the people of Taiwan and that it expects the final resolution of the Chinese civil war to be by peaceful means. In the meantime, economic and cultural contacts between Taiwan and the mainland are steadily increasing. However, the Taiwanese have shown no inclination to accept the PRC's offer of "one country, two systems," under which the ROC would accept the PRC as the legitimate government of China in return for autonomous control over the affairs of Taiwan.

Modern Taiwan

CHINA

Taiwan Strait

Chinkuashih
Keelung
Hsinchu
Taipei
Changhua
Taichung
Ts'aot'un
Hualien
Lukang
Puli
Yüanlin
Nant'ou
Chia-i
Pescadores
Islands
Tainan
P'ing-tung
Kaohsiung

Pacific Ocean

0   100 Kilometers
0   60 Miles

SINGAPORE AND HONG KONG: THE LITTLEST TIGERS

The smallest but by no means the least successful of the "little tigers" are Singapore and Hong Kong. Both contain large populations densely packed into small territories. Singapore, once a British colony and briefly a part of the state of Malaysia, is now an independent nation. Hong Kong was a British colony until it was returned to PRC control in 1997. In recent years, both have emerged as industrial powerhouses, with standards of living well above those of their neighbors.

TO THOSE LIVING IN GLASS HOUSES

Kishore Mahbubani is permanent secretary in the Ministry of Foreign Affairs in Singapore. Previously he served as his country's ambassador to the United Nations. In this 1994 article, adapted from a piece in the Washington Quarterly, the author advises his audience to stop lecturing Asian societies on the issue of human rights and focus attention instead on problems in the United States. In his view, today the countries of the West have much to learn from their counterparts in East Asia. This viewpoint is shared by many other observers, political leaders, and foreign affairs specialists in the region.

KISHORE MAHBUBANI, "GO EAST, YOUNG MAN"

In a major reversal of a pattern lasting centuries, many Western societies, including the U.S., are doing some major things fundamentally wrong, while a growing number of East Asian societies are doing the same things right. The results are most evident in the economic sphere. In purchasing power parity terms, East Asia's gross domestic product is already larger than that of either the U.S. or European community. Such economic prosperity, contrary to American belief, results not just from free-market arrangements but also from the right social and political choices. . . .

In most Asian eyes, the evidence of real social decay in the U.S. is clear and palpable. Since 1960, the U.S. population has grown by 41%. In the same period, there has been a 560% increase in violent crimes, a 419% increase in illegitimate births, a 400% increase in divorce rates, a 300% increase in children living in single-parent homes, a more than 200% increase in teenage suicide rates, and a drop of almost 80 points in [SAT] scores. A clear American paradox is that a society that places such a high premium on freedom has effectively reduced the physical freedom of most Americans, especially those who live in large cities. They live in heavily fortified homes, think twice before taking an evening stroll around their neighborhoods, and feel increasingly threatened by random violence when they are outside.

To any Asian, it is obvious that the breakdown of the family and social order in the U.S. owes itself to a mindless ideology that maintains that the freedom of a small number of individuals who are known to pose a threat to society (criminals, terrorists, street gang members, drug dealers) should not be constrained (for example, through detention without trial), even if to do so would enhance the freedom of the majority. . . . This belief is purely and simply a gross violation of common sense.

My hope is that Americans will come to visit East Asia in greater numbers. When they do, they will come to realize that their society has swung much too much in one direction: liberating the individual while imprisoning society. The relatively strong and stable family and social institutions of East Asia will appear more appealing. And as Americans experience the freedom of walking on city streets in Asia, they may begin to understand that freedom can also result from greater social order and discipline. Perhaps the best advice to give to a young American is: "Go East, Young Man."

The success of Singapore must be ascribed in good measure to the will and energy of its political leaders. When it became independent in August 1965, Singapore's longtime position as an entrepôt for trade between the Indian Ocean and the South China Sea was on the wane.

Within a decade, Singapore's role and reputation had dramatically changed. Under the leadership of Prime Minister Lee Kuan-yew (b. 1923), the government cultivated an attractive business climate while engaging in public works projects to feed, house, and educate its two million citizens. The major components of success have been shipbuilding, oil refineries, tourism, electronics, and finance—the city-state has become the banking hub of the entire region.

As in the other "little tigers," an authoritarian political system has guaranteed a stable environment for economic growth. Until his recent retirement, Lee Kuan-yew and his People's Action Party dominated Singapore politics, and opposition elements were intimidated into silence

The Republic of Singapore

MALAYSIA

SINGAPORE

Singapore R.

Singapore

0   10 Kilometers
0   6 Miles

Singapore Strait

or arrested. The prime minister openly declared that the Western model of pluralist democracy was not appropriate for Singapore (see the box above). Confucian values of thrift, hard work, and obedience to authority were promoted as the ideology of the state.

But economic success has begun to undermine the authoritarian foundations of the system as a more sophisticated citizenry voices aspirations for more political freedoms and an end to government paternalism. Lee Kuan-yew's successor, Goh Chok Tong, has promised a "kinder, gentler" Singapore, and political restrictions on individual behavior are gradually being relaxed.

The future of Hong Kong is not so clear-cut. As in Singapore, sensible government policies and the hard work of its people have enabled Hong Kong to thrive. At first, the prosperity of the colony depended on a plentiful supply of cheap labor. Inundated with refugees from the mainland during the 1950s and 1960s, the population of Hong Kong burgeoned to more than six million. More recently, Hong Kong has benefited from increased tourism, manufacturing, and the growing economic prosperity of neighboring Guangdong province, the most prosperous region of the PRC. Unlike the other societies discussed in this chapter, Hong Kong has relied on an unbridled free market system rather than active state intervention in the economy. At the same time, by allocating substantial funds for transportation, sanitation, education, and public housing, the government has created favorable conditions for economic development.

When Britain's ninety-nine-year lease on the New Territories, the foodbasket of the colony, expired on July 1, 1997, Hong Kong returned to mainland authority. Although the Chinese promised the British that for fifty years, the people of Hong Kong would live under a capitalist system and be essentially self-governing, recent statements by Chinese leaders have raised questions about the degree of autonomy Hong Kong will continue to receive under Chinese rule.

On the Margins of Asia: Postwar Australia and New Zealand

Technically, Australia and New Zealand are not part of Asia, and throughout their short history, both countries have identified culturally and politically with the West rather than with their Asian neighbors. Their political institutions and values are derived from Europe, and their economies resemble those of the advanced countries of the world rather than the preindustrial societies of much of Southeast Asia. Both are currently members of the British Commonwealth and of the U.S.-led ANZUS (Australia, New Zealand, and the United States) alliance.

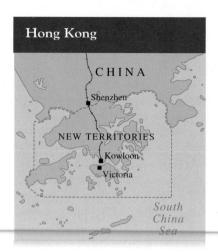

Yet trends in recent years have been drawing both states, especially Australia, closer to Asia. In the first place, immigration from East and Southeast Asia has increased rapidly. More than one-half of current immigrants into Australia come from East Asia, and by early this century, about 7 percent of the population of about 18 million people will be of Asian descent. In New Zealand, residents of Asian descent represent only about 3 percent of the population of 3.5 million, but about 12 percent of the population are Maoris, Polynesian peoples who settled on the islands about a thousand years ago. Second, trade relations with Asia are increasing rapidly. About 60 percent of Australia's export markets today are in East Asia, and the region is the source of about one-half of its imports. Asian trade with New Zealand is also on the increase.

Whether Australia and New Zealand will ever become an integral part of the Asia-Pacific region is uncertain. Cultural differences stemming from the European origins of the majority of the population in both countries hinder mutual understanding on both sides of the divide. But economic and geographical realities act as a powerful force, and should the Pacific region continue on its current course toward economic prosperity and political stability, the role of Australia and New Zealand will assume greater significance.

CONCLUSION

To some observers, the economic achievements of the nations of the western Pacific have come at a high price, in the form of political authoritarianism and a lack

➤THE HONG KONG SKYLINE. Hong Kong reverted to Chinese sovereignty in 1997 after a century of British rule. To commemorate the occasion, the imposing Conference Center, shown here in the foreground, was built on reclaimed shoreland in Hong Kong harbor. The center is surrounded by the gleaming modern skyscrapers of the city of Victoria, with Victoria Peak in the background. The Star Ferry, long a fixture for local residents, plies its way between the island and the peninsula of Kowloon.

Courtesy of William J. Duiker

JAPAN AND THE LITTLE TIGERS SINCE WORLD WAR II

End of World War II in the Pacific	1945
Chiang Kai-shek retreats to Taiwan	1949
End of U.S. occupation of Japan	1950
Korean War	1950–1953
United States–Republic of China security treaty	1954
Syngman Rhee overthrown in South Korea	1960
Rise to power of Chung Hee Park in South Korea	1961
Independence of Republic of Singapore	1965
Death of Chiang Kai-shek	1975
Chung Hee Park assassinated	1979
First free general elections on Taiwan	1992
Return of Hong Kong to mainland control	1997
Financial crisis hits the region	1997
Chen Shuibian elected president of Taiwan	2000

of attention to human rights. Until recently, government repression of opposition has been common in many of these nations. In addition, the rights of national minorities and women are often still limited in comparison with the advanced nations of the West. Recent developments such as the financial crisis of 1997 and the long-lived economic downturn in Japan have also somewhat tarnished the image of the "Asian miracle," raising concern that some of the factors that contributed to economic success in prior years are now making it difficult for governments to develop open and accountable financial systems.

Still, it should be kept in mind that progress in political pluralism and human rights has not always been easy to achieve in the West and even now frequently fails to match expectations. A look at the historical record suggests that political pluralism is often a by-product of economic growth and that political values and institutions evolve in response to changing social conditions. A rising standard of living and increased social mobility should go far toward enhancing political freedom and promoting social justice in the countries bordering the western Pacific.

The efforts of these nations to find a way to accommodate traditional and modern, native and foreign, raise a final question. As we have seen, Mahatma Gandhi believed that materialism is ultimately a dead end. In light of contemporary concerns about the emptiness of life in the West and the self-destructiveness of material culture, can his message be ignored?

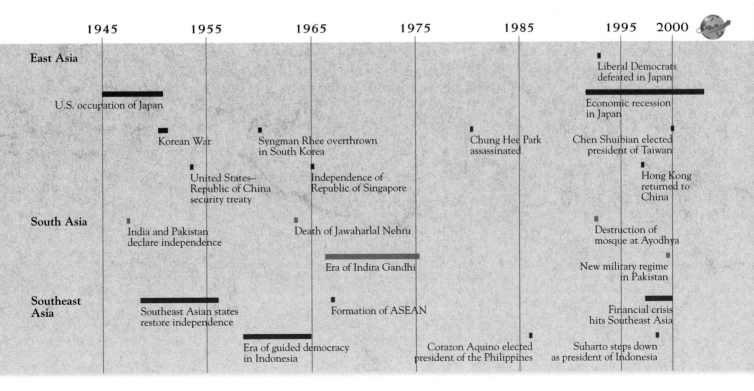

CHAPTER NOTES

1. *New York Times*, May 2, 1996.
2. Quoted in Larry Collins and Dominique Lapierre, *Freedom at Midnight* (New York, 1975), p. 252.
3. Yukio Mishima and Geoffrey Bownas, eds., *New Writing in Japan* (Harmondsworth, England, 1972), p. 16.
4. *New York Times*, January 29, 1996.

SUGGESTED READING

For a recent survey of contemporary Indian history, see S. Wolpert, *A New History of India*, rev. ed. (New York, 1989). Also see P. Brass, *The New Cambridge History of India: The Politics of Independence* (Cambridge, 1990); C. Baxter, *Bangladesh: From a Nation to a State* (Boulder, Colo., 1997); and S. Tharoor, *India: From Midnight to the Millennium* (New York, 1997). On Nehru's government, see D. Norman, ed., *Nehru: The First Sixty Years*, 2 vols. (London, 1965).

The life and career of Indira Gandhi have been well chronicled. Two fine biographies are T. Ali, *An Indian Dynasty: The Story of the Nehru-Gandhi Family* (New York, 1985), and K. Bhatia, *Indira: A Biography of Prime Minister Gandhi* (New York, 1974.) On Indian literature, see D. Ray and A. Singh, eds., *India: An Anthology of Contemporary Writing* (Athens, Ohio, 1983). See also S. Tharu and K. Lalita, eds., *Women Writing in India*, vol. 2 (New York, 1993).

There are a number of standard surveys of the history of modern Southeast Asia. For an introduction, see D. R. Sar Desai, *Southeast Asia: Past and Present*, 2d ed. (Boulder, Colo., 1989). For a more scholarly approach, see D. J. Steinberg, ed., *In Search of Southeast Asia*, 2d ed. (New York, 1985).

There is a rich selection of materials on modern Indonesia. On the Sukarno era, see J. Legge, *Sukarno* (New York, 1972). On the Suharto era and its origins, see M. Vatikiotis, *Indonesian Politics Under Suharto* (London, 1993).

For an overview of women's issues in contemporary South and Southeast Asia, consult B. Ramusack and S. Sievers, *Women in Asia* (Bloomington, Ind., 1999). Articles that focus on the socioeconomic problems of women in India in the 1980s are found in M. Kishwar and R. Vanita, eds., *In Search of Answers: Indian Women's Voices from Manushi* (London, 1991). Of interest on Southeast Asian women's issues is W. Williams, *Javanese Lives: Women and Men in Modern Indonesian Society* (New Brunswick, N.J., 1991).

The number of books in English on modern Japan has increased in direct proportion to Japan's rise as a major industrial power. For a topical approach with strong emphasis on economic and social matters, J. E. Hunter, *The Emergence of Modern Japan: An Introductory History Since 1853* (London, 1989), is excellent. For an extensive analysis of Japan's adjustment to the Allied occupation, see J. W. Dower, *Embracing Defeat: Japan in the Wake of World War II* (New York, 1999).

C. Nakane, *Japanese Society* (Harmondsworth, England, 1979), provides a scholarly treatment, while R. J. Hendry, *Understanding Japanese Society* (Beckenham, England, 1987), is more accessible. On the role of women in modern Japan, see D. Robins-Mowry, *The Hidden Sun: Women of Modern Japan* (Boulder, Colo., 1983), and N. Bornoff, *Pink Samurai: Love, Marriage, and Sex in Contemporary Japan* (New York, 1991).

Books attempting to explain Japanese economic success have become a growth industry. The classic account is E. F. Vogel, *Japan as Number One: Lessons for America* (Cambridge, Mass., 1979). For a provocative response pointing to signs of Japanese weakness, see J. Woronoff, *Japan as—Anything but—Number One* (Armonk, N.Y., 1991). On the costs to society of Japanese economic success, see I. P. Hall, *Cartels of the Mind: Japan's Intellectual Closed Shop* (New York, 1998). Y. Saisho, *Women Executives in Japan* (Tokyo, 1981), discusses women who are trying to find the key to economic success in Japanese business. On Japanese literature after World War II, see the classic D. Keene, *Dawn to the West: Japanese Fiction in the Modern Era* (New York, 1984). On Japanese women authors, see N. M. Lippit and K. I. Selden, eds., *Stories by Contemporary Japanese Women Writers* (New York, 1982).

On the four "little tigers" and their economic development, see E. F. Vogel, *The Four Little Dragons: The Spread of Industrialization in East Asia* (Cambridge, Mass., 1991); J. W. Morley, ed., *Driven by Growth: Political Change in the Asia-Pacific Region* (Armonk, N.Y., 1992); and J. Woronoff, *Asia's Miracle Economies* (New York, 1986).

INFOTRAC COLLEGE EDITION

Visit the source collections at infotrac.thomsonlearning.com and use the Search function with the following key terms.

India history	Nehru
Japan history	Pakistan
Japan women	Southeast Asia
Keiretsu	Sukarno
Korea	

WORLD HISTORY RESOURCES

Visit the *Essential World History* Companion Web Site for resources specific to this textbook:

http://history.wadsworth.com/duikeressentials02/

The CD in the back of this book and the World History Resource Center at **http://history.wadsworth.com/world/** offer a variety of tools to help you succeed in this course, including access to quizzes; images; documents; interactive simulations, maps, and timelines; movie explorations; and a wealth of other sources.

TOWARD A GLOBAL CIVILIZATION? THE WORLD SINCE 1945

As World War II came to an end, the survivors of that bloody struggle could afford to face the future with a cautious optimism. Europeans might hope that the bitter rivalry that had marked relations among the Western powers would finally be ended.

All too soon, however, these hopes were dashed by the emergence of the grueling and sometimes tense ideological struggle between the socialist and capitalist camps, a competition headed by the only remaining great powers, the Soviet Union and the United States. While the two superpowers were able to avoid an open nuclear confrontation, the postwar world was divided into two heavily armed camps in a balance of terror that on one occasion—the Cuban Missile Crisis—brought the world briefly to the brink of nuclear holocaust.

In the shadow of this rivalry, the western European states made a remarkable economic recovery and reached new levels of prosperity. But in eastern Europe, Soviet domination, both politically and economically, seemed so complete that many doubted it could ever be undone. But communism had never developed deep roots in eastern Europe, and when, in the late 1980s, Soviet leader Mikhail Gorbachev indicated that his government would no longer pursue military intervention, eastern European states acted quickly to establish their freedom and adopt new economic structures based on Western models. But although many Europeans rejoiced over the possibility of creating a new, undivided Europe, the ethnic hatreds and tensions that had plagued these nations before World War II reemerged and threatened to divide the continent once again.

Outside the West, the peoples of Africa and Asia had their own reasons for optimism as World War II came to a close. World War II had severely undermined the stability of the colonial order, and by the end of the 1940s, most colonies in Asia had received their independence. Africa followed a decade or two later.

Broadly speaking, the leaders of these newly liberated countries set forth three goals at the outset of independence. They wanted to throw off the shackles of Western economic domination and ensure material prosperity for all of their citizens. They wanted to introduce new political institutions that would enhance the right of self-determination of their peoples. And they wanted to develop a sense of common nationhood within the population and establish secure territorial boundaries. Most opted to follow a capitalist or a moderately socialist path toward economic development.

Regardless of the path chosen, however, the results were disappointing. Virtually all of the former colonies remained economically dependent on the advanced industrial nations or, in the case of those who chose to follow the socialist model of development, were forced to rely on the Soviet Union. Some faced severe problems of urban and rural poverty.

An area of concern for the leaders of African and Asian countries after World War II was to create a new political culture responsive to the needs of their citizens. At first, most accepted the concept of democracy as the defining theme of that culture. Within a decade, however, democratic systems throughout the developing world were replaced by military dictatorships or one-party governments.

The problem of establishing a common national identity has in some ways been the most daunting of all the challenges facing the new nations of Asia and Africa. Many of these new states were a composite of a wide variety of ethnic, religious, and linguistic groups who found it difficult to agree on common symbols of nationalism. Problems of establishing an official language and delineating territorial boundaries left over from the colonial era created difficulties in many countries. As the new century dawns, internal conflicts spawned by deep-rooted historical and ethnic hatreds are proliferating throughout the world.

The introduction of Western cultural values and customs has also had a destabilizing effect in many areas. Although such ideas are welcomed by some groups, they are firmly resisted by others. Where Western influence has the effect of undermining traditional customs and religious beliefs, it often provokes violent hostility and sparks tension and even conflict within individual societies. To some, Western customs and values represent the wave of the future and are welcomed as a sign of progress. To others, they are destructive of indigenous traditions and a barrier to the growth of a genuine national identity based on history and culture. Much of the anger recently directed at the United States in Muslim countries has undoubtedly been generated by such feelings.

From the 1950s to the 1970s, political and economic difficulties led to chronic instability in a number of countries and transformed the developing world into a major theater of Cold War confrontation. During the 1980s, however, a number of new factors entered the equation and shifted the focus away from ideological competition. The growing success of the "little tigers" and the poor eco-

ONE WORLD, ONE ENVIRONMENT

A crucial factor affecting the evolution of society and the global economy at the beginning of the twenty-first century is growing concern over the impact of industrialization on the earth's environment. There is nothing new about human beings causing damage to their natural surroundings, but never before has the danger of significant ecological damage been as extensive as during the past century. The effects of chemicals introduced into the atmosphere or into rivers, lakes, and oceans have increasingly threatened the health and well-being of all living species.

For many years, the main focus of environmental concern was in the developed countries of the West, where industrial effluents, automobile exhaust, and the use of artificial fertilizers and insecticides led to urban smog, extensive damage to crops and wildlife, and a major reduction of the ozone layer in the upper atmosphere. In recent years, the problem has spread elsewhere. China's headlong rush to industrialization has resulted in major ecological damage in that country. Industrial smog has created almost unlivable conditions in many cities in Asia, while hillsides denuded of their forests have caused severe problems of erosion and destruction of farmlands. Destruction of the rain forest is a growing problem in many parts of the world, notably in Brazil and in the Indonesian archipelago. With the forest cover throughout the earth rapidly disappearing, there is less plant life to perform the crucial process of reducing carbon dioxide levels in the atmosphere.

One of the few beneficial consequences of such incidents has been a growing international consensus that environmental concerns have taken on a truly global character. The danger of global warming has become a source of sufficient concern to bring about an international conference on the subject in Kyoto, Japan, in December 1997. If, as many scientists predict, worldwide temperatures should continue to increase, the rise in sea levels could pose a significant threat to low-lying islands and coastal areas throughout the world, while climatic change could lead to severe droughts or excessive rainfall in cultivated areas.

It is one thing to recognize a problem, however, and yet another to solve it. So far, cooperative efforts among nations to alleviate environmental problems have all too often been hindered by economic forces or by political, ethnic, and religious disputes. The fact is, few nations have been willing to take unilateral action that might pose an obstacle to economic development plans or lead to a rise in unemployment. In 2001, President George W. Bush refused to sign the Kyoto Agreement on the grounds that it discriminated against advanced Western countries.

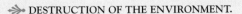

➤ DESTRUCTION OF THE ENVIRONMENT. This stunted tree has been killed by acid rain, a combination of sulfuric and nitric acids mixed with moisture in the air. Entire forests of trees killed by acid rain are becoming common sights in Canada, the United States, and northern Europe.

Judyth Platt, Ecoscene/CORBIS

---

nomic performance of socialist regimes led a number of developing countries to reduce government regulations and adopt a free-market approach to economic development. Similarly, there have been tantalizing signs in recent years of a revival of interest in the democratic model in various parts of Asia, Africa, and Latin America. Free elections have been held recently in South Korea, Taiwan, and the Philippines, while similar developments have taken place in Nigeria, South Africa, and a number of other African countries.

Virtually the entire world has now been transformed as the result of the Industrial Revolution, which began in Europe at the end of the eighteenth century. Not only are countries throughout the world today linked to the economic marketplace put in place by the Western industrialized nations, but many are also adopting political and social institutions and values originally introduced from Europe or the United States.

But the strains produced by these events have been severe in many parts of the world, where the costs of globalization often appear to outweigh the benefits. In Africa and the Middle East, two regions that are rapidly falling behind the rest of the world in terms of per capita income and political development, resistance to Western cultural values and institutions remains strong, not only among the leadership but also from within the rank and file of the population.

Whatever happens to the current economic situation, it has clearly taken on a truly global character. In fact, today we live not only in a world economy, but in a world society, where a revolution in Iran can cause a rise in the price of oil in the United States and a change in social behavior in Indonesia; where the collapse of an empire in Russia can send shock waves as far as Hanoi and Havana; and where a terrorist attack in New York City can disrupt financial markets throughout the world.

One consequence of this process of interdependence is a growing recognition of the common danger posed by environmental pollution (see the box on p. 655). The fact that environmental damage is a common concern suggests the growing need for coordination of efforts on a global scale. Such cooperation, however, has often been hindered by political differences.

Even as the world becomes more global in culture and interdependent in its mutual relations, centrifugal forces are at work attempting to redefine the political, cultural, and ethnic ways in which it is divided. Such efforts are often disruptive and can sometimes work against measures to enhance our human destiny. But they also represent an integral part of human character and human history and cannot be suppressed in the relentless drive to create a world society. What will result is as yet unclear. What is apparent is that the Technological Revolution is proceeding at a dizzying speed that can carry information, ideas, and images around the world in seconds (see the box on p. 657).

What is already apparent is that technological advances will have an enormous impact on human society in coming generations. Although many of these consequences may be welcome, others represent a serious challenge, as individuals raised on television, video games, and the computer find less and less time for human relationships or creative activities. To some, the only antidote to the sense of confusion and alienation afflicting contemporary life is to reject the scientific outlook, with its secularizing implications, and return to religious faith. Others hope that a combination of scientific knowledge and spiritual revival can spark a renewal that will enable people to deal constructively with contemporary alienation and confusion. Still, others believe that, as the common dangers posed by environmental damage, overpopulation, and scarcity of resources become even more apparent, societies around the world will find ample reason to turn their attention from cultural differences to the demands of global interdependence. As the world faces a new century, its greatest challenge may be to reconcile the drive for individual and group identity with the common needs of the human community.

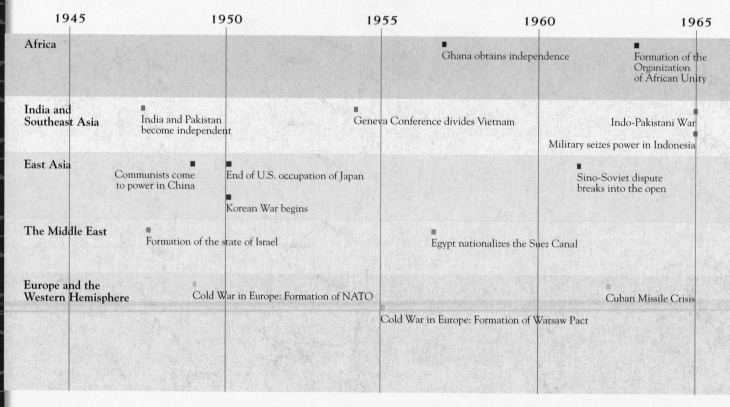

FROM THE INDUSTRIAL TO THE TECHNOLOGICAL REVOLUTION

As many observers have noted, a key aspect of the world economy is that it is in the process of transition to what has been called a "postindustrial age," characterized by a system that is not only increasingly global in scope but also increasingly technology-intensive in character. Since World War II, a stunning array of technological changes—especially in transportation, communications, space exploration, medicine, and agriculture—have transformed the world in which we live. Technological changes have also raised new questions and concerns as well as having unexpected results. Some scientists have questioned whether genetic engineering might result accidentally in new strains of deadly bacteria that cannot be controlled outside the laboratory. Some doctors have recently raised the alarm that the overuse of antibiotics has created supergerms, which are no longer subject to antibiotic treatment. The Technological Revolution has also led to the development of more advanced methods of destruction. Most frightening have been nuclear weapons.

The transition to a technology-intensive postindustrial world, which the futurologist Alvin Toffler has dubbed the Third Wave (the first two being the agricultural and industrial revolutions), has produced difficulties for people in many walks of life—for blue-collar workers, whose high wages price them out of the market as firms begin to move their factories abroad; for the poor and uneducated, who lack the technical skills to handle complex tasks in the contemporary economy; and even for some members of the middle class, who have been fired or forced into retirement as their employers seek to slim down to compete in the global marketplace.

It is now increasingly clear that the Technological Revolution, like the Industrial Revolution that preceded it, will entail enormous consequences and may ultimately give birth to a new era of social and political instability. The success of advanced capitalist states in the second half of the twentieth century has been built on a broad consensus on the importance of two propositions: (1) the need for high levels of government investment in education, communications, and transportation as a means of meeting the challenges of continued economic growth, and (2) the desirability of cooperative efforts in the international arena as a means of maintaining open markets for the free exchange of goods.

As the new century gets under way, these assumptions are increasingly under attack, as citizens refuse to support education and oppose the formation of trading alliances to promote the free movement of goods and labor across national borders. This raises serious questions about the likelihood that the coming challenges of the Third Wave can be successfully met without a growing measure of political and social tension.

ON THE ASSEMBLY LINE. Automation is sometimes cited as one of the key reasons for the vaunted efficiency of the Japanese industrial machine. Mechanical robots, as shown here, perform tasks in Japan that elsewhere are performed by human beings.

© Susumu Takahashi/Reuters

| 1970 | 1975 | 1980 | 1985 | 1990 | 1995 | 2000 |

Release of ANC leader Nelson Mandela from prison

Mandela becomes president of South Africa

United States sends troops to Somalia

Fall of Saigon to North Vietnamese

Assassination of Indira Gandhi

Great Proletarian Cultural Revolution in China

China and United States normalize relations

Hong Kong is returned to China

First oil crisis

Camp David accords

Persian Gulf War

Iranian Revolution

Gorbachev era in the Soviet Union

War in Kosovo

Collapse of communism in Eastern Europe and Soviet Union

Dayton Accords—End of Bosnian War

Reunification of Germany

Terrorist attack on World Trade Center

GLOSSARY

absolutism a form of government where the sovereign power or ultimate authority rested in the hands of a monarch who claimed to rule by divine right and was therefore responsible only to God.

Agricultural (Neolithic) Revolution the shift from hunting animals and gathering plants for sustenance to producing food by systematic agriculture that occurred gradually between 10,000 and 4000 B.C. (the Neolithic or "New Stone" Age).

agricultural revolution the application of new agricultural techniques that allowed for a large increase in productivity in the eighteenth century.

anarchism a political theory that holds that all governments and existing social institutions are unnecessary and advocates a society based on voluntary cooperation.

ANC the African National Congress. Founded in 1912, it was the beginning of political activity by South African blacks. Banned by politically dominant European whites in 1960, it was not officially "unbanned" until 1990. It is now the official majority party of the South African government.

Analects the body of writing containing conversations between Confucius and his disciples that preserves his worldly wisdom and pragmatic philosophies.

anti-Semitism hostility toward or discrimination against Jews.

appeasement the policy, followed by the European nations in the 1930s, of accepting Hitler's annexation of Austria and Czechoslovakia in the belief that meeting his demands would assure peace and stability.

Arianism a Christian heresy that taught that Jesus was inferior to God. Though condemned by the Council of Nicaea in 325, Arianism was adopted by many of the Germanic peoples who entered the Roman Empire over the next centuries.

aristocracy a class of hereditary nobility in medieval Europe; a warrior class who shared a distinctive lifestyle based on the institution of knighthood, although there were social divisions within the group based on extremes of wealth.

Arthasastra an early Indian political treatise that sets forth many fundamental aspects of the relationship of rulers and their subjects. It has been compared to Machiavelli's well-known book, *The Prince*, and has provided principles upon which many aspects of social organization have developed in the region.

Aryans Indo–European-speaking nomads who entered India from the Central Asian steppes between 1500 and 1000 B.C.E. and greatly affected Indian society, notably by establishing the caste system. The term was later adopted by German Nazis to describe their racial ideal.

ASEAN the Association for the Southest Asian Nations formed in 1967 to promote the prosperity and political stability of its member nations. Currently Brunei, Indonesia, Laos, Malaysia, Myanmar, the Philippines, Singapore, Thailand, and Vietnam are members. Other countries in the region participate as "observer" members.

Ausgleich the "Compromise" of 1867 that created the dual monarchy of Austria-Hungary. Austria and Hungary each had its own capital, constitution, and legislative assembly, but were united under one monarch.

authoritarian state a state that has a dictatorial government and some other trappings of a totalitarian state, but does not demand that the masses be actively involved in the regime's goals as totalitarian states do.

auxiliaries troops enlisted from the subject peoples of the Roman Empire to supplement the regular legions composed of Roman citizens.

bakufu the centralized government set up in Japan in the twelfth century. *See* shogunate system.

balance of power a distribution of power among several states such that no single nation can dominate or interfere with the interests of another.

Bao-jia system the Chinese practice, reportedly originated by the Qin dynasty in the third century B.C.E., of organizing families into groups of five or ten to exercise mutual control and surveillance and reduce loyalty to the family.

Baroque a style that dominated Western painting, sculpture, architecture and music from about 1580 to 1730, generally characterized by elaborate ornamentation and dramatic effects. Important practitioners included Bernini, Rubens, Handel, and Bach.

Bedouins nomadic tribes originally from northern Arabia, who became important traders after the domestication of the camel during the first millennium B.C.E. Early converts to Islam, their values and practices deeply affected Muhammad.

benefice in the Christian church, a position, such as a bishopric, that consisted of both a sacred office and the right of the holder to the annual revenues from the position.

bhakti in Hinduism, devotion as a means of religious observance open to all persons regardless of class.

bicameral legislature a legislature with two houses.

Black Death the outbreak of plague (mostly bubonic) in the mid-fourteenth century that killed from 25 to 50 percent of Europe's population.

Blitzkrieg "lightning war." A war conducted with great speed and force, as in Germany's advance at the beginning of World War II.

bodhisattvas in some schools of Buddhism, individuals who have achieved enlightenment but, because of their great compassion, have chosen to renounce Nirvana and to remain on earth in spirit form to help all human beings achieve release from reincarnation.

Bolsheviks a small faction of the Russian Social Democratic Party who were led by Lenin and dedicated to violent revolution; seized power in Russia in 1917 and were subsequently renamed the Communists.

boyars the Russian nobility.

Brezhnev Doctrine the doctrine, enunciated by Leonid Brezhnev, that the Soviet Union had a right to intervene if socialism was threatened in another socialist state; used to justify the use of Soviet troops in Czechoslovakia in 1968.

caliph the secular leader of the Islamic community.

calpulli in Aztec society, a kinship group, often of a thousand or more, which served as an intermediary with the central government, providing taxes and conscript labor to the state.

capital material wealth used or available for use in the production of more wealth.

cartel a combination of independent commercial enterprises that work together to control prices and limit competition.

Cartesian dualism Descartes's principle of the separation of mind and matter (and mind and body) that enabled scientists to view matter as something separate from themselves that could be investigated by reason.

caste system a system of rigid social hierarchy in which all members of that society are assigned by birth to specific "ranks," and inherit specific roles and privileges.

caudillos strong leaders in nineteenth-century Latin America, who were usually supported by the landed elites and ruled chiefly by military force, though some were popular; they included both modernizers and destructive dictators.

censorate one of the three primary Chinese ministries, originally established in the Qin dynasty, whose inspectors surveyed the efficiency of officials throughout the system.

chaebol a South Korean business structure similar to the Japanese keiretsu.

chansons de geste a form of vernacular literature in the High Middle Ages that consisted of heroic epics focusing on the deeds of warriors.

chivalry the ideal of civilized behavior that emerged among the nobility in the eleventh and twelfth centuries under the influence of the church; a code of ethics knights were expected to uphold.

Christian (northern) humanism an intellectual movement in northern Europe in the late fifteenth and early sixteenth centuries that combined the interest in the classics of the Italian Renaissance with an interest in the sources of early Christianity, including the New Testament and the writings of the church fathers.

civic humanism an intellectual movement of the Italian Renaissance that saw Cicero, who was both an intellectual and a statesman, as the ideal and held that humanists should be involved in government and use their rhetorical training in the service of the state.

civil rights the basic rights of citizens including equality before the law, freedom of speech and press, and freedom from arbitrary arrest.

civil service examination an elaborate Chinese system of selecting bureaucrats on merit, first introduced in 165 B.C.E., developed by the Tang dynasty in the seventh century C.E. and refined under the Song dynasty; later adopted in Vietnam and with less success in Japan and Korea. It contributed to efficient government, upward mobility, and cultural uniformity.

class struggle the basis of the Marxist analysis of history, which says that the owners of the means of production have always oppressed the workers and predicts an inevitable revolution. *See* Marxism.

Cold War the ideological conflict between the Soviet Union and the United States after World War II.

collective farms large farms created in the Soviet Union by Stalin by combining many small holdings into one large farm worked by the peasants under government supervision.

collective security the use of an international army raised by an association of nations to deter aggression and keep the peace.

coloni free tenant farmers who worked as sharecroppers on the large estates of the Roman Empire (singular: *colonus*).

Comintern a worldwide organization of Communist parties, founded by Lenin in 1919, dedicated to the advancement of world revolution; also known as the Third International.

common law law common to the entire kingdom of England; imposed by the king's courts beginning in the twelfth century to replace the customary law used in county and feudal courts that varied from place to place.

commune in medieval Europe, an association of townspeople bound together by a sworn oath for the purpose of obtaining basic liberties from the lord of the territory in which the town was located; also, the self-governing town after receiving its liberties.

conciliarism a movement in fourteenth- and fifteenth-century Europe that held that final authority in spiritual matters resided with a general church council, not the pope; emerged in response to the Avignon papacy and the Great Schism and used to justify the summoning of the Council of Constance (1414–1418).

condottieri leaders of bands of mercenary soldiers in Renaissance Italy who sold their services to the highest bidder.

Confucianism a system of thought based on the teachings of Confucius (551–479 B.C.E.) that developed into the ruling ideology of the Chinese state. *See* Neo-Confucianism.

conquistadors "conquerors." Leaders in the Spanish conquests in the Americas, especially Mexico and Peru, in the sixteenth century.

conscription a military draft.

conservatism an ideology based on tradition and social stability that favored the maintenance of established institutions, organized religion, and obedience to authority and resisted change, especially abrupt change.

consuls the chief executive officers of the Roman Republic. Two were chosen annually to administer the government and lead the army in battle.

consumer society a term applied to Western society after World War II as the working classes adopted the consumption patterns of the middle class and installment plans, credit cards, and easy credit made consumer goods such as appliances and automobiles widely available.

Continental System Napoleon's effort to bar British goods from the Continent in the hope of weakening Britain's economy and destroying its capacity to wage war.

cosmopolitanism the quality of being sophisticated and having wide international experience.

cottage industry a system of textile manufacturing in which spinners and weavers worked at home in their cottages using raw materials supplied to them by capitalist entrepreneurs.

cultural relativism the belief that no culture is superior to another because culture is a matter of custom, not reason, and derives its meaning from the group holding it.

cuneiform "wedge-shaped." A system of writing developed by the Sumerians that consisted of wedge-shaped impressions made by a reed stylus on clay tablets.

daimyo prominent Japanese families who provided allegiance to the local shogun in exchange for protection; similar to vassals in Europe.

decolonization the process of becoming free of colonial status and achieving statehood; occurred in most of the world's colonies between 1947 and 1962.

deism belief in God as the creator of the universe who, after setting it in motion, ceased to have any direct involvement in it and allowed it to run according to its own natural laws.

demesne the part of a manor retained under the direct control of the lord and worked by the serfs as part of their labor services.

depression a very severe, protracted economic downturn with high levels of unemployment.

destalinization the policy of denouncing and undoing the most repressive aspects of Stalin's regime; begun by Nikita Khrushchev in 1956.

détente the relaxation of tension between the Soviet Union and the United States that occurred in the 1970s.

dharma in Hinduism and Buddhism, the law that governs the universe, and specifically human behavior.

dialectic logic, one of the seven liberal arts that made up the medieval curriculum. In Marxist thought, the process by which all change occurs through the clash of antagonistic elements.

Diaspora the scattering of Jews throughout the ancient world after the Babylonian captivity in the sixth century B.C.E.

dictator in the Roman Republic, an official granted unlimited power to run the state for a short period of time, usually six months, during an emergency.

diocese the area under the jurisdiction of a Christian bishop; based originally on Roman administrative districts.

direct representation a system of choosing delegates to a representative assembly in which citizens vote directly for the delegates who will represent them.

divination the practice of seeking to foretell future events by interpreting divine signs, which could appear in various forms, such as in entrails of animals, in patterns in smoke, or in dreams.

divine-right monarchy a monarchy based on the belief that monarchs receive their power directly from God and are responsible to no one except God.

domino theory the belief that if the Communists succeeded in Vietnam, other countries in Southeast and East Asia would also fall (like dominoes) to communism; a justification for the U.S. intervention in Vietnam.

dualism the belief that the universe is dominated by two opposing forces, one good and the other evil.

dynastic state a state where the maintenance and expansion of the interests of the ruling family is the primary consideration.

economic imperialism the process in which banks and corporations from developed nations invest in underdeveloped regions and establish a major presence there in the hope of making high profits; not necessarily the same as colonial expansion in that businesses invest where they can make a profit, which may not be in their own nation's colonies.

empiricism the practice of relying on observation and experiment.

enclosure movement in the eighteenth century, the fencing in of the old open fields, combining many small holdings into larger units that could be farmed more efficiently.

encomienda system the system by which Spain first governed its American colonies. Holders of an encomienda were supposed to protect the Indians as well as using them as laborers and collecting tribute but in practice exploited them.

encyclical a letter from the pope to all the bishops of the Roman Catholic church.

enlightened absolutism an absolute monarchy where the ruler follows the principles of the Enlightenment by introducing reforms for the improvement of society, allowing freedom of speech and the press, permitting religious toleration, expanding education, and ruling in accordance with the laws.

Enlightenment an eighteenth-century intellectual movement, led by the philosophes, that stressed the application of reason and the scientific method to all aspects of life.

entrepreneur one who organizes, operates, and assumes the risk in a business venture in the expectation of making a profit.

Epicureanism a philosophy founded by Epicurus in the fourth century B.C.E. that taught that happiness (freedom from emotional turmoil) could be achieved through the pursuit of pleasure (intellectual rather than sensual pleasure).

equestrians a group of extremely wealthy men in the late Roman Republic who were effectively barred from high office, but sought political power commensurate with their wealth; called equestrians because many had gotten their start as cavalry officers (*equites*).

ethnic cleansing the policy of killing or forcibly removing people of another ethnic group; used by the Serbs against Bosnian Muslims in the 1990s.

eucharist a Christian sacrament in which consecrated bread and wine are consumed in celebration of Jesus' Last Supper; also called the Lord's Supper or communion.

evolutionary socialism a socialist doctrine espoused by Eduard Bernstein who argued that socialists should stress cooperation and evolution to attain power by democratic means rather than by conflict and revolution.

fascism an ideology or movement that exalts the nation above the individual and calls for a centralized government with a dictatorial leader, economic and social regimentation, and forcible suppression of opposition; in particular, the ideology of Mussolini's Fascist regime in Italy.

feminism the belief in the social, political, and economic equality of the sexes; also, organized activity to advance women's rights.

fief a landed estate granted to a vassal in exchange for military services.

Final Solution the physical extermination of the Jewish people by the Nazis during World War II.

five pillars of Islam the core requirements of the faith, observation of which would lead to paradise: belief in Allah and his Prophet Muhammad; prescribed prayers; observation of Ramadan; pilgrimage to Mecca; and giving alms to the poor.

folk culture the traditional arts and crafts, literature, music, and other customs of the people; something that people make, as opposed to modern popular culture, which is something people buy.

four modernizations the slogan for radical reforms of Chinese industry, agriculture, technology, and national defense, instituted by Deng Xiaoping after his accession to power in the late 1970s.

free trade the unrestricted international exchange of goods with low or no tariffs.

fundamentalism a movement that emphasizes rigid adherence to basic religious principles; coined to describe Evangelical Christianity, it is often used to characterize Islamic conservatives.

general strike a strike by all or most workers in an economy; espoused by Georges Sorel as the heroic action that could be used to inspire the workers to destroy capitalist society.

gentry well-to-do English landowners below the level of the nobility; played an important role in the English Civil War of the seventeenth century.

geocentric theory the idea that the earth is at the center of the universe and that the sun and other celestial objects revolve around the earth.

glasnost "openness." Mikhail Gorbachev's policy of encouraging Soviet citizens to openly discuss the strengths and weaknesses of the Soviet Union.

Gleichschaltung the coordination of all government institutions under Nazi control in Germany from 1933.

global civilization human society considered as a single world-wide entity, in which local differences are less important than overall similarities.

good emperors the five emperors who ruled from 96 to 180 (Nerva, Trajan, Hadrian, Antoninus Pius, and Marcus Aurelius), a period of peace and prosperity for the Roman Empire.

Great Schism   the crisis in the late medieval church when there were first two and then three popes; ended by the Council of Constance (1414–1418).

guest workers   foreign workers working temporarily in European countries.

guild   an association of people with common interests and concerns, especially people working in the same craft. In medieval Europe, guilds came to control much of the production process and to restrict entry into various trades.

gymnasium   in classical Greece, a place for athletics; in the Hellenistic Age, a secondary school with a curriculum centered on music, physical exercise, and literature.

Hegira   the flight of Muhammad from Mecca to Medina in 622, which marks the first date on the official calendar of Islam.

heliocentric theory   the idea that the sun (not the earth) is at the center of the universe.

Hellenistic   literally, "to imitate the Greeks"; the era after the death of Alexander the Great when Greek culture spread into the Near East and blended with the culture of that region.

helots   serfs in ancient Sparta, who were permanently bound to the land that they worked for their Spartan masters.

heresy   the holding of religious doctrines different from the official teachings of the church.

Hermeticism   an intellectual movement beginning in the fifteenth century that taught that divinity is embodied in all aspects of nature; included works on alchemy and magic as well as theology and philosophy. The tradition continued into the seventeenth century and influenced many of the leading figures of the Scientific Revolution.

hetairai   highly sophisticated courtesans in ancient Athens who offered intellectual and musical entertainment as well as sex.

hieroglyphics   a highly pictorial system of writing most often associated with ancient Egypt. Also used (with different "pictographs") by other ancient peoples such as the Mayans.

high culture   the literary and artistic culture of the educated and wealthy ruling classes.

Hinduism   the main religion in India, it emphasizes reincarnation, based on the results of the previous life, and the desirability of escaping this cycle. Its various forms feature both asceticism and the pleasures of ordinary life, and encompass a multitude of gods as different manifestations of one ultimate reality.

Holocaust   the mass slaughter of European Jews by the Nazis during World War II.

Hopewell culture   a Native American society that flourished from about 200 B.C.E. to 400 C.E., noted for large burial mounds and extensive manufacture. Largely based in Ohio, its traders ranged as far as the Gulf of Mexico.

hoplites   heavily armed infantry soldiers used in ancient Greece in a phalanx formation.

Huguenots   French Calvinists.

humanism   an intellectual movement in Renaissance Italy based upon the study of the Greek and Roman classics.

Hundred Schools   (of philosophy) in China around the third century B.C.E., a wide-ranging debate over the nature of human beings, society, and the universe. The Schools included Legalism and Daoism, as well as Confucianism.

iconoclasm   an eighth-century Byzantine movement against the use of icons (pictures of sacred figures), which was condemned as idolatry.

ideology   a political philosophy such as conservatism or liberalism.

imperialism   the policy of extending one nation's power either by conquest or by establishing direct or indirect economic or cultural authority over another. Generally driven by economic self-interest, it can also be motivated by a sincere (if often misguided) sense of moral obligation.

imperium   "the right to command." In the Roman Republic, the chief executive officers (consuls and praetors) possessed the *imperium*; a military commander was an *imperator*. In the Roman Empire, the title *imperator*, or emperor, came to be used for the ruler.

indirect representation   a system of choosing delegates to a representative assembly in which citizens do not choose the delegates directly but instead vote for electors who choose the delegates.

individualism   emphasis on and interest in the unique traits of each person.

indulgence   the remission of part or all of the temporal punishment in purgatory due to sin; granted for charitable contributions and other good deeds. Indulgences became a regular practice of the Christian church in the High Middle Ages, and their abuse was instrumental in sparking Luther's reform movement in the sixteenth century.

infanticide   the practice of killing infants.

inflation   a sustained rise in the price level.

intendants   royal officials in seventeenth-century France who were sent into the provinces to execute the orders of the central government.

intervention, principle of   the idea, after the Congress of Vienna, that the great powers of Europe had the right to send armies into countries experiencing revolution to restore legitimate monarchs to their thrones.

isolationism   a foreign policy in which a nation refrains from making alliances or engaging actively in international affairs.

jihad   in Islam, "striving in the way of the Lord." The term is ambiguous and has been subject to varying interpretations, from the practice of conducting raids against local neighbors to the conduct of "holy war" against unbelievers.

joint-stock company   a company or association that raises capital by selling shares to individuals who receive dividends on their investment while a board of directors runs the company.

joint-stock investment bank   a bank created by selling shares of stock to investors. Such banks potentially have access to much more capital than do private banks owned by one or a few individuals.

Jomon   the earliest known Neolithic inhabitants of Japan, named for the cord pattern of their pottery.

justification by faith   the primary doctrine of the Protestant Reformation; taught that humans are saved not through good works, but by the grace of God, bestowed freely through the sacrifice of Jesus.

kami   spirits who were worshiped in early Japan, and resided in trees, rivers, and streams. *See* Shinto.

keiretsu   a type of powerful industrial or financial conglomerate that emerged in post–World War II Japan following the abolition of zaibatsu.

kolkhoz   a collective farm in the Soviet Union, in which the great bulk of the land was held and worked communally. Between 1928 and 1934, 250,000 kolkhozes replaced 26 million family farms.

laissez-faire   "to let alone." An economic doctrine that holds that an economy is best served when the government does not interfere but allows the economy to self-regulate according to the forces of supply and demand.

latifundia large landed estates in the Roman Empire (singular: *latifundium*).

lay investiture the practice in which a layperson chose a bishop and invested him with the symbols of both his temporal office and his spiritual office; led to the Investiture Controversy, which was ended by compromise in the Concordat of Worms in 1122.

Lebensraum "living space." The doctrine, adopted by Hitler, that a nation's power depends on the amount of land it occupies; thus, a nation must expand to be strong.

Legalism a Chinese philosophy that argued that human beings were by nature evil and would follow the correct path only if coerced by harsh laws and stiff punishments. Adopted as official ideology by the Qin dynasty, it was later rejected but remained influential.

legitimacy, principle of the idea that after the Napoleonic wars peace could best be reestablished in Europe by restoring legitimate monarchs who would preserve traditional institutions; guided Metternich at the Congress of Vienna.

Leninism Lenin's revision of Marxism that held that Russia need not experience a bourgeois revolution before it could move toward socialism.

liberal arts the seven areas of study that formed the basis of education in medieval and early modern Europe. Following Boethius and other late Roman authors, they consisted of grammar, rhetoric, and dialectic or logic (the *trivium*) and arithmetic, geometry, astronomy, and music (the *quadrivium*).

liberalism an ideology based on the belief that people should be as free from restraint as possible. Economic liberalism is the idea that the government should not interfere in the workings of the economy. Political liberalism is the idea that there should be restraints on the exercise of power so that people can enjoy basic civil rights in a constitutional state with a representative assembly.

limited liability the principle that shareholders in a joint-stock corporation can be held responsible for the corporation's debts only up to the amount they have invested.

limited (constitutional) monarchy a system of government in which the monarch is limited by a representative assembly and by the duty to rule in accordance with the laws of the land.

lineage group the descendants of a common ancestor; relatives, often as opposed to immediate family.

Mahayana a school of Buddhism that promotes the idea of universal salvation through the intercession of bodhisattvas; predominant in north Asia.

mandates a system established after World War I whereby a nation officially administered a territory (mandate) on behalf of the League of Nations. Thus, France administered Lebanon and Syria as mandates, and Britain administered Iraq and Palestine.

manor an agricultural estate operated by a lord and worked by peasants who performed labor services and paid various rents and fees to the lord in exchange for protection and sustenance.

Marshall Plan the European Recovery Program, under which the United States provided financial aid to European countries to help them rebuild after World War II.

Marxism the political, economic, and social theories of Karl Marx, which included the idea that history is the story of class struggle and that ultimately the proletariat will overthrow the bourgeoisie and establish a dictatorship en route to a classless society.

mass education a state-run educational system, usually free and compulsory, that aims to ensure that all children in society have at least a basic education.

mass leisure forms of leisure that appeal to large numbers of people in a society including the working classes; emerged at the end of the nineteenth century to provide workers with amusements after work and on weekends; used during the twentieth century by totalitarian states to control their populations.

mass politics a political order characterized by mass political parties and universal male and (eventually) female suffrage.

mass society a society in which the concerns of the majority—the lower classes—play a prominent role; characterized by extension of voting rights, an improved standard of living for the lower classes, and mass education.

materialism the belief that everything mental, spiritual, or ideal is an outgrowth of physical forces and that truth is found in concrete material existence, not through feeling or intuition.

megaliths large stones, widely used in Europe from around 4000 to 1500 B.C.E. to create monuments, including sophisticated astronomical observatories.

Meiji Restoration the period during the late 19th and early 20th century in which fundamental economic and cultural changes occured in Japan, tranforming it from a feudal and agrarian society to an industrial and technological society.

mercantilism an economic theory that held that a nation's prosperity depended on its supply of gold and silver and that the total volume of trade is unchangeable; therefore, advocated that the government play an active role in the economy by encouraging exports and discouraging imports, especially through the use of tariffs.

Mesolithic Age the period from 10,000 to 7000 B.C.E., characterized by a gradual transition from a food-gathering/hunting economy to a food-producing economy.

mestizos the offspring of intermarriage between Europeans, originally Spaniards, and native American Indians.

metics resident foreigners in ancient Athens; not permitted full rights of citizenship but did receive the protection of the laws.

militarism a policy of aggressive military preparedness; in particular, the large armies based on mass conscription and complex, inflexible plans for mobilization that most European nations had before World War I.

ministerial responsibility a tenet of nineteenth-century liberalism that held that ministers of the monarch should be responsible to the legislative assembly rather than to the monarch.

Modernism the new artistic and literary styles that emerged in the decades before 1914 as artists rebelled against traditional efforts to portray reality as accurately as possible (leading to Impressionism and Cubism) and writers explored new forms.

monotheistic/monotheism having only one god; the doctrine or belief that there is only one god.

mulattoes the offspring of Africans and Europeans, particularly in Latin America.

mutual deterrence the belief that nuclear war could best be prevented if both the United States and the Soviet Union had sufficient nuclear weapons so that even if one nation launched a preemptive first strike, the other could respond and devastate the attacker.

mystery religions religions that involve initiation into secret rites that promise intense emotional involvement with spiritual forces and a greater chance of individual immortality.

nationalism a sense of national consciousness based on awareness of being part of a community—a "nation"—that has common institutions, traditions, language, and customs and that becomes the focus of the individual's primary political loyalty.

nationalities problem the dilemma faced by the Austro-Hungarian Empire in trying to unite a wide variety of ethnic groups including, among others, Austrians, Hungarians, Poles, Croats, Czechs, Serbs, Slovaks, and Slovenes in an era when nationalism and calls for self-determination were coming to the fore.

nationalization the process of converting a business or industry from private ownership to government control and ownership.

nation in arms the people's army raised by universal mobilization to repel the foreign enemies of the French Revolution.

nation-state a form of political organization in which a relatively homogeneous people inhabits a sovereign state, as opposed to a state containing people of several nationalities.

NATO the North Atlantic Treaty Organization; a military alliance formed in 1949 in which the signatories (Belgium, Canada, Denmark, France, Great Britain, Iceland, Italy, Luxembourg, the Netherlands, Norway, Portugal, and the United States) agreed to provide mutual assistance if any one of them was attacked; later expanded to include other nations, including former members of the Warsaw Pact—Poland, the Czech Republic, and Hungary.

natural laws a body of laws or specific principles held to be derived from nature and binding upon all human society even in the absence of positive laws.

natural rights certain inalienable rights to which all people are entitled; include the right to life, liberty, and property, freedom of speech and religion, and equality before the law.

natural selection Darwin's idea that organisms that are most adaptable to their environment survive and pass on the variations that enabled them to survive, while other, less adaptable organisms become extinct; "survival of the fittest."

Nazi New Order the Nazis' plan for their conquered territories; included the extermination of Jews and others considered inferior, ruthless exploitation of resources, German colonization in the east, and the use of Poles, Russians, and Ukrainians as slave labor.

negritude a philosophy shared among African blacks that there exists a distinctive "African personality" that owes nothing to Western values and provides a common sense of purpose and destiny for black Africans.

Neo-Confucianism the dominant ideology of China during the second millennium C.E., it combined the metaphysical speculations of Buddhism and Daoism with the pragmatic Confucian approach to society, maintaining that the world is real, not illusory, and that fulfillment comes from participation, not withdrawal. It encouraged an intellectual environment that valued continuity over change and tradition over innovation.

Neoplatonism a revival of Platonic philosophy; in the third century C.E., a revival associated with Plotinus; in the Italian Renaissance, a revival associated with Marsilio Ficino who attempted to synthesize Christianity and Platonism.

New Course a short-lived, liberalizing change in Soviet policy to its Eastern European allies instituted after the death of Stalin in 1953.

New Culture Movement a protest launched at Peking University after the failure of the 1911 revolution, aimed at abolishing the remnants of the old system and introducing Western values and institutions into China.

New Democracy the initial program of the Chinese Communist government, from 1949 to 1955, focusing on honest government, land reform, social justice, and peace rather than on the utopian goal of a classless society.

New Economic Policy a modified version of the old capitalist system introduced in the Soviet Union by Lenin in 1921 to revive the economy after the ravages of the civil war and war communism.

new imperialism the revival of imperialism after 1880 in which European nations established colonies throughout much of Asia and Africa.

new monarchies the governments of France, England, and Spain at the end of the fifteenth century, where the rulers were successful in reestablishing or extending centralized royal authority, suppressing the nobility, controlling the church, and insisting upon the loyalty of all peoples living in their territories.

Nirvana in Buddhist thought, enlightenment, the ultimate transcendence from the illusion of the material world; release from the wheel of life.

nobiles "nobles." The small group of families from both patrician and plebeian origins who produced most of the men who were elected to office in the late Roman Republic.

Nok culture in northern Nigeria, one of the most active early iron-working societies in Africa, artifacts from which date back as far as 500 B.C.E.

nuclear family a family group consisting only of father, mother, and children.

old regime/old order the political and social system of France in the eighteenth century before the Revolution.

oligarchy rule by a few.

Open Door notes a series of letters sent in 1899 by U.S. Secretary of State John Hay to Great Britain, France, Germany, Italy, Japan and Russia, calling for equal economic access to the China market for all states and for the maintenance of the territorial and administrative integrity of the Chinese Empire.

opium trade the sale of the addictive product of the poppy, specifically by British traders to China in the 1830s. Chinese attempts to prevent it led to the Opium War of 1839–1842, which resulted in British access to Chinese ports and has traditionally been considered the beginning of modern Chinese history.

optimates "best men." Aristocratic leaders in the late Roman Republic who generally came from senatorial families and wished to retain their oligarchical privileges.

orders/estates the traditional tripartite division of European society based on heredity and quality rather than wealth or economic standing, first established in the Middle Ages and continuing into the eighteenth century; traditionally consisted of those who pray (the clergy), those who fight (the nobility), and those who work (all the rest).

organic evolution Darwin's principle that all plants and animals have evolved over a long period of time from earlier and simpler forms of life.

Organization of African Unity founded in Addis Ababa in 1963, it was intended to represent the interests of all the newly independent countries of Africa and provided a forum for the discussion of common problems until 2001, when it was replaced by the African Union.

Paleolithic Age the period of human history when humans used simple stone tools (c. 2,500,000–10,000 B.C.E.).

pan-Africanism the concept of African continental unity and solidarity in which the common interests of African countries transcend regional boundaries.

pantheism a doctrine that equates God with the universe and all that is in it.

paterfamilias the dominant male in a Roman family whose powers over his wife and children were theoretically unlimited, though they were sometimes circumvented in practice.

patriarchal/patriarchy a society in which the father is supreme in the clan or family; more generally, a society dominated by men.

patriarchal family a family in which the husband/father dominates his wife and children.

patricians great landowners who became the ruling class in the Roman Republic.

patronage the practice of awarding titles and making appointments to government and other positions to gain political support.

Pax Romana "Roman peace." A term used to refer to the stability and prosperity that Roman rule brought to the Mediterranean world and much of western Europe during the first and second centuries C.E.

peaceful coexistence the policy adopted by the Soviet Union under Khrushchev in 1955, and continued by his successors, that called for economic and ideological rivalry with the West rather than nuclear war.

Pentateuch the first five books of the Hebrew Bible (Genesis, Exodus, Leviticus, Numbers, and Deuteronomy).

peoples' democracies a term invented by the Soviet Union to define a society in the early stage of socialist transition, applied to Eastern European countries in the 1950s.

perestroika "restructuring." A term applied to Mikhail Gorbachev's economic, political, and social reforms in the Soviet Union.

permissive society a term applied to Western society after World War II to reflect the new sexual freedom and the emergence of a drug culture.

Petrine supremacy the doctrine that the bishop of Rome—the pope—as the successor of Saint Peter (traditionally considered the first bishop of Rome) should hold a preeminent position in the church.

phalanx a rectangular formation of tightly massed infantry soldiers.

philosophes intellectuals of the eighteenth-century Enlighten-ment who believed in applying a spirit of rational criticism to all things, including religion and politics, and who focused on improving and enjoying this world, rather than on the afterlife.

plebeians the class of Roman citizens who included nonpatrician landowners, craftspeople, merchants, and small farmers in the Roman Republic. Their struggle for equal rights with the patricians dominated much of the Republic's history.

pluralism the practice in which one person holds several church offices simultaneously; a problem of the late medieval church.

pogroms organized massacres of Jews.

polis an ancient Greek city-state encompassing both an urban area and its surrounding countryside; a small but autonomous political unit where all major political and social activities were carried out in a central location.

political democracy a form of government characterized by universal suffrage and mass political parties.

politiques a group who emerged during the French Wars of Religion in the sixteenth century; placed politics above religion and believed that no religious truth was worth the ravages of civil war.

polygyny the state or practice of having more than one wife at a time.

polytheistic/polytheism having many gods; belief in or the worship of more than one god.

popular culture as opposed to high culture, the unofficial, written and unwritten culture of the masses, much of which was passed down orally; centers on public and group activities such as festivals. In the twentieth century, refers to the entertainment, recreation, and pleasures that people purchase as part of mass consumer society.

populares "favoring the people." Aristocratic leaders in the late Roman Republic who tended to use the people's assemblies in an effort to break the stranglehold of the *nobiles* on political offices.

popular sovereignty the doctrine that government is created by and subject to the will of the people, who are the source of all political power.

praetorian guard the military unit that served as the personal body-guard of the Roman emperors.

praetors the two senior Roman judges, who had executive authority when the consuls were away from the city and could also lead armies.

predestination the belief, associated with Calvinism, that God, as a consequence of his foreknowledge of all events, has predetermined those who will be saved (the elect) and those who will be damned.

price revolution the dramatic rise in prices (inflation) that occurred throughout Europe in the sixteenth and early seventeenth centuries.

primogeniture an inheritance practice in which the eldest son receives all or the largest share of the parents' estate.

principate the form of government established by Augustus for the Roman Empire; continued the constitutional forms of the Republic and consisted of the *princeps* ("first citizen") and the senate, although the *princeps* was clearly the dominant partner.

proletariat the industrial working class. In Marxism, the class who will ultimately overthrow the bourgeoisie.

purdah the Indian term for the practice among Muslims and some Hindus of isolating women and preventing them from associating with men outside the home.

Puritans English Protestants inspired by Calvinist theology who wished to remove all traces of Catholicism from the Church of England.

querelles des femmes "arguments about women." A centuries-old debate about the nature of women that continued during the Scientific Revolution as those who argued for the inferiority of women found additional support in the new anatomy and medicine.

rationalism a system of thought based on the belief that human reason and experience are the chief sources of knowledge.

realism in medieval Europe, the school of thought that, following Plato, held that the individual objects we perceive are not real but merely manifestations of universal ideas existing in the mind of God. In the nineteenth century, a school of painting that emphasized the everyday life of ordinary people, depicted with photographic realism.

Realpolitik "politics of reality." Politics based on practical concerns rather than theory or ethics.

real wages/income/prices wages/income/prices that have been adjusted for inflation.

reason of state the principle that a nation should act on the basis of its long-term interests and not merely to further the dynastic interests of its ruling family.

reincarnation the idea that the individual soul is reborn in a different form after death; in Hindu and Buddhist thought, release from this cycle is the objective of all living souls.

relativity theory Einstein's theory that holds, among other things, that (1) space and time are not absolute but are relative to the observer and interwoven into a four-dimensional space-time continuum and (2) matter is a form of energy ($E = mc^2$).

Renaissance the "rebirth" of classical culture that occurred in Italy between c. 1350 and c. 1550; also, the earlier revivals of classical culture that occurred under Charlemagne and in the twelfth century.

rentier a person who lives on income from property and is not personally involved in its operation.

reparations payments made by a defeated nation after a war to compensate another nation for damage sustained as a result of the war; required from Germany after World War I.

revisionism a socialist doctrine that rejected Marx's emphasis on class struggle and revolution and argued instead that workers should work through political parties to bring about gradual change.

revolution a fundamental change in the political and social organization of a state.

revolutionary socialism the socialist doctrine espoused by Georges Sorel who held that violent action was the only way to achieve the goals of socialism.

rhetoric the art of persuasive speaking; in the Middle Ages, one of the seven liberal arts.

Rococo a style, especially of decoration and architecture, that developed from the Baroque and spread throughout Europe by the 1730s. While still elaborate, it emphasized curves, lightness, and charm in the pursuit of pleasure, happiness, and love.

sacraments rites considered imperative for a Christian's salvation. By the thirteenth century consisted of the eucharist or Lord's Supper, baptism, marriage, penance, extreme unction, holy orders, and confirmation of children; Protestant reformers of the sixteenth century generally recognized only two—baptism and communion (the Lord's Supper).

samurai literally "retainer"; similar to European knights. Usually in service to a particular shogun, these warriors lived by a strict code of ethics and duty.

sans-culottes the common people who did not wear the fine clothes of the upper classes (sans-culottes means "without breeches") and played an important role in the radical phase of the French Revolution.

sati the Hindu ritual requiring a wife to throw herself upon her her deceased husband's funeral pyre.

satrap/satrapy a governor with both civil and military duties in the ancient Persian Empire, which was divided into satrapies, or provinces, each administered by a satrap.

scholasticism the philosophical and theological system of the medieval schools, which emphasized rigorous analysis of contradictory authorities; often used to try to reconcile faith and reason.

scientific method a method of seeking knowledge through inductive principles; uses experiments and observations to develop generalizations.

Scientific Revolution the transition from the medieval worldview to a largely secular, rational, and materialistic perspective; began in the seventeenth century and was popularized in the eighteenth.

secularization the process of becoming more concerned with material, worldly, temporal things and less with spiritual and religious things.

self-determination the doctrine that the people of a given territory or a particular nationality should have the right to determine their own government and political future.

self-strengthening a late-nineteenth-century Chinese policy, by which Western technology would be adopted while Confucian principles and institutions were maintained intact.

senate/senators the leading council of the Roman Republic; composed of about 300 men (senators) who served for life and dominated much of the political life of the Republic.

serf a peasant who is bound to the land and obliged to provide labor services and pay various rents and fees to the lord; considered unfree but not a slave because serfs could not be bought and sold.

Shinto a kind of state religion in Japan, derived from beliefs in nature spirits and until recently linked with belief in the divinity of the emperor and the sacredness of the Japanese nation.

shogunate system the system of government in Japan in which the emperor exercised only titular authority while the shogun (regional military dictators) exercised actual political power.

skepticism a doubtful or questioning attitude, especially about religion.

Social Darwinism the application of Darwin's principle of organic evolution to the social order; led to the belief that progress comes from the struggle for survival as the fittest advance and the weak decline.

socialism an ideology that calls for collective or government ownership of the means of production and the distribution of goods.

social security/social insurance government programs that provide social welfare measures such as old age pensions and sickness, accident, and disability insurance.

Socratic method a form of teaching that uses a question-and-answer format to enable students to reach conclusions by using their own reasoning.

Sophists wandering scholars and professional teachers in ancient Greece who stressed the importance of rhetoric and tended toward skepticism and relativism.

soviets councils of workers' and soldiers' deputies formed throughout Russia in 1917; played an important role in the Bolshevik Revolution.

sphere of influence a territory or region over which an outside nation exercises political or economic influence.

stateless societies the pre-Columbian communities in much of the Americas who developed substantial cultures without formal nation-states.

Stoicism a philosophy founded by Zeno in the fourth century B.C.E. that taught that happiness could be obtained by accepting one's lot and living in harmony with the will of God, thereby achieving inner peace.

subinfeudation the practice in which a lord's greatest vassals subdivided their fiefs and had vassals of their own, and those vassals, in turn, subdivided their fiefs and so on down to simple knights whose fiefs were too small to subdivide.

suffrage the right to vote.

suffragists those who advocate the extension of the right to vote (suffrage), especially to women.

surplus value in Marxism, the difference between a product's real value and the wages of the worker who produced the product.

Swahili a mixed African-Arabian culture that developed by the twelfth century along the east coast of Africa; also, the national language of Kenya and Tanzania.

syncretism the combining of different forms of belief or practice, as, for example, when two gods are regarded as different forms of the same underlying divine force and are fused together.

Taika reforms the seventh-century "great change" reforms that established the centralized Japanese state.

taille a French tax on land or property, developed by King Louis XI in the fifteenth century as the financial basis of the monarchy. It was largely paid by the peasantry; the nobility and the clergy were exempt.

tariffs duties (taxes) imposed on imported goods; usually imposed both to raise revenue and to discourage imports and protect domestic industries.

tetrarchy rule by four; the system of government established by Diocletian (284–305) in which the Roman Empire was divided into two parts, each ruled by an "Augustus" assisted by a "Caesar."

theocracy a government ruled by a divine authority.

Theravada a school of Buddhism that stresses personal behavior and the quest for understanding as a means of release from the wheel of life, rather than the intercession of bodhisattvas; predominant in Sri Lanka and Southeast Asia.

three-field system in medieval agriculture, the practice of dividing the arable land into three fields so that one could lie fallow while the others were planted in winter grains and spring crops.

three kingdoms Koguryo, Paekche, and Silla, rivals but all under varying degrees of Chinese influence, which together controlled virtually all of Korea from the fourth to the seventh centuries.

three obediences the traditional duties of Japanese women, in permanent subservience: child to father, wife to husband, and widow to son.

tithe a tenth of one's harvest or income; paid by medieval peasants to the village church.

Tongmenghui the political organization—"Revolutionary Alliance"—formed by Sun Yat-sen in 1905, which united various revolutionary factions and ultimately toppled the Manchu dynasty.

Torah the body of law in Hebrew Scripture, contained in the Pentateuch (the first five books of the Hebrew Bible).

totalitarian state a state characterized by government control over all aspects of economic, social, political, cultural, and intellectual life, the subordination of the individual to the state, and insistence that the masses be actively involved in the regime's goals.

total war warfare in which all of a nation's resources, including civilians at home as well as soldiers in the field, are mobilized for the war effort.

trade union an association of workers in the same trade, formed to help members secure better wages, benefits, and working conditions.

transubstantiation a doctrine of the Roman Catholic church that teaches that during the eucharist the substance of the bread and wine is miraculously transformed into the body and blood of Jesus.

trench warfare warfare in which the opposing forces attack and counterattack from a relatively permanent system of trenches protected by barbed wire; characteristic of World War I.

tribute system an important element of Chinese foreign policy, by which neighboring states paid for the privilege of access to Chinese markets, received legitimation and agreed not to harbor enemies of the Chinese Empire.

Truman Doctrine the doctrine, enunciated by Harry Truman in 1947, that the United States would provide economic aid to countries that said they were threatened by Communist expansion.

twice-born the males of the higher castes in traditional Indian society, who underwent an initiation ceremony at puberty.

tyrant/tyranny in an ancient Greek *polis* (or an Italian city-state during the Renaissance), a ruler who came to power in an unconstitutional way and ruled without being subject to the law.

ulama a convocation of leading Muslim scholars, the earliest of which shortly after the death of Muhammad drew up a law code, called the Shari'a, based largely on the Koran and the sayings of the Prophet, to provide believers with a set of prescriptions to regulate their daily lives.

umma the Muslim community, as a whole.

uncertainty principle a principle in quantum mechanics, posited by Heisenberg, that holds that one cannot determine the path of an electron because the very act of observing the electron would affect its location.

unconditional surrender complete, unqualified surrender of a belligerent nation.

untouchables the lowest level of Indian society, technically outside the caste system and considered less than human; renamed harijans ("children of God") by Gandhi and later dalits, they remain the object of discrimination despite affirmative action programs.

utopian socialists intellectuals and theorists in the early nineteenth century who favored equality in social and economic conditions and wished to replace private property and competition with collective ownership and cooperation; deemed impractical and "utopian" by later socialists.

varna Indian classes, or castes. *See* caste system.

vassal a person granted a fief, or landed estate, in exchange for providing military services to the lord and fulfilling certain other obligations such as appearing at the lord's court when summoned and making a payment on the knighting of the lord's eldest son.

vernacular the everyday language of a region, as distinguished from a language used for special purposes. For example, in medieval Paris, French was the vernacular, but Latin was used for academic writing and for classes at the University of Paris.

volkish thought the belief that German culture is superior and that the German people have a universal mission to save Western civilization from inferior races.

war communism Lenin's policy of nationalizing industrial and other facilities and requisitioning the peasants' produce during the civil war in Russia.

War Guilt Clause the clause in the Treaty of Versailles that declared that Germany (and Austria) were responsible for starting World War I and ordered Germany to pay reparations for the damage the Allies had suffered as a result of the war.

Warsaw Pact a military alliance, formed in 1955, in which Albania, Bulgaria, Czechoslovakia, East Germany, Hungary, Poland, Romania, and the Soviet Union agreed to provide mutual assistance. Dissolved in 1991, some former members joined NATO.

welfare state a social/political system in which the government assumes the primary responsibility for the social welfare of its citizens by providing such things as social security, unemploy-ment benefits, and health care.

wergeld "money for a man." In early Germanic law, a person's value in monetary terms, which was paid by a wrongdoer to the family of the person who had been injured or killed.

world-machine Newton's conception of the universe as one huge, regulated, and uniform machine that operated according to natural laws in absolute time, space, and motion.

Young Turks a successful Turkish reformist group in the late nineteenth and early twentieth centuries.

zaibatsu powerful business cartels formed in Japan during the Meiji era and outlawed following World War II.

zamindars Indian tax collectors, who were assigned land, from which they kept part of the revenue; the British revived the system in a misguided attempt to create a landed gentry.

Zen Buddhism (in Chinese, Chan or Ch'an) a school of Buddhism particularly important in Japan, some of whose adherents stress that enlightenment (satori) can be achieved suddenly, though others emphasize lengthy meditation.

ziggurat a massive stepped tower upon which a temple dedicated to the chief god or goddess of a Sumerian city was built.

Zionism an international movement that called for the establishment of a Jewish state or a refuge for Jews in Palestine.

Zoroastrianism a religion founded by the Persian Zoroaster in the seventh century B.C.E.; characterized by worship of a supreme god Ahuramazda who represents the good against the evil spirit, identified as Ahriman.

PRONUNCIATION GUIDE

Abbasid   AB-uh-sid or a-BA-sid
Abu Bakr   a-BOO BAH-ker
Achaemenid   a-KEE-muh-nid
Adenauer, Konrad   AD-n'our-er
Aeschylus   ESS-kuh-lus
Afrikaners   a-fri-KAH-ners
Agamemnon   ag-uh-MEM-nahn
Agincourt   AJ-in-kor
Ahuramazda   ah-HOOR-ah-MAHZ-duh
Akhenaten   ah-kuh-NAH-tun
Akkadian   a-KAY-dee-un
al-Mas'udi   al-ma-SOO-dee
Albigensian   al-bi-GEN-see-un
Albuquerque, Afonso de   AL-buh-kur-kee, ah-FON-soh d'
Allah   AH-luh or AL-uh
Allende, Salvador   ah-YEN-day, SAL-vuh-DOR
al-Ma'mun   al-MAH-moon
al-Rahman, Abd   al-RAH-mun, abd
Amenhotep   ah-mun-HOE-tep
Andropov, Yuri   an-DROP-ov, YOOR-ee
Antigonid   an-TIG-oh-nid
apella   a-PELL-uh
Apennines   A-puh-NINES
Aquinas, Thomas   uh-KWIGH-nus
Archimedes   are-kuh-MEE-deez
Aristotle   ar-i-STAH-tul
Aristophanes   ar-i-STAH-fuh-neez
Arthasastra   ar-tuh-SAHS-tra
Ashkenazic   ash-kuh-NAH-zic
Ashurnasirpal   ah-shoor-NAH-suh-pul
Asoka   a-SHOH-kuh or a-SOH-kuh
assignat   as-seen-YAH or AS-sig-nat
Assyrians   uh-SEER-ee-uns
Attalid   AT-a-lid
Augustine   AW-gus-STEEN
Auschwitz-Birkenau   OUSH-vitz-BUR-kuh-now
Ausgleich   OUS-glike
Avicenna   av-i-SEN-uh
Avignon   ah-veen-YONE
Axum   OX-oom
Bach, Johann Sebastian   BAHK, yoh-HAHN
    suh-BASS-chen
Barbarossa   bar-buh-ROH-suh
Baroque   buy-ROHK
Bastille   ba-STEEL
Beauvoir, Simone de   boh-VWAH, see-MOAN duh
Belisarius   bell-i-SAR-ee-us

benefice   BEN-uh-fiss
Bhagavadgita   bog-ah-vahd-GEE-ta
Blitzkrieg   BLITZ-kreeg
Boeotia   bee-OH-shuh
Boer   BOHR
Boleyn, Anne   BUH-lin
Bólívar, Simón   BOH-luh-VAR, see-MOAN
Bologna   buh-LOHN-yuh
Brandt, Willy   BRAHNT, VIL-ee
Brétigny   bray-tee-NYEE
Brezhnev, Leonid   BREZH-nef, lyi-on-YEET
Briand, Aristide   bree-AHN, a-ree-STEED
Bulganin, Nilolai   bul-GAN-in, nyik-uh-LYE
Bund deutscher Mädel   BUNT DOICHer MAIR-del
Burschenschaften   BOOR-shen-shaft-un
Buthelezi, Mangosuthu   boo-teh-LAY-zee, man-go-SOO-tu
Calais   ka-LAY
caliph/caliphate   KAY-lif/KAY-li-FATE
Cambyses   kam-BY-seez
Camus, Albert   kuh-MOO, al-BEAR
Canaanites   KAY-nuh-nites
Cao Cao   tsau tsau
Capet/Capetian   ka-PAY or KAY-put/kuh-PEE-shun
Carolingian   kar-oh-LIN-jun
carruca   ca-ruh-kuh
Carthage/Carthaginian   KAR-thij/KAR-thuh-JIN-ee-un
Castlereagh, Viscount   KAS-ul-RAY
Castiglione, Baldassare   kass-teel-YOHnay, bahl-dah-SAR-ay
Çatal Hüyük   CHAH-tul HOO-YOOK
Catharism   KA-tha-ri-zem
Catullus   ka-TULL-us
caudillos   kow-THEE-yohz (TH as in the)
Cavendish, Margaret   KAV-un-dish
Cavour, Camillo di   ka-VOOR, kah-MIL-oh
Chaeronea   ker-oh-NEE-uh
Chaldean   kal-DEE-un
Charlemagne   SHAR-luh-mane
Chernenko, Konstantin   cher-NYEN-koh, kon-stun-TEEN
Chiang Kai-Shek   CHANG KIGH-shek
Chirac, Jacques   SHE-RAHK, ZHAHK
Chulalongkorn   CHOO-LAH-LONG-KON
Cicero   SIS-uh-roh
Cistercians   si-STIR-shuns
Cixi   TSE-she
Cleisthenes   KLISE-thuh-neez
Clemenceau, Georges   klem-un-SOH, ZHORZH
Clovis   KLOH-vis

Colbert, Baptiste kahl-BEHR, buh-TEEST

Comneni kahm-NEE,nee

Concordat of Worms kon-KOR-dat of WURMZ or VAWRMZ

condottieri kon-dah-TEE-AIR-ee

consul KON-sul

Copernicus, Nicolaus koh-PURR-nuh-kus, nee-koh-LAH-us

Corinth KOR-inth

Cortés, Hernán kor-TEZ, er-NAHN

Courbet, Gustave koor-BAY, guh-STAWV

Crassus KRASS-us

Crécy kray-SEE

Croesus KREE-suhs

Cruz, Juana Ines de la KROOZ, WAHN-uh ee NAYS de lah

Curie, Marie kyoo-REE, muh-REE

d'Este, Isabella ES-tay

Daimyo die-AIM-yo

Dao De Jing dow duh JING

Darius duh-RYE-us

dauphin DAW-fin

de Gaulle, Charles duh GOLL, SHARL

Delacroix, Eugène del-uh-KWAW, yoo-ZHAHN

Deng Xiaoping DUNG shee-ow-ping

Descartes, René day-KART, ruh-NAY

Dias, Bartholomeu DEE-us, bar-too-loo-MAY

Diaspora die-AS-pur-uh

Díaz, Porfirio DEE-ahz, pah-FEER-yoh

Diderot, Denis DEE-duh-roh, duh-NEE

Diem, Ngo Dinh dzee-EM, NGOH Den

Diocletian die-uh-KLEE-shun

Dorians DOR-ee-uns

Douhet, Giulio doo-EE, JOOL-yoh

Duma DOO-muh

Echeverria, Luis ah-chuh-vuh-REE-uh, loo-EES

Einsatzgruppen INE-zats-groo-pen

encomienda en-koh-mee-EN-dah

Engels, Friedrich ENG-ulz, FREE-drik

Entente Cordiale ahn-TAHNT kor-DYALL

ephor EF-or

Epicurus/Epicureanism EP-i-KYOOR-us/EP-i-kyoo-REE-uh-ni-zem

Erasmus, Desiderius i-RAZZ-mus, des-i-DIR-ee-us

Erhard, Ludwig AIR-hart

Etruscan i-TRUSS-kuhn

Euripides yoo-RIP-i-deez

exchequer EX-chek-ur

Fa Xian fa SHIEN

fasces FASS-eez

Fascio di Combattimento FASH-ee-oh di com-BATT-ee-men-toh

Fatimid FAT-i-mid

Flaubert, Gustave floh-BEAR, guh-STAWV

Friedan, Betty fri-DAN

Friedrich, Caspar David FREE-drik, KASS-par DAHV-eet

Frimaire free-MARE

Fronde FROND

Führer FYOOR-ur

gabelle gah-BELL

Garibaldi, Giuseppe gar-uh-BAWL-dee, joo-ZEP-pay

Gaugamela gaw-guh-MEE-luh

gerousia juh-ROO-see-uh

Gierek, Edward GYER-ek

Gilgamesh GILL-guh-mesh

glasnost GLAZ-nohst

Gleichschaltung GLIKE-shalt-ung

Gomulka, Wladyslaw goh-MOOL-kuh, vla-DIS-lawf

Gorbachev, Mikhail GOR-buh-chof, meek-HALE

Gracchus GRA-kus

Gropius, Walter GROH-pee-us, VAHL-ter

Grossdeutsch gross-DOICH

Guevara, Ernesto "Che" gay-VAR-uh, er-NAY-stoh "CHAY"

Habsburg HAPS-burg

Hadrian HAY-dree-un

Hagia Sophia HAG-ee-uh soh-FEE-uh

hajj HAJ

Hammurabi ham-uh-RAH-bee

Han Gaozu HAHN GOW-ZOO

Hannibal HAN-uh-bul

Harappan har-RAP-an

harijans har-uh-JAHNS

Harun al-Rashid huh-ROON al-ra-SHEED

Hatshepsut hat-SHEP-soot

Havel, Vaclav HAH-vuhl, VAHT-slaf

Haydn, Franz Joseph HIDE-n, FRAHNTS

hegemon HEJ-uh-mon

Hegira huh-JIGH-ruh

Hellenistic hell-uh-NIS-tik

helots HELL-uts

Herzl, Theodor HERT-sul, TAY-oh-dor

Heydrich, Reinhard HIGH-drik, RINE-hart

Hidalgo y Castilla, Miguel hi-DAL-goh ee cahs-TEEL-yuh, mee-GEL

hieroglyph HIGH-ur-oh-glif

Hitler Jugend JOO-gunt

Ho Chi Minh HOE CHEE MIN

Höch, Hannah HOKH

Hohenstaufen HOE-un-SHTAU-fun

Hohenzollern HOE-un-ZAHL-lurn

Homo erectus HOH-MOH i-RECK-tuhs

Homo habilis HOH-MOH HAB-uh-lus

Homo sapiens HOH-MOH SAY-pee-enz

hoplites HOP-lites

Horace HOR-us

Höss, Rudolf HAHSS, roo-DAHLF

Huguenots HYOO-guh-nots

Husak, Gustav   HOO-sahk, guh-STAHV
Hydaspes   high-DASS-peez
Hyksos   hik-SAHS or hik-SOHS
Ibn Khaldun   ib-en-kal-DOON
Ibn Sina   ib-en SEE-nuh
Ieyasu, Tokugawa   ee-eye-AY-soo, toe-koo-GAH-wah
Ignatius of Loyola   ig-NAY-shus of loi-OH-luh
Il Duce   eel DOO-chay
imperator   im-puh-RAH-tor
imperium   im-PIER-ee-um
intendant   in-TEN-duhnt
Inukai Tsuyoshi   EE-NUH-KIGH TSOO-yah-shee
Isis   EYE-sis
Issus   ISS-us
Jacobin   JAK-uh-bin
Jagiello   yah-GYELL-oh
Jaruzelski, Wojciech   yahr-uh-ZEL-skee, VOI-chek
Jiang Qing   JIANG CHING
jihad   ji-HAHD
Jinnah, Mohammed Ali   JEE-nah, moe-HA-mud a-LEE
Judaea   joo-DEE-uh
Junkers   YOONG-kers
Justinian   juh-STIN-ee-un
Juvenal   JOO-vuh-nul
Ka'aba stone   KAH-BAH
Kadar, Janos   KAY-dahr, YAHN-us
Kadinsky, Vassily   kan-DIN-skee, vus-YEEL-yee
kamikaze   kah-mi-KAH-zee
Kangxi   KANG-she
Keiretsu business arrangement   kai-RET-su
Kerensky, Alexander   kuh-REN-skee
Keynes, John Maynard   KAYNZ
Khan, Khubilai   KHAN, KOO-bil-eye
Khatemi, Mohammed   KHAH-tee-mee
Khayyam, Omar   kigh-YAHM, oh-MAR
Khmer Rouge   ka-MEHR roozh
Khoisan   KOY-SAN
Khrushchev, Nikita   KROOSH-chef, nuh-KEE-tuh
Khufu   KOO-FOO
Kita, Ikki   KEE-tah EEk-EE
Knossos   NAH-sus
Koguryo   ko-GOOR-yo
Kohl, Helmut   KOLE, HELL-mut
Kolkhoz   kahl-KAWZ
Kollantai, Alexandra   kawl-un-TIE
Kosovo   kah-suh-VOH
Kraft durch Freude   CRAFT durch FROI-duh
Kristallnacht   KRIS-tal-NAHCHT
Kshatriya   kuh-SHOT-ria
Kuchuk-Kainarji   koo-CHOOK-kigh-NAR-jee
kulaks   koo-LAKS
kulturkampf   kool-TOOR-kahmf
Kundera, Milan   KOON-de-rah, MIL-ahn

Kwasniewski, Aleksander   KWAHS-noo-skee, ah-lek-SAHN-der
laissez-faire   les-ay-FAIR
Lao Tzu   LAUW DZU
latifundia   lat-uh-FUN-dee-uh
Latium   LAY-shee-um
Laurier, Wilfred   LOR-ee-ay
Lebensraum   LAY-benz-roum
Lee Kuan-yew   LEE KWAN YEW
Lévesque, René   luh-VEK, ruh-NAY
Lin Zexu   LIN DZUH-shoo
Livy   LIV-ee
López Portillo, José   LOH-pez por-TEE-yoh, hoh-ZAY
Luddites   LUD-ites
Ludendorff, Erich   LOOD-un-dorf
Luftwaffe   LUFT-vaf-uh
l'uomo universale   l'oo-OH-moh oo-nee-vehr-SAH-leh
Lycurgus   ligh-KUR-gus
Machiavelli, Niccolò   mak-ee-uh-VELL-ee, nee-koh-LOH
Machu Picchu   MAH-CHOO PEEK-SHOO
Madero, Francisco   muh-der-oh, fran-CIS-koh
Magyars   MAG-yars
Mahabharata   MA-HA-bah-rah-tah
Majapahit   mah-ja-PAH-heet
Malleus Maleficarum   mall-EE-us mal-uh-FIK-ar-um
Manchukuo   man-CHOO-KWOH
Manetho   MAN-uh-THOH
Mao Zedong   mau zee-DONG
Marie Antoinette   muh-REE an-twuh-NET
Marius   MAR-ee-us
Marquez, Gabriel Garcia   MAR-kays, gab-ree-ELL gar-SEE-uh
Massaccio   muh-ZAHCH-ee-OH
Mbecki, Thabo   mu-BEK-ee, TYE-bo
Meiji   MAY-jee
Mein Kampf   mine KAHMF
Menander   me-NAN-der
Mendeleyev, Dmitri   men-duh-LAY-ef, di-MEE-tri
Meroë   mer-OH-ee
Mesopotamia   mess-oh-poh-TAME-ee-uh
mestizos   me-STEE-zohs
Metternich, Klemens von   MET-er-nik, KLAY-mens
Michelangelo   my-kell-AN-juh-loh
Mieszko   MYESH-koh
Millet, Jean-François   mi-LAY, ZHAHN-FRAN-swah
Milosevic, Slobodan   mi-LOH-suh-vich, slaw-BAW-dahn
Miltiades   mil-TIGH-uh-DEEZ
missi dominici   MISS-ee doe-MIN-ee-chee
Mitterrand, Francois   mee-ter-AHN, FRAN-swah
Moche   MO-chay
Moctezuma   mahk-tuh-ZOO-muh
Moldavia   mahl-DAY-vee-uh
Monet, Claude   moh-NAY, KLODE

Montesquieu   MONT-ess-skyoo
Montessori, Maria   mon-ti-SOR-ee
Morisot, Berthe   mor-ee-ZOH, BERT
Mozart, Wolfgang Amadeus   MOHT-sart, volf-GANG ah-muh-DAY-us
Muawiyah   moo-AH-wee-yah
Mughal   MOO-gahl
Muhammad   moe-HA-mud
mulattoes   muh-LA-tohs
Muslim   MUZ-lum
Mutsuhito   moo-tsoo-HEE-toe
Mwene Metapa   MWAHN-uh muh-TAH-puh
Mycenaean   my-suh-NEE-un
Nagy, Imry   NAHJD, IM-re
Nebuchadnezzar   neb-uh-kad-NWZZ-ar
Nehru, Jawaharlal   NAY-roo, jah-WAH-har-lahl
Nero   NEE-roh
Neumann, Balthasar   NOI-mahn, BAHL-tah-zar
Nevsky, Alexander   NEW-skee
Ngo Dinh Diem   NGOH din dee-EM
Ngugi Wa Thiong'o   en-GU-ji WA THIE-ong-oh
Nimwegen   NIM-vay-gun
Nkrumah, Kwame   en-KRU-may, KWA-may
Novotny, Antonin   noh-VOT-nee, AN-ton-yeen
Nyerere, Julius   nyay-RARE-ee
Nystadt   nee-STAHD
Octavian   ok-TAY-vee-un
optimates   opp-tuh-MAH-tays
Osiris   oh-SIGH-ris
Ovid   OV-id
Pachakuti   PAH-chah-koo-tee
Pahlavi dynasty   pah-LAH-vee
Palenque   pah-LENG-kay
Paleologus   pay-lee-OHL-uh-gus
Pankhurst, Emmeline   PANK-herst, em-uh-LINE
papal curia   PAY-pul KOOR-ee-uh
Parlement   par-luh-MAHN
paterfamilias   pay-ter-fuh-MILL-ee-us
Peloponnesus   pe-luh-puh-NEE-sus
Pentateuch   PEN-tuh-tuke
perestroika   pair-ess-TROY-kuh
Pericles   PER-i-kleez
Perón, Juan   pay-ROHN, WAHN
Pétain, Henri   pay-TAN, AHN-ree
Petrarch   PE-trark
philosophe   fee-luh-ZAWF
Phoenicians   fi-NISH-uns
Picasso, Pablo   pi-KAW-soh
Pinochet, Augusto   PEE-noh-shay, aw-GOO-stoh
Pisistratus   pi-SIS-truh-tus
Pissaro, Camille   pi-SARR-oh, kah-MEEYL
Pizarro, Francesco   pi-ZARR-oh, frahn-CHASE-koh
Planck, Max   PLAHNK
Plantagenet   plan-TA-juh-net

Plato   PLAY-toe
Poincaré, Raymond   pwan-kah-RAY, re-MOAN
polis   POE-lis
politiques   puh-lee-TEEKS
Polybius   poe-LIB-ee-us
Pompey   POM-pee
pontifex maximus   PON-ti-feks MAK-suh-mus
populares   POP-yoo-lar-ays
praetor   PREE-ter
princeps   PRIN-seps
procurator   PROK-yuh-ray-ter
Ptolemy/Ptolemaic   TOL-uh-mee/TOL-uh-MAY-ik
Punic   PYOO-nik
Pugachev, Emelyan   poo-guh-CHEF, em-ELL-yun
Pyrrhus/Pyrrhic   PIR-us/PIR-ik
Qadhafi, Muammar   gah-DAH-fee, myoo-am-MAR
Qianlong   chee-UN-LUNG
Qin Shi Huangdi   chin SHE hwang-DEE
Qing dynasty   CHING
Quesnay, François   kay-NAY, FRAN-swah
Quetzalcoatl   ket-SAHL-koh-AHT-ul
Quipu   KEE-poo
Quran   kuh-RAN
Rameses   RAM-i-seez
Raphael   RAFF-ee-ul
Rasputin   rass-PYOO-tin
Realpolitik   ray-AHL-poe-li-teek
Reichsrat   RIKES-raht
Ricci, Matteo   REECH-ee, mah-TAY-oh
risorgimento   ree-SOR-jee-men-toe
Robespierre, Maximilien   ROHBZ-pee-air, mak-SEE-meel-yahn
Rococo   ro-KOH-koh
Rosas, Juan Manuel de   ROH-sahs, WAHN mahn-WELL duh
Rousseau, Jean-Jacques   roo-SOH ZHAHN-ZHAHK
Sadducees   SA-juh-seez
Sadi   sah-DEE
Safavids   suh-FAH-weedz
Sakharov, Andrei   SAH-kuh-rof, ahn-DRAY
Saladin   SAL-uh-din
Sallust   SALL-ust
San Martin, José   SAN mar-TEEN, hoh-ZAY
Sartre, Jean-Paul   SAR-truh, ZHAHN-PAUL
satrap/satrapy   SAY-trap/SAY-truh-pee
Schleswig-Holstein   SCHLES-vig-HOLE-stine
Schlieffen   SHLEE-fun
Schmidt, Helmut   SHMIT, HELL-mut
Schroeder, Gerhard   SHROH-der, ger-HART
Schönberg, Arnold   SHURN-burg, ARR-nawlt
Schutzstaffel   SHOOTS-shah-ful
Seleucus/Seleucid   si-LOO-kus/si-LOO-sid
Seljuk Turks   SELL-juke
Seneca   SEN-i-kuh

Sephardic   suh-FAR-dik

sesterces   SES-ters-eez

Sforza   SFORT-zuh

Shari'a   shay-REE-uh

Shari'ya   shay-REE-uh

Sheikh   SHEEK or SHAYK

Shi'ite   SHE-ite

Shotoku Taishi   show-TOE-koo tie-ISH-ee

Siddhartha Gautama   sid-AR-tha guh-TAW-mah

Sieveking, Amalie   SEEVE-king

Sima Qian   suh-MAH chee-AHN or chee-YEN

Sjahrir Sutan   SYAH-rir, soo-TAN

Socrates   SOK-ruh-teez

Solon   SOH-lun

Solzhenitsyn, Alexander   SOLE-zhuh-NEET-sin

Somoza, Anastasio   suh-MOH-zuh, ahn-ash-TAHS-yoh

Sophocles   SOF-uh-kleez

Soyinka, Wole   shah-YIN-kuh, WAH-lay

Spartacus   SPAR-tuh-kus

Speer, Albert   SHPIER

squadristi   sqah-DREES-tee

Sri Lanka   SREE-LAHN-kuh

Srivijaya   sree-vee-JAH-ya

Stoicism   STOH-i-siz-um

Stravinsky, Igor   struh-VIN-skee, EE-gor

Stresemann, Gustav   SHTRAY-zuh-mahn, GUS-tahf

Sturmabteilung   SHTOORM-AP-ti-loong

Sudetenland   soo-DAYT-un-LAND

Suger, Abbot   soo-ZHER

Suleyman I the Magnificent   soo-lee-MAHN

Sumerian   soo-MER-ee-un

Suttner, Bertha von   ZOOT-ner

Tacitus   TASS-i-tus

taille   TAH-yuh or TIE

Tang Taizong   TANG TYE-zawng

Tanzania   tan-zah-NEE-ah

Tenochtitlán   tay-NAWCH-teet-LAHN

Teotihuacán   TAY-oh-tee-WAH-kahn

Tertullian   tur-TULL-yun

Theocritus   thee-OCK-ri-tus

Thermidor   ter-mee-DOR

Thermopylae   thur-MOP-uh-lee

Thucydides   thoo-SID-uh-deez

Thutmosis   thoot-MOH-sus

Tiberius   tie-BIR-ee-us

Tito   TEE-toh

Tlaxcala   tlah-SKAHL-uh

Torah   TOR-uh

Tordesillas   tor-duh-SEE-yus

Toussaint L'Ouverture   too-SAN loo-vur-TOOR

Trajan   TRAY-jun

Trevithick, Richard   TREV-uh-thik

Trudeau, Pierre   TROO-doh, pee-YEHR

Tutankhamen   tuh-tan-KAH-muhn

Tzara, Tristan   TSAH-rah, tri-STAN

Uighur   yu-EE-gur

ulama   oo-lah-MAH

Ulbricht, Walter   UL-brikt, VAHL-ter

Umayyads   oo-MY-ads

Unam Sanctam   OON-ahm SANK-tahm

universitas   yoo-ni-VER-si-tahs

Vaisya   VIGHSH-yuh

Valois   VAL-wah

van Eyck, Jan   van IKE

van Gogh, Vincent   van GOE

Vargas, Getúlio   VAR-gus, zhuh-TOOL-yoo

Venetia   vuh-NEE-shee-uh

Vesalius, Andreas   vi-SAY-lee-us, ahn-DRAY-us

Vespucci, Amerigo   ves-POO-chee, ahm-ay-REE-goe

Vierzenheiligen   feer-tsun-HILE-i-gun

Virgil   VUR-jul

vizier   vuy-ZEER

Volkschulen   FOLK-shool-un

Voltaire   vole-TAIR

Walesa, Lech   va-WENZ-uh, LEK

Wallachia   wah-lay-KEE-uh

Watteau, Antoine   wah-TOE, AHN-twahn

Weizsäcker, Richard von   VITS-zek-er, RIK-art

wergeld   wur-GELD

Winkelmann, Maria   VING-kul-mun

Xerxes   ZURK-seez

Xhosa   KOH-suh

Xinjiang   shin-JI-ang

Xiongnu (Hsiung-nu)   she-ONG-noo

Xuan Zang   SHYAHN ZAHNG

Yahweh   YAH-wah

Yeltsin, Boris   YELT-sun

Yi Song-gye   YEE sohn-GEE

yishuv   YISH-uv

Zapata, Emiliano   zuh-PAH-tuh, ay-mel-YAHN-oh

zemstvos   ZEMPST-voh

Zeno   ZEE-noh

Zhang Xueliang   JANG shwee-lee-ONG

Zhenge   JUNG-huh

Zhou   JOE

Zhu Xi   JOO SHEE

Zhu Yuanzhang   jew whan-JANG

ziggurat   ZIG-guh-rat

Zimbabwe   zim-BAH-bway

Zola, Emile   ZOH-luh, ay-MEEL

zollverein   TSOL-fuh-rine

Zoroaster   ZOR-oh-as-ter

INDEX

racism, 429
Revolutions of 1848, 399–401
scientific advancements, 429
Second Industrial Revolution, 414–17
Socialism, 417
society and social structure, 419
urbanization, 418–19
women's rights, 421–22
World War I (*See* World War I)
World War II (*See* World War II)
after World War II, 590–97, 600–604, 605, 606
European Economic Community (EEC), 593
European Union, 593, 594, 628
Existentialism, 605–6
Expansionism. *See* Imperialism and expansionism
Exploration
England, 305
France, 305
impact of, 303–4
Italy, 297–98
maps, 299
motives for, 298–99
Netherlands, 305
of New World, 302–3
Polos of Venice, 297–98
Portuguese empire, 296, 298, 300–301, 304–5
ship innovations, 300
Spain, 298, 302–3, 305
Eyeglasses, 342–43

F

Factories, 394–95, 397
Falkland Islands, 599
"The Fall of the House of Usher" (Poe), 409
Family
Africa, 617
China, 348–49, 512, 585
Europe, after World War II, 602
Europe, Renaissance period, 274
Europe, 19th century, 420–21
Italy, Fascist regime, 521–22
Japan, 356
Southeast Asia, 315
Soviet Union, 525, 575
U.S., after World War II, 602
Famines, in India, 334
Farming. *See* Agriculture
Farouk (Egypt), 621
Fascism, 521–22, 599
Federal Republic of Germany, 591. *See also* Germany
Feminism, 602–3, 638
Ferdinand of Aragon, 276
Festivals, in Europe, 366
Feudalism
decline of, 273
France, 374, 377
Japan, 356, 469
Russia, 406–7
Fief-holding system. *See* Feudalism

Fillmore, Millard, 468, 469
Film industry, 496, 606
Finland, 490
Firearms, 352
Five Women Who Loved Love (Saikaku), 357
Flaubert, Gustave, 410
Florence, 275, 278
Foot binding, 467
"Forbidden City," 350, 351
Forced labor, 533, 534, 569
Ford, Gerald, 596
Ford, Henry, 414
Fourth Republic (France), 590
Fox, Vicente, 600
France
in Algeria, 612
in China, 462
colonialism, 305, 306, 369, 370
economy, 493, 590, 591
education in, 600
Enlightenment contributions, 364, 365
feudalism in, 374, 377
Great Depression in, 494
Hundred Years' War, 276
in India, 333, 368
industrialization of, 395
invasion of Italy, 278
labor strikes, 600
in Latin America, 370
under Louis XIV, 285–86
military size, pre-World War I, 478
under Napoleon Bonaparte, 379–83
under Napoleon III, 405–6
and Nazi Germany's pre-World War II expansion, 526
North American colonies, 369
occupation of Ruhr, 492
in occupied Germany, 551
political structure, 380, 399–400, 426, 590
Popular Front, 494
pre-World War I alliances, 427
Revolution, The, 363, 374–79
revolution of 1848, 399–400
Second Republic, 399–400
Seven Years' War, 368–69
society and social structure, pre-revolution, 374
Suez Canal, 621
Third Republic, 426
Thirty Years' War, 285
Wars of Religion, 283
wars with England, 368, 369
war with Austria (1792), 377
war with Prussia, 405
witchcraft trial, 284, 285
World War I, 480, 483, 484, 490
after World War I, 492
World War II, 528, 531
after World War II, 590–91
Francis Ferdinand, 478, 479–80
Francis Joseph (Austria), 426
Francis Xavier, 352
Frankenstein (Shelley), 408

Frankfurt, 419
Frankfurt Assembly, 400
Frederick I (Prussia), 287
Frederick II the Great (Prussia), 368, 372, 373
Frederick the Wise (Saxony), 280
Frederick William IV (Prussia), 400
Frederick William the Great Elector (Prussia), 287
French Revolution, 363, 374–79
Freud, Sigmund, 429, 430

G

Galileo Galilei, 292
Gallipoli, Battle of, 483
Gama, Vasco da, 296, 300, 330
Gandhi, Indira, 634, 636, 637
Gandhi, Mohandas "Mahatma," 501–2, 633, 634
Gandhi, Rajiv, 635, 637
Garibaldi, Giuseppe, 404
Gaulle, Charles de, 590, 612
Gender roles. *See* Women, roles of
General Theory of Employment, Interest, and Money (Keynes), 493
Geneva, 281
Geneva Accords, 561
Genghis Khan, 330
German Democratic Republic (GDR), 549, 551–52, 573–74, 578, 591. *See also* Germany
Germanic kingdoms, 428
German Social Democratic Party (SPD), 417
Germany
anti-Semitism in, 429
in China, 460, 462
division of, 551–52
economy, 493, 536, 591
Great Depression in, 492, 493, 494
Green Party of, 605
Holy Roman Empire, 277
industrialization of, 395, 415
map, after World War I, 478
Marxism in, 417
military size, pre-World War I, 478
under Napoleon, 381
nationalism of, 399
Nazi Germany (*See* Nazi Germany)
occupation of after World War II, 538
political structure, late 19th and early 20th centuries, 426
pre-World War I alliances, 427
Protestant Reformation in, 279–80
racism in, 429
reparations owed after World War I, 490, 492
reunification of, 591
and revolution of 1848, 400
Thirty Years' War, 285
unification of, 19th century, 404–5, 428
Weimar Republic, 494
women's rights, 486

Kemal Atatürk, 503–4
Kennan, George, 551
Kennedy, John F., 560, 561, 595, 598
Kent State University, 595
Kenya, 611, 612, 615
Kenyatta, Jomo, 611, 613
Kepler, Johannes, 291
Kerensky, Alexander, 487
Keynes, John Maynard, 493
Khatemi, Mohammad, 624
Khmer Rouge, 642
Khomeini, Ruholla (Ayatollah), 596, 619, 624, 638
Khrushchev, Nikita, 559–60, 561, 563, 569–70
Khubilai Khan, 297, 341
Kim Dae Jung, 648
Kim Il Sung, 647
King, Martin Luther, 595
Kings and queens. *See* Monarchy
Kishore Mahbubani, 649
Kishwar, Madhu, 638
Klerk, F. W. de, 615
Kohl, Helmut, 591
Koizumi, Junichiro, 645
Korea
 division of, 557
 under Japanese control, 359, 472, 535
 after Korean War, 647–48
 U.S. attempts to open country, 472
 World War II Japanese occupation, 535
 Yi dynasty, 357–59
Korean War, 555–57
Kosovo, 319, 595
Kosovo Liberation Army (KLA), 595
Kosygin, Alexei, 564, 571
Kowtow, 346
Kristallnacht, 524
Kritovoulos, 320
Kuala Lumpur, 632
Kundera, Milan, 606
Kurile Islands, 538, 644
Kuroda Seiki, 431
Kursk, Battle of, 531
Kuwait, 624, 628
Kyoto, 351
Kyoto Agreement, 655

L

Labor. *See also* Women in labor market
 children, 395, 397, 398
 in factories, 19th century, 395, 397
 forced labor, 533, 534, 569
 in mines, 19th century, 397
 organization of, 417
Labour Party (Great Britain), 426, 591, 592
The Landing of Marie de' Medici at Marseilles, 291
Land ownership
 Japan, 470
 Latin America, 369
Land reform, in China, 580
Languages
 Afrikaans, 307

of India, 638
 Turkish, 504
Laos, 558
Las Casas, Bartolomé de, 303, 304
Latin America
 agriculture in, 369
 authoritarian governments of, 516–17
 colonial empires in, 369–70
 culture of, 517
 democracy in, 597
 economy, 369, 424, 514–16, 597
 foreign debt, 597
 Great Depression in, 597
 independence movements, 401
 maps, 403, 515
 nation-building, 401–2
 political structure, 369, 402, 424, 516–17
 since 1945, 597–600
 society and social structure, late 19th century, 424
 Spanish-American War, 424
 U.S. investment in, 515–16
 and U.S., 424
Latvia, 490
Laurier, Wilfred, 425
Lavender Mist (Pollock), 605
Law
 France under Napoleon, 380
 Islamic Shari'a, 324
 Mughal Empire, 331
Lawrence of Arabia, 483–84, 503
Lay Down Your Arms (von Suttner), 422
Laye, Camara, 618
League of Nations, 490, 491–92, 526
Leary, Timothy, 601
Lebanon, 491, 505, 621
Lee Kuan-yew, 649
Leisure, 414, 423–24, 600
Lenin, Vladimir, 487–88, 495, 499–500, 506, 549
Leningrad, 531, 536
Leonardo da Vinci, 275
Lepanto, Battle of, 322
Lévesque, René, 597
Lewinsky, Monica, 596
Liberal Democratic Party (Japan), 644–45
Liberalism, 398–99
Liberal Party (Japan), 469
Lightbulb, 414
Lin Biao, 563
Lincoln, Abraham, 407, 408
Lin Zexu, 457
Literacy, 423
Literature
 Africa, 618–19
 China, 349–50, 512, 585–86
 Egypt, 629
 England in Elizabethan era, 290–91
 existentialism, 605–6
 India, 638
 Iran, 629
 Japan, 356–57, 472–73, 513, 647
 Middle Eastern countries, 628–29
 Mughal Empire, 337

postmodernism, 606
 Realism, 410
 Romantic period, 408–9
 Soviet Union, 574–75
 Surrealism, 496
 Symbolism, 430
 "Theater of the Absurd," 605
Lithuania, 490, 576
Liu Shaoqi, 579
Li Zicheng, 343–44
Lloyd George, David, 490
Locke, John, 363
London, 396, 418
Long March, 509
Louis Napoleon, 404, 405–6
Louis-Philippe (France), 399
Louis XI (France), 276
Louis XIV (France), 273, 285–86, 313
Louis XVI (France), 374, 375, 377
Louis XVIII (France), 383
L'Ouverture, Toussaint, 401
Ludendorff, Erich von, 489
Luftwaffe, 528, 537
Lusitania, 484–85
Luther, Martin, 280, 281
Lutheranism, 280
Lu Xun, 512

M

MacArthur, Douglas, 531, 557, 644
Macartney, George (Lord), 347
Macdonald, John, 408
Machiavelli, Niccolò, 279
Madame Bovary (Flaubert), 410
Madero, Francisco, 424
Madras, 333, 368
Magazines, 366
Magellan, Ferdinand, 305
Mahbubani, Kishore, 649
Mahfouz, Naguib, 629
Major, John, 592
Malacca, 297, 301
Malaya, 640
Malaysia, 632–33, 640, 641, 642, 643
Malenkov, Georgy, 569
Mali, 307
Mamluks, 321
Manchuria, 526, 554, 556
Manchus, 343–47
Mandela, Nelson, 615
 Manufacturing. *See* Industrial production and manufacturing
Mao Zedong
 during civil war, 555
 dispute with Soviet Union over authority, 561
 as leader of Communist China, 579–81
 and Long March, 511
 revolution promoted by, 508–9, 510
Maps and mapmaking, 299
Marconi, Guglielmo, 414
Marcos, Ferdinand, 639, 641
Maria Theresa (Austria), 368

New Zealand, 650
Ngo Dinh Diem, 561, 639
Ngugi Wa Thiong'o, 619
Nicaragua, 401, 565
Nicholas II (Russia), 426, 480, 486, 487
Nigeria, 612, 615
Nightingale, Florence, 421
9/11/01, 604, 620
Nixon, Richard M., 560, 562, 564, 595–96
Nkrumah, Kwame, 611, 613
No, 357
Nobility
    Europe, early modern period, 368
    Europe, in Renaissance era, 273
    France, 285, 374
    Japan, 471
    Russia, 373
Nobunaga, Oda, 351
Norman, E. H., 473
North Africa
    Ottoman Empire in, 321–22
    World War II in, 531
North America. *See also* Canada; Mexico;
    United States of America
    colonization of, 305, 369, 370–71
    Seven Years' War in, 368–69
    North Atlantic Treaty Organization
      (NATO), 552–53, 577, 593, 595
Northern Expedition, 508, 509
Northern Ireland, 603
North Korea, 557, 647
North Vietnam, 641
Norway, 287, 528
Novotny, Antonin, 572–73
Nuclear weapons, 537–38, 560, 590, 598, 606
Nur Jahan, 331, 332
Nyerere, Julius, 613, 614

O

Obasanjo, Olusegun, 615
Oda Nobunaga, 351
Oe, Kenzaburo, 647
Oil, 505, 515, 516–17, 564, 625
One Day in the Life of Ivan Denisovich
    (Solzhenitsyn), 575
One Hundred Days of reform, 464
On the Origin of Species by Means of Natural
    Selection (Darwin), 409–10
Open Door policy, 461
Opium War, 457–58
Oppenheimer, J. Robert, 606
Oral tradition, 618
Organization of African Unity (OAU), 613,
    615
Organization of American States (OAS), 597
Orkhan I, 319
Osman, 319
Ottoman Empire
    architecture of, 325
    art of, 324–25
    decline of, 324, 502–3
    defeat of Safavids, 321, 326–27
    end of, 503

    expansion of, 320–22
    maps of, 321, 327, 428, 478
    origins of, 319–20
    political structure, 321, 322–23
    religion of, 323–24
    World War I, 483–84
    after World War I, 478

P

Pahlavi dynasty (Iran), 504
Painting. *See* Art
Pakistan, 633, 634, 635–36
Palestine
    Arab nations' view of, 620–21
    Balfour Declaration, 505
    British control over, 491, 503
Palestine Liberation Organization (PLO),
    621, 622
Palestinians
    in Israel, 621–23, 622
    militancy of, 622–23
    refugees, 621
    terrorism by, 603–4
Pan-Africanism, 613
Pan-Arabism, 621
Pankhurst, Emmeline, 421
Papacy, reform of in 16th century, 282
Paris, 406, 531
Paris Peace Conference, 489–90, 508
Park, Chung Hee, 647–48
Parti Québécois, 597
Pasternak, Boris, 574
Pasteur, Louis, 409
Paul III (Pope), 282
Peace movement, in U.S., 601
Peace of Augsburg, 280
Peace of Westphalia, 285
Pearl Harbor, 530, 531
Pearson, Lester, 596
Peasant rebellions
    in China, 341, 343–44, 345, 458–59
    in Japan, 356
    in Korea, 472
Peasants
    China, 510
    Europe, early modern, 368
    Europe, Renaissance, 273
    France, 374
    Japan, 356
    Korea, 358
    in Russia, 407
    in Soviet Union, 525
Peking University, 508
People's Liberation Army (PLA), 509, 554–55
People's Republic of China (PRC), 555,
    579–86
People's Republic of Korea (PRK), 647
Perestroika, 576
Perón, Eva, 599
Perón, Juan, 599
Perry, Matthew C., 468
Persia, 325–29, 504. *See also* Iran
Peru, independence of, 401

Pétain, Henri, 528
Peter the Great, 288
Petrarch, 275
Petrograd, 486, 487
Philip II (Spain), 283
Philippine Islands
    ASEAN membership, 642
    independence of, 639
    political structure, 639, 641
    U.S. control of, 425
    in World War II, 535
Philosophy. *See also* Confucianism
    Enlightenment, 363–66, 372
    Europe, Renaissance, 273, 275
Photography, 431
Physics, 429
Picasso, Pablo, 431–32
Piedmont, 404
Pilgrimage to Cythera (Watteau), 367
Pissarro, Camille, 430
Pitt, William, 371
Pizarro, Francisco, 303
Plantations, 305, 367
Plassey, Battle of, 333
Poe, Edgar Allan, 409
Poland
    under communist control, 549, 572
    after fall of communism, 593–95
    in fifteenth century, 277
    Nazi Germany's invasion, 526, 528, 533,
      534
    solidarity movement and independence
      of, 577
    after World War I, 490
Police
    in East Germany's Stasi, 573
    in Fascist Italy, 521
    in Nazi Germany, 524, 533
Political philosophy
    Locke, 363
    Machiavelli, 279
    Marxism, 417–18
    Montesquieu, 364
    Rousseau, 365
Political structure
    Africa, 613
    Austria-Hungary, 426
    centralization of, 388
    China, 341, 344, 345
    England, 289
    Europe, early modern, 372–73
    Europe, late 19th and early 20th
      centuries, 414, 426
    France, 380, 399–400, 426, 590
    Germany, 426, 523–24, 533
    Great Britain, 426
    India, 334, 636
    Israel, 622
    Italy, 426, 521–22
    Japan, 354–55, 468–70, 512–13, 514,
      525, 644–45
    Latin American colonies, 369
    Latin American countries, 402, 424,
      516–17

Mexico, 516–17, 600
Middle Eastern countries, 625
Mughal Empire, 331
Ottoman Empire, 321, 322–23
Prussia, 287
Safavid Empire, 327–28
Southeast Asia, 314, 639–41
Soviet Union, 525, 576
Taiwan, 648
Turkey, 625
U.S., 372
Vietnam, 639, 641
Pollock, Jackson, 605
Pollution, 584–85, 605, 637, 655
Polo, Maffeo, 297
Polo, Marco, 297–98
Polo, Niccolò, 297
Pol Pot, 642
Polygamy, in Africa, 617
Popular culture, 606–7
Popular Front, 494
Population growth
    Africa, 614
    China, 347–48, 389, 457
    Europe, early modern, 366–67, 389
    Europe, 19th century, 396
    India, 634, 637
    Japan, 356, 514
Portillo, José López, 600
Portugal
    in Africa, 300, 305–6, 310–11
    in China, 341, 342
    exploration, 296, 298, 300–301, 304–5, 306
    in India, 300, 333
    in Japan, 352, 353
    Latin American colonies, 369, 370
    slave trade, 307
    trade in Southeast Asia, 311
Post-Impressionism, 431
Postmodernism, 605, 606
Potsdam Conference, 538
"Prague Spring," 573
The Prince (Machiavelli), 279
Principia (Newton), 292
Printing, 275, 343
Prisoners of war, 534, 535
Progressive Era, U.S., 425
Progressive Party (Japan), 469
Propaganda
    in Fascist Italy, 521
    in Nazi German, 524
Protestantism, 279–82
Protestant Reformation, 279–80
Protests and demonstrations, 595, 600–601
Prussia
    Congress of Vienna, 397
    and German unification, 400, 404–5
    monarchy, 287, 372
    War of the Austrian Succession, 368
    war with France, 380–81
Psychoanalysis, 429, 430
Ptolemy, 291
Publishing, 365–66

Puerto Rico, 424
Punjab, 634
Purgatory, 282
Puritans, 288, 289
Putin, Vladimir, 577
Puyi (China), 464

Q

Qajar dynasty (Iran), 504
Qianlong, 345
Qing (Manchu) dynasty, 340–41, 344–51, 457–67
Qiu Jin, 467
Quebec, 597

R

Racism, 429, 523, 524
The Radiance of the King (Laye), 618
Radio, 414
Railroads, 394, 396, 415–16
Ramayana, 337
Ramcaritmanas (Tulsidas), 337
Raphael, 275
Rasputin, 486
Reagan, Ronald, 564–65, 596
Realism, 410, 431
Red Army, 488–89
Reed, John, 488
Reformation, Protestant, 279–80
"Reign of Terror," 378–79
Religion. See also Buddhism; Christianity; Islam
    China, 585
    and Enlightenment, 364
    European wars over, 283, 285
    India, conflicts between Hindus and Muslims, 501, 502, 633, 636
    Japan, 646–47
    Marxist view of, 505
    Mughal Empire, 331
    Southeast Asia, 312, 314
    Turkey, 504
Remarque, Erich Maria, 483
Reminiscences (Schurz), 400
Rémy, Nicholas, 285
Renaissance, 273–79
Reparations
    World War I, 490, 492
    World War II, 551
Republic of China. See Taiwan
Retail stores, 415
Revolts and revolutions
    American Revolution, 371
    Austrian Empire, 1848, 400–401
    China, 464, 507–12
    Cuba, 598
    England, 288–89
    France, 363, 374–79, 399–400
    Iran, 623–24
    Latin America, 401
    Mexico, 401, 424, 516
    Russia, 486–87

Revolutionary Alliance (Tongmenghui), 464, 465
Revolutionary War, U.S., 371
Revolutions of 1848, 399–401
Reza Khan, 504
Rhee, Syngman, 647
Rhineland, 526
Ricci, Matteo, 343, 348
Richard II (Shakespeare), 292
Rivera, Diego, 517
Riza-i-Abassi, 329
Robespierre, Maximilien, 377, 379
Rocket, 394
Rococo style, 365
Roman Catholic Church
    condemnation of Copernicanism, 292
    in England, 282, 289
    in France, 283, 377, 380
    missionary activities in China, 342, 343, 344
    missionary activities in Japan, 353–54
    missionary activities in Latin America, 369–70
    missionary activities in New World, 303
    papacy reform in 16th century, 282
    pre-Reformation corruption, 279–80
    reformation of, 282
    religious orders of, 282
    in Spain, 276, 283
Romania, 490, 529, 531, 549
Romanov dynasty, 288
Romanticism, 408–9
Rome, 278, 404, 531
Rommel, Erwin, 531
Roosevelt, Franklin Delano, 494, 516, 538, 549, 554
Roosevelt, Theodore, 425
Rousseau, Jean-Jacques, 365
Rubens, Peter Paul, 290, 291
Rug weaving, 325, 329
Ruhr, French occupation of, 492
Rushdie, Salman, 638
Russia. See also Soviet Union
    under Alexander II, 406–7
    alliance with Germany, 427
    anti-Semitism in, 429
    and Balkan Wars, 427–28
    boundary disputes with China, 346
    capitalism in, 577
    under Catherine the Great, 372–73
    civil war (1918–1921), 488–89
    Congress of Vienna, 397
    Crimean War, 402–3
    end of Soviet Union and emergence of, 577
    expansionism in China, 460, 462
    in fifteenth century, 277–78
    industrialization of, 415–16, 426
    and Iran, 504
    Lenin and the Bolsheviks, 487–88
    maps of, 478, 578
    military size, pre-World War I, 478
    monarchy of, 288